Argumentation and Debate

Critical Thinking for Reasoned Decision Making

THIRTEENTH EDITION

AUSTIN J. FREELEY
Late, John Carroll University

DAVID L. STEINBERG
University of Miami

 CENGAGE

Australia • Brazil • Mexico • Singapore • United Kingdom • United States

CENGAGE

Argumentation and Debate:
Critical Thinking for Reasoned
Decision Making, **Thirteenth**
Edition
Austin J. Freeley, Late
David L. Steinberg

Editor-in-Chief: Lyn Uhl

Publisher: Monica Eckman

Editorial Assistant: Colin Solan

Media Editor: Jessica Badiner

Executive Brand Manager:
Ben Rivera

Senior Market Development
Manager: Kara Kindstrom

Senior Marketing
Communications Manager:
Linda Yip

Rights Acquisition Specialist:
Alexandra Ricciardi

Manufacturing Planner:
Doug Bertke

Art and Design Direction,
Production Management, and
Composition: PreMediaGlobal

For product information and technology assistance,
contact us at **Cengage Customer & Sales Support,**
1-800-354-9706 or support.cengage.com.

For permission to use material from this text or
product, submit all requests online at
www.cengage.com/permissions.

Library of Congress Control Number: 2012953030

ISBN-13: 978-1-133-31160-7

ISBN-10: 1-133-31160-1

Cengage
20 Channel Street
Boston, MA 02210
USA

Cengage is a leading provider of customized learning
solutions with employees residing in nearly 40 different
countries and sales in more than 125 countries around the
world. Find your local representative at: **www.cengage.com**.

Cengage products are represented in Canada by
Nelson Education, Ltd.

To learn more about Cengage platforms and services,
register or access your online learning solution, or purchase
materials for your course, visit **www.cengage.com**.

Printed in Mexico
Print Number: 06   Print Year: 2019

To Dr. Austin J. Freeley and Trudy.
David L. Steinberg

Brief Contents

Contents

Preface

*A*rgumentation and Debate has been an important educational resource for more than 50 years. When Dr. Freeley wrote the first edition, there was a narrow range of accepted conventional argumentation theory and a common approach to academic policy debate modeled after tournament practice. Through 12 editions, the authors have adapted the text to match changing practice in debate and teaching while preserving classical and conventional approaches to learning debate. The new edition continues this tradition. Today there is more diversity than ever before in the approaches used in teaching the argumentation and debate course, as well as in intercollegiate tournament practice. The new edition of *Argumentation and Debate* retains its rhetorical roots with a flexible tone open to a diverse array of debate styles and appropriate in the contemporary context. It recognizes new approaches to argumentation and debate and the need to employ critical thinking skills in a variety of debate formats and argumentative contexts. It values the importance of inclusion and sensitivity to differences of culture, gender, orientation, class, and other factors as they impact communicative choices and argumentation. Finally, the new edition recognizes the growing importance and application of debate in the public sphere, as observed in political campaign debates and other public forum debates. The authors unabashedly employ a preference for evidence-based team topic policy debate; however, the text strives to offer viable tools for a wide range of readers interested in improving their critical thinking for reasoned decision making in unlimited contexts.

In addition to many updates and revisions, readers familiar with previous editions of *Argumentation and Debate* will recognize some substantial new features:

- *Argumentation and Debate: Critical Thinking for Reasoned Decision Making* has been reorganized. The existing chapters have been reordered and new ones added. The Contents begin with foundations and classical traditions, logic and reasoning, and progress to the practice of academic debate, concluding with applied and public debate.

- The section on the history, background, and the organization of academic debate has been expanded (Chapter 2).

- Coverage of classical traditions in rhetoric and argumentation has been expanded (Chapter 3).

- A new chapter on ethics and cultural considerations in argumentation has been added (Chapter 5).

- Updated research chapter, Gathering and Organizing Support (Chapter 10), and new appendix on debate and technology.

- Dedicated chapter on cross-examination (Chapter 13).

- New material on listening (Chapter 15), expanded discussion of Debate as Public Speaking (Chapter 16).

- Coverage of new academic debate formats, including Ethics Bowl, Mock Trial Debate, and Worlds debating, as well as parliamentary and Lincoln–Douglas debate (Chapter 17).

- New chapter on political campaign debates, covering history, impact, and future with discussion of presidential campaign debates from Nixon v Kennedy through McCain–Obama (Chapter 18).

- New chapter on public debating including Long Table Debating (Chapter 20).

- Appendix materials provide a new quick start guide, a sample policy debate, and expanded links to debate resources.

Most chapters provide a miniglossary of terms and conclude with a set of suggested exercises designed to provide experiential learning of the chapter's concepts. Throughout the text many important materials are presented in insets that we hope will prove helpful to the students.

This book is designed for all who seek to improve their critical thinking, reasoned decision making, and advocacy skills. In particular this text is designed for the undergraduate course in argumentation and debate. It is appropriate for any course that empowers students as active citizens participating in the societal demands of democracy.

Austin J. Freeley recorded his thanks to his professors, mentors, and friends in the first edition of this book. The memory of their contributions remains luminous across the years.

We have lost too many friends and important contributors to the field of Debate and Argumentation in recent years. I would like to thank and remember some who personally and positively impacted me—Frank Harrison, Ross Smith, Scott Nobles, Lee Myers, Doug Duke, Gerald Kish, Matt Grindy, and Vince Binder. They are all missed, but live on in the lives they changed through debate.

I would again like to record my thanks to my debate mentors, David Thomas, Norma Cook, Jim Brooks, Warren Decker, and Brenda Logue, and my terrific assistant coaches, for teaching me far more than I could teach them. My sincere thanks go to each of them, including Dan Leyton, Dale Reed, Ernie Querido, David Cram-Helwich, Christopher Cooper, Nicole Colston, Gavin

Williams, Matt Grindy, Nicole Richter, Kenny McCaffrey, Johnny Prieur, Cale Halley, Joe Graziano, and Randall Martinez. Randall and Cale both contributed ideas and were an inspiration to the current edition.

I would also like to acknowledge my boys, Adam and John, who make me very proud, and my supportive and caring wife, Victoria, with much love.

I am grateful to Dr. Freeley for giving me the opportunity to contribute to this project and, thus, to be a small part of his tremendous legacy.

Thanks to all the wonderful people at Cengage who worked hard to make this book a reality, including Monica Eckman and Daisuke Yasutake, who are exceptionally patient, professional, and understanding.

Finally, thanks to the many students we have taught and judged over the years, and those who will carry the tradition into the future. They are our inspiration, helping us refine our thinking and develop more cogent statements on many matters, and have provided many of the examples found throughout this text.

David L. Steinberg

1

Argumentation, Critical Thinking, and Decision Making

In the spring of 2011, facing a legacy of problematic U.S. military involvements in Bosnia, Iraq, and Afghanistan, and criticism for what some saw as slow support of the United States for the people of Egypt and Tunisia as citizens of those nations ousted their formerly American-backed dictators, the administration of President Barack Obama considered its options in providing support for rebels seeking to overthrow the government of Muammar el-Qaddafi in Libya. Public debate was robust as the administration sought to determine its most appropriate action. The president ultimately decided to engage in an international coalition, enforcing United Nations Security Council Resolution 1973 through a number of measures including establishment of a no-fly zone through air and missile strikes to support rebels in Libya, but stopping short of direct U.S. intervention with ground forces or any occupation of Libya. While the action seemed to achieve its immediate objectives, most notably the defeat of Qaddafi and his regime, the American president received both criticism and praise for his measured yet assertive decision.

In fact, the past decade has challenged American leaders to make many difficult decisions in response to potentially catastrophic problems. Public debate has raged in a chaotic environment of political division and apparent animosity. The process of public decision making may have never been so consequential or difficult. Beginning in the fall of 2008, Presidents Bush and Obama faced a growing economic crisis and responded in part with "bailouts" of certain Wall Street financial entities, additional "bailouts" of Detroit automakers, and a major economic stimulus package. All these actions generated substantial public discourse regarding the necessity, wisdom, and consequences of acting (or not acting). In the summer of 2011, the president and the Congress participated in heated debates (and attempted negotiations) to raise the nation's debt ceiling such that the U.S. Federal Government could pay its debts and continue government operations. This discussion was linked to a debate about the size of the exponentially growing national debt, government spending, and taxation. Further, in the spring of 2012, U.S. leaders sought to prevent Iran from developing nuclear weapon capability while gas prices in the United States rose. The United States considered its ongoing military involvement in Afghanistan in the face of nationwide protests and violence in that country sparked by the alleged burning of Korans by American soldiers, and Americans observed the actions of President Bashar Al-Assad and Syrian forces as they killed Syrian citizens in response to a rebel uprising in that nation and considered the role of the United States in that action.

Meanwhile, public discourse, in part generated and intensified by the campaigns of the GOP candidates for president and consequent media coverage, addressed issues dividing Americans, including health care, women's rights to reproductive health services, the freedom of churches and church-run organizations to remain true to their beliefs in providing (or electing not to provide) health care services which they oppose, the growing gap between the wealthiest 1 percent of Americans and the rest of the American population, and continued high levels of unemployment. More division among the American public would be hard to imagine. Yet through all the tension, conflict was almost entirely verbal in nature, aimed at discovering or advocating solutions to growing problems.

Individuals also faced daunting decisions. A young couple, underwater with their mortgage and struggling to make their monthly payments, considered walking away from their loan; elsewhere a college sophomore reconsidered his major and a senior her choice of law school, graduate school, or a job and a teenager decided between an iPhone and an iPad. Each of these situations called for decisions to be made. Each decision maker worked hard to make well-reasoned decisions.

Decision making is a thoughtful process of choosing among a variety of options for acting or thinking. It requires that the decider make a choice. Life demands decision making. We make countless individual decisions every day. To make some of those decisions, we work hard to employ care and consideration; others seem to just happen. Couples, families, groups of friends, and co-workers come together to make choices, and decision-making bodies from committees to juries to the U.S. Congress and the United Nations make decisions that impact us all. Every profession requires effective and ethical decision making, as do our school, community, and social organizations.

We all engage in discourse surrounding our necessary decisions every day. To refinance or sell one's home, to buy a high-performance SUV or an economical hybrid car, what major to select, what to have for dinner, what candidate to vote for, paper or plastic, all present us with choices. Should the president deal with an international crisis through military invasion or diplomacy? How should the U.S. Congress act to address illegal immigration?

Is the defendant guilty as accused? Should we watch *The Daily Show* or the ball game? And upon what information should I rely to make my decision?

Certainly some of these decisions are more consequential than others. Which amendment to vote for, what television program to watch, what course to take,

Miniglossary

Argumentation Reason giving in communicative situations by people whose purpose is the justification of acts, beliefs, attitudes, and values.

Coercion The threat or use of force intended to limit the viable choices of action available to the person threatened.

Critical thinking The ability to analyze, criticize, evaluate, and advocate ideas; to reason effectively; and to reach informed and careful conclusions based on sound inferences drawn from unambiguous statements of knowledge or belief.

Debate The process of inquiry and advocacy; the seeking of a reasoned judgment on a proposition.

Deontological ethics An ethical approach that is process- or act-oriented, and is based on the notion that actions have moral value.

Emotion An internal state or condition attended to by pain or pleasure.

Ethics A set of constructs that guide our decision making by providing standards of behavior telling us how we ought to act.

Ethos A mode of persuasion, the judgment the audience makes of the speaker based on character, sagacity, and goodwill.

Good reasons Reasons that are psychologically compelling for a given audience, which make further inquiry both unnecessary and redundant—hence justifying a decision to affirm or reject a proposition.

Logos A mode of persuasion, the judgment the audience makes of the argument and the reasoning presented. It is a measure of probable truth, not certainty.

Pathos Emotional proof.

Persuasion Communication intended to influence the acts, beliefs, attitudes, and values of others.

Propaganda The use of persuasion by a group (often a closely knit organization) in a sustained, organized campaign using multiple media for the purpose of influencing a mass audience.

Teleological ethics An ethical approach that is results oriented and would focus on the good or bad consequences of an action or a decision.

which phone plan to purchase, and which diet to pursue—all present unique challenges. At our best, we seek out research and data to inform our decisions. Yet even the choice of which information to attend to requires decision making. In 2006, *Time* magazine named YOU its "Person of the Year." Congratulations! Its selection was based on the participation not of "great men" in the creation of history, but rather on the contributions of a community of anonymous participants in the evolution of information. Through blogs, online networking, YouTube, Facebook, Twitter, Wikipedia, and many other "wikis," and social networking sites, knowledge and "truth" are created from the bottom up, bypassing the authoritarian control of newspeople, academics, and publishers. Through a quick keyword search, we have access to infinite quantities of information, but how do we sort through it and select the best information for our needs? Much of what suffices as information is not reliable, or even ethically motivated.

The ability of every decision maker to make good, reasoned, and ethical decisions relies heavily upon their ability to think critically. Critical thinking enables one to break argumentation down to its component parts in order to evaluate its relative validity and strength. And, critical thinking offers tools enabling the user to better understand the nature and relative quality of the message under consideration. Critical thinkers are better users of information, as well as better advocates.

Colleges and universities expect their students to develop their **critical thinking** skills and may require students to take designated courses to that end. The importance and value of such study is widely recognized.

The executive order establishing California's requirement states:

> Instruction in *critical thinking* is designed to achieve an understanding of the relationship of language to logic, which would lead to *the ability to analyze, criticize, and advocate ideas, to reason inductively and deductively, and to reach factual or judgmental conclusions based on sound inferences drawn from unambiguous statements of knowledge or belief.* The minimal competence to be expected at the successful conclusion of instruction in critical thinking should be the ability to distinguish fact from judgment, belief from knowledge, and skills in elementary inductive and deductive processes, including an understanding of the formal and informal fallacies of language and thought.

Competency in critical thinking is a prerequisite to participating effectively in human affairs, pursuing higher education, and succeeding in the highly competitive world of business and the professions. Michael Scriven and Richard Paul for the National Council for Excellence in Critical Thinking Instruction argued that the effective critical thinker:

- raises vital questions and problems, formulating them clearly and precisely;
- gathers and assesses relevant information, using abstract ideas to interpret it effectively; comes to well-reasoned conclusions and solutions, testing them against relevant criteria and standards;
- thinks open-mindedly within alternative systems of thought, recognizing, and assessing, as need be, their assumptions, implications, and practical consequences; and
- communicates effectively with others in figuring out solutions to complex problems.

They also observed that critical thinking "entails effective communication and problem solving abilities and a commitment to overcome our native egocentrism and sociocentrism."[1] Debate as a classroom exercise and as a mode of thinking and behaving uniquely promotes development of each of these skill sets. Since classical times, debate has been one of the best methods of learning

---

1. Michael Scriven and Richard Paul, "Defining Critical Thinking," The Critical Thinking Community, http://www.criticalthinking.org/pages/defining-critical-thinking/410.

Critical Thinking

- Life demands decision making.
- The ability to make reasoned decisions relies on critical thinking.
- Critical thinking enables analysis and evaluation of arguments.
- Critical thinking improves the use of information as well as advocacy.
- Teaching and learning critical thinking are important roles of education.
- Debate teaches critical thinking.

---

and applying the principles of critical thinking. Contemporary research confirms the value of debate.

One study concluded:

> The impact of public communication training on the critical thinking ability of the participants is demonstrably positive. This summary of existing research reaffirms what many ex-debaters and others in forensics, public speaking, mock trial, or argumentation would support: participation improves the thinking of those involved.[2]

In particular, debate education improves the ability to think critically. In a comprehensive review of the relevant research, Kent Colbert concluded, "The debate-critical thinking literature provides presumptive proof favoring a positive debate-critical thinking relationship."[3]

Much of the most significant communication of our lives is conducted in the form of debates, formal or informal. These take place in intrapersonal communications, in which we weigh the pros and cons of an important decision in our own minds, and in interpersonal communications, in which we listen to arguments intended to influence our decision or participate in exchanges to influence the decisions of others.

Our success or failure in life is largely determined by our ability to make wise decisions for ourselves and to influence the decisions of others in ways that are beneficial to us. Much of our significant, purposeful activity is concerned with making decisions. Whether to join a campus organization, go to graduate school, accept a job offer, buy a car or house, move to another city, invest in a certain stock, or vote for Garcia—these are just a few of the thousands of decisions we may have to make. Often, intelligent self-interest or a sense of responsibility will require us to win the support of others. We may want a scholarship

---

2. Mike Allen, Sandra Berkowitz, Steve Hunt, and Allan Louden, "A Meta-Analysis of the Impact of Forensics and Communication Education on Critical Thinking," *Communication Education*, vol. 48, no. 1 (Jan. 1999), p. 28.
3. Kent Colbert, "Enhancing Critical Thinking Ability Through Academic Debate," *Contemporary Argumentation and Debate: The Journal of the Cross Examination Debate Association*, vol. 16 (1995), p. 69.

Good Reasons

- Argumentation relies on good reasons.
- Good reasons are audience-based justifications for or against propositions.
- Good reasons differ by audience and are, therefore, impacted by culture.
- Argumentation guides decision making.

---

or a particular job for ourselves, a customer for our product, or a vote for our favored political candidate.

Some people make decisions by flipping a coin. Others act on a whim or respond unconsciously to "hidden persuaders." If the problem is trivial—such as whether to go to a concert or a film—the particular method used is unimportant. For more crucial matters, however, mature adults require a reasoned means of decision making. Decisions should be justified by good reasons based on accurate evidence and valid reasoning.

Argumentation is reason giving in communicative situations by people whose purpose is the justification of acts, beliefs, attitudes, and values—a definition based on language adopted at the National Developmental Conference on Forensics.[4] British philosopher Stephen Toulmin makes a similar point when he asks, "What kind of *justificatory activities* must we engage in to convince our fellows that these beliefs are based on 'good reasons'?[5] **Good reasons** may be defined as "reasons which are psychologically compelling for a given audience, which make further inquiry both unnecessary and redundant—hence justifying a decision to affirm or reject a proposition."[6]

Note that what constitutes good reasons for one audience may not be good reasons for another. When Taslima Nasrin wrote her novella *Lajja* (*Shame*), she became a target of Muslim fundamentalists. Their fury mounted when she was quoted—or misquoted, she insists—as saying that the Koran should be "revised thoroughly" to give equal rights to women. After all, Islam's central article of faith is that the Koran is the literal word of God and is thus above revision. Nasrin's challenge thus was seen as blasphemy and prompted legal charges and Muslim *fatwas*, or religious decrees, calling for her death:

> A crowd of 100,000 demonstrators gathered outside the Parliament
> building in Dhaka to bay for her blood.... One particularly militant
> faction threatened to loose thousands of poisonous snakes in the capital
> unless she was executed.[7]

---

4. James H. McBath, ed., *Forensics as Communication* (Skokie, IL: National Textbook, 1975), p. 11.
5. Stephen Toulmin, *Knowing and Acting* (New York: Macmillan, 1976), p. 138.
6. David Zarefsky, "Criteria for Evaluating Non-Policy Argument," in *Perspectives on Non-Policy Argument*, ed. Don Brownlee, sponsored by CEDA (privately published, 1980), p. 10.
7. *Time*, Aug. 15, 1994, p. 26.

This incident provides a dramatic example of cultural differences. To Muslim fundamentalists in Bangladesh, even being suspected of calling for a revision of the Koran is a "good reason" for execution.

In most of the world and for most Muslims, "blasphemy" is not perceived as a good reason for death. In America, freedom of the press, enshrined in the First Amendment to the Constitution, is perceived as a good reason for allowing an author to express just about any opinion. A debater needs to discover the justificatory activities that the decision renderers will accept and to develop the good reasons that will lead them to agree with the desired conclusion—or, of course, to reject the reasons advanced by an opponent.

Of course, "good reasons" do not necessarily lead to "good" decisions. Reasons are "good" because they meet the unsaid criteria of the target audience. Therefore, a reasoned decision matches the culture, habits of thought, temporal context, and standards of intellectual application unique to a specific audience or decider within a particular context. Critical thinking is a habit of thought which enables the testing of argumentation potentially leading to informed and thoughtful decision making, but cannot account for all variables (for example, politics or personal agendas). We believe that argumentation leads to better decisions more often than does its alternatives, and it facilitates the application of analytical and evaluative measures guiding effective and careful comparisons and conclusions.

In the following section, we will first consider debate as a method of critical thinking and reasoned decision making. We will then look at some other methods of decision making and see how they relate to argumentation and debate.

I. DEBATE

Debate is the process of inquiry and advocacy, a way of arriving at a reasoned judgment on a proposition. Individuals may use debate to reach a decision in their own minds; alternatively, individuals or groups may use it to bring others around to their way of thinking.

Debate provides reasoned arguments for and against a proposition. It requires two competitive sides engaging in a bipolar clash of support for and against that proposition. Because it requires that listeners and opposing advocates comparatively evaluate competing choices, debate demands critical thinking. Society, like individuals, must have an effective method of making decisions. A free society is structured in such a way that many of its decisions are arrived at through debate. For example, law courts and legislative bodies are designed to utilize debate as their means of reaching decisions. In fact, any organization that conducts its business according to parliamentary procedures has selected debate as its method. Debate pervades our society at decision-making levels.

The ancient Greeks were among the first to recognize the importance of debate for both the individual and society. Plato, whose dialogues were an early form of cross-examination debate, defined *rhetoric* as "a universal art of winning the mind by arguments, which means not merely arguments in the courts of justice, and all other sorts of public councils, but in private conference as well."[8]

Aristotle listed four functions for rhetoric.[9] First, it prevents the triumph of fraud and injustice. Aristotle argued that truth and justice are by nature more powerful than their opposites, so when poor decisions are made, speakers with right on their side have only themselves to blame. Thus, it is not enough to know the right decision ourselves; we also must be able to argue for that decision before others.

Second, rhetoric is a method of instruction for the public. Aristotle pointed out that in some situations scientific arguments are useless; a speaker has to "educate" the audience by framing arguments with the help of common knowledge and commonly accepted opinions. Congressional debates on health care or tax policies are examples of this. The general public, and for that matter the majority of Congress, is unable to follow highly sophisticated technical arguments. Skilled partisans who have the expertise to understand the technical data must reformulate their reasons in ways that both Congress and the public can grasp.

Third, rhetoric makes us see both sides of a case. By arguing both sides, we become aware of all aspects of the case, and we will be prepared to refute our opponents' arguments.

Fourth, rhetoric is a means of defense. Often knowledge of argumentation and debate will be necessary to protect ourselves and our interests. As Aristotle stated: "If it is a disgrace to a man when he cannot defend himself in a bodily way, it would be odd not to think him disgraced when he cannot defend himself with reason. Reason is more distinctive of man than is bodily effort." Similarly, in the nineteenth century, John Stuart Mill placed great emphasis on the value of debate:

> If even the Newtonian philosophy were not permitted to be questioned, mankind could not feel as complete assurance of its truth as they now [in 1858] do. The beliefs which we have the most warrant for, have no safeguard to rest on, but a standing invitation to the whole world to prove them unfounded. If the challenge is not accepted, or is accepted and the attempt fails, we are far enough from certainty still; but we have done the best that the existing state of human reason admits of; we have neglected nothing that could give the truth the chance of reaching us; if the lists are kept open, we may hope that if there be a better truth, it will be found when the human mind is capable of receiving it; and in the meantime we may rely on having attained such approach to truth as is possible in our day. This is the amount of certainty attainable by a fallible being, and this is the sole way of attaining it.[10]

Half a century ago the U.S. Senate designated as Senate Immortals five senators who had shaped the history of the country by their ability as debaters: Henry Clay, Daniel Webster, John C. Calhoun, Robert M. La Follette, Sr., and

---

8. Plato, *Phaedrus*, 261. Translators Cooper and Jowett use slightly different terms in interpreting this passage. This statement draws from both translations.
9. See Aristotle, *Rhetoric*, I, 1.
10. John Stuart Mill, *On Liberty* (New York: Burt, n.d.), pp. 38–39.

Robert A. Taft. The triumvirate of Webster, Clay, and Calhoun especially towered over all the others and were the near-unanimous choices of senators and scholars alike. As John F. Kennedy, then a freshman senator, pointed out, "For over thirty years they dominated the Congress and the country, providing leadership and articulation on all the great issues of the growing nation."[11] For their part La Follette and Taft were selected as the outstanding representatives of, respectively, the progressive and the conservative movements in the twentieth century. In honoring these "immortals," the Senate recognized the importance of debate in determining the course of American history.

Our laws not only are made through the process of debate but are applied through debate as well. Today's trial attorneys cite the famous dictum of attorney Joseph N. Welch as a guide for contemporary legal practices:

> America believes in what lawyers call "the adversary system" in our courtrooms, including our criminal courts. It is our tradition that the District Attorney prosecutes hard. Against him is the lawyer hired by the defendant, or supplied by the court if the defendant is indigent. And the defendant's lawyer defends hard. We believe that truth is apt to emerge from this crucible. It usually does.[12]

Public debate has recently achieved its greatest visibility and popularity through the growth in popularity and frequency of political campaign debates. This is a relatively new phenomenon. The first presidential debates were held in 1960 between Richard Nixon and John F. Kennedy. The next presidential campaign debates were held in 1976 between Gerald Ford and Jimmy Carter, and although not required by law, every presidential campaign cycle since then has featured presidential and vice presidential debates. In 2007–08, there were 47 candidate debates during the primaries (26 for the Democrats, 21 for the Republicans) prior to the general election debates (3 presidential debates and a vice presidential debate). In 2011–12, 20 Republican primary debates had been held prior to the March Super Tuesday primaries. And campaign debates are also gaining popularity at other levels of elections from mayor to governor. These campaign debates introduce us to the candidates and their positions, inform the public about issues of concern and importance ultimately impacting policy, and serve a ritual function of campaign communication.

We need debate not only in the legislature, the courtroom, and on the campaign trail, but in every other area of society as well. Most of our rights are directly or indirectly dependent on debate. As the influential journalist Walter Lippmann pointed out, one of our most cherished rights—freedom of speech—can be maintained only by creating and encouraging debate:

> Yet when genuine debate is lacking, freedom of speech does not work as it is meant to work. It has lost the principle which regulates and justifies it—that is to say, dialectic conducted according to logic and the

---

11. John F. Kennedy, Senate speech, May 1, 1957, from a press release.
12. Joseph N. Welch, "Should a Lawyer Defend a Guilty Man?" *This Week* magazine, Dec. 6, 1959, p. 11. Copyright 1959 by the United Newspapers Magazine Corporation.

rules of evidence. If there is no effective debate, the unrestricted right to speak will unloose so many propagandists, procurers, and panderers upon the public that sooner or later in self-defense the people will turn to the censors to protect them. It will be curtailed for all manner of reasons and pretexts, and serve all kinds of good, foolish, or sinister ends.

For in the absence of debate unrestricted utterance leads to the degradation of opinion. By a kind of Gresham's law the more rational is overcome by the less rational, and the opinions that will prevail will be those which are held most ardently by those with the most passionate will. For that reason the freedom to speak can never be maintained by objecting to interference with the liberty of the press, of printing, of broadcasting, of the screen. It can be maintained only by promoting debate.[13]

We need debate both to maintain freedom of speech and to provide a methodology for investigation of and judgment about contemporary problems. As Chaim Perelman, the Belgian philosopher-rhetorician whose works in rhetoric and argumentation are influential in argumentation and debate, pointed out:

> If we assume it to be possible without recourse to violence to reach agreement on all the problems implied in the employment of the idea of justice we are granting the possibility of formulating an ideal of man and society, valid for all beings endowed with reason and accepted by what we have called elsewhere the universal audience.[14]
>
> I think that the only discursive methods available to us stem from techniques that are not demonstrative—that is, conclusive and *rational* in the narrow sense of the term—but from argumentative techniques which are not conclusive but which may tend to demonstrate the *reasonable* character of the conceptions put forward. It is this recourse to the rational and reasonable for the realization of the ideal of universal communion that characterizes the age-long endeavor of all philosophies in their aspiration for a city of man in which violence may progressively give way to wisdom.[15]

Here we have touched on the long-standing concern of philosophers and political leaders with debate as an instrument for dealing with society's problems. We can now understand why debate is pervasive. Individuals benefit from knowing the principles of argumentation and debate and from being able to apply these principles in making decisions and influencing the decisions of others. Society benefits if debate is encouraged, because free and open debate protects the rights of individuals and offers the larger society a way of reaching optimal decisions.

---

13. Walter Lippmann, *Essays in the Public Philosophy* (Boston: Little, Brown, 1955), pp. 129–130.
14. Chaim Perelman and L. Olbrechts–Tyteca, *Traité de l'argumentation, La nouvelle rhétorique* (Paris: Presses Universitaires de France, 1958), sec. 7.
15. Chaim Perelman, *The Idea of Justice and the Problem of Argument*, trans. John Petrie (New York: Humanities Press, 1963), pp. 86–87.

II. INDIVIDUAL DECISIONS

Whenever an individual controls the dimensions of a problem, he or she can solve the problem through a personal decision. For example, if the problem is whether to go to the basketball game tonight, if tickets are not too expensive and if transportation is available, the decision can be made individually. But if a friend's car is needed to get to the game, then that person's decision to furnish the transportation must be obtained.

Complex problems, too, are subject to individual decision making. American business offers many examples of small companies that grew into major corporations while still under the individual control of the founder. Some computer companies that began in the 1970s as one-person operations burgeoned into multimillion-dollar corporations with the original inventor still making all the major decisions. And some of the multibillion-dollar leveraged buyouts of the 1980s were put together by daring—some would say greedy—financiers who made the day-to-day and even hour-to-hour decisions individually.

When President George H. W. Bush launched Operation Desert Storm, when President Bill Clinton sent troops into Somalia and Haiti and authorized Operation Desert Fox, when President George W. Bush authorized Operation Enduring Freedom in Afghanistan and Operation Iraqi Freedom in Iraq, and when President Obama ordered the killing of Osama bin Laden in Operation Neptune Spear, they each used different methods of decision making, but in each case the ultimate decision was an individual one. In fact, many government decisions can be made only by the president. As Walter Lippmann pointed out, debate is the only satisfactory way the great issues can be decided:

> A president, whoever he is, has to find a way of understanding the novel and changing issues which he must, under the Constitution, decide. Broadly speaking … the president has two ways of making up his mind. The one is to turn to his subordinates—to his chiefs of staff and his cabinet officers and undersecretaries and the like—and to direct them to argue out the issues and to bring him an agreed decision….
>
> The other way is to sit like a judge at a hearing where the issues to be decided are debated. After he has heard the debate, after he has examined the evidence, after he has heard the debaters cross-examine one another, after he has questioned them himself, he makes his decision….
>
> It is a much harder method in that it subjects the president to the stress of feeling the full impact of conflicting views, and then to the strain of making his decision, fully aware of how momentous it is. But there is no other satisfactory way by which momentous and complex issues can be decided.[16]

John F. Kennedy used Cabinet sessions and National Security Council meetings to provide debate to illuminate diverse points of view, expose errors, and

---

16. Walter Lippmann, "How to Make Decisions," *New York Herald Tribune*, Mar. 3, 1960.

Standard Agenda for Group Decision Making

- ■   Define and analyze the problem
- ■   Research the problem
- ■   Establish criteria
- ■   Generate solutions
- ■   Select best solution
- ■   Implement and monitor solution

---

challenge assumptions before he reached decisions.[17] As he gained experience in office, he placed greater emphasis on debate. One historian points out: "One reason for the difference between the Bay of Pigs and the missile crisis was that [the Bay of Pigs] fiasco instructed Kennedy in the importance of uninhibited debate in advance of major decision."[18] All presidents, to varying degrees, encourage debate among their advisors.

We may never be called on to render the final decision on great issues of national policy, but we are constantly concerned with decisions important to ourselves for which debate can be applied in similar ways. That is, this debate may take place in our minds as we weigh the pros and cons of the problem, or we may arrange for others to debate the problem for us. Because we all are increasingly involved in the decisions of the campus, community, and society in general, it is in our intelligent self-interest to reach these decisions through reasoned debate.

When we make an individual decision, we can put it into effect if we control the necessary conditions. If we need the consent or cooperation of others to carry out our decision, we have to find a way of obtaining the appropriate response from them by debate—or by group discussion, persuasion, propaganda, coercion, or a combination of methods.

III. GROUP DISCUSSION

Decisions may be reached by group discussion when the members of the group (1) agree that a problem exists, (2) have compatible standards or values, (3) have compatible purposes, (4) are willing to accept the consensus of the group, and (5) are relatively few in number. When these conditions are met and when all relevant evidence and arguments are carefully weighed, group discussion is a reasoned means of decision making.

---

17. See Theodore C. Sorensen, *Decision-Making in the White House* (New York: Columbia University Press, 1963), p. 59.
18. Arthur M. Schlesinger, Jr., *Imperial Presidency* (Boston: Houghton Mifflin, 1973), p. 215.

In February 1999, after the bitter and divisive House impeachment proceedings and subsequent Senate trial, President Bill Clinton was acquitted on two articles of impeachment. The vote on impeachment in the House occurred on straight party lines. Although there were some Republican defectors in the Senate vote, partisan tensions were heightened by the trial, as were tensions between the legislative and executive branches of the government. Despite the clash of personalities and the difficulties inherent in such partisan and interbranch differences, House and Senate leaders and President Clinton pledged to work together for the good of the country, and were able to implement a number of positive legislative changes. Indeed a strength of American politics is that skilled leaders in both parties traditionally have been able to override political differences and enact at least some important legislation on which both parties could agree. This cooperation has come under attack in the current climate of fragmentation and division. An example of a failure of group decision making in our government is The Joint Select Committee on Deficit Reductions of the U.S. Congress, created by the Budget Control Act of 2011 on August 2, 2011. This group, referred to as the Supercommittee, was a joint committee of the U.S. Congress assigned with generating a recommendation to address the debt-ceiling crisis of summer 2011. Its recommendation would come to a vote of the Congress without the usual process of amendments. This extraordinary structure was an attempt to bypass the partisan gridlock which had prevented resolution of the debt issue. On November 21, the committee issued the following statement, "After months of hard work and intense deliberations, we have come to the conclusion today that it will not be possible to make any bipartisan agreement available to the public before the committee's deadline."[19]

When a group has more than 15 or 20 members, productive discussion becomes difficult if not impossible. A group of senators can discuss a problem in committee, but not on the floor of the Senate. The Senate is too large for discussion; there debate must be used. Of course, informal debate may take place within the discussion process, and discussion may be a precursor of debate.[20] If the differences cannot be solved by discussion, debate is the logical alternative. Or if the group, such as a Senate subcommittee, reaches a decision by discussion, it may be necessary to debate it on the floor to carry the Senate as a whole.

Group decision making is best guided by a systematic procedure for problem solving. The first step requires that group members define and analyze the problem they are to address. They should determine the nature of the problem and its impacts, distinguishing causes from symptoms and measuring the relative importance of each. An important outcome of this step is an agreed-upon statement of the problem. Second, they should research the problem, gathering and

---

19. Statement from Co-Chairs of the Joint Select Committee on Deficit Reduction, Nov. 21 2011, http://www.cfr.org/united-states/statement-co-chairs-joint-select-committee-deficit-reduction-supercommittee-november-2011/p26570.
20. See James H. McBurney, James M. O'Neill, and Glen E. Mills, *Argumentation and Debate* (New York: Macmillan, 1951), p. 67.

evaluating available information relevant to the problem as defined. The third step is perhaps the most important, and most often overlooked: establishing and prioritizing the criteria that will distinguish a successful solution. These criteria may be given numerical value. Its goal is to identify the measures or standards by which competing solutions may be measured, including prioritizing those standards in order of importance. Fourth, the group members should generate a list of possible solutions through a process of brainstorming; and fifth, they should apply the criteria to the established list to select the best solution. Finally, the sixth step is to implement and monitor the solution, leading to reevaluation and in many situations, a return to step one.

Like an individual, a group may act on its decision only insofar as it has the power to do so. If it needs the consent or cooperation of others to carry out a particular plan, the group must use other means to secure their cooperation.

IV. PERSUASION

Purposeful **persuasion** is defined as *communication intended to influence the acts, beliefs, attitudes, and values of others.* Clearly, one method of persuasion is debate. Persuasion is not, however, limited to seeking carefully reasoned judgments, as is debate, nor does persuasion require logical arguments both for and against a given proposition. The "Marlboro Man" advertising campaign, for example, which persuaded customers to purchase Marlboro cigarettes by image advertising, associating the image of a handsome, rugged, and healthy cowboy with their product must have been judged as highly effective persuasion by the company that ran it for many years, but it did not seek the kind of carefully thought-out judgment that one associates with debate. A 2012 ad by Direct TV promoted their product through a TV ad featuring a humorous but fallacious slippery slope argument:

- when your cable company keeps you on hold, you get angry,
- when you get angry, you go blow off steam,
- when you go blow off steam, accidents happen,
- when accidents happen, you get an eyepatch,
- when you get an eyepatch, people think you're tough,
- when people think you're tough, people wanna see how tough,
- and when people wanna see how tough, you wake up in a roadside ditch,
- don't wake up in a roadside ditch, get rid of cable and upgrade to direct TV.

Frequently the persuader hopes to dominate the stage and avoid situations in which another side of the argument might be presented. Consider the cigarette companies, which accepted the ban on TV advertising without the prolonged court battle that many expected. The reason for this may have been that the TV stations were required to give equal time to public service announcements about the hazards of smoking. The tobacco companies apparently found it preferable to direct their advertising dollars to media that did not have an equal-time requirement. President Hugo Chavez of Venezuela recently made international headlines and prompted national protests when he failed to renew the license of Radio Caracas Television (RCTV), a popular television network, likely because it had been critical of him, thus effectively eliminating local opposition to his government.[21]

It is not unusual in the United States for political candidates to agree to interviews only with media individuals with whom they share ideology or position, or with networks or programs sympathetic to their political affiliation and approach. FOX News is more likely to air interviews with conservative Republicans and MSNBC is more likely to be accessible to progressive Democrats.

Persuaders select the type of persuasive appeals they believe to be best adapted to their audience. These may include such diverse communications as a picket line, a silent prayer vigil, a clever negative political commercial on TV, or the stately formality of a debate before the Supreme Court. (Audience analysis is considered in Chapter 16.) In 2011, a group of individuals successfully persuaded many through their mere presence in Zuccotti Park, located in New York City's Wall Street financial district. The protests, termed Occupy Wall Street, were against social and economic inequality, greed, corruption, and the undue influence of corporations on government—particularly from the financial services sector; of course, centered symbolically and geographically at Wall Street.

Aristotle thought of rhetoric as the study of persuasion as it is shaped to impact a particular audience under a unique set of characteristics (the given case). He identified arguments as the means of persuasion available to the rhetor and observed that any argument is given power through the modes of persuasion: ethos, pathos, and logos. Ethos is the proof that is in the speaker, or put another way, the judgment that the audience makes of the speaker. Audience members judge the speaker based on three characteristics. The first of these characteristics of ethos is character. The audience measures the character of the speaker based on their perception of her ethical behavior. Of course, in order to determine the ethical nature of a speaker's actions, the audience must have a point of reference. The speaker's ethics are measured by a set of values, and the audience is likely to favorably receive values that they perceive to be like theirs. So character is essentially a measure of identification; does the speaker represent himself as similar to the audience in life experience and values. The second characteristic of ethos is sagacity, or wisdom. In contemporary usage, this would include consideration of the speakers' expertise and competence specific to the material of the argument. The third characteristic of ethos is goodwill, or the trustworthiness and dynamism of the speaker. The second mode of proof impacting the persuasive impact of an argument is pathos, or emotional proof. This is the audience's judgment of the personal impact of the argument on them as listeners. Aristotle described emotion as an internal condition attended

21. Christopher Toothaker, "Chavez Warns Foreign Critics," *The Miami Herald*, July 23, 2007, p. 8A.

Modes of Persuasion

- Ethos
  1. character
  2. sagacity
  3. goodwill
- Pathos
- Logos

---

to by pain or pleasure. Pathos is employed when persuasive appeals create felt responses by the listener, as a tragic story creates sadness, motivating a greater acceptance of the argument. Finally, arguments are persuasive if they employ logos, or logical proof. Logos is the judgment the audience makes of the argument itself, but it is not a measure of certainty or falsity of an argument, but rather of relative strength or weakness of the persuasion. In other words, rhetorical arguments are not measured as either true or false, as in formal logic or mathematical reasoning, but as probable or not, using a measure of contingency.

Persuaders reach a decision on the problem before they begin the process of persuasion, beginning with the position they wish their audience to hold. Recall that debate is thought of as "inquiry and advocacy," including a component of questioning. Persuaders continue the process of persuasion until they solve the problem by persuading others to accept their decision or until they are convinced that further efforts are pointless. In trying to influence others, they may find it necessary or advantageous (1) to join with other persuaders and become propagandists or (2) to face the opposition and become debaters. Thus they must be familiar with the principles of argumentation and debate. This knowledge is also a defense against the persuasion of others. If we subject their appeals to critical analysis, we increase our likelihood of making reasoned decisions. And if persuaders advocate a decision we believe to be unsound, we may find it necessary to become debaters and advocate the conclusion we favor.

Unintended persuasion occurs when we receive a message not intended for us—for example, we overhear a private conversation in an elevator and are influenced by it—or when we unknowingly communicate to and influence others in an unintended way.

V. PROPAGANDA

Propaganda is the use of persuasion by a group (often a closely knit organization) in a sustained, organized campaign using multiple media for the purpose of influencing a mass audience. Historically propaganda has been associated with religious, social, or political movements. Today the term has been expanded to include commercial advertising campaigns. The term first came into common use in 1622 when Pope Gregory XV established the Sacred Congregation for Propagating the Faith. What, in the view of the faithful, could be more commendable than spreading the faith? In 1933, when Hitler appointed Dr. Joseph Goebbels as his minister of propaganda, the word took on a different connotation. From the standpoint of non-Nazis, what could be more evil than spreading Nazism? Even today *propaganda* often is perceived as a pejorative term. Imagine an official of a women's group saying:

> We've been conducting an extensive educational campaign to inform
> the public of the necessity of making abortion on demand available to
> women on welfare. It was going very well until the churches unleashed
> a bunch of propagandists to work against us.

Thus, in everyday language, *we* educate or give information, while *they* propagandize. Another example is President Chavez of Venezuela. He spoke to the United Nations in 2007, referring to President George Bush as "the devil." Later Chavez threatened to deport international visitors from Venezuela who were critical of him and his government.

Of course, the end does not justify the means. Propaganda, like persuasion, may be viewed as good or bad only to the degree that it is based on true evidence and valid reasoning. Examples of questionable methods may be found in the Allied propaganda in the United States prior to America's entry into World War I. At that time extensive use was made of distorted or false atrocity stories. Other examples may be found in communist propaganda from the former Soviet Union, which made extensive use of the technique of the "big lie." During Middle East crises both Israel and the Arab countries have conducted propaganda campaigns in the United States designed to sway public opinion in their favor. Each side obviously thinks of theirs as good and the others' as bad.

Examples of propaganda used for good purposes include the various campaigns designed to get the public to drive safely, to recognize the symptoms of cancer, and to practice safe sex; these examples are usually based on sound evidence and reasonable inference. Other examples include campaigns by churches to persuade people to act in accordance with the Ten Commandments and by charitable groups to raise funds for the homeless or for people with AIDS. Propagandists reach a decision on a problem before they begin the process of propaganda. They continue their campaign until they solve the problem by persuading others to accept their decision or are convinced that further efforts are pointless. In their efforts to influence others, propagandists may find it necessary or advantageous to confront their opponents and become debaters. In such cases they need knowledge of argumentation and debate. If their evidence is accurate, their reasoning valid, and their appeals chosen carefully, the campaign will have the greatest opportunity for success. If any of the conditions is lacking, however, the chances for success are diminished.

Similarly, knowledge of argumentation and debate is an important defense against the propaganda campaigns we constantly confront. Unless we subject propaganda to critical analysis, we will be unable to distinguish the good from the bad. We will lose our ability to make reasonable decisions and may fall prey to "hidden persuaders."

VI. COERCION

Coercion is defined as the threat or use of force intended to limit the viable choices of action available to the person threatened. Parents employ coercion when they take a box of matches from a baby or punish a child for failure to complete a homework assignment; society employs coercion when it confines criminals to prison or fines violators for driving infractions; the nation employs coercion when it goes to war. A democratic society places many restrictions on the exercise of coercion. Parents may not physically or mentally abuse their children; criminals may be sentenced to prison only after they have an opportunity to defend themselves in court; the United States may declare war only after the advocates of war win consent in Congress. President Bush found it prudent to obtain congressional approval for the use of force in Operation Enduring Freedom in Afghanistan and Operation Iraqi Freedom, and President Obama sought and achieved international cooperation before supporting the opposition in Libya. In a democratic society, coercion as a method of solving problems—by private individuals or the state—is generally prohibited except in special cases in which it has been found necessary after debate. A totalitarian society, by contrast, is characterized by sharply limited debate and by almost omnipresent coercion.[22]

Coercion may be employed to influence a decision. The coercive powers of the state represent a strong logical appeal against a decision to commit a crime, and for some individuals it may be the only effective appeal. In arguing in favor of policy propositions, affirmative debaters often provide for coercion in the plan of action they advocate. They may include an "enforcement plank" providing for fines, imprisonment, or some other penalty for those who do not obey or who try to circumvent the requirements of the plan. Alternatively, they may advocate enforcement of the plan through existing legal structures.

A decision to employ coercion is likely to be socially acceptable and effective when that decision is made after full and fair debate. Baron Karl von Clausewitz's classic definition of war as the "continuation of diplomacy by other means" suggests that war—the ultimate form of coercion—is a method of problem solving to be selected after a careful debate on the possible risks and benefits.

Methods of Decision Making

- Debate
- Individual Decision
- Group Decision
- Propaganda
- Coercion
- Combination of Methods

---

22. See Aleksandr I. Solzhenitsyn, *The Gulag Archipelago* (New York: Harper & Row, 1974).

VII. COMBINATION OF METHODS

It is often necessary to use a combination of methods in making a decision. The social context will determine the most suitable methods in a particular case.

The solution to a problem requiring the consent or cooperation of others may extend over a considerable period of time and may warrant use of all the methods of decision making. For example, through *individual decision* a person might determine that nonrefundable beverage containers cause unacceptable litter and should be prohibited.

Because that person is powerless to implement such a decision alone, he or she must use *persuasion* to influence friends to join in the effort. They may use the process of *group discussion* to decide how to proceed toward their objective. They might find it necessary to organize a group for raising funds and to work together for a period of months or years conducting a *propaganda* campaign directed toward the voters of the state. During this campaign many individuals might play a role in *persuading* or *debating*. Eventually a bill might be introduced into the state legislature.

After *discussion* in committee hearings and a number of *debates* on the floor of the legislature, a final *debate* determines the disposition of the bill. If the bill is enacted into law, *coercion* will be provided to ensure compliance. The validity of the law probably will be tested by *debates* in the courts to determine its constitutionality. When the law is violated, *coercion can* be applied only as the result of *debates* in the courts.

VIII. ETHICAL DECISION MAKING

Effective arguers, persuaders, and debaters have much power in their ability to influence others and to impact important decision making. It is therefore important that they enter the rhetorical sphere with ethical constructs. Quintilian, the great Roman Orator, wrote:

> Since an orator, then, is a good man, and a good man cannot be conceived to exist without virtuous inclinations, and virtue, though it receives certain impulses from nature, requires notwithstanding to be brought to maturity by instruction, the orator must above all things study morality, and must obtain a thorough knowledge of all that is just and honorable, without which no one can either be a good man or an able speaker." [23]

Why is this so? The implications of unethical conduct in speaking are far ranging.

The consequences of a failure to consider ethical constructs when making decisions range from business failures and harm to others (ENRON, the

---

23. Quintilian, Institutes of Oratory, Book 12, Chapter 2, in Bizzell, Patricia, and Bruce Herzberg, *The Rhetorical Tradition: Readings from Classical Times to the Present*, 2nd ed. (Boston: Bedford/St. Martin's, 2001), p. 418.

Great Recession of 2008, invasion of Iraq) to incarceration (Scooter Libby, Jack Abramoff, Tom DeLay, Duke Cunningham, William Jefferson), to the destruction of personal relationships and careers. **Ethics** are a set of constructs that guide our decision making by providing standards of behavior telling us how we ought to act. While ethics may be based on or reflected in laws, they are not the same as laws. Similarly, we learn value systems and thus standards for ethical behavior from our communities and cultures, but that a behavior is a cultural standard or norm does not make it ethical.

According to Thomas White, there are two broad philosophical approaches to understanding ethical choices: **teleological** and **deontological**. The teleological approach is results oriented and would focus on the good or bad consequences of an action or a decision. The deontological ethic is process- or act-oriented and is based on the notion that actions have moral value.[24] Scholars at the Markkula Center for Applied Ethics at Santa Clara University have suggested that in making ethical decisions one ought to follow a framework through the following steps:

- Recognize an ethical issue
- Get the facts
- Evaluate alternative actions from various ethical perspectives
- Make a decision and test it
- Act, then reflect on the decision later[25]

Debate offers the ideal tool for examining the ethical implications of any decision, and critical thinking should also be ethical thinking.

How do we reach a decision on any matters of importance? We are under constant pressure to make unreasoned decisions, and we often make decisions carelessly. But which method is most likely to lead to wise decisions? To make wise judgments, we should rely on critical thinking. In many situations, argumentation's emphasis on reasoned considerations and debate's confrontation of opposing sides give us our best, and perhaps only, opportunity to reach reasoned conclusions. In any case it is in the public interest to promote debate, and it is in our own intelligent self-interest to know the principles of argumentation and to be able to apply critical thinking in debate.

---

24. Thomas White, "Philosophical Ethics," http://www.ethicsandbusiness.org/pdf/ strategy.pdf. Adapted from Thomas White, "Ethics," in *Business Ethics: A Philosophical Reader* (New York: Macmillan, 1993).

25. Manuel Velasquez, Dennis Moberg, Michael J. Meyer, Thomas Shanks, Margaret R. McLean, David DeCosse, Claire André, and Kirk O. Hanson, "A Framework for Thinking Ethically," Markkula Center for Applied Ethics, http://www.scu.edu/ethics/ practicing/decision/framework.html (downloaded July 20, 2007). This article appeared originally in *Issues in Ethics*, vol. 1, no. 2 (Winter 1988).

EXERCISES

1. *Individual decisions.* For one week, keep a journal of decisions you make. Separate them into trivial, somewhat important and very important decisions. How did you make your decisions? Upon what did you base your decisions? Can you identify a pattern based on level of importance?

2. *SPAR debates* (SPontaneous ARgumentation). This is a classic introductory debate exercise.

   Format

Affirmative (Pro side) opening speech	90 seconds
Cross-Examination by Negative (Con side)	60 seconds
Negative opening speech	90 seconds
Cross-Examination by Affirmative	60 seconds
Affirmative closing speech	45 seconds
Negative closing speech	45 seconds

   Procedure
   Debaters step to the front of the room in pairs. One debater calls a coin flip. The winner may either choose the topic (from a list posted on the board) or the side they will defend. After two minutes of preparation time the debate begins. Each debater has a total one minute additional preparation time to be used during the debate. There should always be an on-deck pair of debaters preparing their arguments.

   Possible topics
   Honesty is always the best policy.
   Slavery still exists today.
   True love really does exist.
   Violence is a necessary means to settle disputes.
   Police are necessary for safety.
   People should not eat meat.
   The drinking age should be lowered to 18.
   Smoking should be banned in all public places.
   There is no such thing as Homeland Security.
   Marijuana should be legalized.

3. *Group discussion.* Students should form groups of five to seven and using the standard agenda for group problem solving, complete the following exercise.

   As the most outstanding and well-respected students in your Ethics in Communication course, your professor has asked you to formulate a recommendation to her concerning a problem in the class.

   It has come to the attention of Professor Young that one of the students in the class plagiarized on an assigned paper. Sue M. Moral turned in a paper, more than half of which was actually written by her good friend Ben There. Ben had written the original paper for the same course two years ago, and suggested to Sue that she use his paper for her assignment. Since Professor Old had taught the course (since retired) when Ben took the course, Professor Young would be unlikely to recognize the work. Ben did not know that Professor Old had been so impressed with his paper that he had given it to Professor Young as a sample paper for her to keep on file. Professor Young also found out that Sue's roommate, Bye Stander, also a student in Ethics in Communication, knew about Sue's plagiarism, but did not inform Professor Young. In fact, Bye had agreed to photocopy Ben's paper for Sue, since she was making a trip to Kinko's for other reasons. The assignment counts 10 percent of the course grade. Sue has a "B" average on all other work in the class. Bye has an "A" average. Ben is still a major in the department. His "A" on the paper barely enabled him an "A" in Ethics in Communication. He hopes to graduate next semester with a "C" average.

What, if any, action do you recommend Professor Young take?

4. *Persuasion.* Prepare a two-minute impromptu speech in support of your claim that "People should do _____" or "People should NOT do _____." Offer three reasons in support of your claim.

5. *Ethics.* Identify an ethical dilemma for decision making. Follow the framework suggested in the chapter to make a decision resolving the dilemma. Identify your ethical approach as teleological or deontological. Use one of these scenarios:

-   In researching your debate topic, you find a published study that seems to provide excellent support for your case. You are so excited about the study, that you e-mail the author at his university. When he does not reply, you call the university and speak to a secretary who tells you that the author has been dismissed from the university because it was found that he was falsifying data in his research.

-   Do you reference the study anyway? Why or why not?

-   Your debate partner falsifies evidence and reads it in a debate. What do you do?

-   A boat is sinking and the lifeboat only can seat 20 people, but there are 22 passengers, yourself included. Who gets on the lifeboat and how do you choose? Who should be sacrificed? Should the Captain always go down with the ship? Some additional information:

    1. The water is very cold so it is not an option for someone to be submersed at all and survive.

    2. A person would need to be out of the water and drying off without being re-submerged to survive.

    3. One cannot swim to shore, they would die before they made it halfway.

    These free internet sources provide additional scenarios:

-   http://www.differencemakers.com/swapshop/pdf/dilemma_examples.pdf.

-   http://www.ehow.com/info_8240434_10-ethical-dilemmas.html.

-   http://escalate.ac.uk/resources/careerskills/90.

2

....

Foundations of Debate

On Charles' first day of class in argumentation and debate, his professor asked him why he had chosen the course. Charles responded that "I always argue with my parents and friends. In fact, I often call my favorite radio sports-talk show to argue with the host. My mother is an attorney, and she sometimes practices her openings and summations for me. And I practically live online, defending myself on the Listserv I belong to and my favorite blogs, and networking with my friends on Facebook and other sites. So I know all about argumentation and debate, and I'm good at it!" Charles correctly recognized that the principles of debate are important across many different fields of practical arguing. But he was not yet aware of the richness and diversity of debate practice.

Chapter 1 explored argumentation as a necessary and valuable vehicle for making informed and thoughtful decisions. Critical thinking is both a positive consequence of reasoned argument and a tool necessary for effective argumentation. Debate is the application of argumentation. It occurs in various contexts and for a variety of reasons. These contexts are shaped by a number of variables including the arguer's reasons for participating in engaged discussion, the nature and motivation of the audience to the debate, the subject of the debate, and the nature of the decision called for. All these variables define the nature of debate. The expectations and demands of a particular debate or type of debate will thus be shaped by the fields or spheres within which the debate takes place.

For the purpose of this discussion, we suggest that debate can be classified into two broad categories: applied and academic. **Applied debate** is conducted on propositions, questions, and topics in which the advocates have a special interest, and the debate is presented before a judge or an audience with the power to render a binding decision on the proposition or respond to the question or topic in a real way. **Academic debate** is conducted on propositions in which the advocates have an academic interest, and the debate typically is presented before a teacher, judge, or audience without direct power to render a decision on the proposition.

Miniglossary

Academic debate   Debate conducted under the direction of an educational institution for the purpose of providing educational opportunities for its students.

Applied debate   Debate presented before a judge or audience with the power to render a binding decision on the proposition or to respond to the question or topic in a real way.

CEDA   Cross Examination Debate Association.

Ethical   Being in accordance with the accepted principles of right and wrong that govern the conduct of a profession or community.

Forensics   An educational activity primarily concerned with using an argumentative perspective in examining problems and communicating with people.

Judicial debate   Debate conducted in the courts or before quasi-judicial bodies.

Mock trial debate   A form of academic debate that emulates trial court debating.

Moot court debate   An academic form of judicial debate used by law schools to prepare students for courtroom debate.

NDT   National Debate Tournament.

Nonformal debate   Debate that occurs in various contexts without formal or prearranged procedural rules.

Applied Parliamentary debate   Debate conducted under the rules of parliamentary procedure (see Chapter 19).

Academic Parliamentary debate   A form of competitive academic debate practiced under the auspices of organizations including the National Parliamentary Debate Association and the American Parliamentary Debate Association.

Special debate   Debate conducted under special rules drafted for a specific occasion—for example, presidential campaign debates.

Of course the audience in an academic debate does form opinions about the subject matter of the debate, and that personal transformation may ultimately lead to meaningful action. However, the direct impact of the audience decision in an academic debate is personal, and the decision made by the judge is limited to identification of the winner of the debate. In fact, in academic debate the judge may be advised to disregard her feelings regarding the merits of the proposition and to render her win or loss decision only on the merits of the support and clash as presented by the competing arguers in the debate itself. The most important identifying characteristic of an academic debate is that the purpose of the debate is to provide educational opportunities for the participants.

I. APPLIED DEBATE

Applied debate occurs within structures and organizations wherein decisions may be binding and will have impact in pragmatic ways, which range from imprisonment and even capital punishment in criminal trials to temporary shifts of opinion of radio talk shows listeners. These sorts of debate vary in their level of formality and even importance, but are marked by the motivations of the participants and the conventions and rules governing them. Applied debate may be classified as special debate, judicial debate, parliamentary debate, or nonformal debate. After discussing each of these classifications of debate briefly, we will consider academic debate in more detail.

A. Special Debate

Special debate is conducted under special rules drafted for a specific occasion, such as political campaign debates. Examples include the Lincoln–Douglas debates of 1858, the Kennedy–Nixon debates of 1960, the Bush–Clinton– Perot debates of 1992, the Bush–Gore debates of 2000, Bush–Kerry in 2004, McCain–Obama in 2008, and the series of debates involving the candidates for the Democratic and Republican Partys' nominations during the 2008 and 2012 presidential primary campaigns. These were formal debates, yet they were neither judicial nor parliamentary; they were conducted under special rules agreed on by the debaters. In an article published in the *Seattle Times*, Paul Farhi and Mike Allen described the process that led to the special rules for the Bush–Kerry debates in 2004:

> After weeks of private and reportedly heated negotiations, representatives of President Bush and Sen. John Kerry agreed earlier this week to three televised debates, with another for Vice President Cheney and Sen. John Edwards. The first presidential debate takes place Thursday at the University of Miami.
>
> And now, with the release of a 32-page "memorandum of understanding," we understand why it took so long. The document is crammed with sections and subsections spelling out almost every imaginable rule of engagement and detail about how the debates will look. Or will be prohibited from looking.
>
> In its precision and seeming fussiness, in its attempt at control, it often reads like an agreement between a concert promoter and a particularly demanding pop diva....

While the most important part of such agreements certainly has to do with the details governing the format and nature of questions or topics addressed, all details are considered. The authors continued,

> The agreement, for example, spells out the exact dimensions of the lectern to be used (50 inches high on the side facing the audience, 48 inches on the side facing the candidates) in the first and third debates, and how far apart those lecterns will be (10 feet, as measured from "the left-right center" of one "to the left-right center of the other"). It specifies the type of stools (identical, of equal height, with backs and footrests) that Bush and Kerry will sit on for the second, town-hall-style debate, as well as the arrangement (in a horseshoe) and nature of the audience. It specifies that it will consist of an equal number of "likely

voters who are 'soft' Bush supporters or 'soft' Kerry supporters," soft being a polling term for people who might be willing to change their minds. There are details about the type of warning lights to be used if a candidate runs over his allotted time, about the moderators' conduct, about the coin flip that will be used to determine who goes first (the type of coin or number of flips isn't specified). There's even a codicil that might be called "the perspiration clause," since it alludes to every candidate's worst fear: an outbreak of Nixon-style flop sweat. The clause commits the nonpartisan producer, the Commission on Presidential Debates, to use its "best efforts to maintain an appropriate temperature according to industry standards for the entire debate," although it's unclear what "industry standard" temperature is, or even what industry the agreement is referring to.[1]

Debates between presidential candidates are now well established in the American political scene, and similar debates are often held between candidates in elections at all levels, from student government president to mayor to vice president. While the formats of these debates may leave much to be desired, they at least bring the candidates together and give voters a better opportunity to compare the candidates than they would otherwise have. Although this type of debate is most often associated with political figures and campaign issues, it may be used by anyone on any proposition or set of questions or topics. Opposing advocates merely have to agree to come together under the provisions of a special set of rules drafted for the occasion. Other examples of special applied debates may occur in panel discussions held at academic conferences and on college campuses, and in government hearings about social issues of public concern. They are marked by a set of rules and format uniquely designed for a particular debate, usually as negotiated or coordinated by the participants or parties acting on their behalf. And special debates will usually be presented to a general audience of voluntary listeners. In the case of governmental hearings, parliamentary debates and binding votes may follow; however, the special debates are meant to be informative and precede parliamentary debate.

B. Judicial Debate

Judicial debate is conducted in the courts or before quasi-judicial bodies. Governed by the rules of a court of law, its purpose is the prosecution or defense of individuals charged with violation of the law or the determination of issues of law alleged to be applicable to specific cases before the court. Court TV and other television and even Internet access make courtroom argument easily accessible to interested spectators.

Judicial debate may be observed in any court from the Supreme Court of the United States to a local court. In its academic form, judicial debate is

---

1. Paul Farhi and Mike Allen, "Rules of Engagement: Presidential Debate Details" *The Seattle Times*, Sept. 28, 2004; page updated 02:22 P.M., http://seattletimes.nwsource.com/html/politics/2002048299_webdebaterules28.html.

known as **moot court debate** and is used by law schools to prepare students for courtroom debate. The impeachment trial of President Clinton during the winter of 1999 is a rare example of judicial debate held before the U.S. Congress under special rules establishing the Senate as a jury and presided over by the chief justice of the Supreme Court.

The principles of argumentation and debate apply to judicial debate. Because judicial debate is also concerned with sometimes highly technical rules of procedure—which may vary from federal to state courts, from one state to another, and from one type of court to another within a given state—the specific methods of judicial debate are not considered here. **Mock trial debate**, which emulates the form of trial court debating but without the emphasis on rules of procedure and admissibility, is considered in Chapter 17. Of course, moot court and mock trial debates are academic and not applied, as their judges do not render binding decisions on formal cases; however, they are designed as role-playing exercises employing the rules and conventions of real judicial debate.

C. Applied Parliamentary Debate

Applied Parliamentary debate is conducted under the rules of parliamentary procedure. Its purpose is the passage, amendment, or defeat of motions and resolutions that come before a parliamentary assembly. The practice of parliamentary debate may be observed in the Senate or House of Representatives, state legislatures, city councils, and town governing bodies, and at the business meetings of various organizations, such as the national convention of a major political party or a meeting of a local fraternity chapter. C-SPAN allows television viewers access to parliamentary debate in Congress, and local public television stations and radio stations may offer city or county government and school board meetings for public consumption.

In its educational or *academic* form parliamentary debate may be known as a model congress, a model state legislature, a model U.N. assembly, or a mock political convention. Intercollegiate debaters also compete in parliamentary debate tournaments, adapting the rules of procedure to the tournament context, with two-person teams competing. Of course, these simulations are not *applied debate*, although they are modeled after applied parliamentary debate just as moot court and mock trial are modeled after applied judicial debate.

The principles of argumentation and debate apply to parliamentary debate. The special provisions of parliamentary procedure that also apply to this type of debate are discussed in Chapter 19.

D. Nonformal Debate

Nonformal debate is conducted without the formal rules found in special, judicial, parliamentary, and academic debate. This is the type of debate to which newspapers and television commentators typically are referring when they speak of the "abortion debate," the "immigration debate," and other controversies that arouse public interest. The term *nonformal* has no reference to the formality or informality of the occasion on which the debate takes place. A president's state-of-the-union address—a highly formal speech—may be a part of a nonformal debate. A rap session in a college dormitory or a Twitter exchange—very informal situations—may also be part of nonformal debates.

Examples of nonformal debate can be found in national political campaigns, in community hearings or town hall meetings about water pollution or new school bond issues, in business meetings about corporate policy, in college conferences on matters of educational policy or the allocation of funds, and in election campaigns for student body officers. Nonformal debates occur in scientific and research realms, as in the debate over the ethics and implications of stem cell research. Internet chat, blogs, talk radio and television provide forums for nonformal debate over issues ranging from lifestyle choice to sports, and many individuals participate in nonformal debate through Internet lists, networks, and chatrooms, including YouTube, Facebook, MySpace, and countless blogs and communities. At the family level, nonformal debates may revolve around issues including the choice of a college or whether grown children should move back into the family home.

II. ACADEMIC DEBATE

As noted previously, academic debate is conducted under the direction of an educational institution to provide educational opportunities for students. Many schools and colleges conduct programs of academic debate. The issue here is not whether we will participate in debate—our participation is inevitable, because, sooner or later, most educated people will take part in some form of debate. The issue is whether our participation will be effective. Academic debate can teach us to become effective in this essential art.

A. The Background of Academic Debate

A history of academic debate would fill many volumes, but a few salient facts should be mentioned here. The origins of debate are lost in the remote reaches of history, but we know that people were debating at least 4,000 years ago. For example, Egyptian princes debated agricultural policy at the pharaoh's court (2080 B.C.). Chinese scholars conducted important philosophical debates during the Chou Dynasty (1122–255 B.C.). Homer's epic poems, the *Iliad* and the *Odyssey* (900 B.C.), contain speeches—which the Roman rhetorician Quintilian cited as examples of the arts of legal pleading and deliberation—that may be regarded as embryonic debates. Aristotle's *Rhetoric* (384–322 B.C.) laid the foundation of argumentation and debate and is influential even today.

Although debate exists all over the world, it thrives in the context of democratic Western civilization. Former Secretary of State Henry Kissinger noted that American foreign policy that encourages the spread of democracy faces daunting problems in some cultures, such as Confucianism:

> Unlike democratic theory, which views truth as emerging from the
> clash of ideas, Confucianism maintains that truth is objective and can
> only be discerned by assiduous study and education of which only a rare

few are thought to be capable. Its quest for truth does not treat conflicting ideas as having equal merit, the way democratic theory does.
Since there is only one truth, that which is not true can have no standing or be enhanced through competition. Confucianism is essentially
hierarchical and elitist, emphasizing loyalty to family, institutions, and
authority. None of the societies it has influenced has yet produced a
functioning pluralistic system (with Taiwan in the 1990s coming the
closest).[2]

Of course, Confucianism is not the only culture to put stringent limits on
debate. As we saw earlier, Muslim fundamentalists in Bangladesh favor executing
anyone who debates the Koran.

Academic debate began at least 2,400 years ago when the scholar Protagoras
of Abdera (481–411 B.C.), known as the father of debate, conducted debates
among his students in Athens. Corax and Tisias founded one of the earliest
schools of rhetoric, specializing in teaching debate so that students could plead
their own cases in the law courts of ancient Sicily.

Debate flourished in the academies of the ancient world and in the medieval
universities, where rhetoric was installed as one of the seven liberal arts. What
may have been the first intercollegiate debate in the English-speaking world
took place in the early 1400s at Cambridge University between students from
Oxford and Cambridge. The debating programs at British universities, which
utilize a parliamentary format, have long been a training ground for future members of Parliament.

Debating has always been an important part of the American educational
scene as well. Debating flourished in the colonial colleges; disputations were a
required part of the curriculum, and debates were often a featured part of commencement ceremonies. Almost all the leaders of the American Revolution and
the early national period were able debaters who had studied argumentation in
the colonial colleges or in the community debating "societies," "lyceums," and
"bees" that flourished throughout the country: "From the Spy Club at Harvard
in 1722 to the Young Ladies Association, the first women's debating society, at
Oberlin in 1835, the one common thread in literary societies was student interest
in debating important issues."[3]

Intercollegiate debating began in the late 1800s, and interscholastic debating
soon followed. In the early 1900s, however, intercollegiate debates were relatively rare. Normally a college would schedule only a few intercollegiate debates
during an academic year, and large audiences would assemble to watch the few
students who were privileged to participate in these unusual events.

Academic debate as taught and practiced in the classroom experience often
follows the model offered by students involved in intercollegiate debate practice.
This is predictable, as many of the professional educators teaching the Debate

2. Henry Kissinger, *Diplomacy* (New York: Simon & Schuster, 1994), p. 638.
3. Charles DeLancey and Halford Ryan, "Intercollegiate Audience Debating: Quo Vadis,"
Argumentation and Advocacy, vol. 27 (1990), p. 49.

and Argumentation course are, or have been, intercollegiate debate coaches. In addition, intercollegiate debaters are immersed in the practice of academic and lead innovations and evolutions in practice and thought about debate. Thus, it is worthwhile to understand some of the history or intercollegiate debate and some of the trends, good and bad, associated with that history.

Recognition of the value and importance of academic debate increased steadily during the twentieth century. Tournament debating was introduced in the 1920s, and by 1936 some educators were concerned about its increasing popularity.[4] But tournament debating did not become predominant until the late 1940s. From the 1920s to the 1940s, contract debating prevailed. A college debating team would send out contracts to other teams specifying details such as which team would argue which side of the proposition, how judges or audiences would be selected, and where the visiting team would be housed, and offering to reciprocate as host on some future occasion. The major motion picture, "The Great Debaters" tells the story of Wiley College and their ultimately successful campaign to participate in a contracted debate with Harvard University (in fact, the real-life debate was Wiley College vs. The University of Southern California). The film reveals many of the real issues facing college debate teams during the era of contract debates, including the appropriate role of the coach in preparing strategies and materials, and the difficulty of travel and portrays the drama and excitement of debating in front of large audiences with a decision in the balance.

Typically, teams would work to arrange a series of debates in various locations. When a sufficient number of signed contracts had been returned, teams would depart by car, bus, or train for a few days or a week or two of debating. Usually the schedule called for one debate a day, although in major cities like Boston, New York, Washington, and Chicago, two debates a day might be scheduled. On rare occasions teams traveled coast to coast in private railroad cars.

In the post–World War II era, tournament debate became the predominant mode of debating. A yearlong resolution was selected and announced to facilitate debaters' preparation, although individual tournaments might or might not adhere to the national resolution. In 1947 the U.S. Military Academy began the National Debate Tournament **(NDT)** at West Point. Tournament debating proliferated, and teams soon could choose among many tournaments at nearby or distant colleges on almost any weekend between October and April. Swing tournaments evolved in which two colleges relatively close to each other would schedule back-to-back tournaments during the winter break so that, instead of one or two debates a day, teams could attend two tournaments in a week. A tournament would offer as many as 12 or more debate rounds in a single tournament. The NDT committee (a group of debate coaches representing member schools) served to select and announce the yearlong topic in the summer.

In 1967 the American Forensic Association (AFA) assumed responsibility for the NDT, which has been hosted by a different college each year since then. By

---

4. Alfred Westfall, "Can We Have Too Much of a Good Thing?" *The Forensic of Pi Kappa Delta,* Oct. 1936, p. 27.

1967 the NDT had become the dominant force in intercollegiate debating, and virtually all teams geared their programs to winning a place in the NDT or emulated the practices of teams that were successful in the NDT. Debaters hoping to participate in the NDT debated a proposition announced in the summer before the academic debate season began. As in the NCAA basketball tournament, only a select number of teams are selected to participate in the NDT. The establishment of the NDT became important in shaping the practice of intercollegiate debating. It promoted the establishment of a national circuit of tournaments through the year, an annual topic, and development of a set of practices and conventions shaping the way academic debates occurred.

Tournament debating, as opposed to contract debating, engaged many students representing numerous colleges and universities. Instead of one debate in front of an audience, involving a total of four student debaters, a tournament offered opportunities for dozens or hundreds of students to compete, 2 on 2, in as many as 4 or 5 debates per day over a 3- or 4-day tournament weekend. This served the benefit of expanding opportunities to participate in debate to far more students. The only limits were the number of available classrooms and individuals willing to serve as judges. However, as it would be impossible to assemble the hundreds of audiences needed to decide the many debates in any given tournament, individual judges were assigned to represent audiences and render decisions identifying the winners of each debate. Most judges were faculty coaches or alumni. Since the same people taught, coached, and judged debates repeatedly, and they strove to make objective decisions in the debates based on the content and not the style of debaters, some unique practices emerged. Debaters, relying on judges who were well informed on the topics and experienced in the theory and vocabulary of debate, focused on content over delivery in their presentations. They began to rely on substantial prepared material, including evidence in the form of quoted support and prewritten briefs and cases. Recall that they debated the same topic throughout the academic year. In addition, a technical language specific to tournament debate emerged and was shared by participants, providing shortcuts for participants, but making the debate more technical and inaccessible to casual observers. The content and quality of argumentation became deeper, but traditional delivery gave way to a fast-paced technical presentation. Most noticeably, because debaters found that with "expert judges" as opposed to lay audiences, they would be evaluated on the quality of their evidence and reasoning rather than their speech delivery, and given time limits on their speeches, debaters found that they would succeed in the competition by reading and speaking faster and faster, alienating those outsiders not immersed in the debate activity.

In 1971 the Cross Examination Debate Association (**CEDA**) was established to provide an alternative to NDT debating—in part to meet a perceived need by placing greater emphasis on communication. (The use of cross-examination debating is no longer a distinguishing feature between the two approaches; since 1974–1975 the NDT has used the cross-examination format.) CEDA, which initially employed non-NDT policy propositions, started using value propositions in 1975. Two propositions per year—one for each academic semester—were debated. CEDA also established a sweepstakes system, which recognized the top debate programs in each region and in the nation. A point system was developed to reward successful debaters, both novice and experienced. (The NDT later adopted a similar point system with sweepstakes awards.) In 1986, CEDA established a national championship tournament open to any CEDA member. After a modest start as the Southwest Debate Association, CEDA emerged as the most widely used mode of intercollegiate debating. CEDA began as an attempt to bring intercollegiate debating back to a more audience-centered activity. The CEDA point system was designed to encourage local and regional debating, thus making debate accessible to more institutions, a reaction to the national circuit encouraged by the NDT, and its shared conventions. For some time, CEDA successfully achieved its goals, to create a more accessible activity for college students focusing on good delivery and quality argumentation. Over time, however, students hungry to win found that as judges gained more experience and expertise, they would once again be receptive to the same techniques and styles CEDA had been founded to change. In addition, the national tournament contributed to the reestablishment of a national circuit, again raising the bar of technical debate practice and faster delivery.

Throughout this period, NDT debate continued, with its best debaters developing highly technical and quickly delivered cases and argumentation. The leaders of the NDT always preferred the yearlong policy proposition.

In 1996 the fall CEDA topic was reselected as the spring CEDA topic, thereby creating a yearlong proposition, as was used by NDT. In addition, despite the non-policy or quasi-policy nature of the CEDA propositions from 1975 until 1996, by the mid-1990s most CEDA debates involved discussion of policies. These debates were very similar in content to those occurring among schools debating the NDT topic. Because CEDA debates had also adopted the stylistic characteristics common to NDT debates, the two debate groups differed little in debate practice. During their respective national tournaments in 1996, the NDT leadership communicated to CEDA that if CEDA adopted a yearlong policy proposition announced in the summer, NDT would adopt that proposition as well, creating a shared topic. CEDA did so, and thus the "merger" of CEDA and NDT occurred. CEDA and NDT maintain their separate ranking systems; however, teams now compete in tournaments previously closed to them by style, topic, and membership. Some teams and a majority of member schools in each organization compete in both the NDT and the CEDA National Championship. Participation in the NDT is selective: Teams must qualify through a system of open bids and district competition. The CEDA tournament is open to any team representing a member school (remember that CEDA is an organization, whereas NDT is a tournament).

Other debate organizations sponsoring team debates coexist with CEDA and NDT. The American Debate Association (ADA) was established in 1985 to foster the growth of "reasonable" rule-based policy debate.[5] ADA was concerned with keeping debate accessible to new debaters and new debate programs while maintaining academic integrity in its top-level debating. ADA has always debated

---

5. For a more detailed consideration of NDT, CEDA, ADA, and other debate formats, see "Special Issue: A Variety of Formats for the Debate Experience," *Argumentation and Advocacy*, vol. 27, no. 2 (fall 1990).

within the NDT structure and utilized the NDT proposition. The National Educational Debate Association (NEDA) promotes debate with a focus on communication style and educational practice. NEDA selects its own propositions. The National Parliamentary Debate Association (NPDA) and the American Parliamentary Debate Association (APDA) sponsor competitive intercollegiate debate using a modified parliamentary format and featuring propositions chosen for individual debates or debate rounds. In fact, NPDA is now the largest intercollegiate debate organization and the most popular. Begun in 1991, NPDA is a type of impromptu debate not using prepared materials or directly quoted evidence. It has, however, begun to experience some of the same evolution as NDT and CEDA debate have, as judges become more expert and technical, the nature of the debate has become more technical and less audience-centered.

Lincoln–Douglas, or one-on-one, debate is organized through the National Forensic Association. The International Debate Education Association (IDEA) and the International Public Debate Association (IPDA) also work to promote academic debate. In 1997, CEDA established an additional debate format called "public sphere debate," designed to provide competitive audience-style debate evaluated by nontraditional debate judges. The topic for public sphere debate was a narrowed or alternate version of the CEDA/NDT proposition. In 1999, CEDA eliminated the public sphere proposition and replaced it with a nonpolicy proposition (see Chapter 3). The nonpolicy proposition never gained much popularity and was abandoned in the 2002–2003 academic year.

To be successful, academic debate students must know and adapt to the preferences and expectations of their judges; just as in applied debate, arguers must shape their messages to fit their audiences. While CEDA and NDT have essentially merged as debate communities, new subcultures have developed based in part on styles of judging and debating. Constant change in argumentation styles and approaches create new challenges of adapting to unfamiliar audiences. NPDA and NFA-LD judges represent unique conventions and expectations as well, as does every classroom or lecture hall housing an academic debate. Varying experience levels also affect the preferences and expectations of judges and coaches. Each of the various debate organizations and styles represents a set of unique approaches to the practice of debate. Another important factor contributing to the conventional practice of the various academic debate groups is the manner by which judges are assigned. Even within a pool of expert debate judges, randomly assigned judges present a different challenge than judges who are assigned (as is the convention in most NDT and CEDA tournaments) by "mutual preference." (This is a system whereby debaters rank and rate their potential judges. The tournament then attempts to assign judges who are equally preferred by both teams facing each other in a given debate, allowing debaters to avoid the demand to adapt their advocacy and styles to a wide range of judges.)

B. The Organization of Academic Debate

Academic debate is by no means limited to the classroom and the argumentation course. As the previous discussion outlines, many colleges conduct programs of academic debate by organizing debating teams, which give students opportunities beyond the traditional course offerings. Academic credit is often given for participation in the debate program—a program usually open to any qualified undergraduate. The director of forensics conducts the program to provide training opportunities for students new to debate and to maximize the challenge for more experienced students. CEDA, the American Forensics Association, the National Communication Association, IDEA, and other professional organizations, however, do promote scholarship and development of argumentation theory and teaching for all those interested in academic debate. They support research and learning to be applied in debate and argumentation classes, on-campus debating, and across the curriculum.

As the designation "director of forensics" suggests, many debating programs today have broadened their focus to include other forensic activities. "**Forensics** is defined as an educational activity primarily concerned with using an argumentative perspective in examining problems and communicating with people."[6] Recognizing that many forensics programs have been expanded to include a wide variety of public speaking and individual events in addition to debate, the 1984 definition continues:

> Forensics is viewed as a form of rhetorical scholarship which takes various forms, including debate, public address, and the interpretation of literature. Forensics serves as a curricular and co-curricular laboratory for improving students' abilities in research, analysis, and oral communication. Typically, forensic activities are conducted in a competitive environment so as to motivate students and accelerate the learning process. Forensics remains an ongoing, scholarly experience, uniting students and teachers, in its basic educational purpose.[7]

C. Values of Academic Debate

Because debating is an ancient discipline that is thriving in modern educational institutions, we should consider some of the values of academic debate. Although not all these values are unique to debate, a successful academic debate program is an important means of attaining them. Indeed, for many students it is the best, and sometimes the only, means of obtaining the benefits outlined here.

1. Debate Provides Preparation for Effective Participation in a Democratic Society.   Debate is an inherent condition of a democratic society. Our Constitution provides for freedom of speech. Our legislatures, our courts, and most of our private organizations conduct their business through the medium of debate. Because debate is so widespread at decision-making levels, a citizen's ability to

---

6. This definition, adopted at the Second National Developmental Conference on Forensics in Evanston, Illinois, in 1984, reaffirmed the definition adopted at the First National Developmental Conference on Forensics, held in Sedalia, Colorado, in 1974.
7. Second National Developmental Conference on Forensics.

vote intelligently or to use his or her right of free speech effectively is limited without knowledge of debate. As we know from history, freedoms unused or used ineffectively are soon lost. Citizens educated in debate can hope to be empowered to participate in the shaping of their world.

2. Debate Offers Preparation for Leadership.   The ultimate position of leadership is the presidency of the United States. Historian Arthur M. Schlesinger, Jr., cites two indispensable requirements that an effective president must meet. The first is "to point the republic in one or another direction." The second is to explain to the electorate why the direction the president proposes is right for the nation. Ronald Reagan understood, as Jimmy Carter never did, that politics is ultimately an educational process. Where Carter gave the impression of regarding presidential speeches as disagreeable duties, to be rushed through as perfunctorily as possible, Reagan knew that the speech is a vital tool of presidential leadership. His best speeches had a structure and an argument. They were well written and superbly delivered. They were potent vehicles for his charm, histrionic skills, and genius for simplification."[8] The candidacy and presidency of Barack Obama has been powered by effective oratory, and one of the arguments frequently offered by GOP candidate, Newt Gingrich, in 2012 was that he should win the GOP nomination because he is most qualified to participate in the presidential debates with President Obama.

It is interesting to note that Schlesinger's second requirement echoes our definition of argumentation given in Chapter 1. Although few of you will become president, many will aspire to positions of leadership. And an indispensable requirement of leadership—not only in politics but in almost all areas of human endeavor—is that the leader explains why the direction proposed is right.

3. Debate Offers Training in Argumentation.   From classical times to the present, argumentation teachers have viewed debate as the best method of providing training in this discipline. Debate offers an ideal opportunity for students to apply the theories of argumentation under conditions designed to increase their knowledge and understanding of these theories and their proficiency in their use. As an educational method debate provides excellent motivation for learning, because students have both the short-term goal of winning a decision or an award in a tournament, and the long-term goal of increasing their knowledge and improving their ability. This combination of short-term and long-term motivations provides for an optimum learning situation. The constant monitoring of student achievement with immediate feedback and evaluations by debate judges gives frequent opportunities to encourage growth and progress and to detect and remedy misunderstandings.

4. Debate Provides for Investigation and Intensive Analysis of Significant Contemporary Problems.   Thoughtful educators have long been concerned that students and the general public often have only a superficial knowledge of

---

8. Arthur M. Schlesinger, Jr., *The Cycles of American History* (Boston: Houghton Mifflin, 1986), p. 293.

significant contemporary problems. In addition to acquiring knowledge of the principles of argumentation, debaters also have a chance to investigate and analyze the significant contemporary problems and relevant literature that form the basis of the propositions under debate. In the course of a debating career, students will acquire a better-than-average knowledge of current problems, as well as skill in applying methods that will enable them to critically analyze the problems. As one authority points out, the true aim of rhetoric—the energizing of knowledge—is correlated with inquiry and with policy.[9] Through debate students learn how to acquire knowledge and how to energize that knowledge.

5. Debate Develops Proficiency in Critical Thinking. Through study of argumentation and practice in debate, students participate in an educational process specifically designed to develop their proficiency in critical thinking. A number of studies have investigated whether college courses in argumentation and debate improve critical thinking. One researcher, Kent R. Colbert, found that, after a year's participation in either CEDA or NDT debate, the debaters significantly outscored the nondebaters on critical-thinking tests.[10] Debaters learn to apply the principles of critical thinking not only to problems that emerge in the relative comfort of research or a briefing session but also to problems that arise in the heat of debate.

6. Debate Is an Integrator of Knowledge. Educators are constantly searching for methods of synthesizing knowledge. Debate is one way of achieving this goal:

> The exponents of a synthesis of knowledge and the broader view of a problem can [learn] from the practical experience and method of the arguer and discussant. Almost any problem at which the debater works cuts across these fields of knowledge.[11]

For example, in debating a proposition dealing with the issue of immigration policy, debaters must have at least a minimal familiarity with the principles of argumentation, culture, international politics, economics, political science, sociology, psychology, finance, business management, labor relations, government, history, and philosophy. They will, of course, learn the principles and details of these disciplines through the appropriate departments of the college or through independent study; however, through debate they can integrate their knowledge of these various disciplines and bring them to bear on a significant contemporary problem. Debate offers a uniquely dynamic and energized environment within which students can learn. For many students debate is their first, and often their most intensive and valuable, experience in interdisciplinary studies.

7. Debate Develops Proficiency in Purposeful Inquiry. Debate is defined as a process of inquiry and advocacy. Debaters must be well informed about all the

---

9. See Charles Sears Baldwin, *Medieval Rhetoric and Poetic* (New York: Macmillan, 1928), p. 3.
10. Kent R. Colbert, "The Effects of CEDA and NDT Debate Training on Critical Thinking Ability," *Journal of the American Forensic Association*, vol. 21 (1987), pp. 194–201.
11. Baird A. Craig, "General Education and the Course in Argumentation," *The Gavel*, vol. 38, p. 59.

relevant aspects of the issue to be debated. The extent to which debate motivates students to undertake purposeful inquiry into significant contemporary problems, to apply the principles of critical thinking to those problems, and to integrate the knowledge acquired from various disciplines is suggested by a former college debater:

> In my four years of college debating, we worked on such vital real-world topics as aid for international development, the Constitutional right of privacy, trade policies on the Pacific Rim, and federal energy policies. Each of these big topics was subject to a range of interpretations and required in-depth research on subsidiary issues as well.
>
> Preparing to debate these subjects led me and many other debaters to do our first serious research. Debate introduced me to *Foreign Affairs*, the law reviews and indexes, *Business Periodicals Index*, the *Public Affairs Information Service*, *Dialog*, *Nexis*, *Datatimes*, *Dow Jones News/Retrieval*, and other databases.
>
> While numbers aren't everything, the fact is that the amount of research my partner and I did in just one year of debate exceeded the amount of research I did in preparing my master's thesis. Undoubtedly the research I had done for debate got me up to speed for the pressures of grad school and the competitive world of business.

Indeed, debaters frequently work on the cutting edge of contemporary problems, studying matters before they emerge as subjects of general public concern. As noted previously debaters seek out the web sources and scholarly journals in which significant problems are often first reported and discussed. The general public draws its information from tweets, television, and the popular press, which may not report on these matters accurately, fully, or until months or years later. For example, many environmental concerns, such as the "greenhouse effect" and loss of rain forest were considered "exotic" topics by nondebaters who encountered them in the late 1970s. However, by the mid-1990s, stories on these subjects were common in mass-circulation publications.

An examination of the lists of national intercollegiate debate propositions (see Appendix C) will reveal that debaters do in fact work on the cutting edge, considering major contemporary problems in advance of the general public. Perhaps the most striking example of foresight in discerning future public policy issues may be found in the then highly controversial 1954–1955 NDT proposition on the diplomatic recognition of communist China. It was not until President Nixon's historic visit to China 17 years later that the United States extended diplomatic recognition to China.

Learning how to conduct inquiry in sometimes unfamiliar fields and gaining practical experience in this kind of research will serve you well in many of your later pursuits.

8. Debate Emphasizes Quality Instruction.   Debate is based on a close tutorial relationship between faculty and students as well as experiential learning. Educators are worried about the negative effects of large classes and impersonal teaching, and debate classes offer an alternative by providing a tutorial relationship between faculty and students. Such classes usually are small and offer many opportunities for interaction between students and professor as they prepare for class debates or other class projects. This valuable process is enhanced by the feedback that usually follows such projects. Also, most of the educational activity of the debate program is carried out in a tutorial situation. The director of forensics or an assistant works with the two members of the debate team as they plan their research, develop their affirmative case, and plan their negative strategies. The coach may also work with groups of four students after a practice debate as they critique the debate in depth and plan for further improvement. Because this tutorial relationship is rarely limited to a quarter or a semester, but rather extends over four years, it provides a valuable opportunity for personalized education in the all-too-often impersonal world of higher education. Students benefit as well from interaction with their judges, who are talented educators from other colleges and universities. For example, community college student debaters may have hours of educational interaction with professors representing the nation's finest universities. Finally, in debate, the students are empowered with the direct responsibility for their own learning process. One cannot learn debate or acquire its skill sets without active, engaged participation.

9. Debate Encourages Student Scholarship.   Debate establishes standards of research and scholarly achievement that are rarely equaled in other undergraduate courses. Some students worry that the time they spend on debate may have a negative effect on their grades, but in fact the opposite is true. Intercollegiate debaters report that their work in debate is a significant factor in helping them do better on exams, write better term papers, and score higher on graduate school admissions tests. This, of course, is the predictable result of the benefits considered in this section. The scholarly skills that debaters develop in researching, organizing, presenting, and defending a debate case are directly transferable to many other academic pursuits.

Added to this is the challenge to do one's best that debate provides. In the classroom the professor typically makes "reasonable" assignments that the "average" student can fulfill. In intercollegiate debate, however, one's opponent is rarely "reasonable" or "average." As we noted in Point 7, good debaters will do far more research than the average professor would ever expect for a term paper and will present it with far more skill and defend it far more effectively than would be required on a class assignment. Preparing for and participating in major tournaments can be a mind-expanding experience that encourages students to tap their full capabilities and enables them to realize their full potential.

Argumentation courses and intercollegiate debate are traditional training grounds for pre-law students. One study of 98 law school deans found that 69.9 percent would advise pre-law students to take a course in argumentation and 70.3 percent would recommend participation in intercollegiate debate. The deans also indicated that pre-law students "needed training in the skills of public speaking" (81.9 percent), "practical experience in the use of research techniques" (84.2 percent), "training in the application of the principles of logical reasoning"

(89.6 percent), and "training in the techniques of refutation and rebuttal" (75.8 percent).[12] Not only are such training and experience valuable for pre-law students, they are important assets in many other areas of graduate study and in business and professional endeavors.

10. Debate Develops the Ability to Make Prompt, Analytical Responses.   In the 1988 presidential campaign Michael Dukakis—who had an 18-point lead in the early polls—let George Bush's attacks go unanswered. One of Bush's more effective salvos was to criticize Dukakis for vetoing a bill requiring teachers to lead the Pledge of Allegiance each day. "'Dukakis' strategy of shrugging off attacks suddenly stopped looking presidential and started looking weak,' said a top aide.... Months after Bush first raised the issue, Dukakis finally responded."[13] The failure to respond promptly and analytically to this and other attacks that Dukakis apparently judged to be frivolous was considered by many observers to be an important factor in Dukakis's defeat. In today's world of instant communication, candidates let attacks go unanswered at their peril (see Chapter 3). Politicians, business executives, and ordinary citizens may also find themselves in situations that require a prompt, analytical response. Students learn to do this in debate; cross-examination requires an instant response, and the response to an argument made in an opponent's speech must be prepared during the speech or in the brief time between speeches.

11. Debate Develops Critical Listening.   In their pioneer research on listening, Ralph G. Nichols and Leonard A. Stevens found that "on the average we listen at approximately a 25 percent level of efficiency."[14] If we allow our attention to wander while an opponent speaks, our reply will be ineffective and off the mark. And if we miss 75 percent of our opponents' arguments, we will surely lose the debate. Debaters quickly learn to listen to their opponents with sharply focused critical attention, recording their arguments precisely on a flow sheet (a specialized note-taking system used by debaters) so that their own responses are to the point—adapting the phrasing of their opponents and turning the subtleties and limitations heard to their own advantage. The ability to listen critically is widely recognized as an important attribute of the educated person. Nichols and Stevens found that a top executive of a large industrial plant reported "perhaps 80 percent of my work depends on my listening to someone, or upon someone else listening to me."[15] Debaters begin to develop this important skill of critical listening from their very first debate.

12. Debate Develops Proficiency in Reading and Writing.   Many debates are conducted in writing—for example, the daily "debates" on the editorial page of

---

12. From a paper by Don R. Swanson, "Debate as Preparation for Law: Law Deans' Reactions," presented at the Western Speech Communication Association convention (1970).
13. *Time*, Nov. 21, 1988, p. 47.
14. Ralph G. Nichols and Leonard A. Stevens, *Are You Listening?* (New York: McGraw-Hill, 1957), p. ix.
15. Nichols and Stevens, *Are You Listening?* p. 141.

USA Today. However, as a practical matter we most often think of debate as an oral argument. How then does debate develop proficiency in writing? Don't we merely "talk on our feet" when we debate? As we have seen, debate does indeed develop the ability to make prompt, analytical responses (see Point 10).

However, as we will discover, much of the debate is written prior to delivery. The first affirmative constructive speech is almost invariably a manuscript speech, which means that it is written and rewritten, revised and edited as the advocates try to develop the most effective statement of their position. In the same way many portions of other kinds of speeches and arguments are the products of careful writing and extensive rewriting, as well as skillful adaptation to previous speeches. Debaters must use clear, concise, powerful language to defend their positions. They build an extensive and precise vocabulary and develop a sense of clarity, which they bring to their writing.

The writing proficiency developed in debate pays dividends first by enabling debaters to present arguments more cogently and effectively. The skills learned in writing for debate carry over to many other fields. Students will find that they can apply the writing skills they learn from debate in writing term papers and in writing better answers to essay exams in their other classes. And after graduation, students find that writing proficiency is highly valued in almost any business or profession.

Research conducted on Urban Debate League debaters has evidenced debate as an excellent tool to promote literacy training and development of reading skills. Reading aloud has the effect of building reading skills, even among those with very low reading capabilities. Participation in debate also builds vocabulary, as noted above, as students must learn to navigate complex academic, technical, and challenging resource materials.[16]

13. Debate Encourages Mature Judgment.   Scholars tell us that many problems in human affairs result from a tendency to see complex issues in black-and-white terms. Educational debate gives students a chance to consider significant problems from many points of view. As debaters analyze the potential affirmative and negative cases, they begin to realize the complexity of most contemporary problems and to appreciate the worth of a multivalued orientation. As they debate both sides of a proposition, they learn not only that most contemporary problems have more than one side but also that even one side of a proposition embodies a considerable range of values. Sometimes at the start of an academic year, some debaters may, on the basis of a quickly formulated opinion, feel that only one side of a proposition is "right." After a few debates, however, they usually request an assignment on the other side of the proposition. By the end of the year (or semester), after they have debated on both sides of the proposition, they learn the value of suspending judgment until they have amassed and analyzed an adequate amount of evidence. The need to advocate one side of the proposition in a debate also teaches them that decisions cannot be postponed indefinitely. When

---

16. Linda Collier, "Argument for Success: A Study of Academic Debate in the Urban High Schools of Chicago, Kansas City, New York, St. Louis and Seattle," paper presented at the National Communication Association National Convention, 2004.

they finally formulate their personal position on the proposition, it may or may not be the same as at the beginning of the year. But now it will be a position they have reached after careful consideration, one they can defend logically.

14. Debate Develops Courage.   Debate helps students to develop courage by requiring them to formulate a case and defend it against strong opposition, under pressure. In debate students' cases will come under attack, and they might be tempted to push the panic button, beat a disorderly retreat, and avoid the confrontation. They cannot do this, however. The situation requires that they defend their position. They must have the courage of their convictions. They must discipline themselves, concentrate on the problem, organize their thoughts, and present a refutation. Well-prepared debaters find that they can defend their position, that their opponents are only human; as a result, they gain new confidence in themselves and in their ability to function in a competitive situation.

15. Debate Encourages Effective Speech Composition and Delivery.   Because composition and delivery of the debate speech are among the factors that determine the effectiveness of arguments, debaters need to select, arrange, and present their materials in keeping with the best principles of public speaking. Debating places a premium on extemporaneous delivery, requiring speakers to think on their feet. Typically debaters will speak before many different audiences: a single judge in the preliminary round of a tournament, a group of businesspeople at a service club, or a radio or TV audience. Each of these situations provides new challenges. Constant adaptation to the audience and to the speech situation helps debaters develop flexibility and facility in thinking and speaking.

Nervousness about public speaking is one of the most common fears for students and professionals. It can serve as a real and significant barrier to effective communication and ultimately to academic and professional success. Debate is an ideal arena for students to develop coping mechanisms allowing them to manage their speech anxiety. Because debate both requires and allows for substantial preparation, students develop confidence in their materials and passion for their advocacy. Debate provides a focus on the content over style, so the attention is on the arguments, not on the person. Student debaters may forget to be nervous as they have so much else to think about. And repetition of experience helps the students build confidence and learn to cope with their inevitable nervousness in such a way as to prevent it from impeding their objectives.

16. Debate Develops Social Maturity.   Intercollegiate debate provides an opportunity for students to travel to different campuses and meet students and faculty members from various parts of the country. It is not unusual for a team to participate in tournaments on the East or West Coast, in the Deep South, in the New England states, and in many points in between in the course of a year. Formerly there were eastern, midwestern, southern, and western styles of debating. But mass transportation has allowed debating to take place on a national scale, and so these regional differences have largely disappeared.

Exposure to both the businesslike atmosphere of the debate and the informal social situations that accompany most debates and tournaments helps students acquire social amenities, poise, and self-confidence. In the competition of a tournament or a classroom debate, they learn that they must accept victory or defeat gracefully and that they must respond courteously to the criticism of judge(s) regardless of their decisions. The educational benefits that come from meeting professors from a number of different colleges in informal settings can also be significant. In the college classroom, debaters will directly engage one another more than in most other courses. To debate is to express and to listen, to work together and to build community. One need not travel to encounter others with values and life experiences different from one's own. The interaction afforded in the debate classroom and through the experience of sharing ideas through debate fosters shared understanding and relationship building.

17. Debate Develops Multicultural Sensitivities.   As debaters learn to interact effectively with their colleagues, coaches, and judges in the debate environment, they will have the opportunity to engage individuals representing diverse cultural backgrounds. In the open debate context that celebrates free expression, students learn to communicate with sensitivity in a multicultural environment that may not be available on their home campus. Further, the nature of communication and argumentation demands that to be effective, debaters consider the implications of culture, values, and worldview on their cases and on their strategic approaches. To persuade a judge requires an understanding and sensitivity to their perceptual screen, and it is inescapable that argument premises are based upon foundations built at least in part by culture.

18. Debate Empowers Personal Expression.   In an academic environment, debate offers the participant a unique opportunity to express their ideas, experience, and voice. Rhetorical space—the opportunity to be respectfully heard—is guaranteed to the sincere participant. This opportunity to be heard is empowering and inspiring. Participants are able to learn from each other's experience and develop and grow as individuals and members of larger communities.

19. Debate Develops Problem-Solving Skills.   Policy debate demands that participants investigate and evaluate important social problems and creatively and critically apply solutions to those problems. Experience suggests that these abilities enable debaters to systematically evaluate situations and, by utilizing reasoned measurement and ingenuity, discover appropriate solutions. Research also proves that debate training helps individuals find solutions to their own problems and, in particular, promotes nonviolent solutions to conflict. The National Debate Project reports that debate reduces violence. Important new research is demonstrating that a significant correlation exists between the increased verbal skills associated with debate participation and decreased physical violence in both peer and domestic relations.[17]

---

17. National Debate Project, http://communication.gsu.edu/ndp/benefits.htm, downloaded July 20, 2007.

20. Debate Develops Essential Proficiencies.   As we have seen, debate is an educational activity that provides students with the opportunity to develop proficiency in writing, thinking, reading, speaking, and listening. Educators and educational groups view these competencies as being vital to intellectual development. The consensus among major studies of education in the United States is that proficiency in oral communication is essential to academic competency. Consider the findings of the following studies:

1. The National Commission on Higher Education Issues identified the "fundamental competencies in reading, writing, speaking, mathematical techniques, and reasoning" as the requisite intellectual skills for the pursuit of higher education (*Summary Recommendations of the National Commission on Higher Education Issues*).

2. The National Commission on Excellence in Education echoed the same views and specified the same competencies, including both oral and written communication in its enumeration of necessary skills (*A Nation at Risk*, U.S. Department of Education, National Commission on Excellence in Education).

3. The Education Commission for the States' Task Force on Education for Economic Growth, whose members include governors, business leaders, and educators, assessed the critical needs of the education–commerce nexus and concluded that educational preparation for the "very competitive world of international commerce and trade" must include the essential language competencies of "reading," "writing," "speaking," and "listening" (*Action for Excellence*, Report of the Task Force on Education for Economic Growth, Education Commission for the States).

4. In its 1988 report the College Entrance Examination Board also listed "speaking and listening" among what it termed the "Basic Academic Competencies": "the broad intellectual skills essential to effective work in all fields of college study. They provide a link across disciplines of knowledge although they are not specific to any particular discipline. The Basic Academic Competencies are reading, writing, speaking and listening, mathematics, reasoning and studying" (*Academic Preparation for College*, The College Board).

5. In its proposal for strengthening public education, the Paideia Group specified the requisite intellectual skills for the educational process: "The skills to be acquired are the skills of reading, writing, speaking, listening, observing, measuring, estimating and calculating. They are linguistic, mathematical and scientific skills. They are the skills that everyone needs in order to learn anything, in school or elsewhere" (*Paideia Proposal*, the Paideia Group).

6. The American Association for the Advancement of Science, in a report prepared by the National Council on Science and Technology Education, stated that students should be able to "distinguish good arguments from bad ones" (*Project 2061 Phase 1 Reports*, the American Association for the Advancement of Science).

Debate is distinctive because of its unique dialectical form, providing the opportunity for intellectual clash in the testing of ideas. The creation of an argument is one of the most complex cognitive acts students can engage in. To create arguments, students must (1) research issues (which requires knowledge of how to use libraries and databases), (2) organize and analyze the data, (3) synthesize different kinds of data, and (4) evaluate information with respect to the quality of conclusions it may point to. To form the arguments after this process, students must (1) understand how to reason, (2) be able to recognize and critique different methods of reasoning, and (3) comprehend the logic of decision making. The successful communication of arguments to audiences reflects another cognitive skill: the ability to communicate complex ideas clearly with words. Finally, the argumentative interaction of students in a debate reflects an even more complex cognitive ability—the ability to process the arguments of others quickly and to reformulate or adapt or defend previous positions.[18]

III. ETHICAL STANDARDS FOR DEBATE

Because we use debate as a means of influencing human behavior, the mature, responsible advocate will be concerned with **ethical** standards for debate. To be conducted so that the benefits of debate are achieved, debate must be open, accessible, honest, and fair. Debate empowers its participants, but the power associated with debate participation carries with it personal responsibility. This responsibility includes honest and accurate representation of support materials and fair and open treatment of everyone involved. Debate in a free society demands civil behavior and fair treatment. To promote open participation, debaters should avoid language and behavior that would exclude or discourage the voices of any participants.

A. Ethical Practice

Ethical standards for debate practice occur on multiple levels. Some standards will vary by community and even by individual interpretations. For example, what is considered to be comprehensible or reasonable presentational style will vary. Some standards, however, are agreed upon and provide guidance for practice in all academic debate arenas.

First, the importance of competition must be kept in perspective. Many students enjoy debate largely due to its competitive nature. Because they are motivated to compete effectively, they work hard and immerse themselves in their debate preparation. This intensity of involvement results in great benefits to student debaters in achieving educational objectives and skill development. However, it should be remembered that competition is but a means to the more important educational ends.

---

18. Adapted from "A Rationale for Forensics as Education," adopted at the Second National Developmental Conference on Forensics, Evanston, Illinois, 1984.

Second, honesty and integrity should be maintained at the highest levels. The checks on honesty in the academic debate context are limited. In applied debate, opportunities to evaluate the accuracy of claims and support are available through methods including press coverage and legal checks on evidence history. Academic debate is time bound. For fair evaluation of evidence and reasoning it is vital that the highest standards of honesty be practiced.

Third, all participants should treat each other with respect. This may include appropriate language, nonverbal messages, and even choice of argumentation. The key is to honor each other's right to rhetorical space and to encourage open participation. To do so may require introspection, as disrespect may be communicated in subliminal and unintentional ways. Argumentation should be directed only at opponent's arguments and support, not at individuals or peoples.

Fourth, evidence standards require complete source citations and verbatim quotation. Fairness requires that evidence be gathered from published sources available to all participants. An advocate in debate is at a minimum ethically bound to provide reasons for their claims in the form of some type of proof.

B. Inclusion of All Participants

Debate provides a unique opportunity to learn from and about each other; across gender, culture, class, education, geography, and other differences. The opportunity to build bridges, however, can only be realized if participants become self-aware and work hard to create openness in their communicative behaviors. Socialization is a result of communicative behavior and is insidious. However, the academic debate laboratory offers the opportunity to alter negative socializations and to substitute empowerment and respect. This positive change demands growth in awareness about those behaviors that devalue or discourage equality of participation. Growth of community requires respect and equality.

Research and personal narrative indicate that bias against woman and minorities exists in the community of intercollegiate debate. Any barriers to participation, whether intentional or not, are unethical and counterproductive. Barriers preclude the empowerment of many who would benefit from participation and deny those who do participate the richness of diversity. Discrimination and repression, of course, reflect practice in the academic world, business and industry, and in society at large. Fortunately, debate offers an ideal forum to discuss and change old and deep-seated bias. Tonia Green, a debater for the University of Louisville, presented a portion of her personal narrative as part of a debate at the District 6 National Debate Tournament Qualifier at Georgia State University in 2004.

> People continuously create false solutions for this flawed institution contributing to the pollution of the miseducation of life. I debate not just for competitive success but for a true purpose, by recognizing and not forgetting my social location as an African-American woman. My values as an African-American woman reflect my values as an African-American woman debater. "And that statement is more serious than the atom bomb and Saddam," as Lauryn Hill would say in her song, *Freedom Time*.

EXERCISES

1. View a debate. Many are available online. What type of debate was it (applied or academic, etc.)? You may find debates in many locations, including the Commission on Presidential Debates (http://www.debates.org/index.php?page=debate-history), You Debate (http://www.youdebate.blogspot.com/). The Debate Video Blogspot (http://debatevideoblog.blogspot.com/), 2012 Election Central (http://www.2012presidentialelectionnews.com/2012-debate-schedule/2011-2012-primary-debate-schedule/), and countless other places.

2. *Listening.* Choose a story from the newspaper. Five student volunteers should leave the room, while one remains. Have one volunteer return and have the in-the-room volunteer read the newspaper article aloud. No notes allowed, and after the first reading, the article will be discarded. Then call on the next person to return. The person who has just listened to the reading of the article should recount the story, including all details, to the new student. One at a time, have each student return and repeat the process. The rest of the class should observe. After all five have returned, have the class discuss what details were omitted, changed, or added.

3. Form teams of two to three people each. Each team should identify their candidate for President of the Argumentation and Debate class. Negotiate rules for a campaign debate. What should be the format, layout, etc.?

4. Working in teams, prepare a set of ethical standards to govern the debates in your class.

5. Form an online community consisting of your class. Your instructor may wish to do so through a course website, or you can create one. One easy way to facilitate this is to form a group at Yahoo! (http://www.groups.yahoo.com/). As a class, select a topic for debate and initiate an online debate.

3

....

The Foundations of Argument

The practice of debate and the study of argumentation have a long and rich history. In recent years, you have experienced the emergence of the Internet and digital communication with their many life-changing, exciting, and sometimes threatening new technological opportunities to interact with and to influence others. In a like manner, over 2,000 years ago, the use of spoken language and oral discourse (debate and public speaking) to influence others emerged as a new "technology" to scholars and citizens in ancient Greece. For nearly a millennium, peaking in the fifth century B.C., public oral communication evolved and challenged its users with practical and ethical questions. Those early debate pioneers paved the path for us as contemporary users of the art of rhetoric and the technology of argumentation. In this chapter, we will review the classical traditions and the structures of argument which have shaped our understandings, review a contemporary exploration of the structure of argument, and explore types of reasoning.

I. CLASSICAL TRADITIONS

Our understanding of argumentation and debate is founded in the classical study and practice of rhetoric as it developed in ancient Greece, especially around the fifth century B.C. The Greek tradition in debate was in part a product of their unique geopolitical history and culture. At the crossroads of the ancient world, the Greek city-states became centers for trade, and thus communication. With Athens as their center, the city-states shared religion and language, but generally resisted unified government and common defense. Exemplified by the poet Homer's great epics, the *Iliad* and the *Odyssey*, the Greek Culture was an oral culture. Shared values and knowledge were passed along by the storytelling of the bards. As democratic forums developed during this Golden Age of Greece, citizens were likely to be called upon to defend themselves in legal suits before

Miniglossary

Analogy, reasoning by   The process of making a comparison between two similar cases and inferring that what is true in one case is true in the other.

Backing   Additional evidence and reasoning advanced to support a warrant.

Categorical syllogism   A syllogism in which the major premise is an unqualified proposition. Such propositions are characterized by words like *all, every, each,* and *any,* either directly expressed or clearly implied.

Causal reasoning   The process whereby one infers that a certain factor (a cause) is a force that produces something else (an effect).

Claim   The conclusion we seek to establish by our arguments.

Conditional syllogism   A syllogism in which the major premise deals with uncertain or hypothetical events. Usually identified by *if, assuming, supposing,* or similar terms, either expressly stated or clearly implied. Also known as a hypothetical syllogism.

Deduction   Argument that begins with a broad generalization and moves to a more specific application or conclusion.

Degree of cogency   The extent to which an argument is both sound and intellectually compelling because it is well founded in fact, logic, or rationality.

Dialectic   A method of argumentation and reasoning in which interlocutors engage in a question and answer format in order to arrive at truth.

Disjunctive syllogism   A syllogism in which the major premise contains mutually exclusive alternatives. Usually indicated by such words as *either, or, neither, nor, but,* and *although,* either expressly stated or clearly implied.

Enthymeme   (1) A truncated syllogism, in which one of the premises or the conclusion is not stated. (2) A syllogism based on probability, signs, and examples, whose function is rhetorical persuasion. Its successful construction is accomplished through the joint efforts of speaker and audience.

Ethos   A mode of proof based on the judgment an audience makes of the speaker.

Example, reasoning by   The process of inferring conclusions from specific cases.

Grounds   Evidence and reasoning advanced to establish the foundation of a claim.

Induction   Argument that begins with a specific case and moves to a broader generalization.

Logos   A mode of proof based on the judgment an audience makes of the message itself, based in practical reasoning or logic.

Modal qualification   The degree of cogency we attach to our claim.

Pathos   A mode of proof based on emotional responses engendered within the listener.

Rebuttal   Evidence and reasoning introduced to weaken or destroy another's claim.

Sign, reasoning by   The process of inferring relationships or correlations between two variables.

Sophists   Teachers of rhetoric and other skills needed to participate in the civic life of ancient Greece.

Syllogism   A systematic arrangement of arguments consisting of a major premise, a minor premise, and a conclusion.

Warrant   Evidence and reasoning advanced to justify the move from grounds to claim.

public juries. In Athens, these juries would consist of as many as 500 members. While the wealthy might engage expensive speech writers for representation, most citizens would need to access their own public speaking and argument skills and represent themselves. In addition, citizens were expected to participate in the democratic governance of their community, and as such, they might be called upon at any time to debate or decide on issues of public policy. Thus, an appreciation for and a prevalence of public discourse and debate characterized the Greek community. Skills of rhetoric and argumentation were essential to the citizen of Athens.

A. The Sophists

A group of teachers emerged to satisfy the needs of citizens to develop and utilize oratorical skills and to succeed as free citizens in the civic life of Greece. These "sophists" taught their students practical skills needed for successful citizenship. Chief among these skills was rhetoric. While some of the sophists were known for their manuals and practical "how-to" lessons (Corax and Tisias), others were known for their skills at ghost writing (Isocrates) and others for their powerful and engaging speaking styles (Gorgias and Demosthenes). What the sophists shared was a focus on techniques effective at persuading audiences. Their definition of rhetoric might be the "craftsmanship of persuasion."

Protagoras was a sophist and teacher who relied on debate as a central component to his teaching and public decision making. Thomas M. Conley wrote that:

> Protagoras [invented] "antilogic"—that is, the method of resolving disputes by examining the arguments on both sides of the question, without recourse to some objective criterion of truth or to some traditional standard of behavior. The truth, for all practical purposes, was held by Protagoras to be inaccessible; and matters of prudence, virtue, and honor were all contestable. Thus, only by examining the arguments for and against a given proposition can one come to some determination as to which side is to be believed and acted upon.[1]

Protagoras was therefore referred to as the *father of debate*, and was known for requiring all his students to engage in academic debate over various subjects.

B. Plato

The term "sophist" in ancient Greece was a reference to wisdom or knowledge. As teachers of civic participation, the sophists were generally respected for their skills and objectives. However, today the term "sophistry" is used to describe flawed, manipulative, or dishonest reasoning. This negative interpretation of

---

1. Thomas M. Conley, *Rhetoric in the European Tradition* (New York and London: University of Chicago Press, 1994), p. 5.

sophism is in part a consequence of the philosophical critique offered of the sophists by Plato. Plato, student of Socrates and teacher of Aristotle, was distrustful of public decision making and rhetoric. He considered a most important goal for civic decision making and philosophy to be the discovery of scientific and absolute truth. Plato satirized and criticized the practice of the sophists in his dialog the *Gorgias*. In this work, through the character of Socrates, Plato offered arguments against rhetoric. He argued that rhetoric is not an art, that it allows guilty to escape deserved punishment, that it allows bad men a tool with which they may wrongly manipulate the masses, that it enables the user to disguise the truth, and that it is a false power, as it does not necessarily promote good. He viewed the rhetorical practice of the sophists as a manipulation of uninformed audiences without a concern for real truth. Plato's interpretation of rhetoric as practiced by the sophists might have been, "the knack of persuasion." He also described rhetoric as "cookery," that is, a speech or argument could be concocted by the sophist by combining a mix of compatible ingredients in a recipe producing a pleasing and tasty "meal" or rhetorical message.

In another dialogue, *The Phaedrus*, Plato offered a set of requirements which rhetoric would need to meet in order to become a worthy art. Here he argued that the speaker must first know the truth of what he is going to say so as to avoid being deceived by that which is not true; second, that the rhetorician must be able to define his terms, thus following rules of logic; and third, he must provide principles of organization of arguments. Plato's fourth requirement is that the rhetor must know the souls, or the psychology, of his audience; fifth, that he must understand the importance and nature of delivery and style of presentation; sixth, that cross-examination and interaction is preferable to uninterrupted discourse; and finally, that the rhetorician should have high moral purpose.

Plato's preferred method of discourse was NOT rhetoric but philosophical dialectic, a question and answer format which works from premise to premise. The goal of dialectic is to discover truth. It begins with definition of terms and proceeds through analysis (classification of observations into categories) to synthesis (moving from concrete to abstract, forming universal generalizations). Dialectic is precise, begins with questions, and only advances upon agreement by respondents. It utilizes a rigor of testing only possibly though cross-examination and application of rules of logic. Recall that dialectic seeks absolute truth by asking questions, whereas rhetoric begins with a probable truth and seeks agreement. However, both rhetoric and dialectic involve reasoning, and therefore debate.

C. Aristotle

In his work, *The Rhetoric*, Aristotle may have been (in part) responding to his teacher's requirements for rhetoric to become an art as presented in *The Phaedrus*. As you know from Chapter 1, Aristotle recognized important and valuable functions of rhetoric. A practical scientist, Aristotle valued rhetoric as a means of civic participation and decision making. His view was distinct from that of the sophists or Plato. Aristotle defined rhetoric as "the faculty for observing, for any given case, the available means of persuasion." There are several important components of this definition. First, he viewed rhetoric as a "faculty for observing," that is, a theoretical pursuit, not a knack or even cookery, but a systematic and thoughtful approach requiring academic understanding and theoretical knowledge. Second, the "given case" requires that the rhetor select and construct appropriate appeals for the unique set of demands presented by a specific audience and situation, including audience analysis and adaptation. Finally, the "available means of persuasion" implied a logical structure, identifiable and systematic. Means of persuasion are the arguments available to the arguer.

For Aristotle, rhetoric offered a "counterpart" to dialectic, a parallel method of reasoning and argumentation. Dialectic seeks truths; Rhetoric arrives at probabilities. While dialectic utilizes a deductive form of reasoning termed the "syllogism," rhetoric offers the deductive "enthymeme." Deduction begins with universal generalizations and proceeds to specific applications. Conversely, induction in dialectic is exemplified by the admission of a respondent to specific cases, enough of which can lead interlocutors (those engaged in the back and forth of dialectic) to a general conclusion or generalization. Induction in rhetoric begins with a specific example or instance in order to provide support for a broader generalization.

Aristotle's, "modes of persuasion" were described as supports created by the speaker, which serve to favorably impact the audience. These include ethos, pathos, and logos. Ethos is ethical proof, the judgment made by the audience of the speaker. Ethos may be identified as impacting character, sagacity, and/or goodwill. Character is the measure an audience makes of the ethics and ethical behavior personified by the speaker. An audience will favorably evaluate speakers who live up to their values, but importantly, they are most likely to favor the rhetor that expresses and demonstrates what they consider to be good values. How does the audience determine what values are "good"? They will compare them to their own values. So, if an audience perceives the speaker's values to be similar to their own, they will find their arguments more persuasive. A speaker can emphasize shared values by generating identification with their audience. The more the audience member believes the speaker is like them, the more they have in common, the more likely the speaker is to boost the character component of their ethos. Sagacity is the degree to which the audience perceives the speaker to display wisdom, competence, expertise, or knowledge about the subject. Goodwill is the trust and dynamism generated by the speaker.

It may be said that Plato objected to rhetoric in part because it involved emotional appeals, thus clouding the judgment. Aristotle recognized that emotions, when balanced with other forms of reasoning, actually inform the judgment. Pathos is emotional proof, the proof that is in the listener. In other words, emotions, "those conditions attended to by pain or pleasure," are evoked, and therefore the listener becomes an instrument of persuasion through their own internal reactions. Aristotle identifies the psychology of the listener and offers a list of emotions to which the arguer may appeal. Finally, logos refers to logical proof, the judgment the audience makes of the facts and reasoning provided by the arguer. However, logos is a reference to a practical and probable sort of reasoning, not the rigorous precision of dialectic or formal logic. All three modes of persuasion serve to give persuasive force to any argument (enthymeme or example) offered by an arguer. In fact, they operative synergistically, each impacting the other.

Aristotle also recognized that argumentation occurs within different contexts, generating differing expectations, characteristics, and needs for different types of speeches, specifically, forensic, deliberative, and epideictic rhetoric. Forensic discourse refers to legal speaking, or rhetoric designed for court. It examines past events and seeks to establish what is just or unjust. Deliberative discourse refers to that sort of speaking necessary to guide decision making, as in determination of government action or laws. It focuses on future actions. Epideictic speaking is speaking to praise or blame. It occurs in ceremonial occasions, as in eulogies or celebrations and focuses on the present. Epideictic speaking questions values and virtues.

Contemporary debate formats blend characteristics of both dialectical and rhetorical reasoning. Special debates including presidential campaign debates are rhetorical, even sophistic, whereas classroom academic debates are far more structured and dialectical in their construction. It is useful to consider Plato's objections to sophistry while considering our argumentation within the contexts and guidance provided by Aristotle.

In this chapter we will consider what are now the two most common structures for argumentation. We turn first to the structures of Aristotle, whose syllogism and enthymeme have been standard tools of reasoning for centuries and are still the basis of much reasoning. Next we turn to a contemporary logician, Stephen Toulmin, whose concept of the elements of any argument—claims, grounds, warrants, backing, modal qualifications, and possible rebuttals—has come into common use.

The formal structure of these methods of reasoning gives us special opportunities to make astute analyses of lines of reasoning and to test their validity. The methods and terminologies of both the classical and the contemporary structures are now widely used in argumentation, and students should have a working knowledge of both.

II. THE CLASSICAL STRUCTURES OF ARGUMENT

As introduced above, two special forms of *deductive* reasoning are the dialectical syllogism and the rhetorical enthymeme. As you know, Plato was the student of Socrates and the teacher of Aristotle, and a critic of rhetoric. He was suspicious of the power and influence of rhetoric over unsophisticated people. He preferred the philosophical method of formal inquiry known as "dialectic." Dialectic, in which a question-response process is followed, is guided by rules of formal logic in which interlocutors begin with a set of questions in their search for answers and ultimately, truth. Rhetoric, which involves uninterrupted argumentation or speech, begins with an answer and then provides proof to persuade an audience of the probable truth of that answer. Aristotle recognized the importance and value of both dialectic and rhetoric in a democratic society, and argued that for the dialectical syllogism, there was the counterpart of the rhetorical enthymeme. Both are useful to the debater in different ways.

By understanding the structures of syllogism and enthymeme for the purpose of analysis, we can apply the appropriate tests of formal validity and of rhetoric to the reasoning we encounter as we explore a problem, to the reasoning we develop for our own case, and to the reasoning we meet in our opponent's case.

A. Syllogisms

Syllogisms are deductive forms of argument, proceeding from generalization to specific application. We will discuss three types of syllogisms: (1) categorical, (2) disjunctive, and (3) conditional. First, however, we should consider the structure of all types of syllogisms. The **syllogism** is a systematic arrangement of arguments:

1. A *major premise*, which is a proposition stating a generalization ("All A's are B's")

2. A *minor premise*, which is a proposition stating a specific instance related to the generalization ("C is an A")

3. A *conclusion*, which necessarily must follow from these premises ("Therefore, C is a B")

The following is an example of syllogistic reasoning:

All legally insane persons are incompetent to make binding agreements. (*major premise*)

John Doe is legally insane. (*minor premise*)

Therefore, John Doe is incompetent to make a binding agreement. (*conclusion*)

Note that the argument begins with a sweeping generalization and ends with a specific claim about Doe. In the dialectic method, interlocutors would challenge each premise vigorously in order to ascertain its truth.

In the various examples of syllogisms that follow, assume for now that each premise is absolutely true. We will focus first only on the structure of the argument; later we will consider the truth of the premises (in the section "Formal Validity and Material Truth").

1. The Categorical Syllogism.   In the **categorical syllogism**, the major premise is an unqualified proposition. These propositions are characterized by words like *all*, *every*, *each*, and *any*, either directly expressed or clearly implied. The example above represents the categorical syllogism.

Some scholars object to this aspect of the categorical syllogism, pointing out that it is difficult to make unqualified generalizations. After all, for example, all legally insane persons are not the same; the nature and degree of their illnesses, the types of treatment they require, and their chances of recovery differ widely. They are identical, however, in that they are all incompetent to make legally binding agreements as long as they are legally insane. For practical reasons we treat many matters as identical and make unqualified generalizations about them. Advocates have to try to determine when it is practical or necessary to make unqualified generalizations, within a specific context, and when it is prudent or necessary to recognize the differences in apparently identical matters.

Tests: Categorical Syllogism

---

1. The categorical syllogism must have three terms—no more and no less. These terms may be represented by the letters A (middle term), B (major term), and C (minor term). Here's an example:

   MAJOR PREMISE: All A's are B's.

   MINOR PREMISE: C is an A.

   CONCLUSION: Therefore, C is a B.

2. Every term must be used twice in the categorical syllogism—no more and no less.

3. A term must be used only once in any premise.

4. The middle term must be used in at least one premise in an unqualified or universal sense. In the syllogism on legal insanity (see page 53), the middle term was correctly distributed, referring to all legally insane persons. The middle term is incorrectly distributed in the following example, because (A) is qualified by the word "some."
   (some). Consequently, the conclusion of this syllogism is invalid.

   MAJOR PREMISE: Some politicians (A) are corrupt (B).

   MINOR PREMISE: Calvin Hobbes (C) is a politician (A).

   CONCLUSION: Therefore, Calvin Hobbes (C) is corrupt (B).

5. A term may be distributed in the conclusion only if it has been distributed in the major or minor premise. The following is an example of an illicit major—a major term that is distributed in the conclusion but not in the major premise.

   MAJOR PREMISE: All leftists (A) want the United States to cut defense spending (B).

   MINOR PREMISE: Congressman Zilch (C) is not a leftist (A).

   CONCLUSION: Therefore, Congressman Zilch (C) does not want the United States to cut defense spending (B).

   When the major premise is fully stated—"All leftists are among those who want the United States to cut defense spending"—it becomes apparent that the major term (B) is not used in a universal sense in the major premise and thus may not be distributed in the conclusion. Congressman Zilch might be a pacifist.
   The following is an example of an illicit minor—distributed in the conclusion but not in the minor premise.

   MAJOR PREMISE: All union presidents (A) favor the union shop (B).

   MINOR PREMISE: All union presidents (A) are members of unions (C).

   CONCLUSION: Therefore, all members of unions (C) favor the union shop (B).

   In this example the minor term (C) is distributed not in the minor premise but in the conclusion. When the minor premise is fully stated—"All union presidents are some members of unions," it becomes apparent that the minor term (C) has not been distributed and that consequently the conclusion is invalid. The only conclusion that could be drawn from these premises is that some union members favor the union shop.

Tests: Categorical Syllogism (Continued)

6. At least one of the premises must be affirmative. Obviously no valid conclusion can be drawn from two negative premises. Here is an example:

   MAJOR PREMISE: No Democratic senators (A) will vote for this bill (B).

   MINOR PREMISE: Senator Eliot (C) is not a Democratic senator (A).

   CONCLUSION: Therefore, Senator Eliot (C) will _____?

7. If one premise is negative, the conclusion must be negative. Here's an example:

   MAJOR PREMISE: No Republican senators (A) voted for this bill (B).

   MINOR PREMISE: Senator Eliot (C) is a Republican senator (A).

   CONCLUSION: Therefore, Senator Eliot (C) did not vote for this bill (B).

Certain tests may be applied to validate or dismiss the integrity of the categorical syllogism.

2. The Disjunctive Syllogism.   The **disjunctive syllogism** is a syllogism in which the major premise contains mutually exclusive alternatives. The separation of alternatives is usually indicated by such words as *either, or, neither, nor, but,* and *although,* either expressly stated or clearly implied.

MAJOR PREMISE: Either Congress will amend this bill or the president will veto it.

MINOR PREMISE: Congress will not amend this bill.

CONCLUSION: Therefore, the president will veto it.

The validity and soundness of the disjunctive syllogism may also be tested.

3. The Conditional Syllogism.   The **conditional syllogism**, also known as the *hypothetical syllogism,* is a syllogism in which the major premise deals with uncertain or hypothetical events that may or may not exist or happen. The conditional event is usually indicated by *if, assuming, supposing,* or similar terms, either expressly stated or clearly implied. For example, the following conditional syllogism was used in debates on the proposition "Resolved: That the federal government should adopt a program of compulsory wage and price controls":

MAJOR PREMISE: If the present measures have reduced greenhouse emissions, then we will not need to implement a cap-and-trade system.

MINOR PREMISE: Present measures have not reduced greenhouse emissions.

CONCLUSION: Therefore, we will need to implement a cap-and-trade system.

The major premise of the conditional syllogism contains an *antecedent* statement, which expresses the conditional or hypothetical event under consideration, and a *consequent* statement, which expresses the event that is maintained

---

Tests: Disjunctive Syllogism

1. *The major premise of the disjunctive syllogism must include all of the possible alternatives.* For example, after tribal wars broke out in Africa, some thought severe food shortages might occur and called for the United States to send massive food shipments to Africa. The argument went like this:

   MAJOR PREMISE: We must send food to Africa or millions will die.

   MINOR PREMISE: We don't want millions to die.

   CONCLUSION: Therefore, we must send food to Africa.

   Negative advocates who encountered this syllogism recognized that the major premise did not include all possible alternatives. They pointed out that the African country under consideration not only produced enough food to feed itself but normally had ample food for export. The problem was not a food shortage but a genocidal tribal war. Food was rotting in the fields while rival tribes battled, destroying the transportation system. Thus, unloading food on docks at the country's ports—even if that could have been done—would have been useless, because the ports were under siege and the roads were impassable.

2. *The alternatives presented in the disjunctive syllogism must be mutually exclusive.* Those who opposed sending food to the African country argued that the war and not a food shortage was the major cause of deaths. They argued that only a major effort by the United Nations could end the war. They maintained that sending food without ending the war would merely increase deaths, because the rival tribes would intensify the war to gain control of the food supplies.

3. *The minor premise must affirm or contradict one of the alternatives given in the major premise.* If the minor premise neither affirms nor contradicts one of the alternatives in the major premise, no valid conclusion is possible. Here is an example:

   MAJOR PREMISE: Congress must either raise taxes or reduce federal expenditures.

   MINOR PREMISE: Members of Congress will not cut their own salaries.

   CONCLUSION: Therefore, Congress must _____?

   Because congressional salaries are only a minor part of all federal expenditures, the premise that members of Congress will not cut their own salaries might more accurately be phrased as "Members of Congress will not reduce *some* federal expenditures." Even though congresspersons will not cut their own salaries, it is possible for them to reduce *other* federal expenditures; therefore this premise neither affirms nor contradicts one of the alternatives in the major premise.

---

as necessarily following the antecedent. In the example just given, the antecedent statement begins with the word *if* and the consequent statement begins with the word *then*. The *if-then* relationship is a convenient way of expressing the major premise in a conditional syllogism.

Certain tests may be applied to the conditional syllogism.

Tests: Conditional Syllogism

---

1. *The minor premise must affirm the antecedent or deny the consequent.* If the minor premise affirms the antecedent, the conclusion must affirm the consequent; if the minor premise denies the consequent, the conclusion must deny the antecedent. Consider this example:

    MAJOR PREMISE: If the price of gas continues to rise, more people will ride public transportation.

    MINOR PREMISE: The price of gas will continue to rise.

    CONCLUSION: Therefore, more people will ride public transportation.

    Note that in this case the minor premise affirms the antecedent and the conclusion affirms the consequent. The following example does just the opposite:

    MAJOR PREMISE: Either the American team will qualify for the World Cup, or Americans will not watch it.

    MINOR PREMISE: The American team will not qualify.

    CONCLUSION: Americans will not watch the World Cup.

2. *If the minor premise denies the antecedent or affirms the consequent, no valid conclusion can be drawn.* Here's an example:

    MAJOR PREMISE: If the price of gas continues to rise, more people will ride public transportation.

    MINOR PREMISE: The price of gas will NOT continue to rise.

    CONCLUSION: Therefore, _____?

    In this example the absence of an increase in interest rates will not lead to more of these notes being purchased. However (because a change in any of a number of fiscal or monetary policies might lead to more of these notes being purchased), one cannot conclude that more notes will *not* be purchased. Thus, when the minor premise denies the antecedent, no valid conclusion can be drawn. Now consider this example:

    MAJOR PREMISE: Either the American team will qualify for the World Cup, or Americans will not watch it.

    MINOR PREMISE: The American team WILL qualify for the World Cup.

    CONCLUSION: Therefore, _____?

    Even if the American team does qualify for the World Cup, numerous other factors might prevent people from watching it. Thus, when the antecedent statement affirms the consequent, no valid conclusion can be drawn.

B. The Enthymeme

1. Definitions of the Enthymeme. The rigorous rules of the syllogism make it a valuable instrument for testing arguments. But these rules also limit the situations in which it can be used. We rarely talk in syllogisms; we are more likely to express our arguments in less-than-complete syllogisms. Also there are many situations in which we must deal with probabilities rather than certainties. In these circumstances we make use of the enthymeme. Because there are two discrete concepts involved, there are two definitions of the **enthymeme.**

The first definition of the enthymeme—as a *truncated (shortened) syllogism*—is extremely important to the advocate. As noted, people usually do not talk in syllogisms.

Many arguments are expressed in the form of enthymemes. In a debate on federal aid for higher education, we might hear this argument: "This plan would lead to federal control and is undesirable." Expressed in the form of an enthymeme, this argument would look like this:

MAJOR PREMISE: This plan leads to federal control.

CONCLUSION: Therefore, this plan is undesirable.

As advocates encountering this enthymeme, we would immediately look for the unstated major premise. If the unstated major premise were "*Some* forms of federal control are undesirable," we would recognize that the middle term is not distributed and that therefore the conclusion is formally invalid. If the unstated major premise were "*All* forms of federal control are undesirable," the conclusion would be formally valid, but we might want to question the material truth of the major premise.

Thus, when we encounter enthymemes in an argument—and we will often encounter them—we should look for the unstated premise and determine whether the conclusion logically follows that premise or whether the unstated premise is materially true. In discovering the unstated premise, we may open up important avenues of analysis.

Sometimes advocates may find it psychologically advantageous to omit the conclusion. If the major and minor premises are clearly stated, the audience or judges will draw the conclusion and may hold it more firmly because they reached it "on their own." Or advocates may be able to make an unpleasant point without actually stating it. Thus a professor might say to a student, "Anyone who failed the midterm exam must get a B or better on the final to pass the course. You failed the midterm." The professor would no doubt get the message

---

Two Definitions of the Enthymeme

1. The enthymeme is a *truncated* syllogism in which one of the premises or the conclusion is not stated.
2. The enthymeme is a syllogism based on probabilities, signs, and examples, whose function is rhetorical persuasion. Its successful construction is accomplished through the joint efforts of speaker and audience, and this is its essential character.[*]

[*]Lloyd F. Bitzer, "Aristotle's Enthymeme Revisited," *Quarterly Journal of Speech*, vol. 45, no. 4 (1959), p. 408.

across without verbalizing it; and the student, drawing the inevitable conclusion, might be motivated to put extra effort into preparing for the final.

The enthymeme—as the term is used in the second definition (with the focus on probabilities, signs, and examples and on construction through the joint efforts of speaker and audience)—may or may not omit one of the premises or the conclusion. This definition of the enthymeme is also important to the advocate, who is often concerned with probability rather than certainty and who often wishes to build on premises already established in the mind of the audience.

Affirmative advocates of a policy proposition argue for implementation of some *plan of action*, which they claim will have substantial benefits. Negative debaters may argue that the affirmative's plan should be rejected on the basis of its costs For example, many negative debaters use this objection to the cost of an affirmative plan:

MAJOR PREMISE: All plans that increase the federal deficit should be rejected.

MINOR PREMISE: This plan *may* increase the deficit.

CONCLUSION: Therefore, this plan should be rejected.

In this case the debater hoped the audience was predisposed to oppose deficits and would thus join with the debater in building the enthymeme by accepting the major premise. Syllogistically this argument proves absolutely nothing. It has a formal validity of zero. The syllogism is a logical instrument for dealing with certainty; it is concerned with all of the factors in a certain classification and with matters that necessarily and inevitably follow from certain premises. However, many problems the advocate must consider are not subject to certainty or to absolute proof. If the negative can establish a reasonable degree of cogency for its argument—if it can establish a reasonable probability that the plan will cause an increased budget deficit—it might well win the decision.

Another enthymeme was used in some debates on the democracy assistance proposition:

MAJOR PREMISE: All programs that engage in nation building are undesirable.

MINOR PREMISE: The affirmative's plan of democracy assistance may engage in nation building.

CONCLUSION: Therefore, the affirmative's plan of democracy assistance is undesirable.

In this case the debater hoped the audience was predisposed to oppose nation building and so would join with the debater in building the enthymeme by accepting the minor premise. At the time of these debates, the negative could cite some evidence to support the minor premise, and the affirmative could cite some evidence to refute it. Assuming neither side could establish certainty, the decision on this clash would go to the side establishing a fair preponderance of evidence.

Enthymemes, like syllogisms, may be classified as categorical, disjunctive, and conditional. The same tests used to determine the formal validity of a syllogism may be used to determine the formal validity of an enthymeme. Although the enthymemes just cited are invalid as syllogisms, they are formally valid as enthymemes. Thus, if advocates can establish a preponderance of probability to support their arguments and can get the audience to join with them in the construction of the enthymeme, they may persuade reasonable people to accept their conclusions.

The following enthymeme, however, is formally invalid; thus, regardless of the degree of probability attached to the premise, the conclusion is worthless:

> MAJOR PREMISE: Some domestic industries are not harmed by Chinese imports.
>
> MINOR PREMISE: Textiles are a domestic industry.
>
> CONCLUSION: Therefore, textiles are probably not harmed by Chinese imports.

The fallacy of an undistributed middle term—"*some* domestic industries"— renders the conclusion of this enthymeme formally invalid.

2. Chain of Enthymemes.   Arguments are often stated in the form of a chain of enthymemes. A speaker may state only the conclusion of an enthymeme, use that as one premise of a second enthymeme, state the conclusion to the second enthymeme without indicating the other premise, and continue in this way to build a chain of enthymemes. The omitted portion of the enthymeme sometimes will be evident and uncontestable; other times, however, it may not be apparent or may be subject to refutation. Consequently advocates should recognize and analyze a chain of enthymemes, seek out the omitted portions of the argument, restructure the argument in syllogistic form, and apply the appropriate tests.

Advocates will often find it advantageous to begin to build a chain of enthymemes in the minds of the listeners. As Aristotle advised: "Our speaker, accordingly, must start out from ... the [actual] opinions of the judges [audience], or else the opinions of persons whose authority they accept. And the speaker must make sure that his premises do appear in this light to most, if not all, of his audience. And he must argue not only from necessary truths, but from probable truths as well."[2]

Thus, if the advocate were speaking before a civil liberties group, analysis of the audience might lead him or her to conclude that the group would support the major premise, "Privacy is an important value guaranteed by the U.S. Constitution." Building on this premise in the minds of the audience, the advocate might begin the argument by stating, in effect:

> MINOR PREMISE: The USA Patriot Act violates our right of privacy.
>
> CONCLUSION: Therefore, the USA Patriot Act must be repealed.

Or, if the speaker were addressing a gun club, analysis of the audience might lead him or her to conclude that the group would support the major premise,

---

2. Aristotle, *Rhetoric*, II, 22.

"The right of the people to keep and bear arms shall not be infringed." Building on this premise in the minds of the audience, the speaker might begin the argument by stating, in effect:

MINOR PREMISE: The Gun Registration Act infringes on our right to keep guns.

CONCLUSION: The Gun Registration Act is unconstitutional.

Advocates should analyze their decision renderers carefully and seek out opportunities to build a chain of enthymemes on the premises already established in the minds of the audience or judge (see the Chapter 15 section "Analysis of the Audience").

C. Formal Validity and Material Truth

In the syllogisms and enthymemes considered thus far, we have assumed that each premise of each syllogism is *absolutely* true and that each premise of each enthymeme is *probably* true. If they are true, the conclusions drawn from the formally valid syllogisms are matters of absolute certainty, and the conclusions drawn from the formally valid enthymemes must be accorded the degree of cogency appropriate to the probability found in the premises. If, however, any of these premises is false, then its conclusion is worthless regardless of the formal validity of the construction:

MAJOR PREMISE: Any child can make a website.

MINOR PREMISE: John is a child.

CONCLUSION: Therefore, John can make a website.

This syllogism unquestionably is formally valid. Assume that John really is a child; the minor premise is then materially true. The major premise, however, has no foundation in fact. Obviously the conclusion is worthless.

Note that a materially true conclusion is not proof that the premises are materially true or that the syllogism is formally valid. Consider the following syllogism:

MAJOR PREMISE: All nations that have received direct economic aid from the United States are now military allies of the United States.

MINOR PREMISE: Canada has not received direct economic aid from the United States.

CONCLUSION: Therefore, Canada is a military ally of the United States.

The proof of this conclusion must come from a source other than this syllogism.

To establish the material truth of a premise, the advocate must apply the tests of reasoning and the tests of evidence considered earlier. Because many premises are, in fact, conclusions from other syllogisms or enthymemes that may or may not have been stated in the argument, the appropriate tests of formal validity should be applied to them.

III. THE ELEMENTS OF ANY ARGUMENT
(TOULMIN'S MODEL)

Whereas formal logic provides for rigorous testing of arguments based on almost mathematical rules, most human decisions, even by critical audiences, are made on a basis of more practical reasoning (Aristotle referred to this as logos). Therefore in debate, more often than not, the test of an argument is not whether it is true or false, but rather, is it strong or weak.

Philosopher Stephen Toulmin offers a model for better understanding the structure of practical reasoning that occurs in any argument. He maintains that six elements can be found in any wholly explicit argument: (1) claims, (2) grounds, (3) warrants, (4) backing, (5) modal qualifications, and (6) possible rebuttals.[3] We consider each in turn.

A. Claims

The **claim(s)** element of the argument is the conclusion we are trying to establish by our argument. Our claim might be the proposition itself—for example, "Resolved: That the federal government should significantly strengthen the regulation of mass media communication in the United States" or "Resolved: That the federal government should initiate a new jobs program in the United States." In practice, to establish those claims, we would first have to establish a series of other claims—for instance, "Banning publicity will reduce terrorism" or "Reducing barriers to small business expansion will reduce unemployment in the United States." Of course, a claim without support is only an assertion, and has limited persuasive force.

B. Grounds

Once we have made a claim, we must advance **grounds**—evidence and reasoning to establish the foundation of our claim. We have to provide good reasons to establish that our claim is solid and reliable. The grounds represent what we have to go on. They generally provide concrete and observable "facts" or descriptions, and provide evidence from which the movement to a claim can be based.

C. Warrants

Once we have made a claim and we have indicated the grounds or factual basis for that claim, we must provide a **warrant**—evidence and reasoning advanced to justify the move from the grounds to the claim. We need to establish that the evidence and reasoning we have offered as grounds apply in this particular instance. The warrant is the bridge that supports the movement from data to claim, or put another way, is the foundation upon which the argument is based. It represents the explanation providing reasoning acceptable to the audience.

---

3. Stephen Toulmin, Richard Rieke, and Allan Janik, *An Introduction to Reasoning* (New York: Macmillan, 1979), p. 25.

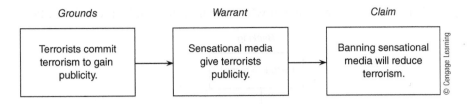

Let's consider how affirmative advocates on the proposition "Resolved: That the federal government should significantly strengthen the regulation of mass media communication in the United States" used these three elements of argument: If the advocates have provided good evidence and reasoning to establish their grounds and to support their claim, they will have taken important steps toward establishing their claim.

Let's continue now with a consideration of the other elements of argument.

D. Backing

Our warrant will not always be accepted merely on our say-so or be intuitive; we may have to provide **backing**—additional evidence and reasoning to support our warrant. Applying this element to our mass media example, we expand our diagram:

We see that the warrants are not self-validating.[4] Therefore, we need to provide additional evidence and reasoning to sustain our warrant in the form of backing.

E. Modal Qualifications

When we have considered the grounds, warrant, and backing offered in support of our claim, we are in a position to qualify that claim—that is, to express the degree of cogency (considered in detail later in this chapter) that we can attach to our claim. The degree of cogency, or **modal qualification**, we can attach to our claim may vary from certainty to possibility.

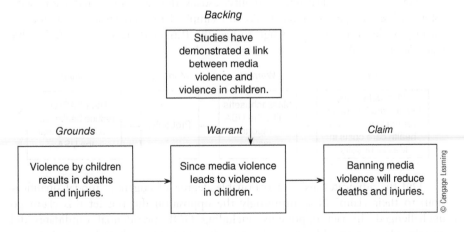

---

4. Toulmin, Rieke, and Janik, *An Introduction to Reasoning*, p. 58.

Let's consider an example in which the modality can be precisely verified:

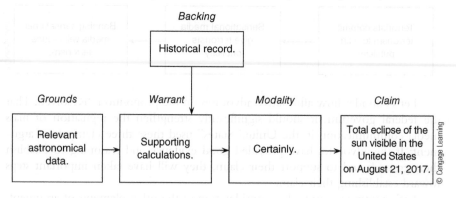

Students are invited to check with the astronomy department of their university: Do the professors there agree with the modality or degree of cogency assigned to this claim? Note that after August 21, 2017, this claim will become a perfect example of judicial notice (see Chapter 6). If "everyone" knows that there was a total eclipse of the sun on that date, we only have to mention the fact to establish the claim. Because the eclipse of 2017 will be the first eclipse of the sun visible in the United States since July 11, 1991, it will undoubtedly be a well-publicized event. Only after a lapse of some time after the event will it be necessary to introduce evidence to support the claim.

Consider another example: Will the United States withdraw its troops from Afghanistan by 2014 as proposed by President Obama? However, an affirmative answer to these questions *cannot* be given with *certainty* until that date arrives. Although eclipses and the orbits of planets can be predicted with certainty far in advance, the decisions of nations—and their ability to carry out these decisions—cannot be predicted with anything approaching the same precision.

Advocates rarely deal with certainty; usually they are concerned with establishing a lesser degree of cogency. As an example, let's consider an argument frequently made during the campaign to pass the Patient Protection and Affordable Care Act (PPACA).

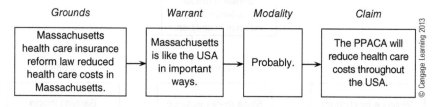

Did the advocates assign a reasonable degree of cogency (modal qualification) to their claim? Not surprisingly the opposition did not let this claim go unchallenged. In fact opponents, including GOP presidential candidates did exactly what we would expect them to do—introduce rebuttal—which brings us to the last of Toulmin's elements of argument.

F. Rebuttals

As is discussed in detail in Chapter 14, **rebuttal** involves introducing evidence and reasoning to weaken or destroy another's claim. In the debate on a jobs bill, the negative introduced rebuttal designed to destroy the degree of cogency that the affirmative assigned to its claim.

With the rebuttal and its backing now before us, we will either have to drop the claim or assign to it a much lower degree of cogency (modality). Depending on the evidence and reasoning the negative has used in its rebuttal, the chance that PPACA ("Obamacare") will reduce health care costs in the United States has now been lowered from a probability to at best a possibility.

Rebuttal, then, may be seen as an element of argument that may block or impede the movement of argument from grounds to claim and force us to reconsider and to define more precisely the degree of cogency we assign to our claim.

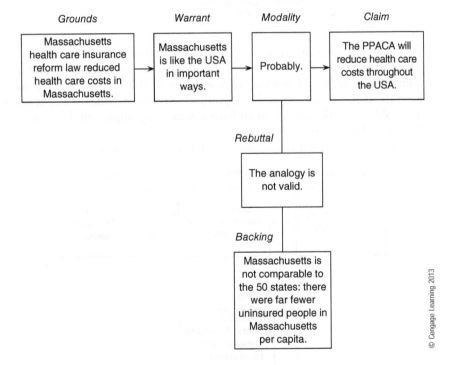

G. Extending the Elements of an Argument

The samples we have considered are brief. In an actual argument or debate, the elements of argument are often extended and complex. In the example just discussed, the opposition built on their backing, "Massachusetts is not comparable to the 50 states: there were far fewer uninsured people in Massachusetts per capita," to establish a disadvantage and advanced a revised version of that backing as grounds, "The PPACA, by extending health care coverage to many more people without generating revenue to cover the increased coverages will increase the federal deficit":

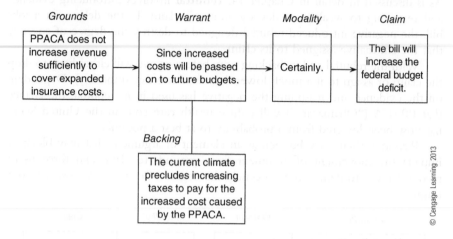

Naturally the proponents responded with rebuttal of their own, challenging the claims that the PPACA savings would not cover the increased costs, and that the current climate would preclude increasing taxes. Still more arguments were built on the deficit argument as the opposition introduced evidence and reasoning to establish that the deficit would have a devastating impact on the economy or that the bill would reduce deficits.

Another example, with more obvious flaws, may help to clarify:

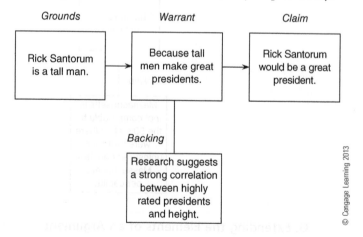

This argument seems outrageous, yet presidential candidates are careful to emphasize their height during campaigns. A major point of conflict occurred during negotiations to arrange the stage for the Obama versus McCain debates of 2008. Obama was significantly taller than McCain. The McCain campaign team preferred debating while seating to equalize height during the debate. So there seems to be at least some validity to the above argument. Is it a strong argument? Santorum's height can be measured. Analysis would isolate the key to this argument as the warrant, and how well it would be received by the intended audience.

Careful evaluation of the elements of argument will allow the advocate to detect flaws in an argument, and thus to launch an attack on an opponent's argument or to replace or repair a flawed argument intended to support the advocate's own position.

IV. TYPES OF REASONING

Reasoning is the process of inferring conclusions from premises. The premises may be in the form of any of the various types of evidence; they may be stated as propositions; or they may be statements of conclusions reached through prior reasoning. They are based in concrete observation and presumably objective observation of phenomena or occurrences. Thus advocates use the premises they have previously established or asserted (and can count on some agreement upon), and by a process of reasoning, they try to establish something new—a conclusion they want their audience to accept. If the audience perceives the premises as well grounded and the reasoning as rhetorically sound, it will be likely to accept the conclusion.

A. The Degree of Cogency

The **degree of cogency** is the extent to which an argument is both sound and intellectually compelling because it is well founded in fact, logic, or rationality. (As we saw earlier, Toulmin used the term *modal qualification* to express this concept.) The degrees of cogency are certainty, probability, plausibility, or possibility. These may be thought of as existing on a continuum, represented by the following diagram.

These degrees of cogency are not discrete compartments; rather, they are terms used to suggest the relative compelling force of various logical proofs.

Cogency Continuum

Absolute truth				A scintilla of truth

Certainty
..................Probability
....................Plausibility
....................Possibility........................ © Cengage Learning

1. Certainty. *Certainty* is associated with absolute truth. If a conclusion is a certainty, all competent observers are in agreement. Relatively little of the advocates' time is concerned with this degree of proof. But few matters of human affairs actually are subject to proof as certainty. Advocates' efforts usually are in the realm of probability; they have to try to demonstrate that their conclusions have a degree of credibility warranting acceptance. In criminal courts, which demand the highest standard of proof, all elements of the case must be proven "beyond a reasonable doubt," or what has been estimated to be over 90 percent certainty. Outside the criminal courts we are often required to make decisions based on a lesser degree of certainty. For example, the secretary of the treasury, even with all of the resources of the federal government at his or her disposal, cannot establish as a certainty the proposition that a given tax bill will raise X dollars in revenue. Advocates who debated Health Care Reform and Federal Support for Higher Education found that estimates of tax revenues and program savings were often inaccurate. Furthermore, matters that are a certainty are, by definition, not appropriate subjects for debate. Matters that are a certainty, however, are often used as part of the evidence and with reasoning are used to establish new conclusions.

We should note that it is not only the evidence itself but the way it is perceived that will determine certainty and the other degrees of cogency. If our ego, politics, finances, or other interests are involved in the matter, our evaluation of the evidence will vary. While the judge or audience may attempt to consider some matters dispassionately and objectively (fortunately, this is usually the case with judges in academic debate and in judicial courtrooms), at all times advocates have to be aware of audience attitudes and adapt their cases, reasoning, and evidence to their listeners' interests or predispositions (see Chapter 15).

2. Probability.   *Probability* is associated with a high degree of likelihood (but *not* certainty) that a conclusion is true. As advocates we will spend much of our time trying to prove that our propositions have a high degree of probability and are more probably true than those of our opponents. For example, no method of contraception is 100 percent effective; even sterilization fails at times, and other methods range from 76 to 97.6 percent in their effectiveness. Thus, in choosing contraceptives, people are basing their decisions on probabilities. In the physical sciences the degree of probability of a proposition being true can be established with great precision; often thousands of cases can be examined under carefully controlled conditions. In other areas, however, it is not always possible to measure as accurately and to control as precisely the variables affecting the proposition. In civil courts the standard of proof is the preponderance of evidence; this means a 51 percent chance of being true. Outside the civil courts the necessary degree of cogency depends on the situation. For example, the secretary of the treasury, in seeking to establish the proposition that a given tax reform bill will raise X dollars in revenue, will have to qualify his or her statement. That is, he or she will have to say that if the present level of employment is maintained, if spending is continued at the present level, if there isn't an international crisis, and if various other relevant factors don't change, then it is reasonable to assume that the tax bill will raise X dollars.

3. Plausibility.   *Plausibility* is associated with a lesser degree of likelihood that a proposition is true. Advocates will use arguments having this degree of proof only when no better arguments are available. The ancient Sophists often used this type of proof; modern propagandists do so as well. Arguments of this type are sometimes superficial or specious and have limited probative force for the thoughtful listener or reader. Sometimes, of course, we are forced to make decisions simply on the basis of plausibility, if this relatively low degree of cogency is the best available. Many life-or-death surgical decisions are made on this basis. When a new surgical procedure is first developed (heart transplant, for example), the surgeon tells the patient, in effect, "If you go on as you are, all our experience indicates that your condition will continue to deteriorate and you will die within a few months. We've developed a new surgical procedure that *could* help you. We've had some successes with this new procedure, but frankly it's still experimental and we don't have enough data to make firm estimates." Given this set of circumstances, would you take the gamble?

4. Possibility.   *Possibility* is associated with a low degree of likelihood that a proposition is true. The advocate has only limited use for proofs with this degree of cogency and will always seek proofs having greater logical force. Until the closing weeks of the baseball season, for example, a mathematical possibility usually exists that the last-place team could win the division pennant. If such a possibility requires, however, that the last-place team win all its remaining games and that the top three teams lose all their remaining games, this possibility would not warrant serious consideration. Sometimes, of course, we are forced to make decisions when proofs with this low degree of likelihood are the best available. When debating the proposition "Resolved: That the federal government should establish a national program of public work for the unemployed," some affirmative teams argued that the proposition should be adopted because a major recession might occur in the future and that such a program should be established in case it needed to be put into effect at the onset of the recession. At the time the proposition was debated, the country was enjoying a period of prosperity and there was no evidence of a recession in the foreseeable future (hard to recall such a time!). But some affirmative teams argued successfully that on the basis of all our previous experience a recession was a possibility for which we should be prepared.

Consider an example regarding a debate on the proposition to increase space exploration: "The chemical substance which can only be produced in space *could* be a one-shot cure for diabetes." As we saw, this evidence as presented is useless. But let's assume for a moment that a pharmaceutical company hoped to develop such a substance; after all, that's entirely *plausible*, indeed *probable*. Let's assume further that the company had conducted exhaustive studies indicating that, by using certain techniques in the zero gravity of space, such a substance *could* be produced. Yet, prior to actual testing in space, one can only say "could." Until the experiment was actually performed in zero gravity and the results carefully evaluated, no one could say positively that the substance would in fact be a one-shot cure for diabetes. Yet, given the rewards that would come from such a discovery, it's entirely reasonable to believe that investors would risk large sums of money on the long odds.

The effort to develop the next generation of computer technology provides another example. Although it is generally agreed that new computer capabilities will come about, highly competent engineers have different ideas about designs and possibilities. At this time no one actually knows how or what will be developed, but the cost-benefit ratio of being the first to develop a new-generation computer application is so great that billions of dollars are being poured into research on this project.

The rest of this chapter will consider the types and uses of the tests of reasoning. We first discuss general tests applicable to all types of reasoning. Then we cover specific tests for (1) reasoning by example, (2) reasoning by analogy, (3) causal reasoning, and (4) sign reasoning.

B. Tests of Reasoning and Their Uses

Obviously all reasoning does not have the same degree of cogency. Therefore, it's important to test reasoning to determine the degree of probability of the conclusions. Often more than one type of reasoning is involved in a given line of argument, making it necessary to apply all the appropriate tests to each piece of reasoning. There are three uses for the tests of reasoning.

1. To Test the Validity of One's Own Reasoning.   Validity in reasoning is the measure to which the claim or conclusion forwarded by its advocates is indeed supported by the evidence and reasoning offered for it. In the construction of a case, advocates will discover much reasoning advanced by others and will develop tentative lines of reasoning of their own. Before incorporating any of this reasoning into their cases, they must apply the tests of reasoning so that they may reject invalid reasoning and include only what will stand up under scrutiny. By applying the tests of reasoning, they can anticipate the probable lines of refutation by their opponents and prepare their counter refutation. These tests of reasoning should also be applied outside the debate situation. For example, as college students weigh the propositions that they should enter law school, or medical school, or a certain field, their future happiness and success require that they carefully apply the tests of reasoning to the arguments supporting these propositions.

2. To Test the Validity of the Reasoning Advanced by the Opposition.   In preparing cases, advocates have to try to discover the probable lines of reasoning their opponents will use, apply the appropriate tests to this reasoning, and plan refutation of it. In the course of the debate, they should be prepared to apply the appropriate tests as their opponent's actual lines of reasoning are presented and to develop their refutations accordingly.

3. To Test the Validity of Reasoning Advanced for a Decision.   Often we may seek neither to advance our own arguments nor to refute arguments of others; rather, we function as decision renderers to whom various lines of reasoning are directed. As citizens, we are the target of arguments advanced by political parties. To function as responsible citizens, we have to apply the tests of reasoning to these arguments. If we plan to buy a car, or stock, or a house, or make any other significant purchase, our own self-interest compels us to apply the tests of reasoning to the arguments advanced by the salesperson. In fact any time we have to make a decision of any significance, common sense dictates that we apply the tests of reasoning to the factors relating to that decision with a degree of rigor directly related to the importance of the decision.

In the course of the debate, we and our opponents are presenting reasoning to the audience or judges for their decision. The audience or judges will make a judgment as to what degree of cogency they assign to the conflicting arguments. We must be in a position to advance good reasons that they should accept our arguments and reject the reasoning of our opponents.

C. General Tests of Reasoning

The general tests that should be applied to all types of reasoning are drawn from Toulmin's model of arguments. Once a claim is advanced, we may apply these general tests to the supporting elements of the argument. The tests, of course, must be specific to the particular argument being considered. An affirmative answer to the following test questions implies that the reasoning is sound; a negative answer may imply the presence of a fallacy.

1. *Are the grounds solid?* Have good reasons been given to establish the foundation of this claim? Have reliable evidence and reasoning been provided to establish grounds for the claim?

2. *Does the warrant justify the claim?* Have sufficient evidence and reasoning been given to provide good reasons justifying the movement from grounds to claim in this specific instance? Does the assumption upon which this reasoning is provided make sense and hold up to scrutiny?

3. *Is the backing adequate?* In many cases the warrant or rebuttal is not sufficient to stand alone. Have additional evidence and reasoning been provided to establish adequate backing? The same tests applied to data should be applied to the backing.

4. *Has the rebuttal been properly evaluated?* Almost any argument is subject to rebuttal. Have sufficient evidence and reasoning been provided to offset or minimize the rebuttal? Has the rebuttal been properly evaluated?

5. *Has the degree of cogency (modal qualification) been properly determined?* As we have seen, the degree of cogency or modal qualification that may be attached to a claim may vary from certainty to possibility. Has the degree of cogency assigned to this particular claim been established accurately and precisely?

D. Types of Reasoning and Tests for Each Type

Reasoning is often classified as deductive or inductive. *Deductive* reasoning moves from generalization to specific application. Syllogisms are deductive forms of argument. For example, the classic syllogism offered by Plato posits: all men are mortal (broad generalization or premise), Socrates is a man (more specific), Socrates is mortal (most specific). Deductive reasoning claims to establish the certainty of a conclusion. *Inductive* reasoning moves from specific cases to generalizations. For example, "I had Pad Thai at the new Thai Restaurant last night and it was very good" (one specific case of my meal at the new restaurant); "I can therefore safely conclude that this is an excellent restaurant" (refers to a broader number of cases), and in fact, "I would have to say that Thai food is excellent!" (even broader). Inductive reasoning claims to establish a lesser degree of cogency for its conclusion. Irving Copi points out:

> Although every argument involves the claim that its premises provide evidence for the truth of its conclusion, only *deductive* argument involves the claim that its premises provide *conclusive* evidence.... An inductive argument, on the other hand, involves the claim not that its premises give conclusive evidence for the truth of its conclusion, but only that they provide *some* evidence for it.... Inductive arguments may, of course, be evaluated as better or worse, according to the degree of likelihood or probability which their premises confer upon their conclusions.[5]

As a practical matter, advocates use both **deduction** and **induction**, moving back and forth from one to the other many times while developing or analyzing an argument. The intermingling of deduction and induction will become apparent as we consider the principal types of reasoning and their related tests.

1. Reasoning by Example. The process of **reasoning by example** consists of inferring conclusions from specific cases. This process may be represented as follows:

$$\left.\begin{array}{l} \text{Case}_1 \\ \text{Case}_2 \\ \text{Case}_3 \\ \text{Case}_n \end{array}\right\} \text{Conclusion}$$

© Cengage Learning

Sometimes a single case may be used to establish the conclusion or generalization. More often a number of cases will be offered as the basis for the conclusion. Reasoning by example is a form of inductive reasoning and involves either cause or sign reasoning, because the advocate is trying to show that the examples or cases are a cause or a sign of the conclusion presented.

Advocates make frequent use of reasoning by example. In debating the proposition "Resolved: That the United States should discontinue direct economic aid to foreign countries," some affirmative teams may try to establish the argument that recipient nations resented direct economic aid. They may offer as

---

5. Irving M. Copi, *Introduction to Logic*, 3rd ed. (London: Macmillan, 1968), pp. 20–21.

examples statements by various foreign leaders, maintain that these statements express resentment toward direct economic aid, and from these cases draw the conclusion that resentment against such aid is widespread or likely. Other affirmative teams debating this proposition could maintain that direct economic aid is wasteful or unaffordable under current conditions of deficit spending and budget crises. They may offer examples of expenditures of direct economic aid monies, maintain that these expenditures have been unwise, and from these cases draw the conclusion that direct economic aid is wasteful or counterproductive.

The following questions serve as tests for reasoning by example:

1. *Is the example relevant?* Advocates should determine whether the cases offered are relevant to the matter under consideration. For example, the statements of foreign leaders representing resentment toward the United States and quoted by the affirmative support cuts to economic aid may have been criticisms of U.S. foreign policy generally, not of direct economic aid specifically. They may also reflect criticisms of U.S. *military* aid, rather than direct economic aid. These objections may demonstrate that the examples offered by the affirmative are not relevant examples of criticism of direct economic aid, however accurate they might be as examples of criticism of other aspects of U.S. foreign policy. In this way they may refute the conclusion drawn from the examples.

2. *Is there a reasonable number of examples?* Although a single example may be used to establish a generalization or conclusion, the advocate's position is usually stronger with supporting examples. Even a carefully controlled laboratory experiment is usually not accepted as establishing a conclusion until it has been repeated with the same results by other competent scientists—and, in medicine, not until thousands of cases have been studied.

    How many cases are enough? One method of obtaining enough cases is to make a complete enumeration. For example, you could ask all the students in your argumentation class whether they own iPads and then draw the conclusion that X percent of the students own iPads. Complete enumeration, however, has obvious limitations, because it is often difficult or impossible to consider every case. Therefore, advocates have to present enough cases to convince a reasonable person that there is a high degree of probability that a conclusion is correct.

    It could be argued in response to the foreign aid example that while direct economic aid may have been wasteful in some cases, three or four examples of waste among thousands of projects is not sufficient to justify the conclusion that such aid, as a whole, is wasteful. An opponent might carry this refutation a step further; and introduce reports of congressional committees that have studied large numbers of projects and found that such projects were, on balance, useful. Thus, although time limitations will often prevent our citing a large number of examples directly, we may give a few examples to illustrate our point and then, to substantiate our conclusion further, offer the testimony of persons who have studied large numbers of cases.

3. *Do the examples cover a critical period of time?* In many cases the time at which the examples were studied or the time period covered by the examples may be critical. The advocate should try to find examples representative of the period of time critical to the argument. Suppose, in debating direct economic aid, the affirmative had chosen all of its examples of waste from the first year or two of the operation of an aid program. The negative might maintain that some errors in administration could be expected at the start of a new program and that the affirmative offered no examples of waste in the recent, current, or longer term operation of a program. Public opinion polls taken during election years often provide dramatic evidence of the importance of obtaining examples from the critical period of time. After the first Persian Gulf War, President George H.W. Bush's popularity in the polls soared to near unprecedented highs. Many of the front-runners for the Democratic nomination dropped out of the race, apparently believing Bush was unbeatable. The critical period of time, however, was November 1992. By then, Bush had dropped to second place in a three-way race, and Clinton won by a plurality. Opposition to President Obama's Affordable Health Care Act was high during the period of GOP campaign's blistering the program, but before most of its mandates and benefits had kicked in.

4. *Are the examples typical?* The advocate must determine whether the cases offered are really representative. In 2011–2012, a number of laws were passed to prevent voter fraud by limiting early voting, increasing documentation and requirements upon those registering themselves or others to vote, and requiring photo identification at the polls. Yet cases of fraud were exceedingly rare. Pennsylvania, upon passage of a new restrictive law, admitted that the number of cases of fraud they had prosecuted in the last five years was zero.

5. *Are negative examples noncritical?* Advocates must discern whether the negative examples they discover are critical or noncritical. In matters of policy, it is unlikely that all of the examples will support one conclusion. Some examples may well be negative or contrary to the conclusion. In considering direct economic aid, advocates will find examples of waste and examples of excellent management; in considering employment practices, advocates will find examples of firms that practice discrimination and examples of firms that do not. They should remember that they are concerned more often with probability than certainty. They should not attempt to show that *all* direct economic aid projects are wasteful; rather, they should try to show that the examples of wastefulness warrant the conclusion that waste is inherent in the program and that direct economic aid should be discontinued. On almost any proposition the opponents are likely to have negative examples; advocates must anticipate these examples and be prepared to offer adequate evidence that the examples are noncritical and do not invalidate their conclusion.

Reasoning by example may also be analyzed by laying out the argument as outlined in the section "The Elements of Any Argument" earlier in this chapter.

For example, assume the advocate claims there are practical alternatives to nuclear power, as the following diagram shows.

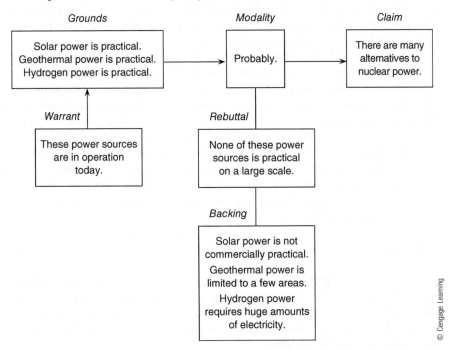

2. Reasoning by Analogy.   The process of **reasoning by analogy** consists of making a comparison between two similar cases and inferring that what is true in one case is true in the other. Reasoning by analogy is a form of inductive reasoning, in which the advocate seeks to show that the factors in his or her analogy are either a cause or a sign of the conclusion presented. This process may be represented as follows:

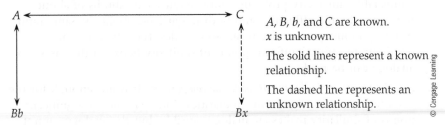

In this diagram *A* might represent Megalopolis, *Bb* might represent the type of city income tax in effect in Megalopolis, *C* might represent Gotham, and *Bx* might represent the type of infrastructure program proposed for Gotham. An advocate using reasoning by analogy might argue that, because a certain type of infrastructure program was desirable in Megalopolis, a similar program would be desirable in Gotham. Similarly, advocates might demonstrate that democracy assistance programs have been successful for some emerging democracies and would therefore, be effective for others, or that because some states have successfully reduced their deficit crises by limiting the rights of public employees to collective bargaining, increasing limitation on public unions to collective bargaining would be wise policy for other states.

Analogies may be literal or figurative. The analogy is *literal* when the cases compared are in the same classification, as are Megalopolis and Gotham (if we accept these as metropolitan cities for the purposes of our illustration) or the various state governments. The analogy *is figurative* when the cases compared are in different classifications—as in the statement "This car is a lemon!" A book reviewer made clever use of a figurative analogy when he noted, "Writing about the business of baseball is like writing about the music in topless bars." However fascinating the thrust and parry of management and labor, however clever the stratagems and costly the miscalculations of the opposing sides, they are not why people go to baseball games.[6] This comment was obviously made before the success of *Moneyball*!

These analogies have zero value as logical proof. They do, however, make their points effectively by utilizing *imagery* (a factor of style considered in detail in Chapter 16).

Carefully developed literal analogies may be used to establish a high degree of probability. Figurative analogies, on the other hand, have no value in establishing *logical* proof. If well chosen, however, they may have considerable value in establishing *ethical* or *emotional* proof, in illustrating a point, and in making a vivid impression on the audience.

The following questions provide tests for reasoning by analogy:

1. *Are there significant points of similarity?* Advocates should determine whether significant points of similarity exist between the cases compared. In making an analogy between Megalopolis and Gotham, the advocate might be able to discover a number of significant points of similarity. For instance, both might have approximately the same population; both might have comparable inner-city problems; both might have suburbs of about the same size and affluence; and both might have about the same ratio of heavy industry to service businesses. Unless the advocate can demonstrate some significant points of similarity between the cases, no analogy can be made.

2. *Are the points of similarity critical to the comparison?* It is not enough for the cases to have some significant similarities. The existence of significant points of similarity makes an analogy possible, but the analogy cannot have a reasonable degree of cogency unless it can be demonstrated that the cases are similar in critical points. We could easily demonstrate, for example, some points of similarity between a water pump and the human heart. We would not conclude, however, that a mechanic is qualified to

---

6. Alan Abelson, "Barbarians at the Ball Park,"*New York Times Book Review*, Apr. 10, 1994, p. 3.

repair both. Similarly, as indicated, we could find many significant similarities between Megalopolis and Gotham; however, in arguing that a certain type of city income tax is equally desirable in both cities, we would find these similarities noncritical. To support an analogy involving a city income tax, we would have to determine, for example, whether similar state income tax laws applied in both cities or whether there were similar state and city sales taxes in effect in both cities, similar reciprocity provisions for suburban city income taxes, similar taxes of other types, or similar financial policies. It might also be important to consider the political viability of new taxation based on local politics and party affiliation. In other words, we would have to demonstrate that the two cities were similar in critical points.

3. *Are the points of difference noncritical?* Advocates will discover that no two cases are identical in every respect. Even when two cases are similar in critical points, there will still be certain points of difference. Advocates need to determine whether the points of difference are critical or noncritical. This often depends on the context in which the comparison is made. For example, "identical" twins are usually similar in many respects, yet they have different fingerprints. This apparently minor difference might become critical and outweigh all similarities in a case in which the identity of one of the twins was the issue and fingerprint evidence was available. As another example one might point to a low level of malpractice suits against British physicians and the soaring rate of malpractice suits against American physicians and argue that British physicians must be providing much better medical care. In support of this one could argue that an injured British patient would be just as willing to sue as an injured American patient, so the only possible reason for the difference in the ratio of malpractice suits must be the quality of medical care. But there are critical differences in British and American law. In Britain the contingency fee is prohibited; in America it is almost the sole means of financing malpractice suits. Another critical difference is that in Britain all malpractice suits are held before a judge; in America almost all such suits are heard by juries. To defend an analogy, the advocate must be prepared to demonstrate that the similarities outweigh the differences in the cases compared and that the differences are not critical to the matter at issue.

4. *Is the reasoning cumulative?* An analogy is strengthened if it can be demonstrated that more than one comparison can be made in support of the conclusion. For instance, in defending the proposition that a city income tax would be advantageous in Gotham, the advocate would strengthen his or her case by making analogies not only between Gotham and Megalopolis, as mentioned, but also between Gotham and other comparable cities having city income taxes. If we were able to demonstrate that the similarities between the cities compared were critical and that the differences were noncritical, we would strengthen our case by using cumulative analogies.

5. *Are only literal analogies used as logical proof?* Advocates should remember that only literal analogies may be used to establish logical proof.

Figurative analogies are useful as illustrations, but they have no probative force. When confronted with a figurative analogy, advocates should be prepared to demonstrate its shortcomings as logical proof.

Reasoning by analogy may also be analyzed by using the elements of any argument. For example, assume the advocate claims that British medical care is better than American medical care, as the following diagram shows.

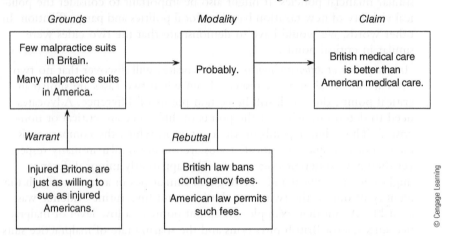

3. Causal Reasoning.   In the process of **causal reasoning**, one infers that a certain factor (a cause) is a force that produces something else (an effect). This process can be represented as follows:

$$C \atop \text{(inferred)} \xrightarrow{\hspace{2cm}} \begin{matrix} E \\ \text{(known)} \end{matrix}$$

© Cengage Learning

The same process can be used in reverse. That is, if an effect is known to exist, it may be reasoned that it was produced by a cause. This process may be represented as follows:

$$C \atop \text{(inferred)} \xleftarrow{\hspace{2cm}} \begin{matrix} E \\ \text{(known)} \end{matrix}$$

© Cengage Learning

Causal reasoning, whether cause-to-effect or effect-to-cause, usually involves generalization. In using causal reasoning the advocate tries to show *why* the proposition is valid. The National Weather Service, for example, regularly reports the existence of low-pressure areas and other phenomena (causes) and predicts that we will have rain (an effect) tomorrow. The fact that the weather service is not always right emphasizes the point considered earlier: We often deal with matters in the realm of probability because we cannot establish certainty. Recall that in order to debate the discontinuance of direct economic foreign aid, some advocates may try to show that this aid causes resentment among recipient countries. Continuing this argument, those advocates may reason that if direct economic aid (the cause) were discontinued, then criticism (the effect) would also be eliminated. Conversely, the proponents of such aid would argue that the aid was producing desirable effects.

Advocates must, of course, recognize that many causes are at work in any problem under consideration; at the same time they should try to discern the practical, effective cause or causes in the matter at issue. Many debates on human affairs revolve around causal matters. The supporters of a national jobs program, for example, may see such a program as a cause that would produce many desirable effects, whereas opponents may see it as a cause that would produce many undesirable effects. Causal reasoning influences our thinking on personal matters as well. Students may go to college because they see a college education as a cause that they hope will produce desirable effects in later life.

The problem, as we apply the tests of causal reasoning, is to discern the significant, practical, and effective causes in the matter at issue. The following tests of reasoning may be applied either to cause-to-effect or to effect-to-cause reasoning:

1. *Is the alleged cause relevant to the effect described?* Some observers have claimed that an increase in sunspot activity causes a rise in the stock market. Is there a relevant cause-and-effect relationship between these two phenomena? Most competent authorities have not been able to discern it. One college debater recently informed her professor that she expected to win because it was snowing the day the tournament began and she had previously won a tournament when snow had fallen at the start of the event. Her remark was facetious, of course, because she recognized that there was no causal relationship between snowfall and winning a tournament. Yet this kind of reasoning has formed the basis of many superstitions. The superstition that breaking a mirror will cause seven years of bad luck, for example, is based on the assumption that a cause-to-effect relationship exists when in fact there is no such relationship. Unless and until a causal link can be established between an alleged cause and an alleged effect, one cannot hope to develop causal reasoning.

2. *Is this the sole or distinguishing causal factor?* Advocates should determine whether the alleged cause is the only causal factor in producing the effect under consideration or, if not, whether it is the distinguishing causal factor. In debates on the proposition "Resolved: That the federal government should significantly strengthen the regulation of mass media communication in the United States," some affirmative advocates may use cause-to-effect reasoning to argue that television commercials for fast food cause children to demand to their parents that they should be able to eat these products, which in turn had deleterious effects on their health. In countering this line of reasoning, some opponents may argue that children naturally like the foods served by fast food restaurants and that parents appreciate the convenience of the restaurants, so even if commercials for these products were banned from television, the families would still eat just as much fast food.

Negative advocates might extend their argument by claiming that, if television commercials for these products were banned, the manufacturers would simply shift their advertising to Internet, texting, newspapers, magazines, and billboards (that is, media not affected by the affirmative's plan) and that these media would produce the same effect as the television commercials had. Thus the negative advocates could claim that television commercials are neither the sole nor the distinguishing causal factor in children's consumption of fast foods. The advocate should therefore be prepared to demonstrate that the alleged cause is the sole or distinguishing causal factor.

3. *Is there reasonable probability that no undesirable effect will result from this particular cause?* Usually a given cause will produce various effects in addition to the effect under consideration. Will these other effects be desirable, unimportant, or undesirable? If desirable, they will aid those advocating this particular cause; if unimportant, they will have no adverse impact; if undesirable, they may provide good reason for rejecting the arguments in support of this cause. In debating the mass media proposition, opponents could develop a disadvantage argument by maintaining that, if an advocate's plan of banning television commercials for fast food restaurants were put into effect, it would drastically reduce the demand for certain types of food products and would therefore cause widespread unemployment among food producers; the harms resulting from this unemployment would far outweigh any harms uniquely related to fast food consumption.

   Some readers of this book can verify the following example from their own experience: Penicillin is a very effective cause for producing certain very desirable effects in some types of illness. Yet in some persons penicillin causes effects that are so undesirable that its use is contraindicated. The possible good effects are outweighed by the undesirable effects. Thus advocates have to determine what other effects will be produced by the cause they speak for and be prepared to demonstrate, at the least, that these other effects are not undesirable.

4. *Is there a counteracting cause?* When an effect that will take place in the future is the factor under consideration, it is necessary to determine that no counteracting cause, or causes, will offset the alleged effect. In debating the mass media proposition, some advocates may argue for restrictions on the sale or distribution of pornographic material. Opponents could reasonably argue that the sale of pornographic materials would continue virtually undiminished under the affirmative's plan because of certain counteracting causes. Specifically they argued that (1) the courts would find it difficult or impossible to define pornography; (2) the affirmative's figures on the sales of pornographic material proved that a vast market exists for such materials, which means that the criminal elements that produced it would have a strong incentive to circumvent the law; (3) prosecutors would be reluctant to prosecute pornography cases, because prosecuting cases with little hope of obtaining convictions would be a waste of tax dollars; and (4) regulation of pornography on the Internet would be impossible and counterproductive. Thus advocates must be prepared to demonstrate that other causes at work in the situation will not counter the effect they claim a certain cause will produce.

5. *Is the cause capable of producing the effect?* Often various factors occur prior to a given event, yet these factors cannot be considered as causing the effect until it can be established that they are capable of producing it. For example, did the assassination of Archduke Ferdinand at Sarajevo cause World War I? Although this incident did immediately precede the outbreak of that war, assassination of members of European royalty was not an unusual occurrence, and such occurrences typically did not cause wars. Most thoughtful historians do not regard this assassination as a cause capable of producing World War I, and so they assign other causes to that war.

In debating about a jobs bill, advocates may argue that a plan requiring improvements and repairs in infrastructure would have the effect of creating jobs, thus guaranteeing the employment opportunities called for by the proposition. Of course, affirmative advocates would have to prove that their plan would be capable of generating several million *new* jobs.

When Sarah Palin became the Republican vice presidential nominee in 2008, many supporters believed that her presence on the ticket would cause large numbers of women to vote for John McCain. This causal reasoning turned out to be faulty; Barack Obama won a majority of women's votes.

In debating, as in politics and many other contexts, a plan is often proposed as a cause that will produce a particular desired effect.

6. *Is the cause necessary and sufficient?* A *necessary* cause is a condition that is essential to producing the effect. Oxygen, for instance, is a necessary condition for fire. Oxygen alone will not cause fire, but we cannot have fire without it. Once we have identified the necessary condition for an event, we can *prevent* that event from occurring by removing one of the necessary conditions.

A *sufficient* cause is a condition that automatically produces the effect. As the inventor of the guillotine well knew, decapitation is sufficient cause for death. The difference between a necessary and a sufficient cause is that, although a necessary condition must be present, it will not by itself produce the effect. The sufficient cause is by itself enough to produce the effect. Most often a sufficient cause is a collection of necessary causes all present at one time and place. For instance, oxygen, a combustible material, and the combustion point are all necessary conditions to fire. Together, all three constitute the sufficient cause for a fire. Once we have identified the sufficient conditions for an event, we can *produce* the event by bringing the sufficient conditions together. For example, President Obama's Affordable Health Care Act sought to make insurance coverage available to more Americans, assuming that insurance is a necessary requirement to accessible health care. However, insurance alone does not provide the sufficient number of health care professionals to deliver needed services, therefore insurance alone may be necessary, but is not sufficient to overcome a lack of health care facilities or doctors.

7. *How does a new cause affect the system?* In debates on health care reform, advocates might identify the need for better medical care for inner city residents by citing tragic cases of children bitten by rats as a need for

providing medical care to inner city residents. A reasonable counter might be to argue that there would be little point in treating a rat bite and then sending a child back to the substandard home to be bitten again by another rat. Instead of spending the money on medical care, they might argue, it would be better to spend money on providing better housing, better food, and other improved conditions for poor dwellers of substandard housing.

Causal reasoning may also be analyzed by using the elements of an argument. For instance, assume the advocate claims that the cost-of-living index will go up because of a recent increase in the cost of meat, as the diagram indicates.

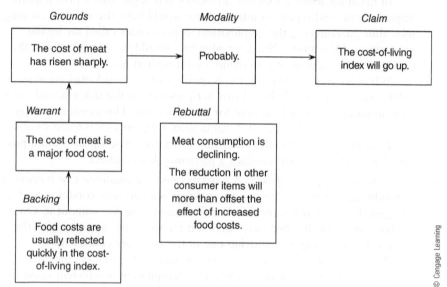

4. Reasoning by Sign.   The process of **reasoning by sign** consists of inferring relationships or correlations between two variables. Here one argues that two variables are so closely related that the presence or absence of one may be taken as an indication of the presence or absence of the other.

Reasoning by sign involves reasoning by analogy, by example, or from effect to effect as the advocate seeks to show that a proposition is valid. (In causal reasoning, you will remember, the advocate seeks to show *why* a proposition is valid.) We use reasoning by sign when we note that the leaves are falling from the trees and take this as a sign that winter is coming, or if we conclude that unemployment is low because the city park benches are empty during the day. The attribute is a part or a characteristic of the substance or totality with which we are concerned. In reasoning by sign the advocate may reason either from the attribute to the substance or from the substance to the attribute.

If one variable may be taken as a sign of another, the relationship between the variables is *reciprocal*. The relationship between the variables is *nonreciprocal* when one variable may be taken as a sign of the other but the second variable is not a reliable sign of the first. For instance, if a person is president of the United States, we may take this as a sign that he or she is at least 35 years old. Obviously, we cannot take the fact that a person is 35 years old as a sign that he or she is president of the United States.

In debating the proposition "Resolved: That the United States should extend diplomatic recognition to Cuba," some negative advocates argued that we should not adopt the proposition because diplomatic recognition was a sign of approval of the government in question.

The following questions serve as tests of reasoning by sign:

1. *Is the alleged substance relevant to the attribute described?* It is necessary to determine whether there really is a sign relationship between the substance and the attribute under consideration. Some affirmative advocates, in meeting the argument that diplomatic recognition would be a sign of approval, maintained that diplomatic recognition is not a sign of approval. In support of this, they pointed out that the United States extended diplomatic recognition to many regimes that followed policies we did not approve of; they maintained that no sign relationship exists between approval of a government and diplomatic recognition of that government. Unless and until advocates can demonstrate that a sign relationship exists between the substance and the attribute under consideration, they cannot develop sign reasoning.

2. *Is the relationship between substance and attribute inherent?* Advocates have to determine whether the relationship between substance and attribute is inherent or merely incidental. A political commentator once noted that the Cubans greatly increased the number of attachés at their embassy in a certain Central American country. He took this action as a sign that the Cubans were planning to increase their aid to forces seeking to overthrow that country's government. But was the relationship inherent? On some occasions this type of action has been a sign of an attempt to overthrow a government. More often, however, it has merely meant an increased propaganda or trade campaign.

3. *Is there a counterfactor that disrupts the relationship between substance and attribute?* It is necessary to determine that no counterfactor or factors disrupt the relationship. An increase in the number of attachés that one country assigns to another may under some conditions be a sign that the country increasing its embassy personnel plans to invade. For example, when the United States expanded its embassy in the People's Republic of China, no one took this as a sign that the United States planned to overthrow the People's Republic; too many counterfactors disrupted that sign relationship.

4. *Is the sign reasoning cumulative?* Reasoning by sign is strengthened by a demonstration that more than one sign relationship can be presented in support of the conclusion. An upturn in durable-goods orders might be a sign that an economic slump is ending. But this sign by itself is a relatively weak indicator. If other signs can be found—such as increases in a number of indicators (productivity rate, orders for plants and equipment, orders for consumer goods, and new residential building permits)—the accumulation of a series of signs may add up to a conclusion with a high degree of cogency.

Sign reasoning can also be analyzed by using the elements of any argument. For instance, assume the advocate claims that the economy will improve in the next few months, as in the accompanying diagram.

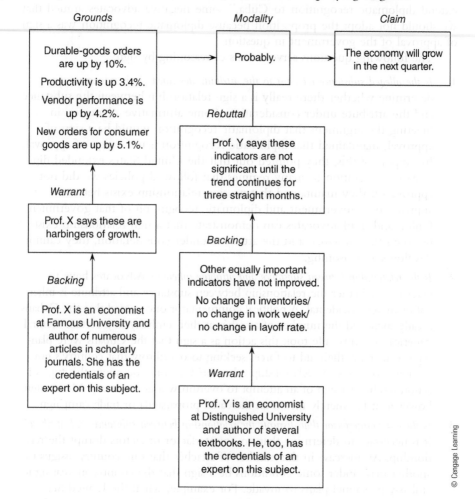

EXERCISES

1. Find an argumentative editorial published in a daily newspaper within the past month. Restate the arguments in the form of syllogisms or enthymemes. Analyze these arguments. Show why they are or are not formally valid.

2. Find an argumentative editorial as in Exercise 1. Lay out the major arguments using Toulmin's model of Argument (the elements of any argument.) Does the warrant justify the movement from grounds to claim? Has the writer established the modality of the claim accurately? Has sufficient backing been provided when needed? Have possible rebuttals been considered?

4

Obstacles to Clear Thinking

Clear thinking is essential to all intelligent decision making. From the moment we begin to explore a problem until the end of the final debate on that problem, we have to constantly be on guard against obstacles to clear thinking. Argumentation, requiring a clear thought process which tests the reasoning process between premise, or grounds, and claim, or conclusions, challenges us to question carefully these links. Obvious obstacles are readily detected. One type of obstacle, however, that is more subtle, and hence more deceptive, is called a fallacy. At first glance the error, unreasonableness, or falseness of the fallacy is not apparent, for the statement has the appearance of truth or reasonableness. Richard Whately defined a **fallacy** as "any unsound mode of arguing, which appears to demand our conviction, and to be decisive of the question in hand, when in fairness it is not."[1] In *The Rhetoric*, Aristotle warned of nine types of enthymemes which seem to be based in sound reasoning, but are not, sometimes referred to as "sham" enthymemes (Book II, Chapter 24).

Recall that dialectical argumentation relies on rule-based structures of formal reasoning based in certainty and that rhetorical reasoning, as it relies on *logos* and practical reasoning, may be less formal and is based in a relative determination of degree of cogency or strength of argument. Dialect measures an argument as true or false, whereas rhetoric measures an argument as relatively strong or weak. While in formal reasoning and dialectic, fallacious reasoning warrants rejection of arguments, in rhetorical discourse, fallacies or flaws in reasoning will likely weaken the rhetorical or persuasive force of an argument but not demand its rejection. We are constantly bombarded with, and forced to make decisions on the basis of fallacies. Being aware of these unsound approaches can improve our ability to construct more compelling advocacy,

---

1. Richard Whately, *Elements of Logic* (Boston: James Munroe, 1848), p. 143.

Miniglossary

Ambiguity Arises when the meaning of a word, phrase, or passage may reasonably be interpreted in two or more ways.

Appeal to ignorance Advocates maintain that something cannot be so because they, or the audience, have never heard of it.

Appeal to tradition Support for an argument is based on customary and historical support for the argument.

Arguing in a circle Occurs when one assumes as a premise for the argument the very conclusion one intends to prove.

Bandwagon Support for an argument based on its popular support by a large number of people.

Fallacy Any unsound mode of arguing, which appears to demand our conviction, and to be decisive of the question at hand, when in fairness it is not.

Denying a valid conclusion Advocate admits or cannot refute the premises of an opponent, yet denies the conclusion that logically follows from these premises.

Grammatical structure Reasoning based on meaning distorted by incorrect or imprecise grammar.

Hasty generalization Argument from example in which the inference, or movement from specific example to generalization, is made on the basis of insufficient evidence, either nonrepresentative example(s) or an insufficient number of examples.

Incomplete comparison A type of grammatical fallacy in which the point of comparison is missing or not clearly identified.

Irrelevancy An argument in which proof is carried beyond its reasonable limits, and therefore does not pertain to the claim.

Loaded language Use of emotionally charged words in an effort to establish a conclusion without proof.

Non sequitur A conclusion that does not follow from the premises or evidence on which it is based.

Popular appeal An advocate tries to win support for a position by maintaining that he or she is merely an "ordinary person" like everyone else.

Post hoc Assuming a causal relationship where none has been proved.

Pseudoargument Fallacy created (by accident or design) by distortion, confusion, manipulation, or avoidance of the matters at issue or by substitution of matters not germane to the issue.

Pseudoquestion An advocate asks an unanswerable, "loaded," or ambiguous question or series of questions, or asks a question based on a false assumption.

Repeated assertion An argument is presented as proof for itself.

Special pleading Urging that an exception be made to an accepted line of reasoning.

Straw argument Setting up an issue merely so it can be knocked down.

Structured response A pattern is established leading to an improper or unsupported conclusion.

Verbalism The abundant use of words without conveying much meaning.

to speak to the weaknesses in our opponents' positions, and to be better critical consumers of argumentation.

Fallacies are usually easy to detect in isolation, but woven into the context of an argument, they may go unnoticed unless we are on guard. Debate gives those who render decisions one of the strongest protections against fallacies. Not only do they have the opportunity to detect fallacies themselves, but there is the added safeguard that the opposing advocates are motivated to point out fallacies in one another's cases.

Fallacies may be used accidentally or deliberately. Some advocates intentionally introduce fallacies into their arguments to exploit their listeners or readers and secure an unfair decision. Contemporary examples of apparently deliberate use of fallacies can be found in any international crisis as the hostile parties create propaganda to sway world opinion. Much of this propaganda is prepared by persons intelligent enough to recognize the fallacies they are using. But some fallacies may be introduced into arguments unintentionally by well-meaning people. Advocates must be alert for obstacles to clear thinking at all times and from all sources.

For convenience, fallacies are classified here under various groupings and subgroupings. In actual argument fallacies often are interwoven, and a fallacious argument may be a complex of several fallacies. It is inevitable that the classifications of fallacies will overlap and that examples may not fit cleanly into a single typology. In exposing fallacies in our opponent's case, we will do little good by exclaiming, "Aha! In his last statement my opponent committed the fallacies of circulus in probando and per negationem consequentiae!" Although we may wish to identify and classify a fallacy for our own convenience, our task in the debate is not to name the fallacy but to show those who render the decision how or why the matter in question is fallacious. This task is complicated by the fact that fallacies are often field dependent—that is, they must be considered in context. As Stephen Toulmin points out, "Most disturbingly to some people, arguments that are fallacious in one context may prove to be quite solid in another context. So we shall not be able to identify any intrinsically fallacious forms of argument; instead we shall try to indicate why certain kinds of argument are, in practice, fallacious in this or that kind of context."[2]

One helpful way of exposing fallacies is to focus attention on the warrants (considered in Chapter 3) and see whether the expressed or implied warrant justifies the claim made.

Some hold that there is no such thing as a fallacy; rather there is a failure to apply the appropriate tests of evidence or reasoning or language. In this chapter some of the conventional fallacies are discussed and some appropriate tests recommended. The use of the concept of fallacies provides us with a means of double-checking our arguments and those of our opponents, but is not a doomsday weapon guaranteeing success over all fallacious argumentation.

---

2. Stephen Toulmin, Richard Rieke, and Allan Janik, *An Introduction to Reasoning* (New York: Macmillan, 1979), p. 157.

I. FALLACIES OF EVIDENCE

Much argumentation in applied and academic debate relies on premises or grounds built upon the presentation of quoted material, or evidence. Theater or film advertisements sometimes provide examples of fallacious use of evidence. One critic wrote of a Broadway musical:

> *Interlude* represented an inept effort to make a dull story palatable by adding music. Unfortunately one brilliantly executed dance number in the first act was not enough to keep the show moving. Lavish costuming could not overcome the basic fact that the female lead simply does not have an adequate voice for the theater. The comedy routines showed brief flashes of inspiration, but they could not relieve the overall pedestrian pace of *Interlude*.

The newspaper advertisements quoted the reviewer as saying, "*Interlude* ... brilliantly executed ... lavish costuming ... flashes of inspiration." We can guard against this kind of fallacious use of evidence by asking, "Is any evidence omitted?" Taking evidence out of context, also referred to as quote mining, contextomy, suppressed evidence, or cherry picking, may offer a convenient way to find the quotes and conclusions which will support a claim, or to avoid consideration of parts of the evidence which are counter to your conclusion, but it is intellectually dishonest and when brought to light is likely to be a counterproductive strategy. During the 2012 Presidential election campaign, Senator Rick Santorum gave a speech in which he said, "The issue in this race is not the economy. The reason the economy is an issue in this race is because the federal government is oppressing its people and taking away your freedom and the economy is suffering as a result." Ads in support of his opponent, Governor Mitt Romney quoted only the first sentence, suggesting that Santorum's point was that "The issue in this race is not the economy." This was a distortion of Santorum's point.[3] Scientific and scholarly writing and even thorough political commentary frequently offers the exceptions, alternative explanations, or arguments and evidence against the conclusion ultimately arrived at by an author. However, for an advocate to quote an author or source offering such statements (the material after a transition like, "opponents may argue...") is likely to be flawed use of the evidence.

One study about global climate change observed in its introduction that:

> Global climate change is a controversial issue. Many people believe that global climate is warming, due to human activities. Some scientists and civilians, however, argue that present global warming is a natural fluctuation which was not caused by human activities (natural law, i.e., change of solar radiation, El Nino, La Nino, etc.). Global warming is facing an inconvenient challenge after the release of new temperature data showing the planet has not warmed for the past 15 years and figures suggest that we could even be heading for a mini ice age.

---

3. http://2012.talkingpointsmemo.com/2012/03/romney-camp-attacks-santorum-without-of-context-quotes.php.

Fallacies of Evidence

- An unsupported assertion is often presented as if it were a complete argument
- Violation of the tests of evidence discussed in Chapter 9 reveal fallacies of evidence

---

An unscrupulous advocate arguing against the threat of global warming might evidence mine by quoting, "Global climate change is a controversial issue … scientists and civilians … argue that present global warming is a natural fluctuation which was not caused by human activities … new temperature data (show) … the planet has not warmed for the past 15 years and figures suggest that we could even be heading for a mini ice age." Of course, this would take the introductory material completely out of context. The same study concludes "Whatever the scenario is, the varied and extreme climate around the world caused by destructive human activities will certainly destroy our environment and livings in the future."[4]

One of the most common fallacies of evidence is the use of the unsupported assertion. Here the speaker offers no evidence to support a statement; he or she asks us to assume that something is so merely because he or she says it is so. The high-pressure used car salesperson may tell a customer, "This car is in perfect condition. You'd better buy it now before someone else gets it." The prudent buyer would not accept this unsupported assertion but would look for evidence of the condition of the car. We can guard against this fallacy by asking, "Is the contention an unsupported assertion?"

The tests of evidence discussed in Chapter 9 can help us identify other fallacies of evidence.

II. FALLACIES OF REASONING

Not only must we guard against fallacies of evidence, but we must also be alert to possible fallacies in each of the types of reasoning we considered earlier.

A. Example

Argument by example is an inductive process calling upon us to reason that based on one or more specific cases we should conclude a broader generalization, or apply the experience of one case to another. Based on a single positive

---

4. Zhang, WenJun and Liu, Chunhua (Published online 10 March 2012), "Some Thoughts on Global Climate Change: Will it Get Warmer and Warmer?" *Environmental Skeptics and Critics,* 2012, 1(1): 1–7, http://www.iaees.org/publications/journals/environsc/articles/2012-1(1)/some-thoughts-on-global-climate-change.pdf.

experience dining at a new restaurant, we are willing to recommend the restaurant to others or return to it. However, we may have been lucky, and received the only good meal served so far by that establishment. A speaker who maintains that the public schools are failing to educate our children may offer as proof the following examples of their "failure":

> Last year 23 percent of the graduates of North High School who went to Omega State University were required to take remedial English; 37 percent of the North High graduates at Omega were required to take remedial math. I could cite dozens more examples of the failure of our schools, but this is enough to prove that we need a statewide system of competency testing before we grant high school diplomas.

Are you willing to accept this as an accurate picture of conditions statewide? Are the North High students typical of all students in the state? Are the North High students who go to Omega State typical of North High students in general? We can quickly expose this fallacy by asking, "Are the examples given typical of the whole?" Statistical methods offer quantitative measures for this test, but generally we are left to analyze and evaluate the reasoning with nonnumeric measures.

Another common fallacy of reasoning by example is committed by the person who knows two or three motorcyclists who have criminal records and concludes, "They're all drug dealers." Here one should ask, "Have sufficient examples been given?" A **hasty generalization** based on insufficient evidence often leads to unsound conclusions that will not be accepted by those who render the decision.

Recall the tests for argument by examples offered in Chapter 3:

1. Is the example relevant?
2. Is there a reasonable number of examples?
3. Do the examples cover a critical period of time?
4. Are the examples typical?
5. Are negative examples noncritical?

Unsatisfactory answers to any of these questions raise doubt about the validity or the reasoning upon which the argument by example relies.

B. Analogy

Argument by analogy offers a comparison of parallel cases. A Russian leader once told an American visitor: "With the death of communism, Russia is now completely democratic. We even have competing candidates running for some offices." The American exposed the fallacy in this analogy by replying, "You have started toward democracy, but you still have a way to go. In America we have at least two well-established political parties and we are ruled by laws, not by decrees." In this case the American applied the question, "Are there critical differences in the factors compared?" Her answer pointed out two essential differences between American and Russian governments. Chapter 3 offered this list of questions as tests for analogical reasoning:

1. Are there significant points of similarity?
2. Are the points of similarity critical to the comparison?
3. Are the points of difference noncritical?
4. Is the reasoning cumulative?
5. Are only literal analogies used as logical proof?

C. Cause

Many causal factors are at work in most situations. Gasoline prices rose steeply in the spring of 2012. President Obama, in speeches and ads, pointed some of the blame at oil companies while the GOP candidates for the presidency argued that the policies of the president were to blame. These causal arguments were effective as campaign rhetoric because they suggested artificially simple causal reasoning. Of course, multiple causes contributed to the rise in gas prices, including global demand, supply disruptions related to instability within middle eastern countries who supply oil, the threat related to Iranian sanctions for developing a nuclear program, supply bottlenecks due to reduced refining capabilities, the relative cost of the dollar, the 2011 earthquake and tsunami in Japan, and many other factors. That the U.S. president (or the oil companies) could significantly impact gas prices was an overly simplistic and probably fallacious line of reasoning. Fallacies of this type may be detected by asking, "Is a partial causal relationship treated as the sole or distinguishing causal factor?" In addition, the questions offered in Chapter 3 are helpful.

1. Is the alleged cause relevant to the effect described?
2. Is this the sole or distinguishing causal factor?
3. Is there reasonable probability that no undesirable effect will result from this particular cause?
4. Is there a counteracting cause?
5. Is the cause capable of producing the effect?
6. Is the cause necessary and sufficient?
7. How does a new cause affect the system in evaluating casual reasoning?

D. Sign

The ability to use reasoning by sign effectively is an essential part of the work of all who seek rational decisions. The physician, for example, must constantly be on guard against fallacies in interpreting signs. In diagnosing a case, the neurologist may look for the Babinski sign, a certain type of movement of the toes after

---

Fallacies of Reasoning

For each, the fallacy represents a violation of the tests identified for each category in Chapter 3.

- ■ Example
- ■ Analogy
- ■ Cause
- ■ Sign

---

stimulus. This sign is apparently inherent in certain types of illness and, when found in adults, is taken as an indication of the presence of disease of the corticospinal pathway. The Rossolimo sign, a certain type of flexing of the toes after stimulus, indicates disease of the pyramidal tract. It is a much less reliable sign, however, because it is sometimes absent when the disease is present and it is sometimes found in healthy individuals. All who use reasoning by sign should be on guard against fallacies that might lead to false conclusions. Consider the questions offered in Chapter 3:

1. Is the alleged substance relevant to the attribute described?
2. Is the relationship between substance and attribute inherent?
3. Is there a counterfactor that disrupts the relationship between substance and attribute?
4. Is the sign reasoning cumulative?

III. FALLACIES OF LANGUAGE

The fallacies of language are often interwoven with other fallacies. Some of the more common fallacies of language that advocates should guard against are discussed here.

A. Ambiguity

Ambiguity arises when the meaning of a word, phrase, or passage may reasonably be interpreted in two or more ways. For example, what does a speaker mean when saying, "I favor the American way of doing things"? A candidate for public office once campaigned on the slogan of "more teamwork in government." "Teamwork" may sound good, but what does it mean? A government official recently testified that he had not received any "improper" gifts from a constituent and that he had not made any "unreasonable" requests of governmental agencies on behalf of this constituent. His opponents viewed these same activities as "corruption" and "influence." Such terms as *feminist, family values, egalitarian, multi-cultural, liberal, conservative,* and *middle of the road* have so many different meanings to so many different people that they are often ambiguous. President Clinton famously made the claim, "I did not have sexual relations with that woman, Miss Lewinsky," relying on the ambiguity of the term "sexual relations."

B. Verbalism

Verbalism refers to the abundant use of words without conveying much meaning. There is a story of a politician who, seeking to avoid taking a position on gun control legislation, said, "The question is not a simple one. Indeed anyone could say—and they would be more or less right—that it is complex. In the second instance there is the First Amendment to the Constitution. I mean in the first place there is the Second Amendment—or whatever. This is perfectly clear until you get to the part that isn't. About the militia that is. And I wonder what the Founding Fathers would say about that? And why it isn't. When I was a boy my father took me hunting and fishing. And I was duck hunting only last month. I think fathers should take their sons hunting unless they have daughters. And more recently the Tenth Amendment business. And, of course, daughters should go hunting too. And we need to look at this thing from the law and order point of view as well also." The National Council of Teachers of English (NCTE) offers an annual "Doublespeak" award. Doublespeak, a term coined by George Orwell in his novel *1984* is a form of verbalism, "using language that is grossly deceptive, evasive, euphemistic, confusing, or self-centered."[5] Their 2011 award winner was Cherokee Principal Chief Chad Smith, for saying "It's a basic, inherent right to determine our own citizenry. We paid very dearly for those rights" when speaking of the recent final decision to expel the Freedmen Cherokee from the tribe in Oklahoma. In 2008, they recognized the term "aspirational goal." As the NCTE wrote, "'Aspirational goal' is both a tautology and a paradox. Aspirations and goals are the same thing; and yet when the terms are combined, the effect is to undermine them both, producing a phrase that means, in effect, 'a goal to which one does not aspire all that much.' The goal of 'aspirational goal,' clearly, is to disguise inaction and thwart legitimate aspirations."

C. Loaded Language

Loaded language provides many possibilities for obstacles to clear thinking. **Loaded language** involves the use of words which in addition to their denotative meanings, or objective, descriptive meanings, also have a secondary meaning, which is emotionally charged and therefore seeks to establish a conclusion without proof. In a recent political campaign one candidate declared, "The time has come to throw this do-nothing, corruption-riddled administration out of office." Obviously such an administration should be thrown out of office, but the mere use of

---

5. http://www.ncte.org/volunteer/groups/publiclangcom/doublespeakaward.

these labels did nothing to prove that the administration was guilty of either of the charges. When appearing on the *Today Show*, Governor Sarah Palin referred to the Presidency of President Obama as entailing "failed socialist policies" while the candidates for the GOP nomination for the Presidency all claimed to be "true conservatives." These terms, "socialist" and "conservative" condemn or celebrate without specificity or support, thus they interfere with the reasoning process.

Loaded language, or name-calling, is too often used in political campaigns. The *New York Times* reported this example:

> What's in a name? When it comes to winning elections, it could be everything. In fact, here is some choice advice for candidates about names to call your campaign opponents and yourselves.
>
> Call your opponent a "sick, pathetic, liberal, incompetent, tax-spending traitor." Reserve for yourself the label "humane, visionary, confident, candid, hard-working reformer."
>
> Saying good things about yourself and bad things about your opponent may seem basic, in life as much as in politics. But now, this specific advice on which names to use has been drawn up and a list is being distributed to Republican state legislative candidates across the country.[6]

A more creative example of loaded language was reported from a Florida senatorial campaign by *Time* magazine:

> [George] Smathers used fancy language to convey sinister meanings to benighted rural listeners. "Are you aware that Claude Pepper is known all over Washington as a shameless extrovert? Not only that, but this man is reliably reported to practice nepotism with his sister-in-law, and he has a sister who was once a thespian in wicked New York. Worst of all, it is an established fact that Mr. Pepper before his marriage habitually practiced celibacy."

Pepper was defeated by 67,000 votes. "On election night people came up to our house in cars, shouting obscenities, cheering the fact that I had been defeated," Pepper recalls. "They wanted to destroy me and just about did."[7]

Fallacies of Language

- Ambiguity
- Verbalism
- Loaded Language
- Grammatical Structure

---

6. *New York Times*, national edition, Sept. 9, 1990, p. 18.
7. *Time*, Apr. 25, 1983, p. 29.

D. Grammatical Structure

Grammatical structure can, and often does, alter the meaning of a sentence. At a recent Republican convention the first draft of the party platform contained the sentence "[Republicans] oppose any attempts to increase taxes which would harm the recovery and reverse the trend to restoring control of the economy to individual Americans." A harmless bit of political rhetoric; of course everyone would oppose *harmful* tax increases, yet the door was left open to *unharmful* tax increases. The party's conservatives fought "The Battle of the Comma" and changed the sentence to read, "oppose any attempts to increase taxes, which would harm the recovery and reverse the trend to restoring control of the economy to individual Americans." The sentence, as punctuated with the comma, held *all* tax increases to be harmful. When the sentence was read aloud, the presence or absence of a pause would indicate the presence or absence of a comma.

Incomplete comparison is another grammatical fallacy—for example, "The present foreign aid program is unquestionably more effective." More effective than what? The advocate must guard against these hazards of grammatical usage.

IV. FALLACIES OF PSEUDOARGUMENTS

Pseudoarguments are fallacies created (by accident or design) by distortion, confusion, manipulation, or avoidance of the matters at issue or by substitution of matters not germane to the issue. Some common fallacies are considered here.

A. Offering Irrelevancy

The fallacy of **irrelevancy** carries an argument beyond its reasonable limits. For example, some opponents of "right-to-work" laws argued that these laws did not provide jobs for the unemployed. These laws were intended not to provide jobs but merely to eliminate the requirement of union membership as a condition of employment. It would be just as reasonable to criticize the polio vaccine because it does not prevent pneumonia.

B. Arguing in a Circle

The fallacy of **arguing in a circle** occurs when one assumes as a premise for the argument the very conclusion one intends to prove, or put another way, the conclusion is derived from premises that presuppose the conclusion. This is also referred to as "begging the question." For example, consider this exchange: "Tupac Shakur is a greater rapper than Vanilla Ice because people with good taste in rap prefer Shakespeare." "How do you know who has good taste in rap?" "Why, that's simple; people with good taste in literature prefer Tupac to Vanilla Ice." Even though Tupac is undoubtedly a greater writer than Vanilla Ice, this circular argument does not prove the claim.

C. Ignoring the Issue

This may also be referred to as ignorance of refutation (*ignoratio elenchi*) or ignoring the counterevidence, and may be presented as a "Red Herring" argument. In a debate on the proposition "Resolved: That the United States federal government should significantly increase exploration and/or development of space beyond the Earth's mesosphere," an affirmative team proposed a particularly weak and ineffective plan. In a thoughtful, closely reasoned refutation, the negative demonstrated that the affirmative's plan was completely unworkable as the cost of the program was prohibitive in the current environment and that the technology called for by the plan's advocates had not been developed. In their remaining speeches the affirmative debaters completely ignored the issue of the workability of their plan; instead they spent their time claiming the great advantages that would come from their plan if it were workable. The Red Herring is a reference to fox hunting, wherein a smoked fish (herring) is rubbed across the fox's trail to draw the dogs off the fox's scent. In argumentation, a debater may offer an irrelevant argument thus distracting the audience, and perhaps their opponents, from the issue in question. This may happen during debates when the central issue or proposition is not clear, so arguers will apply arguments in which the premises are logically irrelevant to the conclusion. In the space example, the advocates ignored the arguments about plan workability, instead drawing the audience's attention to the benefits of their program.

D. Baiting an Opponent

Sometimes advocates will bait their opponents by insulting them, attacking them personally, criticizing their friends, or doing anything that will cause them to lose their temper. Once advocates lose their cool, they are likely to lose control of the argument and make reckless statements that will undermine their case. Advocates can defend themselves against this kind of baiting only by holding their temper during the argument. It was anticipated that in the 2008 Vice Presidential debate between Senator Joe Biden and Governor Sarah Palin, Palin would attempt to bait Biden, causing him to respond aggressively, thus damaging the public's perception of him. This would have played to Biden's reputation for aggressive debating and possibly benefited empathy for Palin as a female candidate. This was ultimately not the case as the debate was cordial and Governor Palin did not seem to make attempts at baiting her opponent.

E. Repeating an Assertion

The fallacy of **repeated assertion** occurs when an argument is repeated, with the repetition treated as proof. In a debate on guaranteed annual wages, members of the affirmative team stated repeatedly, without offering any proof, that American working persons need a guaranteed annual wage. A negative speaker, exposing this fallacy, pointed out that saying something three times did not make it true. This fallacy is not always so easily brushed off, however. Adolf Hitler developed to a fine art the technique of repeating a "big lie" so often that many came to believe it.

F. Structuring a Response

The fallacy of **structured response** is often found in cross-examinations or any other situation in which the advocate has an opportunity to ask a series of questions. The advocate first asks a series of unimportant questions, which the respondent must answer in a predetermined way, until the pattern of a response has been established. Then the critical question is asked. An old routine of insurance salespersons, for example, goes something like this: "You love your spouse, don't you?" "You love your children, don't you?" "You want your children to go to college, don't you?" "You want your family to continue to live in this lovely house, don't you?" "If something should happen to you, you want your family to be provided for, don't you?" "You would still want your children to go to college, wouldn't you?" "You want to provide protection for them, don't you?" "To be safe, don't you feel you should sign your name on this routine form today?" Any prospects who have been lulled into a series of "yes" responses may find that they have signed an application for insurance without fully realizing the commitment they have undertaken.

The structured response was used effectively by Senator Edward Kennedy at the 1988 Democratic Convention, when after each recitation of supposed Republican shortcomings he asked, "Where was George?" (The Republican candidate, Vice President George Bush, had stated that he was not present when certain controversial decisions were made.) The partisan audience quickly picked up the theme and chanted "Where was George?" along with Kennedy as he continued the list.

Another application of the structured response is the "false dilemma" or "false dichotomy." The arguer presents a set of choices, suggesting that one and only one may be selected. However, the implied forced choice is a false one; it is possible to select all, both, or none of the choices offered.

G. Special Pleading

The fallacy of **special pleading** occurs when advocates accept a line of reasoning and its conclusions but urge a special exception for their case. The reasoning applies principles inconsistently. Examples of special pleading are sometimes found in Congress. Members of Congress are likely to support balancing the budget, but not at the expense of cutting items of special interest to their constituents.

H. Substituting the Person for the Argument

This is also referred to as ad hominem, or "to the man." This fallacy involves attempting to have an argument accepted or rejected not because of any merit or defect intrinsic to the argument but because of the character of the person advancing the argument. For example, some people said that health care reform should be rejected because Socialists favor it. Conversely it may be argued that because someone is good in some respect, his or her arguments on some other matter must also be good. To counter the prosecution's claim that his or her client shot a business rival, the defense attorney in a murder trial might try to present the client as, for example, a kindly man who helps old ladies across busy streets, who is good to his wife and his children, who gives generously to charities, and who sings in the church choir. Traditionally the country rallies behind the president at the time of an international crisis, the theme being, "We must support the president during this crisis." Thus Roosevelt during World War II, Kennedy at the time of the Cuban missile crisis, and Bush during Operation Desert Storm enjoyed great initial support for policies that later came under criticism. President George W. Bush relied on such support when he began his presidential reelection campaign in 2004 with spot advertisements reminding voters of the ongoing war on terrorism by presenting images of the twin towers of the World Trade Center.

Note that an argument about a person is legitimate when the character of the person is intrinsic to the matter at issue. Evidence that John Doe was a child molester would be legitimate if the issue were his employment as a teacher. Evidence that Jane Roe was a convicted embezzler would be germane if the issue were her employment as an accountant. These examples emphasize the point made at the beginning of this chapter that fallacies are often field dependent. Doe's sexual activities or Roe's criminal record are critical, legitimate evidence in the context considered here; they would be irrelevant and thus fallacious in many other contexts.

I. Substituting Bombast for Argument

When no evidence or reasoning is available, advocates may sometimes attempt to support their argument by sheer noise and histrionics, and language full of long or pretentious words, used to impress others. In a debate on the mass media proposition, for example, a debater claimed that the federal government had a moral obligation to mandate a massive increase in the number of hours of closed-captioned programs that television stations provided for the hearing impaired. The opposing speaker, asked her to define "moral obligation." Caught in her error (the vague and unsupported assertion of a moral obligation), she replied with more hope than confidence, "My partner will define that in the next speech." The partner, now on the spot, frantically searched his evidence files but was unable to find a single scrap of evidence defining moral obligation or any notion of lines of argument that he could use to support his colleague's claim. There may have been some arguments to support this assertion, but they were not available at that moment. In desperation he decided to bluff his way by *bombast*. In a voice seemingly choked with outrage and emotion, he said, "The negative has asked us to define 'moral obligation.'" Eyes flashing with apparent righteous indignation, he glared at his opponents: "We all know what 'moral obligation' is!" Pounding the lectern with his fist, he cried, "A 'moral obligation' is a 'moral obligation,' the undeniable responsibility and demand that an empathetic society is obliged to, required to, by divine expectation and deontological mandate, provide essential facilitative structures advancing and supporting deleterious expediencies for those existential beings encumbered and enunciated by the need for empowerment" (he continued to rant). The negative, cowed by these histrionics, never dared mention the subject again. Had the next negative speaker, in sharp contrast to the bombast of the affirmative, calmly and thoughtfully pointed out the absurdity of the affirmative's definition, he might well have punctured the balloon the affirmative speaker had used so effectively to conceal his lack of an adequate answer to a reasonable question.

J. Denying the Antecedent

This occurs when reasoning relies on an "if-then" statement (a conditional claim where an antecedent is framed as the if-statement, and the consequent is the then-statement) wherein the arguer wrongly assumes that denying the antecedent will then necessarily deny the consequent. For example, "If she came to class every day, she will surely make an 'A' on the exam. She did not come to class every day. Therefore, she will not make an 'A.'" This may be fallacious reasoning, as the student may yet make an "A" on the exam.

K. Using Popular Appeal

The fallacy of **popular appeal** occurs when an advocate tries to win support for a position by maintaining that he or she is merely an "ordinary person" like everyone else. This approach was popular with rural politicians at the turn of the nineteenth century and is still common today. During the 1988 presidential campaign, Michael Dukakis liked to contrast his "son of immigrants" background with the "preppy" image of Vice President George Bush by proclaiming, "My friends, there is only one country on the face of the earth where this son of immigrants could aspire to be the president of the United States, and that's the United States." As the governor of Massachusetts, the son of a millionaire physician, and a Harvard Law School graduate himself, Dukakis was, of course, not exactly a typical son of immigrants. And one might be forgiven for asking where else but the United States could one reasonably aspire to be president of the United States?

Another aspect of the same fallacy is the **bandwagon** technique—arguing that something should be done because "everybody" is doing it. In many political campaigns, both candidates will proclaim their confidence that they will win by an overwhelming majority. They hope by this method to induce many undecided voters to vote for them simply because they are going to win anyway. Only one brand of cigarettes or soap or any other type of product can be the most popular, yet note the number of companies that claim their product is the most popular. They hope their product will be bought because "everyone" is buying it.

L. Offering a "Straw Argument"

The fallacy of the **straw argument** occurs when advocates set up an issue merely so they can knock it down. Sometimes they attack a minor argument of their opponents and claim that they have refuted the whole case. Or they might refute an argument their opponents did not advance and claim that they have thus refuted their opponents' position.

In the debate about the Dream Act, a proposed law which would provide some limited educational benefits and legal status to certain undocumented children of immigrants who have entered the United States illegally, some opponents argued that there must be better control of immigration at the border, and that there should not be a "path to citizenship" for the over 11 million immigrants currently within U.S. borders who have entered illegally. The proponents of the Dream Act had not opposed stricter controls at the borders nor had they advocated a "path to citizenship" for undocumented immigrants, including the beneficiaries of the Dream Act. The opponents had raised these issues so they could argue against them. The claims offered by no one engaged in the debate were straw person arguments, set up by the opponents of the Dream Act so that they could be defeated.

M. Appealing to Ignorance

The fallacy of the **appeal to ignorance** occurs when advocates maintain that something cannot be so because they, or the audience, have never heard of it. There are two types: (1) if there is no evidence or knowledge to support the truth of a statement, it is pronounced false, and (2) if there is no evidence to prove a claim false, it is presumed true. Uninformed persons, for example, at one time declared the telephone to be an impractical gadget because "Everyone knows you can't talk over wires."

Unfortunately the appeal to ignorance is sometimes successful with an uninformed audience. The defense against this fallacy is to provide the audience with the knowledge necessary to understand the argument. But this is not always easy. Before the moon landings, it would have been almost impossible to refute the argument "Of course, you can't get to the moon, that's science fiction" before a popular audience without giving a lengthy technical explanation. In fact the explanation would have probably had to be so lengthy and technical that it could not be presented within the available time.

N. Asking Pseudoquestions

The fallacy of the **pseudoquestion** occurs when an advocate asks an unanswerable, "loaded," "leading," or ambiguous question; or a question based on a false assumption; or so many questions that an opponent cannot possibly answer them adequately within the available time. An example of this type of question is, "Have you stopped cheating on examinations?" This fallacy may also be used by the advocate who rather than making a positive claim, implies a conclusion by asking a question. For example, rather than arguing that solar power generation is not economically viable for most individual citizens, and providing evidence and reasoning in support of that, the arguer would ask a series of questions like "Could you or your family afford a $50,000 investment for a technology of limited reliability?" The question makes and proves no claims, but the advocates intend their audience to arrive at the conclusion that solar power generation is not viable for them.

O. Appealing to Tradition

The fallacy of the **appeal to tradition** occurs when the advocate maintains that we should follow a certain policy because we have "always" done things that way. Thus a negative speaker, in a debate on a proposition on comprehensive medical care for all citizens argued against the affirmative's plan by saying it was unnecessary because physicians and hospitals had always provided free medical care for the indigent. The fact that something has been a longstanding tradition does not prove its merit. As a famous senator once pointed out, murder and larceny have been practiced in all nations in all ages, but this does not make either murder or larceny meritorious.

P. Posing a Non Sequitur

A non sequitur is an argument which "does not follow," in other words, the conclusion is not supported by the premises or evidence offered for it. Most fallacies can be described as non sequitur. One headache paid product advertised its pills based on the research claim that it was "90% more effective than its competitors for pain OTHER THAN HEADACHE PAIN." This evidence did not provide support for the product as a headache remedy, and was therefore a non sequitur. College athletes make lots of money for their institutions, therefore, the NCAA should have football playoffs for its top level institutions. Again, the evidence does not support the claim.

Thus far we have avoided the Latin names of fallacies, but the **non sequitur**—which is simply a conclusion that does not follow from the premises or evidence on which it is based—is best known by its Latin designation. In health care debates, some advocates affirmatives cite evidence showing that many people could not afford medical care and then argued that the government should provide free medical care for all citizens. In other debates some negatives argued that the affirmative plan would be administered by a government agency and so would be inefficient. Bureaucracy does have a bad reputation—but it does not follow that all government agencies are inefficient.

Q. Arguing Post Hoc

This title is shorthand for the longer Latin phrase *post hoc ergo propter hoc*, meaning "after the fact, therefore because of the fact." The fallacy of **post hoc** lies in assuming a causal relationship where none has been proved. American history provides one of the best known illustrations of this fallacy. Every American president elected at a 20-year interval since 1840 died in office (Harrison, Lincoln, Garfield, McKinley, Harding, Roosevelt, and Kennedy) until Ronald Reagan broke the morbid chain of coincidence (in 1980). A remarkable coincidence, surely, but their election in a particular year was hardly the cause of their death. Superstitions are sometimes based on arguing post hoc. It is said that Michael Jordan superstitiously wore his Carolina blue shorts under his Chicago Bulls uniform, and that he believed he could not win unless he was wearing the shorts. Of course, since he always wore them, he was wearing them for all his championships, but also, all his losses!

V. ARISTOTLES SHAM ENTHYMEMES

As referenced earlier, Aristotle identified a list of nine types of enthymemes, which he wrote "look genuine but are not." These will seem familiar to some of the categories and specific examples of fallacies offered above. The first of these is based in diction, or language, and includes an attack on false choice and antithesis as a figure of speech. Second is to assert of the whole what is true of the parts. Third is the use of indignant language in lieu of proof, and fourth is to mistake a sign, or single instance, as proof. Fifth is the accidental, or coincidental sign, and sixth is argument from consequence or circumstance, which is described as an example of fallacy by omission, as they imply a condition based on insufficient consideration of variables. The seventh sham enthymeme offered by Aristotle is the post hoc propter hoc, falsely assuming that because B happens after A, it happens because of A. Eighth is time and manner, additional variables which must be considered in determining relationships, and finally, ninth, is the confusion of the absolute with the particular, or inappropriately swift application of a generalization to a specific case.

VI. CONCLUSION

The preceding list is by no means comprehensive. The value of reviewing and considering both categories of fallacious reasoning and specific fallacies is to develop a habit of thought rather than to apply a particular checklist. Obviously there are many fallacies, and the possibility of their being introduced into arguments is almost unlimited. As advocates, refutants, and decision makers, we are well advised to constantly be on guard against these obstacles to clear thinking, not only in statements of others but in our own statements as well.

Fallacies of Pseudoarguments

- Offering irrelevancy
- Arguing in a circle
- Ignoring the issue
- Baiting an opponent
- Repeating an assertion
- Structuring a response
- Special pleading
- Substituting the person for the argument
- Substituting bombast for argument
- Denying the antecedent
- Using popular appeal
- Offering a "straw argument"
- Appealing to ignorance
- Asking pseudoquestions
- Appealing to tradition
- Posing a non sequitur
- Arguing post hoc

EXERCISES

1. Find the full text of a recent speech by a public figure. Find the speech online and listen to it as you follow along with the text. You may also wish to compare this with excerpts of the speech printed in the newspapers or newsmagazines. Do you find a fallacy of omitted evidence? Remember, there is a big difference between an accurate condensation and the fallacy of omitted evidence.

2. Analyze some newspapers and newsmagazines published within the last month. Locate five fallacies in the editorial or news sections of these publications, and locate five fallacies in the advertisements.

3. Some of the following statements contain one or more fallacies. List the fallacies you discover in these statements.

    a. The Championship Kennels use Wags Dog Food exclusively. Get Wags Dog Food for your dog today!

    b. Canada has nationalized its health care. The same system would work well in the United States.

    c. Gun control laws are bad; that's how Hitler came into power in Germany.

    d. Q: What will be the cost of this plan during its first five years of operation? A: Our country owes a debt of gratitude to the farmer. The farmer represents the American way of life. Farmers are good people. They live close to the soil. They have not come under the influence of Socialist union bosses or Eastern intellectuals.

    e. Why is it that the Democratic Party always leads this country into war and the Republican Party always leads us into depression?

4. Create or find an example of each type of fallacy identified in the chapter.

5

Ethical and Cultural Considerations in Argumentation and Debate

In Chapter 1 we introduced the notion of ethics within the context of decision making (p. 19–20) and in Chapter 2 we discussed ethical practice in debate (p. 44–45). This chapter will provide a broader consideration of ethical and moral constructs as they may impact the practice and understanding of argumentation and debate. Such ethical considerations are founded in philosophical studies, and have direct and indirect implications for debate. Many debates, academic and applied, engage in direct debate about ethical questions. Such debates challenge the nature of people as naturally lazy or industrious, the role of government in limiting individual or corporate action, the relationship of animals to humans, and of human activity to the environment, and so many other foundational ethical concerns that it is impossible to list or even identify them all. All debates, whether the ethical frameworks are questioned or assumed, rely on ethical principles and constructs as their base premises. For example, advocating military intervention to solve humanitarian crises relies on a set of ethical assumptions, which may be challenged. Finally, all arguments are weighed by some measure of impact, and ethical models offer perceptual screens through which the relative importance and value of impacts may be measured.

This chapter will provide an overview of ethics and ethical constructs, and a brief introduction to cultural studies.

Miniglossary

Agency   The ability and opportunity for marginalized groups and individuals to resist domination.

Anthropocentrism   A human-based ethic, considering the natural environment important as an instrument for the happiness and survival of humans.

Critical Theory   A theory of how cultural entities execute dominance and suppression of other cultural groups through their actions including communication.

Culture   The collective programming of the mind which distinguishes the members of one group or category of people from another.

Deep Ecology   An ethical philosophy which measures the value of the natural environment as its own value, not as an instrument for the happiness or survival of humans.

Hegemony   The existence of dominance of one social group over another.

Categorical Imperative   According to the moral philosophy of Immanuel Kant, an unconditional moral law applying to all rational beings and independent of all personal desires and motives; representative of deontology or duty-based ethics.

Metaethics   The attempt to understand the metaphysical, epistemological, semantic, and psychological, presuppositions and commitments of moral thought, talk, and practice.

Normative ethics   The study of ethical action.

Shallow Ecology   An ethical philosophy which fights against pollution and resource depletion to maintain resources and standards of living for human quality of life.

I. ETHICS

So what is "ethics"? In Chapter 1 we defined "ethics" *as a set of constructs that guide our decision making by providing standards of behaviour telling us how we ought to act.* While this is a useful definition, it is incomplete. Consider the following different ways of conceptualizing ethics:

1. Ethics may be thought of as a complex foundation of morally based rules, as might be adhered to within a culture or group.

2. Ethics may provide specific guidelines for individuals or groups engaged in similar activities or with occupational concerns, for example, business ethics or sportsmanship.

3. Ethics may characterize the way people think of themselves and the self-applied measures for right behavior based in personality or experience which guide them to virtuous or appropriate behavior.

4. Ethics may construct a general and universal set of values, guiding a broader understanding about the human condition born of philosophical commitment, constructs and motives.

Each meaning is useful to our understanding of the term and concept. As a complex foundation of morally based rules ethics provides a foundation upon which premises rely and, therefore, upon which arguments are ultimately based. This system of principles also serves as a paradigm through which audiences and debaters think about and understand their argumentation. As a set of rules, field specific ethics provide measurements and applications through which debaters and audiences can measure the impacts and ethical implications of their advocacies and examples. Such rules may also, however, be brought into question, providing necessary opportunities for debate, which challenges the rules themselves. Individual moral principles help to describe one of the three approaches to normative ethics, virtue ethics, and certainly the consideration of rightness and wrongness, goodness and badness of actions and impacts provide the conceptual framework for decision making in debate and argumentative situations. Scholars at the Markkula Center for Applied Ethics provide the following discussion:

> Ethics is two things. First, ethics refers to well-founded standards of right and wrong that prescribe what humans ought to do, usually in terms of rights, obligations, benefits to society, fairness, or specific virtues. Ethics, for example, refers to those standards that impose the reasonable obligations to refrain from rape, stealing, murder, assault, slander, and fraud. Ethical standards also include those that enjoin virtues of honesty, compassion, and loyalty. And, ethical standards include standards relating to rights, such as the right to life, the right to freedom from injury, and the right to privacy. Such standards are adequate standards of ethics because they are supported by consistent and well-founded reasons.
>
> Secondly, ethics refers to the study and development of one's ethical standards. As mentioned above, feelings, laws, and social norms can deviate from what is ethical. So it is necessary to constantly examine one's standards to ensure that they are reasonable and well-founded. Ethics also means, then, the continuous effort of studying our own moral beliefs and our moral conduct, and striving to ensure that we, and the institutions we help to shape, live up to standards that are reasonable and solidly-based.[1]

Debate will inevitably rely on, apply, and question issues of right and wrong, including applications of standards of ethics, and will challenge individuals to examine their own standards of ethics.

When you break down any argument, inevitably you will find assumptions within the reasoning and/or evidence to support the claims of the argument. We use the word *inevitably* because the skeptic philosophers teach us that perceived universal truths about the physical world around us can be misinformed, a product of deception or even beyond our ability to comprehend. If we want to have a debate about aviation, for example, we at least have to assume certain things

---

1. Velasquez, M., Andre, C., Shanks, T., Meyer, M., & Meyer, M. (2010). Scu.edu. Retrieved from http://www.scu.edu/ethics/practicing/decision/whatisethics.html.

such as the laws of gravity, aerodynamics, and history of aviation used as evidence truly did happen and is not just the product of a clever ruse.

Some assumptions about the physical world are made without vocalized debate. Prior assumptions and shared understandings enable debates, giving us foundations and a starting point. Debates and arguments would take ages if we made sure to discuss and eventually come to agreement on each assumption or premise upon which an argument relies. We can debate about airline travel accepting in advance that there is such an industry. The most fundamental assumptions of one's philosophic ethical beliefs, however, should be of great concern to anyone involved in the resolution of a dilemma or supposition of an argument within the realm of ethics and morals. Accepting too many givens as "prior assumptions" will lead to poor decision making, avoiding essential questions.

Every argument we make and every belief we have is a product of ethical assumptions we have about the world. Recognizing some of the important ethical dilemmas faced by people, and differing ways of thinking about them can help you recognize the assumptions in all arguments about what one ought to do in any given situation. In this section, we'll explore the most widely used and historically significant advances in ethical theory.

The study of ethics is generally divided into three levels of operation: metaethics, normative ethics, and applied ethics.

A. Metaethics

The authors of the Stanford Encyclopedia of Philosophy define *metaethics* as "the attempt to understand the metaphysical, epistemological, semantic, and psychological, presuppositions and commitments of moral thought, talk, and practice."[2] Clearly, the mission of metaethics is an exceptionally broad mission. It deals with the highest levels of abstraction and seemingly unanswerable moral puzzles and questions about fundamental understandings regarding morals and human behavior. To some degree, the aim of metaethics is procedural. It seeks to identify or establish views and assumptions which are or may be shared by those engaged in more concrete or applied debate. This discipline is more concerned with identifying general principles and even base definitions than application of specific constructs or specific sets of rules or principles.

Metaethics is concerned with understanding the inherent nature of ethical properties. For instance, what *is* goodness or justice? Or how do we know what is good or bad? To what extent is human behavior chosen? What is the relationship between freedom and responsibility? Is freedom by its nature good? These are "meaning of life" sort of questions which set the table for subsequent debate. As explained by Fieser in *The Internet Encyclopedia of Philosophy*, "Metaethics investigates where our ethical principles come from, and what they mean. Are they merely social inventions? Do they involve more than expressions of our

---

2. Sayre-McCord, Geoff, "Metaethics," *The Stanford Encyclopedia of Philosophy (Spring 2012 Edition)*, Edward N. Zalta (ed.), http://plato.stanford.edu/archives/spr2012/entries/metaethics/.

individual emotions? Metaethical answers to these questions focus on the issues of universal truths, the will of God, the role of reason in ethical judgments, and the meaning of ethical terms themselves."[3] Unlike the other branches, metaethics is less concerned with what should or ought to be done, but instead focuses on questions of why do we choose the values we choose to influence, how we decide what should or ought to be done. It is easy and normal to take for granted the considerations of metaethics in the discussions we have in our everyday lives. In nuanced debate, some of the metaethical assumptions inherent in the arguments presented could hold the key to the best way to engage your opponent's claims.

As explained by Robert Cavalier in *The Online Guide to Ethics and Moral Philosophy*, "Metaethics talks about the nature of ethics and moral reasoning. Discussions about whether ethics is relative and whether we always act from self-interest are examples of meta-ethical discussions. In fact, drawing the conceptual distinction between Metaethics, Normative Ethics, and Applied Ethics is itself a "metaethical analysis."[4] Dr. Fieser places the schools of thought in metaethics into two categories: metaphysical and psychological. Metaphysics questions the nature of the universe: What exists independently of human conception and what is invented by humans? The first metaphysical approach to metaethics suggests that moral values may be objectively measured as they exist in nature and/or have been issued by God. This is the "other-worldly" notion that ethics exist and it is up to us, as humans, to discover and follow them. A second metaphysical approach to metaethics denies the universal existence of moral values as objective absolutes, but adopts the view of skeptical philosophy and assumes that moral values are human inventions. This does not suggest that there are no moral values or that they are unimportant, but only recognizes the human involvement in defining and understanding them. This position may be referred to as *moral relativism*. In turn, moral relativism may be thought of as *individual relativism*, which holds that each person creates their own moral principles, and *cultural relativism*, which places the credit for generation of values and moral principles within the culture or community. These metaethical questions become vitally important when considering the impact of argumentation across cultures and even as applied to diverse populations and groups.[5]

The psychological approach to metaethics questions what motivates a person to pursue ethical behavior and construct or understand moral guidelines. Three approaches, or categories of questions regarding the nature of ethical standards, include egoism and altruism, emotion and reason, and male and female morality. Thomas Hobbes believed that human actions are largely guided by selfish objectives. Joseph Butler agreed, but also recognized that we may also be motivated by a nature of benevolence, thus the school of thought regarding personal

---

3. Fieser, J., *Psychological Issues in Metaethics*, June 29, 2003. Retrieved from http://www.iep.utm.edu/ethics/.

4. Cavalier, R., *Online Guide to Ethics and Moral Philosophy*. N.p., 2002. Web. 8 June 2012. http://www.phil.cmu.edu/Cavalier/80130/part2/II_preface.html.

5. Fieser, J., *Psychological Issues in Metaethics*, June 29, 2003. Retrieved from http://www.iep.utm.edu/ethics/.

approaches to ethics through egoism and altruism are measured by individuals' commitments to themselves and others. The second psychological approach to metaethics, emotion, and reason weighs the contribution of reasoning and emotion to moral decision making. Hume and others come down on the side of emotions. Hume stated "reason is, and ought to be, the slave of the passions." More rationally focused thinkers, including, for example, Immanuel Kant, have argued that emotions cloud the judgment and that reason and rationality should prevail. The third such approach takes a feminist viewpoint and suggests that traditional metaethics is male dominated and represents a patriarchal or male ethic, based in categorical division and hierarchy. These feminist philosophers advocate an alternative and feminine perspective which is more holistic, less accepting of domination, property, and power as fundamental premises, and more committed to nurturing, empowering, and spontaneity with less commitment to rigid sets of rules and expectations.[6]

B. Normative Ethics

Normative ethics refers to the study of ethical action. It may also be referred to as *prescriptive ethics*. Normative ethics is distinct from metaethics because it is concerned with the application of standards or criteria that influence and guide our understanding of the rightness and wrongness of action and, therefore, our behavior. It is concerned with what we *ought* to do. Normative ethical theories influence the policies of governments and the lessons we teach our children. Cavalier observes, "Normative ethics is interested in determining the content of our moral behavior. Normative ethical theories seek to provide action-guides; procedures for answering the Practical Question ("What ought I to do?")."[7] The theories of normative ethics are many, and an understanding of the most popular and influential theories will help you recognize the ethical assumptions inherent in your opponent's arguments. Constructs of normative ethics provide to the debater and the decision rendered a framework or set of measures through which to evaluate competing claims, advocacies, and policies. The most frequently discussed sets of normative ethical theories include the two introduced in Chapter 1 (consequentialism, or teleological approaches, and deontological approaches), as well as the classical notion of virtue. Consequentialism focuses on the outcome or end result of action in measuring its ethicality, deontology bases its measure of ethics on rules and duties which guide action, and virtue ethics focus on the actor. In the famous novel *Les Misérables*, by Victor Hugo, the protagonist Jean Valjean is imprisoned for the crime of stealing a loaf of bread to feed his ill and starving niece. His antagonist, the police inspector Javert pursues Valjean, dedicated to his belief that justice, as embodied by the law, is the only right guidance for action. Throughout his life, which he reconstructs

---

6. Fieser, J., *Psychological Issues in Metaethics*, June 29, 2003. Retrieved from http://www.iep.utm.edu/ethics/.
7. Cavalier, R., *Online Guide to Ethics and Moral Philosophy*. N.p., 2002. Web. 8 June 2012. http://www.phil.cmu.edu/Cavalier/80130/part2/II_preface.html.

with a new identity, Valjean (Monsieur Madeleine) faces a number of ethical dilemmas. In stealing to feed his niece, he follows a consequentialist ethic. As the narrative progresses, Valjean is called upon to make additional decisions, recognizing that relying solely on the measure of consequences provides insufficient guidance for his life decisions. He then employs a virtue-based ethic to become a man of character. Javert maintains, to the end, an unwavering commitment to the rule of law as right behavior, exemplifying a deontological approach to ethics.[8]

1. Virtue Ethics.   While discussed in ancient China and central to concerns of Confucius, the contemporary western study of Virtue Ethics begins its lineage in the discussions of Socrates, Plato, and Aristotle in the 4th century B.C. in Greece. Recall that the Roman orator, Quintilian, demanded that the orator be an ethical actor (repeating the maxim of Cato, "... [a] Good man speaking well: Speech must treat that which is just and honorable, or is to be opposed." A man must (a) be free from all vice, (b) be a lover of wisdom, (c) a sincere believer in his cause, (d) a servant of the state and its people.[9] This reflected an important measure of ethics in the virtues of the individual. Virtues are the habits of the individual that become indistinguishable from identity or behavior. They define you, direct you to good actions, and stand in contrast to vice and wrong behavior. For virtue ethics, the *character* of the agent is paramount as the driving force for ethical behavior. This means that in order to determine whether or not an action is just or right, one must examine the agent in relation to the circumstances of the case. Motives are important and supersede rules or measures of consequences. Remember the example of Jean Valjean, who struggles with the question of what sort of man he will be, what actions and choices will define his character. Such are the measures of virtue.

Aristotle argued that virtues are "good habits that we acquire, which regulate our emotions." For example, in response to my natural feelings of fear, I should develop the virtue of courage, which allows me to be firm when facing danger.[10] Virtue ethics as discussed by Aristotle focus on three essential concepts: virtue, moral wisdom, and happiness. Virtue, or excellence, termed *arête* in Greek, is more than an attitude or favorable predisposition to act rightly, and cannot be evaluated on the basis of a single act, or the observable action of the person. It requires a complexity of thought and spirit and embodies the whole nature of the person. It recognizes interaction among behaviors and dispositions, emotional reactions, and commitments. Such a conception of virtue also considers the relative nature of this commitment. While it is admirable to fight one's weaker inclinations and ultimately make a right decision about what to do, thus employing "continence" or strength of will, it is more virtuous to do the right thing without any internal struggles or temptations to do otherwise.

---

8. Aquinas, T. (2009), *Everyday Thomist*. Retrieved from http://everydaythomist. wordpress.com/2009/08/20/learning-ethics-from-les-miserables/.

9. Quintilian & Butler, H. E. (1920), *The Institutio Oratoria of Quintilian*. Cambridge, Mass: Harvard University Press.

10. Fieser, J., *Psychological Issues in Metaethics*, June 29, 2003. Retrieved from http://www. iep.utm.edu/ethics/.

Practical or moral wisdom (*phronesis*) recognizes that virtues must be tempered and balanced, employing common sense born of experience and perspective. While honesty is certainly a virtue, being "honest to a fault" might lead a person to hurt another's feelings in expressing negative opinions about them ("you look like you've gained weight..."). Generosity is virtuous until it creates hardship for one's family or self. Finally, the concept of *eudaimonia*, which is a sort of happiness and flourishing, is a measure of virtue. This must be considered as abruptly distinct from a hedonistic happiness or pleasure, but rather is a reference to contentment in living a virtuous life. The virtuous person lives a good life, and suggests a satisfaction and coherence to right thought and action.

2. Consequentialism.   Consequentialism is the class of normative ethical theories holding that the consequences of one's conduct are the ultimate basis for any judgment about the rightness of that conduct. Thus, from a consequentialist standpoint, a morally right act is one that will produce a good outcome, or consequence.

Consequentialism is usually regarded as the philosophical opposite of Deontology and is sometimes referred to as Teleological ethics. The word comes from the Greek *telos,* which means "an end purpose." A thing, process, or action is teleological when it is for the sake of an end, that is, a telos or final cause. Regardless of the value's intrinsic or extrinsic nature, under teleological ethics or consequentialism, it is the final end result of an action that determines the moral fortitude of said action.

So in the case of lying, the consequentialist would not on-face deny the morality of the action in the same way a deontologist or virtue ethicist might argue. Instead, for the teleological ethicist, we must determine whether the lie created positive outcomes consistent with values and morals considered good. Would you lie to a Nazi to protect the identity of a Jewish person? Would you lie to the IRS to avoid paying taxes, which will support governmental activities you oppose? This view allows the same action to be justified in one instance and unjust in another. For consequentialism a lie to save the lives of others without harm to anyone else would be considered a good action, regardless of whether the lie itself violated a moral value; in this case, telling the truth. However if the lie was told for greedy or otherwise morally negative ends, then the same act of lying is deemed unethical. So if the genuine reason for lying to the IRS was to avoid paying taxes so one could buy a new flat screen television, the consequentialist would likely find that an immoral act. Justifications for moral measurement by consequentialist approaches may be placed into one of three schools of thought. First, *ethical egoism* would deem behavior morally acceptable if the consequences of the act in question are more favorable than unfavorable to the person doing the act. Second, *ethical altruism* would consider an action right if the consequences are more favorable than unfavorable to others, NOT to the actor (as in Jean Valjean's theft of bread). Third, *utilitarianism* could measure the action morally right if the consequences of the action are more favorable than unfavorable to everyone, including, but not limited to, the actor.

Utilitarianism is the most common refined ethical theory commonly associated with consequentialism. Utilitarianism holds that the proper course of action is the one that maximizes the overall "happiness". It is thus a form of consequentialism, meaning that the moral worth of an action is determined only by its resulting outcome, and that one can only weigh the morality of an action after knowing all its consequences. Another commonly attributed explanation of Utilitarianism is that it holds that the right action is the one that maximizes the greatest good, for the most agents, over the longest amount of time. The two most influential contributors to the Utilitarian theory are Jeremy Bentham who described it as the "pleasure principle," and John Stuart Mill who used the term, "the greatest happiness principle." Bentham proposed a sort of cost–benefit measure by which each individual case is considered for its moral rightness or wrongness based on the relative benefits and costs of the individual act. Hence, this approach is referred to as *act-utilitarianism*. Bentham also proposed that the consequence of each act be measured by the degree to which we experience pain or pleasure (or that others experience pain or pleasure) as a result of the act. This measure is referred to as *hedonistic utilitarianism*, and explains the term "happiness principle."

Rule utilitarianism, as articulated by John Stuart Mill, advocates a set of basic rules generated to benefit society as measured by what acts produce "the greatest good for the most people." Rule utilitarianism posits that overall happiness (utility) is best achieved in a rule-based system, and each situation need not receive special treatment according to its unique nature, but society can apply moral "rules" to bring more predictability and continuity to decision making.

Social Contract Theory.   Recall that Hobbes advocated the metaethical theory of psychological egoism, that our actions are selfishly motivated. Based on that foundation, Hobbes developed the view that a set of moral *rules* is important to manage selfish action for the good of the society. Without rules, that which we value is at risk to those who would take it, including our property, our families, our freedoms, and even our lives. Therefore, civilized society, motivated as it should be by selfish desires for security, demands that we enter into a social contract, an agreed-upon set of rules which may be enforced in order to protect the individual from the selfish acts of others.

Some view consequentialism's adaptability appealing for their ethical world view. Others view this adaptability as inconsistency and a weakness for an objective ethical theory. Some even argue that consequentialist and deontological theories are not necessarily mutually exclusive. Robert Nozick, for example, argues for a predominantly consequentialist framework but also incorporates and relies on deontological restricts toward the actions agents are permitted to do.

3. Deontology or Duty Theories.   Inspector Javert, in *Les Misérables*, is motivated by a sense of duty to enforce the law. Duty, or deontological, theories base their moral foundations on "specific, foundational principles of obligation."[11]

---

11. Fieser, J., *Psychological Issues in Metaethics*, June 29, 2003. Retrieved from http://www. iep.utm.edu/ethics/.

The term "deontological" comes from the Greek word *deon*, or duty. These basic duties may be bound in spiritual commitments to one's God and understanding of religious rules for behavior, or other accepted sets of responsibilities to one's self and others. They may include commitments to do no harm to others, to treat others with respect and equality, and to promote the welfare and good of others. Based in part on these duties, we will identify three approaches to deontology: rights theory, the categorical imperative, and prima facie duties.

First, duty-based ethics may be built on *rights* theory. A "right" may be thought of as a protection or claim against the behavior of another. Rights and duties are symbiotic: they are dependent on one another. If I have a right to be respected by you, then you have a duty to respect me! If I have a right to be paid by you for services rendered, you have a responsibility to provide payment. In the Declaration of Independence, Thomas Jefferson recognized natural rights, as had been articulated by philosopher John Locke, including life, liberty and the pursuit of happiness, and their more specific rights as implied, property, movement, speech, and religious expression. These were deemed natural rights as they are given to us by God. Fieser identifies the fundamental characteristics of moral rights:

> First, rights are natural insofar as they are not invented or created by governments. Second, they are universal insofar as they do not change from country to country. Third, they are equal in the sense that rights are the same for all people, irrespective of gender, race, or handicap. Fourth, they are inalienable which means that I cannot hand over my rights to another person, such as by selling myself into slavery.[12]

Rights theory, thus, identifies right action by a set of rules that recognize the existing rights and resultant responsibilities of people.

A second approach to duty-based ethics is represented by Immanuel Kant and his *Categorical Imperative*. Kant embraced the notion that we operate within the framework of a set of specific duties to ourselves and to others and that the moral nature of an act could not be measured solely by its consequences. He rejected the consequentialist criteria of utilitarianism by embracing the maxim that motives and duties behind acts, not the resulting consequences, should guide ethical decision making. Kant argued that groups could not determine and impose a morality of action based on their results, in part because there would be disagreement on how to interpret these results. In addition, he did not feel that specific situation-based rules were sufficient to guide coherent right action. Kant argued that there is a more basic obligation of duty that defines even specific application. It is a "single, self-evident principle of reason" that he calls the categorical imperative. A categorical imperative, he argued, is fundamentally different from hypothetical imperatives. Two prongs of the categorical

12. Fieser, J., *Psychological Issues in Metaethics*, June 29, 2003. Retrieved from http://www.iep.utm.edu/ethics/.

imperative are key to our understanding. First is the test of universalizability, "what if everyone acted how I am about to act?" or "am I prepared to allow or even require everyone to do the same thing I am doing?" The second, and more fundamental, requirement for Kant is that one treats people as ends in themselves, and not a means to an end. People should always be treated with dignity, and never used as mere instruments. So, I would not lie to the IRS, as I would only be using them (and other law-abiding taxpayers) as instruments to my own happiness. Kant believes that the morality of all actions can be determined by appealing to this single principle of duty.

The third approach to duty-based ethics which we will discuss is the theory of *Prima Facie Duties* of British philosopher W.D. Ross. Ross adheres to the importance of individual responsibilities as natural and universal, but offers a shorter list than his predecessors. They reflect our moral convictions, and are:

- Fidelity: the duty to keep promises
- Reparation: the duty to compensate others when we harm them
- Gratitude: the duty to thank those who help us
- Justice: the duty to recognize merit
- Beneficence: the duty to improve the conditions of others
- Self-improvement: the duty to improve our virtue and intelligence
- Nonmaleficence: the duty to not injure others.[13]

Of course, situations will generate forced choices between conflicting duties. Ross argues that our *actual* duties become clear to us when these cases emerge. For example, even though I promised to never interfere in my teenage child's self-directed use of my power tools, I will intervene when I see her threatening injury to herself.

In general, all the duty-based, or deontological, approaches to normative ethics rely on ethical theory supporting that the decision process should be the primary considering factor when determining morality. Rather than measuring the ethical rightness based on the end result and measured success (consequentialism) or the character of the decider (virtue), deontology or duty-based ethics rely on the decider to "do the right thing" in the act of decision making, as guided by one of a set of available decision processes.

C. Applied Ethics

The third branch of ethical study's title is self-explanatory. Applied ethics is a term used to describe the attempt made to identify the morally correct action as it pertains to various aspects and fields of human life. Some common examples of applied ethics are medical or bioethics, business ethics, environmental ethics, animal ethics, and sexual

---

13. Fieser, J., *Psychological Issues in Metaethics*, June 29, 2003. Retrieved from http://www.iep.utm.edu/ethics/.

ethics. What marks these as applied ethical arenas are potential for controversy, that is, there are at least two sides to be considered, and that it is a distinctly moral issue.

Debaters will often have the opportunity to explore cases or areas of applied ethics in exploring specific propositions. Applications of ethics may not employ unique bodies of content material or theory, but rather they are likely to apply normative and even metaethical theories and principles to specific and concrete decision contexts. Following are some normative ethical principles which may be applied in some specific scenarios. This list is by no means exhaustive, and it borrows from theories of virtue, consequentialism, and duty.

- The **Principle of Autonomy** instructs us to respect the personal freedoms of others and to refrain from inhibiting individual self-determination.

- The **Harm Principle** is the belief that liberty or freedom may be restricted, when doing so prevents harm to others.

- The **Offense Principle** is the belief that liberty or freedom may be restricted, when doing so prevents offense to others.

- The **Principle of Paternalism** is the belief that a person's liberty or freedom may be limited to prevent that person from committing actions that could harm themselves.

- **Social Justice** is the belief that liberty or freedom may be restricted when doing so can promote social goals, like equality or security.

- **Legal Moralism** is the belief that liberty or freedom is justifiably circumscribed to prevent a person from committing actions that run contrary to the collective morality of society. Related to *majoritarianism*, which posits that liberty or freedom of a person may be limited when doing so conforms to the wishes of the majority.

- **Beneficence** is the belief that it is morally wrong to fail to increase the good of others when one is in a position to do so. Related to *benevolence*, which is the duty to help those in need.

- **Compensatory Justice** is the principle that victims of injury should receive fair compensation for harm done, ideally compensation, which restores an individual to the position they would have occupied had the injury not occurred.

- **Distributive Justice** is the belief that society should distribute benefits and responsibilities fairly, using impartial criteria.

- **Due Process** and **Retributive Justice** are commitments to a just and fair process, wherein the state respects all of the legal rights that are owed to a person and when delivered, punishments and consequences are proportionate to the transgressions committed.

- The **Principle of Nonmaleficence** is the belief that one should not harm others. It is linked to the Latin phrase *primum non nocere*, which means, "*first, do no harm.*"

- The **Golden Rule** is one of the most widely accepted and known moral principles, advocated by most of the world's great religions, establishes the standard that one should behave toward others as they would wish to be treated. Of course, not everyone wishes for the same treatment!

▪ **Veracity** is the belief that it is important to disclose critical information and to tell the truth about all things relevant to the decision.

Again, these principles represent a representative range of concepts which may be applied in situations calling for ethical decision making, but the list is far from comprehensive. The principles may not always offer guidance, particularly when they contradict within a given application. In addition to considering application of normative issues in applied ethics, ethicists and arguers are interested in specific areas of applied ethics. A few examples are identified here, but the complete list would be much longer. *Biomedical ethics* or *bioethics* focuses on a range of issues which arise in clinical settings. Issues considered include (but are not limited to) questions related to end of life decisions, human cloning, genetic screening, stem-cell research, abortion, privacy of medical records, mandatory drug screening, provision (or denial) of medical care, and many other issues fundamental to decisions made by patients, doctors, providers, researchers, insurance companies, governmental officials, and others. The field of *business ethics* considers practices, responsibilities, and consequences of action by business organizations within the capitalist business environment including issues like deceptive advertising, insider trading, accounting and finance principles and transparency (or secrecy and deception), employee rights, job discrimination, affirmative action, whistle-blowing, and drug testing. In the aftermath of Enron's "cooking the books," deceptive and secretive credit card policies by financial institutions, excessive financial bonuses for top executives, reckless trading behaviors and predatory lending practices contributing to the "great recession," dangerous drilling practices by BP Oil contributing to the Deepwater Horizon Oil Spill, and so many more consequential and publicized events by business, much attention has been given to business ethics.

Environmental ethics consider the relationship of humans to the earth and the natural environment. Our world has limited resources and human behavior has a substantial, mostly deleterious effect on it. Water, land, and air suffer the consequences of human activity, and we face crises of shortages, extinctions, climate change, and toxicity. Some would recognize these negative consequences to the natural environment as they increase hardship for human survival. People who are human centered in their consideration of this relationship between people and the environment, who assign intrinsic value primarily to humans and consider any need to protect the environment to be justified based on the need humans have to use natural resources and survive are *anthropocentric*. Their ecology is a *shallow ecology* that fights against pollution and resource depletion to maintain resources and standards of living for human quality of life. This is likely to be a utilitarian ethic, focused on the consequences of failing to preserve the environment. *Deep ecology* attributes per se values to animals and the environment, and considers humans as only another component of the living environment, no more important than the other components. It is more likely to rely on a deontological ethic, ascribing a duty to protect and sustain the natural environment. *Animal Ethics* stems from the concept that animals, as sentient beings, also have rights. Issues of concern include the production of meat as food, preservation of species, ethical and humane treatment of animals and animal testing. Additional ethical studies include government ethics, ethics of war, marriage and sexual ethics, ethics of race, and many more.

II. CULTURE AND CULTURAL STUDIES

Culture is probably the single most important factor influencing our communication and thus our argumentation approaches. Our learned culture establishes for us that set of rules, norms, values, and conceptions that we model and that color our understandings of the world. It therefore hardwires at least some of the ethical foundations upon which our moral principles are based. It shapes our understandings and our perceptions. What we choose to argue, and how we argue is shaped by culture, and how we understand and interpret what we receive and perceive is shaped by culture. So what is culture, then? Geert Hofstede defines culture as "the collective programming of the mind which distinguishes the members of one group or category of people from another."[14] Therefore, as the title of his book infers, culture is a sort of "software of the mind." Hofstede continues, "culture is learned, not inherited, it derives from one's social environment, not from one's genes." To argue across cultures is both inevitable and extraordinarily challenging. A starting point for such argumentation is a position of *cultural relativism*, as described by Claude Levi-Strauss and translated by Hofstede, "Cultural relativism affirms that one culture has no absolute criteria for judging the activities of another culture as 'low' or 'noble'. However, every culture can and should apply such judgment to its own activities, because its members are actors as well as observers."[15] So in order to understand and relate to cultural ethics, one must be both self-aware of their own culture ethic and sensitive to and open to the cultural ethic of others. Of course, culture exists on a number of layers, including national culture, regional, ethnic, and/or religious groups, gender, generation, social class and education, and

Dimensions of Culture
1. Power distance 2. Collectivism versus individualism 3. Femininity versus masculinity 4. Uncertainty avoidance

14. Hofstede, G., *Cultures and Organizations: Software of the Mind*, 1991. London: McGraw-Hill, p. 5.
15. Hofstede, G., *Cultures and Organizations: Software of the Mind*, 1991. London: McGraw-Hill, p. 7.

occupational groupings. These co-cultures all impact our own set of values and communication habits, as well as what we perceive to be our cultural identities. Hofstede further defines some key identifying criteria or characteristics of culture, the dimensions of culture, as power distance (small to large), collectivism versus individualism, femininity versus masculinity, and uncertainty avoidance (weak to strong). In other words, each culture can be identified based on how it scores on this set of criteria. Power distance refers to the extent to which a culture accepts authoritarian and hierarchical power structures. Large power distance means the culture is accepting of a large discrepancy in power. The United States tends to be very low on this scale, preferring equality to large power distance. Collectivism describes commitment to groups such as family, church, and community. Americans tend to be more individualistic, with less commitment to groups. The next set of criteria measures differences between feminine and masculine societies; for example, in a feminine culture the dominant values are caring for others and preservation, and people and warm relationships are important, whereas in a masculine culture the dominant values are material success and progress, and money and things are important. Finally, uncertainty avoidance describes the extent to which the culture is tolerant of ambiguity and difference, for example, one criteria for weak uncertainly avoidance is "what is different is curious" whereas strong uncertainty avoidance might say "what is different, is dangerous."

Critical Theory.   Given this backdrop, it is useful to understand that critical philosophers, in the tradition of Marx, have considered the importance of culture and, more importantly, how cultural entities execute dominance and suppression of other cultural groups through their actions including communication. These critical theorists are most concerned with generating voice and emancipation for repressed and silenced groups. For them, what distinguishes an ethic as *critical* is that it strives to empower and emancipate those who experience domination. An adequate critical theory must "meet three criteria, it must be explanatory, practical, and normative, all at the same time. That is, it must explain what is wrong with current social reality, identify the actors to change it, and provide both clear norms for criticism and achievable practical goals for social transformation."[16]

Cultural Studies.   Cultural studies is a subset of critical theory. Developed and organized out of the work of Richard Hoggart and Stuart Hall, in reaction to changing cultural politics of England in the 1960s and 1970s, it borrows from the earlier work of Antonio Gramsci, who recognized that the dominant political groups not only benefited from employment of means of brute force and capital to suppress the masses, but also utilized what he termed *cultural hegemony* to penetrate the everyday culture of working people. Hegemony is the existence of dominance of one social group over another. It is a form of power based on dominance by a group across many types of activities, so that its exercise garners widespread consent and seems natural and inevitable. According to Gramsci, social groups struggle in many

---

16. Bohman, J., *The Stanford Encyclopedia of Philosophy*, March 8, 2005. Retrieved from http://plato.stanford.edu/entries/critical-theory/.

different ways, to win the agreement of other groups to gain dominance in thought and practice over them. He argued that the power is controlled by an economic elite, and that hegemony enables a diverse culture to be repressed and controlled, propelled by complex systems of domination. *Cultural hegemony* then is a systematic and hierarchical set of social structures. A nuanced and effective hegemony is sustained by many people living in it, with their compliance, but not always their recognition of complicity. Gramsci observes that since power in a democracy results from persuasion, it is never completely or permanently achieved. A dominant group has to acknowledge the existence of those whom it dominates by winning the consent of competing or marginalized groups in society. Gramsci's notion of cultural hegemony was distinct from prior descriptions of class-based hegemony in that it focused on structures of cultural groups in concert rather than class as a primary determining factor in domination. Therefore, *agency* is a key term for cultural theorists. Agency refers to the ability and opportunity for marginalized groups and individuals to resist domination.

Ziauddin Sardar introduces Cultural Studies as defined by the following five essential defining characteristics:

- Cultural studies aims to examine its subject matter in terms of cultural practices and their relation to power. For example, a study of a subculture (such as white working class youth in London) would consider the social practices of the youth as they relate to the dominant classes.

- It has the objective of understanding culture in all its complex forms and of analyzing the social and political context in which culture manifests itself.

- It is both the object of study and the location of political criticism and action. For example, not only would a cultural studies scholar study an object, but she/he would connect this study to a larger, progressive political project.

- It attempts to expose and reconcile the division of knowledge, to overcome the split between tacit cultural knowledge and objective (universal) forms of knowledge.

- It has a commitment to an ethical evaluation of modern society and to a radical line of political action.[17]

Cultural studies investigates the ways in which meaning is generated, disseminated, and produced through various practices, beliefs, and institutions. It also considers the political, economic, and social structures within a given culture which contribute to domination. Cultural theorists include advocates of feminism, critical race theory, orientalism, whiteness, and some forms of postcolonial criticism. Among the goals of cultural theory is to give voice to suppressed peoples, to uncover means of domination and to employ agency to empower the marginalized. So, cultural theory has ethical constructs as its underpinnings, and normative ethical theory as its modus operandi.

---

17. Sardar, Z., & Van Loon, B. (*Introducing Cultural Studies*, Cambridge, UK: Icon Books, 1999. Retrieved from http://en.wikipedia.org/wiki/Cultural_studies.

EXERCISES

1. Look up the honor code (or equivalent) for your institution. What meta-ethical assumptions are revealed by the authors? What principles of normative ethics and what general ethical construct?

2. Visit the website for the Intercollegiate Ethics Bowl: http://www.indiana.edu/~appe/ethicsbowl.html#national_cases_rules.

   Click on the button marked *the national championship cases and rules.* Choose a case. Apply each of the three normative ethical constructs identified in the chapter. How does the application differ by each approach?

3. Visit the website for the Markkula Center for Applied Ethics: http://www.scu.edu/ethics/practicing/focusareas/cases.cfm. Click on the button marked *ethics cases* and follow the instructions.

4. Identify cases of ethical decision in today's newspaper. How would you resolve the issue(s)?

5. See the movie *Les Misérables* and discuss the ethical decisions made by Jean Valjean and Inspector Javert.

6

The Debate Proposition

Debate is a means of settling differences, so there must be a controversy, a difference of opinion, or a conflict of interest before there can be a debate. If everyone is in agreement on a fact or value or policy, there is no need or opportunity for debate; the matter can be settled by unanimous consent. Thus, for example, it would be pointless to attempt to debate "Resolved: That two plus two equals four," because there is simply no controversy about this statement. *Controversy is an essential prerequisite of debate.* Where there is no *clash* of ideas, proposals, interests, or expressed positions on issues, there is no debate. Controversy invites decisive choice between competing positions. Debate cannot produce effective decisions without clear identification of a question or questions to be answered. For example, general argument may occur about the broad topic of illegal immigration. How many illegal immigrants live in the United States? What is the impact of illegal immigration and immigrants on our economy? What is their impact on our communities? Do they commit crimes? Do they take jobs from American workers? Do they pay taxes? Do they require social services? Is it a problem that some do not speak English? Is it the responsibility of employers to discourage illegal immigration by not hiring undocumented workers? Should they have the opportunity to gain citizenship? Does illegal immigration pose a security threat to our country? Do illegal immigrants do work that American workers are unwilling to do? Are their rights as workers and as human beings at risk due to their status? Are they abused by employers, law enforcement, housing, and businesses? How are their families impacted by their status? What is the moral and philosophical obligation of a nation state to maintain its borders? Should we build a wall on the Mexican border, establish a national identification card, or enforce existing laws against employers? Should we invite immigrants to become U.S. citizens? Surely you can think of many more concerns to be addressed by a conversation about the topic area of illegal immigration. Participation in this "debate" is likely to be emotional and intense.

Miniglossary

A burden of proof   The obligation to prove what one asserts. Applies to both the affirmative and the negative, as any advocate forwarding a claim must provide support sufficient to overcome the natural presumption against that claim.

The burden of proof   The risk of the proposition; the obligation of the affirmative, in order to overcome the presumption against the proposition, to give good and sufficient reasons for accepting the proposition.

Burden of refutation   The obligation to refute, or respond to, opposing arguments. Applies to both the affirmative and the negative. Failure to fulfill the burden of refutation results in the acceptance of the unrefuted argument.

Presumption   A predisposition favoring a given side in a dispute. Describes a psychological state in which listeners and decision makers are predisposed to favor or oppose one side of a debate or an argumentative position.

Proposition   A statement of judgment that identifies the central issue in a controversy. May be a proposition of fact, value, nonpolicy, or policy.

Proposition of Fact   Descriptive claims addressing qualities of condition or causation.

Proposition of Value   Evaluative claims, identify qualities of relative goodness or badness of a thing or condition.

Proposition of Policy   Advocative claims calling for action and including identification of an actor and the prescribed act.

Quasi Policy Proposition   Expresses a value judgment about a policy.

Status quo   The existing state of things; the present system.

However, it is not likely to be productive or useful without focus on a particular question and identification of a line demarcating sides in the controversy. To be discussed and resolved effectively, controversies are best understood when stated clearly such that all parties to the debate share an understanding about the objective of the debate. This enables focus on substantive and objectively identifiable issues facilitating comparison of competing argumentation leading to effective decisions. Vague understanding results in unfocused deliberation and poor decisions, general feelings of tension without opportunity for resolution, frustration, and emotional distress, as evidenced by the failure of the U.S. Congress to make substantial progress on the immigration debate.

Of course, **arguments** may be presented without disagreement. For example, claims are presented and supported within speeches, editorials, and advertisements even without opposing or refutational response. **Argumentation** occurs in a range of settings from informal to formal, and may not call upon an audience or judge to make a forced choice among competing claims. Informal discourse occurs as conversation or panel discussion without demanding a decision about a dichotomous or yes/no question. However, by definition, **debate** requires "reasoned judgment on a **proposition**." The proposition is a statement about which competing advocates will offer alternative (pro or con) argumentation calling upon their audience or adjudicator to decide. The proposition provides focus for the discourse and guides the decision process. Even when a decision will be made through a process of compromise, it is important to identify the beginning positions of competing advocates to begin negotiation and movement toward a center or consensus position. It is frustrating and usually unproductive to attempt to make a decision when deciders are unclear as to what the decision is *about*. The proposition may be implicit in some applied debates ("Vote for me!"); however, when a vote or consequential decision is called for (as in the courtroom or in applied parliamentary debate) it is essential that the proposition be explicitly expressed ("the defendant is guilty!"). In academic debate, the proposition provides essential guidance for the preparation of the debaters prior to the debate, the case building and discourse presented during the debate, and the decision to be made by the debate judge after the debate. Someone disturbed by the problem of a growing underclass of poorly educated, socially disenfranchised youths might observe, "Public schools are doing a terrible job! They are overcrowded, and many teachers are poorly qualified in their subject areas. Even the best teachers can do little more than struggle to maintain order in their classrooms." That same concerned citizen, facing a complex range of issues, might arrive at an unhelpful decision, such as "We ought to do something about this" or, worse, "It's too complicated a problem to deal with." Groups of concerned citizens worried about the state of public education could join together to express their frustrations, anger, disillusionment, and emotions regarding the schools, but without a focus for their discussions, they could easily agree about the sorry state of education without finding points of clarity or potential solutions. A gripe session would follow. But if a precise question is posed—such as "*What* can be done to *improve* public education?"—then a more profitable area of discussion is opened up simply by placing a focus on the search for a concrete solution step. One or more judgments can be phrased in the form of debate propositions, motions for parliamentary debate, or bills for legislative assemblies. The statements "Resolved: That the federal government should implement a program of charter schools in at-risk communities" and "Resolved: That the state of Florida should adopt a school voucher program" more clearly identify specific ways of dealing with educational problems in a manageable form, suitable for debate. They provide specific policies to be investigated and aid discussants in identifying points of difference. This focus contributes to better

---

The Debate Proposition

- A proposition is a statement of judgment that identifies the central issue in controversy
- Those arguing in favor of the proposition present the *affirmative* side
- Those arguing against the proposition present the *negative* side

and more informed decision making with the potential for better results. In academic debate, it provides better depth of argumentation and enhanced opportunity for reaping the educational benefits of participation. In the next section, we will consider the challenge of framing the proposition for debate, and its role in the debate.

I. DEFINING THE CONTROVERSY

To have a productive debate, which facilitates effective decision making by directing and placing limits on the decision to be made, the basis for argument should be clearly defined. If we merely talk about a **topic**, such as "homelessness," or "abortion," or "crime," or "global warming," we are likely to have an interesting discussion but not to establish a profitable basis for argument. For example, the statement "Resolved: That the pen is mightier than the sword" is debatable, yet by itself fails to provide much basis for clear argumentation. If we take this statement to mean that the written word is more effective than physical force for some purposes, we can identify a problem area: the comparative effectiveness of writing or physical force for a specific purpose, perhaps promoting positive social change. (Note that "loose" propositions, such as the example above, may be defined by their advocates in such a way as to facilitate a clear contrast of competing sides; through definitions and debate they "become" clearly understood statements even though they may not begin as such. There are formats for debate that often begin with this sort of proposition. However, in any debate, at some point, effective and meaningful discussion relies on identification of a clearly stated or understood proposition.)

Back to the example of the written word versus physical force. Although we now have a general subject, we have not yet stated a problem. It is still too broad, too loosely worded to promote well-organized argument. What sort of writing are we concerned with—poems, novels, government documents, website development, advertising, cyber-warfare, disinformation, or what? What does it mean to be "mightier" in this context? What kind of physical force is being compared—fists, dueling swords, bazookas, nuclear weapons, or what? A more specific question might be, "Would a mutual defense treaty or a visit by our fleet be more effective in assuring Laurania of our support in a certain crisis?" The basis for argument could be phrased in a debate proposition such as "Resolved: That the United States should enter into a mutual defense treaty with Laurania." Negative advocates might oppose this proposition by arguing that fleet maneuvers would be a better solution. This is not to say that debates should completely avoid creative interpretation of the controversy by advocates, or that good debates cannot occur over competing interpretations of the controversy; in fact, these sorts of debates may be very engaging. The point is that debate is best facilitated by the guidance provided by focus on a particular point of difference, which will be outlined in the following discussion.

II. PHRASING THE DEBATE PROPOSITION

In argumentation and debate a **proposition** is a statement of judgment that identifies the central issue in controversy. The advocate desires to have others accept or reject the proposition. Debate provides for organized argument for and against the proposition: Those arguing in favor of the proposition present the affirmative side; those arguing against it present the negative side. To promote intelligent and effective argumentation, a debate proposition must have certain characteristics.

A. Controversy

As stated at the beginning of this chapter, controversy is an essential prerequisite of debate. Thus an effectively worded debate proposition should begin with a subject of public dispute, or potential dispute, and clearly state the controversy or reference the point of the relevant controversy.

B. One Central Idea

The most elegant proposition provides for the best debate and ultimately the most useful decision making. There should be a clear-cut yes or no answer to a single point of controversy to enable productive and sensible debate. Even though complexity is inevitable and many smaller questions will need to be answered to provide an answer to the broader propositional question, if a proposition has more than one central idea, it will lead to confusion. Consider the proposition "Resolved: That the Philosophy Club deplores abortions and lotteries as immoral." While some people certainly would agree with this proposition, there are really two subjects for argument here. Some might deplore abortions and approve of lotteries; others might take the opposite view. Two central ideas like these should be placed in separate propositions and debated separately. If this resolution were introduced into the Philosophy Club's parliamentary debate, any member of the club could move to amend the original motion into two separate motions. If the amendment were seconded and passed, then the two motions could be debated separately. The proposition addresses two controversies.

C. Unemotional Terms

The proposition should be stated in unemotional terms, without loaded language that might give a special advantage to the affirmative or the negative. Consider the proposition "Resolved: That cruel, sadistic experimenters should be forbidden to torture defenseless animals pointlessly." The heavily loaded, emotional language gives the affirmative an unreasonable advantage. "Resolved: That vivisection should be illegal" states the proposition in dispassionate terms. Although emotionally loaded terms have persuasive value, they have no place in a debate proposition.

Although probably no word is completely neutral to everyone, one can and must try to minimize the evaluative aspects of a proposition. The wording of the proposition must be such that reasonable participants on either side will accept it as accurately and dispassionately describing the controversy to be debated.

D. Statement of the Affirmative's Desired Decision

The policy proposition should represent a statement of the decision the affirmative desires. It should set forth the decision clearly and precisely so that, if adopted, the affirmative advocates will have achieved their purpose, yet maintain sufficient lee-way for the affirmative to address a range of possible interpretations. The proposition "Resolved: That the power of the federal government should be increased" is vague and indefinite. If the affirmative should win a debate on such a proposition, what would have been accomplished? Nothing specific enough to guide policy making or inform the participants about a particular policy question. After it was agreed that the powers of the federal government should be increased, another debate on the specific powers in question would be needed. For example, people who favored increasing the power of the federal government by allowing it to make military appropriations for three, rather than two, years might oppose an increase in the power of the federal government that would allow it to abolish the states. The phrasing of the proposition should be clear, specific, devoid of ambiguous terms, and precise in the statement of the desired decision. In particu-lar, the direction of change should be identified, to draw a clear distinction for preparation and debating as to which side occupies which argumentative ground. For example, should there be more regulation or less?

Although the decision desired by the affirmative must be stated with preci-sion, the proposition sometimes gives the affirmative considerable latitude in its analysis of the **status quo**—the existing state of things—and allows for the pos-sibility of several plans in implementing that decision. For example, the proposi-tion "Resolved: That the federal government should grant annually a specific percentage of its income tax revenue to state governments" indicates the general plan but allows the affirmative considerable latitude in analyzing the status quo and in developing the details of the plan. Thus some affirmatives might call for the plan to improve the financing of state and local services. Others might focus on specific problems, such as improved financing of roads and bridges, the crimi-nal justice, or health care system. Still others might develop a quite different analysis and call for the adoption of the proposition as a means of checking the power of the military–industrial complex.

Such "open-ended" propositions realistically reflect the fact that different persons may support the same policy for a variety of reasons. As the saying goes, "Politics makes strange bedfellows," and in applied debate we often find unlikely combinations of legislators supporting a bill for widely different reasons.

The statement of the proposition should be affirmative in both form and intent. The proposition "Resolved: That the United States should not give direct economic aid to foreign countries" is in negative form. The use of negative phrasing is potentially confusing and needlessly complicates the advocates' task in presenting their case. By contrast, "Resolved: That the United States should offer foreign aid in the form of developmental assistance programs" allows affir-matives to clearly advocate particular aid programs.

The proposition "Resolved: That the jury system should be abolished" is negative not in its form but in its intent. The flaw here is that the proposition

---

Characteristics of an Effectively Worded Debate Proposition

- Controversy
- One central idea
- Unemotional terms
- Precise statement of the affirmative's desired decision

---

represents an interim goal and does not provide a clear, precise statement of the decision desired by the affirmative. If the jury system was abolished and nothing provided in its place, all accused criminals would go free, because there would be no means of trying them. But the proposition "Resolved: That juries should be replaced by a panel of three judges" represents a statement of a decision some affirmatives might advocate.

An important challenge for the framers of debate propositions is to find an appropriate balance between a very loosely worded proposition that fails to provide sufficient guidance for preparation and an overly restrictive or tightly worded proposition that overlimits the creativity of the advocates in interpreting the action required by the proposition. Considerations in selecting the appropriate degree of specificity may include the format, the context for debate, the nature and expertise of the participants, availability of support materials, the intended audience, and so on.

In addition to the criteria for a debate proposition, there are additional requirements for propositions in academic debate. (See the inset "Phrasing the Proposition for Academic Debate" on pages 132–133.) For CEDA and NDT debate, once several well-phrased propositions have been offered to the forensic community, a choice is made. (See the inset "Choosing the Proposition for Academic Debate" on page 134.) Individual tournament hosts design propositions to be debated in parliamentary debate rounds, and the National Forensic Association (NFA) and National Educational Debate Association (NEDA) choose their own propositions for Lincoln–Douglas and team debate, respectively.

III. TYPES OF DEBATE PROPOSITIONS

Debate propositions may deal with controversies of fact, value, or policy. We will first consider propositions of fact, then value, and finally policy.

A. Propositions of Fact

A proposition of fact is a type of descriptive claim. In a debate on a proposition of fact, the affirmative maintains that a certain thing is true, whereas the negative maintains that it is false. Our law courts are almost entirely concerned with propositions of fact. Examples of typical propositions of legal debates include

"Resolved: That Richard Roe is guilty of robbery," "Resolved: That this is the last will and testament of John Doe," and "Resolved: That the plaintiffs constitutional rights were violated in this trial." Examples of typical debates on propositions of fact outside the courtroom include "Resolved: That the stock market will decline next year," "Resolved: That life begins at conception," "Resolved: That human activity causes greenhouse warming," and "Resolved: That others conspired with Lee Harvey Oswald to assassinate President Kennedy." This latter proposition of fact had been the subject of extensive public debate for years, and interest in it surged to new heights following the release of Oliver Stone's film *JFK*. Obviously a debate over a proposition of fact is not necessarily easy and may be a rich and important debate. In 2002 and 2003, the debate over the question of Saddam Hussein's ability to produce weapons of mass destruction was a debate of earth-shaking importance, and in 2012, the causal relationship between presidential action (or inaction) and gas prices at the pump was an important issue of fact considered by Americans.

Propositions of fact also may be debated as precursors, or as a part of debates on propositions of value or propositions of policy, because it is frequently essential to establish relevant facts before reaching decisions about values or policies. In general, propositions of fact address existence of conditions (the climate of the earth has warmed during the past century) or causation (human behavior has contributed to global warming).

B. Propositions of Value

A proposition of value is a type of evaluative claim. Values are our beliefs about right and wrong, good and bad. So a proposition of value essentially makes a statement that something is good or bad. In a debate on a proposition of value, the affirmative maintains that a certain belief, value, or fact is justified, that it conforms to the definition or criteria appropriate to evaluate the issue. Examples of typical propositions of value include "Resolved: That abortion is immoral" and "Resolved: That television is a vast wasteland." One of the most prominent differences between a proposition of value and a proposition of policy is that the policy proposition requires the affirmative to propose a plan to implement the policy. The proposition of value does not provide for a plan. Rather, the affirmative seeks support for a claim that (1) endorses a value (for example, "Resolved: That compulsory national service for all qualified U.S. citizens is desirable") or (2) chooses one value over another (for example, "Resolved: That the federal deficit is a greater threat to American society than is unemployment") or (3) rejects a value (for example, "Resolved: That the emphasis on competitive athletics is deleterious to American society").

Quasi-policy propositions are propositions that express a value judgment about a policy. Examples of typical quasi-policy propositions include the "compulsory national service" proposition just cited and many CEDA propositions prior to 1996, such as "Resolved: That a unilateral freeze by the United States on the production and development of nuclear weapons would be desirable." Although a plan is not explicit in quasi-policy propositions, it is implicit, and the debaters may need to debate the policy implications of the proposition. Between 1999 and 2002, CEDA selected both a policy and what they termed a "nonpolicy" resolution for each academic year. They defined a nonpolicy resolution as one "phrased so as to generally affirm the truth or value of an idea, condition, or action, but not to simply affirm the desirability or worth of future change."

A value may be a precursor of a policy. Once we have endorsed a value, the next logical step in most cases is to support policies consistent with that value. The intensity with which a value is endorsed or rejected will determine whether we adopt a *personal* policy or urge a *public* policy. A woman who favored the "abortion is immoral" proposition mentioned earlier might say, "Others may follow their own conscience; my values would never permit me to choose abortion." Intense partisans on both sides take a more activist stance and seek to have their values enacted into law. Of course, debaters might engage in a pleasant disputation on values that have no discernable policy implications—for example, "Resolved: That Washington was a greater president than Lincoln." A negative win on this debate implies no policy that we should tear down the Washington Monument or build Lincoln another memorial.

If we decide that "television is a wasteland," we might adopt a personal policy of watching much less television. If, however, we urge that the public support the value we have chosen, then a certain type of programming should, as a matter of policy, be eliminated from television and replaced with programming more beneficial to the public interest. The implications of such a policy are clearly a subject for examination by debaters and those who render the decision.

An example of fact and value judgments leading to policy considerations occurred in the first Bush–Dukakis presidential campaign debate in 1988. George H. W. Bush, who was known to favor the "sanctity of life" (a value proposition) and to regard abortions as "killings" (a fact position), was asked, "If abortions were to become illegal, do you think women who have them should go to jail?" (a policy position). Bush replied, "I haven't sorted out the penalties... I'm for the sanctity of life, and once that illegality is established, then we can come to grips with the penalty side, and of course, there's got to be some penalties to enforce the law." This response was judged to be weak and ineffective by some observers. Michael Dukakis promptly focused on the policy implications of Bush's values: "Well, I think that the vice president is saying that he's prepared to brand a woman a criminal for making this decision." [1]

While we may sometimes debate facts, values, or policies by themselves, we will find that on many occasions it is necessary to consider all of them together.

C. Propositions of Policy

A policy proposition is a type of advocate claim. It calls for change. CEDA defines policy resolutions as those "phrased so as to affirm the value of future

---

1. See the *New York Times*, Sept. 26, 1988, p.11, for the full text of this exchange.

and specific governmental change, and suggesting a broad but predictable array of potential affirmative plans." Of course, in other forums, policy propositions may call for change by nongovernmental actors. (I should have a pizza for dinner!) In a debate on a proposition of policy, the affirmative maintains that a policy or course of action should be adopted. Most debates in legislative bodies are on propositions of policy. Examples of typical debates in Congress, state legislatures, and city councils include "Resolved: That the proposed tax bill should be enacted" and "Resolved: That the Senate should advise and consent to the nomination of Joseph Doakes as ambassador to France." In private organizations as well, most debates are on propositions of policy—for example, "Resolved: That the National Communication Association should hold its annual convention in Chicago" or "Resolved: That Compact Motors should pay a quarterly dividend of 50 cents per share of common stock" or "Resolved: That more dormitories should be established on this campus."

Recall that a plan to implement the policy is an essential part of the affirmative's case. In debates on policy propositions, propositions of value often arise as important issues. For example, in debates on the proposition of policy "Resolved: That the federal government should significantly strengthen the regulation of mass media communication in the United States," it was sometimes necessary to debate as essential issues "Resolved: That First Amendment rights are the most important of all our rights" and "Resolved: That pretrial publicity denies a fair trial to defendants in criminal trials" (both propositions of value).

The O. J. Simpson murder case in 1995 raised many issues of fact, value, and policy. Was O. J. guilty of murder? This was a question of fact the trial intended to answer. During the pretrial hearings a friend of O. J.'s slain ex-wife wrote a book. Did this create prejudice against O. J.? While in jail awaiting trial, O. J. also wrote a book. Did this create prejudice in favor of O. J.? The media—from the tabloids to the mainstream press, from Court TV to the major networks—reported all of the events, gossip, rumors, and opinions surrounding the trial. Did the media's First Amendment right to report about the trial and events surrounding it outweigh O. J.'s right to a fair trial? Had O. J. been convicted, his lawyers might have sought to argue some of these questions of fact and value before the Supreme Court. Another case with sensational media coverage was the Casey Anthony murder trial in 2011. Casey was accused of the murder of her 2-year-old daughter Caylee. The trial proceeded amidst a barrage of media publicity with Casey eventually being found not guilty of murder charges (although she was guilty on four counts of providing false information to the police officers investigating the case). What happened? Was Casey guilty (question of fact)? Did the pretrial publicity negatively impact her right to a fair trial or impair justice for Caylee (value)? What should be the verdict and punishment for Casey (policy)?

Had the prosecution sought the death penalty in either case, the issue of whether to apply it would have become a question of policy to be debated by the jury in separate proceedings following a guilty verdict.

As another example, consider the Monica Lewinsky–Bill Clinton scandal, also in 1995–2000. The House impeachment proceedings against President Clinton focused on propositions of fact. For its part the Senate considered the magnitude of the value implications and, finally, the appropriate policy action: Should President Clinton be removed from office? Just as questions of fact, value, and policy are interwoven in one of the twentieth century's most highly publicized murder trials and the historic proceedings against a president, they are also interwoven in the great debates on public policy and in the unpublicized debates that influence our everyday lives. When Senator John Edwards was tried in 2012 for violations of campaign finance law for the money provided by his political supporters which he used to support the lavish lifestyle of his mistress, Rielle Hunter, questions of fact were not contested. Edwards had conducted an extramarital affair that resulted in the birth of a child, and contributors had provided financial support for Ms. Hunter. What was contested was application of law (which constitutes a rights-based interpretation of values) and the policy questions of ultimate verdict and potential penalties (should he be found guilty and punished?)

IV. PRESUMPTION AND BURDEN OF PROOF

A. The Status Quo

In debates about propositions of policy, affirmative advocates support change, usually favoring new governmental policy. Policy propositions call for an agent (often the U.S. Federal Government) to actively do something new (depart from the existing set of actions in favor of different action, such as new law). Such supported change requires departure from the status quo, usually described in terms of currently existing structures, stated policies or laws. The status quo is the current system or the way things are now. For example, at one time capital punishment was legal throughout the United States; it was the status quo. Then the Supreme Court ruled that existing capital punishment statutes were unconstitutional. The status quo then became one of no capital punishment. Subsequently some states enacted new capital punishment laws that met the Supreme Court's criteria, and executions resumed in those states. Thus the status quo is that some states permit capital punishment under specific circumstances. But partisans on both sides are seeking to change this status quo: Some want to expand capital punishment to all states, whereas others want to abolish it. While propositions of fact and value do not address consideration of a "status quo" as they do not call for *change*, they do operate from a parallel notion: that participants in the debate begin with a prior assumption regarding the proposition, that it is false. So as the status quo represents a system under attack, prior assumptions represent beliefs under attack, as critical listeners or judges reject the positively worded claim forwarded by the proposition of fact or value until it is proven true.

Phrasing the Proposition for Academic Debate

The additional requirements for propositions used in academic debate involve significance, fairness, length, and ambiguity.

Significant Contemporary Problem

In choosing an issue for educational debate, educators not only look for a well-phrased proposition but also try to select one that will provide an opportunity for exploring a significant problem of current interest to students, judges, and audiences. Because the topic should be one on which information is readily available, national debate propositions deal with matters of current national or international concern. Some debate coaches favored the civil rights proposition selected by CEDA/NDT in 1998–1999 because they believed it helped to attract students, especially minority students, to debating. The 2003–2004 CEDA resolution, however, was criticized as too diffuse and obtuse to be interesting at first glance to new debaters. The 2011–2012 Arab Spring topic was timely, and addressed events in constant news rotation.

Educators also seek an issue that will remain in the news and stay interesting during the academic year or semester so that debaters can continue to find new evidence and arguments. When the Supreme Court's right-to-privacy decisions were the subject of a national debate proposition, the educators who chose this issue did not expect that these decisions would be overruled during the year the proposition was being debated. But had this happened, the status quo on privacy might have changed so substantially as to render the proposition unsuitable for academic debate.

Sometimes the status quo may change dramatically and require substantial changes in affirmative cases without necessitating a change in the proposition. During the academic year in which the proposition concerning "federal control of the supply and utilization of energy" was debated, a number of such changes occurred. Early in the season some affirmative teams argued that "the Arab nations might embargo oil." Negative teams confidently denied this possibility, but the Arabs did in fact embargo oil early in the season. Some affirmative teams then argued for gas rationing as the only means of dealing with the oil embargo. As the academic year went on, however, it became apparent that, although some states had imposed limitations on gas sales, no real-world support existed for federal rationing. During that year many teams found it necessary to redraft their affirmative cases for almost every tournament, for the status quo changed repeatedly as new policies became operative or as new evidence became available. During the 2002–2003 academic debate season, a portion of the resolution became undebatable before the end of the debate year, as the SORT agreement, one of the policy actions called for in the proposition, was ratified by the U.S. Senate on March 6.

Equal Conflicting Evidence and Reasoning

In applied debates the evidence and reasoning may strongly favor one side. In the courts, attorneys may defend clients when the evidence against them is almost overwhelming. In legislatures the minority leader may fight for an almost hopeless cause. In academic debate, however, the objective is not to secure or to prevent the adoption of a proposition. Rather, it is to use the proposition to provide opportunities to learn about argumentation and debate, as well as about the subject itself. For educational purposes preference is given to propositions that give both sides an approximately equal opportunity to build a strong case.

Phrasing the Proposition for Academic Debate (Continued)

Single Declarative Sentence

In the interests of clarity, and because of the limited amount of time available, academic debate propositions should be limited to a single declarative sentence. In applied debates the proposition may be as long as necessary; for instance, a bill in Congress is a specialized form of debate proposition and may extend for many pages. Recent CEDA/NDT resolutions have violated this to some degree by offering lists of options to the affirmative. The trend has been for those options to be increasingly specific as to policies to be advocated, thus offering clarity for individual debates. Criticism has been directed at the failure of some resolutions (for example, the 2003–2004 CEDA/NDT resolution) to offer a consistent theme and of some resolutions to be overly restrictive in dictating affirmative advocacy.

Avoidance of Ambiguity

Those wording a proposition for academic debate should seek to avoid excessive ambiguity while not unnecessarily limiting the debaters' opportunities to be creative in their interpretation of the terms of the proposition. The framers challenge, then, is to achieve a balance between being too vague and too prescriptive. It is generally more effective to provide a clear direction of change in the wording of the proposition (for example, *increase* gun control, rather than *change* gun laws). The Second National Developmental Conference on Forensics made the following recommendations specifically for academic debate:

1. Take care when using any encompassing term such as *all, every,* or *any.*
2. Take care when using vague or compounding words or phrases such as *greater* or *any and all.*
3. Consult linguistics experts on the phrasing and interpretation of debate propositions.
4. Specify clearly the nature and direction of the change or decision.
5. Seek wording that will balance the need for maintaining interest over a period of time with the need to limit the topic in order to create a meaningful level of research and discussion.

B. Presumption

In debate **presumption** is a predisposition favoring a given side in a dispute. It describes the psychological predisposition of a listener or decision maker. Presumption may also be thought of as that prior assumption held by the audience or judge that the proposition is false, requiring that its advocates present convincing and compelling proof to compel its acceptance. Presumption may be viewed from two perspectives: the judicial perspective and the policy perspective. The judicial perspective offers a constant understanding of presumption by rule: It always favors the status quo, a presumed condition (for example, presumption of innocence), or the inverse of the positively worded proposition (that is, the statement is presumed *false*). The judicial perspective may be considered when the option exists of continuing the structure of the status quo. With this option there may, of course, be

---

Choosing the Proposition for Academic Debate

Each year, CEDA solicits topic papers from members of the debate community. Each topic paper provides an overview of a topic area, with discussion of the available literature, possible topic linkages and phrasings, and the relative merits of debating that topic area. In the spring the topic selection committee of CEDA, utilizing the topic papers to generate ideas, identifies at least three topic areas to be presented to the membership of CEDA. The membership votes for their preference among the problem areas, and the committee goes back to work to frame no fewer than three policy propositions within the chosen topic area, to be presented to the CEDA membership for final selection. The yearlong proposition, to be used by CEDA and the NDT, is announced in July. The ADA uses the CEDA/NDT proposition. NEDA and NFA select their own propositions. Parliamentary tournament debaters, as represented by APDA and NPDA, use topics selected for each round of a given tournament as framed by the tournament hosts.

Research-based team debating in the tournament context makes use of national debate propositions indispensable. If students had to debate a different proposition for each tournament, or even if they attempted to debate a number of different propositions during the year, they would acquire considerable experience in research methods but might sacrifice the depth of research and experience in evidence-based debating. The first few academic debates on a new proposition are often tentative and experimental. After a number of debates on a proposition, the learning situation provides more depth.

Of course, alternative debate forums, including Parliamentary Debate (NPDA and APDA) offer different educational experiences and skill sets based on impromptu development of ideas and broad-based reading and research about a wide range of issues. Although such approaches may not offer the depth of research and argumentation, they are certainly valuable experiences in public advocacy and critical thinking.

Because much academic debating is on a national intercollegiate debate proposition, it is useful to know how such propositions are chosen. The care devoted to the selection of these propositions suggests something of the care that individual debaters should exercise in phrasing propositions for their own use. Similar standards should also be applied to resolutions for extemporaneous style debates such as those practiced in parliamentary debate tournaments.

---

minor repairs and other modifications, but the essential features of the status quo will continue until good and sufficient reason is given to justify a change. This perspective is mandated in the courts, for example, where the accused must be presumed innocent (the status quo) until proved guilty. As a defendant is presumed innocent, the status quo is presumed acceptable until and unless a compelling case is offered to the contrary.

From the judicial perspective, presumption favors the status quo. That is, the existing state of affairs will continue until good and sufficient reason is given for changing it. In debates using the judicial perspective, the presumption favors the status quo and the affirmative has **the burden of proof**—the risk of the proposition. Because change involves risk (and cost), the advocates of change must prove that it is worthwhile to take that risk. The advocates who affirm the proposition are required to prove their case. They must provide good and sufficient reason for adopting or accepting the proposition, and they must convince those who render the decision. If they do not fulfill the burden of proof, they will lose all that they hoped to gain from adoption of the proposition. These concepts are aptly summed up in the maxims "If it ain't broke, don't fix it."[2]

The policy perspective is used when change is inherent in the status quo. For example, in 2004 President Bush, the incumbent president, ran for reelection. That year the voters had the option of voting for Bush (the status quo) or for his opponent, John Kerry. Constitutional restrictions barred Bush from running for a third term in 2008; thus change was inevitable. Voters in the year 2000 did not have the option of supporting the status quo (voting for Clinton) but chose between two or more departures from the status quo, as in 2008. Of course in 2008, Senator John McCain may have had some "presumption" in his favor, as he represented the incumbent party (Republican). However, given a sense of high risk in maintaining the policies of the Bush administration due to economic and foreign policy crises, this presumption was weak. In 2012, Barack Obama also faced a weak economy, so even as the incumbent, and therefore benefiting from some presumption in his favor due to incumbency, this advantage was weakened by consideration of risk. As is typical in such cases, one choice represents a greater change in the status quo than the other, as in 2000 the Republican candidate (Bush) was perceived as more substantially different than the Democratic candidate (Gore), and in 2008, the Democratic challenger (Obama) represented more of a departure from the status quo than did the Republican (McCain).

From the policy perspective, presumption favors the position that provides the greatest advantages while incurring the least disadvantages, or incurs the least risk due to the lesser degree of change. Put another way, presumption favors the position that is less risky or that incurs the least risk of harmful consequences. In debates on value propositions the presumption favors the position of the greater over the lesser value. For example, in debates on the "testing for controlled substances" proposition, the issue in many debates is whether "privacy" concerns outweigh "safety" concerns. The same question may be asked with reference to debates about TSA Body Scanners, wherein travelers sacrifice their personal privacy in exchange for safety and security.

How does one determine the burden of proof in such cases? The classic rule of burden of proof applies: One who asserts must prove. Let us now look at a few examples to see how these concepts work. We will first consider some examples from the judicial perspective.

Do you favor a constitutional amendment defining marriage as the legal union of a man and a woman? A school prayer amendment to the Constitution? A right-to-life amendment to the Constitution? A balanced budget amendment? The status quo is the Constitution as it now exists. If you want to advocate a change to the Constitution, you have the burden of proof. In this case you must convince both branches of Congress to pass your amendment and then

---

2. "Taxing News," *Newsweek,* July 8, 1991, p. 8.

you must convince 38 states to ratify it. This is the burden of proof we place on those who want to change our Constitution.

The concept of presumption is a vital part of our legal system. Did Richard Roe rob the Cook County National Bank? Our laws explicitly require that a person be presumed innocent until proved guilty. The status quo is that Richard Roe is innocent, and the police department and the district attorney must convince a jury that he is guilty before he can be sentenced. (Unfortunately this principle of law is sometimes distorted. The accused in a well-publicized case may have a "trial by news media" and be "proved guilty" in the minds of the prospective jurors before the courtroom trial begins. British law is much stricter than American law in prohibiting pretrial publicity about the accused.)

The Richard Roes of this world move through the criminal justice system in relative anonymity; their cases rarely attract the attention of the media. The O. J. Simpson murder trial, however, drew unprecedented, worldwide attention. One TV reporter, commenting on the problem of choosing a jury for the trial, quipped; "Only someone who has been in a coma for the past few months hasn't heard about the O. J. case." The trials of Scott Peterson, Kobe Bryant, Martha Stewart, Phil Spector, Robert Blake, Zacarias Moussaoui, and Casey Anthony have drawn similar attention.

There are, however, some exceptions to this concept of presumption of innocence. For many years in contested tax cases, the taxpayer was in effect guilty until proved innocent—a clear violation of the presumption of innocence. This inversion of principle, however, had become the status quo and stood until, in a major ruling, the Fifth Circuit Court of Appeals put the burden of proof on the Internal Revenue Service (1RS).[3] The 1RS Restructuring and Reform Act of 1998, also known as the "Taxpayer's Bill of Rights," legislatively shifted the burden of proof in certain legal proceedings from individual taxpayers to the 1RS.

C. The Burden of Proof

Advocates for positively worded propositions, therefore, have the challenge to overcome the presumption, or predisposition, against their side. They fulfill this challenge, the "burden of proof" by providing a "prima facie" case for the proposition. A prima facie case is one that is coherent and whole, makes sense on its face to a reasonable, thinking person, and thus, provides sufficient proof to overcome the presumption against it. Legal proceedings may send a case to a Grand Jury to consider whether or not the prosecutor has a prima facie case worthy of sending to trial. Of course, in our law courts different standards prevail for the burden of proof in different circumstances. Before a grand jury only "probable cause" need be proved to secure an indictment; in a criminal trial the prosecutor must establish proof "beyond a reasonable doubt" to secure a guilty verdict; in a civil case the verdict commonly is based on a "preponderance of evidence."

---

3. *New York Times*, May 2, 1989, p. 1.

Outside the courtroom reasonable persons usually apply this standard and base their decisions in important matters on a "preponderance of evidence." The judge in legal proceedings will instruct the jury as to what constitutes "probable cause" or "reasonable doubt."

The concepts of burden of proof and presumption made the front page of the *New York Times* and other newspapers across the country when the Supreme Court ruled that in gender discrimination cases "an employer has the legal burden of proving that its refusal to hire or promote someone is based on legitimate and not discriminatory reasons." In the same decision the Court ruled that the employer has to show only by "a preponderance of evidence" that its reasons were legitimate, and not by the more rigorous standard of "clear and convincing proof" as required by a lower court.[4] Outside the courtroom we do not have predetermined definitions of what constitutes a "preponderance of evidence." Therefore a definition of that phrase may become a critical issue in the debate as the debaters try to convince the decision makers that theirs is a satisfactory definition within the context of the debate.

In certain situations in parliamentary debate, the affirmative must obtain a two-thirds or three-quarters majority to carry its burden of proof. In 1995 the proposal was advanced that Congress should require a three-fifths vote to enact new taxes. By contrast, to convict Richard Roe of robbing the Cook County National Bank, the prosecutor must convince 100 percent of the jury. If one juror is not convinced of Roe's guilt, he cannot be convicted.

Sometimes the burden of proof may be greater than expected. In 1994 a majority of California voters thought they had won a victory when they approved Proposition 187, the anti-illegal immigration initiative. Their opponents, however, persuaded a federal court to delay enforcement of the initiative, arguing that federal, not state, laws governed the status of immigrants. A federal district court judge struck down the law as unconstitutional.

The burden of proof in enacting a new federal law is greater than that of obtaining a majority of one state's votes. To enact a new federal law, one must convince a majority of the House, a majority of the Senate, and the president. If the president vetoes the law, then the proponents must convince two-thirds of the House and two-thirds of the Senate. If the law is challenged in the courts, then its supporters may have to convince a majority of the Supreme Court. Let us now consider a few examples from the policy perspective.

In some cases, again, change may be inherent in the status quo. In such cases there is a presumption in favor of *a* change but not in favor of any *particular* change. A typical example may be found in the automobile industry, in which most companies make annual model changes. Even though new models come out every year, the designers advocating model X have the burden of proof to convince their company that model X is better than model Y or model Z or any other model under consideration. In some situations there is no status quo; for

---

4. A conservative English statesman, Viscount Falkland, expressed this famous dictum in 1641 in more stately prose: "When it is not necessary to change, it is necessary not to change."

example, when it comes time to elect freshman class officers, there are no incumbents.

Thus, when the status quo provides for a change or when a change is inherent in the status quo, the advocates of a new policy or of possible change have the burden of proof. Similarly the advocates of a specific value (as in a debate on a proposition of value in which the affirmative advocates the specific value called for in the resolution) have the burden of proof. Again, the classic rule of burden of proof applies to all of these situations: One who asserts must prove.

The affirmative—the one advancing an assertion, or supporting the proposition—has the burden of proof. The question then arises: What amounts to satisfactory proof? The answer depends on the rules governing the debate and the judgment of the person or group empowered to decide. At a minimum the affirmative must go more than halfway in convincing the decision makers. Thus, for example, if 49 percent of the members of your club vote for a motion and 51 percent vote against it, the motion fails. If 50 percent vote for the motion and 50 percent against it, the motion fails. In debate, the negative will seek to poke holes in the prima facie case advanced by the affirmative, thus weakening their case below a minimally acceptable level of proof.

Note that there is a distinction between *the* burden of proof and *a* burden of proof, and that this distinction applies to both the judicial and the policy perspective. The burden of proof always rests on the affirmative, who must prove that the proposition should be adopted or accepted. However, **a burden of proof** may rest on either the affirmative or the negative. Whoever introduces an issue into the debate has a burden of proof. The advocate must support the argument he or she introduces. During a trial, for example, the prosecution may allege that Richard Roe committed a robbery in Chicago. Richard Roe may claim that he was in New York at the time of the robbery. Richard Roe now has assumed a burden of proof; he must prove his alibi. In a debate on the "testing for controlled substances" proposition, if the negative introduces the argument that "privacy" concerns outweigh "safety" concerns, they have assumed a burden of proof.

D. The Burden of Refutation

Both sides in a debate will have a **burden of refutation**—the obligation to refute, or respond to, opposing arguments. This burden also referred to as the burden of "clash" rests on the advocate whose case is weakened by an argument advanced by an opponent. The advocate must refute that argument or suffer damage to the case. In Richard Roe's case, if Roe introduces evidence to establish that he was in New York at the time of the robbery, the prosecution has a burden of refutation. That is, the Chicago district attorney must refute that evidence or Roe will go free. In the "controlled substances" case the affirmative must refute the negative's "safety" argument or face a serious loss.

A tie is thus impossible in academic debate. The affirmative either carries its burden of proof or it does not. Even in a debate with one judge, a common situation in academic debate, a tie is impossible. If the judge discerns that both teams have done an equally good job, he or she must render a decision for the negative because the affirmative has failed to carry its burden of proof. Reasonable people follow this principle in making individual decisions. If the arguments pro and con are equal—if they simply cannot make up their minds—they decline to support the affirmative's proposal.

EXERCISES

1. Examine the following "propositions." Which are well phrased? Which violate the criteria of a well-phrased proposition? What criteria do they violate? Rephrase the incorrect propositions so they meet the requirements for academic debate.

   a. Inadequate parking facilities on campus
   b. The obesity epidemic
   c. Should our college abandon intercollegiate athletics?
   d. The present method of electing the president of the United States should be improved
   e. Affirmative action in college admissions
   f. Gay/lesbian rights
   g. Is politically correct speech a violation of free speech?
   h. Our college should not adopt a multicultural curriculum

2. Phrase one proposition of fact, one of value, and one of policy for each of the following areas:

   a. Health Care
   b. Education
   c. Civility
   d. The War on Terror
   e. Tuition

3. From the newspapers, newsmagazines, radio and television broadcasts, and Internet discussions of the past week, identify what problems are currently being debated in Congress or in the nation. Phrase propositions of fact, value, and policy on five problems currently being debated nationally. Phrase these 15 propositions in a manner suitable for academic debate.

4. From the newspapers, newsmagazines, radio and television broadcasts, and Internet discussions of the past week, find five examples of quasi-policy propositions currently being debated in Congress or in the nation.

5. Prepare a five-minute speech for delivery in class in which you state a proposition of policy and demonstrate how it meets the criteria of a well-phrased proposition for academic debate.

6. Consider the 2007–2008 NDT/CEDA debate proposition (see Appendix D). Reword it to better meet the criteria for an effective proposition.

7

Analyzing the Proposition

As we discussed in Chapter 6, effective debate begins with the identification of a controversy from which a proposition emerges or is framed. The proposition provides debaters a focus for preparation and argumentation, and allows the audience or judge a guideline for their decision. The proposition focuses clash and ensures that arguments are pertinent to decision making. The proposition for debate may be formulated by one of the advocates in the debate, by agreement between the opposing advocates, or by someone other than the actual advocates. If a student at a business meeting of a college organization introduces the motion "Resolved: That the dues of this organization should be increased twenty-five dollars a semester," he or she is formulating a proposition for debate. Before Abraham Lincoln and Stephen Douglas held their famous debates, they agreed on the propositions they would use. The proposition may also be expressed in the form of a motion in parliamentary debate, and in our current political environment, candidates involved in campaign debates are presented propositions in the form of questions from moderators, audience members, or even YouTube contributors. Frequently an attorney first learns of the proposition to be debated in a court case when he or she is retained by a client in the form of formal legal charges or claims.

Regardless of how the proposition is chosen, our first task as advocates is to analyze the proposition and the area of controversy from which it is derived. When a chemist analyzes a compound, he or she breaks it down into its most basic elements to identify its makeup. Similarly, as debate advocates we must break the proposition down into its component parts, define the terms of the proposition, and then identify the issues involved. Words or terms in the proposition must be defined *within the context of the proposition*. For example, we cannot define, or even pronounce, the word *polish* until we know the context in which it is used. Analysis of the proposition's relationship to the problem area—the political, legal, social, or other relevant contexts from which it arises—may reveal

---

Miniglossary

Definition of terms   The advocate's supported interpretation of the meaning of the words in the proposition.

Fiat   The convention in academic policy debate that, for the sake of argument, participants may assume implementation of a reasonable policy. This allows debaters to focus on the question of whether a policy *should* be adopted and to avoid as irrelevant arguments about whether the policy *would* be adopted.

Issues   Critical claims inherent in the proposition. Questions identifying points of controversy.

Stock issues   Those issues common to most debates on given types of propositions. In value debate they are definitive and designative; in policy debate they include harm, inherency, and solvency.

Presumption   A predisposition favoring a given side in a dispute. From the judicial perspective the presumption favors the status quo. From the policy perspective the presumption favors the position that provides the greatest advantages while incurring the least disadvantages. In value debate, the presumption favors the greater over the lesser value.

Harm   The stock issue that identifies an imperfection within the status quo, marked by urgency and characterized by important deleterious consequences of inaction.

Inherency   The stock issue that identifies a probability for future harm, based in the embeddedness of the harm within the status quo and predicting that absent affirmative policy action, the harm will continue.

Solvency   The stock issue that identifies the ability of the plan to work and to reduce the harm.

---

other terms that require definition and new concepts that will aid in the development of issues.

I. THE IMPORTANCE OF DEFINING TERMS

The **definition of terms**—the advocate's supported interpretation of the meaning of the words in a proposition—is an essential part of debate. In some instances the opposing advocates will agree right away on the definition of terms, and the debate will move on to other issues. In other cases the locus of the debate may be the definition of a key term or terms, and definitions become the "voting issue" or central concept that decides the debate. In all debates, however, a shared understanding of the interpretation of the proposition is necessary to guide argumentation and decision making.

Many intercollegiate debate propositions call for the "federal government" to adopt a certain policy. Often the term is self-evident in the context of the proposition, and no definition is necessary. In debates on the 2001–2002

CEDA proposition, "Resolved: That the United States Federal Government should substantially increase federal control throughout Indian Country in one or more of the following areas: child welfare, criminal justice, employment, environmental protection, gaming, resource management, taxation," the affirmative merely designated the appropriate federal agency (for example, The Bureau of Indian Affairs or the Environmental Protection Agency) to carry out its policy, and the debate moved on to other issues. This identification of the specific agent, for example, which agency within the Federal Government will create and/or implement the policy change, in some cases may be important to the debate, at other times it is not in question. However, sometimes other terms in the proposition (for instance, *Indian Country*) become critical issues of the debate. Not infrequently the negative will raise the issue of topicality and argue that the affirmative's plan is not the best definition, or interpretation, of the proposition. In debates on propositions of value, the clash over definitions or criteria may be crucial to the outcome.

In debates outside the educational setting, the same situation prevails. In some debates the definition of terms is easy and obvious—they need only be stated "for the record," and the debate proceeds to other issues. In other debates, however, the definition may be all-important. For instance physicians, clerics, and ethicists conduct long, hard-fought debates on the critical issue of when life begins: At conception? When the fetus becomes capable of surviving outside the womb? When the brain begins to function? Or at the moment of birth?

Exactly the opposite problem arose, and continues, in debates over the use of organ transplants. Does death occur when breathing stops? When the heart stops? Or when the brain ceases to function? Some states have debated this issue and adopted new definitions of death; in other states the debate continues. Similarly, environmentalists seeking protection from development for valued resources debate the definition of *wetlands* in public hearings; owners of sports franchises work to redefine players' salaries to fit within predetermined salary caps; and customers considering new product purchases study competing definitions of *value*. In February 2004, President Bush called upon the Congress to "promptly pass and send to the states for ratification, an amendment to our Constitution defining and protecting marriage as a union of a man and a woman as husband and wife." This advocacy by the president was an attempt to *define* "marriage" in such a way as to limit it to heterosexual couples. A public debate about the meaning of marriage, and its alternative, "civil union," ensued and continues. Definitional debates have political, moral, and personal implications. What is poverty? Obesity? Adulthood? In 2007, the meaning of the term "surge" in reference to the U.S. military action in Iraq, and again in 2012, the "surge" of U.S. troops in Afghanistan, was hotly contested. Were these expansions of the wars or simply provision of necessary resources to achieve existing objectives? Proposals for immigration reform have offered the opportunities for illegal immigrants working in this country to achieve citizenship or benefits through a cumbersome and expensive process. Some proposals for reform legislation have failed in part because the "path to citizenship" for undocumented aliens, or even provision of limited benefits was termed "amnesty" by its opponents. Likewise, the definition of "terrorism" creates significant problems in our foreign policy. It has long been the history of the U.S. Federal Government to express certain powers over the states by defining the "Commerce Clause" of the U.S. Constitution ("... to regulate Commerce with foreign Nations, and among several States ...") in such a way as to favor, in certain circumstances, federal power over the states. The Supreme Court heard in 2012 the case that warranted a personal mandate to purchase health insurance based on this clause. In part, the court's challenge was to define commerce in relation to American's access to or compelled purchase of health care as required in the Affordable Care Act.

Terms that do not actually occur in the proposition itself but that an advocate expects to use in the course of the debate may also require definition. For example, the words *classical, cyclical, involuntary, full, structural, frictional, long term,* and *hidden* did not appear in the proposition "Resolved: That the federal government should establish a national program of public work for the unemployed." Yet, because references to these types of unemployment likely recurred in debates on the proposition, the debaters needed to define them.

In debates on this same proposition, dictionary definitions of the individual words *public* and *work* would have done little to clarify the meaning of the proposition or to furnish a basis for argument. Advocates define the phrase *public work* rather than the individual words, and, by referring to the use of this phrase in legislation, they were able to provide a useful definition.

In analyzing the problem, advocates must carefully consider all possible definitions of all the terms. In presenting their cases, however, they will define only the terms that might be unfamiliar to their audience or about which they and their opponents might differ. In debating the proposition "Resolved: That Congress should be given the power to reverse decisions of the Supreme Court," it would probably be unnecessary to define *Congress* and *Supreme Court*. But it would be necessary to define *reverse* and *decisions*, because legal usage of these terms differs from popular usage, and opposing advocates sometimes interpret these words differently within the context of this proposition.

Consider the old brainteaser—when a tree falls in a forest but nobody hears it, does it make a sound? The answer, of course, is totally dependent on your definition of *sound*. If you define it as waves in the air, the answer is yes; if you define it as the subjective experience of hearing, the answer is no. The terms of a debate proposition may be defined in a variety of ways. To make the basis of the argument explicit, advocates should choose the method or combination of methods best suited to the requirements of the proposition and to the interests of the audience. It is important to define terms carefully to ensure a profitable debate.

II. METHODS OF DEFINING TERMS

A. Basic Methods

1. Example.   Giving an example is often an effective method of defining terms. In debates on the "national program of public work" proposition, affirmative teams sometimes defined their terms by saying, "By a national program of public work, we mean a program similar to the WPA of the 1930s, putting people to work in government jobs building roads, repairing bridges and in countless other ways, building and restoring our national infrastructure." In this way they gave their audience a specific example of the type of program they proposed. Examples are generally discovered by debaters in the course of researching their issues and thus, they tend to appear in the literature related to the proposition or topic area.

2. Common Usage.   In the interest of accuracy and precision, debate propositions sometimes contain technical terms. Often these terms can be defined effectively by referring to common usage, or "common person" or "person on the street" definition. For example, in debates on the proposition "Resolved: That the requirement of membership in a labor organization as a condition of employment should be illegal," some affirmative teams defined an important term by saying, "By *labor organizations* we mean the type of organization popularly referred to as unions." This reference to common usage usually served to establish a definition acceptable to both teams and clear to the audience. Although the word *unions* would have served well as a definition, it would not have been an acceptable term for use in the proposition. Many important "unions" operate under the legal title of *brotherhoods, associations, federations,* or other names; and most important legislation regulating unions speaks of *labor organizations.* Had the word *unions* been used in the proposition, it might have led to some pointless quibbles as to whether such legislation would apply to organizations such as the railroad brotherhoods.

To qualify as common usage, a term must be commonly understood across lines of gender, age, and culture. The Senate confirmation hearings on Supreme Court Justice Clarence Thomas triggered an extensive public debate about "sexual harassment." Both men and women opposed it, but in many cases they had substantially different definitions of the term. The hearings, which dominated prime-time television and the front pages of newspapers, were generally ignored or given minimal coverage elsewhere in the world. This seems to indicate a cultural difference between the United States and many other countries in which sexual harassment is not a crime and the sexual behavior of politicians and other public figures is considered off limits to the media. It also offers an example where the legal definition of sexual harassment, which is precise and well established in law, policy, and case-law, did not match the public perception of the act.

Similarly, when denying his involvement in a "sexual relationship" with White House intern Monica Lewinsky, President Clinton argued that, for him, oral sex did not constitute *sex* or a *sexual relationship.* He based his argument on the assumption that, for many (including himself), there is a clear distinction in common usage between the terms *oral sex* and *intercourse,* and that a definition of the terms *sex* and *sexual relationship* would refer only to the latter.

Of course, we do not require common global understanding for a term to be in popular usage in the United States. However, living in a multicultural society, we must be aware that cultural differences may influence how a term is perceived.

Sometimes terms in common usage are widely misunderstood. For instance, the *New York Times* called 12 A.M. and 12 P.M. "the trickiest times on the clock." Does 12 A.M. designate midday or midnight? Is 12 P.M. lunchtime or bedtime? Railroads avoid the problem by using schedule times such as 12:01 A.M. and 11:59 P.M. The military, too, avoids the problem by using 24-hour time; noon is 1200 and midnight is 2400. According to the nation's highest authority on time, the U.S. Naval Observatory, "there is no 12 A.M. or 12 P.M., only noon and midnight."[1] When time is critical, as it may be in contracts, on birth or death certificates, and in interpretations of other documents, it is advisable to use terms that are defined by a recognized authority.

Sources of common usage must be evaluated with care. One person's common usage may differ with another's for many reasons. An appeal to the judge or audience may fail if their sense of common interpretation differs from the debaters'. One source of common usage definitions is a general dictionary, including, for example, *Webster's, Oxford Collegiate*, and *American Heritage* dictionaries. Wikipedia or other "wiki" sources may provide useful references for common usage definitions, as they are generated and edited by a community of Internet users, not necessarily scholars or experts.

3. Authority.   Some terms may be defined most effectively by referring to an authority qualified to state their meaning and usage. Such definitions, which may be referred to as *Field* definitions, because they are developed by experts in the relevant field, are offered by content area scholars and professionals and generally reflect important study and critical consideration by those most immersed in the study of the topic area. In the case of legal or legislative definitions, much time and effort, as well as argument, is likely to have contributed to the established definitions. Field-specific dictionaries, encyclopedias, and books and articles by recognized scholars are often used as authority for a particular definition. In some cases, legislation and/or legal case law may offer definitions endorsed by the parliamentary or judicial process, and academic literature will often establish carefully framed interpretations designed for precision and effective application. In debates on whether "advertising degrades the quality of life in the United States," some debaters turned to the *American Heritage Dictionary* for their initial definitions of *degrades* and *quality of life*. Failure to consult the proper authority can lead to unexpected results. In one instance *Time* magazine chided the Nebraska legislature for failure to consult a recognized authority in drafting drug legislation, which resulted in a drug offender going free:

> Burling was acquitted on largely lexicological grounds. The state legislature misspelled the drug's chemical name when it passed the bill that outlawed it in 1986. Thus Burling could not be convicted of possessing the substance specified by the lawmakers. The correct spelling is

---

1. *New York Times*, Nov. 29, 1987, p. 19.

methylenedioxymethamphetamine, not methylenedioxyethampheta-mine [note the omission of the letter *m*] as the law had it. Next time they ban a drug in Nebraska, they'd better consult a pharmacological dictionary.[2]

What is the definition of AIDS? The federal Centers for Disease Control (CDC) are the defining authority on matters of diseases. In 1993 the CDC adopted a broader definition of AIDS to include those infected with HIV who also had tuberculosis, pneumonia, or other illnesses. Under the new definition the number of AIDS cases increased overnight by 111 percent. The power to define a disease can create an epidemic or "eradicate" the disease. Definitions of autism, obesity, and even specific ethnicities will impact research results and policy.

We often hear that an appalling number of Americans are illiterate. What are the facts? Who can provide an accurate picture? The U.S. Census Bureau says that 95 percent of Americans are literate. (Of course, the Census Bureau can make mistakes, but no other source even remotely approaches the ability of the Census Bureau to gather population data.) Certainly this is primary evidence. But should we accept it as conclusive evidence? We could never question millions of individuals ourselves. But we might ask: How does the Census Bureau define *literacy?* The answer might surprise you: Anyone who said they attended school through the fifth grade was counted as literate![3] No effort was made to deter-mine if these people could actually read or write. If we changed the definition to people who said they attended school through the third grade, the literacy rate would probably jump to 99 percent. If we required people to prove they could read and write at the fifth-grade level, who knows what the figure would be? The power to define literacy can change our nation's literacy rate to serve the interests of whoever defines the term. What is an "A" school or an "F" school? Tests and other "objective" measures have been devised in many states and districts to determine the performance of a school, and these definitions have substantial impacts on salaries, merit pay, and resources for schools.

Courts struggle every day to interpret the meaning of terms. Their precision in defining words important to enforcement of statutes can provide a powerful source of definition to the debater. In legal matters the only definition that counts is the one upheld by the Supreme Court. For example, what does *request* mean? Section 1915(d) of Title 28 of the U.S. Code states that federal district judges may "request" lawyers who practice before the federal courts to under-take uncompensated representation of the poor. Justice John Paul Stevens, in a dissenting opinion, held that *request* should be understood to mean "respectfully command." Justice William J. Brennan, Jr., held in the 5–4 majority opinion that "in everyday speech request means to ask, petition or entreat, not to require or command."[4]

2. *Time,* Dec. 12, 1988, p. 33.
3. John Silber, "Illiteracy and the Crisis of Our Society," *Bostonia* (spring 1994), p. 48.
4. *New York Times,* May 2, 1989, p. 8.

Another problem of legal definition is exemplified by application of the term "obscenity" by courts in freedom of speech cases. To some extent, the term is defined by local standards, which are open to interpretation and application by the courts. Sources of definitions by authorities are wide and varied. Terms may be defined within the text of laws, court decisions, books, articles, websites, and other materials produced by experts and agencies. Field-specific dictionaries may often be helpful.

4. Operation.   Some terms are best defined if the advocate provides an operational definition and explains the function or special purpose represented by the terms in a specific context. Debates on the proposition "Resolved: That the nonagricultural industries should guarantee their employees annual living wage" required careful definition of the phrase *guarantee ... a living wage*. Some affirmative advocates might choose to provide an operational definition, defining these terms by presenting their plan. For example:

> We propose a plan whereby the employer provides that a person working forty hours a week, with no additional income, should be able to afford a livable quality and quantity of housing, food, utilities, transport, health care, and recreation, no less than the wage equivalent to the poverty line for a family of four. The use of operation as a method of definition is often linked with the presentation of a plan and is a helpful way of explaining a complex matter.

5. Negation.   Sometimes a term may be defined effectively by indicating what it does *not* mean. In debates on the nationalization of basic industries, some teams defined *basic industries* by combining negation with example. That is, they said, "We do not mean the corner drugstore, we do not mean retail businesses, we do not mean service businesses; we mean steel, autos, transportation, mining, oil, and gas." Debaters considering regulation of mass media might advocate increased regulation of traditional broadcast media including TV and Radio, but exclude regulation of the Internet.

6. Comparison and Contrast.   Some terms may be best understood if they are compared to something familiar to the audience or contrasted with something within the common experience of the audience. In debates on the "mass media" proposition, some negative teams offered a counterplan alternative proposing the creation of an agency "similar to the National Association of Broadcasters" to regulate newspapers. They then claimed an advantage from the fact that their plan called for voluntary regulation in contrast to the affirmative's proposal of federal regulation.

7. Derivation.   One of the standard methods of defining words is to trace their development from their original, or radical, elements. Thus, in a debate on fair employment practices, it would be possible to define the word *prejudice* by pointing out that the word derived from the Latin words *prae* and *judicium*, meaning

---

Methods of Defining Terms

- Example
- Common Usage
- Authority
- Operation
- Negation
- Comparison and Contrast
- Derivation
- Combination of Methods

"before judgment." Definition by derivation has limited use in argumentation and debate, because the advocate is usually concerned with the contemporary use of the word within a specific context.

8. Combination of Methods. Because most propositions of debate contain several terms that must be defined, no single method is likely to be satisfactory for the definition of all of the terms. If any term is particularly difficult to define, or if it is of critical importance in the debate, the advocate may use more than one method of definition to make the meaning clear.

B. Providing a Satisfactory Definition

A satisfactory definition is one that meets the expectations of those who render the decision and provides reasonable guidance in interpreting the proposition. It recognizes that there is no single interpretation of any given term or statement, but proposes that for various reasons the definition(s) offered by the affirmative are most acceptable for the unique demands of the specific debate context within which they are offered.

In academic debate a judge may expect that a definition be *reasonable* or that it be the *best definition* in the debate. These standards offer different demands: it is easier to be reasonable than it is to be the best! In applied debate the decision makers often have different expectations about decisions in different situations. As we saw in Chapter 6, the courts have different standards for defining the burden of proof in different situations. In our personal lives, too, we frequently apply differing standards. For example, our definition of "satisfactory medical care" would no doubt vary depending on whether we had a sprained ankle or a life-threatening illness.

In academic debate advocates sometimes offer unusual definitions—definitions that are not consistent with the expectations of the opposing advocates. The use of "trick" definitions to catch an opponent off guard or to gain some other advantage is specifically *not recommended*. A trick definition or the resultant case is one that the affirmative hopes in the first instance will find the negative unprepared and in the second instance will convince the judge to accept. One example of this occurred in debates on the proposition "Resolved: That greater controls should be imposed on the gathering and utilization of information about U.S. citizens by government agencies." Early in the season, most negatives expected that the affirmative cases would deal with abuses of computerized credit information. But one trick case called for legislation to prohibit the gathering and utilization of information about citizens who used marijuana. (The affirmative argued that if the police and prosecutors were prohibited from gathering and utilizing such information, they would devote their time and energies to more important crimes.) Of course, once this case became well known, it lost an essential characteristic of the trick case—it no longer found negative teams unprepared. Advocates who depend on trick cases will find that usually they are quickly exposed and defeated by competent opposition. Not every unusual definition, however, should be regarded as a trick definition. The apparently unusual definition might take the opposing team by surprise only because they failed to thoroughly analyze the proposition. On the 2011–2012 CEDA proposition, the U.S. Federal Government should substantially increase its democracy assistance for one or more of the following: Bahrain, Egypt, Libya, Syria, Tunisia, and Yemen. Some debaters argued that the best way to facilitate the growth of democracies was noninterference, thus they defined "democracy assistance" as the removal of democratic assistance or aid. This often did not make for good debates, as the affirmative definition tended to usurp the negative's ground, putting them in the position of opposing the resolution by defending democracy assistance.

Debaters are sometimes advised to look for the "original understanding" of the proposition. Such advice draws on important precedent: Attorneys arguing a case involving a constitutional issue before the Supreme Court may consult the debates that surrounded the adoption of the Constitution or the relevant amendment to discover the original understanding of the Founding Fathers. Most debate propositions, however, do not stem from constitutional issues, and there may be little or no record to provide evidence of the original understanding. Thus this well-intentioned advice is frequently of little value in academic debate.[5]

How, then, can one prove that a definition is satisfactory? The key is to give the decision makers good reasons to accept that definition.

What are some of the good reasons one might advance to prove that a specific definition is satisfactory? The reasons will differ with different propositions and different decision renderers, but some of the most frequently used criteria are listed in the inset on pages 151–152.

---

5. The extent to which "original understanding" should be used in legal debate is itself a subject of debate within the legal community. See Robert H. Bork, *The Tempting of America* (New York: Free Press, 1990). Throughout the book, Bork makes his argument for the use of "original understanding" and offers his critique of other methods.

To prove that a definition is *reasonable*, one must establish that the definition meets the relevant criteria or standards. To prove that a definition is the *best in the debate* one must establish that the definition meets the relevant criteria in ways that are superior to opposing definitions.

C. The Meaning of Should and the Convention of Fiat

Most propositions on matters of policy contain the word *should (or ought)*—for example, "Resolved: That such-and-such should be done." In a debate on a policy proposition, **should** means that intelligent self-interest, social welfare, or the national interest prompts this action and that it is both desirable and workable. When the affirmative claims a policy "should" be adopted, it must show that the policy is practical—but it is under no obligation to show that it would be adopted. The affirmative must give enough detail to show that if implemented, it would work. It may be impossible, within the time limitations of the debate, for the affirmative to give all the details, but it must at least show the outline of its policy and indicate how the details could be worked out. For example, in a debate on federal funding for education, the affirmative could not reasonably be expected to indicate how much money each state would receive under its plan, but it would be obliged to indicate the method by which the amount of the grants would be determined. It would be pointless for the negative to seek to show that the affirmative's plan could not be adopted by demonstrating that public opinion is against it or that the supporters of the plan lack sufficient voting strength in Congress.

Consider that, at one time, public opinion and a majority of Congress were opposed to the income tax, yet when the advocates of the income tax demonstrated that it should be adopted, the Sixteenth Amendment was enacted. In the same way it could be demonstrated that, at a given time, the Eighteenth, Nineteenth, Twenty-first, and Twenty-sixth Amendments to the Constitution could not possibly have been passed. Too many people were opposed to prohibition, opposed to women's suffrage, opposed to the repeal of the Eighteenth Amendment, or opposed to lowering the voting age to 18. Yet all these amendments were passed after the advocates of these measures won debates showing they *should* be adopted. Thus in an academic debate on a policy proposition, *constitutionality is never an issue*. If the affirmative proves that a certain policy should be adopted, it has also proved that, if necessary, the Constitution should be amended. In the same way, if the affirmative's proposal is currently illegal or outside the scope of existing law, it has, by showing that its proposal should be adopted, demonstrated that the necessary enabling legislation should be enacted.

Thus in academic debate the negative cannot argue that "Congress will never pass the affirmative's plan" and proceed to prove that, because of attitudinal barriers, political interest, or some other reason, the affirmative can never get enough votes to enact its proposal. The affirmative may simply call upon "fiat," where for the sake of the argument they will assume the hypothetical enactment of the proposal and focus on their advocacy that Congress *should* enact the plan. The affirmative need only demonstrate that its proposal ought to be adopted; it need not consider the political or attitudinal barriers that so far have prevented its enactment, although it may have the obligation of defending the merits of its proposal against the potential political and/or attitudinal consequences of enactment.

The negative must avoid the "should–would" argument, which is pointless in academic debate.[6] The point is not **would**—but *should*—the affirmative's proposal be adopted. The negative may, of course, focus on the workability of the policy and try to demonstrate that a given policy, if adopted, would not work or would produce significant disadvantages.

For example, in debating the "government control of the supply and utilization of energy" proposition, the negative could not argue that Congress would not pass gasoline rationing because it is so unpopular with members of Congress and their constituents. The affirmative could simply fiat rationing—that is, argue that it *should* be passed and assume, for the sake of argument, that it has been implemented. However, the negative could argue that, because rationing is so unpopular, it would not work; that there would be widespread violations and black markets; that the system would break down; and thus that the affirmative could not achieve any advantage.

Fiat is the convention in an academic policy debate that, for the sake of argument, participants may assume implementation of a reasonable policy. This allows debaters to focus on the question of whether a policy *should* be adopted and to avoid as irrelevant arguments about whether the policy *would* (or *will*) be adopted. The purpose of fiat is to require the debaters to debate the merits of the proposition, and not the political machinations of how one might garner

---

Criteria to Prove a Satisfactory Definition

Debate often focuses on the relative merits of competing definitions. Standards that support the definitions offered as satisfactory provide valuable measures for comparison of differing interpretations. The debater is well advised to choose definitions that meet valid criteria.

1. *Prove that your definition is officially stipulated as the correct one for this resolution.* This criterion is of great value in the law courts, where many definitions are stipulated by statute and have been upheld by the highest courts so often that appeal is pointless. Elsewhere a *kilogram* is defined by an international agreement; a *watt* is a standard unit of measure in the United States; *drugs* are defined by official pharmacopoeias. Less common terms like *black hole*, *gigaflop*, *pulsar*, and *quasar*, although not officially defined, have universally accepted definitions in the scientific community. Of course, any definition could be changed, but changes in official or universally accepted definitions come only after exhaustive debate.

---

6. "Should–would" arguments may be of considerable importance in applied debate. A political leader might feel that a certain policy should be adopted but, recognizing that it would be impossible to marshal sufficient support, decide not to fight for it, preferring to conserve energy and credibility for more viable policies. For example, some of President Reagan's advisors urged that the Constitution should be amended to ban abortions and to permit school prayer. Reagan sympathized with their proposals but declined to lead an all-out legislative battle for them, apparently feeling Congress would never enact them.

Criteria to Prove a Satisfactory Definition (Continued)

2. *Prove that your definition is grammatically correct.* Presumably the framers of the proposition are knowledgeable in the conventions of English grammar and syntax, each word in the proposition is there for a good reason, and each word further refines the meaning of the sentence. Thus you must prove that your definition considers all the terms of the proposition and that none of the terms is redundant or contradictory.

3. *Prove that your definition is derived from the appropriate field.* Many propositions contain specialized terms. If the subject is nuclear weapons, you must prove that your definition is the one used by nuclear physicists. If the subject is economics, you must prove that your definition is the one used by economists.

4. *Prove that your definition is based on common usage.* Many of the terms in debate propositions are words in common usage. Because debate is a public activity, you must be able to prove that your definition is consistent with the common usage of the general public.

5. *Prove that your definition is consistent with policy makers' or value makers' usage.* Debaters are arguing that we, the public, should adopt or reject a certain policy or value. You must prove that your definition is consistent with the usage of the makers of policy and value in the public forums; for example, you would need to prove that your definition is consistent with the definition used in congressional debates on the subject.

6. *Prove that your definition meets the original understanding of the proposition's framers.* (Cautions against this method are given in the section "Providing a Satisfactory Definition.") This criterion may be compelling to some judges and to some legal scholars in applied debate in the courtroom. But the original understanding of the people who framed a proposition for academic debate or for applied debate outside the courtroom is often elusive, and it may even be impossible to discover.

7. *Prove that your definition provides a clear distinction between what legitimately fits within the definition and what is excluded by the definition.* It is important that definitions clearly distinguish between affirmative ground and negative ground.

8. *Prove that your definition would provide a fair division of ground.* That is, prove that, if interpreted as you suggest, there would be fairly equal ground for both affirmatives and negatives to use for development of their plans, counterplans, and argumentative positions. Included here might be justification for your definition based on the educational merits of such a definition: Is it better to provide a narrow but deep interpretation of propositional terms or a broad but shallow interpretation? In addition, you may want to suggest that, in the interest of fairness and prior notice, a definition should provide clear and predictable limits within which advocates may analyze and interpret the resolution.

Note that the debater will rarely use all these criteria to prove that the definition used is satisfactory. In fact, some of the criteria will contradict others. Initially the definition is stated succinctly with only the minimum evidence essential to establish the claim. Only if the definition comes under attack does the debater move to a full-scale justification of the definition. The most important function of these criteria is to provide a way for judges to weigh competing definitions and decide which is most satisfactory for a given debate.

To successfully attack an opponent's definition, one must prove that the definition does not meet one or more of the criteria just discussed. Note, too, that the criteria listed here, although widely used, are not all-inclusive. Depending on the nature of the proposition, other criteria may be discovered and applied to prove or disprove the claim that the definition is satisfactory.

the votes necessary for enactment. However, the political fallout of plan adoption may be subject to debate. Fiat is generally thought to assume that the plan has been implemented through "normal means." Of course, what is "normal' varies by the subject of legislation and the context. Some policy initiatives are implemented by legislation, others by administrative promulgation or executive action. Normal means in our governmental system, nonetheless, includes deal making and compromise. Implementation of an affirmative proposal might be argued to require use of political capital, which would then be lost at the cost of the potential implementation of other policies or actions. So fiat is limited to the action identified in the proposition, and the interpretation offered by the affirmative of the method and logistics of implementation.

Note, too, the limitations of fiat: Fiat is not a real power. The affirmative may use fiat to focus on *should*, but fiat goes no further. The affirmative may not "fiat" that advantages will flow from its plan; the advantages must be proved. The affirmative may not "fiat" attitudes; for example, the affirmative may not "fiat" that all citizens will love gas rationing and will eagerly comply with the plan. Fiat is not a magic wand; it may not be used to make a plan work.

Another way to approach fiat is to consider it as it relates to the "agency" or ability to invoke change held by the debaters as activists and advocates. Such an approach recognizes that the traditional use of fiat is hypothetical; at the end of a debate when a judge votes for the affirmative, of course, the plan does not in reality become law. The true agency or power of the debaters as advocates is to influence the participants in the immediate debate itself. Therefore, the debate as an act of advocacy should be the focus of the participants, and the decision rendered by the judge is about the debaters rather than the hypothetical plan they are debating. Based on such an approach, critical and philosophical implications of the rules and contexts of the debate itself, the performances of the debaters (including their advocacy and language use), and the underpinnings of the structural framework of policy advocacy and debate practice are all subject to debate. Critical and performance-based approaches built on the idea that "fiat is illusionary" have grown in popularity in tournament practice. Proponents point to debates that are more relevant to the lives of participants (judges and debaters) and to a greater sense of involvement and activism by debaters. Opponents note that debates may lack clear points of clash or concrete comparison (as is provided by the policy comparison facilitated by traditional fiat).

III. ISSUES

Issues are those critical claims *inherent* in the proposition that the affirmative must establish. They may also be thought of as places where groups of arguments converge or points of clash subordinate to the proposition. Issues also suggest checklists or categories of arguments to be addressed by the participants in a debate or argumentative situation. The Greek rhetoricians observed that for any argument or case, there exists *STASIS*, a set of issues to be addressed or questions to be answered in order to determine the validity of the case. Stasis may be shared within a genre of similar cases, or may emerge from the subject matter. For contemporary debaters, stasis tends to be discovered in the stock issues.

In a traditional policy debate, the negative must defeat at least one "stock" issue to win (although the stock issues will be measured in relation to one another). **Stock issues** are those issues common to all debates on similar types of propositions, or standard claims that are applicable to many propositions. Issues may be readily recognized, because they are questions with answers that directly prove or disprove the proposition. If the issues are established, then the proposition must prevail. As debaters begin analysis of the proposition, they phrase the issues as questions—for example, "Did John Doe kill Richard Roe with malice?" Issues in the analysis stage are phrased in the form of questions to which the affirmative must answer yes. Of course, the negative must answer no to at least one issue or there is no debate. When the issues are presented in a debate, the advocate phrases them as declarative sentences—for example, "John Doe killed Richard Roe with malice." Stock issues will be considered in detail in the following sections.

Potential issues are all of the possible answers to the stock issue questions. In any given debate, however, it is unlikely that all of the potential issues will be used.

Admitted issues are issues that one side concedes, or chooses not to challenge. For example, in debates on the proposition "Resolved: That the federal government should implement a program that guarantees employment opportunities for all U.S. citizens in the labor force," some affirmatives introduced the issue "millions of U.S. citizens are unemployed." In view of the evidence the affirmative could have produced to support this issue, many negative advocates readily admitted this issue. Some negatives introduced the issue "millions of unemployed do not suffer economic hardship." In view of the evidence the negative could have produced to support this issue, many affirmatives quickly concede this issue. It is usually a wise policy for debaters to concede those issues they cannot win and concentrate on those issues they have a chance of winning.

The *issues of the debate* are the issues that actually are introduced into the debate and on which the opposing advocates clash. For example, the potential issues on a certain proposition might be: A, B, C, D, E, F, G, H, I, and J. The affirmative might introduce issues A–F. The negative might admit issues B and C, introduce issue G, and seek to refute issues A, D, E, and F. The potential issues H, I, and J were not introduced by either side and thus did not enter into this debate. The issues of this debate were A, D, E, F, and G.

The *ultimate issue* or *voting issue* arises when there is only one issue remaining in dispute, or when all remaining issues rest upon that single voting issue. In some debates the clash may narrow down to one contended issue, which becomes the ultimate issue. In the preceding example the affirmative might have won issues A, D, E, and F early in the debate, leaving only issue G in dispute. Issue G thus would become the ultimate issue of this debate.

Contentions are statements offered in support of an issue. (Contentions may also be referred to as observations or even "main points.") Pertinent evidence is organized into cogent arguments to support each issue. Usually several contentions are offered in support of an issue. The affirmative may fail to establish some of the contentions and still win its case, provided that the remaining contentions have enough substantiating force to establish the issue.

A. Discovering the Issues

One of the first problems confronting the advocate in preparing to debate a proposition is discovering the issues. In a courtroom debate the issues are often stated explicitly in the law applicable to the case before the court. For example, if the proposition before the court was, in effect, "Resolved: That John Doe murdered Richard Roe," in most jurisdictions the issues would be:

1. Richard Roe is dead.
2. John Doe killed Richard Roe.
3. John Doe killed Richard Roe unlawfully.
4. John Doe killed Richard Roe following premeditation.
5. John Doe killed Richard Roe with malice.

If the prosecution failed to prove any one of these issues, John Doe could not be convicted of murder. However, he might be convicted of manslaughter or some other lesser charge if some of the issues were proved.

In debates outside the courtroom, the issues are seldom so explicitly stated. It is up to the advocates to discover them using one of several methods. First, a careful definition of the terms of the proposition will aid the advocate in discovering some of the issues of the debate. As the terms are defined, important aspects of the proposition will become apparent and reveal at least some of the issues. For example, in debates on "a national program of public work for the unemployed," the definition of the word *unemployed* was important. If unemployed was defined as including homemakers who were seeking part-time work, this definition suggested the issue question "Do the unemployed have the skills necessary for a public work program?"

Second, stock issues—the standard questions applicable to many propositions— may be used profitably in the early analysis of the problem. As standard questions they are not sufficiently specific to the issues of a particular proposition, but they often aid the advocate in the formulation of the actual issues.

1. Stock Issues on Propositions of Fact or Value.   The stock issues in a debate on a proposition of fact or value are drawn from the two basic elements of the affirmative case: definition and designation. Because academic debate is more often concerned with propositions of value than with propositions of fact, we will refer to propositions of fact only briefly and consider propositions of value in much more detail.

In their briefest form the stock issues may be phrased as follows:

1. Definitive issues
   a. What are the *definitions* of the key terms? As discussed above, the terms in the proposition must be defined in order to establish an interpretation

of the proposition itself. This will necessarily include definition of the value(s) explicitly or implicitly identified as points of controversy. For Propositions of Fact and Value, definitions are the first point of stasis or "stock issue." They provide the primary focus of the case. What is "privacy," "life," "global warming"? Definitions should be offered for words and phrases in isolation, but also compiled to deliver an interpretation of the proposition as a whole statement. The advocates must provide their interpretation of, considering key definitions, what is the meaning of the statement that is the proposition.

b.   What are the *criteria* for the values (or for interpretation of definitions)? The values provide the points of clash for the debate, but in order to consider competing values, criteria or devices for measurement of the values must be provided. In the case of fact-based or descriptive definitions, some method for testing the definitions may be called for. The criteria are measures for the definitions, providing a practical and systematic way of comparing argumentation on each emerging point of note. So they offer a taxonomy or measurable and organized set of concepts by which the definitions and interpretations are operationalized.

2.   Designative issues
   a.   Do the facts *correspond* to the definitions? Examples provided in support of or in opposition to the proposition are relevant only inasmuch as they are relevant to the terms as defined in 1-a; advocates must present proof that their examples or explanations are indeed consistent with the definitions and interpretations they have provided. Designative issues apply examples or premises to the criteria established in 1-b, thus engaging direct comparison on a systematic set of criteria. They filter the proof through the measurement screen established by the criteria issue.
   b.   What are the *applications* of the values? At this point, debaters must apply the criteria established in 1-b to the facts presented in 2-a.

With this brief outline in mind, we can proceed to a more detailed consideration of the stock issues.

Let us turn first to the murder trial of John Doe that we just considered. This trial, of course, is a debate on a proposition *of fact*. The definitive issue in this trial

---

Stock Issues on Propositions of Fact or Value
1.   Definitive Issues
a.   Definitions
b.   Criteria
2.   Designative Issues
a.   Correspondence
b.   Application

is the legal definition of murder. The designative issues in this trial are the five issues—Richard Roe is dead, John Doe killed Richard Roe, and so on—that the prosecuting attorney must prove in order to establish that the facts correspond to the definition of murder, thus proving that Joe Doe is guilty of murdering Richard Roe.

In a trial court debate on a proposition of fact, the issues are often neatly spelled out in the applicable law. In most debates outside the courtroom, however, the issues must be discovered by a careful analysis of the proposition. Consider the value proposition "Resolved: That commercial television is more detrimental than beneficial to American society." What are the definitions of the key terms? We will certainly have to define *commercial television* and *American society*. What are the criteria by which to define the value terms *detrimental* and *beneficial*? (You may want to refer to the discussion on how to provide a satisfactory definition.)

As we consider the application of the values, we may discover additional issues. The affirmative might argue that "detrimental" applies to programming that emphasizes sports, soap operas, and escapist entertainment, whereas "beneficial" applies to programming that emphasizes classical drama, classical music, and scholarly lectures. The negative might reply that the application of such values would drive viewers away, which in turn would drive sponsors away. With little or no advertising revenue, the television stations would have to turn to the government for revenue; thus the government should become the arbiter of television programming. Such government control, the negative might argue, would be far more detrimental than the programming the affirmative indicted. The affirmative might respond by arguing that the application of its values would raise the intellectual level of American society, that in time the public would come to appreciate its "beneficial" programming, and that the quality of American society would be improved.

Note that as the debaters began to consider the policy applications of the values, they moved into a quasi-policy debate. In such debates the negative may well offer "value objections" that are very similar to the policy issue of "disadvantages." Additional issues long associated with policy debate become essential in quasi-policy debate. Because quasi-policy debate involves policy issues, we will consider them next.

2. Stock Issues for Propositions of Policy.   The stock issues for the proposition of policy are drawn from the three basic elements of the affirmative case: harm, inherency, and solvency. In their briefest form, the stock issues may be phrased as follows:

1. Harm
   a. Does a compelling problem (an imperfection marked by urgency) exist in the status quo?
   b. Is the problem quantitatively important?
   c. Is the problem qualitatively important?

A harm is established when the affirmative advocate convinces the judge or audience that the quantity and/or quality of life for a significant number of people is severely at risk. Harms are consequences of inaction within the status quo, which have impact. Qualitative harms relate to diminished quality of life, and are likely to be value based; they are intangible yet important. Quantitative harms are concrete, objective, and measurable.

2. Inherency
   a. Are the causes of the problem built into the laws, attitudes, and/or structures of the status quo?
   b. Absent a significant change in policy action, is the problem likely to continue?

   Inherency refers to the barriers preventing solution of the harm within the status quo, or the structures which imbed the things causing the harm within the status quo. Due to inherency, absent affirmative action, the harm will continue into the future.

3. Solvency
   a. Is there a workable plan of action?
   b. Does the plan solve the problem?
   c. Does the plan produce advantages?
   d. Do the advantages outweigh the disadvantages?

Solvency is often the most challenging issue to support. It challenges advocates to prove that their plan of action is not only workable, but that if implemented, it will reduce the harm identified and not cause substantial disadvantages, or harmful consequences upon implementation and operation.

With this brief outline in mind, we can proceed to a more detailed consideration of the stock issues.

Is there a justification for a change in the status quo? That is, are there specific needs, problems, undesirable factors, shortcomings, unmet goals or criteria, unattained advantages, or alternative justifications that constitute good reasons for changing the status quo? Are these conditions significant enough to warrant a change in the status quo? (Significance may be demonstrated either quantitatively or qualitatively, or, best of all, in both ways.) The HARM issue addresses existing evil in our world. We would not act to implement change unless we are convinced that there is a cost to not acting. Harm requires advocates to address the importance and compelling nature of existing problems, that is, their *IMPACT*.

The INHERENCY issue considers the likelihood that absent our positive action, the HARM will continue. Advocates may need to address questions including: Are these conditions inherent in the status quo? Are they caused by the status quo? (Inherency may be demonstrated as being structural, attitudinal, or, again best of all, in both ways.) Is it impossible to eliminate these conditions by repairs, adjustments, or improvements within the framework of the status quo? Is any negative proposal to repair or adjust the problems of the status quo unsatisfactory? And most importantly, if we do not act, will the harms continue into the future?

The issue of SOLVENCY considers the proposed solution and focuses on policy comparison. Is there a plan to solve the problems cited as justification for

---

Stock Issues for Propositions of Policy

1. Harm
2. Inherency
3. Solvency

---

adopting the proposition? Is the plan topical—that is, is it directly related to the proposition? Is the plan workable? Does the plan have solvency—that is, will it solve the problems? Is any possible negative counterplan topical and thus capable of being absorbed into the affirmative's plan? Is any counterplan unworkable or lacking in solvency?

Will the plan achieve the claimed advantages? That is, will it satisfy the justification offered by the affirmative, meet the needs cited by the affirmative, and attain the goals or criteria cited by the affirmative? Will the plan produce no disadvantages as great as or greater than those existing in the status quo? Will any possible negative counterplan produce greater disadvantages than the status quo or the plan? Are the advantages inherent in the plan—that is, will they necessarily flow from the adoption of the plan? Are the advantages unique to the plan—that is, can they be obtained without adopting the plan? Are the advantages significant? Do they outweigh the disadvantages?

3. Using Stock Issues. After carefully defining the terms of the proposition and the related terms from the area of controversy, and applying the appropriate stock issues, the advocate will formulate a preliminary statement of the potential issues of the debate.

Both the affirmative and the negative use stock issues in their analysis. Affirmatives use stock issues as they seek to discover the issues they will advance. Negatives use stock issues as they seek to anticipate the issues they must refute and the issues they will advance, such as disadvantages.

A practical method for the advocate to follow in beginning analysis involves two basic steps. Note that this is a checklist for the process of preparation, not for actually debating the issues.

1. Phrase the stock issue as a question: Is there a justification for a change in the status quo of the type called for in the resolution? Is the problem inherent in the status quo? And so on.

2. Answer each of these questions with the statement of a potential issue of the debate.

The following example shows how the stock issues may be used.

Some debaters started their analysis of the proposition "Resolved: The United States Federal Government should establish an energy policy requiring a substantial reduction in the total nongovernmental consumption of fossil fuels in the United States." Their preliminary research helped them quickly identify many problems related to energy use. These problems included the risks inherent in nuclear power generation, the dangers of reliance on foreign oil, and the harms to the environment caused by the burning of fossil fuels, including air pollution and contributions to global warming. In addition, they found many advocates for various solutions to these problems. As they defined the terms in the proposition, they recognized that they would have to select an agent of implementation from within the U.S. Federal Government, and that they would need to advocate a set of actions built specifically around energy policy. For example, new tax credits to encourage use of alternative energy sources might not be considered "ENERGY" policy. And, their policy must reduce the CONSUMPTION of a particular type of resources: FOSSIL FUELS.

As these debaters continued their preliminary research, they decided that a major evil in the status quo was that through their unnecessarily high consumption of gas, private automobiles needlessly generated excessive emissions of greenhouse gases and created a dangerous reliance on imported oil. They also found that even though a federal government policy existed to decrease consumption of fossil fuels by placing CAFE (Corporate Average Fuel Economy) limits on the fleets of automobile manufacturers, those standards were too low and there was an important loophole: Light trucks that exceed 8,500 lbs gross vehicle weight rating (GVWR) did not have to comply with CAFE standards. These vehicles included very popular pickup trucks, sport utility vehicles, and large vans, thus undermining the existing energy policy. Establishment of a new policy in the form of stricter CAFE standards was warranted. This research led them to formulate the following potential harm issue.

Excessive consumption of fossil fuels is a major problem. In analyzing the harm, they recognized that although it was still debatable, in general, it was the conclusion of a consensus of scientists that by creating auto emissions, humans contributed to global warming, and that the consequences of that would be catastrophic. In addition, human health was negatively impacted by the air pollution created by auto emissions, and independently, relying on a largely foreign supply of oil put the United States at greater risk of economic disruption and foreign policy danger, including wars.

They found these problems to be inherent, since the American economy was dependent on the use of personal automobiles for transportation, and because the attitudes of consumers tended to favor less efficient cars. Therefore, some regulation was called for, but existing restrictions had proved insufficient, and were circumvented by the loophole on light trucks. More research indicated that auto manufacturers could comply with a higher standard, including the closing of the light truck loophole. The plan would work, and it would reduce consumption of fossil fuels in the form of gas, thus reducing incrementally the reliance on foreign oil and contributions to greenhouse warming.

These potential issues represented the debaters' preliminary analysis of the problem. At this point they had moved from general stock questions to potential issues specifically adapted to the proposition. Their next task was to test these potential issues by further research to determine whether the evidence would in fact support the claimed issues. The debaters had to discover whether there

---

Issues (Critical Claims Inherent in the Proposition)

- *Stock issues* are those issues common to all debates on similar types of propositions or standard claims that are applicable to many propositions.
- In a traditional policy debate, the negative must defeat at least one stock issue to win.
- *Potential issues* are all of the possible answers to the stock issue questions.
- *Admitted issues* are issues that one side concedes or chooses not to challenge.
- The *issues of the debate* are the issues that actually are introduced in the debate and on which the opposing advocates clash.
- The *ultimate issue* or *voting issue* arises when there is only one issue remaining in dispute or when all remaining issues rest upon that single voting issue.
- *Contentions* are statements offered in support of an issue.

---

were effective objections to their plan—whether their plan would produce disadvantages greater than the claimed advantages. There would certainly be disadvantages to increasing CAFE standards. American automakers were behind their foreign competitors in the production of high mileage cars. And, some safety and convenience might be sacrificed in order to reduce emissions. On the basis of further study, the debaters no doubt modified their potential issues and tried them out in a few practice debates. Experience led them to rethink some or all of the potential issues. They had, however, taken the essential first step: They had moved from the general to the specific and had begun a meaningful analysis of the proposition.

EXERCISES

1. Working in pairs, find competing definitions for each of the terms listed below. Have a debate in which you each defend one of the definitions as superior to your opponent's. Alternate with four speeches, none to exceed one minute.

   Terrorism
   Marriage
   Poverty
   Sufficient Health Care
   Family Values
   Middle Class
   Responsibility
   Respect
   Adult
   Freedom

Privacy
Obesity
Beauty
Leadership
Quality of Life
Life

2. Working in teams, select a policy proposition (this could be one you for-mulated in exercise 2 from Chapter 6). Define key terms and prepare an interpretation of the proposition. Then outline a case addressing potential harms, inherency, and solvency.

3. From recent newspapers, newsmagazines, or news websites, find an example of an argumentative speech on a proposition of policy by a public speaker. A candidate's answer to a moderator's question in a political campaign debate would be an excellent choice. Identify the "proposition" or central argu-ment made by the speaker and state the issues set forth. If necessary, rephrase the speaker's words to form a clear and correct statement of the proposition and issues; be careful, however, to preserve the speaker's ideas. Do you agree with the speaker's choice of issues?

4. Prepare a three-minute speech for delivery in class in which you (a) state a proposition of policy or value as determined by your instructor, (b) define the terms, and (c) state the issues. The class will be asked to evaluate the three parts of your presentation. Prepare an outline of this speech to give to your instructor.

8

....

Evidence and Proof

In order to justify the invasion of Iraq rather than to continue a U.N.-sponsored inspection regime in Iraq, President Bush in 2002 and 2003 offered evidence of Iraqi-sponsored programs to develop and stockpile weapons of mass destruction (WMDs), in violation of U.N. resolutions. This evidence included claims of intelligence information that could not be detailed. Was the evidence offered by the Bush administration sufficient? The war ensued with the support of the majority of the American people, even in the face of opposition by many of our allies including France and Germany. After the end of major combat was declared, when weapons of mass destruction had not been discovered, contenders for the Democratic nomination to the presidency and other opponents of the war offered that failure to find WMDs was evidence that the war was unwarranted. Was their argumentation well founded?

Evidence is the raw material of argumentation. It consists of facts, opinions, and objects that are used to generate proof. The advocate brings together the raw materials and, by the process of reasoning, produces new conclusions. We cannot undertake critical thinking without a sound basis of evidence. The use of evidence is not limited to debates—although debates give us an excellent means of learning about evidence. Even in unstructured disputes in informal settings, we must necessarily seek out evidence. Who won the first Heisman trophy? Just what does your warranty cover? Did the campus paper really say that? Those and countless other matters are best settled by referring to the appropriate evidence.

The impact that the evidence will have on the decision renderers will depend on their perceptions and values. In intercollegiate debate, judges are expected to evaluate evidence coolly and dispassionately, setting aside any preconceived notions and weighing the data critically. This is a good model for us to follow when we are called on to make important decisions. Yet we must recognize that, in almost any situation, the judge or the audience will be influenced by the *source* of the message (that is, the advocate or the publication the advocate quotes), the *message* itself, and

---

Miniglossary

Casual evidence That which is created without an effort being made to create it and is not designed for possible future reference.

Conclusive proof Evidence that is incontrovertible, either because the law will not permit it to be contradicted or because it is strong and convincing enough to override all evidence to the contrary and to establish the proposition beyond reasonable doubt.

Corroborative proof Strengthening or confirming evidence of a different character in support of the same fact or proposition.

Direct evidence That which tends to show the existence of a fact in question without the intervention of the proof of any other fact.

Evidence Consists of facts, opinions, and objects used to generate proof.

Evidence aliunde Evidence that explains or clarifies other evidence.

Extrajudicial evidence Evidence that is not admissible in court; such evidence may be used outside the court.

Indispensable proof Evidence without which a particular issue cannot be proved.

Judicial evidence Evidence that is admissible in court.

Judicial notice Evidence introduced into argument without the necessity of substantiation; it is assumed to be so well known that it does not require substantiation.

Negative evidence The absence of evidence that might reasonably be expected to be found, were the issue in question true.

Partial proof Used to establish a detached fact in a series of facts tending to support the issue in dispute.

Prearranged evidence That which is created for the specific purpose of recording certain information for possible future reference.

Presumptive evidence Evidence that tends to show the existence of a fact by proving other related facts.

Primary evidence The best evidence that the circumstances admit; original or first-hand evidence that affords the greatest certainty of the matter in question.

Public records All documents compiled or issued by or with the approval of any governmental agency.

Public writings A frequently used source of evidence that includes all written material, other than public records, made available to the general public.

Secondary evidence Evidence that by its nature suggests the availability of better evidence in the matter in question.

---

the *channel* (for example, face-to-face communication, radio, or television). The judge will be affected by all these factors as a *receiver* (that is, the receiver's values and perceptions affect his or her evaluation of evidence). This is no less true in the academic debate than in other argumentative contexts, despite judges' best efforts to divorce themselves from their own personal judgments.

We probably could establish, after some debate, that the unemployment rate in the United States exceeds 8.2 percent. Once that fact was established, we would proceed to the more difficult matter of establishing that under the circumstances, and evaluated in the context of global trends and international economies, 8.2 percent was an acceptable or unacceptable rate of unemployment. The college professor serving as debate judge would probably feel empathy for the scholarly opinion of a professor of economics. An unemployed audience member might attach the most weight to a labor leader's view. A banker in the audience might be most impressed by a statement from the chair of the Federal Reserve Board. A student in the audience might evaluate the evidence on the basis of personal experience: Is unemployment a remote concept considered only in economics classes, or was one of the student's parents just laid off at the auto plant or will the student soon graduate and enter the job market?

In previous chapters we considered how controversies are discovered and framed, and how argumentation is built to support cases and address key issues in dispute. Recall the place of evidence in debate; it is the most fundamental element upon which argumentation is constructed. In this chapter we will consider the evidence itself, and we will consider some tests to be applied to evidence. Subsequent chapters will consider the composition of the case and the delivery of the case thereby highlighting the interrelationship of evidence with source, message, channel, and receiver. By understanding evidence and its interrelation with communication, we will be in a better position (1) to evaluate arguments presented for our decision and (2) to construct good reasons to serve as justification for the decisions we desire to secure from others.

Evidence may be classified as direct or presumptive. **Direct evidence** is evidence that tends to show the existence of a fact in question without the intervention of the proof of any other fact. For example, in a debate on "tax sharing," the claim that "43 states now have state income taxes" could be established or refuted by reference to the Internal Revenue Service, or some other reliable source. In argument direct evidence is most frequently used to establish supporting contentions rather than to prove the proposition itself. If irrefutable evidence existed in proof of the proposition, there would be no point in debating it. At one time, for example, the proposition "Resolved: That the United States can land men on the moon" was debatable. Today there is simply no point in debating the proposition (although a quick web search will turn up numerous websites making the claim that the landing was a hoax).

Presumptive evidence, or indirect or circumstantial evidence, is evidence that tends to show the existence of a fact in question by proving other, related facts—facts from which the fact in question may be inferred. In debates on the "hazardous waste" proposition, for example, students had many occasions to argue presumptive evidence. When someone lived (usually unknowingly at the time) near a site where hazardous waste had been buried and contracted cancer years later, could it be presumed that the hazardous waste was the cause of the cancer? Many civil suits turned on this issue, and many state legislatures enacted laws addressing this question. In many cases the courts ruled that the presumption was strong enough to justify a verdict for the plaintiff.

Evidence

- *Evidence* is the raw material of argumentation.
- *Direct evidence* tends to show the existence of a fact in question without the intervention of the proof of any other fact.
- *Presumptive evidence*, or indirect or circumstantial evidence, is evidence that tends to show the existence of a fact in question by proving other, related facts, from which the fact in question may be inferred.

As a practical matter much time and effort is spent on presumptive evidence. "But you can't convict a person on circumstantial evidence!" students sometimes protest. On the contrary, many people *are* convicted on the basis of circumstantial evidence. If there is strong direct evidence of the guilt of the accused, the case seldom comes to trial; under such circumstances the accused usually finds it advisable to "plea bargain" (plead guilty to a lesser charge in exchange for a lighter sentence).

I. SOURCES OF EVIDENCE

Evidence is introduced into an argument from various sources. By understanding the uses and limitations of the sources of evidence, we will be more discerning in reaching our own decisions and in developing arguments for the decisions of others.

A. Judicial Notice

Judicial notice is the quickest, simplest, and easiest way of introducing evidence into an argument. **Judicial notice** (the term is borrowed from the courts) is the process whereby certain evidence may be introduced into an argument without the necessity of substantiation; it is assumed to be so well known that it does not require substantiation. This is the predominant form of evidence in academic parliamentary debates. In almost any argument it is necessary to refer to various matters of common knowledge in order to lay the foundation for other evidence to be introduced later and to set the argument in its proper context. Certain matters, which we might reasonably expect any well-informed person to know, may be presented as evidence simply by referring to them. Certain cautions, however, must be observed in the use of judicial notice.

1. The Evidence Must Be Introduced.   Advocates cannot expect those who render the decision to build a case for them; they cannot plead, "But I thought everybody knew that." If certain evidence is important to an understanding of the case, then the advocate must introduce that evidence. The Supreme Court summed up this principle, which applies to legal pleadings and to other types of argumentation, when it ruled, "A judge sees only with judicial eyes and knows nothing respecting any particular case of which he is not informed judicially."

2. The Evidence Must Be Well Known.   The instrument of judicial notice may be used only for those matters that are truly common knowledge. For example, when the "energy" proposition was debated, the existence of an oil shortage could be established by judicial notice; the extent of the shortage was another matter, however. To establish this, the debater had to produce evidence that would likely be attacked with conflicting evidence. If advocates introduce little-known evidence merely by judicial notice, they may anticipate some doubt in the minds of those who render the decision. The Supreme Court made this sound principle of argumentation a part of our legal structure when it ruled, "Courts should take care that requisite notoriety exists concerning the matters on which they take judicial notice, and every reasonable doubt upon the subject should be resolved in the negative." Note that well-known evidence is often perishable. For example, the bombing of Pearl Harbor is burned indelibly in the minds of one generation of Americans; the assassination of President Kennedy is firmly implanted in the minds of another generation of Americans. They can tell you where they were, who they were with, and what they were doing at the time they learned of these events. But you may or may not remember the dates or any details of these events from reading about them in school years after they occurred. You may, however, recall the date of the terrorist attacks on the World Trade Center in New York City and the Pentagon. Those events are well known to you.

3. The Evidence May Be Refuted.   Evidence offered by judicial notice is usually presented in the expectation that it will be accepted without question by the opposition. But such evidence, like all evidence, is subject to possible refutation. In debates on "right-to-work" laws, for instance, some affirmative debaters sought to establish by judicial notice that "there is widespread corruption in labor unions." Negative debaters, however, usually refused to allow this claim and introduced evidence designed to refute it.

In presenting evidence through judicial notice, the advocates ask, in effect, that their opponents and those rendering the decision suspend the tests of evidence and accept their assertion as an established fact not requiring proof. Opposing advocates allow such evidence to go unchallenged at their peril. If the evidence actually is irrefutable, there is no point in raising an objection. But if the evidence is refutable and the opposing advocates fail to raise an objection, then they have only themselves to blame if those who render the decision accept the evidence as an established fact.

The use of judicial notice is not uncommon in academic debate. It is most likely to be found toward the end of the academic year, when a certain body of evidence and argument related to the current national debate proposition has become common knowledge in the forensic community. In these circumstances judicial notice will be effective if (1) the evidence is so well known to the opposing team that it will concede the point by not attempting to refute it and (2) the evidence is so well known to the judge(s) that it will weigh in the decision as if it were fully developed rather than merely asserted.

Judicial notice is not limited to the courtroom or academic debate, however. It may be used in any circumstances in which the evidence is, in fact, well known to those who render the decision. Thus an executive at a board meeting might argue, "We can't use this incentive plan—remember Jones' report on how it would affect our tax situation?" If the report is well known to the board, and if all members accept its conclusion that the incentive plan would hurt the company's tax position, the proposal may well be defeated by this brief use of judicial notice. The advocate must remember that what is well known to the "in-group" may be unfamiliar to others. Thus the use of a critical piece of evidence by judicial notice might be devastating in the final round of a major tournament but ineffective in an exhibition debate before a Kiwanis club. Similarly, the brief reminder that might clinch an argument before knowledgeable board members might be meaningless at a stockholders' meeting; the stockholders of a large corporation could not be expected to be familiar with the details of every report submitted to the board of directors.

B. Public Records

Public records are often used as a source of evidence. On many matters they are the most important evidence, because private individuals or organizations lack the authority or resources to assemble much of the evidence that can be found only in public records.

Public records include all documents compiled or issued by or with the approval of any governmental agency. In this category are such diverse materials as the *Congressional Record*, federal and state statute books, birth certificates, deeds, reports of congressional hearings, and the minutes of a town meeting. Official records are usually highly regarded. The fact that they are public records, however, does not mean that they should be accepted uncritically. A public record containing the report of a congressional committee might be the best possible source of information on the amount of money the United States spent on direct economic aid to foreign countries in a certain year, because the committee has the power to compel officials to produce their records and testify under oath. The same report might contain the testimony of witnesses on the value of this economic aid. Their testimony would not necessarily be the best possible expert opinion on that subject, however: they might be impartial authorities, or they might be highly prejudiced lobbyists.

C. Public Writings

Public writings, another frequently used source of evidence, include all written material, other than public records, made available to the general public. In this category are such diverse materials as the *Encyclopedia Britannica* and the *Weekly World News*, a college textbook and the campus humor magazine, the *World Almanac* and *The Great Gatsby*, and a Brookings Institution report and an astrologer's chart. Some public writings command high prestige and are likely to be accepted readily; others are more likely to be disbelieved than believed. Obviously the value of public writings varies tremendously. Professional or scholarly peer-reviewed journals and Wikipedia all fall into this category!

D. Private Writings

Caution: Private writings and testimony of witnesses, like interviews and correspondence, will provide both *leads* to evidence and evidence that is *admissible* in the debate. As noted previously, the advocate needs to know the distinction.

Private writings include all written material prepared for private rather than public use. Some private writings are designed to become public records at a later date. Wills, for example, become public records when they are probated; contracts become public records if they are brought into court for adjudication. Any private writing may become a public record if it is included in the records of a court or a governmental agency, or it may become a public writing if it is made available to the general public. Most private writings, however, are prepared for a limited circulation among selected individuals. In this category are such diverse materials as a privately owned company's financial statement prepared by a certified public accountant, a student's class notes, a diary, and a personal letter.

Private writings may be carefully prepared documents designed to report events with great precision and to reflect considered judgments, or they may be incomplete and studded with offhand comments or facetious remarks. Because private writings constitute an important source of evidence, care should be taken to determine who prepared the document and under what circumstances. Note that personal letters are not customarily introduced as evidence in academic debate. The reason may be that it is usually impossible to authenticate a personal letter within the limitations of an academic debate. Thus, if private writings become public writings, they are clearly admissible in the form of public writings. If they remain private writings, they are leads that may guide one to admissible evidence.

Computers have created a gray area of public or private writing. E-mail or comments on an electronic bulletin board are similar to postcards. That is, they're public in the sense that many people have easy access to them, but they're private in the sense that they are often intended for one person or a small group of people. The test here is the context in which the evidence is found. If it is stored in a database available to the general public, it is clearly a public writing and admissible as evidence. If the evidence is only fleetingly available, it must be treated as a lead. Note, too, that there is the problem of verifying such evidence.

E. Testimony of Witnesses

The testimony of witnesses is one of the most common sources of evidence. Testimony in court or before a governmental body is usually given under oath and is subject to penalties for perjury or contempt. Testimony outside the courtroom or hearing room is not subject to the same legal restrictions and is usually more informal. For example, management officials usually give testimony on the operation of their company at a stockholders' meeting; the president of a company may ask the plant superintendent for an oral report on the utility of a new machine; the college freshman may ask a sophomore for advice on what courses to take. In fact, much of our day-to-day business and social activity is based on the testimony of witnesses.

Sources of Evidence
■ Judicial Notice ■ Public Records ■ Public Writings ■ Private Writings ■ Testimony of Witnesses ■ Personal Inspection

The value of such testimony may vary considerably. Clearly the testimony of a witness at a congressional hearing is readily admissible by citing the hearings. The "testimony" of your political science professor in a classroom lecture is *not* admissible in academic debate unless published, but it may constitute a valuable lead that will enable you to find admissible evidence.

F. Personal Inspection

When personal inspection is used as a source of evidence, something is presented for examination to the persons rendering the decision. For instance, the automobile sales person may invite customers to lift the hood and inspect the motor; a stockbroker may show the financial statement of a company to a client; or a senator may bring a bag of groceries into the Senate chamber for use during a speech on nutrition. College students frequently are asked to perform personal inspections. For example, the geology professor may offer a sample of rock for the class to examine; the economics professor may sketch a supply-and-demand curve on the board; or the music professor may play a portion of a recording for a music appreciation class.

Personal inspection is frequently used in courtroom debates: Attorneys show juries and judges the murder weapon, arrange for them to visit the scene of the crime, or show them the plaintiff's injuries. Evidence presented through personal inspection has been carefully selected and arranged by someone to support a particular argument; it must therefore be examined with care.

II. TYPES OF EVIDENCE

A. Judicial or Extrajudicial Evidence

Evidence is usually classified as judicial or extrajudicial. **Extrajudicial evidence** is also known as "extralegal" or "incompetent" evidence. The word *incompetent* has no negative connotation when used in this sense, but merely means "not admissible in court"; such evidence may be used outside the court. Thus extrajudicial evidence is used to satisfy persons about the facts requiring proof in any situation other than a legal proceeding and is subject only to the usual tests of evidence. **Judicial evidence**, also known as "legal" or "competent" evidence, is evidence that is admissible in court. Such evidence must satisfy not only the usual tests of evidence but also the various technical rules of legal evidence.

In legal proceedings certain otherwise perfectly good evidence is excluded. For example, if we are trying to decide whether a certain man's testimony is trustworthy, we are interested in knowing whether he has a criminal record. Such evidence, however, is often excluded from courtroom debates. Thus, if someone says, "That evidence couldn't be admitted in court," the objection is irrelevant unless the debate actually is taking place in court.

The famous O. J. Simpson murder case educated the public on these terms. For weeks there was intensive media coverage of the pretrial hearings. During these hearings the defense and prosecuting attorneys debated whether the results of DNA testing, O. J.'s history of spousal abuse, and other matters were judicial evidence. If judicial, such evidence would be admissible to the trial. Similarly, the admissibility of the prior sexual history of the alleged victim in the Kobe Bryant rape trial was an issue for the court to consider and drew public attention, as did evidence of Casey Anthony's social behavior during the 31 days her daughter Caylee was missing before a missing person report was filed and a JibJab animation depicting Casey as a dancing monster.

B. Primary or Secondary Evidence

Evidence is often classified as primary or secondary. **Primary evidence** is the best evidence that the circumstances admit. It affords the greatest certainty of the matter in question, and it is original or firsthand evidence. **Secondary evidence** is evidence that falls short of this standard, because by its nature it suggests there is better evidence of the matter in question. Thus an examination of this chapter of this book is primary evidence that the book contains a chapter on evidence; someone's statement in a review that this book contains a chapter on evidence is secondary evidence.

In debates on a law enforcement proposition, for example, students came across many newspaper and magazine stories quoting the FBI as reporting that the crime rate had gone up 16 percent that year. These stories, of course, were secondary evidence of the FBI's report. Thoughtful debaters checked the primary evidence: the FBI's report itself. There they found the caution that the statistics should not be used for year-to-year comparisons. One reason for this caution was that, in 1995, many police departments across the country switched from the Uniform Crime Report (UCR) system of reporting crimes to the national incident-based system. The incident-based system required the police to report each crime that occurs during an incident. Under the UCR system police reported only one crime per incident—the most serious crime. Thus, if someone broke into a home and robbed and raped a woman the UCR would report that event as a rape. In the incident-based system it is reported as three separate incidents: as breaking and entering, as grand theft, and as a rape—and possibly other crimes as well. Indeed, up to 10 separate crimes could be reported for a single occurrence in the incident-based system. The fact that the incident-based system reported and counted many more crimes was not statistically valid evidence of any change in the number of crimes actually committed. Many secondary sources omitted this caution, and debaters who depended on this secondary evidence sustained embarrassing defeats at the hands of debaters who had sought out the primary evidence.

Primary evidence is stronger than secondary evidence because there is less possibility of error. Secondary evidence is weaker than primary evidence because it does not derive its value solely from the credibility of the witness, but rests largely on the veracity and competence of others. In any argument the prudent advocate seeks to use primary evidence whenever possible.

C. Written or Unwritten Evidence

Written evidence is evidence supplied by writings of all kinds: books, newspapers, and magazines, as well as less frequently used types of writing, such as Roman numerals carved on the cornerstone of a building. *Unwritten evidence* includes both oral testimony and objects offered for personal inspection.

In arguments outside the courtroom, written evidence generally is given greater weight than oral evidence, because it is easier to substantiate. In a recent intercollegiate debate a negative speaker introduced unwritten, secondary evidence by saying:

> Last week I had the opportunity to talk with the senator when he visited in my hometown, and he told me that …

Then the negative debater quoted a statement strongly critical of the affirmative's position. An affirmative speaker replied to this by using written evidence:

> We have no way of knowing how accurately the negative quoted the senator or of knowing what the senator said in a private interview. However, we do have a record of the considered opinion of the senator on this subject as he expressed it in an article in the *New York Times Magazine* of last week when he stated …

The affirmative debater then quoted a carefully qualified statement that indicated only minor reservations about the affirmative's position. Which of the speakers quoted the senator correctly? Perhaps both. The senator may have changed his mind; or, more likely, the two statements represented the difference between an offhand comment and a considered opinion. In any event the judge accepted the statement of the affirmative speaker, because he could better substantiate his evidence.

On the other hand, we often accept and act on oral evidence even when it is hearsay. If a professor says to some students, "Last night the dean told me that the president told him that the trustees have decided to raise the tuition next year," the students might well decide immediately that they will have to raise more money for next fall's tuition. As noted in Chapter 10, although unwritten evidence is not used in academic debate, it may provide valuable leads to written evidence, which can be used in academic debate.

D. Real or Personal Evidence

Real evidence is furnished by objects placed on view or under inspection. In the courtroom real evidence may consist of fingerprints, scars, or weapons. Outside the courtroom a farmer may be asked to inspect test plots in which different types of seed are used; a customer might be invited to taste a new food product; a student might be invited to examine a famous painting in a museum; or a customer might be asked to test drive a new car.

We are constantly offered pseudo- or real evidence in the form of print advertisements and TV and radio commercials. Vast sums of money are lavished on producing evidence designed to convince us to buy a product or vote for or against a candidate. Pictures of a car effortlessly speeding along a mountain road or of an opposition candidate caught at a particularly inept moment are offered as "real" evidence of the performance of the car or of the candidate's qualifications. It is important to realize that such "real" evidence is selected and prepared by someone. Consequently, if we hope to make a critical judgment about this evidence, we must apply the appropriate tests of evidence both to the evidence itself and to the persons who prepared it.

Personal evidence is evidence furnished by persons, and it may be in the form of oral or written testimony. The credibility we attach to personal evidence depends in large part on the competence and honesty we attribute to the person providing the testimony.

E. Lay or Expert Evidence

Evidence is usually classified as either lay or expert. As a practical matter, however, it is often difficult to distinguish between the well-informed layperson and the expert. Representatives and senators, for example, may or may not be experts on the subjects they speak about. However, because their official position gives them unusual opportunities to acquire special knowledge on many subjects, audiences often regard them as experts. The able intercollegiate policy debater who has spent an academic year in a superior forensic program studying a national debate proposition might be qualified as a minor expert on that proposition.

Lay evidence is provided by persons without any special training, knowledge, or experience in the matter under consideration. Such evidence is useful in areas that do not require special qualifications. For example, in debates on "right-to-work" laws, the testimony of "rank-and-file" union members or managers of small businesses was frequently important. These people often had no special knowledge of law, economics, sociology, or even unions. But they were able to give important evidence as to how certain union practices had affected them.

In general the courts will allow laypersons to testify on matters of fact, but will not allow them to testify as to their opinions. This limitation may apply in argumentation outside the courtroom as well. Laypersons, assuming they meet the qualifications of a good witness, are usually competent to testify on a matter of fact they have observed; however, their opinion of the significance of the fact is another matter. Thus the testimony of a rank-and-file steelworker as to how many members of his or her local attended the meeting at which a strike vote was taken would be good evidence, assuming that the steelworker was an honest and competent person. However, his or her opinion about the effect of a steel strike on the national economy could not be considered as more valuable than that of any other layperson of comparable education and intelligence. Only an expert, in this case probably an economist, could give a meaningful opinion.

Expert evidence is evidence provided by persons with special training, knowledge, or experience in the matter under consideration. In the courtroom expert testimony is permitted only when the inference to be drawn requires something more than mere everyday experience. For example, an expert would be required to infer the mental state of an accused person based on the accused's behavioral characteristics. Similarly, in argumentation outside the courtroom, expert testimony should not be used unnecessarily.

The courts further require that the special competence of experts be established before they are allowed to offer opinion evidence. It is advisable to follow this practice in all argumentation. Remember that an expert is a maven in certain areas only and is a layperson in all other areas. Debaters should introduce the expert's credentials and establish the credibility of the information or conclusions provided.

The qualifications of a witness should be studied carefully before that individual is accepted as an expert. That persons are well known or that their views appear in print does not establish them as experts. Intercollegiate debaters are constantly required to distinguish between the expert and the pseudoexpert. Each year the national debate proposition deals with some subject of contemporary significance, about which a number of articles appear in the press. Some are thoughtful analyses written by experts; others are superficial treatments turned out under the pressure of a deadline by writers who may know less about the subject than the typical college debater. Even more are biased and uninformed opinions offered in blogs or other Internet outlets.

In any matter likely to be the subject of a debate, there will probably be expert opinion on both sides. Economists will differ on the merits of a certain tax policy; physicians will differ on the merits of a certain drug; lawyers will differ in their opinion about whether a certain merger violates the antitrust laws; advertising people will differ on the merits of a certain advertising campaign. An important task in both applied and academic debates is establishing a preponderance of expert opinion—not by simply marshaling *more* experts than the opposition but by using testimony from *better qualified* experts whose opinions may be related directly to the matter at hand, and by providing comparisons of the experts' credentials.

The scientific study is a form of expert evidence that advocates eagerly seek out in an effort to establish greater credibility for their claims. Arguments about the credibility of studies are often crucial to the outcome of a debate. Debate educator Sara Newell maintains that a study is unique in that we are provided not only with opinions (the conclusions of the study) but also the facts (observations/data) on which those opinions are based; we are provided not only facts but also with an explanation of how the observations were made; and we are provided not only statistics but also with an expert interpretation of the statistics. A study then is evidence which includes an argument for its own credibility. This unique combination gives a study the potential to "carry more weight," to be more conclusive and more credible than other types of evidence.[1]

Advocates who introduce studies into a debate must be prepared to give good reasons that the studies should be accepted; those whose case is harmed by the studies must be prepared to give good reasons that the studies should be rejected. Newell offers these recommendations:

> Reasonably, the person who introduces the study into the round needs to give some standard or warrant for the credibility of the study. Three major factors determine the extent of proof necessary: (1) the controversial nature of the study's conclusion, (2) the existence of counterstudies, and (3) the importance or controversy of the policy claim. The warrant may range anywhere from general qualification of the expertise of the researcher, to evidence from other sources proclaiming the study to be good or acceptable, to specific explanation and support for the external and internal validity.... The arguments indicating a study are generally of five types. In hierarchical order, according to persuasive power, they are (1) counterstudies disprove, (2) the study is flawed— specific indictments by experts, (3) the study is flawed—general indictments by experts, (4) the study is flawed—specific indictments by the debater, and (5) general indictments by the debater. "The study is flawed" just means that something is wrong with either the internal or external validity.[2]

F. Prearranged or Casual Evidence

Prearranged evidence is created for the specific purpose of recording certain information for possible future reference. Many public records and public writings are of this type. Political leaders often try to get their views "on the record," so that at election time they will have evidence that they supported measures of interest to their constituents. The average person has a considerable amount of prearranged evidence: birth certificates, driver's licenses, marriage certificates, deeds to property, social security cards, insurance policies, receipts, canceled checks, contracts, military discharge papers, transcripts of college records, and so on. Prearranged evidence is valuable because it is usually created near the time that the event in question took place; also, because it is intended for future reference, it is usually prepared with care. At the same time, because this kind of evidence is *arranged*, it may be subject to the influence of those arranging it.

Casual evidence is created without any effort being made to create it and is not designed for possible future reference. For example, when a newspaper

---

1. Sara E. Newell, "The 'Study' as Evidence and Argument in Academic, Policy Debate," in *Proceedings of the Summer Conference on Argumentation*, eds. Jack Rhodes and Sara Newell (sponsored by the Speech Communication Association and the American Forensic Association) (privately published, 1980), p. 296.
2. Newell, "The 'Study' as Evidence and Argument in Academic, Policy Debate," p. 302.

photographer snapped a human-interest picture of a "Good Samaritan" helping a motorist whose car had broken down and was blocking rush-hour traffic, he had no intention of creating evidence. It simply happened to be a light news day, and the editor decided to run the picture with the names of the motorist and the Good Samaritan together with a brief story about the traffic tie-up. Some months later that casual evidence became important evidence in a criminal trial in which the Good Samaritan was accused of bank robbery. The circumstantial evidence against the Good Samaritan was strong: His car matched the description of the robber's car, even to a similar dent on the left rear fender; his physical description matched that of the robber; he had no alibi; and he could not remember where he had been at the time of the robbery four months earlier. His future looked bleak until his attorney, doing research on an unrelated case, happened to come across the newspaper story, which established that, at the time of the robbery, his client had been in a city 100 miles away. This casual evidence led to a prompt acquittal.

Casual evidence is valuable because the party concerned did nothing to create the evidence, so it will not appear manipulated or contrived. In the robbery trial example the accused did not know a photographer was coming to the scene of the traffic jam, and he did not ask to have his picture taken or published. As the accused did nothing to create the evidence, the jury was all the more ready to believe it was genuine and not a prepared alibi. The weakness of casual evidence is that its value is usually not known at the time it is created, often no effort is made to preserve it, and later efforts to recall events may be subject to uncertainty. In this case it was sheer luck that the picture appeared in the paper together with the accused's name and the fact that it was taken at the height of the morning rush hour on a particular day.

Caution: Databases contain both prearranged and casual evidence. LexisNexis, for example, may carry the text of a Supreme Court decision. This decision was prepared with care by the justices and transcribed with care by a staff familiar with legal usage and terminology. This is prearranged evidence prepared with every expectation that it will be quoted in serious debate.

By contrast, a comment on that decision found on a blog might be very casual evidence—a flamingly indignant, off-the-cuff, impassioned outburst offered immediately upon the announcement of the court decision, without a sufficient opportunity to reflect or consider the decision. The author, if one could be found, might well disavow it as a momentary outburst not intended as a serious, scholarly, for-the-record critique of the decision.

G. Negative Evidence

Negative evidence is the absence of evidence that might reasonably be expected to be found, were the issue in question true. For example, if the name of a person cannot be found in an official list of graduates of your college, this is negative evidence that he or she did not graduate from the school. Negative evidence played an important part in at least one presidential election. In 1884 a New York clergyman called the Democrats the party of "rum,

Romanism, and rebellion" in a speech at a reception attended by James Blaine, the Republican candidate. Blaine's failure to repudiate this statement was taken by many voters as negative evidence that he agreed with it. Some historians regard this as the critical turning point in the election in which Blaine was defeated and Grover Cleveland elected. Failure to oppose new taxes by refusing to sign Americans for Tax Reform chairman Grover Norquist's pledge to that effect is likely to cost any Republican candidate for elected office their election or reelection. Failure to sign would serve as negative evidence of their opposition to taxes!

Negative evidence was highly important in the investigations of the assassination of President Kennedy. Official investigations established that *no evidence* of a conspiracy existed. Yet rumors of conspiracies persist and have spawned many books, articles, and television programs, as well as the controversial Oliver Stone film *JFK*. Is the absence of any evidence of a conspiracy proof that there was no conspiracy? Or is it proof that the investigators were not thorough enough?

Negative evidence must be introduced into the argument with care. Advocates should claim negative evidence only when they are certain there is an absence of the evidence in question.

Even if careful investigation establishes that the evidence is indeed missing, is it missing for the reason claimed? This difficulty of negative evidence can be illustrated by a case from World War II. Germany developed and stockpiled huge amounts of the deadly nerve gases Tabun, Sarin, and Soman.[3] German scientists who studied Allied scientific journals found no reference to these chemicals. Because this absence of any reference to these chemicals was exactly what one would expect to find as the result of efficient censorship, the Germans concluded that the Allies also had developed the gases and probably had large supplies on hand. The fear of retaliation apparently led the Germans to decide not to use their gases during the war. Actually the chemicals were not mentioned in the Allied journals simply because no Allied scientist had discovered them. Their existence was unknown until Allied troops stumbled on the German supplies after VE Day.

Richard Bernstein's commentary on historian David Irving's *Hitler's War* considers a perplexing problem of negative evidence.[4] In his book Irving made the extraordinary assertion that the Nazi's extermination of the Jews was carried out without the Führer's knowledge. Irving argued that Hitler never committed to writing any order implementing the "Final Solution." In the absence of evidence that Hitler did know, Irving concluded that he did not—a classic case of negative evidence. Other historians have argued that this is a biased view because Hitler used code words to make his wishes known to his followers.

A more recent problem of negative evidence arose when many veterans of the Gulf War complained of a mysterious malady, the Persian Gulf syndrome,

---

3. These compounds are designated GA, GB, and GD in the United States; their less volatile liquid counterparts are known as V-agents.
4. Richard Bernstein, "Culling History from Propaganda," *New York Times*, Apr. 24, 1994, sec. 4, p. 4.

which they attributed to Iraq's use of chemical or biological weapons. When questioned by a congressional committee, representatives of the Department of Defense and the CIA testified that they had no convincing evidence that such weapons had been used, but they were not willing to guarantee that exposure had not occurred.

> The intelligence community has an expression, "Absence of evidence is not evidence of absence," said John T. Kriese, chief officer for ground forces at the Defense Intelligence Agency. I cannot say there was no CW [chemical warfare] use or BW [biological warfare] contamination. From everything I know my judgment is that it was not used. [But] I think it's impossible to prove a negative.[5]

Failure to discover evidence of Saddam Hussein's development and stockpiling of weapons of mass destruction in Iraq after Operation Iraqi Freedom was used to argue that American intervention had not been justified.

Fortunately we are rarely faced with such complex tasks as those that confront intelligence agencies seeking to discover an enemy's capabilities. Consider this typical use of negative evidence in everyday affairs: An executive receives a tempting offer to purchase some merchandise from an out-of-town firm. The price is favorable, but she does not know whether the firm will really deliver merchandise of the quality claimed. The executive directs an assistant to look into the matter. The assistant calls the Better Business Bureau in the firm's city and inquires. The reply indicates that the firm has been doing business in that city for 25 years and that only six complaints have been received about the firm in the past year, with all adjusted to the satisfaction of the customers. The executive would probably take this lack of unsettled complaints as satisfactory negative evidence that the firm is reputable.

H. Evidence Aliunde

Evidence aliunde, also known as "extraneous" or "adminicular" evidence, explains or clarifies other evidence. Often the meaning or significance of evidence is not apparent on the presentation of the evidence per se; therefore, that evidence must be explained by the presentation of other evidence. In debates on free trade, for example, some debaters introduced as expert evidence the opinion of certain economists that free trade would be beneficial because it would permit the operation of the principle of comparative advantage. Unless those who rendered the decision understood the principle of comparative advantage, this evidence would be of little value until the debaters introduced additional evidence to explain the concept.

Evidence is used in extraordinarily complex combinations in argumentation. One piece of evidence may often be classified under several types. For example, in a debate on the "increase exploration and/or development of space"

---

5. *New York Times*, May 26, 1994, p. A12.

proposition, one affirmative speaker offered the following evidence from *Time* magazine to establish an advantage:

> One of the six crew members [of the aborted *Discovery* mission] is Charles Walker, 35, an engineer with McDonnell Douglas and the shuttle's first ambassador for private enterprise. Walker's in-flight task is to concoct a mystery drug for Johnson & Johnson, using a technique called electrophoresis, which in the zero gravity of space can separate biological compounds 700 times as efficiently as on earth. Judging by the many clues the principals have dropped, the substance *could be a one-shot cure for diabetes.*

The identification of the types of evidence represented by this statement will help us to analyze it. Obviously it is written evidence from a public record—that is, *Time*. Clearly it is secondary evidence, because *Time* isn't telling who the "principals" are. It *may* be expert evidence, as suggested by the use of the word *principals*, but we don't know who made the statement or what the credentials of the principals are. It is probably unwritten evidence; "clues" tend to be "dropped" in off-the-record comments. Certainly, had the clues appeared in, say, the *New England Journal of Medicine*, *Time* would have cited such a prestigious source. This evidence in its current form is useless, as the affirmative debater who used it—just once—quickly found out. Clearly evidence aliunde is needed to clarify this evidence before it will have real impact in establishing the value of preparing biological compounds in space.

I. Alternative Forms of Evidence

If the development of argumentation is considered outside the traditional logical construct, importance of emotional content and alternative viewpoints may become relevant. Classroom and tournament debaters derive most of their evidence from published sources. These sources represent well-educated experts from academe, particular content fields, government, and other privileged

---

Types of Evidence

- Judicial or Extrajudicial Evidence
- Primary or Secondary Evidence
- Written or Unwritten Evidence
- Real or Personal Evidence
- Lay or Expert Evidence
- Prearranged or Casual Evidence
- Negative Evidence
- Evidence Aliunde
- Alternative Forms of Evidence

positions. In other words, the sources of most quoted evidence are economic and social elites within their respective societies. Thus, they have access to traditional publication in academic journals, periodicals, and other materials. They may be perfectly qualified to offer opinions and conclusions about problems of general concern, but their viewpoints may be limited by standpoint. Therefore, it is beneficial at times for debaters to offer their own nontraditional forms of proof, and those of marginalized or disenfranchised persons. The form of such evidence may be in narrative, poetry, prose, art, music, or hip-hop. The content, although challenging to measure, can be powerful and emotional, and can offer viewpoints excluded by traditional standards. Further, visual evidence may provide argumentative support through pictorial evidence, and even the performance of the arguers may support reasoning and claims offered.

III. THE PROBATIVE FORCE OF EVIDENCE

We are concerned not only with the sources and types of evidence but also with its *probative force*. Evidence may only partially substantiate an issue, or it may be strong enough to justify the claim conclusively in the minds of those who render the decision. Baseball fans engaged in a pleasant disputation on the question "Who won the Most Valuable Player award last year?" will probably settle the matter conclusively by reference to a standard almanac. But if the question is, "Who was the greatest baseball player of all time?" a conclusive answer is probably impossible; the game has changed too much over the years. Ty Cobb and Babe Ruth unquestionably are greats of yesteryear, but there is no practical way of comparing them with today's greats. Thus the standards necessary to establish a conclusive answer probably could not be agreed on. The debate over the 2003–2004 NCAA Division I-A national football championship would be no less challenging. Both Louisiana State and Southern California made claims to the championship, and the standards of the NCAA and its Bowl Championship Series did not resolve the issue. If all involved could agree on the standards, there would have been only one champion.

The often-heard question "If we can put a person on the moon, why can't we solve the problem of homelessness or clean up the inner cities?" provides an excellent example of the probative force of evidence. Once the political decision was made to spend the money to put a person on the moon, the problem was limited to its scientific and engineering aspects. The scientific and engineering communities had developed agreed-upon standards that allowed them to establish conclusive proof that a moon landing could be made, and the mission was accomplished. Solving homelessness or cleaning up the inner cities, however, depends not only on accepted scientific and engineering facts but also on complex political and social problems involving conflicting values and perceptions. Thus the decision renderers will determine the probative force of evidence, and the task of the advocates remains that of discovering evidence that will have the desired impact in justifying their claim.

A. Partial Proof

Partial proof is used to establish a detached fact in a series of facts tending to support the issue in dispute. In debating the proposition of "providing a living wage," affirmative debaters might introduce evidence of seasonal fluctuations in employment as partial evidence in support of their harm issue. In a murder trial the prosecution usually has to introduce evidence to prove malice on the part of the accused toward the murdered person—partial evidence in the series of facts the prosecution will seek to establish in order to prove the charge of murder. Evidence that only partially substantiates the advocate's contention is of little value in itself. However, when several pieces of partial evidence are combined, their effect may be powerful. Indeed, taken together they might become conclusive. Malice, in the murder trial, provides necessary, but not sufficient evidence to support the case against the accused.

B. Corroborative Proof

Corroborative proof, also known as "cumulative" or "additional" proof, is strengthening or confirming evidence of a different character in support of the same fact or proposition. For example, in debates on "free trade," some advocates sought to show that free trade would harm domestic industry. Evidence showing a specific industry that would be harmed was of some value in establishing this contention. Evidence that a number of industries would be harmed made the contention stronger. Similarly, a defendant in a trial might claim that he was out of town on the day the crime took place. One witness who saw him in another city on the day in question could furnish evidence of his alibi, but his alibi would be stronger if he could produce several witnesses to corroborate his story. Finding that a scientific conclusion is supported by a number of researchers, or better yet, a "consensus of experts" is compelling evidence.

C. Indispensable Proof

Indispensable proof is evidence without which a particular issue cannot be proved. In courtroom debates it is relatively easy to identify indispensable evidence. In a murder trial, for example, the prosecution must introduce evidence to establish the actual death of the person alleged to have been murdered.

In argumentation outside the courtroom, the indispensable evidence necessary to establish the proposition is usually less well defined than in legal

---

The Probative Force of Evidence

- Partial Proof
- Corroborative Proof
- Indispensable Proof
- Conclusive Proof

proceedings, but careful examination of the proposition will indicate certain matters that must be proved. In the case of academic debate case, the stock issues may comprise a template for required and indispensable proof.

D. Conclusive Proof

Conclusive proof is evidence that is incontrovertible, either because the law will not permit it to be contradicted or because it is strong and convincing enough to override all evidence to the contrary and to establish the proposition beyond reasonable doubt. Evidence that may not be contradicted in legal proceedings varies from one jurisdiction to another. Outside the courtroom no evidence is safe from refutation, and no evidence is conclusive or acceptable on its merits alone. The advocate always seeks to find such evidence, but on matters likely to be the subject of debate, conclusive evidence that applies directly to the proposition is seldom available. Obviously, once conclusive evidence is presented on a proposition, that proposition is no longer debatable. More often such evidence is found to support subsidiary matters related to the proposition. In debates on "right-to-work" laws, for example, some advocates were able to introduce conclusive evidence of corruption in labor-management relations; they were not able, however, to introduce conclusive evidence that "right-to-work" laws would eliminate such corrupt practices.

Evidence is an essential ingredient in all argumentation. We cannot make intelligent decisions without evidence. The value of one piece of evidence, however, may differ considerably from that of another. Therefore, when we evaluate evidence presented to us for our decision, we must accept the good and reject the defective. Likewise, when we seek the decision of others, we must evaluate evidence carefully so that we use sound evidence in our case. We must also be able to evaluate the evidence of our opponents so that we can expose their defective evidence. Those seeking to reach a reasoned decision on evidence will find it desirable to apply the tests of evidence considered next.

EXERCISES

1. Select one contention related to the current CEDA/NDT national intercollegiate debate proposition, as your instructor specifies. Bring to class two examples of each of the following classifications of evidence:

    a.   Direct evidence to prove this contention
    b.   Presumptive evidence in support of this contention

2. From newspapers or newsmagazines published within the past week, find examples of the use of the following sources of evidence to support a contention:

    a.   Judicial notice
    b.   Public records

    c.   Public writings

    d.   A source that was originally a private writing

    e.   Testimony of a witness. Write a brief paper in which you classify the evidence, identify the contention advanced by the writer, and attach a clipping of the supporting evidence.

3.   Obtain the text of a recent public speech by a well-known national figure or an editorial in a newspaper or newsmagazine on a matter of current importance. Classify the evidence:

    a.   By type

    b.   By the probable probative force the evidence had on the audience addressed by the speaker

4.   Attend an intercollegiate debate and take careful note of the evidence presented in the debate. Prepare a brief paper in which you classify evidence:

    a.   By type

    b.   By the probable probative force it had on the judge

    Compare this with the paper you prepared for Exercise 3. Who used more evidence, the public figure or the debaters? Why? Who did the better job of giving the audience good reason for accepting the evidence?

9

Tests of Evidence

Evidence provides the building blocks with which the advocate constructs the case. If the evidence is accurate, the advocate can construct a strong case; if the evidence is weak or flawed, the case can never be sound. Furthermore the advocate is often confronted with conflicting evidence. For instance, as the "University of California–Berkeley Wellness Letter" once observed, studies have shown that caffeine raises, lowers, or does not alter blood pressure; increases, decreases, or does not alter heart rate; stimulates respiration or does not affect it; raises or does not raise metabolic rate; raises or does not raise glucose concentration; raises or does not raise cholesterol levels.[1]

A Harvard University researcher found no evidence that normal caffeine consumption poses any sort of health hazard. A Stanford University study found that decaffeinated coffee caused a 7 percent increase in cholesterol. And a Boston University study suggested that five or more cups of coffee a day—regular or decaf—can cut the risk of developing colon cancer by 40 percent. Conflicting evidence is not limited to medicine but can be found in every field of human affairs. Thus we must consider the tests of evidence.

I. USES OF TESTS OF EVIDENCE

Thus far we have considered the sources and the types of evidence; we next consider tests that may be applied to evidence. These tests have three important uses.

---

1. *AARP Bulletin*, vol. 31, no. 1 (Jan. 1990), p. 6.

Miniglossary

Clear evidence   Proof that supports exactly what it is intended to support with precision and definitional clarity.

Counterintuitive rejection of evidence   Evidence the audience rejects in the first instance because they "know" it is wrong—for example, that employment causes harms.

Intuitive acceptance of evidence   Evidence the audience accepts in the first instance because they "know" it is right—for example, that unemployment causes harms.

Psycho-facts   Beliefs that, though not supported by hard evidence, are taken as real because their constant repetition changes the way we experience life.

Reliable evidence   Evidence from a trustworthy source, with a reputation for honesty and accuracy in similar matters and consistency in commenting on the matter.

Sufficient evidence   A fair preponderance of evidence.

Verifiable evidence   Evidence which may be authenticated, confirmed, and/or substantiated.

A. Testing the Credibility of One's Own Evidence

In constructing their cases advocates will discover a great deal of evidence. Before they use any of it, they should apply the tests of evidence, rejecting weak and inconclusive evidence and retaining only what stands up under examination. By applying the tests of evidence, they may also anticipate the probable refutations of their opponents and prepare to meet them. One can only choose the "best" available evidence if there is a body of evidence from which to choose, so after the research process, it is incumbent upon the prepared debater to select the most effective evidence. And one can only prepare to defend their case when they are well aware of the relative strengths and weaknesses of their support.

The tests of evidence should also be applied to problems outside the debate situation. For instance, the political leader must weigh intelligence reports; the executive must evaluate reports of market trends; and the college student must appraise studies of employment opportunities in various fields. Throughout life we all have to formulate propositions, gather evidence related to those propositions, and evaluate that evidence as a part of the process of making decisions. Intelligent self-interest and our sense of responsibility to those affected by our decisions require that we apply the tests of evidence with care.

B. Testing the Credibility of Evidence Advanced by an Opponent

While preparing their own cases, advocates must also look for evidence that opponents will find useful, apply the appropriate tests to it, and plan a refutation. As a debate develops, advocates will discover the actual evidence used by

---

Questions for Testing Evidence Credibility

In general, affirmative answers to these questions imply that the evidence is credible; negative answers imply a weakness in the evidence.

Is there enough evidence?

Is the evidence clear?

Is the evidence consistent with other known evidence?

Is the evidence consistent within itself?

Is the evidence verifiable?

Is the source of the evidence competent?

Is the source of the evidence unprejudiced?

Is the source of the evidence reliable?

Is the evidence relevant?

Is the evidence statistically sound?

Is the evidence the most recent available?

Is the evidence cumulative?

Is the evidence critical?

---

opponents and be prepared to test and refute it during the debate. Any debate will require that a judge or audience select between or among competing evidence. If a debater can point to weaknesses in their opponents' evidence while defending their own, they can be in a better position to persuade the audience to choose theirs.

Note that the responsibility for applying the tests of evidence and for refuting evidence rests on the party whose case is damaged by the evidence. If certain evidence used by our opponents adversely affects our case but we do not refute it, the decision renderers may accept even weak evidence at face value. The absence of refutation may actually enhance the value of the adverse evidence.

C. Testing the Credibility of Evidence Advanced for a Decision

Although we may participate in only a few debates over a lifetime, we constantly have to make decisions. As citizens, as consumers, and simply as social beings, we are confronted with evidence that we must evaluate almost daily. Thus, if we do not properly evaluate the evidence of a political candidate's qualifications, we may share the responsibility for a poor government; if we do not evaluate the evidence of the merits of a product, we may be inconvenienced or may lose money. In fact, whenever we fail to apply the tests of evidence, we run the risks inherent in an unwise decision. The rewards of applying these tests are correspondingly great. As we apply them, we increase our opportunities for making sound decisions and gaining all the benefits that come with wise decisions.

II. TESTS OF CREDIBLE EVIDENCE

The tests of credible evidence considered have their roots in the long history of argumentation and should give advocates a reliable system for evaluating evidence. The tests of evidence can be stated in the form of questions; the inset on page 186 lists these questions. As indicated previously, all evidence obviously does not have the same degree of cogency, and thoughtful persons test the degree of cogency that decision renderers are likely to assign to the evidence. Let's now discuss the tests in detail.

A. Sufficient Evidence

The advocate must provide enough evidence to support the issue being disputed. How much is enough? When we begin our research, we may find some credible evidence in support of our position. But in debatable matters there will be credible evidence on the other side as well. Advocates therefore must provide evidence that is more convincing than the opposing evidence. Naturally they seek conclusive evidence, but because this is often unavailable, they have to settle for **sufficient evidence**—that is, for a fair preponderance of evidence. In the civil courts the verdict is based on a "preponderance of evidence." In important matters outside the civil courtroom, reasonable people also apply this standard in making decisions. The national intercollegiate debate propositions, for example, always have some evidence—but less than conclusive evidence—available for each side. Usually the ability of the advocates determines which side will establish a fair preponderance of evidence. Remember that in an argumentative situation the advocates try to convince those who render the decision rather than to convince their opponents.[2] They need to persuade only those who judge the debate that they have a fair preponderance of evidence.

B. Clear Evidence

The advocate must provide evidence that is clear or that, by means of evidence aliunde, can be made clear. For instance, in a classroom debate on the "mass media" proposition ("Resolved: That the federal government should significantly strengthen the regulation of mass media communication in the United States"), an affirmative team built a case to ban violence on television. The debaters were delighted to discover a newspaper article by a psychiatrist and research director of the National Coalition on Television Violence in which he said: "The surgeon general's expert panel concluded the evidence is overwhelming. Violent

---

2. In some argumentative situations the opponent may render the decision by conceding. For example, in a civil suit for personal injury damages, the defense attorney may try to convince the plaintiff's attorney that his or her case is so weak that it would be better to accept a modest out-of-court settlement than to run the risk of the jury's awarding no damages—or, of course, vice versa.

entertainment has a harmful effect on viewers."[3] At first the debaters thought they had found an excellent source that seemed to be saying exactly what they wanted. But was the evidence clear? Without evidence aliunde it is not clear. What is meant by violence? Professional football or professional hockey? Saturday morning cartoons? A drama featuring a few murders? Nor is it clear what "harmful" meant—something trivial or something catastrophic? The negative would have quickly pointed out the lack of clarity in this particular piece of evidence. The affirmative debaters wisely decided to seek additional evidence to clarify this evidence in the mind of the judge. Their further research turned up evidence that the surgeon general's report was 26 years old. They decided that if Congress had not acted on the report in 26 years, they must have found the evidence unconvincing. The affirmative decided they would seek evidence that was clear, primary, and recent.

C. Evidence Consistent with Other Known Evidence

Advocates must determine whether their evidence is consistent with other known evidence. If it is, they may be able to strengthen their evidence by corroborative evidence. If it is not, they have to be prepared to show that their evidence is more credible than other known evidence or that other known evidence is not applicable in this particular case. For instance, if business executives offer evidence that the unit cost of a certain product will decrease as production increases; their evidence is consistent with the experience of many manufacturing firms. Thus this evidence will be consistent with other known evidence.

This test, however, clearly does not prohibit the advocates from using or considering evidence inconsistent with other known evidence. For example, in debating the "guaranteed employment opportunities" proposition, some students found evidence indicating, as we would expect, that unemployment was correlated with ill health, divorce, child abuse, crime, and suicide. This finding was consistent with other known evidence and provided the students with recent studies on the very point they wanted to make. Other students, researching the same proposition, came across other studies indicating that the stress associated with employment and the hazards of on-the-job accidents were also correlated with ill health, divorce, child abuse, crime, and suicide. Given the widespread acceptance of the work ethic in American society, based on **intuitive acceptance of evidence**, most audiences would probably accept the evidence because they "know" that employment is good and unemployment is bad. When offered such evidence, we tend to nod in agreement and think, "Sure, that's obvious." Those debaters who used the second piece of evidence likely encountered **counterintuitive rejection of evidence**, whereby audiences reject the evidence because they "know" it is wrong. When debaters find it necessary to use counterintuitive evidence, they must

---

3. Thomas E. Radecki, "We Must Curb TV Violence," *USA Today*, Oct. 24, 1988, p. A10.

demonstrate to the decision renderers that their experts' credentials are superior and that their experts' evidence is more recent. They also have to supply other good reasons why the counterintuitive evidence—evidence inconsistent with other known evidence—should be accepted in the particular case.

Psycho-facts are related to intuitive and counterintuitive evidence. Economist Robert Samuelson defines **psycho-facts** as "beliefs that, though not supported by hard evidence, are taken as real because their constant repetition changes the way we experience life."[4] For example, many people believe that asbestos in schools poses a health hazard to schoolchildren. But as Supreme Court Justice Stephen Breyer showed, the asbestos panic was a costly mistake.[5] Samuelson noted that the risk of police dying on the job was 1 in 4,500, the risk of dying from an airplane crash was 1 in 167,000, and the risk of dying from lightning was 1 in 2 million—while the risk of dying from asbestos in schools was 1 in 11 million. (All data are annual.)

Advocates should not disregard evidence simply because it is inconsistent with other known evidence or considered counterintuitive. Many beliefs now widely held were once considered counterintuitive. However, the advocate should recognize that this evidence has to be considered especially carefully. The advocate must be prepared to have the evidence attacked by opponents and must anticipate possible audience resistance. In most fields, of course, some known evidence is available on either side of a proposition. For example, with regard to trends in the stock market, there is probably some evidence indicating a rise and some indicating a decline.

In this era of immediate access to unlimited information through Internet search, it must also be remembered that misinformation may have a multiplier effect. When secondary evidence is presented in unedited locations, such as websites or blogs, it may be repeated. Those who repeat the evidence do so as if they were providing a secondary report of primary information, when in fact, the original information may be flawed or inaccurate, and the original source becomes invisible, but the information generates a life of its own. So all evidence is to be considered with careful and critical evaluation.

D. Evidence Consistent within Itself

Advocates should study the evidence carefully and determine whether it is consistent within itself. For example, in debating the proposition "Resolved: That United States law enforcement agencies should be given significantly greater freedom in the investigation and/or prosecution of felony crime," some affirmative debaters cited evidence of an alarming increase in the number of rapes (going on to argue that the affirmative's plan for a change in the way rape trials

---

4. Robert J. Samuelson, "The Triumph of the Psycho-Fact," *Newsweek*, May 9, 1994, p. 73.
5. Stephen Breyer, *Breaking the Vicious Circle Toward Effective Risk Regulation* (Cambridge, Mass.: Harvard University Press, 1994), p. 26.

were conducted was necessary). Well-prepared negative debaters turned to the same source and quoted the following:

> The rates are for reported crimes only. In many cases society's attitude about a crime is a significant factor in whether or not it will be reported. Rape is a classic example; only a few years ago the woman was assumed "to have asked for it" and vast numbers of women were too ashamed to report the crime. Today Rape Crisis Centers are widely available to help and counsel the victim; "date rape," a term unheard of until recently, is now a recognized phenomenon.

Thus, while the statistical tables did show an increase in the crime of rape, the text of the document itself contained a serious disclaimer about the accuracy of the statistics. The evidence was not consistent within itself. The negative argued that the increased reporting proved that women were now willing to go to trial and that the affirmative's plan to change the way rape trials were conducted was unnecessary.

Here's another example: A group campaigning for a higher tax rate for a local school district issued a pamphlet in which they maintained that the additional revenue would go for increased teachers' salaries—an increase they argued was necessary to maintain quality education in the school district (quality education was a popular issue in this school district). Examination of the proposed budget printed in the pamphlet, however, showed that most of the additional tax revenue would go for the purchase of additional school buses and to pay bus drivers and bus maintenance workers (busing was an unpopular issue in this school district).

A newspaper editor's nightmare may be found in the following example, which appeared in a major metropolitan newspaper:

U.S. Report Riles Currency Market

Yen Falls to Post-War Low on News from Treasury

WASHINGTON—The dollar fell to a post–World War II low against the yen yesterday after the U.S. Treasury issued a report saying a strong yen would help reduce the swelling U.S. trade deficit with Japan.

Clearly the headlines and the text of the story are inconsistent with one another.

E. Verifiable Evidence

Advocates must always be able to verify their evidence—that is, authenticate, confirm, and substantiate it. In gathering evidence advocates should carefully check evidence against other sources to satisfy themselves about its validity before presenting it, and they should present whatever supporting evidence may be necessary to their audience. They should also carefully identify the source of their evidence with accurate and complete source citations, so that those who render the decision can verify it themselves if they wish. For example, in a debate on economic policy, a speaker might say, "According to *Newsweek*, December 26, unemployment fell from 11 percent to 8.2 percent during the last three years." The audience could then consult *Newsweek* and verify that the magazine did make that statement. In most debates this would probably be enough to establish the claim about unemployment. If the audience were skeptical or doubted the magazine's accuracy, the speaker might want to offer a further opportunity for verification by citing the appropriate reports. Verification of a claim, of course, is more impressive if one can demonstrate that various independent sources verify the claim. (We discuss cumulative evidence in a later section.)

Caution: Some evidence from databases is easily verifiable; other such evidence is highly perishable and may be impossible to verify. Suppose, for example, that the critical piece of evidence in a debate is a quotation from last week's *Wall Street Journal.* The affirmative has a printout of the quote; the negative challenges the accuracy of the printout. If the matter is really crucial, the judge can call up the quotation on a computer and determine the accuracy of the affirmative's printout. If, however, the quotation in question is from a week-old comment on a blog, it will probably be impossible to verify. Such comments are routinely deleted after 48 hours. Thus we offer this admonition: *Never use evidence that cannot be verified.*

F. Competent Source of Evidence

Advocates must determine whether the source of the evidence is actually qualified to testify on the matter at issue. When the source of evidence is a *layperson,* the following tests should be applied.

1. *Did the witness have an opportunity to observe the matter in question?* A popular journalist once spent a week in Cuba and on his return wrote an article entitled "Castro's Secret Plans for Central America." One might reasonably ask if the writer, who was an experienced journalist but a layperson on matters of foreign policy and espionage, actually had an opportunity to learn about secret decisions made by a tightly controlled totalitarian regime.

2. *Was the witness physically capable of observing the matter in question?* A trial witness once claimed that he would be able to identify a robber he had seen at a distance of approximately 100 yards, yet he was unable to read a clock in the courtroom 30 yards from the witness stand. One might reasonably ask if the witness was physically capable of seeing the person he claimed he saw.

3. *Was the witness mentally capable of reporting his or her observations?* A defendant at a certain trial testified in great detail about the routine events of a business day five years earlier, but he was unable to recall any details of other business days at approximately the same time. One might reasonably ask if the witness was mentally capable of recalling all of the details he claimed he remembered.

A person's power of observation may be influenced by circumstances surrounding the event. A standard psychology class experiment involves two individuals who rush into the classroom, fight, and then rush out. When asked to describe the incident, students often give widely differing reports. We must know, too, whether the witness had any interest in making a mental effort to observe and remember the event. How many people attended last year's commencement ceremonies at your college? Ask a few people who were present. Probably very few made any effort to count the audience. Research on eyewitness testimony consistently suggests that as humans we are imperfect, impacted by selective perception and memory.

When the source of evidence is an *expert*, the following tests would be applied in addition to the tests applicable to a lay witness.

4. *Does the witness have official signs of respectability?* If claiming to be a physician, does the witness have a medical degree? If claiming to be an economist does the person have a doctorate in that field? In other words, does the witness have expert credentials? The fact that a physician has all the proper credentials of a surgeon does not, of course, guarantee that the operation will be a success. However, even though some persons without proper credentials have performed successful surgery, few of us would care to entrust our lives to an amateur brain surgeon.

5. *Is the witness well regarded by other authorities?* If an expert witness is highly regarded by others in the field in which he or she claims special competence, then the opinions have added weight. If a physician is an officer of the appropriate medical associations, is accredited in a specialty, has presented papers at medical conventions, and is a professor of medicine at an accredited medical school, then it is reasonable to conclude that this person is well regarded by other authorities in medicine. Advocates should look for similar signs of professional regard for other types of experts.

G. Unprejudiced Source of Evidence

Advocates must determine whether the source of evidence is prejudiced. In many cases people testify about matters in which they have an interest, and in some cases those who have a personal stake in the matter are the only witnesses available. Are these individuals free from prejudice? Do they report matters objectively, or do they slant them in a manner favorable to their own interests? The advocate must determine whether the witness has an interest in the matter at issue and whether this interest is likely to influence his or her testimony. Research questioning the global warming hypothesis is often the conclusion of studies or testimony of experts employed by or funded by the oil industry. For many years, conclusive proof of the harmful health consequences of cigarette smoking was colored by the predominance of the tobacco industry as funder of that research. Of course, many people compelled to write or speak about a subject have a bias about that subject, that is what motivates their interest in the issue at hand.

Traditionally presidents are evaluated after their first 100 days in office. When President Clinton reached that landmark, one major city newspaper ran the front-page headline "Clinton Has Good Marks for His First 100 Days." Sounds impressive, doesn't it? The critical question, of course, is who gave Clinton the good marks? The first paragraph of the story gave the answer: "President Clinton acknowledged yesterday that he had underestimated the power of the Republicans who killed his jobs bill but gave himself good marks overall for his first 100 days in office." Obviously Clinton is not an unprejudiced source of evidence on the question of how he did in his first 100 days in office. If students were permitted to assign their own grades, membership in Phi Beta Kappa would grow by several thousand percent.

In the famous Rodney King case in Los Angeles, King was arrested for speeding and resisting arrest and was taken to a hospital after being beaten by the police. King charged police brutality. The police responded that he was resisting arrest and that they had to use reasonable force to restrain him. Another man, who had no connection with King or the police and who just happened to witness the arrest, videotaped the event. The tape was the *crucial* piece of evidence in this case. In the lengthy legal proceedings that followed this incident, two different juries interpreted the incident differently. No one, however, challenged the fact that the man who videotaped the event was unprejudiced. Note also that this is an example of casual evidence (see Chapter 8). The man with the camcorder did not set out to collect crucial evidence; he was merely trying out a newly acquired gadget.

Whenever possible, it is best to seek out evidence from an unprejudiced source. Academic or scientific writing may be a helpful resource in this respect, as authors are more likely to guard against being influenced by their own biases, and will openly describe their involvement with the subject. In addition, they will use scientific tools designed to guide objective observations. However, even academics are not immune to personal biases, and they may also be more likely to receive favorable reviews for their work when they emphasize significant results. The *reluctant witness* is the witness who furnishes evidence against his or her own interests or prejudices. This evidence, of course, is even stronger than that from a disinterested source. For example, throughout his long fight against impeachment, President Nixon had counted on Republican loyalists who had ably defended him in the House Judiciary Committee proceedings. When new evidence was released after the committee hearings concluded, Nixon at first glossed over its importance. But within hours of the release of the transcripts, all Republican members of the committee indicated that the new facts "were legally sufficient to sustain at least one count against the president" and that they would vote for impeachment. Apparently this reluctant reversal of their previous position was a major factor in convincing Nixon his case was hopeless. Three days later he resigned.

H. Reliable Evidence

Advocates must determine whether the source of evidence is trustworthy. Does the source have a reputation for honesty and accuracy in similar matters? Presidential elections afford interesting examples of the reliability of sources of evidence. Official results of presidential elections are not known until several days after the election. But the national news services have established such a reputation for reliability in reporting results that we invariably accept and act on their unofficial returns, which are announced the night of or the day following the election. While the final result of the 2000 election was long delayed, the media coverage of the historic court battles was generally considered to be reliable. Similarly the polls predicting the results of presidential elections have earned a reputation for accuracy and are generally considered to be **reliable evidence**. By contrast, evidence offered by the candidates themselves predicting the outcome of elections is notoriously unreliable. Typically front-runners in the polls will downplay the importance of the polls for fear their supporters will become overconfident and fail to turn out the vote, which could lead to a defeat. Candidates who are trailing in the polls also minimize the importance of the predictions for fear their supporters will become discouraged and fail to turn out to vote, leading to a crushing defeat.

If advocates can demonstrate that the source of their evidence is reliable, they increase the credibility of that evidence. If they can demonstrate that the source of their opponent's evidence is not reliable, they have cast doubt on that evidence.

I. Relevant Evidence

Advocates must determine whether the evidence is actually related to the matter at issue. Sometimes evidence is offered that is not relevant to the issue or that only seems to be relevant. For instance, the popular phone-in polls using the 900 area code generate dubious evidence. The public is asked to call different numbers to register yes or no votes, or to express preferences for different candidates. The deficiency is that only those who feel strongly enough to pay for this toll call are likely to phone in, and, of course, those who feel *very* strongly can make multiple calls—not exactly relevant evidence of how the general public would vote.

J. Statistically Sound Evidence

Occasionally advocates may find it necessary to use evidence in the form of statistics; however, such evidence should be introduced into a speech only when absolutely necessary. President Reagan, for example—who could draw on all the resources of the federal government for statistical evidence—would use statistics in a speech only if he could not make his point without them. When he did use statistics, he would "round off" and simplify the figures and dramatize them as much as possible. This is a sound practice for all speakers to follow, because most audiences find statistics uninteresting, difficult to follow, and easy to forget. Statistical evidence is always prepared by someone, is almost always written evidence, and is usually expert or allegedly expert; it is therefore subject to the usual tests of evidence. Strictly speaking, there are no special tests for statistics that are not implied in the other tests of evidence. However, because the form of statistical evidence is specialized, certain tests will help advocates evaluate this evidence.

1. Have Accurate Statistics Been Collected?   Many people are reluctant to appear socially unacceptable or uninformed. When a pollster calls, they tend to give what they think is a socially acceptable response—they say they intend to vote when they don't, offer what they believe to be less controversial opinions, or express some arbitrary view to cover up their ignorance of an issue. In one study almost a third of the respondents offered an opinion when asked about the nonexistent "Public Affairs Act." With regard to phone surveys, it should be noted that women answer the phone 70 percent of the time. A poll that doesn't take this into account by making extra calls to get enough men is likely to be skewed. Advocates have to search for evidence that will establish the accuracy of the statistics collected.

2. Have the Statistics Been Classified Accurately?   If you want the best place to go skiing, what do you look for? The folks at Rand McNally once ignored Colorado's world-class resort areas in their list of the 10 best cities for skiing, ranking Detroit first, Los Angeles second, and Akron-Canton, Ohio, third. "This is insane!" protested Colorado ski resort owners. Six of their state's ski resorts are among the nation's 10 busiest, with Vail the top pick of skiers. But the author of *Sports Places Rated: Ranking America's Best Places to Enjoy Sports* said the rankings made "perfect sense." They were based on federally defined metropolitan statistical areas, and all of Colorado's world-class ski resorts are just outside such areas. The scoring was based on the total ski lift capacity within the metropolitan area where the city was located. Detroit has five ski areas in its three-county metropolitan area, but none of them are on mountains. Should we classify the best places for skiing by chairlift capacity in metropolitan statistical areas or by the size of the slopes?

   Students debating a proposition on direct foreign economic aid learned the importance of accurate classification of statistics. Some sources listed foreign aid expenditures as amounting to billions of dollars; others listed these expenditures as $700 million, $500 million, or other amounts. The difference depended on how the person preparing the statistics classified military aid, defense support, technical assistance, and other types of aid.

3. Has the Sampling Been Accurate?   Statistical methodology enables researchers to generalize about large populations based on very small samples of the larger populations. So instead of interviewing 200 million Americans, researchers systematically select 100 or 1000 representative individuals from whom they can project their findings. While the quantitative tools available to the research facilitate such a process with extremely sophisticated accuracy, the generalization is still based on the assumption that the small group selected represents the larger population.

   The ratings of television programs are based on such tiny samples that some congressional observers wonder if they are not meaningless. Some statisticians claim they can predict a presidential election with only a few thousand respondents—if they have just the right proportion of urban residents, farmers, northerners, women, African Americans, college graduates, manual laborers, naturalized citizens, and so on.

   Getting such a representative sample, however, is difficult. Many pollsters would rather interview prosperous-looking people who live in good residential areas than go into the slums to find the requisite number of unskilled laborers. Some ghetto dwellers view pollsters as representatives of "the Establishment" and refuse to reply to questions or give misleading answers. A number of psychological studies are based on responses given by college sophomores—mainly because many sophomores are enrolled in psychology classes, and it is convenient to test them. But are college sophomores representative of the general public? So it is important to consider how the sample was selected and what degree of confidence is afforded by the sample and the statistical measures employed.

4. Have the Units Been Accurately Defined?   A kilowatt-hour is a reasonably well-defined unit, but what is a "work week"? Students debating a proposition on annual living wage might discover that there are many different definitions for this term. How many hours or days comprise the work week? Changing what is an acceptable measure for cholesterol or body mass index (BMI) may significantly alter considerations of public health and even projections of the costs of a health care policy. Even such seemingly familiar and easily understandable units as "the family" require accurate definition: That unit is defined one way for tax purposes, another way in housing statistics, and in still other ways in other statistics.

5. Are the Data Statistically Significant?   Almost any set of statistics will show certain variations. Are the variations significant? Statistical differences are considered significant only if the sample is sufficiently large and representative, and if allowance has been made for the necessary margin of error, seasonal fluctuations, and other factors. If one student scores 120 on an IQ test and another student scores 121, the difference is not statistically significant. If you toss a coin 10 times and it comes up heads 8 times, the result is not statistically significant. Figures showing the extent of unemployment in December and June are not significant unless seasonal differences have been taken into account.

6. Is the Base of the Percentage Reasonable?   Whenever statistical evidence is reported in percentages, the advocate must discover the base from which the percentage was determined. Has the value of the American dollar gone up or down? It all depends on the date used as the base. During the Summer Olympics in Los Angeles in 1984, things were so peaceful that the police insisted that crime in certain sections had somehow dropped 250 percent. *Newsweek* noted wryly, "Anything over 100 percent seems to imply that some lawbreakers had switched to performing good deeds."

7. Do the Visual Materials Report the Data Fairly?   Statistical evidence is often reported in visual form. Visual materials are helpful in overcoming audience apathy toward statistics and, when prepared correctly, in clarifying complex data. However, visual materials can distort statistical evidence. Therefore the advocate must determine whether the various charts, diagrams, and other visual materials really interpret the data fairly. For example, assume that the following figures for the production of widgets are absolutely accurate:

	United States	Japan
Last year	1,000,000	5,000
This year	1,010,000	10,000

Visual Materials: Examples

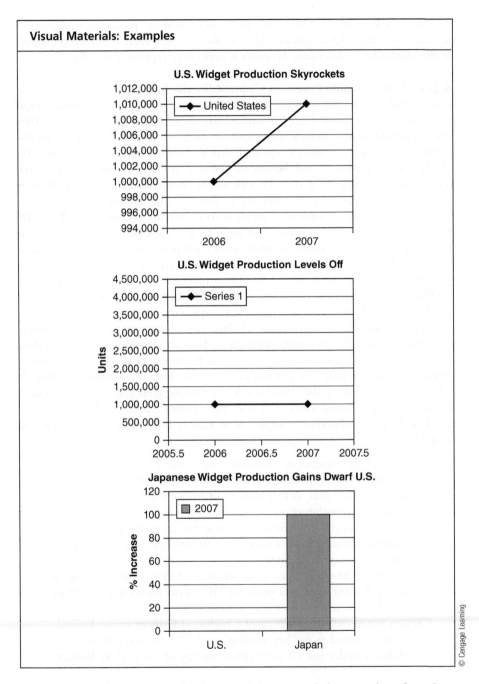

Now consider the graphs in the box on this page and the way they slant these figures. In the first two the choice of units for the vertical axis of the graph produces two quite different pictures; in the third one the height of each bar is reasonably accurate, but a distorted picture is created by using a much wider bar for Japan. The caption above each graph adds to the distortion.

These few simple examples only begin to suggest the possibility of distortion in visual materials. Advocates should carefully examine each visual aid presented in the argument to determine whether it accurately represents the data.

8. Is Only Reasonable Precision Claimed for the Statistics?   If greater precision is attributed to the statistics than they deserve, it may lead to unwarranted conclusions. How many battered women are there in the United States? *Time* once reported that 4 million American women are assaulted by a "domestic partner" each year. *Newsweek* reported that the number of women beaten by "husbands, ex-husbands and boyfriends" was 2 million a year. As *Newsweek* noted, this is terrible. Not only because of the implication that either *Time* or *Newsweek* was wrong by a factor of 2, but because the divergence reflects society's actual state of ignorance on such an important and theoretically verifiable statistic. Nor is this a problem unique to the question of how many men beat their wives. Great issues of public policy are being debated by people who have no idea what they're talking about.[6] Both *Time* and *Newsweek* acted in good faith and used credible sources. The problem was that even apparently credible sources can arrive at widely different statistical conclusions.

In their desire to satisfy the demand for quantification, journalists, legislative reference clerks, supposedly serious scholars, special interest groups, and others often provide us with "imaginary numbers."[7] Thus we should view with a healthy suspicion statistics that come from sources less interested in precisely measuring a given problem than in showing that it's even worse than anyone thought. "People who want to influence public policy have a real strong feeling that the end justifies the means," says Cynthia Crossen, a *Wall Street Journal* reporter and author.[8]

Consider the following examples of imaginary numbers that have appeared in the media:

> Estimates of the number of homeless range from 223,000 to 7 million.
> A U.S. senator announced that 50,000 children are abducted by strangers each year. A Department of Justice study found fewer than 5,000 stranger abductions a year.
> One source claimed that 150,000 women die annually of anorexia. Another source reported there are 150,000 cases of anorexia a year, almost none of them fatal.
> The American Medical Association announced that family violence kills nearly 10,000 women a year. An FBI report found that a total of 4,000 women were murdered a year.
> Crossen noted that the "Survey of Childhood Hunger in the United States" offered as its "key finding" that 11.5 million American children under age 12 were either hungry or "at risk" of hunger.

---

6. "The Numbers Game," *Newsweek*, July 25, 1994, p. 56.
7. This term is used here to indicate numbers that come from the writer's imagination, with little or no warrant from the real world. In higher mathematics an imaginary number is a multiple of the square root of −1.
8. "The Numbers Game," p. 57.

The "at risk" category is often a fruitful one for social action groups seeking to magnify a problem. The term *at risk* can easily be defined to raise or lower the number by several million.

When you read about such wide discrepancies in the statistics on such important matters as these, do you wish you could find the truth of the matter?

9. Are the Data Interpreted Reasonably? Sometimes "the thing speaks for itself" and no interpretation is necessary.[9] Usually, however, someone reports the data and draws conclusions from them—and that someone may support a particular point of view. For example, assume that the following figures on the cost of widgets are absolutely accurate:

Month	Cost of Widgets	Increase (%) from January	Increase (%) from Previous Month
January	$1.00	—	—
February	$1.10	10	10.0
March	$1.20	20	9.6
April	$1.30	30	9.1
May	$1.40	40	7.8
June	$1.50	50	7.1
July	$1.60	60	6.7
August	$1.70	70	6.2

With these data before them, the advocates may make a number of accurate but different statements. On the one hand they might say, "The price of widgets has increased by 70 cents in eight months." Or they might say, "The price of widgets soared a staggering 70 percent in runaway inflation in just eight months." On the other hand, the advocates might take a more sanguine view and say, "Last month the price of widgets rose only 6.2 percent." Or they might report, "Inflation is ending; for the sixth consecutive month there has been a decreasing rate of increase in the cost of widgets."

As another example, consider which is safer, travel by air or travel by car? The statistical method favored by the airlines examines passenger-miles traveled. To reach this figure, multiply the number of passengers in a plane or car by the

---

9. The legal maxim is *res ipsa loquitur*. A classic example would be a surgical operation, after which a sponge is found in the patient's abdomen. The patient, who was under anesthesia at the time, cannot testify that the surgeon did anything wrong. Usually there are no witnesses to the wrongdoing; if any of the other physicians or nurses present at the operation had noticed the error, they would have told the surgeon, who would have corrected the situation before the incision was closed. The plaintiff's lawyer would argue *res ipsa loquitur*: Sponges simply are not supposed to be left in a patient's abdomen; therefore the surgeon must have done wrong. The *res ipsa loquitur* argument, although powerful in this case, is not necessarily conclusive. Now, however, the surgeon's lawyer would have the burden of proving that the sponge had somehow been introduced into the patient's abdomen by some other surgeon at some other time.

number of miles flown or driven by each vehicle. Viewed this way, scheduled commercial airline travel had 0.06 deaths for each 100 million passenger-miles flown in the most recent 10-year period; cars had two fatalities for each 100 million passenger-miles driven in the same period. This suggests that commercial airplanes are 33 times safer than cars.

However, if you prefer driving to flying, you might prefer the vehicle-miles method, which completely ignores how many people are in the vehicle. Viewed this way, commercial airplanes had 6.6 fatalities per 100 million vehicle-miles, while cars had only 3 fatalities for each 100 million vehicle-miles. This method suggests that cars are more than twice as safe as commercial airplanes.

Clearly the advocate should review statistical data in as much detail as possible and determine if the interpretation is reasonable or if other equally reasonable interpretations are possible.

10. Are the Questions Unbiased? Even polls taken by highly regarded professional pollsters at almost the same time can produce dramatically different results depending on how the question is phrased. A recent survey was reported in the *Texas Tribune*:

> Fifty-nine percent of likely Texas voters oppose Gov. Rick Perry's efforts to keep Planned Parenthood out of the joint state-federal Women's Health Program, while 38 percent approve, according to a new poll from Public Policy Polling.
>
> But the poll—released as the reproductive health program circles the drain—is likely to have critics. It was sponsored by Planned Parenthood, whose clinics currently provide reproductive health care for 40 percent of the low-income women in the program.
>
> And some of the language in the poll questions is hotly debated by Republican lawmakers and abortion opponents, who say they are following federal law—not breaking it—by excluding from the Medicaid waiver program Planned Parenthood and other clinics under the same organizational umbrella as abortion providers.[10]

Wording of survey questions can "push" responses, or measure specific reactions unrelated to the subject of concern to the debater.

GOP pollster Fabrizio McLaughlin found that Americans gave "Hillary Clinton" a favorable or unfavorable rating of 56.8 percent to 25.6 percent, while "Hillary Rodham Clinton" got 49.4 percent to 30.6 percent—almost a 13 percent difference.[11]

The perspective, or spin, given to a question may have a profound effect on the response elicited. We might be surprised and worried if the same person expressed radically different judgments depending on how the question was put

10. Emily Ranshaw, "Poll: Voters Want to Keep Planned Parenthood in WHP," *The Texas Tribune*, Mar. 5, 2012, http://www.texastribune.org/texas-health-resources/ abortion-texas/poll-voters-want-keep-planned-parenthood-whp/.
11. *Time*, Apr. 5, 1993, p. 15.

to him or her. Yet that happens frequently. For example, a group of doctors was asked:

> Imagine that the United States is preparing for the outbreak of an unusual disease, which is expected to kill 600 people. Two alternative programs to combat the disease have been proposed. Assume that the exact scientific estimate of the consequences of the program is as follows: If program A is adopted, 200 lives will be saved. If program B is adopted, there is a ⅓ probability that 600 people will be saved and a ⅓ probability that no people will be saved. Which of the two programs do you favor?

The vast majority of doctors (72 percent) opted for program A. Another group of doctors was given the same "cover story" as the first, but they were asked to choose among the following alternatives:

> If program C is adopted, 400 people will die. If program D is adopted, there is a ⅓ probability that nobody will die, and a ⅔ probability that 600 people will die. Which of the two programs do you favor?

Only 22 percent of the doctors opted for program C. The odd thing is that C is merely a different way of phrasing A.[12] And D, of course, is only a different way of phrasing B. So the spin can really make a difference. Advocates should be aware of spin control and give careful consideration to how the question is phrased.

11. Are the Statistics Meaningful to the Audience? Tournament debaters speak of millions, billions, and trillions as casually as if they were members of the House Appropriations Committee. This is accepted in tournament debates, because the evidence is usually familiar to all. Before a general public audience, however, an effort must be made to make these numbers meaningful to the layperson. Consider this example:

> It takes only about 11½ days for a million seconds to tick away, whereas almost 32 years are required for a billion seconds to pass. And a trillion? The Neanderthal man finally disappeared about a trillion seconds ago. Thus when we speak of $2 trillion, we're talking the dollar equivalent of twice the length of the existence of human-kind, compared with the 11½ days worth of dollars most of us aspire to win in the lottery.[13]

As we saw earlier, statistics may be interpreted in a number of ways. Naturally the advocate will want to put a favorable spin on the statistics When columnist George Will opposed legislation that would have put a limit on the amount of money that could be spent on political campaigns, he deprecated the proposal by saying that "in 1992 congressional races involved a sum equal to 40 percent of

---

12. Leo Katz, *Bad Ads and Guilty Minds: Conundrums of the Criminal Law* (Chicago: University of Chicago Press, 1987), pp. 4–5.
13. Molly Ivins, "Getting It Sort of Right—By the Numbers," *Cleveland Plain Dealer*, Apr. 30, 1993, p. C6.

what Americans spent on yogurt."[14] Most Americans spend only a trivial sum for yogurt—and 40 percent of trivial really is inconsequential. Thus Will's spin suggested that there was hardly any need for the legislation he opposed.

K. The Most Recent Evidence

Old evidence may sometimes be more valuable than recent evidence. If we want to know certain facts about the voyage of the *Mayflower*, a document dating from 1620 may be more valuable than one dating from 1920. A map made in A.D. 1000 was important evidence supporting the claim of many scholars that Leif Ericson's Norsemen reached Labrador, the New England coast, and Martha's Vineyard long before Columbus "discovered" the New World.

Often, however, the most recent evidence is the best evidence. If the facts of a situation can change, or if opinions about a certain matter tend to be revised, we want the most recent information available. For instance, this month's Bureau of the Census estimate of the population of the United States is more valuable evidence of the size of the population than a report issued by the same bureau a year ago.

In many cases more recent evidence, simply because it is more recent, is enough to refute older evidence. In debates on the "mass media" proposition, some affirmative teams called for a ban on the advertising of diet drinks containing saccharin. Their justification was that a several-year-old Canadian study indicated a 60 percent greater risk of bladder cancer among saccharin users. The value of this evidence sharply depreciated when, three-quarters of the way through the debate session, a series of new studies appeared that reported "there is no saccharin-induced epidemic of bladder cancer in this country" and that people who use moderate amounts of saccharin "can be assured that their excess risk of cancer, if present at all, is quite small and little cause for concern." Finally, in 2010, it was reported that "The EPA has officially removed saccharin and its salts from their list of hazardous constituents and commercial chemical products. In a December 14, 2010 release, the EPA stated that saccharin is no longer considered a potential hazard to human health."[15] Because new evidence is constantly appearing on matters that are likely to be subjects of debate, advocates should make a special point of gathering the most recent evidence and allowing for it in their case.

L. Cumulative Evidence

Although one piece of evidence is sometimes enough to support a point, advocates are usually in a stronger position if they can offer several pieces of evidence from different sources or of different types to substantiate their contentions. In debates on the issue of nuclear power plant safety, for example, the opinion of one eminent scientist might be offered to establish a certain contention. This

---

14. George Will, "So, We Talk Too Much?" *Newsweek*, June 28, 1993, p. 68.
15. Richard Yost, News Release, United States Environmental Protection Agency, 12/14/10.
http://yosemite.epa.gov/opa/admpress.nsf/d0cf6618525a9efb85257359003fb69d/ea895a11ea
50a56d852577f9005e2690!OpenDocument.

contention would be more firmly established, however, if the advocate could show that the same conclusion was shared by, say, the Nuclear Regulatory Commission, the Union of Concerned Scientists, the Institute of Nuclear Power Operations, and the National Academy of Sciences.

M. Critical Evidence

We may have much evidence, but do we have the critical evidence—the evidence we really need in a particular situation? In many cases evidence made available to us is distorted. That's the reason the Food and Drug Administration has phased in new regulations governing food labeling and advertising. *Time* magazine reported the following:

> Budget Gourmet Light and Healthy Salisbury Steak, which are labeled "low fat," derive 45% of its total calories from fat.
> Diet Coke contains more than one heavily advertised calorie per can (so does Diet Pepsi).
> There is no real fruit—just fruit flavors—in Post Fruity Pebbles.
> Honey Nut Cheerios provide less honey than sugar and more salt than nuts.
> Mrs. Smith's Natural Juice Apple Pie contains artificial preservatives.
> The word *natural* refers to the fruit juice used to make the pie.
> If you can't trust Mrs. Smith, whom can you trust?[16]

In the first Persian Gulf War *the* critical question for Iraq was where the coalition would attack. General Norman Schwarzkopf provided ample evidence, in the form of air and naval bombardment, that the attacks would come from the south and the east. Saddam Hussein thus concentrated his forces to meet attacks from these directions. While escalating the bombardment in the south and the east, Schwarzkopf, in what he later called his "Hail Mary play," moved more than 200,000 troops across as much as 300 miles of desert in 10 days without Saddam Hussein's knowledge and attacked on Iraq's weak western flank. In this case "evidence" was a decoy.

In April, 2012, President Obama proposed "The Buffett Rule." According to the *Washington Post*, "The Buffett rule proposal would boost tax rates paid by households with incomes between $1 million and $2 million, phased up to a 30 percent minimum tax rate for those making more than $2 million a year."[17] As posted by the White House, "The Buffett Rule is a simple principle that everyone should pay their fair share in taxes. No household making more than a $1 million should pay a smaller share of their income in taxes than middle-class families pay. For the 98 percent of American families who make less than $250,000, taxes should not go up."[18] The justification for the rule was thus

---

16. *Time*, July 15, 1991, pp. 52–53.

17. The *Washington Post*, " 'Buffett Rule' could combat income inequality, White House says,"

4/11/2012. http://www.washingtonpost.com/business/buffett-rule-could-combat-income-inequality-white-house-says/2012/04/11/gIQABXHIAT_story.html.

18. http://www.whitehouse.gov/economy/buffett-rule.

fairness more than revenue. Opponents of the Buffett Rule responded with evidence that the revenue generated by the rule would not make a substantial dent in the federal budget deficit, and that new taxes should not be imposed upon middle-income taxpayers. This evidence was not critical to the arguments in favor of the rule. (Other arguments providing evidence that *was* critical suggested that the richest Americans would be able to circumvent the rule thus avoiding a leveling of tax rates, and that if successful, the rule would have a deleterious impact on job creation and investment.)

III. TESTS OF AUDIENCE ACCEPTABILITY

In addition to tests of evidence credibility, the advocate must also apply tests of audience acceptability. Some evidence that might appear credible may not be acceptable to the audience; therefore the advocate must consider not only how the audience views the credibility of the evidence but also the acceptability of the evidence to the audience. The audience, of course, may be a single judge in an academic debate, the whole voting population of the United States in a presidential election, or any group of decision renderers.

A. Evidence Consistent with Audience Beliefs

A negative answer to the tests of evidence previously considered implies some weakness in the evidence. A negative answer to the question of consistency with audience beliefs, however, does not carry such an implication; advocates occasionally have to use evidence inconsistent with audience beliefs and hope to persuade their audience to change or incrementally shift beliefs. When they use such evidence, advocates should anticipate audience resistance and take steps to overcome this resistance. This means that they must analyze their audiences and determine their beliefs on the various pieces of evidence they plan to use.

An excellent example of how the audience's beliefs condition their response to political candidates occurred in the 1988 presidential election. In the Democratic primaries Michael Dukakis proudly *boasted* that he was "a card-carrying member of the American Civil Liberties Union." The liberal Democrats who voted in the primaries saw this as evidence that Dukakis's views were consistent with theirs. This evidence was credited with contributing to his winning the nomination. But in the general election George Bush *accused* Dukakis of being "a card-carrying member of the ACLU." In the general election many more conservative voters saw this as evidence that Dukakis's views were inconsistent with theirs. This evidence was credited with contributing to Bush's victory. In 2012, Governor Mitt Romney, in his campaign for the GOP nomination for president, made the claim that as governor of Massachusetts, he was a "*Severely Conservative Governor.*" This description served him well among republican core voters during the primaries, but at least for some potential voters, may have represented a departure from moderate identities or affiliations.

The importance of audience beliefs is not limited to political campaigns; there are ardent partisans for nonpolitical issues as well. Experienced advocates

> **Questions for Testing Audience Acceptability**
>
> In general, affirmative answers to these questions indicate that the evidence will probably be acceptable to audiences; negative answers indicate that it probably will not be acceptable.
>
> Is the evidence consistent with the beliefs of the audience?
>
> Is the source of the evidence acceptable to the audience?
>
> Is the evidence suited to the level of the audience?
>
> Is the evidence consistent with the motives of the audience?
>
> Is the evidence consistent with the norms of the audience?
>
> Is the evidence documented for the audience?

recognize that many audiences will contain partisans who will interpret evidence from the point of view of their own beliefs. Advocates need to find evidence that will be acceptable to as many members of the audience as possible.

B. Source Acceptable to the Audience

The level of source acceptability does not imply any weakness in the evidence itself; rather, it indicates a problem advocates have to overcome. We know that audiences tend to believe some sources more than others. If evidence comes from a source that has high prestige in the minds of audience members, they are likely to accept it automatically; if it comes from a source without special prestige for the audience, it has to stand on its own merits; if it comes from a source the audience has little or no respect for, it may be discredited regardless of its intrinsic merits. Advocates, then, should try to use sources of evidence that are acceptable to the audience. If they find it necessary to use sources with low prestige, they must establish the credibility of the sources, at least in this special case. When they find it absolutely essential to use sources the audience is hostile to, they have to overcome this hostility.

An excellent example of this problem occurred when the proposition "Resolved: The federal government should control the supply and utilization of energy" was debated. When the Arabs embargoed oil and raised prices in the 1970s, many parts of the country experienced serious shortages, and prices rose sharply. How much of the shortage was due to the embargo? How much of the price increase was caused by the increase in the price of imported oil? The oil companies had one answer; governmental agencies had another; consumer advocates had a third answer. Which source would the audience believe? It depended almost entirely on the audience's attitude toward the various sources. One debater solved the problem by citing figures from consumer advocate Ralph Nader and argued that, because even Nader admitted that imports were down X percent, the audience should accept that figure as accurate. The pro-consumer members of the audience felt they had to agree with their hero; and the pro-business members of the audience, while believing the actual figure to be much higher, were pleased to see an old rival admit there was some truth on their side. As Carl Hovland and his colleagues pointed out:

> The debater, the author of scientific articles, and the news columnist all bolster their contentions with quotations from figures of prestige ...
> When acceptance is sought by using arguments in support of the advocated view, the perceived expertness and trustworthiness of the communicator may determine the credence given them.... Sometimes a communication presents only a conclusion, without supporting argumentation, and its acceptance appears to be increased merely by attributing it to a prestigious or respected source.[19]

If, for example, advocates wished to cite certain evidence that had appeared in the *New York Times*, *National Geographic*, *Ladies Home Journal*, and *Field and Stream*, they would be well advised to cite the source with the highest prestige for their audience. Hovland and colleagues found that the credibility of a message seems related to the particular magazine in which it appears.[20] Students debating the "law enforcement" proposition found confirmation of this fact. Some excellent articles relating to the proposition, written by highly regarded, well-qualified sources, appeared in *Playboy* magazine. When the debater said, "As Superintendent Parker said in last month's *Playboy* ...," audiences usually interrupted the quotation with chuckles. Apparently the audiences associated the magazine more readily with the pictures of naked women for which it is famous than with the quality articles it sometimes publishes. President Carter learned that lesson when an interview he had granted appeared in *Playboy* shortly before the presidential elections. The interview generated more negative publicity for Carter than almost any other single incident in the campaign and led him ruefully to admit during the third television debate of the campaign, "If I should ever decide in the future to discuss my deep Christian beliefs ... I'll use another forum besides *Playboy*."[21]

C. Evidence Suited to Audience Level

It's important that the evidence not be too technical or too sophisticated for the audience to understand. In debates on the issue of nuclear power plant safety, some of the primary evidence was so technical that it could be understood only by a physics maven. When debating before lay audiences, the advocates were forced to discard the primary evidence and turn to secondary evidence that made approximately the same point in simpler terms. One debater summed up such evidence by saying, "You don't have to be a rocket scientist to understand that if a nuclear plant blows up, there goes the neighborhood—Maine, Vermont, New Hampshire."

---

19. Carl I. Hovland, Irving L. Janis, and Harold H. Kelley, "Credibility of the Communicator," in *Dimensions in Communication*, 2nd ed., ed. James H. Campbell and Hal W. Hepler (Belmont, Calif.: Wadsworth, 1970), p. 146.
20. Hovland, Janis, and Kelley, "Credibility of the Communicator," p. 147.
21. See Paul F. Boller, Jr., *Presidential Campaigns* (New York: Oxford University Press, 1984), p. 352.

D. Evidence Consistent with Audience Motives

Advocates occasionally have to use evidence not in keeping with the values and attitudes of the audience. In these cases they should expect audience resistance. Some advocates debating the "mass media" proposition used cases calling for restraints on publication of information about the identity of CIA agents (giving as their justification that events in Iran and Afghanistan necessitated increased U.S. intelligence-gathering capabilities). Some judges, thinking of earlier CIA abuses, ignored the affirmative's carefully qualified plan and said, "I simply cannot vote to give the CIA unchecked powers."

E. Evidence Consistent with Audience Norms

Certain audiences have well-defined norms for evaluating evidence, and the advocate must be aware of and adapt to these norms. Someone arguing a point of law before a group of lawyers will find that they have definite ideas about how legal arguments should be made. In the same way scientists, physicians, accountants, policymakers, philosophers, and others usually impose specific standards for evaluating evidence. For example, the norms that a group of scientists imposes on evidence used to establish a scientific hypothesis will be much more rigorous than the data needed to establish a proposition before a lay audience.

F. Evidence Documented for the Audience

We saw earlier that evidence must be verifiable. To give the audience the opportunity to verify evidence, a speaker has to provide documentation within his or her speech at the time of evidence presentation. In an academic debate the judge expects this documentation, and a good debater will fulfill the judge's expectations. In fact, the NDT, the ADA, the AFA, and the CEDA provide guidelines for ethical and fair use of debate evidence. CEDA's constitutional bylaw (bylaw XVII, Section B–C of the CEDA Constitution, revised March, 2012) is particularly clear:[22]

1. "Evidence" is defined as material that is represented as published fact or opinion testimony and offered in support of a debater's claim.

2. "Fabricated" evidence refers to the citing of a fact or opinion that is either from a source that is found to be non-existent or not contained in the original source of the material in question.

3. "Distorted" evidence refers to the misrepresentation of the actual or implied content of factual or opinion evidence. Misrepresentations may include, but are not limited to, the following:

    a. Quoting out of context: selecting text from an article in such a way that the claim made with the selected text is clearly inconsistent with the author's position as that position is manifest in the article,

---

22. http://cedadebate.org/files/2012%20Spring%20Constitution.pdf.

    book, or other source from which the quotation is drawn, when that material is taken as a whole.

    b.   Internally omitting words from a quotation or adding words to a quotation in such a way that the meaning evident in the resulting modified quotation deviates substantially in quality, quantity, probability or degree of force from the author's position as manifest in the quotation in question prior to modification.

    c.   Internally omitting words from a quotation or adding words to a quotation without indicating, either on the written form of the quotation or orally when the quotation is delivered to an opponent or judge, that such a deletion or addition has been.

4.   Fabricated and distorted evidence are so defined without reference to whether or not the debater using it was the person responsible for originally misrepresenting it.

5.   Competitors shall allow their judges and opponents to examine the evidence on request, and provide on request sufficient documentation on the source of the evidence, which would allow another person to locate the quotation in its original form.

To avoid any misunderstanding, the full source information should be presented *in the speech*. As any student of communication theory knows, not only the debate judge but the general public as well reacts to documentation. As Paul Rosenthal points out:

> Verifiability is the primary linguistic factor in enforcing a statement's credibility, not because the listener *will* verify the statement but because he or anyone else *can* verify it…. This opens up the possibility that measurement of the degree of verifiable content in a message may provide an index of its credibility to the receiver.[23]

An experimental study by Helen Fleshler and her colleagues led them to conclude:

> It is evident that message documentation was the primary variable that determined evaluations of message and speaker. Concrete message documentation resulted in significantly more positive evaluations of the message and the speaker.[24]

    Here's an example of how people respond to documentation: Peggy Noonan, a speechwriter for Presidents Reagan and George H. W. Bush, used the image of

---

23. Paul I. Rosenthal, "Specificity, Verifiability, and Message Credibility," *Quarterly Journal of Speech*, vol. 57 (Dec. 1971), p. 400. Italics in original.
24. Helen Fleshler, Joseph Ilardo, and Joan Demoretcky, "The Influence of Field Dependence, Speaker Credibility Set, and Message Documentation on Evaluations of Speaker and Message Credibility," *Southern Speech Communication Journal*, vol. 39 (summer 1974), p. 400.

"a thousand points of light" in the elder Bush's acceptance speech. The phrase captured the public's imagination, and for months the media speculated about its origin. Noonan described her reaction to a newspaper story about the phrase:

> C. S. Lewis had used the phrase "a thousand points of light" in one of his science-fiction books, which did surprise me. I hadn't read it, but *I assume the* Times *was right because it cited the page number of a specific edition, a show of confidence that suggests the writer had the book in his hands as he wrote.* People ask me now if that's where it came from. I say no.[25]

EXERCISES

1. Find three advertisements in newspapers published during the past week in which advertisers use evidence to support their arguments. Apply the appropriate tests of evidence to the advertisements. Attach copies of the ads to your paper.

2. Find three editorials in newspapers published within the past week in which the writer uses evidence to support his or her argument. Apply the appropriate tests of evidence to the editorials.

3. Find three examples of the use of statistical evidence in newspapers or newsmagazines published during the past week. Apply the appropriate tests of evidence to the statistics.

4. Find three examples of the use of graphic aids to present statistical evidence in newspapers or newsmagazines published in the past week. Apply the appropriate tests of evidence to the visual aids.

5. Prepare a three-minute speech for presentation in class in which you develop an argument supported by carefully chosen evidence. Other class members will be invited to apply the tests of evidence to see if your evidence is sound. Prepare an outline of your speech in which you indicate the types of evidence used, and give this outline to your instructor.

6. One point debates. Divide into teams of two. The first debater will make a claim supported by evidence (select one of your cards blocked in the previous chapter). The second speaker (the opposing team) will challenge your evidence applying the appropriate tests of evidence to discredit it. The third speaker will defend the initial card against the challenges made, supporting the original point, and the fourth debater will answer the arguments made by the third debater.

---

25. Peggy Noonan, *What I Saw at the Revolution* (New York: Random House, 1990), p. 313. Emphasis added.

10

Gathering and Organizing Support

Once the controversy has been analyzed and the statement of the potential issues has been formulated, the next step is to explore the controversy. Advocates who want to present their position intelligently and to convince others to concur with them must be thoroughly familiar with the controversy. They must undertake an organized program of research so that they can explore fully all relevant aspects of the issues. Careful research will provide a firm foundation for the case they will build. And the potential issues formulated in the analysis of the controversy will help to give direction to their exploration of it. The processes of analyzing and exploring the controversy are interwoven, and advocates will move from one to the other as long as they are concerned with the proposition. They must be innovative and creative in their search for evidence and issues, and they must be coolly and dispassionately analytical in evaluating findings and planning further research. On the basis of their exploration, they may find it necessary to rephrase the issues they originally developed or to develop new issues, or even to revise the proposition. Research includes the process of reading and learning about the issues pertinent to the proposition and case building, but it is also the process of finding evidence, the "raw material" of debate, and organizing it for use in supporting arguments, issues, positions, and cases.

In formal debate, a restatement of the proposition cannot be done unilaterally; it requires the consent of all parties concerned. While advocates may interpret the proposition, they are obliged to use it as their starting point and focus for debate. The intercollegiate debater, the trial attorney, and other advocates often must debate a proposition not subject to revision. In informal debate in government and business, advocates—for persuasive purposes—often attempt to change the wording and meaning of the proposition unilaterally. For example, opponents of

---

Miniglossary

Blog   Literally "Web Logs," blogs began as a sort of online diary. They are websites or pages containing regular postings by authors and may include invited comments or articles by readers and guests.

Brainstorming   A method of shared problem solving in which all members of a group spontaneously contribute ideas. Individuals may use brainstorming by rapidly generating a variety of possible solutions.

Boolean Search Operators   The words *and, or, not,* and *near* when used to define the relationships between keywords in a web search using a search engine.

Brief   An organized set of prepared arguments with supporting evidence.

Card   Debate jargon for a single item of quoted material used in support of an argumentative claim.

RSS (Really Simple Syndication)   A format for delivering regularly changing web content.

Search engine   A computer program that works to retrieve and prioritize information within a computer system.

Think tanks   Groups of experts who conduct research and prepare reports in support of their inquiry and advocacy concerning issues of various concerns including public and governmental policy, business, science, and education.

Wikis   The term "wiki" is Hawaiian for *quick*. Wikipedia is the most famous. Groups of readers contribute to the development of materials, including contribution of content as well as editing.

---

abortion prefer to speak of the "right to life," and supporters of euthanasia prefer to state their proposal as "death with dignity" rather than as "mercy killing." In parliamentary debate the proposition may be amended by a simple majority vote; in many conference and discussion situations, the problem may be revised by informal action. In any event advocates continually explore the issues and revise the case on the basis of new information.

A systematic process of gathering and organizing information should proceed through a series of steps, keeping in mind that the road forward may require some steps back. First, the debaters must consider what they already know about the topic and generate lists of interpretations and subtopics. This step includes self-reflection and brainstorming. The second step is to read and learn about the topic. Next, debaters gather evidence, and finally, they organize what they have found.

I. REVIEWING AND GENERATING IDEAS

Remember that research begins with a systematic review of what you already know. Debate propositions usually focus on issues of important and timely controversy, so it is rare that they are completely unknown to the academic student debater. It is worthwhile to generate lists of topics, issues, stories, and known information about the topic(s) to begin the process of investigation. Such a process is helped by interaction with others, leading to the process of brainstorming.

Traditionally advocates try to develop cases by a careful, orderly, deliberate, logical process. Although the case they ultimately present must be logically sound, advocates sometimes find it advantageous to shorten the logical processes while gathering ideas for their case. Sometimes the solution to a problem is found by means of an "intuitive leap," a "hunch," a "lucky break," an "inspiration," or "serendipity." The advocate might simply happen to look into an obscure reference and make a critical inference or find exactly the piece of evidence needed to complete a chain of reasoning. The advocate might consider a seemingly improbable plan "just for the fun of it" and find that it meets his or her needs perfectly. Or the advocate might follow up an apparently irrelevant lead and uncover an important precedent, or consider an impractical proposal that will lead to a highly practical solution.

A dramatic example of how one may use inferences to make a creative leap from sketchy data occurred when an inference reader in the CIA was assigned to read native-language newspapers of a hostile regime. The reader noted that a small town's soccer team, perennial losers, suddenly began winning games and catapulted to the top of their league. At the inference reader's urging, an overflight was made of the town, revealing a nuclear installation. The regime had carefully camouflaged the installation but had forgotten that its technicians would notably improve the town's soccer team. Thus skilled inference reading revealed an important secret.

It is for the express purpose of uncovering ideas that might otherwise be ignored or delayed that the advocate uses **brainstorming**: a method of shared problem solving in which all members of a group spontaneously contribute ideas. Individuals also may use brainstorming by rapidly generating a variety of possible solutions. Many situations arise in which it may be profitable to use brainstorming: in defining terms or discovering issues, in finding materials for an argument, in connection with the problems of evidence or reasoning, and in building the case. Although brainstorming is not a substitute for the ways of dealing with problems considered in other chapters, it is a supplement that can help in many situations.

In a typical brainstorming session the participants make a deliberate effort to create an informal atmosphere in which everyone is encouraged to contribute and no one is permitted to criticize. They are usually most successful when following certain guidelines; the inset on page 213 summarizes the process.

Brainstorming is often deceptively simple—the ideas generated may evoke the comment that "anyone could have thought of that." This is often true. The point is that, in many cases, no one had thought of the idea earlier, and perhaps no one would have thought of that particular idea had it not been for the brainstorming session. Many of the ideas that emerge in brainstorming sessions are pure "fluff." However, if only one important idea evolves that otherwise might never have been considered, the time has been well spent.

One group of college students debating a "national program of public work for the unemployed" found early in the season that their affirmative

Guidelines for Brainstorming

1. *Limit the size of the group.* Brainstorming has been found to work better in small groups. Fifteen is usually considered to be the maximum workable size, and groups with as few as two or three members have been effective. It is even possible for an individual to brainstorm alone.

2. *Limit the time devoted to a brainstorming session.* Because the objective of brainstorming is to produce a large number of ideas and to avoid any critical evaluation during the session, it is usually desirable to limit a session to one hour or less. Many profitable sessions have been limited to between 20 and 40 minutes.

3. *Announce the problem in advance.* The person calling the brainstorming session should state the problem he or she wants the group to consider, either at the start of the session or a day or two in advance.

4. *Encourage all participants to contribute.* Because the objective is to secure the maximum possible number of ideas, everyone should participate. The leader can encourage contributions by creating a friendly, informal atmosphere. Participants should not only originate ideas but also modify and extend ideas presented by others.

5. *Don't follow any organized pattern.* Whereas traditional discussion follows a careful pattern of reflective thinking, brainstorming deliberately follows no pattern. The objective is to provide an atmosphere for the trigger effect, in which an idea, even a bad or irrelevant one, once expressed, may trigger a good idea.

6. *Don't permit any criticism or evaluation of ideas.* Because criticism at this stage tends to discourage contributions and decreases the possibility of the trigger effect, the leader must suppress criticism and strive to maintain an atmosphere in which everyone feels free to contribute.

7. *Record all ideas.* In the most widely used method, two or three members of the group write ideas on a blackboard as rapidly as they are expressed. Other methods include the "idea tree"—whereby a short pole is set in the center of the table and participants write out their ideas and attach them to the "tree" with adhesive tape—and the "cracker barrel"—whereby a basket is placed on the table and participants write their ideas on pieces of paper and toss them into the "barrel." Whichever method is used, all ideas should be recorded and forwarded to the person or group responsible for evaluation.

8. *Subject all ideas to rigorous evaluation.* Only when the brainstorming session is over and the ideas have been recorded in some usable form should they be subjected to thorough evaluation. Sometimes the ideas are duplicated and sent to the participating individuals for their evaluation. In many cases they are forwarded to a policy-making group or to the individual responsible for making decisions for screening and testing. The ideas gathered during brainstorming may serve as springboards for concepts that will be developed more fully during evaluation.

teams were having difficulty with their plan, which called for a massive program of urban renewal to provide jobs. Their negative opponents were defeating the plan by pointing out that few of the unemployed had the skills necessary for construction work. The debaters held a brainstorming session from which evolved the idea that the affirmative plan did not have to call for construction work. Then they proceeded to develop a new plan that called for

---

Questions to Ask in Locating References

1. *Who is concerned with the proposition?* Persons and organizations concerned with a problem might include those with an academic interest in it, those interested in the potential influence of the proposition, and even those currently unwilling to take a public stand on the problem. For example, in seeking information on a "higher education" topic, the answer to the question "Who is concerned with the proposition?" might include the various associations of educators, economists, political scientists, businesspeople, labor organizations, and organizations in other related fields. The scholarly associations and their journals seldom take an official position for or against legislation, but their journals contain important articles about contemporary problems in the area of their special interest. The education journals, in particular, would yield a number of significant articles on this proposition.

2. *Who is interested in securing the adoption of the proposition?* The answer to this question will often lead to one of the most prolific sources of information. A search for information on "higher education" would lead an advocate to the Department of Education, for example, which took the lead in presenting the administration's arguments in favor of the proposition.

3. *Who is interested in preventing the adoption of the proposition?* The answer will often lead to another prolific source of information. The advocate interested in "higher education" might find, for example, that the National Association of Manufacturers published a good deal of material opposed to the proposition.

---

conservation, service, and maintenance work that unskilled persons could easily perform. This plan might have evolved by some other means, of course, but this particular group of advocates was unable to develop an effective plan until they brainstormed the problem.

An excellent place to start when brainstorming and beginning research on a CEDA/NDT resolution is the topic paper and surrounding discussions produced during the topic selection process. These papers are readily accessible through the CEDA forums (http://www.cedadebate.org/forum/index.php?board=135.0). The topic paper reflects the brainstorming and research already done by others and provides a bibliography of primary sources relevant to the proposition. The forums also record the community brainstorming and discussions guiding topic selection and wording.

II. THE RESEARCH PROCESS

In evidence-based team topic policy debating, the ultimate goal of having files filled with evidence (statistics, research-based expert conclusions, expert testimony and examples, and more) begins with brainstorming and reviewing prior knowledge, and then proceeds through some general background reading designed to enable the debaters to gain an overview and general knowledge about the topic. For debaters preparing for nonevidence-based debates, such as academic parliamentary debates, debaters brainstorm to generate lists of possible debate propositions, and prepare by conducting ongoing research at the level of reading and learning about the topic.

Whether in the library or elsewhere, research today generally begins on a computer. Online research through Internet sources and databases can be productive, and libraries generally have online research capabilities, which often can be accessed from remote sites. But one way or another, advocates are well advised to turn to the library for their first sources of material. Because library, computer facilities, resources, physical arrangements, and loan policies vary enormously, advocates are well advised to familiarize themselves with their library's collections and organization so that subsequent searches for information will be purposeful and effective. Librarians are usually eager to assist individuals doing serious research and can provide valuable aid.

A. Background Material

Gather background material to give you direction and help you learn about your topic. Encyclopedias and dictionaries, including Wikipedia, can provide a good start. The free online English dictionaries, http://www.yourdictionary.com and http://dictionary.reference.com/, provide excellent resources and services including definitions, thesaurus entries, spelling, pronunciation, and etymologies. The *Oxford English Dictionary* and *Oxford Reference* are also available online, as is *Merriam-Webster's Collegiate Dictionary*. The objective of the researchers in this stage is not to gather proof for argumentation, but to learn about the terms and issues relevant to the proposition and develop ideas about their future research. Find relevant resource materials in the reference section of your library, and test out various combinations of keywords across different search platforms. Exploration usually begins with the acquisition of general information on the problem. As the advocate acquires some general knowledge of the problem, he or she is in a position to develop more specific lines of inquiry and to seek more specialized information.

At this point in the research process, general search engines such as Google, Yahoo, Bing, and Ask (this is not a complete list!) are useful to guide one to sources providing background information about the topic under consideration. While it should not be considered as a source of quoted material, Wikipedia (http://en.wikipedia.org/wiki/Main_Page) can also provide guidance.

B. Books

The richest, deepest, and most complete analysis of topic areas is likely to be available in scholarly books about the subject. Books have the advantage of depth, and also may provide extensive bibliographies leading the researcher to more valuable sources of information and evidence. Because they are broad in their coverage, books may offer excellent means of gaining general knowledge about the topic. Of course books, compared to many other sources of evidence, may be long and cumbersome to digest and navigate. In addition, as the process of researching and writing a book and having it published and disseminated may be quite time-consuming, books will probably not provide the most current information available on the topic. Finally, books may be difficult to access than some other sources. While some books are available in electronic form online, such accessibility is far from universal, and thus, the researcher must rely on availability in their local library or through the more time-consuming process of interlibrary loan.

Use catalogs to find books. Every library will have its own catalog, and you may wish to access the Library of Congress catalog (http://catalog.loc.gov/) to help you discover relevant books. Another excellent resource is WorldCat (http://www.worldcat.org/), self-described as the world's largest network of library resources. In addition, you may visit commercial online bookstores (Amazon and Barnes & Noble are two such vendors) to identify books and even read reviews then find links to other related books. Once you have secured some relevant books, they can lead you to more. Follow the footnotes and seek out the materials listed in the bibliographies of relevant books.

C. General Periodicals

General reading periodicals may include newspapers and magazines. Use indexes, databases, and specialized search engines to seek out periodicals. Because advocates are most often concerned with a proposition of current interest, they may expect that information relating to the proposition will appear from time to time in the daily newspapers, weekly newsmagazines, and monthly magazines. Online availability makes information dissemination possible immediately. In fact, in some cases debaters may wish to subscribe to e-mail delivery of newspapers or relevant bulletins, or RSS feeds (discussed later). Resourceful advocates constantly scan current publications for articles related to their problem. Major newspapers include the *New York Times*, the *Washington Post*, the *Wall Street Journal*, the *Guardian*, and the *Financial Times* (of London). Weekly reading should include newsmagazines like *Time*, *Newsweek*, *U.S. News & World Report*, and the *Economist*. If the proposition is related to a particular field, advocates should add the special publications of that area to their research list. For example, if they are concerned with a business problem, they should read the *Wall Street Journal*, *Business Week*, *Fortune*, the *AFL-CIO News*, and the *Monthly Labor Review*, together with some of the trade papers and newsletters of the specific area under consideration.

Advocates should make a special point of reading publications with different editorial policies. Much of their opponents' evidence and argument may come from publications with which they disagree. If they study this information in its original source, they will be in a better position to deal with it in the debate.

Most major journals and periodicals are available (at least in part) on the Internet. In addition, a number of quality journals are only available online. The list of available sources is practically endless. For example:

The Daily Beast/ Newsweek	http://www.thedailybeast.com/ newsweek.html
CNN	http://www.cnn.com/
New York Times	http://www.nytimes.com/
Salon	http://www.salon.com/
Slate	http://slate.msn.com/
The Economist	http://www.economist.com/
The New Republic	http://www.tnr.com/
Time Magazine	http://www.time.com/time/
Truthout	http://www.truthout.org/
U.S. News & World Report	http://www.usnews.com/
Wall Street Journal	http://www.wsj.com/
Washington Post	http://www.washingtonpost.com/

A more productive way to locate periodical information is through a subject or keyword search through one or more of your library's general indexes. These indexes will guide you to a wide range of newspapers, magazines, journals, e-journals, and other sources. There are quite a few available services, but they generally require membership for access, so you will have to investigate your own access. Even when index services overlap, they each have their own unique collections and idiosyncrasies. It is wise to conduct a variety of searches in different locations. Some very good indexes include Academic OneFile, InfoTrac, Lexis-Nexis, NewsBank, Alternative Press Index, World News Connection, Wilson Web, and EBSCOhost (various collections, including Readers' Guide Full Text and Readers' Guide Retrospective), ProQuest Research Library, Public Affairs Information Service (PAIS) International, LegalTrac, OCLC FirstSearch, and Expanded Academic ASAP. To locate what your library has to offer, visit the library's web page, locate the list of databases and indexes, and browse. The list above is only exemplary, it is far from exhaustive. In some cases, these tools will enable a "one-stop" research facilitator, providing links to full text immediately available online, and citation functions, providing helpful citation formatting.

More specific indexes are available to guide you to more focused discipline-specific materials and scholarly journals. Scholarly publications are distinct from publications offering substantive or general interest news and are more credible and usually more specific. One can often recognize a scholarly journal in a number of ways. Often its title includes the name of a specific professional organization (*Journal of the American Medical Association*) and may even include the word "journal." Articles are likely to include an abstract, which is a descriptive summary of the article contents at the beginning of the article, and they will have an academic appearance without exciting photographs or color graphics. They will always cite their references in the form of footnotes and endnotes, and will list a number of editors and reviewers. Articles in scholarly journals are "peer reviewed" and competitively selected for publication. They therefore represent extensive and high-quality research and careful evaluation. This helps to ensure a higher level of credibility and believability than other periodicals. Numerous field-specific indexes, like Communications & Mass Media Complete and Family & Society Studies Worldwide may guide researchers to scholarly journals in their areas of interest. Be sure to check your library for available indexes in the disciplines appropriate to your topic. General indexes for scholarly publications include JSTOR: The Scholarly Journal Archive, Google Scholar, and ERIC (Educational Resources Information Center).

D. Journals

Journals are academic and professional publications that are published at regular intervals. They are generally peer reviewed. The peer review process means that materials are edited and reviewed by experts and then competitively selected for publication. This process ensures a high level of credibility and specificity regarding the subject matter and conclusions. While they may be difficult to read, as they are prepared in scientific academic style, they will be useful for locating believable conclusions and data about the topic area. Peer-reviewed research is also published in proceedings of scholarly or professional meetings and sometimes at the websites of think tanks, government agencies, interest group, and other locations. They may be best located by use of indexes available through your library, including (but certainly not limited to) JSTOR, ERIC, and discipline-specific databases and indexes. In addition, Google Scholar, and other special Internet search engines can help to locate scholarly and professional publications.

E. Government Sources

Access government documents. Much useful research, information gathering, policy analysis, and debate sponsored by and conducted by the U.S. federal government are easily available and extremely useful to the academic debater. By some measures, the U.S. federal government is the largest publisher in the world. By law, government publications must be made available to you (unless classified), and most are available free online. To begin the process of researching government documents, use the Archives Library Information Center at http://www.archives.gov/research/alic/reference/govt-docs.html, and the very accessible U.S. federal government information portal (http://www.usa.gov/). Government documents include the debates and hearings held by Congress, white papers and studies commissioned by the federal government, and much more data, research, and opinion available and relevant to the debater.

F. Databases

Seek out databases. Databases collect information from various locations and organize them for access and use. The debater is most interested in those databases, accessible through libraries, in which publications and sources of information are organized for easy access. A particularly helpful database for academic debaters is CQ Researcher Plus Archive. CQ stands for *Congressional Quarterly*. This source provides excellent information by collecting reports about issues of public policy and presenting them in a useful and readable format.

G. Think Tanks

Access **think tanks**. These are groups of experts who conduct research and prepare reports in support of their inquiry and advocacy concerning issues of various concerns including public and governmental policy, business, science, and education. For some think tanks, their mission is primarily research; others are unabashed promoters and lobbyists. They may be funded as nonprofit organizations, in which case they avoid political affiliation, or privately. Some well-known think tanks (certainly not an exhaustive list), categorized by their political inclinations are:

Conservative
- American Enterprise Institute
- Claremont Institute
- Competitive Enterprise Institute
- Project for the New American Century
- Heritage Foundation

Liberal
- Brookings Institution
- Center on Budget and Policy Priorities
- Center for American Progress
- Center for Economic and Policy Research
- Center for Progressive Reform

Libertarian
- Cato Institute
- Ayn Rand Institute

Nonpartisan
- Aspen Institute
- Atlantic Council of the United States
- Center for Strategic and International Studies
- Council on Foreign Relations
- Woodrow Wilson International Center for Scholars

H. The World Wide Web

Search the Web. Many students are tempted to *begin* their research with an Internet search. This is ill-advised. The World Wide Web, or the Internet, is the cumulative collection of images, text, video, and other materials that have been organized and stored on computers called web servers by a wide range of individuals, businesses, and organizations. The output of any keyword search is likely to be huge. Web pages or websites range from collections of high-quality research materials posted by nonprofit think tanks and academic associations to social networking sites, personal diaries, and commercial materials. Much useful information is available to the web searcher, but the challenge (and it is a huge challenge) is to efficiently locate and identify material of worth and to critically evaluate its quality. A debater accessing an article in a scholarly journal knows the article has been carefully reviewed and edited and represents some level of reliability and credibility. This is not so for a website. In this section, we will consider how to search the Web, how to assess the credibility of a website, and some dangers to avoid.

Searching the Web begins with a **search engine**. This is a computer program that works to retrieve and prioritize information within a computer system, in this case, the Internet. There are literally hundreds of available search engines; as of 2012, 83 percent of users rely on Google for their Internet searches.[1] A useful source of special search engines that will guide you to more specific information than general web searches is Colossus, available at http://www.searchenginecolossus.com/Academic.html. This is a valuable tool also available without library access. To use a search engine, begin with a keyword search. Enter relevant terms into the search space. Use the "Boolean search operators" AND and OR to limit your search in different ways. For example, Obama AND "gay marriage" will find material that contains references to both President Obama and to gay marriage; using OR will find materials with references either to the president or to gay marriage, or to both the president and gay marriage. Please note that without the quotation marks, the above search will also turn up references to Obama and gay, and to Obama and marriage. Many engines will also allow use of NOT as an operator. This typically is offered as BUT NOT or AND NOT. For example, Obama BUT NOT gay marriage will turn up materials including references to President Obama, but excluding any materials that also reference gay marriage. Another Boolean operator is the word NEAR. Obama NEAR Syria should turn up materials in which Obama appears within 10 or 25 (depending on the search engine) words of Syria in the text of the article. Even more useful are the characters + (for the word AND), − (for the word NOT), and "" (to enclose a phrase).

Websites are not equal in their credibility. Here are some types of websites:

- Personal home pages. These are developed and posted by individuals. They may include family pictures and hobbies, but they may also offer opinions and even academic or research papers, resumes, and other informative

---

1. Purcell, K., Brenner, J., & Rainie, L, *Search Engine Use 2012*, Mar. 9, 2012. Retrieved from http://www.pewinternet.org/~/media/Files/Reports/2012/PIP_Search_Engine_Use_2012.pdf.

materials. Personal home pages may include blogs (weblogs, or journals) or social networking sites.

- Special interest sites. These may be posted by clubs, community organizations, or special interest groups. They are inherently biased, as they are created to promote or facilitate their interest. For example, they may promote a political issue (gun control), and community initiative (a proposed dog park), or a hobby (paintballing).

- Professional sites. Such websites are official functions of professional organizations, institutions, or individuals. They may provide useful information about the work of the web poster, and may offer quality research, advice, information, and opinion. While they may exist to promote a for-profit business, the information at the site is free and offered as a service.

- Commercial sites. A large number of websites are advertisements, portals for online sales, or catalogs. These include giant online businesses (Amazon.com), brick and mortar businesses with web presence (Barnes & Noble), and at-home entrepreneurship.

- Publications. Newspapers, journals, and magazines generally publish online in addition to their hard copy publication, and some journalistic publications are strictly online (e-zines). For many, the Web is simply another medium for their credible journalism. However, anyone can publish his or her own material to the Web. The line between a personal home page and a respected blog is a fine one.

- Wikis. The term "wiki" is Hawaiian for *quick*. Wikipedia is the most famous. Groups of readers contribute to the development of materials, including contributions of content as well as editing. They can be extremely helpful in understanding a concept, but are not necessarily credible as sources of qualified information, research, or opinion.

- Blogs. Literally "Web Logs," blogs began as a sort of online diary. They are websites or pages containing regular postings by authors and may include invited comments or articles by readers and guests. They offer a wide range of content from rants of angry readers to interesting, credible, and relevant observations by experts. None, however, offer substantial editing or reviewing. Blogs range from personal blogs (including "microblogs" like Twitter) to corporate, subject, and media blogs. They may be attached to news publications to offer opportunities for reader's comments or stand alone as essays. Recall that these sources, even when the author's are credible, are seldom verifiable. They do not offer very productive material for debate evidence, but can help the researcher looking for background and general information.

- RSS (Rich Site Summary or Really Simple Syndication) is a format for delivering regularly changing web content. Many news-related sites, weblogs, and other online publishers syndicate their content as an RSS feed to whoever wants it. It's an easy way for you to keep up with news and information that's important to you, and helps you avoid the conventional methods of browsing or searching for information on websites. Now the content you want can be delivered directly to you without cluttering your inbox with e-mail messages. This content is called a "feed." RSS is facilitated by most web browsers.

How does one navigate this wide range of varied information? Some standards for all evidence have been explored in Chapter 8. Some things to look for include: Is the author of the information clearly identified? What can you learn about her or him? Are the author's credentials sufficient to lend credibility to the subject? Is the corporate author or sponsoring organization clearly identified? What is their likely bias or reputation regarding the topic? Are the date of publication and the date of the information available? Is it current? Is there a list of works cited? What type of website is it? Are they selling a product or service? Can you learn anything relevant about the site from its Web address? For example, the last three letters will indicate the following: .edu (education sites), .gov (government sites), .org (organization sites), .com (commercial sites), and .net (network infrastructures).

Finally, do not assume that because a website looks professional that it is credible. Graphics are easy to navigate, and the Internet is accessible to everyone, regardless of integrity. For example, if you click on http://www.wto.org/, you will visit the legitimate website of the World Trade Organization (WTO). If you visit http://www.gatt.org/, you will visit a sham website that has been made to look like the WTO site, but offers subtle (and not so subtle) false stories in an attempt to ironically criticize the WTO. If you happened onto the sham site without any other knowledge about the WTO, you would read stories that, among other things, promote formalized slavery. While the fake site is a clever criticism of the WTO, it is not factually representative.

I. Direct Communication

Information may also be obtained through interviews and correspondence. The answers to the three questions in the inset on page 214 will suggest people the advocate should try to interview or correspond with.

Caution: Interviews and correspondence will provide both leads to evidence and evidence that is admissible in the debate. It is important to know the difference between the two types.

1. Interviews.   Interviews with subject-matter experts can be valuable sources of information. The value of any interview depends to a considerable extent on our advance preparation; carefully planned preliminary research will enable us to ask meaningful questions. The student debater is in an excellent position to secure interviews with faculty members. Furthermore, interviews often can be arranged with members of Congress, business executives, labor leaders, and others who have special knowledge of the subject of the debate proposition.

Consider a hypothetical case: In the course of an interview with Dr. Hamilton, an economics professor on your campus, you might ask about a study that your opponents cited and that you found particularly difficult to refute. If Dr. Hamilton replies, "The Back Bay Study is seriously flawed because it failed to consider ...," you have a *lead*. You can't quote Dr. Hamilton's statement in a debate because, within the limitations of academic debate, you cannot prove you are quoting this professor accurately. At the first opportune moment, ask Dr. Hamilton, "How can we document the flaws in this study?" If Dr. Hamilton replies by citing a scholarly article in an economics journal, and if your examination of the article provides a detailed statement of the flaws in the Back Bay Study, you are covered. By citing the article to which the economics professor gave you a lead, you now have evidence that is admissible in the debate.

There are many other important interviews the advocate can study. Radio and television stations often present interviews with national or world figures on problems of contemporary importance. (*Meet the Press, Hardball,* and *Face the Nation* are examples.) Magazines also often publish interviews in which prominent persons are *quizzed* about important problems; these can serve as important sources of information. Websites and blogs offer interviews as well as personal statements by noted experts. Note that the same distinction between leads and admissible evidence applies here. An interview in a magazine clearly is admissible evidence; it is available in the public record and may be used without any question on that score. However, your recollection of what the secretary of the treasury said on *Meet the Press* last Sunday is just that—your recollection. As such it constitutes a lead and nothing more. Of course, if the Monday newspapers quote the secretary's statement, you have admissible evidence. Otherwise you must request a transcript of the program, and you cannot use the evidence until the transcript arrives.

In academic debate, convention wisely requires that the advocate document evidence from sources available in the public domain.

2. Correspondence. Correspondence, including written communication and e-mails, is often a fruitful source of information, but NOT evidence. A helpful starting point in the search for information is the list of associations and societies in the United States published in Associations Unlimited. Hundreds of organizations are listed, ranging from "Abolish Capital Punishment, American League to" through "Zoologists, American Society of." Most of these organizations, as well as many other special interest groups, will respond to thoughtful letters or e-mail correspondence asking intelligent questions in the area of their concern.

Often advocates will discover organizations that strongly support or oppose the proposition under consideration. Some of these groups maintain elaborate propaganda agencies. Through correspondence advocates may obtain press releases, special papers, data sheets, pamphlets, booklets, and other materials not ordinarily available through libraries. Here, too, it is important to note the distinction between a lead and admissible evidence. For example, suppose that, in response to your request for a transcript of the House Hearings on Unemployment, your representative not only sends you a copy but adds a personal note stating, "I feel these hearings are unnecessarily gloomy. My view is that we will see a substantial drop in unemployment beginning in the next quarter." The hearings, of course, are admissible evidence. But the letter is not because, within the limitations of academic debate, it is impossible to authenticate the letter. It is,

---

Sources of Debate Materials

- Background Materials
- Books
- General Periodicals
- Journals
- Government Sources
- Databases
- Think Tanks
- The World Wide Web
- Direct Communication

---

however, a valuable lead. Call your representative immediately and ask whether the prediction can be documented. If your representative refers you to a recent think-tank study that has gone unnoticed in the press, you may—when you get a copy of the study—have valuable admissible evidence. Do not quote an e-mail or personal correspondence that is not published in a manner so as to be publically available to all participants in the debate.

III. READING WITH A PURPOSE

Advocates can make brainstorming work by preparing a carefully drafted outline of the ideas and sources suggested in brainstorming. From this list they should develop a bibliography to use in research and a list of publications to monitor. While doing research and monitoring, they can revise and refine the bibliography and list of monitored publications. This process of brainstorming, research, and revising will continue until the first debate, which will often trigger further brainstorming and research that will continue as long as the proposition is debated.

When students are asked to monitor the daily press or weekly newsmagazines, they sometimes protest, "But I don't have time to read all those newspapers and magazines." Perhaps they do not have time to read an entire newspaper every day, but when they read for the purpose of finding information on a specific problem, they do not need to read the entire paper. It takes only a few minutes to scan the bulky *New York Times* to determine whether it contains an article on, say, inflation, unemployment, population stabilization, or an international conflict.

Whether research is conducted in through an online index, database, or search engine, effective use of *keywords* is critical to productive gathering of information. The advocate must be familiar with the jargon of the relevant field and the workings of the index or search aid to know what keywords to look for, how to combine them, and how to broaden or narrow a search. The researcher also must become familiar with the language used by those writing about the controversy. As the researcher becomes more familiar with the relevant literature, he or she will know better how to limit searches by dates and types of materials and thus how to more efficiently zero in on relevant data.

Try to map out the argument as best you can before you start researching. Keep a physical map of it (either on the computer or written down), and add to it as your research progresses. The point is to be aware of all the different components of the argument, so you recognize a card when you see it. Develop a list of keywords or phrases that go along with your argument. Try to determine if the literature uses any other words or phrases interchangeably. This will give you different options when you are looking for articles. Copy and investigate the footnotes. Sometimes you might randomly find a title that looks interesting. Or, if you find some helpful information, and there is a footnote for it, look it up as it will probably help you. Search for similar articles by the same author. Find their website, or the website of the publication they write for or organization they represent. Or, just Google their name and explore. But if an author writes about an issue, odds are there is more of their work somewhere.

IV. READING CRITICALLY

More literature is available on any contemporary, controversial problem than advocates could possibly read in the time available. Research, then, must be planned for both breadth and discrimination, so that time is used efficiently. Advocates must seek out sources representative of the various points of view related to the problem in order to understand possible lines of argument. Because much writing on any contemporary problem is likely to be a restatement of other writings, or a superficial treatment, discriminating advocates will seek out original sources, articles in scholarly or professional journals, writings by qualified authorities, and reports by competent and objective persons, giving preference to sources with established reputations for accuracy.

An article on nuclear weapons appearing in the *Bulletin of the Atomic Scientists*, for example, is more likely to contain accurate and significant information than is an article on the same subject in the Sunday supplement of a local newspaper. The full text of the secretary of state's speech on a foreign policy problem may contain some carefully phrased qualifications that are omitted in the brief summary appearing in a newsmagazine.

Advocates cannot read everything written about the problem. So they must be critical in their reading to select representative, authoritative, accurate, and significant material for careful, detailed study.

V. RECORDING MATERIALS

In the early exploration of a problem, advocates should adopt a systematic method of recording materials so they may readily use the information assembled from many different sources. Advocates may use any method—index cards, legal pads, filing cabinets, computer data files—that their needs dictate and their resources permit. Many advocates develop a portable library that they can take with them on the campaign plane or into the boardroom, the courtroom, or the classroom. Intercollegiate debaters developed a successful method of recording materials by using thousands of file folders (or dozens of accordion-style expandable files) stuffed with letter-sized briefs, assembled in boxes or tubs carried with the aid of hand trucks or carts. Now, these substantial files are generally stored in electronic form, via word files, dropbox, or the "Cloud." Although the advocate may use only a relatively few briefs in any one debate, experienced CEDA/NDT debaters find it desirable to have thousands of pieces of information immediately available to meet the many possible arguments presented by their opponents.

At one time intercollegiate debaters stored their material on index cards, filed in recipe boxes or long file drawers. With the advent of easily accessible photo-copying, it became more efficient to organize page-sized **briefs** into file folders and expandable files. Now, these briefs are electronic, however, they often still refer to one item of information as a **card** even though it is generally a quotation or statistic read from a full-sized sheet of paper. As you conduct your research, your goal is to accumulate *cards*, and to organize cards so as to construct argument briefs.

How much evidence does one need in applied debating? The short answer is: whatever it takes to win the argument. In a class debate a few dozen well-chosen evidence cards may be sufficient. By contrast, some lawsuits have required literally truckloads of evidence. Most advocates prefer to have too much rather than too little evidence available to them. In academic debate, if some seldom-used evidence becomes critical, you must either have it with you or lose whatever issue the evidence might win for you if it were available.

While researching and reading source material, advocates should have a system on which to record (1) all information that may help in supporting their stand on the proposition and (2) all information that may be of help to opponents. Begin by organizing cards.

There are three parts to a card. The tag (a one sentence explanation of the card), the citation or cite (the source of where the card comes from, including author and publication), and the card itself. Make sure to get the full or complete citation. This includes the author, where it was published, the date of publication, the volume or issue number, and the website if it is online. If you are referencing a book, include the editor (if there is one). If it is one chapter of a book, include the chapter name as well as the book name.

Make sure to get the person's qualifications. Newspapers will often just have a staff writer, which is their qualification. But in books or journals, those people usually have credentials. Even if the credentials are not listed, search for them online. Do a Google search for the name, or look in *Who's Who*. If five minutes of looking saves you a debate because your key evidence comes from a Ph.D. professor of physics at Cornell University instead of some dude from the *Pittsburgh Post Gazette*, it is well worth it.

If you are on an Internet source with no apparent date, look closely on the website. Often there is a copyright symbol at the bottom and a year, indicating when the material was last updated or "published." If nothing is available after rigorous searching, use the Date of Access (DOA). Make it clear in the citation that the date referenced is the date that the material was accessed, and not necessarily when it was published.

Put brackets around the beginning and end of the material to be quoted in the card. This will help you process it later. If you are "cutting" cards on the computer, when you are finished cutting the card, paste the citation above it immediately. Do not put a tag that the card does not support. It is better to acknowledge the card for what it is, and connect it with other cards that together tell a story. That is much better than trying to claim that one card says the whole thing, and then you look like a fool in a debate. If you are cutting cards from a hard copy source (not on computer), you have to process them, which involves printing up a list of citations, cutting out the cards, and pasting or taping them to the appropriate cites. This is called *processing*. Make sure to process your evidence shortly after you cut it.

You should tag your evidence as soon as you cut it. Don't just leave it with brackets on the side. If you are on the computer, you can type a tag right after you cut the card. If you are reading a printed source, write the tag to the side. You still have the option to change the tag before you print or block the card (adding it to a brief), but having some sort of tag there is necessary to categorize and sort.

VI. ORGANIZING MATERIALS

Not only must advocates have a wealth of information, but that information must be instantly available to them. The method considered here is used by intercollegiate debaters, but it may be adapted to any type of advocacy.

First, the advocate should classify information as *affirmative* or *negative*, and classify the type of argument (disadvantage, case/solvency, counterplan, and so on), perhaps indicating these classifications by an abbreviation placed on each card or by different colors of cards. Next, the advocate should classify the cards according to the issues developed. The affirmative file will consist of the issues necessary to develop the affirmative case together with the evidence necessary to establish the case in the first affirmative speech and to defend and extend the case in the second affirmative speech and rebuttals.

A system of indexing the files should be developed to enable the advocate to locate any brief quickly. After evidence has been "cut" (tagged and marked) and "processed" (attached to its relevant citation), it is ready to be "sorted." Here, you go back to your map of the argument or file. Make sure you have categories for as much of the argument as possible. Make separate piles for every category (even for different subcategories), and organize your big stack of cards into each pile. Sometimes a card will not fit under any category, and you have to create a new one. It is important to physically see the file laid out so you can tell if there are any holes to fill. Once the file is sorted, you are ready to block.

Blocking is the creation of argument briefs, prepared and evidenced arguments ready to be presented in a debate. You may wish to begin by putting your name in the top left corner. Put the title of the block in the top center of the page. Put the name of the file on the top right of the brief. Put your tag, cite, and card down on the page.

Make an index for the file on the top right, place the number for that page in the block. For instance, if it is the first piece of paper under a four-page impact extension block, put 1/4. If it is the second page in a six-page answers to block, put 2/6. Place the page number on the bottom right of the file. Do not number until you are certain the file is finished, or until you have produced an index.

The objective is to provide as many subheadings as necessary (separate files) while keeping related information together (within files and among groups of related files) to make essential information instantly available. Color coding may be used to indicate subdivisions, and highlighting and underlining will indicate "cards" (selected quoted material) and portions of cards with particularly important information. The examples shown here are drawn from the files of student debaters, but any advocate who must organize a large mass of data must develop some comparable system.

In some cases advocates will find that a given piece of information might appropriately be placed under more than one classification. Multiple cards recording the same information should be prepared and inserted in the proper places, with cross-references to other locations to avoid repetition.

Careful exploration of the problem is essential to intelligent advocacy. Reasonable and prudent people will give little time and less credence to advocates who don't seem to know what they're talking about. Debaters who thoroughly study the appropriate sources of information, carefully conduct their research, read purposefully and critically, record materials accurately, and organize effectively are taking an important step toward responsible and effective advocacy. Only well-prepared advocates can hope to gain and hold the attention of a critical audience, perform well against well-informed opponents, and secure a decision from reasonable judges.

EXERCISES

1. *Brainstorming.* Working in groups of five, brainstorm a list of causes and possible solutions to the problem of childhood obesity (or substitute any significant social issue; you may wish to brainstorm an issue for classroom debate). This should culminate in a "map" for your research.

2. Find one card from each of the seven sources of debate materials (excluding direct communication) relevant to issues identified in Exercise 1 (or identify a social issue and collect one relevant card from each type of source).

3. *Treasure hunt.* Find a recent book or scholarly article about the topic identified in Exercise 1 (or choose a topic of social importance). Use the bibliography to identify another source, go to that source, and find another relevant source in its bibliography. Continue until you have visited five sources.

4. Begin with a topic of social importance. Identify as many keywords and combinations of keywords as you can to guide your online research of the topic.

5. Begin with a topic of social importance. Locate one of the six types of websites relevant to the topic. Evaluate the quality of each as a source of debate information.

11

Arguing *For* the Proposition

Affirmative debaters support the proposition. Recall that presumption is a predisposition opposing the proposition. Presumption opposes the proposition for a number of reasons. These reasons include our natural skepticism to accepting a positively worded statement or new belief, our reluctance to expose ourselves to the risk of the unknown, and our inclination to find comfort in retaining the status quo until given reason not to. So before the debate, the negative side, because they oppose the proposition, enjoys the advantage of presumption. Put another way, the affirmative is behind. In order to overcome this presumption, the affirmative must fulfill the burden of proof by presenting a prima facie case for the proposition. That case is the subject of this chapter.

In this chapter on the affirmative case and in the next chapter on the negative case, we will begin with value propositions and conclude by considering policy propositions. You will notice that, in this chapter and the next, more space is devoted to policy debate than to value debate. The reason is simple: Most team topic debaters participate in policy debate. Also debating policies requires advocates to address issues of fact and value in addition to fundamental policy questions.

Team topic policy debate as now exemplified by debate at the NDT has been around since 1920 (the first NDT was in 1947). CEDA did not begin using value propositions until 1975 and adopted only policy topics beginning in spring 1995. Since the 1996–97 academic year CEDA and NDT have shared the same yearlong policy topic. Not surprisingly, given policy debate's 55-year lead, more research and writing have been done in the policy area. Lincoln–Douglas debaters sometimes use policy or quasipolicy topics, and parliamentary debaters also use a variety of types of topics, including policy ones.

The CEDA national proposition "Resolved: That United States military intervention to foster democratic government is appropriate in a post cold war world" is an excellent example of the blurring of the value–policy distinction.

Miniglossary

Advantages   The benefits or gains that the affirmative claims will result from adopting its plan, which must be shown to outweigh the disadvantages.

Application   In debating a proposition of value case; the measure of effect in accepting the value, or concrete implication of the value.

Attitudinal inherency   Suggests that attitudes prevent solution of the identified problem within the status quo.

Comparative advantage case   The affirmative argues that its plan will produce greater advantages than the status quo.

Criteria   The standard or the basis upon which a decision is to be made. A major issue in value debate; sometimes used in policy debate.

Intrinsic   A factor is intrinsic if it is embedded within the essential nature of a thing or is an inherent characteristic or consequence of the thing.

Impact   A substantial measure of importance.

Plan   The affirmative's method of solving the problems claimed in the justification as needs or harms. It must produce the advantages claimed by the affirmative.

Qualitative significance   The compelling nature of a harm as diminished quality of life or denial of some important value.

Quantitative significance   Numerical, observable, and concrete measure of the harm.

Structural inherency   Demonstrates that the harm is permanently built into the status quo; consists of law, court decisions that have the force of law, and societal structures.

Turnaround argument   Converting a negative's disadvantage into an affirmative advantage. In common usage any statement that one turns against the originator.

This *quasipolicy* proposition prompted most affirmative teams to use policy paradigms and in many cases to offer plans. Plans, as we will see, are a hallmark of policy debate. This is a clear example of debaters broadening their horizons and reaching out to previously untapped sources of argumentation theory.

Knowledgeable negative teams meeting such cases wisely responded by also turning to policy debate theory and offered disadvantages—which, as we will learn, are another hallmark of policy debate—as well as counterplans to the affirmative's case. One observer of CEDA debate in the early 1990s notes: "At those tournaments meeting the characterization of the national circuit virtually every round will feature an affirmative defending more or less specific policies … while the negative articulates equally specific [disadvantages]."[1] We can enrich

---

1. Kenneth Broda-Bahm, "Community Concepts of Argumentative Legitimacy: Challenging Norms in National-Circuit CEDA Debate," *Forensic of Pi Kappa Delta*, vol. 79, no. 3 (spring 1994), p. 30.

our knowledge of argumentation and debate if we draw on both value and policy paradigms and apply them as appropriate in our debates. In the real world of applied debate as well, we do not have the luxury of saying, "I do only value debate" or "I do only policy debate." As value debate tended to incorporate policy argumentation in the early 1990s, current policy debate practice relies heavily on critical and philosophical considerations of value.

In applied debate, we must be prepared to debate both value and policy or more likely to debate propositions in which both are interwoven. An understanding of both types of debate empowers us to play an effective role in the complex world of applied debate, where arbitrary distinctions between value and policy are not usually made.

We cannot intelligently and effectively debate the great issues of domestic or foreign policy without considering both value and policy. Nor can we use critical thinking to arrive at an individual decision (see Chapter 1) without considering both value and policy. Outside academic debate, of course, all of us will have occasion to debate both value and policy propositions as we apply the process of critical thinking to the problems of reasoned decision making.

I. OBJECTIVES OF THE AFFIRMATIVE CASE

Both value and policy debate are usually in the area of probability, not certainty, and time limitations—not only in academic debate but in informal debate as well—do not make it possible to introduce all the relevant evidence and arguments regarding any topic. The affirmative, therefore, is not required to establish its case as a matter of certainty. Such a degree of cogency is rarely attainable in life. Instead the affirmative has to establish a *prima facie case* that provides the highest possible degree of probability, giving those who render the decision *good reasons* to accept the resolution. For example, in debating the proposition "Resolved: That the American judicial system has overemphasized freedom of the press," the affirmative does not have to prove its position absolutely; it merely has to establish sufficient good reasons to justify the judges' accepting its position. In the same way, in debating the proposition "Resolved: That the United States should reduce substantially its military commitments to NATO member states," the affirmative is not required to establish its position as a certainty; it merely has to provide sufficient good reasons to justify the judges' accepting its position.

II. PROPOSITION OF VALUE AFFIRMATIVE CASES

As we saw in Chapter 6, in a debate on a proposition of value, the affirmative maintains that a certain belief, value, or fact is justified and that it conforms to the definition or criteria appropriate to evaluate the matter at hand. In developing the affirmative case on a proposition of value, the advocate needs to present a prima facie case, made up of argumentation in support of the stock issues.

Stock Issues: Proposition of Value

1. Definitive issues
   a. What are the definitions of the key terms?
   b. What are the criteria for the values?
2. Designative issues
   a. Do the facts correspond to the definitions?
   b. What are the applications of the values?

A. Requirement to Provide a Satisfactory Definition

As we saw in Chapter 7, advocacy of a proposition of value requires a reasonable definition of terms. In debating value propositions, definition is a stock issue essential to proving a prima facie case and is considered in that context here. Definition, however, involves more than providing definitions of the terms in the resolution. Definition provides the affirmative's interpretation of the meaning of the propositional statement.

In debating the proposition "Resolved: That federal government censorship is justified to defend the national interest of the United States," it was essential to define *censorship, justified, and national interest.* Our two military involvements in Iraq, and one in Afghanistan have provided an interesting variety of definitions. American correspondents, for the most part, have voluntarily cooperated with the U.S. government's *requests* not to report certain matters. British correspondents were *prohibited* from mentioning anything their government did not want mentioned, and this ban was enforced by harsh penalties. Other coalition governments had *even more stringent control* over their media. Clearly, there is a vast difference between these interpretations of censorship.

In debating the proposition "Resolved: That individual rights of privacy are more important than any other constitutional right," it was clearly necessary to define *rights of privacy.* Actually there is no explicitly identified constitutional right to privacy, yet in many cases the courts act as if there were. What is the best definition in these circumstances? For many years, the sex life of a political figure was considered to be a private matter. Times change, however, and President Clinton's sexual activities were extensively reported in the media before and during the impeachment proceedings. Almost everyone is in favor of privacy. Yet we recognize that the public interest requires some exceptions. What exceptions can you justify as part of your definition?

B. Requirement to Provide a Satisfactory Criterion

In debates on value propositions, the affirmative must provide a reasonable criterion for each of the value terms in the proposition and for the primary value defended. **Criteria** offer a measure of the values and a method of comparing competing values. The negative must also carefully consider the criterion offered by the affirmative and be ready either to offer a better criterion or to take advantage of any error of the affirmative.

In debating the proposition "Resolved: That American television has sacrificed quality for entertainment," it is essential for the affirmative to provide carefully considered criteria for the value term *quality*. How would one measure this term? If the criteria are properly chosen, they create a sound basis for the affirmative's case and greatly increase the affirmative's chances of winning the debate. But if the criteria are not well chosen, they open up opportunities for the negative to defeat the affirmative by providing better criteria or to turn the criteria against the affirmative by providing value objections.

C. Requirement to Provide Application

Here the affirmative must address the question "What is the application of this value?" **Application** is the measure of effect in accepting the value, or concrete implication of the value. If the value set out in the proposition is accepted, what will happen? In debating the proposition "Resolved: That increased restrictions on the civilian possession of handguns in the United States would be justified," the affirmative had to be prepared to demonstrate that increased restrictions would indeed be justified—that they would, for example, reduce crime. Reducing crime is a highly desirable value application. But would increased restrictions on handguns actually contribute to this goal? The negative would certainly argue that restrictions would have little impact on crime—most crimes don't involve guns (for example, white-collar crimes), and criminals could always get guns if they wanted them. The negative would no doubt also argue that, on balance, other values were more important than reducing crime—for instance, the constitutional right to bear arms. The affirmative in value debates has to develop and defend its application issue in a way very similar to the development and defense of the advantage issue in policy debate, in that both must establish a compelling impact. As in policy debates, the impact may be qualitative and thus philosophically based. Application of the value should be demonstrated as having a significant impact through qualitative and/or quantitative means.

D. Requirement to Prove the Intrinsic

In value debates the advocates must sometimes prove that certain factors are **intrinsic** to various elements of the case or to the relationship between certain elements of the case. A factor is intrinsic if it is embedded within the essential nature of a thing or is an inherent characteristic or consequence of the thing. In debating the "right-to-privacy" proposition considered previously, debaters often had to establish just what was intrinsic, or essential, to the right to privacy and why that was more important than other constitutional rights. In debating the censorship proposition also considered previously, debaters tried to establish that certain factors intrinsic to censorship were critical to the defense of the national interests of the United States.

E. Requirements of Significance

As in policy debate, the advocates in value debate have to prove that the essentials of their case are significant. The values they advocate must be proved to be significant values, and the application of those values must be significant. In the gun control example, reducing crime would certainly seem to be a significant application, but *how much* would crime be reduced? Enough to offset the negative's claim of lost constitutional rights? Thus, as in policy debate, significance is often established by weighing the application *on balance* against the value objections. Significance is also an important issue in policy debate and will be considered in more detail later in the chapter.

F. Putting the Case Together

Typically the debate case is the product of several debaters working together. Once the outline of the case is satisfactory, the next step is to prepare a manuscript of the first affirmative speech. The final draft of the manuscript should be the product of extensive rewriting and editing and should reflect the maximum skill of the advocate (or advocates, if the manuscript is a group effort) in speech composition. It must be so written that, when the speech is presented, the advocate can achieve maximum effectiveness in delivery. (You may find it helpful to review Chapter 16 when building and presenting an affirmative or negative case.)

Once the manuscript for the affirmative speech is completed, the advocates have to prepare *briefs*—short speech segments—that they will use to refute negative attacks and to extend affirmative arguments. Because these briefs must be adapted to the specific negative case met, they cannot simply be read from a manuscript; rather, they have to serve as carefully planned outlines for an extemporaneous presentation. Successful debaters also will be able to produce well-executed extensions. *Extensions* consist of new evidence and analysis to carry forward arguments introduced earlier; they are not simply repetitions of previously introduced evidence and argument.

III. PROPOSITION OF POLICY
AFFIRMATIVE CASES

As we saw in Chapter 6, in a debate on a proposition of policy, the affirmative maintains that a certain policy or course of action should be adopted. In developing the affirmative case on a proposition of policy, the advocate is responsible for presenting a prima facie case.

The prima facie case is made up of a number of issues just as issues are made up of a number of arguments. In deciding whether or not to adopt a new policy, any reasonable person is likely to ask three questions:

1. Do I perceive a need for a change? Is there some harm or exigency in the world that urgently needs to be eliminated?

2. Is this problem likely to go away by itself or does some action really need to be taken? Is it inherent to the world as it is? Absent affirmative action, is it likely to continue?

3. If this policy is adopted, will it really help? Will it solve the problem and not cause too many new problems?

These three questions make up the *stock issues* of policy debate. In order to establish a prima facie case for a policy resolution, an affirmative team must provide convincing arguments that answer each of these questions in the affirmative. In debate, these questions or issues are referred to as **harm**, *inherency*, and **solvency**. The affirmative must address all three in order for debate to begin and most of the clash in the debate will revolve around them.

A. Requirement to Prove the Harm

The first stock issue is harm. If there is no harm in the world, there is no reason to change things. Harm may be absence of a greater good (for example, things are OK now, but they could be a whole lot better) or a real, observable, existing evil. Existence of harm helps establish the need for change. To be persuasive, the harm identified by the affirmative should be *significant, compelling*, and *widespread*. It is important to remember that harm alone does not warrant an affirmative ballot, but without harm, there is no justification for a resolution change.

Significance asks the question, "How much harm is there?" Advocates strive to demonstrate quantitative significance, a numerical, observable, and concrete measure of the harm. This may be established by observing a numerical measure of the harm: by identifying the number of people affected negatively by the harm and/or by measuring the statistical probability of risk (how likely is it that the harm will actually occur?). Although big numbers are certainly impressive and serve an important persuasive function, it must be remembered that statistics can prove that a harm is significant without providing a head count. We do not know exactly how many homeless people there are in the United States or how many individuals have contracted HIV/AIDS, but there is little doubt that these are both significant problems. Affirmatives are wise to provide some realistic estimates of the extent of the harm and present evidence that such estimates are likely to be understated.

Harm must above all be *compelling*. As with all arguments, the key to a compelling harm is **impact**. If a reasonable person can be aware of the harm and ask, "so what?" the harm is probably not very compelling. The problem of male pattern baldness is quantitatively significant, but not compelling to all bald men. Baldness may not be thought to substantially reduce an individual's quality of life or violate any important human value (except perhaps vanity). In order to establish a compelling harm, the affirmative must establish a qualitative harm, one that points to diminished quality of life or denial of some important value.

Qualitative significance is important by definition and significant by implication. The U.S. Supreme Court establishes policy based on the denial of a single individual's rights because important values are at stake; that is, qualitative harm is established. **Quantitative significance**, on the other hand, is not compelling if it is not tied to a qualitative harm. That thousands of people are dying of diabetes warrants action not just because of the number of people affected, but more importantly because we place a great value on human life and avoidance of suffering. It is generally accepted that human life is valuable and thus death is a per se harm, and that avoidance of pain is valuable, and thus suffering is harmful. That a condition is harmful should not be taken for granted. The degree of harm must be examined with utmost scrutiny. Economic harm, for example, is not persuasive unless it is shown to diminish the quality of life for a number of individuals in a substantial way or lead to an increased risk of death. Qualitative harm establishes the impact of the harm and to have impact is to be compelling.

Finally, it is generally accepted that a harm should be demonstrated to be *widespread*. This depends somewhat on the nature of the resolution. Most policy resolutions call for national or international action. If a problem is local or regional, national or international, action may not be called for. It is up to the advocates of change to prove the widespread and pervasive nature of the harm.

Although advocates are usually in a stronger position if they can provide both quantitative and qualitative needs, and indicate the widespread nature of the harms, it is not always possible to do this. In debating the proposition "Resolved: That the federal government should significantly strengthen the regulation of mass media communication in the United States," some affirmatives called for greater governmental control of the mass media's reporting of criminal trials on the grounds that sometimes mass media coverage led to unfair trials. Debaters using this case found that they could document few instances in which media coverage had influenced juries. But they argued that the Sixth Amendment right to an impartial jury was qualitatively so important that this right should be protected even if it was violated in only one out of thousands of trials.

B. Requirement to Prove the Inherency

Inherency may be thought of as a *propensity for future harm*. Once it has been established that there is a harm that needs to be corrected, a decision maker considers alternatives. If the problem is likely to go away without a major overhaul of the status quo, then substantial change is unwarranted. Inherency looks to the causes of a problem. Unfortunately, causes are seldom simple. Most problems have many interrelated causes, some of them unidentifiable. If the causes of a problem are relatively permanent fixtures within the status quo and a major reform on the level of resolutional change is needed to alter them or overcome them, then inherency is established. Inherency is tricky, however, as systems are in a constant state of change. Description of the status quo, then, must predict the direction of change and indicate that the problems identified in the harm are not likely to disappear without resolutional action. Thus inherency asks, "Will the problem go away by itself, or do we need to do something major about it?"

The strongest form of inherency is **structural inherency**. Structural inherency demonstrates that the harm is permanently built into the status quo and that major revisions of the status quo are needed to in order to eliminate the harm. Structural inherency consists of law, court decisions that have the force of law, and societal structures. Prison construction is inherently difficult because it requires public approval and public funding by law. Public funded abortions may be banned because the Supreme Court allows the states to do so; the American flag can be burned as symbolic speech because the Court has so ruled. Marijuana smokers go to jail because there are law against illicit drug use and possession. In some states, labor unions have created closed shops through legal and social structures. If the affirmative can prove that laws, court decisions, or societal structures prevent the solution of its harm, then it has demonstrated structural inherency.

Inherency may also be based on the attitudes of people who have authority that affects decisions bearing on the harm. **Attitudinal inherency** suggests that attitudes prevent solution of the identified problem within the status quo. Racist and sexist attitudes in our society work to prevent equal rights and opportunities for women and minorities. Fear of crime prevents extensive use of prison work-release and furlough programs; ironically, even the construction of new penal institutions is feared because few communities welcome such facilities. It is useful to examine the core motives behind such attitudes. For instance, problems with drug distribution and crime are generally tied to profit or power. Once the core motive behind the harmful action is revealed, the attitudes can be clearly examined.

It is sometimes argued that because a harm exists and there is no sign of it going away, it is inherent. This analysis, referred to as *existential inherency*, is usually based on inadequate research. If it is true that the problem will not easily go away, then it is probable that there is a reason. This reason is either a structural or an attitudinal barrier to solving the problem within the status quo. Existential inherency is "pseudo" inherency. It is a way of copping out and saying, "We know there is a harm, we just don't know why." If you cannot identify the reasons behind the harm, you cannot hope to solve that harm. In order to be prima facie, the affirmative must present either a structural or an attitudinal barrier to solving the harm within the status quo. When it has done so, it has met the burden of inherency.

In the example involving mass media reporting of jury trials, affirmative advocates had an easy time establishing structural inherency. The First Amendment provides a formidable barrier to any government regulation of the press. The affirmative's plan could be put into effect only by amending the Constitution and giving the federal government powers specifically denied it by the First Amendment.

In this same case the affirmative was often able to prove attitudinal inherency as well. It argued that sensationalism increased newspaper circulation and increased TV ratings. For this reason, it maintained, newspapers and television stations were predisposed to seek out and present lurid and often unproven or inadmissible (in court) news that might prejudice jurors.

C. Requirement to Prove the Solvency

Once the affirmative has established that there is a significant, compelling, and widespread harm and that the harm is not likely to go away without some radical change in the present system, it must provide a plan of action for solving that harm. This *plan* must meet the burden of solvency: It must solve the harm better than the status quo does. It is not expected that the affirmative will eliminate the harm, only that it can demonstrate a **comparative advantage**. In other words, the plan compared to the status quo is a superior system; it is comparatively advantageous. In order to do this, the affirmative must address the issue of solvency by proving that its plan would work, that it would solve the problem better than the status quo would, and that it would avoid side effects that would be worse than the harm itself.

The first requirement of solvency is workability. The affirmative is allowed to employ **fiat** in assuming implementation of its plan. Fiat is not magic; it only allows the affirmative to assume for the sake of argument that if its plan were shown to be desirable, it would be adopted through a normal legal procedure. Debate thus centers on whether or not it would be adopted. If debaters had to prove that their plan would be adopted, they would have to spend all their time arguing about the political feasibility of getting votes for the plan. This would prevent the policy analysis that is the core of the debate. Thus, fiat assumes hypothetical implementation, but not workability. The affirmative must prove that its plan could eliminate or overcome the structural and attitudinal barriers identified in inherency and that it could reasonably be expected to work in the real world. It may not invent magical technologies or create funding out of thin air, nor may the affirmative assume that it has demonstrated a feasible plan. Only then has it met the burden of workability.

The plan is the focal point of a policy debate, providing the connecting link between the needs and the advantages. The **plan** must solve the problems claimed in the justification as needs or harms, and it must produce the advantages claimed by the affirmative. The affirmative's plan has to be developed in sufficient detail to demonstrate that it can meet the alleged needs and that it can produce the claimed advantages. But it must be simple enough to be presented and defended within the time limits of academic debate.

Even though the plan should be tailored to fit the resolution and the specific case of the affirmative, it should be a reasonable policy with real-world advocates. In searching for plan ideas, debaters should look to experts who have produced relevant public statements, literature, and, in some cases, studies to support the efficacy of plan adoption.

Beginning debaters should master a basic format; advanced advocates can make reasonable variations in this basic format that they feel are desirable and defensible. The major parts of a plan are, in common usage, designated as *planks*. The following inset shows the basic plan format.

The essential components of the plan, or plan planks, should be "topical." It is considered an illegitimate strategy to insert "extratopical" plan planks. These are parts of the plan from which advantages may be claimed but that are not essential

Basic Plan Format

PLANK 1—AGENCY

In this plank the affirmative specifies who will be responsible for administering its plan. This may include identifying who will enact the plan and/or who will do the work of the plan. Does the affirmative require an existing agency of the federal government to administer its plan? Does it create a new agency? Here's where the affirmative must provide the essential details of the agency that will put its plan into effect.

PLANK 2—MANDATES

In most debates this is the essence of the plan. In this plank the affirmative specifies the mandates given to the agency that administers the plan. The affirmative must specify exactly what it requires the agency to do. If new legislation is needed to carry out the affirmative's plan, this plank is the place to provide for it.

PLANK 3—ENFORCEMENT

This may not be necessary; however, it is occasionally helpful to facilitate the functioning of a plan by identifying how it will be enforced. In the harm and inherency issues, the affirmative has provided many reasons people will resist its plan. Now it must provide a means of making people behave the way it wants them to. The affirmative may find it necessary to advocate the imposition of fines, prison terms, or other forms of coercion or incentives to make people act in the way necessary for its plan to work. In some circumstances the affirmative may be able to demonstrate that under the new conditions created by its plan, people will act in the desired way because it is now in their self-interest to do so. Most often enforcement will be through "normal means," meaning it is not specified by the plan.

PLANK 4—FUNDING AND STAFFING

Again, often unnecessary, however, in this plank the affirmative specifies how it will get the funds and staff to permit the agency to carry out its mandates. Some cases on the proposition "Resolved: That the United States federal government should significantly increase exploration and/or development of space beyond the earth's mesosphere" would likely require billions, maybe trillions of dollars in increased taxes in a time of budget deficits and rising national debt. By contrast, some cases on the "regulation of mass media communication" proposition required only a nominal increase in staff and funding to allow an existing agency to carry out the mandates. Again, these actions usually occur through "normal means."

PLANK 5—ADDENDUM

In this concluding plank, the affirmative adds such further provisions as may be necessary to complete the implementation of its plan. For example, it might provide for the repeal of any conflicting legislation, indicate the intent of the plan, and provide other details that could help make the plan comprehensive and readily understandable.

to the policy action embedded within the resolution. For example, in debating the employment opportunities proposition, most affirmative cases necessarily caused an increase in income for the people who gained employment. This argument opened the way for the negative to run a "grain-fed beef" disadvantage. The argument indicated that with increased income people had a propensity to consume more grain-fed beef; and grain-fed beef, the negative argued, caused an increase in cardiovascular disease, thus killing off the very people the affirmative wanted to help. (This generic slippery slope disadvantage applied to many affirmative plans. It was sometimes called the "meatballs" disadvantage; later all big-impact generic disadvantages were termed "meatballs.") Some affirmatives, anticipating this attack, stated that their plan would be partly financed by a tax on grain-fed beef. This tactic either discouraged the negative from running the disadvantage or allowed the affirmative to answer it by claiming that the increased cost of the now-taxed grain-fed beef would hold consumption of it to present levels, thus incurring no new disadvantage. Such a plan plank would likely be considered extratopical, and thus an unfair strategy. The affirmative action may only implement or enable the policy action essential to the resolution.

The affirmative is not required to demonstrate that its plan will be adopted, but it does have to demonstrate that its plan, if adopted, would be workable. The affirmative may employ the concept of fiat to enable the enactment of its plan over the inherency it identifies. It may not, however, fiat, or assume, the workability of its plan. If the plan calls for an increase in personal income taxes and a reduction in property taxes, it does not make sense for the negative to raise the workability issue; the status quo has effective means of enforcing tax collections. In some cases, however, workability may become an all-important issue. In debates on comprehensive medical care for all citizens, one affirmative plan called for annual physical examinations of all citizens. The affirmative sought to evade its responsibility by claiming that this provision of its plan would be "enforced by all necessary means." The negative established that millions of citizens—through fear, ignorance, or apathy—would not volunteer for the physical examinations and argued that the affirmative must provide an effective enforcement mechanism or lose its claimed advantage. The inexperienced affirmative debater, in a moment of excess, responded that this provision of the plan would be enforced by "drawing and quartering." The next negative speaker argued that the method of enforcement provided by the affirmative—drawing and quartering—was not only counterproductive to health but so repugnant to contemporary standards of law enforcement that it constituted grounds for rejecting the proposition. The judge agreed; drawing and quartering may have been accepted practice in the Middle Ages, but it was an unacceptable and unworkable plan provision for contemporary America.

Fiat assumes that the plan is adopted through "normal means"—typically the usual policymaking procedure of the relevant decision-making body, most often the U.S. federal government. Occasionally teams may have to debate just what constitutes *normal means* for a given situation. However, affirmatives may not fiat past the implications of the decision-making process. For example, they may not fiat that there would not be political costs of plan implementation (although they may be able to turn to their plan advocates to prove that there would not be such costs).

Affirmatives also may not fiat unreasonable provisions for their plan. For example, in a debate on consumer protection, the affirmatives may not fiat that their administrative body will be headed by Ralph Nader; in a debate on crime control, they may not fiat that the members of their administrative body will be incorruptible;[2] if they designate a congressional committee to investigate the CIA, they may not fiat that all of the committee members will be liberal Democrats. In short, the affirmative plan is subject to normal political processes, and its members are subject to normal human frailties. Thus the affirmative may not appoint Gandalf the White and Harry Potter to its administrative body and stipulate that magic will be enacted to overcome attitudinal inherency and any other problems that prevent the status quo from functioning perfectly.

In addition, the plan need only provide sufficient information as to the workings of the policy as advocated. In debating the proposition "Resolved: That the federal government should annually grant a specific percentage of its income tax revenue to the state governments," the affirmative was not obliged to specify how much money would be given to each state. But it was obliged to present a policy by means of which such amounts could be determined.

The second requirement of solvency is that the plan solve the harm to a greater extent than the status quo. This component is known as the "plan meet need" or "plan meet advantage." The affirmative, to meet its prime facie burdens, must guarantee some advantage, and if possible, provide some measure of probable success. It should be able to indicate how much of the harm the plan can reasonably be expected to eliminate.

In building the plan, the advocate should keep solvency in mind. In the research process it is a good idea to begin with the solvency advocates—those experts who support the particular policy. It is important to provide the appropriate agency to administer the plan. In debates on the development of outer space, for example, some affirmatives chose to have their plan administered by NASA, because NASA had the expertise to work in space. These affirmatives were prepared to defend NASA as the best agency to solve the problem.

The mandates should be carefully drafted to achieve the desired objective. In debates on the "guaranteed employment opportunities" proposition, the affirmative could not say, "The government will increase employment by 3 percent." Instead it had to specifically indicate what the government must do to achieve a 3 percent increase in employment. Some affirmatives mandated a reduction of the standard work week under the Fair Labor Standards Act and found that they had to spell out their mandate in great detail to demonstrate that the plan would solve the problem.

---

2. Of course, one may attempt to provide for desirable qualities in appointees. The mayor of Cleveland once appointed a special committee of clergy—promptly dubbed "The God Squad" by the media—to investigate crime. The mayor's supporters hailed the appointments on the ground that clergy would be incorruptible; his opponents scoffed that clergy led sheltered lives and did not know enough about crime to investigate it.

The enforcement plank has to provide incentives or coercive measures to make people behave in the desired way, and it must be realistic and supported by expert advocacy. The enactment of legislation to increase the drinking age to 21 provides an interesting example of plan building to provide for enforcement. The minimum drinking age is determined on a state-by-state basis. The proponents of the 21-year-old minimum recognized that it would take years of lobbying to get all 50 states to enact the legislation they desired, so they chose to lobby the federal government. They succeeded in getting the federal government to enact legislation requiring the states to raise the minimum drinking age to 21 or lose a substantial percentage of federal highway construction funds. This mixture of coercion and incentive provided the enforcement necessary to make the states pass the desired legislation. The proponents of the legislation felt that the states were doing a satisfactory job of enforcing drinking laws; what they wanted to change was the age at which the laws were enforced.

Funding and staffing must be balanced. That is, they must be sufficient to achieve the affirmative's objectives, yet not so great that they can easily be turned into disadvantages. In debates on the "development of space" proposition, many affirmatives found it necessary to provide for multibillion-dollar tax increases to fund their program and multibillion-dollar tax incentives to encourage private corporations' participation in their program. In these cases, they had to be ready to prove that these vast sums could be raised. The age-21 drinking law, of course, required no funding plank; to enforce states' compliance, the federal government merely threatened not to distribute funds already appropriated. The addendum plank has to supply any provisions needed to make the plan operate effectively. Sometimes an affirmative plan is against existing laws or constitutional provisions. Remember, as we saw in Chapter 7, constitutionality is never an issue in academic debate. However, the plan must take appropriate action to make its provisions legal. People who wanted to lower the voting age to 18 clearly were proposing an unconstitutional action. The solution came in the form of the Twenty-Sixth Amendment. Thus, if the affirmative's plan is unconstitutional, illegal, or extralegal (not regulated by existing law), the addendum plank should include the necessary provisions to legalize its proposal, consistent with normal means. If the negative can successfully argue that the plan is either illegal or so unclear that lengthy court battles will result, the affirmative will lose solvency.

Solvency must be unique to the plan. In developing this portion of the case, the affirmative must demonstrate that only this plan can solve the problem in the most advantageous way. If the needs can be solved by some means other than the plan, there is little reason to adopt the plan. In debates on the mass media proposition, some affirmatives built cases claiming that violence on television was harmful and called for a plan whereby the federal government would regulate television to ban violence. Some negatives meeting this case claimed that the National Association of Broadcasters (NAB) (a voluntary agency) could solve the problem without federal intervention. The affirmative responded by arguing that not all television stations belonged to the NAB and that not all NAB members followed all provisions of the NAB code. Thus the affirmative claimed that only its plan could guarantee full solvency of the needs by mandating that all television stations adhere to its regulations governing violence on television.

Ideally, the affirmative is able to rely on expert solvency advocates, real-world supporters of the affirmative plan. The affirmative is on far safer ground if it can refer to these experts who have designed the proposal and published their advocacy of it as opposed to being creative and designing its own plan. In many cases, the plan may also have been implemented in other areas or smaller jurisdictions as a pilot project or other policy, providing empirical evidence of its desirability.

Affirmatives are strongest when they can present ideas supported by one or more "solvency advocates." These are scholars, policy experts, or other researchers or professionals who are immersed in the problem area under discussion through professional activity or study. They are knowledgeable experts who have considered the issues addressed by the affirmative and by the proposition, and have written or spoken in favor of the affirmative plan. They provide the strongest and most credible support for the plan. In some cases, it is feasible to demonstrate from empirical experience that a plan will work, because it has succeeded elsewhere. For example, solvency evidence for a single-payer (government provider) health care system for the United States may be secured from the much studied Canadian experience, and evidence supporting legalization of marijuana and heroin can be gotten from the Netherlands' experience.

Finally, the affirmative advocates must be prepared to compare the benefits of their proposal to any possible negative consequences or disadvantages. Any change has costs. The affirmative need not point these out, but it must be prepared to answer the negative's arguments that the cost of the plan is greater than its benefits. This third component of solvency is not a prima facie issue, as it need not be discussed until the negative raises the question of disadvantages.

D. Requirement to Prove the Advantages

The advantage portion of the affirmative case must be developed in sufficient detail to demonstrate that the plan meets the need and corrects the deficiencies and weaknesses that the affirmative has found in the status quo. **Advantage** refers to the benefits or gains that the affirmative claims will result from adopting its plan, which must be shown to outweigh the disadvantages. The affirmative also must be careful to link the advantages to the plan and demonstrate that the advantages are caused by the plan, are unique to the plan, and cannot be obtained by other factors outside the scope of the plan.

The advantage(s) should have a clearly identified impact or a substantial measure of importance so that they can be weighed positively against disadvantages. In fact, all arguments should be measured by their impact, both strategically in terms of their importance vis-à-vis all other arguments in the debate, and with regard to measurement of importance. The impact of an affirmative case is the importance and measured value of its advantages.

The advantages should be integrated with the needs. In a debate on the "guaranteed employment opportunities" proposition, if an affirmative argues that millions are unemployed and that these unemployed people suffer from poor health, have high rates of suicide, and commit many crimes, the affirmative must prove as its first advantage that it will provide employment opportunities for millions, that their health will improve, and that suicides and crime will be reduced as a result. The affirmative is most compelling if it is able to prove that increased employment, improved health, and reduction in suicide are a direct result of the plan action, and that the same benefits are *not* available through other programs.

Every policy action has costs. The affirmative's plan will almost invariably create some significant problems. Thus, it is in the negative's interest to discover and present the strongest possible set of disadvantages it can find and to prove that these disadvantages are inherent in the plan. The affirmative must, of course, be prepared to refute or minimize these disadvantages. Realistically, however, some disadvantages cannot be refuted. The affirmative must be able to prove a net gain; that is, it must prove that the advantages outweigh the disadvantages.

An everyday example of the need to prove that the advantages outweigh the disadvantages involves contact lenses. If you or some of your friends wear them, you are aware of a disadvantage—there is the risk of losing them. But those who wear contact lenses have decided that this disadvantage is outweighed by the advantages of convenience and appearance. They have chosen on balance to opt for contact lenses. The idea of balancing advantages against disadvantages is important to the debater. The affirmative seeks to show that on balance the advantages outweigh the disadvantages; the negative seeks to show that the disadvantages outweigh the advantages.

In debating the "guaranteed employment opportunities" proposition, some negatives argued that employment causes more health problems than unemployment does. They cited the number of injuries caused by industrial accidents and the number of illnesses caused by working with hazardous materials, and they claimed that on balance the affirmatives' plan caused more ill health than unemployment did. Affirmatives meeting this disadvantage often responded that they were providing employment opportunities for the unemployed, not forcing them to take jobs. Thus, they argued, on balance it is better for a person to have the opportunity for a job and to have the freedom to choose whether to accept the potential hazards of the job.

Another method of demonstrating that the advantages outweigh the disadvantages is risk analysis. This involves estimating the probability (likelihood) of occurrence of some negatively evaluated state of affairs. The impact of the negatively evaluated state of affairs also has to be determined. We are all familiar with the evidence showing that wearing seat belts saves lives. Death certainly is a high impact disadvantage to not wearing a seat belt. However, the evidence also shows that millions of drivers and passengers have decided that the likelihood of being involved in an accident in which a seat belt might save their lives is remote, so they don't wear seat belts.

In debating the "guaranteed employment opportunities" proposition, some affirmatives presented a plan that mandated a cutback on imported oil and the conversion of all possible industries to fossil fuel. (They argued that the high cost of imported oil caused unemployment and that the development of domestic fossil fuel would increase employment. Development of domestic fossil fuel production would necessarily rely on growth of the labor-intensive coal industry. Coal emissions, however, have an even greater impact on the environment than do oil emissions.) In response some negatives developed the disadvantage that the affirmative's plan would melt the polar ice caps by increasing coal emissions into the upper atmosphere and cause flooding of all the world's coastal cities, which, in turn, would cause trillions of dollars of damage. Certainly the negative had high impact—trillions of dollars of damage is an awesome disadvantage. Some affirmatives meeting this disadvantage, however, were able to demonstrate that these events had a very low likelihood of occurring. Melting of the polar ice caps would require a quantum increase of coal-based fossil fuel emissions on a worldwide scale, whereas the affirmative proposed only that the United States increase its use of fossil fuel. Because the negative was usually unable to establish any threshold—the point at which burning a million more tons of coal would actually melt the polar ice caps— the affirmative was usually able to demonstrate that the likelihood of the disadvantages occurring was remote and thus that the advantage outweighed the disadvantage.

A particularly effective way for an affirmative to answer a disadvantage argument against its plan is the turnaround. In common usage a **turnaround argument** is any statement that one turns against the originator. In debate usage the term is usually applied to the affirmative's turning around a negative's disadvantage and converting it into an advantage or to the negative's turning around an affirmative's advantage and converting it into a disadvantage. Thus both teams in a debate must seek to develop their arguments so as to avoid turnarounds of their own position. At the same time they must be alert for opportunities to provide turnarounds for their opponent's arguments. Turnaround arguments may be "link turns" based on the links to the negative disadvantage arguments (that is, the plan not only does not cause the disadvantage, it actually prevents it!) or "impact turns" based on the impacts (the consequence of the disadvantage is not really a bad thing; in fact, it is a very good thing). Of course, the affirmative should be careful to avoid making both sorts of "turn" arguments at the same time, or it may fall into the trap of a "double turn" (if it argues that its plan better avoids the disadvantage impact, and that the disadvantage impact is actually good, it is offering a reason why the plan is bad).

In debates on the guaranteed employment proposition, some affirmatives claimed as an advantage that their plan would "raise millions out of poverty." Some negatives meeting this case countered with the disadvantage that the affirmative plan would "increase cardiovascular disease" (arguing that with increased income people would drink more alcoholic beverages, which would lead to more cardiovascular disease). Some affirmatives meeting this disadvantage were able to turnaround the argument and claim the additional advantage of "improved health" (arguing that a moderate increase in consumption of alcohol actually reduced the risk of cardiovascular disease—the negative had merely shown that more people would drink alcohol, not that anyone would drink to excess).

The disadvantages just cited were used frequently by negative constructive speakers. But did they represent a hard-nosed assessment of the real world, or were they merely strategic ploys of little merit? Such arguments are made in real-world policy debates, and all of the evidence comes from reputable sources. The "real world" is a mixture of insightful and farfetched arguments, and the advocate must be prepared to respond to both. Only careful risk analysis will allow us to assess the merits of the argument and to demonstrate to those who render the decision whether the grounds, and the supporting arguments or intermediate conclusions, constitute good reasons for accepting the conclusion.

A familiar example of a turnaround is the prelaw student who considered taking an accounting course as an undergraduate because she felt she would need knowledge of accounting in law school. A friend advised her, "Don't take accounting now—it will take too much time from your other courses." The prelaw student decided that this argument was a turnaround. She chose to take the accounting course as an undergraduate on the grounds that she could better afford the time it would take as an undergraduate than as a law student.

E. Requirement to Defend Topicality

Topicality is sometimes mistaken for a prima facie issue. It is not. Topicality is certainly a critical issue, often the single most important issue in the debate, but it is considered independently of the stock issues. Topicality is an a priori issue. This means it must be decided first. After the debate, the judge first considers topicality. If the plan is topical, the judge will then evaluate the stock issues. If the plan is not topical, the judge need not examine the stock issues. Hence, it is a priori. Although presumption on the stock issues is generally negative because the negative opposes change, presumption on the issue of topicality is generally affirmative: Judges consider the plan to be topical unless and until the negative makes persuasive arguments that it is not. The affirmative need not prove that its plan is topical in order to be prima facie.

F. Preparation

Once the manuscript for the affirmative speech is completed, the advocates have to prepare *briefs*—short speech segments—that they will use to refute negative attacks and to extend affirmative arguments. Because these briefs must be adapted to the specific negative case met, they cannot simply be read from a manuscript; rather, they have to serve as carefully planned outlines for an extemporaneous presentation. Successful debaters also will be able to produce well-executed extensions. *Extensions* consist of new evidence and analysis to carry forward arguments introduced earlier; they are not simply repetitions of previously introduced evidence and argument analysis.

IV. BUILDING FOR OPTIMUM CAPABILITY

Affirmative advocates of both value and policy propositions have the burden of proof; they must take the offensive and mount a strong attack to advance their case. Much of what we have considered so far has to do with the affirmative's offensive position. Remember, though, that debate does not take place in a vacuum and that an able negative will mount strong attacks against the affirmative. The affirmative has to build its case and deploy its evidence so as to achieve the optimum balance of offensive and defensive capabilities.

In building their case, advocates have to anticipate the probable areas of negative attack. They frequently can adjust their case to avoid or blunt many negative attacks before they can be made. In developing cases on an "improved access to medical care for all citizens" proposition, affirmative advocates (foreshadowing the Obama proposal) might have called for a "single-payer plan." As they studied possible negative attacks, they might discover that the enormous cost and complexity of the single-payer plan provided the negative with myriad plan attacks. After considering the difficulty of answering the potential attacks, the affirmative team might reject the single-payer plan and opt for plans that provided for health insurance exchange and incremental increases in the number of people covered through Medicaid and Medicare. The incremental plans would benefit fewer people. However, even though some of the same negative attacks would apply because the market forces and incremental plan would cost billions of dollars less than a universal plan, it would be easier to defend.

Imagine that on the same proposition, affirmative advocates thought it would be a good idea to provide annual physical examinations for all citizens as a plank in their plan. Initially they would discover a good deal of evidence supporting the idea. But later they discovered evidence—which they were sure their opponents would also find—indicating that these examinations for the whole population were counterproductive when subjected to cost-benefit analysis. (The argument went that it would take so much time to give over 250 million physical examinations a year that physicians would not have time to do anything else.) Thus affirmatives eliminated what had initially seemed a desirable plank for their plan and provided instead for multiphasic testing for the population. This method would check for many, but not all, diseases. Because the tests would be administered by physicians' aides and analyzed by computers, their cost would be much lower, in terms of both dollars and physicians' time.

Although it is defensively sound to choose a plan that avoids the strongest negative attacks, advocates are cautioned that they still must provide a plan that will produce significant advantages. Obviously it is easier to answer the cost attacks on a $1 billion plan than on a $70 billion plan. Given the context of the proposition, however, does the $1 billion plan produce significant advantages? The task of the affirmative advocates is to build a plan that achieves the optimum balance of offensive and defensive capabilities.

President Reagan once called his speechwriting staff together to plan a series of campaign speeches. He summed up his objective by saying, "Anyway, what I want is the kind of speech there ain't no rebuttal to."[3] Reagan's request is every debater's dream. And his graceful eulogy of the *Challenger* astronauts certainly evoked no rebuttal. But no team of speechwriters, no matter how talented, could produce a campaign speech that would face no rebuttal. Indeed, no speech on a debatable subject can be presumed to be safe from rebuttal.

Prudent affirmatives will consider the most likely and effective attacks against their case and build in reasonable defensive provisions. An axiom of debate is that a good case defends itself, and the well-planned case is built to provide for the maximally effective self-defense.

V. ALTERNATIVE DEBATE APPROACHES

As has been discussed earlier in this book, one thing intrinsic to debate is self-examination and change. Although what you have read thus far in this chapter will provide a sound traditional framework for policy and value debate, the traditions are slowly evolving. An unbounded creativity in practice has evolved, with new conceptions of fiat as the reflexive authority of those participating in the debate round itself, and with critical examination of the battle to give rhetorical space to marginalized voices and open the debate experience to more viewpoints, standpoints, and cultures. Debate approaches may disregard the traditional frameworks in favor of storytelling, hip-hop, music and film, poetry, and other novel challenges to the conventional approaches. In more subtle structures, debaters can build their comparative advantage cases with philosophical foundations. More radical challenges to tradition may offer argumentation (sometimes in aesthetic forms) to defend the resolution and/or to challenge the framework of policy debate. Critical approaches focus on philosophical and value-based interpretations of prepositional terms, and performance-based approaches find clash in music, visual communication, role-playing, and other creative forms of self-expression. Elizabeth Jones of Louisville University presented the following rap as a part of her affirmative case in favor of U.S. withdrawal from NATO:

Roma people feel just like me, tired of being deprived of their liberty.

Relegated to ghettos, held as slaves, poor health care leading to early graves.

Prison scars, from prison bars, walking round the prison yard.

No running water, no heat, no jobs, and everything you've seemed to love, you've lost.

While the rich get richer, who's paying the cost?

---

3. Peggy Noonan, *What I Saw at the Revolution* (New York: Random House, 1990), p. 146. Used by permission of Elizabeth Jones.

George Soros, Bill Clinton, to Dick Cheney, the so-called bearers of
  democracy.

NATO represents the military wing, of the all-powerful capitalist regime.

While you think gangsters listen to rap and sag,

They really wear suits and carry leather bags.

Politicians with the power to pick, define, and choose who will win and
  who will lose.

Not hearing the Roma or Palestine,

I guess it depends how genocide is defined.

Source: used by permission of Elizabeth Jones.

EXERCISES

1. Prepare the full manuscript for a first affirmative speech on a value proposition. Include all the evidence and reasoning necessary to establish a prima
   facie case.

2. Prepare the full manuscript for a first affirmative speech on a policy proposition. Include all the evidence and reasoning necessary to establish a prima
   facie case.

3. Write a rap in support of a proposition of value or policy.

12

....

Arguing *Against* the Proposition

The job of the negative is to negate, that is, to prevent the triumph of the proposition by raising doubt about the affirmative's prima facie case for the proposition. Because presumption generally favors the negative, a "tie," which is descriptive of a debate where neither side clearly prevails, will result in a decision for the negative. To achieve at least a tie, it is to the advantage of the negative to point to flaws or weaknesses in the affirmative's case. The negative may elect a strategy of "running refutation" wherein they work to defeat one or more of the stock issues offered by the affirmative. This strategy presents as many arguments against each of the affirmative case claims as possible, without necessarily considering a negative position any more thematically linked than "the affirmative is wrong."

A negative decision is a rejection of the proposition, not an endorsement of an "antiproposition." Some, however, may describe this approach as throwing a bunch of stuff against the wall to see what sticks. While running refutation may successfully defeat the affirmative, the negative will generally be more persuasive if, in arguing *against* the proposition, they offer a coherent case or advocacy, the acceptance of which will result in rejection of the proposition.

The negative case requires flexibility in planning. A careful analysis of the proposition will probably enable the negative to determine the issues the affirmative is most likely to advance. The affirmative establishes the initial ground for debate by introducing their case. So until the debate is actually underway, the negative team may not know what type of case the affirmative is advocating; it will not know what weight the affirmative attaches to each issue or what evidence and argument it uses in developing its issues. This uncertainty places a high premium on the negative's ability to adapt to the affirmative's case as it is presented. Of course, the affirmative must also be prepared to adapt their argumentation to the negative's attacks once they have heard them. Nonetheless, the affirmative will always have the advantage of going first, thus determining through their definition of terms and presentation of the case, the argumentative ground and focus of the debate.

I. OBJECTIVES OF THE NEGATIVE

Because presumption opposes the proposition and therefore its advocates, the burden of proof rests with the affirmative. In theory the negative does not even have to speak until the affirmative has presented a prima facie case. The prudent advocate will recognize, however, that audiences sometimes equate silence with consent and may accept a proposition on the basis of less than a prima facie case.

Miniglossary

Burden of rebuttal   The obligation of the negative to refute at least one of the issues of the affirmative. Otherwise the affirmative will prevail, and the obligation of all debaters to refute arguments forwarded by their opponents, or the argument will be considered cogent for the weight of that argument.

Conditional counterplan   Argument by the negative that it may abandon advocacy of the counterplan if certain conditions prevail.

Case turn   Offensive negative strategy designed to demonstrate that the needs identified by the affirmative are not needs but, in fact, benefits to the status quo.

Counterplan   A plan presented by the negative that is competitive with the affirmative's plan and is a superior policy alternative.

Disadvantages   The undesirable consequences that the negative claims will flow from the affirmative's plan. These must be shown to outweigh the advantages.

Generic disadvantages   Disadvantages that may be applied to a number of possible affirmative plans.

Kritic   An argument which challenges the philosophical foundations, or applies ethical constructs to the opponent's advocacy and its implications.

Permutation   A test of competition of a counterplan offered by the affirmative. The hypothetical illustration of plan and counterplan, or plan and Kritic alternative operating together.

Shells   Brief versions of arguments to be expanded upon later in the debate.

Slippery slope argument   The argument that a seemingly harmless proposal in the affirmative's plan would be an irreversible first step leading inevitably to the most deleterious disadvantages.

Topical counterplan   A counterplan that might be used as an affirmative plan under some definitions of the resolution but is nontopical with regard to the operational definition the affirmative has chosen to use. Once the affirmative has parametrically defined the resolution, almost any mutually exclusive plan may constitute grounds for a counterplan.

Topicality   The state of conformity to the intent of the debate resolution. A plan is topical if it justifies the full intent of the resolution, the needs are solved, or the comparative advantages are gained as a direct result of the planks in the plan that implement the resolution.

Value objections   In value debate, the negative argument that undesirable consequences will flow from adoption of the affirmative's case. Similar to a disadvantage in policy debate.

Therefore, the advocate has to be prepared to reply to any affirmative case, even if it does not meet all the logical requirements of a prima facie case. In the courtroom the defense may move that a case be dismissed on the ground that the prosecution or plaintiff has not presented a prima facie case. But this option is not generally available outside the courtroom.

While the burden of proof rests on the affirmative, once the affirmative case is presented, the negative assumes the **burden of rebuttal (or burden of refutation)**; that is, the negative has the obligation to refute at least one of the issues of the affirmative, or the affirmative will prevail. In fact, any argument forwarded by an advocate and unanswered by their opponent will be considered cogent for the weight of that argument. As the debate progresses, each subsequent debater acquires a new burden of rebuttal on each argument addressed, so refutation alternates from side to side throughout the debate. So, the negative may choose simply to point to holes in the affirmative case, hoping to damage the affirmative's ability to defend all issues. However, the negative will be much more effective if it constructs a coherent position, integrating its arguments into a policy advocacy that competes with the affirmative's advocacy. We will discuss first the proposition of value negative case and then the proposition of policy negative case. The discussion of the policy negative case will include a consideration of many issues critical to both value and policy negative cases.

II. PROPOSITION OF VALUE NEGATIVE CASES

The negative has the burden of rebuttal and has to attack the case that the affirmative presents. The negative knows that the affirmative will present definitive and designative issues. The negative has to refute at least one of the affirmative issues, or else carry one of the issues the negative introduces, to win. Again, negatives will be much more persuasive if their arguments are integrated into a coherent, comprehensive negative position. In developing the negative case, the value debaters select the most appropriate combination of the various available options.

A. Attack Topicality or Definitions

Topicality, in a debate over a resolution of fact or value, refers to the state of conformity to the intent of the debate resolution. When advocates argue that a matter is not topical, they maintain that it is not related to or does not directly stem from the proposition being debated, that is, it is not a fair or sound interpretation of the proposition. In a debate on a proposition of fact or value, topicality is an attack on the affirmative's definitions as they come together to provide an interpretation of the proposition. For example, in a debate on the proposition that increasing foreign investment in the United States is detrimental to this nation, one negative debater argued that the affirmative's definition of terms must be consistent with its grammatical use in the proposition. The debater noted that whether a word is used as a noun, a verb, an adjective, or an adverb will substantially alter the meaning of the proposition. Thus the negative concluded that the affirmative's was not topical, because its definition of the word *increasing* did not stem from the term as used in the proposition.

Topicality is an "a priori" issue—that is, it is considered separate from and prior to other issues. If the negative can convince the judges that the affirmative's case is not topical, it may win regardless of the strength of the case—the implication being that the affirmative case does not support the resolution being debated. If the affirmative can convince the judges that its case is topical, it will have won that issue but not the debate. Even when the negative argues that the affirmative's interpretation is not topical, the debate continues, but at the end of the debate, the judge will consider the issue of topicality first in making her decision.

Definitions were discussed in some detail in Chapter 7. As noted there, in value debate the affirmative is required to present at least a reasonable interpretation of the proposition. If the affirmative's definition is perceived to be unreasonable, the negative may choose to attack the definition. The likely implication of a successful negative attack on the definitions of the affirmative is that the case is nontopical, which means the negative wins the debate.

Since defining the terms in a debate about a proposition of fact or value is a necessary stock issue, the negative may win the debate not only on the issue of relevancy, but also on the merits of the definitions and interpretations themselves. The negative may argue that the definitions offered by the affirmative are inaccurate or harmful. Definitions may be harmful if the implication of accepting the definition outside the debate context would result in negative consequences. For example, to define "democracy assistance" broadly enough so that it would include military support could be argued to encourage violence solutions to social problems, or to refer in a definition to those individuals who have entered the United States without legal process or documentation as "illegals" dehumanizes people and minimizes consideration of them to one negative aspect of their behavior.

B. Attack Criteria

To successfully attack the affirmative criteria, the negative should offer reasons the criteria initially presented are flawed or dangerous and also offer a *counter-criterion*. In a debate on the proposition "Resolved: That significantly stronger third-party participation in United States presidential elections would benefit the political process," one affirmative argued that "survival" was the ultimate value—that is, the most important criterion. A negative meeting this case argued that "democracy" was the ultimate value. As the debate developed, the negative was able to sustain its position that democracy was the most important criterion and so won the decision ("give me liberty or give me death!"). Accepting the countercriterion as superior will force the judge to measure the competing values and applications by the negative standard. If the negative can establish that other criteria are more important than those advanced by the affirmative and show that the affirmative does not meet these criteria, the negative will usually prevail.

C. Attack Significance

The negative's objective in attacking significance is to prove that at least some of the essential elements of the affirmative's case are not significant enough to justify adopting the resolution. If the affirmative can establish the significance of its case, it is in a strong position to counter other negative attacks. Thus the negative must find ways to minimize the significance of at least some of the essential elements of the affirmative's case.

D. Attack Uniqueness

The negative's objective in attacking uniqueness is to prove that at least some of the essential elements of the affirmative's case are not unique to the resolutional terms, and thus do not warrant accepting the resolution. In a debate on the third-party proposition mentioned previously, one affirmative argued that significantly stronger third parties would intrinsically lead to beneficial applications in the American political system. The affirmative cited the income tax, direct election of senators, women's suffrage, labor legislation, and social security as examples of desirable legislation originating with third parties. The negative meeting this case pointed out that these laws were enacted under the status quo and thus were not unique to strengthened third parties. If the negative can prove that some elements of the affirmative case are not unique to the case or could be obtained without adopting the resolution, it has successfully attacked the uniqueness claim of the affirmative.

E. Attack Application

In attacking application the negative tries to prove that the value or quasipolicy advocated by the affirmative will not be applied to the problem, that the implication of the value is not positive, or that the application offered is not a legitimate application of the values being upheld. In a debate on the third-party proposition, one affirmative claimed that the application of the resolution would result in strengthened third parties able to enact important legislation perceived as extreme by complacent majorities. A negative meeting this case attacked the application by arguing it would not function as the affirmative claimed it would. The negative maintained that a third party could not enact any legislation until it grew to major-party size, and to attract enough voters to do that, it would have to drop its extreme position.

F. Attack Solvency

Of course, in a debate over a proposition of value, the affirmative is not required to present a plan (although at times they may offer a plan or something like it as an illustration to represent the implications of their value position). However, it is often effective for the negative to point to the concrete implications of affirmative advocacy in order to challenge the benefits or reasons to accept the value(s) promoted by the affirmative. In attacking solvency the negative argues that, even if the application functions as the affirmative wants it to, it will not solve the problem, or achieve the good things implied by value advocacy. This is really a policy argument applied to the value or quasipolicy context. In debates on the proposition on foreign investment in the United States mentioned previously, some affirmative teams argued as follows:

1. Foreign investors would build coal-burning factories in the United States that would substantially increase the amount of carbon dioxide released into the atmosphere.

2. This increase of carbon dioxide would cause a greenhouse effect.

3. The greenhouse effect would warm the earth's atmosphere.

4. This would cause disastrous changes in the earth's climate, which would threaten life on earth.

Negative teams meeting this type of case often responded by arguing in this way:

1. If all U.S. coal-burning plants were shut down, the greenhouse effect would be delayed for only three or four years.

2. China, with 50 percent of global coal reserves, intends to increase coal consumption substantially in the near future.

3. Other countries are eager to increase industrialization and will use more coal.

The negative team then concluded that the affirmative's plan would not solve the greenhouse problem, which it gave as the justification for accepting the resolution. If the negative wins the solvency argument, there is no reason to adopt the resolution.

G. Provide Value Objections

Value objections are the negative arguments that undesirable consequences will flow from adoption of the affirmative's case. In other words, they are reasons the criteria and/or values upon which the affirmative case relies are philosophically or pragmatically bad. In providing value objections the negative argues that the affirmative's proposal or acceptance of the affirmative's values and advocacy will produce something so objectionable—in effect, a disadvantage—that we should reject the affirmative's case. In a debate on the third-party proposition, one negative argued that multiple parties rather than a lone third party would result. Multiple parties, she claimed, inherently lead to unstable governments and domestic chaos, which in turn could lead to a totalitarian regime. Note that value objections are introduced by the negative. When the negative introduces them, the affirmative must be prepared to demonstrate that they are not significant and that they are outweighed by other issues.

III. PROPOSITION OF POLICY NEGATIVE
APPROACHES

As in value negative cases, in policy debates the negative has the initial burden of rebuttal and must attack the case that the affirmative presents. The negative knows that the affirmative will present harm, inherency, plan, solvency, and advantage issues. The negative must refute at least one of the affirmative issues, or else prevail on at least one of the issues the negative introduces in order to win. Of course the negative will be in a much stronger and more persuasive position if it can create a consistent and coherent advocacy to compete with the affirmative's advocacy. The specific development of the case and the particular issues the negative uses in any given situation obviously will depend on the resolution under debate, the available evidence and arguments, the actual case of the opposition, the dynamics of the occasion, and the attitudes, interests, and intellectual capabilities of the audience.

Each negative strategy should be custom built and adapted to the specific affirmative case it must oppose. The negative selects among its arsenal of potential issues and develops those best suited to a particular situation. Although carrying one issue—workability, for instance—could win for the negative, advocates should remember that a competent affirmative will have anticipated and prepared for all possible attacks. Thus, because the negative can rarely be sure of winning an issue until the debate is over, its best strategy generally is to attack all vulnerable areas of the affirmative case. It should concentrate its major attacks on the most vulnerable areas—for example, not only attacking workability but also providing minor repairs or a counterplan and proving that disadvantages outweigh advantages.

A. Attack Topicality

If your professor assigns you to write a paper about the works of Chaucer, and you turn in a superb paper about Shakespeare, you are not likely to receive good marks. Your paper is not "topical," that is, it does not conform to the parameters established by the assignment. Topicality is the procedural question asking whether the plan offered by the affirmative conforms to the parameters (limits and opportunities) offered by the proposition.

All other arguments in a debate are weighed together, relative to one another; topicality is a stand-alone issue. Because topicality is considered a priori, if the judge determines that the plan is not topical, he or she will usually not consider the other issues in the debate. In debate over policy propositions, the question of topicality is strictly a question of the plan and whether it represents the action called for in the language of the proposition. If the negative wins the topicality issue, it generally wins the debate. It is the one issue that if won by the negative usually means the debate is won by the negative. Other issues are measured in relation to each other, but topicality stands alone.

When advocates argue that a plan is not topical, they maintain that it is not a legitimate or appropriate embodiment of the action called for in the proposition being debated. In the courts an attorney may object to a piece of evidence, a question, or an argument on the ground that it is not relevant to the case before the court. If the judge sustains the objection, the matter is excluded. In parliamentary debate the chair can rule as "out of order" any remarks or proposed amendments that are not germane to the business before the house. (The stringency with which this rule is enforced varies; for example, the U.S. Senate does not require that a senator's remarks be germane.) In academic debate the topicality issue usually becomes an absolute voting issue, and the judge awards the decision to the negative if it wins the issue. In less formal situations, reasonable individuals tend to dismiss irrelevant arguments.

1. Topicality of the Plan.   Recall that topicality refers to whether the plan is a legitimate and fair interpretation of the policy action called for in the resolution. The primary test for topicality is the *plan in a vacuum*. The plan, absent arguments about justification, solvency, and advantages, must itself be topical. If the plan advocated by the affirmative is not topical, they are advocating something other than the resolution, and therefore, should be disqualified based on topicality.

The proposition "Resolved: That the federal government should grant annually a specific percentage of its income tax revenue to the state governments" provides an interesting example. This proposition mandated four specific things for the affirmative's plan: (1) an annual grant, (2) a specific percentage of the revenue, (3) funds coming from federal income tax revenue, and (4) funds distributed by the federal government to state governments. If any one of these items had been missing, the negative would have had grounds for arguing "not topical." The affirmative may add some nontopical provisions to its plan to provide for a reasonable implementation of its proposal. For example, in debating the revenue-sharing proposition, some teams provided that the funds could not be used for (1) matching federal funds for federal categorical grant programs or (2) highway construction. The argument by the affirmative is that these are necessary and essential components to facilitating the policy action called for by the proposition. The negative is well advised to argue that portions of the plan are nontopical; thus any advantage gained by them is extratopical and should not be considered.

2. Extratopicality of the Advantages.   The advantages must be a direct result of implementation of a topical plan. If the negative can prove an advantage is extratopical, that advantage should be rejected as a reason for adopting the resolution. It may also be argued, that since the affirmative may not "sever" portions of their plan once presented, if an essential portion of the plan is not topical, the plan as a whole should be rejected.

If the advantages come from a nontopical provision of the plan, the affirmative is in trouble. On the revenue-sharing proposition some affirmative teams argued that the states should be *required* to give funds to public schools and claimed the advantage of better education. Negatives meeting this case were usually able to prove that the provision mandating education was nontopical and that the advantage of better education came from giving the money to the

---

Topicality

1. *Definition(s):* The negative presents its definition(s) of terms or phrases in the resolution.
2. *Violation(s):* The negative argues that the affirmative plan violates or fails to meet the negatives' definition(s).
3. *Reasons to prefer:* The negative offers standards or criteria by which definitions should be judged and argues that its definitions more completely meet these criteria than do the affirmatives definitions; therefore, its interpretation is superior and should be preferred.
4. *Impact (voting issue):* The negative explains why the affirmatives failure to present a topical plan means the judge should vote for the negative.

---

schools and not from any of the four items mandated in the resolution. They also demonstrated that the advantage was "not unique" to the resolution. The same advantage could be achieved by having the federal government give money (and not necessarily income tax revenue) directly to the schools. (The affirmative might have been in a stronger position to win if they could prove that upon receipt of funding from the topical revenue-sharing plan, states would, without federal mandates, prioritize spending on education thus accruing the advantages of better education. This would require evidence proving that education was the first priority states would satisfy.)

As we have just seen, the advantage of "better education" as argued was non-topical, as it resulted from a nontopical portion of the plan, the mandate that states increase funding on education. As we have also noted, nontopical plan planks may be added to the plan to facilitate reasonable implementation. However, any advantage that comes from a nontopical plank of the plan is itself nontopical. For example, the provision that no revenue-sharing funds be used for highway construction was a reasonable nontopical constraint. If, however, the affirmative claimed as an advantage that it would reduce waste in highway construction, such an advantage would clearly be nontopical; it would stem from adoption of a nontopical plank of the plan. Of course it would also be "not unique," in that any waste in highway construction could be eliminated by legislation other than revenue sharing.

B. Attack the Harm

The objective of the negative here is either to challenge the harm issue by demonstrating that the affirmative has not proved the existence of a harm, by proving that there is no harm, by minimizing the harm, or by arguing that the harm is, in fact, a benefit.

1. No Harm.   In rare circumstances, the negative may be able to argue successfully that there is no harm to the conditions identified by the affirmative. In debating the proposition "Resolved: That the federal government should control the supply and utilization of energy in the United States," some affirmatives called for the federal government to ban any further construction of nuclear energy plants to generate electricity. They pointed out that the status quo was committed to the construction of such plants and argued, as their harm issue, the claim that, when we had 100 or more such plants, there would be an unacceptable risk of radiation leakage or explosion. Many negatives argued that no harm existed or would exist. They maintained that nuclear power plants were perfectly safe and that any leakage or explosion was impossible. They cited evidence that no fatality had ever been caused by a civilian nuclear power plant and extended their argument by citing the elaborate safety precautions already in existence. The disaster at Chernobyl was irrelevant, the affirmative maintained, because the plant had been built to a design inferior to U.S. standards, and the 2011 earthquake off the Pacific coast of Tōhoku, Japan, was not comparable because American reactors are not built in such vulnerable locations. Debates on this issue provided excellent examples of the clash of evidence. Solid evidence was available to both sides, and the debate inevitably was won by the team that could provide the most recent evidence from the best-qualified authorities, who could be quoted most directly in support of the point under dispute.

2. Harm Not Significant.   The negative objective in attacking significance is to prove that the harms or advantages of the affirmative (when weighed against the disadvantages of plan adoption and the advantages of a counterplan or modified status quo) are not sufficiently significant to warrant adopting the resolution. In many debates, this is synonymous with arguing existence of the harm issue, as discussed above. However, when the measure of importance of the harm is in question, the significance of the harm is the appropriate target of the negative.

The negative will usually find it advisable to examine the affirmative's harm for both quantitative and qualitative significance, and attack the affirmative if either or both are not proved. In debates on the proposition "Resolved: That the federal government should significantly strengthen the regulation of mass media communication in the United States," some affirmatives argued that television commercials for sugar-laden food products caused cavities in children. Negatives meeting this case readily proved that an unknown number of cavities were not sufficient justification for government regulation of the mass media. On the same proposition some affirmatives argued that violence on television "affected children adversely." Again, negatives quickly refuted the significance of the harm—no significant numbers of children were proved to have been adversely affected, and no qualification was provided for "adversely affected."

In debates on the "guarantee employment opportunities" proposition, affirmatives could usually readily show that millions were unemployed, thus establishing quantitative significance. Negative advocates may grant this argument and respond that while unemployment is not a desirable condition, if it is temporary and those experiencing it have savings and support from public and private programs, the consequence may not justify massive new government spending programs, and thus, the affirmative had not proved a qualitative harm from unemployment. In fact, at least while unemployed, citizens are able to avoid the stress of work and danger of workplace accidents. They continued this argument by introducing evidence to show that many unemployed persons received unemployment compensation, food stamps, and other welfare benefits. Thus, they maintained, the affirmative had not proved that the unemployed persons were harmed by their unemployment.

The negative may attack the affirmative for failing to prove quantitative significance, qualitative significance, or, in some circumstances, both quantitative and qualitative significance. Most often, of course, the affirmative will successfully establish some significance. The task of the negative then is to prove that the significance established by the affirmative is not sufficient on balance to outweigh the disadvantages the negative will try to prove.

3. Harm Overstated. A well-prepared affirmative is usually able to identify an important harm area and to find expert evidence that portrays the harm in the most compelling way possible. It is the job of the negative to argue that the affirmative's estimation of the harm is overstated and to offer evidence to prove that point. Successfully done, this mitigates the magnitude of the impact won by the affirmative.

4. Case Turns. The most effective way to argue against the affirmative's harms is to use the classic turnaround argument, or *case turn*. This is an offensive negative strategy designed to demonstrate that the harms identified by the affirmative are not harms but, in fact, benefits to the status quo. For example, during debates on the proposition "Resolved: That the United States federal government should amend Title VII of the Civil Rights Act of 1964, through legislation, to create additional protections against racial and/or gender discrimination," many affirmatives identified broad cases of discrimination occurring within the status quo. Negatives turned this issue by claiming that, although discrimination is harmful, its existence motivated repressed people to organize movements and mobilize grassroots action, which would be far more effective in creating meaningful social change than the top-down solution mandated by the plan. In debating expansion of health care access, negatives may answer the harm of lack of access to health care by arguing that expanding access to health care also increases exposure to potentially harmful vaccines, x-ray radiation, and exposure to overmedication. Or, it may be argued against a jobs program, that new building programs to employ people through the building of infrastructure projects require use of resources including the burning of fossil fuels, which may in turn contribute to accelerated global warming. The harm then becomes a reason to oppose the affirmative, or put another way, the harm becomes an advantage of the negative's alternative.

C. Attack Inherency

Inherency is the stock issue which forwards that due to the nature of the status quo and absent affirmative reform, there is a probability that the harm identified will indeed continue into the future. Inherency may be described as a barrier to solvency which is structurally embedded within the status quo, or a set of prevailing behaviors and attitudes which preclude positive reform. Most importantly, inherency identifies the root cause(s) resulting in harms and predicts that these causes will make the continuation of the harm likely. Negatives may address inherency claims in several ways.

First, the negative may argue that the affirmative has either failed to identify the barrier or incorrectly identified the inherent cause or failed to recognize the importance of alternative causes of the harm within the status quo. For example, the affirmative may argue that Americans are in bad health and present evidence that 52 million Americans do not have health insurance. Negatives may counter that while it is true that many do not have health insurance, this does not prevent them from receiving necessary care from clinics and other free sources, that the majority of sick Americans actually have insurance, and that a majority of uninsured are so by choice. They may also offer low-cost structures within the status quo which serve to remedy the harm, including free health information available on the Internet and through other media sources and free local screenings and educational programs. In addition, they may be able to prove that for many, the barrier to having health care is not cost or availability, but information and marketing, which can be easily remedied without implementation of the affirmation plan.

Remember that if the affirmative inherency is very strong, it may "swamp" solvency; that is, no plan may be able to overcome the inherency. Fiat will allow implementation, but not workability. In addition, fiating affirmative action over strong attitudinal biases or disrupting existing governmental structures may result in substantial disadvantages. Finally, if the affirmative has not clearly identified the reasons the plan has not been implemented or the root causes of the problem, it may be missing the hidden disadvantages that are the real reasons the harm continues to exist. A second set of negative arguments against inherency may be identification of trends or systematic adjustments naturally occurring within the status quo which will solve the problems identified in the harm issue without legislative or policy action. For example, it may be argued that increasing gas prices will naturally cause a shift to alternative and renewable energy sources, thus solving the generation of greenhouse gases through existing market forces and without new rules, laws, or programs. Minor repairs offer additional opportunities for negative argumentation. These are the introduction of small actions not requiring the major changes required by the affirmative plan which could reduce the harm. For example, consumers may boycott companies who are major polluters and producers of greenhouse gases, thus creating economic incentives for those companies to reduce their carbon footprints.

D. Attack Solvency

Typically the negative will seek to minimize the affirmative advantage by arguing issues of harm and inherency, and then prove that the plan will not achieve the benefits claimed by the affirmative.

In developing solvency arguments, the negative attempts to prove that the plan will not work, that even if it works exactly as the affirmative wants it to, it will not solve the harm or achieve the advantages claimed, and that the advantages are not significant or compelling. For example, in debates on the "guaranteed annual wage for nonagricultural workers" proposition, some affirmatives argued as their harm issue that the purchasing power of unemployed persons must be maintained. They cited evidence that millions of persons were unemployed annually and then presented a plan that would provide a guaranteed annual wage for employees with one year's seniority. Negatives argued that the plan did not provide solvency because millions of the unemployed cited in the affirmative's harm were agricultural workers, who were not covered in the plan (they were excluded by the resolution). Negatives then introduced evidence to show that most unemployed persons had less than one year's seniority in their last job and so would not receive the guaranteed annual wage provided for in the plan. The plan would work for the relatively few unemployed persons with one year's seniority, but not for the millions cited by the affirmative in its need issue.

In debates on the "guaranteed employment opportunities for all U.S. citizens" proposition, some affirmatives proposed a plan to rebuild the inner cities and claimed as their advantage that this plan would provide jobs for all. Negatives meeting this case were quick to point out that the jobs created by this plan did not "guarantee employment opportunities" for workers unskilled in the building trades or for people who could not handle the physical demands of unskilled construction work.

1. Workability. The negative's objective here is to block adoption of the resolution by proving that the plan proposed by the affirmative is unworkable. Those advocating a ban on personal ownership of handguns would have to prove that such a law would be enforceable given the likely inherency, that many gun owners would elect to keep their guns, and that in order to apply the ban, law enforcement agencies would have to violate privacy rights beyond their ability to do so. Advocates of nuclear fission as a method of energy production or manned space travel beyond the solar system would have a hard time proving the efficacy of the technologies. To argue workability, the negative should present a series of concisely stated, closely reasoned arguments. In preparing for this, as with other negative issues, advocates often develop a series of briefs against potential affirmative plans. When they hear the plan the affirmative is actually presenting, they pull the appropriate briefs from their file and adapt them to the specific plan presented by the affirmative.

Debating the energy proposition, one affirmative team cited the energy shortage as its harm and proposed to solve the harm by a plan that called for the federal government to require electric plants to phase out the use of oil and coal and to build solar, geothermal, and nuclear plants to produce electricity. Well-prepared negatives usually had briefs of arguments prepared for each of these energy sources. One negative argued against this plan by introducing evidence to establish the following:

> First, solar energy is unworkable because (1) it has never been proven in commercial use; (2) its potential is geographically limited by cloud cover; (3) the fuel cell method is prohibitively expensive—it would increase the cost of electricity one thousand times; and (4) the reflector

method is prohibitive in land cost—it would require an area equal to the size of 21 states to solve the affirmative's needs.

Second, nuclear energy is unworkable because (1) there will be a long time lag before reactors can be built—all present nuclear plants are two to seven years behind schedule, and future plants will be delayed even more because of lengthy lawsuits and hearings where the dangers to life and environment will be argued; and (2) there is now a shortage of uranium necessary to operate the present plants—there just will not be enough uranium to operate the number of plants proposed by the affirmative.

Third, geothermal is unworkable because (1) there are very few potential sources of commercially useful size; (2) these are located in earthquake-prone areas, where drilling for the hot water might in itself cause earthquakes, or in areas remote from any population to use the electricity they might produce; and (3) there is a shortage of copper, which makes it commercially impractical to transmit electric power over great distances.

The negative concluded its workability argument by demonstrating that all three of the energy sources proposed by the affirmative could not solve its harm.

2. Plan Will Not Accrue Claimed Advantages.   In developing this argument, advocates concentrate on attempting to prove that the plan—even if it works exactly as the affirmative wants it to—will not accrue the advantages claimed by the affirmative. Often reasons why the case is inherent also provide reasons why the plan cannot succeed. Negative debaters seek to identify the reasons and mechanisms that will allow plans to be circumvented.

In debating the law enforcement proposition, some affirmatives proposed as their plan that wiretapping be legalized for state and local police forces and claimed as their advantage that there would be more convictions of criminals because wiretaps would produce direct evidence of crimes. Negatives meeting this case argued that the plan would not accrue the advantage, because criminals would assume their phones were tapped and take countermeasures to circumvent the plan. They argued that criminals would (1) reduce the use of phones, (2) use scrambler phones, (3) use electronic devices to discover untapped phones and use those phones, (4) use randomly chosen public phones, (5) use frequently changed codes, (6) use frequently changed slang or code, and (7) use fragmentary references and identification.

In debating the "comprehensive medical care" proposition, one affirmative provided in its plan for free medical care for all citizens and claimed as one of its advantages "better medical care for the poor." The negative argued that the plan could not accrue this advantage because (1) few physicians practice in the rural and urban areas where most poor people live; (2) the poor lack the money to pay for transportation to travel to the areas where the physicians practice; (3) many poor people are not aware of the value of early medical care and will not seek it; (4) many poor people are afraid of medical care and will not seek it until their condition is critical; and (5) many of the working poor cannot afford to take time off to obtain medical care and do so only when their condition is critical.

Affirmative plans may also offer opportunities for circumvention. If there is a strong attitudinal inherency for the harm, there is motive and often the ability for people to avoid the mandates of the plan. This is a criticism of the Affordable Care Act. While it does mandate purchase of health insurance, the penalty of noncompliance is more than the cost of compliance. So people who have the motive may elect to accept the fines and not purchase insurance.

3. Impact of Advantage.   Negative teams may also wish to argue that even if an advantage is achieved, it is not a compelling or significant advantage. In debates on the energy proposition, some affirmatives presented a plan providing for a ban of offshore drilling for oil and claimed the advantage of protecting the environment by (1) preventing unsightly oil rigs, (2) protecting fish life, and (3) preventing ecological damage from possible oil leakage. Some negative teams meeting this plan argued that the advantages were not significant, because (1) the oil rigs would be miles offshore so no one could see them from the shore; (2) oil rigs provided a feeding ground for fish, so the fish population actually increased in this area (note this negative case turn, in which the affirmative claimed that banning oil rigs protected fish life, and the negative turned this argument around, claiming that oil rigs increased the fish population); and (3) oil leakage was rare, and even in those few cases in which it occurred, the wildlife population returned to normal in two years. They concluded their argument by maintaining that the affirmative had provided neither quantitative nor qualitative significance for its advantage; that is, offshore wells did no harm to the environment, and, in any event, the need for oil clearly outweighed the insignificant environmental considerations the affirmative presented.

Recall the asbestos example mentioned in Chapter 9. Many people argued that asbestos in school buildings posed a life-threatening danger to schoolchildren. The negative might argue that only 1 in 11 million children were at risk. As economist Robert Samuelson notes, "The standard retort is: a rich country like ours can afford absolute safety. No we can't. Regulatory costs raise prices or taxes. Our incomes are lower than they might be. That's OK if we receive a lot of benefits—much cleaner air or healthier food. But it's not OK if the benefit is trivial or nonexistent."[1]

Saving even one child's life could hardly be called trivial. Is one life a significant advantage for a multibillion-dollar expenditure? Could that sum be used in other ways that might save or improve thousands or millions of lives?

E. Prove Disadvantages

Unless topicality is being argued, disadvantage arguments are the most important negative arguments in most policy debates. This is because they are the negative's offense: They offer reasons that adoption of the affirmative plan would be bad. When negatives argue against the harm, inherency, or solvency issues, they are

---

1. Robert J. Samuelson, "The Triumph of the Psycho-Fact," *Newsweek*, May 9, 1994, p. 73.

for the most part (excepting case turns) making arguments that the benefit of the affirmative is not as great as claimed, that is, they are "playing defense." These are strategically sound approaches, but by themselves are not reasons to reject plan implementation. Every policy action entails risk and has some sort of costs. The negative's objective with disadvantage arguments is to block the adoption of the resolution by offering reasons that the plan proposed by the affirmative will produce disadvantages (substantial costs) and that these disadvantages (costs) outweigh any possible advantage (benefit) the plan may achieve.

In debating the energy proposition, one affirmative, having established as its need that strip mining damaged the environment, provided a plan that banned all strip mining and claimed the advantage of a better environment. A negative meeting this case argued that banning strip mining (which it called surface mining) would produce the following disadvantages: It would (1) cause a shortage of copper (most copper comes from surface mines, and copper wire is essential for the transmission of electricity from generators to users); (2) cause a shortage of iron (most iron comes from surface mines); (3) exacerbate the oil shortage (because oil would be used as a partial replacement for surface-mined coal); (4) increase the cost of electricity (because scarce oil and more expensive deep-mined coal would be used to replace surface-mined coal); (5) increase inflation (as a result of 1–4); (6) increase unemployment (as a result of disadvantages 1–5); (7) increase black-lung disease (because more people would work in deep mines under the affirmative's plan); (8) increase the number of mine accidents (because working in deep mines is inherently more dangerous than working in surface mines); (9) cause dependence on unreliable foreign sources for coal (because present domestic deep mines could not meet the demand for coal and foreign sources might embargo coal, as the Arabs embargoed oil); and (10) exacerbate the balance-of-payments problem (because dollars would flow out of the country to buy coal). The negative then concluded this portion of its case by arguing that these disadvantages far outweighed whatever aesthetic advantages might be gained by viewing a landscape untouched by surface mining as contrasted with a landscape reclaimed after surface mining.

In debates on U.S. trade policies with China, some affirmative plans called for ending China's "most favored nation" status to force it to improve its human rights record. Some negatives meeting this plan argued the disadvantage: increased human rights violations. They maintained that China could easily shift its trade to nations that did not link trade and human rights, and with no incentive to improve, conditions would become worse.

Of course, the negative must prove the disadvantage. As we saw in Chapter 6, whoever introduces an issue or contention into the debate has *a* burden of proof.

1. Prove the Slippery Slope. When the affirmative's plan is not bad per se, the negative may try to prove that the plan includes a seemingly harmless proposal that would be an irreversible first step down a **slippery slope** to the most deleterious consequences. In debates on the mass media proposition, an affirmative plan to ban advertising of sugar-laden food products would probably have the advantages of reducing children's cavities and improving their general health. Certainly these are desirable things in themselves. Negatives meeting such cases argued that this seemingly benign plan would lead us down a slippery slope to abridgement of the First Amendment; that is, if we banned advertising for foods with a high sugar content, what would be next? It would set a dangerous precedent that could lead to the banning of advertising for books and for political candidates and would create unacceptable barriers to free speech. In short, the negative said, we should avoid taking the first step down the slippery slope that could lead to clearly disadvantageous consequences. The affirmative then had the burden of demonstrating that its proposal was a limited step and that its plan included safeguards to avoid the slippery slope. Republicans argue that a rule nominally increasing taxes on the richest Americans (the Buffett rule) would lead to increased taxes on all sectors of society, gradually but sequentially eroding. Constitutionally granted liberties and leading eventually to a totalitarian government.

Note that the slippery slope argument is not unique to the negative, nor is it limited to policy debate. In debates on the proposition "U.S. colleges and universities have inappropriately altered educational practices to address issues of race or gender," some affirmatives noted that many campuses had adopted rules to enforce "politically correct speech." Such rules were intended to reduce racist or sexist slurs. However, some affirmatives argued that rules enforcing "politically correct speech" would lead us down the slippery slope to abridgement of the First Amendment; that is, if we banned slurs, what would be next? It would set a dangerous precedent that could lead to all of the harms cited in the mass media example. The affirmative argued that, although we might deplore racist or sexist slurs, the far greater (more significant) value was the preservation of the First Amendment.

2. Provide Generic Disadvantages.   The disadvantages we have just considered were specific to the cases being attacked. Often, as we have noted, the negative will not know the affirmative's case until the debate is actually underway—and then it is too late to conduct specific research to refute the opponent's case. To provide for this situation, experienced negative advocates develop **generic disadvantages** that may be applied to a number of possible affirmative plans; that is, after careful analysis of the proposition, they discover certain provisions that an affirmative must almost certainly include in its plan. Although they cannot be certain in advance exactly what form these provisions will take, they can make realistic estimates. For example, in debating the "guaranteed employment opportunities" proposition, some negative teams developed a series of generic disadvantages to any affirmative plan that would increase income. (By providing jobs for unemployed people, of course, the affirmative's plan usually did increase their income.) We have previously described the "meatballs" disadvantage. Negative teams argued: (1) When Americans' income increases, they eat more beef; (2) eating more beef increases cardiovascular disease, causing millions of deaths; (3) because farmers would find it more profitable to feed cattle grain to produce more beef, there would be less grain for export to the less developed countries (LDCs); (4) millions of people in the LDCs would die, because they would be unable to get grain; (5) this would cause the LDCs to start World War III in order to obtain needed grain; and (6) World War III would cause the end of life on Earth—a truly Brobdingnagian disadvantage! Would an increase in employment in the United States really cause the end of life on Earth? The advocate must be prepared to demonstrate that the cause is capable of producing the effect under consideration.

As we noted in discussing the slippery slope, the negative debating the mass media proposition could develop effective arguments against banning advertising for sugar-laden foods. Negatives found that arguments used against this specific case could be adapted as generic disadvantages for use against many affirmative cases that imposed limitations on free speech. The negative could not know in advance what the affirmative would argue in favor of banning—saccharin ads, pornography, violence on TV, or any of the other myriad variations available to the affirmative. Against many of these bans, however, the negative could run a slippery slope First Amendment disadvantage and claim that the affirmative's seemingly benign ban would result in the disadvantage of violating First Amendment rights—the point being that the disadvantage of violating free speech outweighed any advantage claimed by the affirmative. The ability to convert a specific disadvantage, with appropriate adaptation, into a generic disadvantage is an important weapon in the negative's arsenal.

A very accessible area for generic negative argumentation is the political process. Because any policy requiring action by the federal government entails political actions, and most policy propositions in academic debate identify the U.S. federal government as their actor, the political cost of affirmative action is a potential arena for negative disadvantage argumentation. Fiat allows the affirmative to assume, for the sake of argument, implementation of their plan "by normal means." However, normal means may require political compromise, utilization of political capital, reordering of legislative agendas, and thus important legislation may suffer in order to facilitate passage of the affirmative plan. The argument may also work in the other direction.

3. Watch for Turnarounds. The wise affirmative will be alert for opportunities to "turnaround" disadvantages and convert them into advantages. Negative advocates, as they build disadvantages, should be aware of this affirmative strategy and consider whether a disadvantage can be turned against them—in which case they should not use it. A successful turnaround means not only that the negative loses the disadvantage but also that the affirmative gains an advantage.

Consider an argument made by a negative speaker that work sharing would cause strikes. These strikes, the negative could argue, would be a disadvantage to the affirmative plan. The affirmative could attempt to "turn around" the disadvantage by citing evidence that unions have gone on strike to obtain work sharing. This evidence would seek to prove that the likelihood of strikes would not occur and, in fact, would be reduced. The affirmative could then claim an additional advantage: Labor relations would be more peaceful under the affirmative plan, because unions would not have to go on strike to obtain work sharing. Of course new issues may not be introduced in the rebuttal speeches. But if the negative had introduced the issue of strikes, it would be perfectly proper for the affirmative to turn around that issue.

In debates on increasing taxes on oil imports, some affirmative teams claimed the advantage of reducing dependence on foreign oil sources. Some negative teams, meeting this type of case, argued a turnaround. They claimed that if oil was more expensive, more nuclear energy plants would be built. This, they argued, would create a disadvantage—increased risk of a nuclear disaster.

4. Prepare Disadvantage Shells.   To allow more time to develop and extend their arguments, negative advocates should present the entirety of their argumentation in some form at their first opportunity: the first negative constructive. **Shells** are brief versions of arguments to be expanded upon later in the debate. Offering their initial argumentation in brief form allows the negative strategic choices later in the debate; they may expand upon those arguments which attract the least response by the affirmative or have the best opportunity to prevail, which saving time on other arguments which are less likely to be successful.

F. Develop the Counterplan

The counterplan is a strong negative strategy because it releases the negative from the need to defend the status quo and it shifts some of the argumentative ground in the debate to the negative. The **counterplan** is a plan presented by the negative—one that is competitive with the affirmative's plan and is a superior policy alternative. Acceptance of the counterplan mandates rejection of the plan, and thus a negative decision. Negatives may offer a counterplan as a superior way to solve the affirmative need or as a superior policy that would be blocked by affirmative plan adoption. A benefit of the counterplan is that it may offer a way to solve the affirmative problem that uniquely avoids the disadvantages offered by the negative.

The essential components of a prima facie disadvantage argument are as follows:

1. *Threshold:* This is the brink, or the point at which the disadvantage begins to happen. The negative argues that affirmatives plan action will push us over that threshold.

2. *Uniqueness:* The disadvantage, if a reason to reject the plan, must be uniquely caused by the plan. If it would occur absent the plan, it is not a reason to reject the plan.

3. *Link:* The disadvantage must link to the plan and be caused by the specific plan action called for. Even generic disadvantages should have links specific to the affirmatives plan.

4. *Impact:* The disadvantage must have a quantitative and/or qualitative impact to be weighed against the affirmatives advantage.

5. *Probability:* Many disadvantages have a huge impact (global nuclear war, for example) but a small probability of occurring. To be a reason to reject the affirmative, the disadvantage must have a genuine chance of happening.

1. Competition.   The counterplan must compete with the affirmative plan or it is not a reason to reject the plan. That is, endorsement of the counterplans means rejection of the plan. Competition may be demonstrated in two ways.

a. The Affirmative Plan and the Counterplan Are Mutually Exclusive.   This means that the plan and the counterplan cannot simultaneously coexist.

   Here's an example: Following the collapse of communism in Eastern Europe, some argued that the United States should withdraw its troops from Eastern Europe. They maintained that, because the Cold War was over, the troops were no longer needed, and the money saved could be used to reduce the national debt. The negative team disagreed with the affirmative's justification and offered a redefined justification. It noted that the Cold War may be over but claimed that the threat of war was greater than ever. As a counterplan against this case, it argued that America should increase its troops in Europe. It held that the collapse of communism created a volatile situation and that wars might break out in the newly liberated nations. The presence of increased U.S. military forces in Europe, it maintained, would be a deterrent to such wars. It argued that, when the advantages and disadvantages of the plan and counterplan were weighed, there was a net benefit in favor of the counterplan. Obviously the United States cannot simultaneously withdraw its troops from Europe and increase its troops in Europe. The plan and counterplan are mutually exclusive.

   The affirmative may seek to illustrate noncompetition of the counterplan by *permuting* its plan to adapt to the counterplan and argue that adoption of both the plan and the counterplan is feasible. A **permutation** is a test of competitiveness; it is the illustration (not the advocacy) that the plan and counterplan can be combined. The affirmative will win if it can establish that the plan and counterplan are not mutually exclusive *and* that adopting both is superior to adopting the counterplan alone.

b. The Counterplan Alone Is Superior to Simultaneous Adoption of the Affirmative Plan and the Counterplan.   It is often impossible to construct a counterplan that cannot simultaneously exist with the affirmative plan. Another measure of competition is the *net benefits* standard. Here the negative seeks to demonstrate that it would be better to adopt only the counterplan than it would be to adopt the combination of counterplan and plan. This might be the case if the counterplan better solves the affirmative need. In addition, the counterplan alone may be superior if it uniquely avoids disadvantages presented by the negative.

   For example, the affirmative might argue that heart disease is the nation's leading killer and so we should appropriate $1 billion for research on heart

---

Formula for Net Benefit

CP > CP + P (the counterplan alone is better than the counterplan plus the plan)

disease. The negative might argue that the government has already spent billions on heart disease, but with only modest results. AIDS, it might maintain, is a more urgent problem and so we should spend the $1 billion on AIDS research. An affirmative meeting this counterplan might agree that both diseases are terrible and permute its case by proposing the appropriation of $2 billion for research: $1 billion for heart disease, and $1 billion for AIDS. If the affirmative can show that simultaneously adopting its plan and the counterplan is possible (they are not mutually exclusive) and more desirable (they provide a greater net benefit) than adopting the counterplan alone, it will win. Given the size of the federal budget, it probably would be possible to add $2 billion without making disastrous cuts in other desirable programs or raising taxes to a level that would damage the economy. For the negative to win, it must establish that funding AIDS research alone would provide a greater net benefit. It could do so if it could demonstrate that funding in excess of $1 billion would be uniquely disadvantageous. In meeting affirmative permutations of this sort, the negative must be able to argue permutation standards and present good reasons that the affirmative cannot permute its case to include the counterplan or prove that the counterplan alone is superior.

The negative may establish that its counterplan is mutually exclusive in a number of ways. It may argue that the counterplan should be carried out by a different level of government than the resolution calls for (for example, the states rather than the federal government), or that a different agency should carry out the counterplan (for instance, it should be voluntary rather than mandated by law), or that finite funds should be used in a different way (for example, the funds available for space research should be used to send a probe to Mars rather than to Venus). In debates on the mass media proposition, negative counterplans often called for a voluntary agency such as the National Association of Broadcasters (NAB), rather than an agency of the federal government, to regulate television. Similarly, in debates on the "consumer product safety" proposition, some negative counterplans called for action by the states rather than the federal government.

The negative has to demonstrate that its counterplan provides the best balance of risks and advantages when compared to the plan of the affirmative. In debates on the mass media proposition, negatives calling for the NAB to regulate television violence often argued that the risk of loss of First Amendment freedoms would be reduced if a voluntary agency, and not the federal government, regulated television violence. On the "consumer product safety" proposition, negatives using a "states" counterplan argued that the states rather than the federal government should regulate a particular consumer product. If a plan turned out to be undesirable, less harm would be done than if the plan were nationwide. And if the plan turned out to be desirable, other states would adopt it.

2. Conditional and Dispositional Counterplans.   The **conditional counterplan** is a counterplan offered as part of an if-then statement by the negative: If the status quo cannot solve the problem, then the counterplan can; or, if the counterplan fails, we will rely on the status quo. In developing this type of case, the negative argues that (1) the status quo can solve the problem, and (2) if the status quo can't solve the problem, it will advocate the negative counterplan. Such a strategy allows the negative to discard advocacy of the counterplan or the status quo depending on how the argumentation plays out in the debate.

Student debaters should consider two important constraints before selecting this approach. First, the time constraints of academic debate may make it extremely difficult to adequately develop both the defense of the status quo and the counterplan. Second, conditional arguments have to be presented with great clarity. This requirement for clarity, when combined with the difficult-in-itself counterplan, makes for a doubly complex problem for the debater.

The negative may also offer its counterplan as a *dispositional* counterplan. This is a special type of conditional argument in which the conditions for advocacy are predetermined. If a counterplan is dispositional, the negative may abandon advocacy of it unless it is turned—that is, unless it is compelled to answer disadvantages to the counterplan.

3. Other Counterplans.[2]   Other forms of counterplans include (1) the delay counterplan, (2) the exceptions counterplan, and (3) the plan-inclusive counterplan. The *delay* counterplan advocates waiting some period of time before adopting the affirmative plan. The rationale for delay is based on avoiding a disadvantage that would uniquely occur from immediate plan adoption. The *exceptions* counterplan advocates that the plan be adopted but that some jurisdiction or group of people be excluded from the plan mandates. For example, during the civil rights debates negatives advocated that affirmative plans be adopted but exclude regulations that would apply to Puerto Pico, Japan, or Native American jurisdictions. These counterplans claimed to avoid disadvantages unique to those groups or states so regulated. Both of these counterplans were types of *plan-inclusive* counterplans, which incorporate the good portions of the plan into a competitive counterplan.

4. Counterplans and Fiat.   It is generally (but not universally) accepted that negatives have some ability to assume fiat for implementation of their counterplans. One approach to negative fiat is to assume that it is reciprocal: If the affirmative can fiat federal government action, so can the negative. Another is to assume that the negative's fiat ground is based in alternative agents: If the affirmative uses the federal government, the negative can use the states or the United Nations. Remember that fiat is not a magic wand, that fiat must assume some normal means of implementation, and that one cannot fiat workability.

5. Counterplans and Presumption.   There are also several ways to view the convention of presumption as it applies to counterplan debates. In a debate in which the negative defends the status quo, it is generally accepted that presumption favors the negative. But what happens if the negative defends a counterplan? One well-accepted theory holds that presumption lies with the policy incurring the least risk or the lesser change. Another is that presumption always opposes the resolution.

---

2. For a more detailed discussion of Utopian counterplans, see the *Journal of the American Forensic Association*, vol. 24 (fall 1987), pp. 95–136, which presents four essays under the heading "Point-Counterpoint: Essays on Utopian Fiat."

Some traditional theorists would argue that, when the negative chooses to counter-plan, it abandons presumption, which then ceases to exist or shifts to the affirmative.

If presumption is considered to oppose the proposition, as is the predominant view of presumption, the negative will always retain the advantage of presumption, even when proposing a counterplan. Thus, if the counterplan is at least as good in merit as the affirmative plan, the judge would opt to reject the affirmative plan, allowing presumption to break the tie. Another way to measure presumption is based on degree of risk. Based on this conception, the policy which represents the greatest change from the status quo entails the most risk. Presumption, then, would favor the smallest degree of change. So an affirmative calling for a program to increase carbon taxes would probably be considered a smaller change than a counterplan to ban the gas burning internal combustion engine, thus retaining presumption for the affirmative.

G. Developing the Kritic (Critique)

The **kritic** (sometimes abbreviated to "K") is a popular form of argument usually (but not always) initiated by the negative team in a debate. It is an argument that challenges the philosophical foundations, or applies ethical constructs to the opponent's advocacy and its implications. In essence the kritic is a value objection used in a policy debate. The argument is structured much like a disadvantage and is argued as an absolute voting issue. Kritics may be based on attacks on some aspect of the opposing advocates' performance, such as language use or on the underlying presuppositions of the resolution or their proposal.

In general, when argumentation is considered "critical," it challenges traditional power structures. Marx offered critical analysis based on economic elites. Some postmodern critics suggest that the paradigm or worldview with which one considers their world (including reflection on activities such as debate, as well as examination of larger social problems) colors what one sees. Thus, existing paradigms, or ways of arguing and understanding, serve to reinforce institutional frameworks and thus reinforce existing power hierarchies. Because they favor inclusion over exclusion, and seek ways to break down repressive regimes, critical scholars often advocate deconstruction of those traditional paradigms in favor of new ways of knowing and thinking. Such arguments tend to be very compelling in their criticism of existing approaches, but less persuasive in their offering of alternatives to the conventions.

One form of kritic argument begins with the recognition that fiat is only a debate convention and that, even when the affirmative wins a debate, the plan is not implemented. Hence, it is important and more immediate to consider the in-round impact of debater behavior and language use on the participants and observers than hypothetical policy implementation. For example, a negative might pick up on the affirmative's use of the generic *he* and suggest that the judge reject the affirmative for furthering the sexist thinking of those present in the debate. Similar arguments may be based on the tendency of the opponents' language, evidence, and/or argumentative positions to "otherize" peoples or groups by isolating them based on their victimization or characteristics, their use of "nukespeak" (talk about the impact of nuclear war) or other language-based approaches to discussion of public policy that might numb listeners to the importance of various issues. Criticism of fast or technical talk in a debate, linear modes of thinking, simplistic cause effect analysis, and many other objections might be offered based on such a critical approach.

Another form of kritic argument questions the premises upon which the resolution, and therefore the affirmative plan, is based. For example, the negative might argue that the resolution (and the affirmative) relies on governmental solutions to social problems. It could then argue that it is governments that cause most of the world's problems and that reliance on the state to solve social problems is philosophically wrong. It then follows that the affirmative should be rejected, because it relies on the state.

Negatives advocating the kritic strategy must be careful to be consistent. To attack the philosophical notion of the state and to offer a world government counterplan, or to criticize use of the generic male pronoun while reading evidence using the term *mankind*, would be inconsistent and would likely result in a negative loss. Negatives should avoid the implied contradiction or hypocrisy of presenting arguments or positions of advocacy that are inconsistent with their kritic. In addition, as with all generic negative strategies, it is important to explain the application of the kritic to the particular round and affirmative (that is, the link). The negative offering a kritic argument should clearly identify its "alternative." The alternative may be a counterplan that embodies the philosophical commitment. However, a more likely critical alternative is a clear explanation of the new ethical foundation or premise(s) advocated by the negative. It is important for the negative to provide a competing mode of thinking, framework, or approach to debating the issues involved if the kritic is to offer a choice that justifies rejection of the affirmative advocacy. So, negatives offering a kritic must explain clearly why acceptance of their kritic philosophy results in affirmative rejection (that is, impact).

EXERCISES

1. Work in pairs of teams. Exchange your affirmative cases (prepared for the previous chapter). For your opponent's case, prepare briefs. If you are debating a value proposition, prepare briefs on topicality, criteria, value objection, and case-specific arguments. If you are debating a policy proposition, prepare briefs on topicality, harm, circumvention, and disadvantage.

2. Continue Exercise 1 by preparing a counterplan argument, including all necessary support.

3. Have a debate. Divide the class in half. Assume that you all normally eat at the cafeteria. The first debater should offer a plan to eat somewhere else (specify the plan). The first negative debater should offer a counterplan (eat at yet another location). Continue back and forth until everyone has participated.

13

....

Cross-Examination

Academic debate involves not only the presentation of uninterrupted advocacy and clash in alternating individual speeches by debaters, but most competitive debate formats also offer opportunities for direct interaction by opposing speakers. **Cross-examination** in debate is the interactive process, usually dedicated to designated and timed speech periods, wherein participants engage in the asking of questions and providing of answers pertinent to the arguments, cases, evidence, and other matters relevant to the debate. In the typical cross-examination format as practiced in evidence-based team topic policy debate and Lincoln–Douglas debate, one debater is designated for each cross-examination period as the questioner and one debater from the opposing team is the answerer. In academic parliamentary formats, debaters may rise to "points of information" in order to ask the speaker pertinent questions during a speech. While cross-examination does not afford debaters the opportunity to introduce new argumentation into a debate, it is often the most dynamic and engaging portion of the debate for the audience (judge) and when done effectively can produce significant strategic and psychological advantages.

Cross-examination in contemporary academic debate practice began as "cross-questioning" "in the Oregon Style of debate introduced in the 1920s by J. Stanley Gray."[1] Gray was concerned that debaters relying on scripted speeches, often written by their coaches or teachers, did not reap the educational benefits offered by debate participation, and that debates as series of uninterrupted speeches were not entertaining or interesting to audiences. Gray said of his innovation:

> The period of cross-questioning is sufficient stimulus for thorough preparation. Aside from the first two speeches, memorized speaking is

---

1. Gray, J., "The Oregon Plan of Debating," *Quarterly Journal of Speech Education*, 1926; 12(2), 175.

Miniglossary

Cross-examination The interactive process in debate, usually dedicated to designated and timed speech periods, wherein participants engage in the asking of questions and providing of answers pertinent to the arguments, cases, evidence, and other matters relevant to the debate.

Direct questions Call for a brief and concrete answer and are generally questions to which the questioner already knows the answer.

Leading questions Questions that imply or contain their own answer and encourage that answer.

Loaded questions Questions based on prior assumptions, and are worded such that when the respondent answers the question directly, they are confirming the assumption.

---

impossible. The debater must learn to adjust himself and his ideas to the new situations which every debate presents. We have found that the audience is always intensely interested in the periods of cross-questioning and many attend the debates just for this feature. (Gray, p. 179)

A similar format was devised a decade later by Darrell Parker at Montana State University, utilizing the legal language "cross-examination."[2] Parker noted a number of advantages of the cross-examination format:

> … the cross-examination represents an improvement over the orthodox style of debate. For one thing, it places a greater premium upon thorough study and preparation of the question by the participants. The first practice will impress upon the debate the necessity of knowing his subject from its every possible angle. He will learn that he must be ready instantly to defend himself every inch of the way. He will have to support and verify his authorities, facts and reasoning. His cross-examiner may attach his case at any point and he must be prepared. Questions will come in fairly rapid succession and to deliberate for long before making a reply is to admit uncertainty. There is little chance of concealing the fact of inadequate preparation from a cross-examiner who is alert and he prepared.… Answering questions affords practice in impromptu speaking.… The use of the cross-examination is a safe-guard against failure on the part of the speakers to reach a definite clash of opinion.… The use of the cross-examination increases audience interest in the debate … [and] provides excellent opportunity for the injection of wit and humor into the debate. (Parker 98–99)

---

2. Parker, D. R., "The Use of Cross-Examination in Debate," *Quarterly Journal of Speech*, 1932;18 (1), 97.

Parker also observed that cross-examination forces speakers to take clear stands on issues, as he put it, "Verbal Camouflage, which has so often been found convenient, loses its potency." Both of these debate innovators were convinced that direct interaction improved the quality of debate even within the constructive and rebuttal speeches, and that the addition of face-to-face questioning made the debate a more enjoyable experience for audience members. As Parker suggested, "Every audience loves a conflict, whether it be a football game or a battle of words...."

Nonetheless, it was not until 1971, with the formation of the Southwest Cross-Examination Debate Association (later to become CEDA), that cross-examination was formally incorporated into intercollegiate debate formats. In 1976, the NDT added cross-examination to its format, and most intercollegiate evidence-based policy debate tournaments and organizations followed suit.

As Gray and Parker discovered 80 years ago, cross-examination is an exciting and rewarding process which creates drama, interest, and clarity for judges and other audience members and strategic, logistic, and persuasive opportunities for debaters. At its best, it offers opportunities to make the arguments forwarded in the constructive speeches more clear and compelling, sets up rebuttal strategies, and offers debaters the opportunity to build ethos and positive relationships with their judges. Confident, knowledgeable, and prepared debaters benefit from effective cross-examination.

Most judges do not consider arguments revealed in the cross-examination period to have been entered into the debate for consideration in their decision unless subsequently made as arguments in a constructive speech. However, it is generally thought that admissions, claims, and clarifications offered within the cross-examination period are binding. In other words, debaters are held to what they said in cross-examination. They should not purposefully mislead or misinform, and they should take care to offer answers which they can defend. So the purpose of cross-examination is NOT to make arguments, but debaters are bound to any information or position offered in the cross-examination.

I. PURPOSES OF CROSS-EXAMINATION

1. To Clarify. The most fundamental purpose of cross-examination is clarification. At its most simple level, this quest for clarification may include questions like "what was your second answer to the disadvantage argument?" Debaters may use the cross-examination period to fill in gaps on their flow sheet and have their opponents repeat things they may have missed. More importantly, debaters can use the cross-examination period to have their opponents explain positions, evidence, claims, policies, and logic not made clear when presented in the preceding constructive speeches. Such clarifications help to prevent misapplication of answers to arguments or misinterpretation by the judge. First, the questioner wants to check their understanding of the positions taken by their opponents so their responses will make sense and be, in fact, responsive.

This will guide them in making good strategic choices as the debate proceeds. Second, the questioner wants to make sure the judge understands the opponent's argumentation, so the opponent cannot begin with a vague or unclear argument, and later in the debate, "morph" the argument into a more specific answer or extension based on misrepresentation or misunderstanding.

2. To Expose Flaws, Mistakes, or Drops.   The cross-examination period offers careful and prepared debaters the opportunity to bring attention to omissions from their opponent's cases, unsupported claims, and failure to fulfill the burden of refutation by answering key arguments. When evidence is biased or weak, questioners may ask about the evidence. "Who was the source of that evidence?" "And who do they work for?" "What is the methodology behind that study?" "What is the date on your evidence?" These sorts of questions may reveal the weakness of evidence offered in support of important claims. Cross-examination also offers the opportunity to point to non-responsive answers or answers that don't make sense. Often, an argument is made which has been preempted, that is, evidence read or arguments made earlier in the debate provide the answer to the attack. On occasion, arguments or evidence presented in support of one position run counter to what has been presented by the same side on another issue. Questions can point to this. "So your argument is that passing a no-texting while driving law will anger voters?" "Yes, that's right." "But on the politics disadvantage, doesn't your evidence demonstrate that voters support the law?" When arguments have been dropped (opponents have failed to address or answer key points), cross-examination offers the opportunity to bring attention to the dropped argument ("... so, what was your answer to our circumvention argument?").

3. To Set Up Strategies.   Questions may seek to pin down an opponent or cause them to clarify their position and its implications in order to set up a later argument or position to be entered into the debate. Debaters may call on opponents to specify exactly what their plan action (or counterplan action) will be so as to support links to disadvantage arguments they intend to make. Philosophical or value-based premises upon which an advocacy is built can be made clear so as to support the link to kritic arguments. Inherencies may be made more explicit as they may provide immovable barriers or mechanisms circumventing solvency.

4. To Build Ethos.   Specific informed questions demonstrate deep knowledge of a content area, and comfort and assertiveness in asking or answering questions can boost the judge's perception of the debater's ethos. Through effective questioning or answering, a debater can display a persona of confidence and competence as well as superior knowledge about the subject area, the proposition, the case, or the literature being referenced in the debate. While for most judges, this perceived advantage will not directly enter into the decision in the debate, it may impact speaker points, and will also impact the judge's perception when comparing competing claims and evidence. The debater who shows herself more prepared and expert about the specific evidence and arguments in the debate, and more familiar with the debate context itself will have an implicit advantage. Judges are more likely to deem her evidence superior or her claims more relevant than the debater who presents himself as less familiar with the literature and knowledge being discussed.

II. STRATEGIES FOR CROSS-EXAMINATION

Edward Bennett Williams, once called "the country's hottest criminal lawyer," gave this tough but practical advice on the most difficult of trial techniques, cross-examination:

> It is ... the art of putting a bridle on a witness who has been called to do you harm, and of controlling him so well that he helps you. You must think of him as a man with a knife in his hand who is out to stab you, and you must feel your way with him as if you were in a dark room together. You must move with him, roll with him. You must never explore or experiment during cross-examination. *You must never ask a question if you do not already know the answer.* If you do know it and the witness refuses to say what you know, you can slaughter him. Otherwise he may slaughter you. Never attack a point that is unassailable.
>
> And if you hit a telling point, try not to let the witness know it. Keep quiet and go on. The time to dramatize it to the jury is during your closing argument.[3]

As Williams observed, cross-examination is an art of war. Some general strategies are identified in the next section.

1. Be Prepared.   While the cross-examination period will appear spontaneous, it should be thoroughly planned. As with every other part of the debate, winning debaters are prepared. Debaters should map out their strategies and objectives prior to the debate and confer immediately prior to the questioning period to prioritize or anticipate questions. While the cross-examination period should not and cannot be completely scripted, debaters should have lists of possible questions prepared in advance based on what arguments they anticipate hearing and what positions they intend to present in response. Debaters are well advised to study their affirmative cases and negative positions as if they are studying for a final exam. Complete preparation means reading and remembering the important articles and reports upon which cases and arguments are based. The cross-examination serves as an oral examination of the debater's familiarity with the arguments in which they are engaging. Of course, debaters should engage in the asking and answering of questions prior to debating.

2. Observe Protocol.   Some of the rules and practices for cross-examination may vary. The traditional cross-examination places questioner and respondent

---

3. *Life* magazine, June 22, 1959, p. 116. Copyright 1959. The Picture Collection Inc.

side by side, standing, in the front of the room facing the judge. One person speaks at a time. One debater is designated to ask and one to answer the questions. Partners remain quiet and do not participate. In some debate contexts, a practice of "open cross-examination" or "tag-team cross-examination" is appropriate. This enables all four debaters to participate in questioning and answering during each questioning period. Debaters should ask the judge, their coach, their teacher, or other administrative officials to clarify the specific rules for the tournament or location. If all are taking part in the cross-examination, it is challenging but important that one debater ask or answer at a time and that each debater avoid speaking over the other participants.

Recall that even in cross-examination, which is more interactive than individual speeches, the audience is still the judge (or other audience members not participating in the debate). Face the judge even when questioning or answering your opponent. And be courteous. It is appropriate to address opponents by first name. Being assertive is positive, being overly aggressive is not. Avoid becoming angry or agitated, and avoid sarcasm, disrespectful references, inappropriate language and grandstanding.

Cross-examination is designed to discuss what has already been entered into the debate during constructive speeches. It is not appropriate to introduce new evidence or arguments in the cross-examination, and it is not helpful to preview answers that are to come or evidence you have available but have not read in a previous constructive speech.

3. Control the Cross-Examination Period. Time is limited in cross-examination. By virtue of being the one asking the questions, the questioner has primary control of the period. However, the challenge faced by the questioner is to manage that time efficiently, accomplishing desired objectives when the respondent is working equally hard to occupy the time. Step one for the questioner in controlling the cross-examination is to ask questions to which you know the answer. Step two is to offer questions which are direct and closed or limited. Avoid open-ended questions ("Could you please explain your case...?"), which allow the respondent to give another constructive speech. Step three is to appropriately cut off the respondent who is grandstanding or filibustering. Do not demand a yes or no answer when that is unreasonable. However, quickly and confidently, but with a courteous tone, interrupt with a follow-up question when the respondent begins to give a speech rather than offering a concise answer to a reasonable question. Step four is to maintain a vigorous pace. Questioners do not effectively manage the cross-examination if they are not prepared with sets of relevant questions; long pauses allow the respondent to take over. As a respondent, you will gain little by ignoring the questions or giving irrelevant speeches. Step one for the respondent is to use prepared answers to anticipated questions. Just as the questioner should be prepared with questions, the effective respondent is prepared with well-thought-out answers which support their positions and arguments. Step two is to demand, in a respectful manner, the opportunity to provide a complete answer, or draw attention to the exchange such that the judge is aware that there is more to the answer than you were allowed to offer. Step three is to be willing to answer "I don't know" when that is the honest answer. If you have prepared and done your homework, the question to which you do not know the answer is likely irrelevant or unimportant. Even if it is important, you do not help your position by making up an answer which will be disproven. Step four is to answer in a clear and concise manner, all reasonable questions to the best of your ability, not wasting the time of the questioner or the judge, and demonstrating your knowledge about the issues and your confidence in your strategy.

4. Manage Nonverbal Factors Effectively.   Cross-examination is an excellent opportunity to provide a direct, simultaneous contrast between yourself and your opponent. The debater will be most challenged in cross-examination by opponents who are aggressive, obnoxious, unreasonable, sarcastic, demeaning, or dismissive. In some cases, these characteristics are reflections of situation-based anxiety in the heat of the competitive moment, sometimes they are reflections of the debater's (flawed) personality, and occasionally they are intentional strategies intended to bait the opponent into responding in kind. Remember that the judge will be more favorably impressed by the respectful, courteous, confident, and assertive debater. Image management during cross-examination can benefit the cool and confident debater and increase the likelihood that his arguments will be well received and favorably compared to those of his opponent by the judge.

5. Consider Question Types.   Low-risk questions are those easily verified within the debate. "Did you offer an answer to the solvency argument?" or "Did the authors of your solvency evidence conclude in their study that a plan like yours would be a good idea?" These may be **direct questions** calling for a brief and concrete answer and are generally questions to which the questioner already knows the answer. Questioners should demand yes or no answers only when appropriate; explanations are often reasonable. High-risk arguments offer respondents the opportunity to strengthen their positions, they may be open ended and their answer is not known to the questioner. "Are there other experts who agree with the authors you quote on the solvency issue?" Of course, if the answer is yes, the question may backfire. **Loaded questions** are based on prior assumptions, and are worded such that when the respondent answers the question directly, they are confirming the assumption. For example, whichever way the respondent answers the question, "have you stopped using illicit drugs?" will confirm the assumption that the respondent was previously using illicit drugs. A leading question is a question that implies or contains its own answer and encourages that answer. "Your plan is an example of increased regulation, isn't it?" Questioners should prefer low-risk questions and avoid open, loaded, and **leading questions.**

1. Questioner Considerations.   The competing roles of questioner and respondent offer some demands unique by role. Following are some implications specific to the role of questioner:

1. Clarification. Some portions of your opponent's speech may have been unclear—either by accident or design. Cross-examination affords an opportunity to clarify them. Here's an example:

   Q: Your plan calls for placing a space station in orbit. What sort of an orbit will that be?

   A: Geosynchronous. That way we will be able to....

   Q: Thank you. That's what I wanted to know.

This brief exchange clarified the affirmative's plan. The negative now knows that the affirmative is going to use a high orbit that will be far more costly than a low orbit and will present many technical difficulties. With the now-clarified plan before them, the negative can begin to develop plan attacks specific to the type of orbit the affirmative is now committed to using in its plan. Clarification may even include questions such as "I missed your third answer on the disadvantage, what was that again?" "Who was the source of your evidence about the dangers of long-term presence in space?" or "May I please see the text of your plan?" And, clarification may also be for the benefit of the judge. Even though you know the answer, you may wish to make sure the judge is aware of it.

2. If you know of a defect in your opponent's evidence, cross-examination gives you an excellent opportunity to expose it. Consider this example:

   Q: You justify your plan for greater freedom for law enforcement agencies by claiming that crime increased 16 percent last year?

   A: Yes, and not only last year; it has been a steady trend.

   Q: And the source of your evidence was?

   A: The *Boston Globe*.

   Q: And where did the *Globe* get its figures?

   A: [Consulting card] From, err, let me see. From the FBI study. Yes, from an FBI report.

   Q: From the 2011 FBI report. Thank you; we'll come to that later. Now....

The questioner has now established the source of the affirmative's evidence. In the next speech the negative will certainly emphasize the flaw they know to be in that evidence. The negative is now confident, since they know that the FBI had warned against using these statistics to make year-to-year comparisons. Let's consider another example:

   Q: You claim industry will move to escape environmental controls?

   A: Right. They certainly will.

   Q: Would you please read that card? I think it was the....

   A: "*State Street Report*.... When faced with unreasonably high taxes and excessive regulation, industry will give serious consideration to their option to move to a location that offers a more favorable business climate."

Q: That specifically says a combination of high taxes and unreasonable regulations, doesn't it?

A: Well, err, yes, but I think the focus is....

Q: Does the evidence say that any industry has ever moved because of environmental regulations alone?

A: Err, no, I don't think so. Not in this report, but environmental controls are a part of it.

Q: Does the *State Street Report* specifically mention environmental controls?

A: It cites "unreasonable regulations" and many of the....

Q: No mention of environmental controls. Thank you. And it said industry would consider moving, didn't it?

A: Yes, and they have moved.

Q: Does your evidence say so?

A: Well, no, not this evidence. We have other evidence that my partner will read....

Q: We'll be looking for it in her speech. But so far there is no evidence of industry moving; no evidence about environmental controls. Thank you.

This cross-examination gave the questioner an opportunity to point out important flaws in the evidence. If the respondent's partner fails to provide the promised new evidence in her speech, the questioner's colleague should be prepared to point that out.

3. Cross-examination may be used to advance your position. Here's an example:

Q: What was your answer to our #4 argument that unemployment will persist in Spain?

A: Uh, I guess I didn't get to that, but....

Q: Thank you.

This brief exchange allowed the debater to emphasize that the other team had dropped an argument. The "development of space" proposition provides another example:

Q: Our evidence says that industry will make billions in the new space station, doesn't it?

A: Yes, but industry is reluctant to go into space.

Q: You mean industry is reluctant to make billions in profits?

A: No. They're reluctant because they're not certain that the station will be built.

Q: Our plan mandates that the space station will be built, doesn't it?

A: Yes, but....

Q: And industry will certainly want those billions of dollars of profit, won't they?

A: Well, once it's built....

Q: Thank you.

4. Cross-examination may be used to establish your response to an attack made on your position. Consider this example:

Q: In your workability attack you said our plan wouldn't work because the people in the new space station would get sick.

A: Right. The evidence shows they develop low blood pressure and lose bone marrow. Both Russians and Americans. And it takes three months....

Q: They get low blood pressure. So what?

A: Low blood pressure isn't good for you.

Q: Does the evidence say that?

A: Well, no, but everybody knows that low blood pressure....

Q: The evidence doesn't say it's low enough to do any harm, does it?

A: It says they develop low....

Q: The evidence doesn't say it gets low enough to stop them from working, does it?

A: Well, no, but everyone knows low blood pressure....

Q: No significance shown in low blood pressure. Now, about the bone marrow—so what?

A: They lose 5 percent of their bone marrow, and it takes three months to get it back to normal. Both Russians and Americans.

Q: Again, no significance. The evidence doesn't say that they can't work, does it?

A: It does say that it takes them three months to....

Q: And they're back to normal. But the evidence doesn't attach any significance to a 5 percent loss, does it?

A: I certainly think it's significant.

Q: Do the physicians who made the report say it's significant?

A: Well, what they say is ... they report ... they report low blood pressure and loss of bone marrow.

Q: And in neither case do they say it's significant. Thank you.

Here the debater defended his case by establishing that the workability attack had no significance.

5. You should avoid "open-ended" questions that allow the respondent freedom to roam at will. Look at this example:

Q: Do you think your plan will reduce fuel consumption?

A: Absolutely. The Petroleum Study proves our carbon tax will effectively reduce consumption. The hearings prove we have the technology. The

Berkeley Report says that this combination of increased taxes and already proved technology will reduce oil imports by at least 20 percent within....

The "do you think" opening gives respondents license to say anything they want to. Of course, they think their position is favorable and will use this opportunity to advance it.

Lawyer and best-selling author Scott Turow, echoing Edward Bennett Williams' sage counsel, admonishes, "A good trial lawyer never asks why, unless he knows the answer."[4] Like the "do you think" opening, a "why" question invites respondents to give the best possible reasons for their position.[5]

Further considerations of the questioner include the following:

6. Questioners should try to elicit brief responses (although questioners may not require a "yes" or "no" answer if a fair answer includes an explanation). They may not cut off a reasonable qualification, but they may cut off a verbose response with a statement such as "Thank you, that gives us enough information" or "That's fine, thank you. That makes your position clear."

7. Questioners should not make arguments during cross-examination. Cross-examination is a time for asking questions and getting responses. The significance of the responses should be argued in the constructive speeches or in rebuttal.

8. Questions should be brief and easily understandable. Rambling, ambiguous questions may confuse the opponent, but they may also confuse those who render the decision. Respondents would certainly ask for a clarification of such questions, and the resultant waste of time would reduce the number of questions that could be asked.

9. Questioners may set the stage for a question—for example, "You know, of course, that President Obama has announced his support for..."

10. Questioners should avoid asking a question unless they already know the answer. Remember the advice of Edward Bennett Williams.

11. Questioners should not attempt to attack unassailable points. Some of the arguments in the respondents' case will probably be so well established as to be irrefutable. An unsuccessful attack on them will merely make their strength more obvious to those who render the decision. Questioners should focus on the points they can carry.

12. Questioners should always remember that the primary purpose of asking questions in cross-examination is to obtain information that they can use to their advantage in their next speech. On the flow sheet, questioners can make notes of their questions and the responses they receive—the judge will be doing this as well—so that they can refer to them directly. Rather than assume that the

---

4. Scott Turow, *Presumed Innocent* (New York: Farrar, Straus, & Giroux, 1987), p. 324.
5. *Life* magazine, June 22, 1959, p. 116. Used by permission of Edward Bennett Williams and *Life*. (Emphasis added.)

significance of an opponent's response is self-evident, questioners can drive the point home to the audience in their next speech. Here are some examples:

In cross-examination, Gail admitted that their space station would be in geo-synchronous orbit. Let's see what that really means in terms of cost....

Roger admitted in cross-examination that their figures on increased crime came from the FBI. Now I'm going to tell you what the FBI itself said about using those figures for year-to-year comparisons....

Remember when I asked Mark about the significance of his claim that people get sick in space stations? He couldn't give you any significance of low blood pressure. None. Again, on the bone marrow, Mark couldn't give you any significance there either. There's no significance shown in their workability attack....

2. Respondent Considerations.   Considerations for the respondent include the following:

1. Respondents must keep in mind that each question is designed to weaken their case or to advance the case of their opponents. Consequently they must constantly be on guard. Consider the motivation or strategy behind the question and try to diffuse it.

2. Respondents must answer any reasonable question in a cooperative fashion. Your attitude as well as the content of your answer are important in the audience and judge's evaluation of your credibility. As noted earlier, however, they can refuse to give a "yes" or "no" answer and can add reasonable qualifications. Here's an example:

   Q: The report adopted the recommendations of the chemical companies, didn't it? Yes or no.

   A: There were Democrats and Republicans on the committee, and the report was adopted by a unanimous vote.

3. Respondents may refuse to answer ambiguous or "loaded" questions. Consider this example:

   Q: Have you stopped cheating on examinations?

   A: I quit the same day you stopped snorting cocaine.

   Q: But, but, but I never snorted cocaine.

   A: Bingo!

4. Respondents may qualify their response. The "Yes, but" qualification is weak. It is better to give the qualification first and then give a direct response, as in this example:

   Q: Do you believe that all branches of government should be responsive to the will of the people?

   A: I believe that the Supreme Court is responsive to the will of the people by protecting their constitutional rights. With this important

---

Questioner Considerations

---

1. Clarification
2. Expose defects in opponent's evidence
3. Advance your positions
4. Respond to an attack
5. Avoid "open-ended" questions
6. Elicit brief responses
7. Ask questions, do not make arguments
8. Keep questions brief
9. Set the stage for the question
10. Ask questions to which you know the answer
11. Do not attack the unassailable
12. Use information gained in c-x in the next speech

---

constitutional safeguard, I would say that government should be responsive to the will of the people.

5. Respondents must answer from their perspective. Former Governor Mario Cuomo of New York provided an example:[6]

REPORTER: Aren't you pretty thin-skinned about that, Governor?

CUOMO: If by thin-skinned you mean very, very quick to respond—that's what I've done for a lifetime. I'd been a lawyer for more than twenty years. You can't let the comment from the witness pass. If [by thin-skinned] you're talking about being personally sensitive to criticism, that's a lot of [expletive].

Caution: Expletives, even mild ones, are out of order in academic debate, and the judge may penalize any debater who uses them. More importantly, effective and polished language use boosts the professionalism of the debater's presentation, enhancing credibility. Use nonverbal communication techniques and carefully chosen language rather than cursing to express emotion.

6. Respondents should be willing to admit not knowing the answer to a question, as in this example:

Q: Do you know what methodology Kwarciany and Langer used in their study?

A: They're reputable scholars. I'm sure they used an appropriate methodology. But, no, I don't know their exact methodology.

---

6. William Safire, "On Language," *New York Times Magazine*, Dec. 22, 1991, p. 10.

7. Respondents should not attempt to defend an indefensible point. It is better to yield a point immediately than to allow questioners to wring admissions from the respondents in a series of questions that will only fix the point more firmly in the minds of those who render the decision.

3. Considerations of Both Questioner and Respondent. Next we will examine some considerations that apply to both questioners and respondents.

1. The questions should focus primarily on arguments developed in the speech of the respondent just completed. However, questions about arguments in a previous speech by the respondent's colleague, or any matter relevant to the proposition, are admissible.

2. The questioner and the respondent should treat each other with courtesy. Sarcasm, "browbeating," or obvious evasion will boomerang to the discredit of the one using them.

    If your opponent comes on too strong and seeks to goad you into losing your temper, keep your cool. Counter this aggression by adopting a friendlier, quieter, slower style. You will appear more confident and competent by comparison. The judge will take note and award points accordingly.

3. Both the questioner and the respondent should bear in mind that they are not conducting a private conversation, but are asking questions and giving responses designed to have an effect on the judge and audience. To facilitate communication with the audience, both speakers should stand and face the audience during the question period.

4. As a general rule, once the questioning has begun, neither the questioner nor the respondent may consult a colleague. In some cases, however, courteous and limited participation by both colleagues may be acceptable. It is wise to know the judge's predisposition on "tag team" or "open" cross-examination. Even when it is possible to do so, it is bad practice to conduct or participate in a chaotic group questioning period. Prefer the one questioner, one respondent format. If partners have questions or important information to offer as answers, they should provide courteous nonverbal cues to indicate that.

Respondent Considerations

1. Be on guard
2. Answer reasonable questions
3. Do not answer unreasonable questions
4. Qualify responses
5. Answer from your perspective
6. If you do not know the answer, admit it
7. Do not defend the indefensible

5. Finally a special consideration for both questioners and respondents is to prepare and *practice*. Once you have prepared your affirmative case or your negative briefs, prepare sets of questions, anticipate opponents' questions, prepare possible answers, and practice for cross-examination. Consider the questions that a skilled opponent will ask. What are the points of your case that are most vulnerable to attack? What questions can hurt you most? What are the questions you will have the most difficulty answering? Plan your answers to such questions, and rephrase them until you have concise, convincing, and effective responses.

In the same manner plan in advance the questions you will ask of your opponent. What arguments is your opponent most likely to advance? What questions will you ask? How will your opponent most likely respond to those questions? How will you follow up on that response? Will a skilled opponent give a response that will help or hurt you? If it will help you, plan how you will follow up on it with further questions or with analysis and argument in your speech.

In summary, when cross-examination is used, it is an essential part of the debate, and advocates must prepare for it with the same care given to all other parts of the debate. This preparation should include careful planning for and actual phrasing of the questions and answers they anticipate using, as well as an analysis of those who will render the decision. In 1987, Governor Dukakis had apparently anticipated and planned for a question about capital punishment in his second debate with then–Vice President Bush. His preparation, however, apparently did not include an analysis of how the audience would react to his calm and dispassionate response.

Advocates preparing for cross-examination might find it helpful to arrange with friends to simulate the preparation that is used to prepare for congressional cross-examination. Presidential nominees to the U.S. Supreme Court are advised to prepare for the rigorous questioning they will receive from members of Congress by undergoing intensive practice sessions:

> Each day for a week, Ruth Bader Ginsburg sat at a table in Room 108 of the Executive Office Building, fielding questions from a panel of lawyers on legal questions....
>
> The question-and-answer sessions for Judge Ginsburg, President Clinton's nominee to the Supreme Court, are part of what the modern

---

Considerations of Both Questioner and Respondent

1. Focus questions on previous speeches
2. Be courteous
3. Face the judge and audience, not each other
4. One person asks, one person answers
5. Prepare and practice

nomination process has become, a full-throttle effort, much like preparing a candidate for a presidential debate.

A senior White House official involved in the process said, "If
when she goes before the committee and every question they ask her is
one we've already asked her in practice sessions, we'll have done our job
well...."

In a famous example in 1987, Judge Robert H. Bork, President
Reagan's choice for the Supreme Court, insisted that he had no need
for practice sessions. Bork, a federal appeals judge and a former law
professor, told the White House that such sessions would be a waste of
time because he was fluent in constitutional give-and-take.

After Bork's nomination was defeated by the Senate after a tumul-
tuous set of hearings ... it has become fixed political law in Washington
that no one should forgo practice sessions.[7]

As Bork's disastrous experience proved, it is folly to face determined opponents
in cross-examination without intensive preparation. The debater's objective in
preparing for cross-examination is to anticipate every question an opponent
might ask and to develop an effective answer.

EXERCISE

1. Practice cross-examination. After one side reads their 1AC, conduct untimed
    cross-examination until you run out of questions. Variations are to form a
    circle, and go around the circle having each person ask a question. Or have
    each individual write down their secret goal for cross-examination on an
    index card, pass it to their neighbor, and have that person ask a series of
    questions designed to achieve the goal (for example, "I want to reveal that
    their link card disproves the brink.")

7. Neil A. Lewis, "Ginsburg Gets Set for Her Most Public Law Exam," *New York Times,*
July 15, 1993, p. B9. © 1993 by the New York Times Co. Reprinted by permission.

14

....

Refutation

A single speech offers argumentation. Two or more consecutive speeches on opposing viewpoints may comprise a panel discussion involving argumentation. Debate requires *clash*. It involves the juxtaposition of competing claims, recognition by opponents defending opposite sides of a proposition of each other's arguments with direct comparisons and critical evaluations concluding with a forced choice among these competing arguments. Debate demands that each side respond to their adversaries' argumentation and defend their own in the face of opponent's responses. In 2012, former Alaska governor Sarah Palin invited (via Twitter) "peaceful New Yorkers to *REFUDIATE* a plan to build a Mosque near the former site of the World Trade Center's Twin Towers."[1] In fact, she meant to challenge readers to refute arguments made by those in support of the Ground Zero Mosque. The process of making, answering, defending, and extending arguments is known as *refutation*.

Strictly interpreted, *refute* means "to overcome opposing evidence and reasoning by proving it to be false or erroneous." The **rebuttal**, strictly interpreted, refers to argumentation meant "to overcome opposing evidence and reasoning by introducing other evidence and reasoning that will destroy its effect." In practice and in most of the chapters, the terms *refutation* and *rebuttal* are used interchangeably, except that the second speech by each advocate in most formats for academic debate is designated as rebuttal speech.

In academic debate advocates are required to refute only the specific arguments advanced by their opponents. In applied debate advocates must refute any evidence and reasoning that may influence the decision renderers.

---

1. Stephanie Condon (July 19, 2010, 9:54 A.M.) PrintText. Palin's "Refudiate" Tweet on Mosque Near Ground Zero Draws Fire (for Substance and Style), *CBS News* Political Hotsheet, July 19, 2010, http://www.cbsnews.com/8301-503544_162-20010892-503544.html.

Miniglossary

Flow sheet An outline of a debate, with the arguments presented in each speech recorded in vertical columns and arranged so that a person can follow horizontally the flow of each argument as it evolves progressively through all the speeches in a debate.

Rebuttal Argumentation meant to overcome opposing evidence and reasoning by introducing other evidence and reasoning that will destroy its effect. Also, the second speech by each advocate in an academic debate.

Refutation Argumentation meant to overcome opposing evidence and reasoning by proving that it is false or erroneous.

I. THE SHIFTING BURDEN OF REBUTTAL

As discussed in the preceding chapters, the burden of proof always remains with the affirmative, whereas the burden of rebuttal initially belongs to the negative. This burden of rebuttal shifts back and forth between the opponents in the course of the debate and is finally placed on one side or the other. The side that bears the burden of rebuttal at the conclusion of the debate may find themselves the loser. In the typical academic debate (policy, parliamentary, and Lincoln–Douglas) the first speaker for the affirmative side establishes his or her case sufficiently well to place the burden of refutation on the negative. The first negative speaker then attempts to shift that burden back to the affirmative. The next affirmative speaker, by rebuilding and extending the case, seeks to shift the burden to the negative again. The burden of rebuttal alternates throughout the debate, with the burden always resting on the side who has yet to answer an argument or response made by their opponents.[2]

Debaters will generally not have time to answer every argument offered by their opponents in any given speech, but they should carefully select which arguments to talk about based on a number of factors, including the importance of the issue to the outcome of the debate, the quality of refutation offered by opponents, and the amount of time required to defend the position. In policy and parliamentary debate formats, it is generally accepted that debaters must fulfill their burden of refutation at the first opportunity, or at least during a designated constructive speech. *New arguments, or responses to arguments not previously addressed, are not allowed during the rebuttal speeches.* This convention provides that arguments are presented early enough in the debate to fairly allow the opponents to respond. When arguments are left unattended by the opposition, advocates will say that the argument has been "dropped," allowing it to fall to the team keeping it alive. However, as will be discussed more later in this chapter, even when one's opponents *drop* an argument, it is up to the opponents to take advantage of the miss by the other side by repeating and expanding on that argument.

---

2. See Chapter 17 for an outline of the speaking sequence and time allotments used in intercollegiate debating.

II. PURPOSE AND PLACE OF REFUTATION

The process of refutation has to be included in every speech of the debate after the first one. Obviously the first affirmative speech, which opens the debate, cannot include direct refutation because no opposition has preceded it. But even this speech may include a certain amount of anticipatory refutation. However, this anticipatory refutation should be directed to issues that the negative must inevitably support and not against "straw arguments" that the affirmative hopes the negative will advance. (See the inset below for a summary of processes of refutation.)

In general advocates should refute an important issue at their first opportunity to do so, rather than allow it to stand unchallenged for any length of time. Occasionally, an advocate might ignore an issue temporarily while waiting for the opposition to commit itself further on the issue. Or advocates might advance a limited refutation, encouraging the opponents to pursue a given line of argument that will commit them to a position the advocates will refute later. Thus the advocates are able to bring into the debate arguments their opponents might prefer to avoid. Every debater will make choices about which arguments to spend time answering and which to allow to stand by not fulfilling their burden of refutation on an individual argument. These decisions about which arguments to answer and which not to answer is an inevitable consequence of the time limits imposed on debater's speeches as well as the strategic benefit of arguing each point. Efficient debaters allocate their precious time wisely, investing it on the arguments which will best benefit their strategy and advocacy and on which they are most prepared.

The Process of Refutation

1. Overthrow the opposition's evidence by demonstrating that it is invalid, erroneous, or irrelevant.
2. Overthrow the opposition's evidence by introducing other evidence that contradicts it, casts doubt on it, minimizes its effect, or shows that it fails to meet the tests of evidence.
3. Overthrow the opposition's reasoning by demonstrating that it is faulty.
4. Overthrow the opposition's reasoning by introducing other reasoning that turns it to the opposition's disadvantage, contradicts it, casts doubt on it, minimizes its effect, or shows that it fails to meet the tests of reasoning.
5. Rebuild evidence by introducing new and additional evidence to further substantiate it.
6. Rebuild reasoning by introducing new and additional reasoning to further substantiate it.
7. Present exploratory refutation—preliminary refutation offered for the purpose of probing the opponent's position and designed to clarify the opponent's position or to force the opponent to take a more definite position.
8. Present counterargumentation that competes with the opposition's.

For example, in debates on the proposition "Resolved: That the nonagricultural industries of the United States should guarantee their employees an annual wage," some affirmative advocates argued that significant numbers of persons were unemployed at the time this proposition was being debated. In using *exploratory* refutation, some negative advocates advanced a deliberately weak refutation—introducing evidence that some unemployed persons had built up substantial savings during the years they had worked—and drew the conclusion that some workers did not need a guarantee of annual wages. Some affirmative advocates responded to this refutation by claiming that the vast majority of unemployed persons did not have substantial savings, because low-seniority workers were the first to be laid off and many had worked for only a few months prior to their unemployment. Once the negative advocates had obtained such an admission from the affirmative as a result of its exploratory refutation, they were able, later in the debate, to focus on their main line of refutation. They then argued that, because the wage guarantees proposed by the affirmative required at least a year's seniority before becoming effective, the proposed plan did not meet the needs of the low-seniority workers, who, according to the affirmative, made up the largest group of unemployed. Exploratory refutation may also serve the purpose of costing the opposition time to answer it, thus creating a positive time exchange for the initiators of the exploratory or "decoy" arguments, which they do not intend to extend later in the debate. Of course, if such "decoy" arguments are not answered at all, the initiator of the unanswered argument may be able to capitalize on this unanswered or "dropped" argument, extending it as exceedingly important for their side.

III. PREPARING FOR REFUTATION

As advocates we should prepare our refutation with the same care that we prepare other portions of our case. Effective refutation is rarely the result of improvisation, but rather results from careful analysis and preparation.

We should be as thoroughly familiar with all evidence and reasoning related to the proposition under debate as is possible. Our knowledge of the subject should not be confined to our own case or to the case we expect the opponent to use; instead it should include all possible aspects of the resolution. In CEDA/NDT policy debate, this process is facilitated by sharing of information. The cases and arguments made by debate teams in tournaments are posted to an openly available Wiki, and teams generally disclose in advance what they will argue. We should therefore make certain that our research on the subject has been sufficiently detailed that we will not be taken by surprise by new evidence or reasoning introduced by the opposition. We should recognize that on most propositions the evidence is seldom complete; new evidence, or new interpretations of evidence, may appear frequently. In other words, we should never assume that our research is complete but should continue it until the very moment of the debate.

Advocates should have a broad perspective in preparing their refutation. They should never limit themselves to one point of view or to one philosophy.

They should try to analyze both sides carefully and should consider all possible positions that may be taken on the proposition. Student debaters will find that one of the best means of improving their refutations is to debate both sides of a proposition, even both sides of the same case. This approach allows them to gain a broader perspective and avoid the danger of seeing only one side. Advocates in nonacademic debates draft the strongest possible cases their opponents might use and prepare refutations for each of these cases. Advocates should consider not only the evidence their opponents may use but also the lines of argument that may be introduced and the philosophical position that may form the basis of the opposition's case.

In planning answers to the possible cases advanced by an opponent, advocates should give careful consideration to the phrasing of any refutation. If an advocate's thinking has proceeded merely to the stage of "If the opposition quotes expert A, I will quote expert B," the refutation is likely to be verbose, uncertain, and lacking in specificity. Rather, the advocate should plan the phrasing of the refutation, making sure that the words are sharp and specific and that the reasoning is cogent. Organized and prepared briefs offer "answers to" a wide range of potential arguments and issues which may be encountered.

After an appropriate signpost (for example, "argument number 1 …") arguments should be presented with the claim first, in the form of a *tag line* or *slug*. This is the point of the argument or claim, phrased positively in seven words or less. Keeping the tag line brief increases the control the debater has over what the judge writes down on their *flow sheets*. The **flow sheet** is an outline of the debate, with the arguments presented in each speech recorded in vertical columns and arranged so that a person can follow horizontally the flow of each argument as it evolves progressively through all the speeches in a debate. Longer tags require the judge to paraphrase or interpret the debater's words. It is important to use powerful and compelling language in framing the tag line. It is much like the *sound bite* political candidates strive for in campaigns. These are the words most likely to be remembered by the judge.

After the tag line debaters should present their evidence or support. This is the data for the argument. Next the debater offers a summary of the warrant, or the reasoning that links the data to the claim. In other words the *warrant* is an explanation of why the evidence supports the claim. Finally the debater should summarize the impact of the argument in the debate. All of this is done quickly with no wasted words. Word economy is a key to effective debating.

IV. PREPARATION: ARRANGING MATERIAL
FOR REFUTATION

Until the debate is actually under way, the advocates cannot be certain what position their opponents will take. Thus they have to have a broad store of materials from which to draw refutation. These materials should be arranged in such a way that they are readily available.

It is essential to prepare refutation briefs in the form of *frontline answers*, or initial answers to an opponent's argumentation, and *extensions*, or defenses of the frontline answers and probable responses in subsequent speeches. These briefs may be filed in folders or accordion files or in readily accessible computer files for easy access.

The brief should provide the debater with the flexibility to make it fit the organization and unique structure of the opponent's argumentation, and will include more evidence and answers than the debater using it is likely to have time to present. Just anticipate potential arguments you will need to respond to, and list as many answers as possible. Find and attach evidence in support of those answers wherever possible. Order the "bullets" or listed answers in order from strongest to weakest, keeping in mind that such an evaluation may change in a given debate. Conscientious student debaters make a habit of constructing detailed briefs and files for every possible argument they may hear. The debater who is thinking too much on their feet did not do enough work in preparation! Preparation is essential.

V. SELECTING AND EXTENDING EVIDENCE AND REASONING

Just as our refutation file should contain more material than can be used in any one debate, our opponents' speeches will contain more evidence and reasoning than we can possibly refute in the allotted time. The problem before us, then, is one of *selection*. The fundamental concept underlying refutation is that we have to try to refute the case of our opponent. This will also involve defending our own positions. To do so, we must have an accurate picture of the case as it is presented and accurate record of every argument and bit of evidence uttered during the debate. The flow sheet enables us to create such a record.

Charting the debate is one of the most important and also one of the most difficult skills the student must master. As discussed previously, the flow sheet is a detailed record of the debate created by systematic note taking. An accurate flow sheet will reflect every argument as it progresses through the eight speeches in the debate. It will record evidence and will show which arguments were answered and which ones were dropped or not answered. The flow sheet is an indispensable tool for the debaters during a debate. More debates are decided because a debater capitalizes on an opponent's drop (or missed argument) than for any other reason. Learning to keep a complete and accurate flow sheet will also help students learn to be more effective critical listeners.

Consider the sample flow sheet presented in this chapter. This is a handwritten flow sheet; many debaters and judges will flow debates using a template created for Excel, or some other computer program, and flow on their laptop computer. Our sample debate is on a policy proposition, and so the arguments are recorded in two parts—*case* arguments and off-case (plan) arguments. Typically debaters and judges record the flow of argument on multiple sheets of

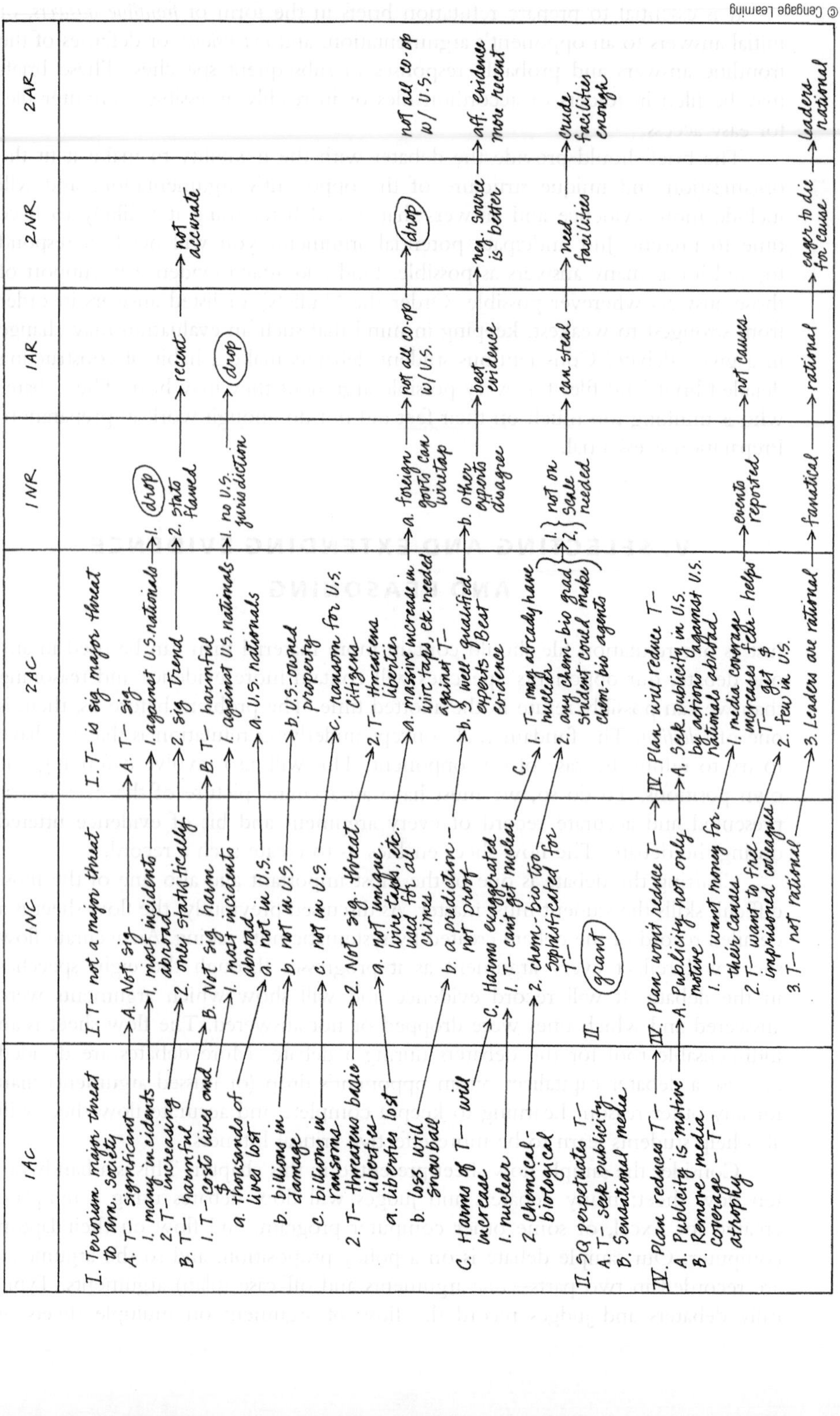

The following is a handwritten debate flow sheet. Columns, left to right: 1AC, 1NC, 2AC, 1NR, 2NR, 1AR, 2NR, 2AR.

1AC

I. Terrorism major threat to Am. society
  A. T- significant
    1. many incidents
    2. T- increasing
  B. T- harmful
    1. T- costs lives and $
      a. thousands of lives lost
      b. billions in damage
      c. billions in ransom
    2. T- threatens basis liberties
      a. liberties lost
      b. loss will snowball
  C. Harms of T- will increase
    1. nuclear
    2. chemical-biological
II. SQ perpetrates T-
  A. T- seek publicity
  B. Sensational media
IV. Plan reduces T-
  A. Publicity is motive
  B. Remove media coverage - T- atrophy

1NC

I. T- not a major threat
  A. Not sig.
    1. most incidents abroad
    2. only statistically
  B. Not sig harm
    1. most incidents abroad
      a. not in U.S.
      b. not in U.S.
      c. not in U.S.
    2. Not sig. threat
      a. not unique - wire taps, etc. used for all crimes
      b. a prediction - not proof
  C. Harms exaggerated
    1. can't get nuclear
    2. chem-bio too sophisticated for T-
II. (grant)
IV. Plan won't reduce T-
  A. Publicity not only motive
    1. T- want money for their cause
    2. T- want to free imprisoned colleagues
    3. T- not rational

2AC

I. T- is sig major threat
  A. T- sig
    1. against U.S. nationals
    2. sig Trend
  B. T- harmful
    1. against U.S. nationals
      a. U.S. nationals
      b. U.S.-owned property
      c. ransom for U.S. citizens
    2. T- threatens liberties
      A. massive increase in wire taps, etc. needed against T-
      b. 3 well-qualified experts. Best evidence
  C.
    1. T- may already have nukes
    2. any chem-bio grad student could make chem-bio agents
IV. Plan will reduce T-
  A. Seek publicity in U.S. by actions against U.S. nationals abroad
    1. media coverage false - helps
    2. few in U.S.
    3. Leaders are rational

1NR

1. (drop)
2. stats flawed
1. no U.S. jurisdiction
  a. foreign govts can wiretap
  b. others experts disagree
1.} not on
2.} scale needed
events reported
fanatical

1AR

recent
(drop)
not all co-op w/ U.S.
best evidence
can steal
not causes
rational

2NR

not accurate
(drop)
neg. source is better
real facilities
eager to die for cause

2AR

not all co-op w/ U.S.
aff. evidence more recent
crude facilities enough
leaders rational

III. Plan	2NC	1AR	2NR	2AR
1. Adm. by Criminal Justice Div. = DOJ	I. Plan won't work	→I. Plan will work; media fears fines		
	A. Inherency proves motive to circumvent			
2. Fed. legislation to limit media coverage of T— to event: no names or causes	B. Media has resources: will litigate for years		→B. will litigate	
	C. Courts overloaded: will take years to reach S.C.	→C. Not unique. Courts overcrowded now	C. proves Plan not work	→C. not unique
3. fines — 25% to 50% of gross annual income	D. SC sensitive to liberties: will dismantle off plan	→D. SC conservative; will uphold plan	→D. SC pro free press	→D. SC more conservative now
4. funding — gen. rev.	II Disadvantages	→II. Plan does not prevent publics knowing		
5. A. IRS give records to DOJ	1. If Plan works, it destroys publics right to know — names and causes of T—	→1. Legitimate causes can get publicity w/o T— . Aff inherency proves media loves sensational		
B. conflicting laws repealed	A. some causes may be legitimate	(Drop)		
C. Const. amend	B. Gov't is covering up illegal or unwise activities abroad	→2. Evidence comes from Congressional committees, not T—		
	2. If Plan works, it destroys free media	III. Not destroy media	III	
	A. Becomes precedent	→A. Plan strictly limited	→A. Precedent slippery slope	A. Plan strictly limited
	B. Gov't wants to restrain media	→B. Courts will check Gov't		
	C. Destruction of free media greater threat than T— Society than T—	→C. Not destroyed because of A ≠ B	→C. Destroy free media	
	3. If Plan works, it escalates T—	IV. T— won't escalate	IV.	
	A. T— escalate to force media coverage	→A. Plan blocks	→A. Incentive to escalate	→Plan blocks
	B. Lack of news about T— means no public support for anti-T— measures	→B. Full news of events only, no names of causes		
		→C. With full news of events public will support anti- T— measures		

legal-sized paper. The case arguments are usually recorded in seven columns on one side of a set of sheets of paper; this represents the case debate. (The heading *1AC* indicates the first affirmative constructive speech; *1AR*, the first affirmative rebuttal; *1NC*, the first negative constructive speech; and so on.) The plan and plan arguments are usually recorded on another group of sheets—thus the name "plan side"—in five columns. If counterplans or topicality arguments are used, they are also recorded on separate sheets, one for each major argument. (Once students have mastered the basic concept of a flow sheet, they will find it easy to provide additional sheets to record these arguments.) Typically the affirmative speakers prepare the outline represented in the first column of the flow sheet prior to the beginning of the debate. This way they can have a more complete, neat, and organized "flow" of the first affirmative speech than would be possible if recorded in real time during the speech. This is called a *preflow*. Negative debaters may prepare partial preflows in advance as well. If they will present generic disadvantage or counterplan arguments, or if there has been complete disclosure by the affirmative about their case in advance of the debate, so that the first negative speech is well prepared in advance, they may have some or all of the 1NC columns completed in a like manner. When there is not prior disclosure, some parts of the negative's argumentation may be preflowed on Post-It notes to be attached to the appropriate column for the debate.

Tips for Keeping Flow Sheets

1. Concentrate! The key to creating useful flow sheets is listening and understanding.
2. Practice! Create flow sheets every chance you get—for the evening news, your classroom lectures, even movies.
3. Use plenty of paper. Record a limited number of arguments on each sheet.
4. Use two colors, one for the affirmative and another for the negative.
5. Be efficient. Use shorthand and symbols, and record only tag lines (the short claim statements) and evidence.
6. Use preflows. Preflow every brief and case you have on sticky note or similar gummed paper. Save the paper by sticking it to the inside of the folder holding the relevant argument, and place it in the appropriate spot on your flow sheet when you present the argument.
7. Use cross-examination and preparation time to fill in the gaps on your flow sheet.
8. Write small, keep columns narrow, and leave plenty of vertical white space. More and more debaters and judges have begun keeping their flow sheet with the help of a laptop computer. To learn more about this technique, visit www.wcdebate.com/1policy/9-edebate.htm.
9. Use arrows to indicate the relationships among arguments and answers.
10. When you miss something, indicate that by leaving a blank space or using some other symbol to remind you to fill in the missing material later.

Debaters and judges use arrows and other symbols to record the flow of the argument and identify on-point clash. Different-colored pens may be used to identify affirmative from negative arguments and to record cross-examination data or to identify other items. To save time, debaters and judges develop a system of abbreviations and symbols. On the sample flow sheet T is used to represent topicality, SQ stands for the status quo or present policies, s for significance, and $SCOTUS$ for the Supreme Court of the United States, and arrow up may mean "increase" or the delta sign can be used in place of the word "change." Important or unanswered arguments should be circled or highlighted. Each column on the flow sheet should be the most accurate and detailed outline possible of that speech. An outline of this type helps debaters detect dropped arguments or weak links in the structure. It takes time and practice to learn how to keep an effective flow sheet, but debaters find it worthwhile to develop this essential skill. With appropriate adjustments the flow sheet can be adapted to any type of argumentative situation. For instance, a college senior confronted with the happy problem of weighing two job offers might find it helpful to prepare a flow sheet weighing the merits of the two offers. A corporate purchasing agent charged with the responsibility of making a major purchase for the company might prepare a flow sheet to help evaluate the advantages and disadvantages of competing products or services.

The flow sheet provides a tool for debaters to use in selecting the most important arguments to extend, and enables wise choices about arguments which may be conceded. No debater wants to give up an argument to their opponents; however, time and strategy demand that they do so. The most successful debaters make the most strategic choices as the debate progresses. When opponents' arguments have limited impact, it is less important to spend precious time answering them. For example, if a negative argument on the harm issue serves to reduce or mitigate the magnitude of the harm, but is not a case turn or a disadvantage (that is, is not an offensive position), the affirmative rebuttalists need not prioritize it. If the affirmative harm is based on an examination of the violent crime and murder rate that results from high unemployment, and the negative response provides evidence suggesting that crime rates have not risen as much as the affirmative projects, the affirmative can easily answer, yes, but they have risen. There is no need to delve into the details of the negative's evidence. On the other hand, if the negative argument is that unemployment actually reduces violent crime (an offensive argument), the affirmative better answer that!

VI. THE STRUCTURE OF REFUTATION

A. Basic Structure

It is to the benefit of the debaters to make the debate easy to follow for themselves, their opponents, and most importantly, for their audience or judge. Being clear allows all participants to track the debate and the clash easily on their flow sheet, thus giving you credit for answering and extending arguments. Within each speech, debates should reveal their outline or brief organization. When answering opponent's arguments, it is important to identify the points of clash. Remember that each argument should be presented with a signpost. This may be a number or a transition like "my next argument is ..." which draws all listeners' attention to the subsequent presentation of the argument. Next, each arguer presents their claim, the tag line, which should be very brief (seven words or less) and easy to record, repeat and remember verbatim. Next evidence will be presented along with necessary explanations and impact.

The basic structure of refutation involves five distinct stages:

Basic Structure of Refutation

1. *Reference:* Identify clearly and concisely the argument you are attacking or defending.
2. *Response:* State your position succinctly (this is the counterclaim, expressed as a tag line).
3. *Support:* Introduce evidence and argument to support your position.
4. *Explanation:* Summarize your evidence and argument.
5. *Impact:* Demonstrate the impact of this refutation in weakening your opponent's case or in strengthening your own case.

As time is the most important and finite resource available to the debater, it is critical to be efficient and economical. When listeners are flowing the debate, little repetition will be necessary in any given speech. The final stage is perhaps the most critical and is the stage beginning advocates most often overlook. Refutation loses its effectiveness unless we tie it in with the case of the opposition or our own case.

B. Extensions and Impact

A debate is a progression of successive speeches through which arguments evolve. Some arguments draw lots of attention and others slip away. The effective debater tracks the debate so that arguments are selected and attended to throughout the debate by choice, not by accident or failure of organization. A debate will rarely be decided by the first couple of speeches, but rather, by the arguments still alive at the end of the debate. That is why the flow sheet is such an important tool for the debater. It enables the debater to watch the progress of each argument, issue, and position as it proceeds horizontally through the speeches (8 in a standard policy format) in the debate. Extending an argument keeps it alive and gives it importance so that it may be considered as a contributor to the judge's decision at the end of the debate.

The first step in extending an argument is to track it on the flow sheet. Find it, and reference it. Next, answer any arguments offered against it. Ideally, single arguments are answered with multiple arguments, especially for those arguments which are central or strategically important to the debater's advocacy. The third step is to repeat, or keep alive, the initial claim offered by your side. When the other side has not answered the argument it is important to capitalize on their failure by extending it into the next column. Recall that if they do not answer the argument at their first opportunity, they are generally not allowed to (no new arguments in rebuttals!) Next, as possible, magnify the argument. Add to it with additional evidence, explanation, or impacts. Impact is the most important function of winning an argument; it answers the question of "so what?" Impact occurs on two levels. First, impact is a measure of the real-world importance of the issue at hand, as the consequence of unemployment on the psychological well-being of millions of Americans, or the increased risk of nuclear detonation generated by Iran's acquisition of nuclear weapons. Second, impact is a measure of the importance of the argument or issue within the debate itself; for example, the affirmative cannot prove that their plan for infrastructure jobs will create a net increase in the number of people employed, therefore, they do not provide any solvency for the harm of unemployment and do not fulfill their burden to present a prima facie case. Perceptually, arguments are likely to be more compelling to the judge's decision if late in the debate, they occupy more space on the flow sheet (more "ink on the flow"), more time is dedicated to them in the later rebuttal speeches, and they have grown in impact through the debate.

C. General Considerations

In addition to the basic structure of refutation, we should be aware of the following general considerations of refutation.

1. Begin Refutation Early. It is usually to our advantage to begin refutation early—both early in our speech and early in the debate. The purpose of beginning refutation early in the speech is to immediately offset the effect of some of the opponents' arguments. This does not mean, however, that the first portion of the speech should be reserved for refutation and the balance devoted to a constructive presentation. The skilled debater will interweave refutation and constructive materials throughout the entire speech. It is usually not desirable to allow a major contention to go unrefuted for too long in the debate. Generally an argument should be refuted in the next available speech. Thus an attack made in the first negative speech must be answered in the second affirmative speech. If the affirmative waits until the final rebuttal to answer this argument, the judge will weigh the answer lightly or even dismiss it, thinking, "Well, yes, they did finally get around to it, but it was so late that the negative had no chance to reply." That would constitute an inadmissible new argument in the rebuttal speeches. In parliamentary debate, this is a rule violation, and opponents may rise to a point of order to call for adjudication on the violation.

2. Conclude with Impact. Usually we want to conclude a speech with positive material designed to advance our own case. After giving the listeners reasons for rejecting the opponents' position, we give them positive reasons for concurring with our position. Tell the story with a look at the big picture, weighing the relative impacts of competing narratives.

3. Incorporate Refutation into the Case.   Although it is usually a good idea to open a speech with refutation, refutation is by no means confined to the first part of the speech. Because the well-planned case meets many of the objections of the opposition, we will often find it advisable to incorporate refutation into our case. For example, in debating the proposition "Resolved: That the federal government should grant annually a specific percentage of its income tax revenue to the state governments," some negative teams objected to the adoption of the resolution on the grounds that it would place an additional burden on taxpayers. In refuting this objection, some affirmative teams made use of built-in refutation by pointing out that the gross domestic product was rising (as, indeed, it was at the time this proposition was debated); thus incomes would rise and more revenue would be derived from the same tax rate.

4. Evaluate the Amount of Refutation.   Advocates often ask, "How much refutation is necessary?" Unfortunately no definitive answer is available; the amount varies from one occasion to another and depends on the judge, audience, and situation. When presenting refutation, in order to adapt to the audience more effectively, be sure to watch the judge or audience closely, looking for both overt and subtle signs of agreement or disagreement. At a minimum the refutation should progress through the five basic stages discussed previously. The goal is to introduce enough refutation to satisfy a reasonable person. Advocates should avoid the too-brief statement of refutation, such as "The recent Brookings Institution study disproves this contention." Such a statement may suggest a line of refutation, but until this line of refutation is actually developed within the context of the debate, it has little value. In general, provide *at least two* answers to your opponent's one.

5. Use Organized Refutation.   Advocates must use a clear, concise, carefully organized pattern of refutation that enables those who render the decision to follow the refutation readily. The objective is to make it easy for judges to "flow" the argument. Skilled advocates clearly identify the specific arguments of their opponents that they are refuting, so that the judge will know exactly where they want their arguments to apply. The basic speaker responsibilities indicate an organized pattern of refutation and a clear division of speaker responsibilities. Once debaters master this basic pattern, by prearrangement with their colleagues they may develop variations.

In informal situations in which we may not have a colleague and there is no judge with a flow sheet, it is still important to have a clear and precise pattern of refutation. We want to make it easy for those who render the decision to follow our arguments.

6. Make Use of Contingency Plans.   Advocates should prepare contingency plans; that is, they should compile briefs of evidence and arguments in advance to raise against issues they believe will be fundamental in meeting the opposing case. In fact, advocates should have a number of contingency plans available. In the course of the debate, they will determine which contingency plans are applicable to the case presented by the opponents; then, of course, they have to adapt the contingency plan to the specific argument used by the opposition.

For example, in debates on a national program of public work for the unemployed, the negative could have safely assumed that the affirmative would have to argue that unemployment is harmful. A negative team prepared contingency plans to meet affirmative arguments on "frictional unemployment," "cyclical unemployment," "long-term unemployment," and so on. In its contingency plan on "long-term unemployment" (unemployment of 15 weeks or more), it assembled evidence to establish that (1) a large percentage were elderly people with retirement incomes, (2) a large percentage were teenagers seeking part-time jobs, and (3) only a small percentage were heads of families, and many of them operated home businesses so they still had income.

VII. METHODS OF REFUTATION

Toulmin's model offers a good method for providing answers to an opponent's arguments (see Chapter 3). First, consider offering a counterclaim to answer your opponent's claim. Generally, if you make a counterclaim, you must provide evidence to support it. Next, consider your opponent's data. Can any of the tests of evidence discussed in Chapter 9 be applied so as to discredit or reduce the strength of the evidence? Finally take a look at the warrant, or the logical reasoning that links the data to the claim. Can any of the tests of reasoning discussed in Chapters 3 and 4 be effectively applied to diminish the strength of the argument? Further refutation techniques involve evidence, reasoning, and fallacies.

A. Evidence

Evidence is refuted by applying the tests of evidence and demonstrating that the evidence advanced by the opposition fails to meet these tests. (See the tests of evidence considered in Chapter 9.) Counterrefutation against attacks on one's own evidence consists of demonstrating that the opposition has applied the tests of evidence incorrectly.

B. Reasoning

Reasoning is refuted by applying the tests of reasoning and demonstrating that the reasoning advanced by the opposition fails to meet these tests. (See the tests of reasoning considered in Chapters 3 and 4.) Counterrefutation against attacks on one's own reasoning consists of demonstrating that the opposition has applied the tests of reasoning incorrectly.

C. Fallacies

Fallacies are refuted by exposing the arguments of the opposition as fallacious. (Fallacies and methods of refuting fallacies are considered in Chapter 4.) Counterrefutation against attacks on one's own arguments as fallacies consists of demonstrating that the arguments are in fact valid.

T A B L E 14.1 Responsibilities of the Speakers: Value Debate

	1AC	1NC	2AC	2NC/1NR
	It is the responsibility of the first affirmative constructive speaker (1AC) to present the affirmative's prima facie case for the resolution, usually read from a manuscript. It should include all the elements of the affirmative case. Here is an example:	It is the responsibility of the first negative constructive speaker (1NC) to present the negative arguments to be developed throughout the debate. This includes off-case (topicality, value objections) and on-case attacks on the affirmative's case. On-case attacks are presented on-point in exactly the same order as the issues are presented by the first affirmative constructive, with clear references to the affirmative claims. The actual order has to be adapted to the affirmative case. This speaker should do the following:	The basic responsibilities of the second affirmative constructive speaker (2AC) are to refute the negative off-case and on-case attacks, to reestablish the initial affirmative claims, and to extend affirmative case arguments.	It is important in the second negative constructive (2NC) and the first negative rebuttal (1NR) to efficiently divide labor. The second negative constructive speaker should "pick up" or extend an appropriate number of the negative arguments presented in the first negative constructive. The negative may elect not to extend all of their arguments at this point. For each position or argument, the speaker should do the following:
1. Definitions		1. Give an overview of the negative position or philosophy for the debate.	1. Address the negative's off-case attacks (which may include topicality, countercriteria, and value objections or, in the case of a quasipolicy debate, may include counterplan and disadvantages).	1. Respond to the second affirmative's answers to the argument.
2. Criteria		2. Present the negative topicality argument, if vulnerable.	2. Answer the negative's on-case attacks in first affirmative constructive order, and defend and extend the case proper:	2. Reestablish the initial first negative claims.
3. Value		3. Present shells of off-case arguments (value objections, disadvantages, counterplan arguments, kritics).	a. Refute the first negative constructive's attacks on each point.	3. Add to or magnify, if possible, the negative argument.
4. Significance		4. Attack vulnerable portions of the case, on-point, in affirmative order.	b. Reestablish the first affirmative constructive's claims and evidence on each point.	
5. Uniqueness				
6. Application			c. Extend or magnify the initial claims with additional evidence	

1AR

The basic responsibilities of the first affirmative rebuttal (1AR) speaker are to answer off-case and on-case attacks extended through the negative block (the second negative constructive and first negative rebuttal) and to extend the case arguments.

1. Refute the negative's off-case arguments.

2. Refute the negative's on-case attacks and case arguments, and extend case arguments from the second affirmative constructive.

Note that this speech requires careful budgeting of time. The first affirmative rebuttalist has to efficiently answer the previous two negative speeches and will not have time to expand on constructive arguments.

1NR

The second negative rebuttalist should be selective in extending those arguments the negative has the best opportunity to win. This speaker should leave out some arguments so as to maximize the time spent on the most promising ones. Specifically, this speaker should do the following:

1. Begin with an overview previewing the reasons to vote for the negative.

2. Reestablish and clinch the few most important arguments in the negative's case.

3. Conclude by presenting the best reasons to justify a decision for the negative and recounting the negative.

2AR

The second negative rebuttalist should be selective in extending those arguments the negative has the best opportunity to win. This speaker should leave out some arguments so as to maximize the time spent on the most promising ones. Specifically, this speaker should do the following:

1. Begin with an overview that encapsulates the reasons the affirmative should win the debate and previews the key issues.

2. Refute the off-case attacks extended by the second negative rebuttalist.

3. Extend the affirmative case.

4. Refute the second negative rebuttalist's attack on the case and extend case arguments.

5. Conclude by presenting the best reasons for justifying a decision for the affirmative by telling the affirmative "story."

TABLE 14.2   Responsibilities of the Speakers: Policy Debate

1AC	1NC	2AC	2NC/1NR
It is the responsibility of the first affirmative constructive (1AC) speaker to present the affirmative's prima facie case for the proposition, usually read from a manuscript. It should include all the elements of the affirmative case. For example:	It is the responsibility of the first negative constructive (1NC) speaker to present the negative arguments to be developed throughout the debate. This includes off-case (topicality, value objections) and on-case attacks on the affirmative's case. On-case attacks are presented on-point in exactly the same order as the issues are presented by the first affirmative constructive, with clear references to the affirmative claims. The actual order has to be adapted to the affirmative case. This speaker should do the following:	It is the job of the second affirmative constructive speaker (2AC) to answer all of the first negative constructive (1NC) arguments, reestablish the initial claims of the affirmative (extend), and magnify the impact or importance of the affirmative arguments by adding onto them.	It is important in the second negative constructive (2NC) and the first negative rebuttal (1NR) to efficiently divide labor. The second negative constructive speaker should "pick up" or extend an appropriate number of the negative arguments presented in the first negative constructive, and the first negative rebuttalist should extend those arguments presented in the first negative constructive not extended by the second negative constructive. The negative may elect not to extend all of their arguments at this point. For each position or argument chosen, the speaker should do the following:
1. Harm	1. Overview of the negative position	1. Answer topicality	1. Respond to the second affirmative's answers to the argument
2. Inherency [Plan]	2. Topicality	2. Answer all off case arguments	2. Reestablish the initial first negative claims.
	3. Shells of off-case arguments (value objections, disadvantages, counterplan arguments, kritics)	3. Answer on-point case attacks and extend 1AC claims	
3. Solvency	4. On-point case attacks	4. Add new impacts or arguments as time allows.	3. Add to or magnify, if possible, the negative argument.

1AR	1NR	2AR
The basic responsibilities of the first affirmative rebuttal speaker (1AR) are to answer off-case and on-case attacks extended through the negative block (the second negative constructive and first negative rebuttal) and to extend the case arguments.	The second negative rebuttalist should be selective in extending those arguments the negative has the best opportunity to win. This speaker should leave out some arguments so as to maximize the time spent on the most promising ones. Specifically, this speaker should do the following:	The basic responsibility of the second affirmative rebuttal speaker is to reestablish and clinch the affirmative's case arguments.
1. Refute the negative's off-case arguments.	1. Begin with an overview previewing the reasons to vote for the negative.	1. Begin with an overview previewing the reasons to vote for the negative.
2. Refute the negative's on-case arguments.	2. Reestablish and clinch the few most important arguments in the negative's case.	2. Refute the off-case attacks extended by the second negative rebuttalist.
3. Extend case claims from the 2AC.	3. Conclude by presenting the best reasons to justify a decision for the negative and recounting the negative.	3. Extend the affirmative case.
		4. Refute the second negative rebuttalist's attack on the case and extend case arguments.
		5. Conclude by presenting the best reasons for justifying a decision for the affirmative by telling the affirmative "story."

D. Affirmative and Negative Refutation

In general, the affirmative side in the debate must answer all or most of the negative's arguments and defend its entire case to win. The negative has the strategic advantage of being able to choose which arguments to extend, or keep alive, until the last rebuttal speech. All advocates are well advised to be strategic: Present evidence and argumentation early in the debate, which will serve you well later. This is to make your evidence work for you. If an argument made by your opponents may be answered by an argument you made earlier in the debate, you should not spend time reading new evidence or explaining a new argument. Instead, apply the earlier argument as your answer.

If the negative argues topicality, the affirmative can defend the topicality of its plan by arguing that it meet the definitions offered by the negative and/or that its definition is superior to the negative one. It will be important for the affirmative to convince the judge that the negative's definitions are overly restrictive or inappropriate. If the negative offers a counterplan, the affirmative should argue that the counterplan is not competitive, that it fails to solve the harm identified by the affirmative, and/or that there are unique disadvantages to the counterplan, and thus the plan is a superior option to the counterplan.

E. Responsibilities of the Speakers

There are eight speeches in the two-person policy debate format (excluding the four cross-examination periods), and each has a fairly standard set of expectations and responsibilities (see Tables 14.1 and 14.2).

EXERCISES

1. Practice flowing by flowing the evening news, sports center, or any talk show.

2. Revisit the Spar Debates, this time debating a policy proposition with a plan, and following the standard responsibilities of the speakers.

3. Each student should make an argument (support with cards or briefs, if available). An assigned respondent should refute the argument following the basic structure of refutation. A third student should use the same method to beat back the attack and defend the original point.

4. Organize one-issue debates on Topicality, Disadvantages, Harm, or any other single issue.

5. Refutation drills. Divide the class in half. The first student will begin a debate on any issue in the news. Continue back and forth, pro or con as long as you can keep going.

15

Listening and Evaluation

As human beings, we tend to be arrogant about our listening skills. While anxiety about speaking is almost universal, overconfidence about listening is just as common. An accurate understanding of the communication process recognizes that in all settings, communication is a two-way process. Listeners are *not* passive observers or obedient sponges, absorbing the ideas offered by debaters, speakers, and other sources of symbolic messages, but rather they are active participants in the creation of shared understanding. The speaker cannot communicate *to* the listener, she must communicate *with* the listener. Because we have ears and can hear does not make us listeners!

As debate judges or audiences to a debate, it is vital that we first recognize our own involvement in interpreting and understanding the arguments, cases, and evidence presented to us. Strive as we might to be objective and unbiased, as humans, our attention and perception is shaped by our personal life history, knowledge, culture, experience, mood, and many other factors. Selective exposure means we avoid messages with which we are uncomfortable or which are not supportive of our lifestyle, interests, curiosities, biases, memberships, or beliefs. More importantly, we choose to hear messages which are consistent with what we already know and believe. The debate culture, by its very nature, imposes an open-minded ethic welcoming all ideas, so it is likely that we have successfully overcome selective exposure when we participate in debate. Selective perception may be more challenging. Our self-system creates a lens through which we understand and interpret the arguments, evidence, and appeals presented to us. We are incapable of being fully dispassionate, although we strive to be so. The act of judging debates, if done effectively, is a powerful and effective exercise which can improve our listening skills across all communicative contexts.

309

Miniglossary

Activist judge   Judges in this approach see themselves as active participants in the debate process, and view the debate not as a game, but as an act.

Evaluator of argument   This judge recognizes the inevitability of intervention, but strives to determine the quality of logic, clash, and evidence presented by debaters in order to choose the superior case or argumentative advocacy.

Hypothesis-testing judge   A judge who focuses on testing the affirmative case and requires that the affirmative overcome any negative attack to win the decision.

Issues judge   A judge who focuses on the stock issues and requires the affirmative to win all the stock issues to win the decision.

Policymaker judge   A judge who contrasts the affirmative's and negative's policy systems and requires that the affirmative's policy system be viable and better than the negative's policy system in order to win the decision. This judge tends to evaluate competing policies on a basis of cost versus benefit.

Skills judge   A judge who focuses on the skills listed on the AFA ballot—analysis, reasoning, evidence, organization, refutation, and delivery—and awards the decision to the team that has done the best debating with regard to these skills.

Tabula rasa judge   A judge who takes no position and allows and expects the debaters to decide the theoretical framework for the decision. If no judging philosophy emerges in the debate, the judge may choose whatever judging philosophy seems most appropriate as a basis for the decision.

Ethical listening, according to Joseph DeVito, requires giving a message a complete and honest hearing without prejudgment, and offering honest responses.[1]

I. STEPS IN EFFECTIVE LISTENING

A. Prepare to Listen

Listening is work! It is not a passive exercise, wherein the speaker exerts all the energy. To be effective as listeners we must be willing to exert the effort required to be fully engaged, observant, and attentive. When possible, we are better listeners when we are familiar with the material we are to hear. Just as the student understands a lecture more completely if he has completed the assigned readings, the debate judge or audience is better prepared if she is knowledgeable about the topic. In intercollegiate policy debate, many of the best judges are coaches who are actively involved in the research process and thus know the material being discussed.

---

1. DeVito, J. A., *Essentials of Human Communication*, 7th ed. (New York: Pearson Education, Inc, 2011), p. 58.

B. Eliminate Distractions

Physical noise and psychological noise can interfere with effective listening. Whenever possible, it will benefit the listener to reduce the distance between herself and the speaker(s) and to clear one's head of other thoughts, concerns, and worries.

C. Limit Multitasking

A debate judge is likely to be multitasking by taking a flow sheet while listening. Additional activities, including texting or surfing the Internet while debaters are speaking, will both limit the listener's ability to completely absorb and critically evaluate the message and offer messages of disconfirmation to the speakers. Disconfirmation messages tell someone that they are unimportant or less important than other concerns. Such messages contribute to ineffective communication and impact the effort expended by the speaker. Attending to the speaker and *only* to the speaker offers courtesy and respect which facilitate improved communication results.

D. Exert Energy and Focus

Listening takes concentration, and in debate, information can come quickly. It takes effort to attend to the speaker and the complex arguments, proof, and clash offered within any debate. The listener must generate the energy to eliminate distractions and receive the messages offered by the speaker. Focus also enables the listener to be aware of all available cues and clues that will assist in understanding the message, including attention to nonverbal and verbal emphasis and signposting, as well as the literal verbal message offered by taglines, evidence, and explanations. And, the effort of listening must be sustained. Once the listener takes a break from listening, it is inevitable that content is lost, and it becomes more difficult to reenter the listening exercise.

E. Suspend Judgment

Our natural biases cause us to make an immediate judgment of quality, acceptability, consistency, and accuracy of information and ideas presented to us as we hear them. These "snap" judgments then may color or impact our evaluation and perception of subsequent appeals. Your evaluation is more accurate when you are able to hear the speaker out, wait for responses and competing claims, and analyze and evaluate all arguments upon their complete presentation.

F. Be Courteous and Offer Feedback

Communication is two way, and you cannot *not* communicate. In their effort to suspend judgment, debate judges may wish to avoid demonstrating agreement or disagreement, or even support for a specific argument or position as it is presented; however, this should not preclude nonverbal immediacy behaviors (head nods, eye contact, and so on) indicating understanding or need for clarity. Positive personal feedback can be encouraging and promote a better communication process. Of course, the comments that follow the debate offer the most direct and explicit feedback.

G. Record the Debate

Flowing the debate has been discussed in Chapter 14. In all debate contexts, it is valuable and important to keep a record of the debate so as to limit the influence of selective retention upon the debate decision. Flowing or detailed and complete note-taking helps keep the listener focused and demands the exertion of energy and effort, all contributing to more effective and productive listening.

II. JUDGING THE DEBATE

We often ask, "What was the vote?" "What was the verdict?" "Who won?" Members of Congress put their voting cards into electronic slots, the electronic scoreboards on the gallery walls light up, and we learn the fate of legislation. The judge in the courtroom asks the jury to state the verdict, and we learn the outcome of the trial. In academic debate the judge announces the decision or writes it on a ballot available to the debaters at a later time. Everything we have considered thus far builds to this climactic moment—the decision.

There is no competitive academic debate without the judge. Debaters compete to win, and the most important focus of their activity is the judge who will determine whether they win or lose. Judges facilitate debate and generate the educational value of debating through their analysis of debates, decisions of winners, comments and evaluation, and debriefing of the debates.

How does a judge evaluate a debate? What is their basis for decision? The decision should be based either on the proposition of debate or on the debate itself. In applied debate the decision should be rendered on the proposition itself; in academic debate the decision should be based on the debate itself—that is, on the comparative merits of the arguments and evidence presented by the opposing teams, not on the merits of the proposition. Of course, it is not quite that simple. Here we consider the role of the judge in academic debates.

III. FUNCTIONS OF THE JUDGE

Judges in academic debates have three functions: to be (1) decision makers, (2) critics, and (3) educators. As decision makers they have to serve as referee and discern which team won the debate; as critics they should report their decisions and the rationale for them with accountability and clarity, keeping in mind that the manner in which they arrive at their decision is important and impacts the way debate is; as educators they will consider the pedagogical implications of their work as debate judge and teacher. Decisions and comments of debate judges have substantial impact on debate practice and on the learning experience of participating debaters. The role of being a debate judge is a challenging and demanding one. Individuals serving in this capacity will contribute to a meaningful learning experience through their expertise and effort expended in the process.

Judge interaction with the debaters during the debate tends to be relatively limited. Judges may keep time for the debaters, even calling out by minute the time remaining in each speech and during preparation. Judges may occasionally call out "Clearer" if the debater is being unclear, or even more infrequently, "Explain" or "What was that?" if they wish to give the speaker an opportunity to clarify something. Parliamentary debate engages a higher level of judge–debater interaction during the debate and some formats even call for the judge to participate by asking questions or determining procedure and rules applications. As discussed earlier in this chapter, some judges make it a point to give nonverbal feedback about the arguments as they are presented; others work just as hard not to provide visual reactions that could influence the debate or negatively affect the debaters. It will contribute positively to the communication context of the debate if the judge will actively offer some feedback confirming they hear and understand arguments made, and nonverbal immediacy confirming and supporting the effort of the debaters.

A. Discerning Which Team Won the Debate

First and foremost, the debate judge is an adjudicator, determining who won the debate. The hard work and preparation put in by the student debaters raises the intensity of learning offered by the debate, and that preparation is motivated by the competition and drive to win the judge's ballot. Judges have a responsibility to make a reasoned decision, guided by careful and thoughtful reflection and complete attention to the performance and arguments of debaters, and clearly articulated to the debaters so as to reinforce and reward their positive debate practice. These principles are consistent applications of the steps of effective listening.

1. Judges Should Apply Their Total Knowledge of Argumentation and Debate and Their Knowledge about the Proposition. In debates an almost infinite range of possibilities may become factors in the decision-making process. Therefore judges must be able to bring to bear a comprehensive knowledge of the principles of argumentation and debate in order to evaluate the arguments advanced. Judges should do their best to make substantive decisions based upon the content and quality of the evidence and reasoning as presented during the actual debate. The First National Developmental Conference on Forensics stated:

> As decision maker the judge is called upon to make choices among alternatives emerging out of the proposition. The judge should value content

above delivery and substance above technique. The stronger position on the issue should prevail, and the more credible evidence should prevail over a greater quantity of evidence having less probative force.[2]

This standard imposes a judgment that debate judges should render decisions based on critical analysis and evaluation of the arguments, issues, cases, and evidence as constructed and employed by debaters in the given round of debate. To reinforce sound debate practice, the judge must be well versed in what constitutes that practice. If debate judging is to teach reasoned decision making, the debate judge must be able to recognize and understand the principles of argumentation upon which the decision is to be based. And in addition to expertise in the discipline of argumentation, the judge is in a better position to fairly evaluate the claims, evidence, and reasoning forwarded about a proposition if they have familiarity about the subject matter and literature of that proposition.

2. Judges Strive to Set Aside Biases Derived from Their Special Knowledge of the Subject for the Duration of the Debate.   The effective debate judge will evaluate the single debate in a vacuum, making their decision not based on their biases and predispositions about the matters under discussion, or on what they know or believe to be the case, but only on the argumentation as presented by the debaters during the debate. The best prepared judges for academic debate have read about the proposition and heard many debates. They are familiar with the literature and in a position to fairly evaluate the quality of the debaters' analysis and use of expert information. This additional knowledge may generate certain attitudes, stereotypes, anticipations, or even distortions in their thinking on the proposition. Their responsibility as judges is to apply this knowledge and be informed by it, while setting aside for the duration of the debate their personal biases. In rendering the decision, most judges will work to consider only the evidence and reasoning actually introduced into the debate. For example, one team may introduce some evidence found in an article by source A. The judge may know that source A's position is superficial and that it could easily be refuted by evidence found in a scholarly book written by source B. However, the judge should not enter into the debate except to evaluate the relative merits of competing claims as supported by the evidence presented. Unless and until the opposing team refutes the weak evidence drawn from source A's article, that evidence should be accepted at its face value within the context of the debate. Subject-matter experts ordinarily do not make good judges for academic debates. Because of their expertise, they have usually formed judgments on the proposition after long and careful study, and find it difficult to set aside these judgments for the duration of the debate (and they may not have the expertise and familiarity of debate theory and argumentation practice discussed above in step 1).

---

2. James H. McBath, ed., *Forensics as Communication* (Skokie, IL: National Textbook, 1975), p. 30.

Judges should draw on their special knowledge of the subject in their post-round discussions to suggest ways the debaters can improve their arguments. Here judges assess the debaters' subject-matter knowledge and reflect their findings in the speaker points on the ballot. When judges discover a deliberate misuse of evidence, they may impose an appropriate penalty. The National Debate Tournament (NDT) has adopted a rule stipulating the following: "If a judge determines that distortion and/or falsification [of evidence] has occurred, the judge shall award the offending team a loss and award zero speaker points to the offending speaker(s)."

3. Judges Must Base Their Decisions on the Debate as It Is Presented. Because they are experts on argumentation and debate, judges could easily refute some of the arguments advanced in the debate. They might know that one team could have taken a much stronger position than it actually did. However, they should never require the students to debate them rather than the opposing team. They must never ask, "Could *I* refute a particular argument?" but rather, "Did the opposing team refute that argument?" They do not ask whether a team's position was weak or strong in relation to the ideal position, but whether the team's position was weaker or stronger than that of their opponents. For example, in debating the proposition "Resolved: That executive control of U.S. foreign policy should be significantly curtailed," an affirmative team took the position that the United States should adopt an isolationist foreign policy. In the opinion of one educator who was asked to judge this debate, such a foreign policy would be disastrous for the United States. His opinion, however, was irrelevant to his function as a judge. The issue was not whether isolation would be good or bad for the United States but whether the affirmative team, within the context of the debate, supported its case for curtailing executive control of U.S. foreign policy.

In fact, because a debate has to be judged within its own framework, almost any statement made or position taken by either team stands until refuted. The sole exception is the last affirmative speech, when the judge may take judicial notice of the validity of the evidence or of the introduction of a new concept. If a team fails to ask the judge to take judicial notice of an obvious error or contradiction in the opponent's case, the judge must assume that the team failed to detect the error; therefore, it must stand against them.

Judges, of course, take note of the strengths and weaknesses in a debate case and refer to them in their post-round discussions and reflect their findings in speaker points and ballot comments.

4. Judges Take Comprehensive Notes during the Debate. Experienced judges are known for the care with which they take notes during a debate. (Note, some judges have abandoned the flow sheet and either do not take notes, or take limited notes in a nonlinear fashion. These judges choose to approach the debate experience in a nonlinear fashion in order to be more inclusive of those who may not have the skill, experience, training, or "privilege" to flow a debate.) The above caveat notwithstanding, all judges should develop a comprehensive note-taking system so that they can record all of the significant developments during the debate in order to evaluate the debate effectively.

Experienced educators judging academic debates find the flow sheet to be the most convenient method of taking comprehensive notes. Judges using the flow sheet method seek to record the development of each issue throughout the debate. This method is similar to the debater's flow sheet considered in Chapter 14 but with one difference: The debater may make notes on a flow sheet to aid in planning future speeches; the judge, of course, will record only the arguments actually presented by the debaters.

Although the methods suggested in Chapter 14 are designed specifically for use in judging the academic debate, they may be adapted for use in rendering a decision on an applied debate. Many trial judges and attorneys use a comparable method to follow courtroom debates, and many business executives use a comparable "balance sheet" to help them weigh arguments in debates on corporate policy. Whenever it is necessary to render a decision on an important debate, some system should be developed to facilitate the process of analyzing and weighing the arguments.

Because the flow sheet is never a verbatim record of the debate, many tournament debate judges will examine evidence, or even the text of arguments, plans, and counterplans, before making their decision. These judges must keep in mind that, although reading material after the debate may clarify their understanding of what was said during the debate, it is not a substitute for paying careful attention and keeping an effective flow sheet during the debate. In addition, most tournament situations demand that the judge make a decision in a timely manner to facilitate the tournament schedule.

5. Judges Should Declare Their Approach to Judging Prior to the Debate. Debate is a communication exercise grounded in rhetorical exchange. Debaters must select and design their strategies and argumentation in order to adapt to and therefore persuade their audience. Of course for most academic debates, the audience is the debate judge. In order to adapt their message to the judge, the debaters should not simply guess about the judge's preferences, biases, and method of judging. The judge may have the opportunity to make their philosophy of judging available to debaters in advance, and it is always appropriate for debaters to ask, or for judges to volunteer such key information prior to the beginning of a debate.

B. Reporting the Decision in an Educationally Useful Manner

The decision, as part of the educational process of debate, should be reported in a way that will contribute to the students' educations. This reporting may be done either by means of an oral critique, a carefully prepared ballot, or, ideally, a combination of these two methods.

1. The Post-Round Critique.   Upon completion of the debate, the judge will typically take some time to review their flow sheet and reflect on the debate before rendering a decision. When evidence has been presented, the judge may call for certain items of evidence to reread its content. Once the judge makes their decision, they report it to the tournament administrators by completing a paper ballot or reporting the results on an electronic ballot to be sent immediately to the tabulation management. The judge will report both speakers' points, which are a rating of each debater's individual performance, and a decision, indicating which *team* won the debate. Next, the judge may have the opportunity to announce and explain their decision to the debaters and engage in a post-round discussion about the debate. Some formats and debate contexts preclude this opportunity for direct engagement either by rule or by scheduling. However, when allowed, the post-round discussion can be an important and valuable function of the competitive debate tournament experience. The best judges strive to offer meaningful and thorough comments and to answer questions about the debate and the debater's performances to engage an interactive learning exchange. The effective critique should do the following:

1. Review the progress of the debate.
2. Cite examples of effective application of the principles of argumentation and debate.
3. Offer suggestions for improvement.
4. Cite the factors most significant in determining the decision.
5. Announce the decision (this is the norm in CEDA/NDT debate, but not universal; in some tournaments may even be prohibited by tournament or league rules; some judges prefer to offer suggestions and feedback to the debaters but to report the decision only on the ballot).
6. Offer an opportunity for questions and interaction with the debaters.

When the oral critique is used, adequate time should be allocated for its presentation.

2. The Ballot.   Whereas oral critiques and decision disclosures are the norm in tournament debating, a written ballot or electronically submitted ballot is generally required to facilitate tabulation. At a minimum, the ballots report the decision and points. Ideally, they offer comments and a record of the judge's reasons for decision (RFD). Even when decisions are orally discussed, it is desirable to have a written record of the decision. When a ballot is used, an oral critique may be presented as well. The judge will generally be asked to prepare a written critique on the ballots that will be handed to the participating teams. An effectively designed ballot should facilitate the following:

1. Record the decision of the debate.
2. Record the name, team affiliation (if relevant), side, speaker position, rank, and points for each debater.

3. Record the name (and affiliation if relevant) of the judge, and provide a signature line.
4. Provide a place for a written critique and reason for decision.
5. Provide a record of the debate for each team.
6. Provide a record of the debate for the tournament director.

Four traditional ballots meeting these requirements are shown in insets. These ballots for the most part are anachronistic; most tournaments now either use their own simple paper ballots or electronic form ballots. However, these ballots are informative, as they reflect a set of criteria formerly used in assigning speaker points and for some judges, in awarding decisions, they outline the necessary components of any ballot.

The AFA Form A ballot (shown below), one of several ballots once published by the AFA, was originally designed for use in CEDA or cross-examination debates; Form W (shown on page 320) was designed for use in NDT debates. Of course, the two are now interchangeable. The Form H ballot (shown on page 321) is meant for Lincoln–Douglas debates.

A ballot for shift-of-opinion debating, which may be prepared locally and distributed to the audience, is shown on page 322.

FORM A

CROSS EXAMINATION
DEBATE ASSOCIATION

DIVISION [   ] ROUND [   ] ROOM [   ] JUDGE [   ]

AFF. [   ] **NEG.** [   ]

INSTRUCTIONS: Fill out ALL shaded areas of the ballot (even if ballot label is attatched). RATE all speakers on a scale from 30 (superior) to 1 (poor). RANK each speaker in order of excellence (1-4; ties are not permitted). If you are awarding the decision to the team with fewer speaker points, check the appropriate box. The boxes should be checked according to the following scale (the boxes do NOT have numerical significance):

P - poor/needs improvement   F - fair   A - average   E - excellent   S - superior

1st Affirmative	2nd Affirmative		1st Negative	2nd Negative
P F A E S	P F A E S		P F A E S	P F A E S

Analysis/Definition
Evidence
Refutation/Rebuttal
Cross-Examination
Organization
Delivery
Language/Style

NAMES

Pts. (30 max) [ ] Rank [ ]   Pts. (30 max) [ ] Rank [ ]   Pts. (30 max) [ ] Rank [ ]   Pts. (30 max) [ ] Rank [ ]

I am persuaded to vote for team [   ] REPRESENTING: [   ] CODE: [   ]
(aff. or neg.)

Low point win? [ ]   [   ] AFFILIATION [   ]
JUDGES SIGNATURE

REASON FOR DECISION/COMMENTS:

IV. JUDGING PHILOSOPHIES

All qualified judges for academic debate agree that the decision must be based on the answer to the question "Which team won the debate?" However, different judges use different philosophical, theoretical, or pedagogical approaches—or different decision-making paradigms—in answering this question.[3] A paradigm is a worldview or general set of principles and understandings. The judge's paradigm colors their perception of the arguments and presentations by debaters, and provides a set of rules or norms the judge will employ in rendering their decision. Identifying judging paradigms is now somewhat historical, as tournament debate judges have evolved beyond the labels which identified their approach in the 1970s and 1980s. At that time, judges tended to fall into the following characterizations.

A. Skills Judge

The **skills judge** focuses on the skills listed on the AFA Form W ballot—analysis, reasoning, evidence, organization, refutation, and delivery—and carefully evaluates which team has performed better with regard to each of these skills. The judge in this case does not merely assign points and add up the score to "find out who won." The ballot is an instrument the judge uses to report decisions. Skills judges base their decisions on their total knowledge of argumentation and debate, and they recognize that, although the skills are given equal weight in the ballot in an actual debate, one or two skills might outweigh all the others and constitute the reason for the decision. For example, one team's use of evidence or its analytic skill in developing a particular critical issue might be decisive. Ultimately, the skills judge works to evaluate the public-speaking qualities of the debate and identify the team that did a better job of blending form and content, style, and material. In contemporary application, many judges, while not singling out the specific list of skill-based criteria as are listed on the old form ballots, do determine their decision in part or completely on their impression of the overall performance of debaters, based on the power of their advocacy, delivery, manner, and consistency. These judges may be termed "performance" judges, and their paradigm a performance paradigm, although the study and understanding of performance as symbolic activity is far more complex than only considering delivery.

B. Issues Judge

The **issues judge** focuses on the affirmative case, and specifically the stock issues. To win the decision from such a judge, the affirmative has to win all the stock issues, harm, inherency, and solvency, whereas the negative needs to win only one stock issue. The affirmative is not required to win every argument and every

3. John D. Cross and Ronald J. Malton, "An Analysis of Judging Philosophies in Academic Debate," *Journal of the American Forensics Association*, vol. 15, no. 2 (fall 1978), pp. 110–123.

American Forensic Association Debate Ballot   FORM **W**

Division _____ Round _____ Room _____ Judge _____

Affirmative _____ Negative _____

Check the column on each item which, on the following scale, best describes your evaluation of the debator's effectiveness:

1-poor	2-fair	3-average	4-excellent	5-superior

1st Affirmative	2nd Affirmative	1st Negative	2nd Negative
(Name)	(Name)	(Name)	(Name)

1 2 3 4 5	1 2 3 4 5		1 2 3 4 5	1 2 3 4 5
		Analysis		
		Reasoning		
		Evidence		
		Organization		
		Refutation		
		Delivery		

Total_____ Rank_____   Total_____ Rank_____   Total_____ Rank_____   Total_____ Rank_____

Rank each debater in order of excellence (1st for best, 2nd for next best, etc.)

In my opinion, this debate was won by_____ representing _____
(Aff. or Neg.)   (School and/or #)

_____
(Judge's Name)   (School)

contention in the debate, but it must win each stock issue. Note that issues are won or lost in comparison to the arguments of the opposing team. A negative team might establish that the affirmative's plan will cause substantial disadvantages. To win this issue, however, the negative must demonstrate that the disadvantage has greater impact than the significance of the need itself. For example, a disadvantage to TSA full-body scanners in screening air travelers is the invasion of privacy. However, if the scanners do contribute to increased safety of air travel, the advantage of safety and security may outweigh the disadvantage of lost privacy. Win to the affirmative favoring scanners. On the other hand, the negative could argue that the harm issue is not compelling by proving that terrorist threats have shifted away from airline targets or that full-body scanners do not discover new chemical explosives, thus not solving the risk of terrorist attacks, in which case the stock issues judge would favor the negative because the issues of harm and solvency were lost by the affirmative. The central tenet of the issues judge was the identification of the issues as a sort of checklist to be identified as necessary elements in their decision. Presumption to the issues judge is a rule, favoring the status quo. To the issues judge, topicality is a critical procedural question preceding consideration of the affirmative case and its strength in addressing the stock issues. If the affirmative loses topicality, they lose by rule.

AMERICAN FORENSIC ASSOCIATION

FORM **H**

LINCOLN-DOUGLAS DEBATE BALLOT

Round _____ Room_____ Date _____ Judge_____

	Name-Code	Points		Name-Code	Points

Aff. _____   _____   Neg. _____   _____

Scale: 12-15   16-19   20-23   24-27   28-30
Below Average   Average   Excellent   Outstanding   Exceptional

COMMENT/RECOMMENDATION (REGARDING ANALYSIS, SUPPORT, REFUTATION, DELIVERY):

AFF.   NEG.

REASONS FOR DECISION (MIGHT INCLUDE ISSUES, REASONABLENESS OF POSITION, PERSUASION):

IN MY OPINION, THE BETTER DEBATING WAS DONE BY _____ REPRESENTING _____
CODE   AFF./NEG.

_____   _____
SIGNATURE OF JUDGE   AFFILIATION

C. Policymaker Judge

The policymaker focuses on the affirmative plan as compared to available alternatives, and through a sort of cost-benefit analysis, compares the merits of the competing policies, simply asking, "which one is better." Topicality is a jurisdictional question, considered prior to consideration of competing policies. If the affirmative is deemed not topical, they will lose. Presumption is reflexive, belonging to the side advocating the policy proposal offering the least risk. Like a legislator evaluating competing pieces of legislation, the **policymaker judge** evaluates the affirmative's policy system (that is, its plan) as it represents a departure from the status quo, contrasts it with the negative's policy system (the status quo or a counterplan), and then decides whether the affirmative has offered a desirable plan. If the affirmative's plan is viable (desirable), the judge will also require that it be better than the negative's policy system. The focus of this paradigm is the direct comparison of competing policies. Stock issues inform the policymaker judge in evaluating the comparison of advantages to disadvantages; however, they are considered not as absolute, or as rules, but as arguments within the affirmative advocacy, and are considered relative to each other. For example, if

---

Shift-of-Opinion Ballot

UNIVERSITY DEBATING TEAMS
Audience Shift-of-Opinion Ballot

INSTRUCTIONS TO THE AUDIENCE:

The debaters will appreciate your interest and cooperation if you will, *both before and after the debate,* indicate on this ballot your *personal opinion* on the proposition of debate.

The proposition is: ''Resolved: That (the proposition of debate is stated here).''

BEFORE THE DEBATE
FILL OUT THIS SIDE
(Check one)

AFTER THE DEBATE
FILL OUT THIS SIDE
(Check one)

_____ I believe more strongly in the affirmative than I did.

_____ I believe in the affirmative of the resolution.

_____ I believe in the affirmative of the resolution.

_____ I am undecided.

_____ I am undecided.

_____ I believe in the negative of the resolution.

_____ I believe in the negative of the resolution.

_____ I believe more strongly in the negative than I did.

the solvency of the affirmative plan is mitigated (many new explosives will escape detection of full-body scanners), then the negative will require less impact of their disadvantage argument in order to outweigh the mitigated advantage. In addition indirect impacts are important to consider, so slippery slope arguments or disadvantages involving multiple links are more important to consider than in some other approaches. Negatives could argue that if a new law requiring full-body scanners at all check points was passed, such a law would be expensive to TSA, thus forcing TSA to lay off human workers, creating more unemployment and therefore damaging the ability of those workers to provide health care to their families, thus increasing the likelihood that they will avoid doctors' visits and therefore not receive flu vaccines, contributing to a new flu epidemic, from which some deaths will occur. The impact of increased flu deaths, even though having a low level of probability, would need to be considered by the policymaker and weighed against the mitigated benefits of scanning as a potential cost to affirmative implementation.

D. Hypothesis-Testing Judge

While the focus of the issues judge is the affirmative case and the issues upon which it is built, and the focus of the policymaker judge is the comparison of competing policies, the focus of the hypothesis testing judge is the proposition. The proposition is viewed as the researcher's hypothesis, a statement of truth to be tested against alternative explanations. The affirmative case is the embodiment or proof in favor of the proposition (hypothesis), and the negative's job is to test the affirmative against possible alternative explanations (defense of the status quo or one or more counterplans). If any of the alternative explanations offered by the negative are equal to or better than the affirmative, the researcher's hypothesis (the affirmative) is rejected. The **hypothesis–testing judge** takes the perspective of a scientist seeking to determine the probable truth of a hypothesis. Unlike the policymaker judge the hypothesis-testing judge does not seek to compare two policy systems. He or she tests the hypothesis—that is, the proposition as exemplified by the affirmative case—alone. Thus the negative is free to defend anything or everything that is nontopical, because alternative explanations (defense of the status quo, or any number of counterplans) offer null hypotheses, the alternative explanations, against which the hypothesis is to be tested. Because the focus of the debate is the proposition, topicality is particularly important to the hypothesis-testing judge. The affirmative seeks to justify the terms in the proposition, and negative arguments, if they are to be reasons to reject the proposition, must be intrinsically counter to these terms. So the multilink disadvantage is less important to the hypothesis tester, as the spreading flu epidemic is far removed from use of full-body scanners and is thus not intrinsic to increasing security checks. As such, it is not a reason to reject the truth of the proposition. The hypothesis-testing judge considers all argument to be conditional, that is, a test of truth; therefore, she tends to be receptive to conditional or hypothetical counterplans. Since the proposition is viewed as a researcher's hypothesis, it is considered false until proven true and, therefore, presumption always opposes the proposition. The main point of this paradigm is a primary focus on the statement that is the proposition. Debate occurred as a means of testing the probable truth of the proposition as embodied in the affirmative team's example.

E. Tabula Rasa Judge

Most debate judges profess to being to a lesser or greater degree, tabula rasa. The **tabula rasa** (or clean-slate) **judge** works to avoid the imposition of his or her own debate philosophy and allows and expects the debaters to decide the theoretical framework for the decision as the debate evolves. If the affirmative is using a stock issue case and argues successfully that the debate should be decided on stock issues, this judge will vote for the affirmative if it carries the stock issues. If the negative offers a conditional counterplan and argues successfully that the judge should function as a hypothesis tester, the judge will vote for the negative if it carries the conditional counterplan. If neither team chooses to argue the judging philosophy, the judge may decide that a certain type of judging philosophy is implicit in the way the debate evolves and choose that philosophy as the basis for decision. Most judges work to be tabula rasa to some degree, striving to make their decisions based on the arguments offered by the debaters in the debate round, and not based on their predispositions about the topic and the materials presented.

F. The Evaluator of Argument

Somewhat like the tabula rasa judge; however, the **evaluator of argument** recognizes that he or she has an expertise and special knowledge in evaluating argumentation and that given the nature of debate, some degree of interpretation or "intervention" by the judge may be necessary. The evaluator of argument will apply standards of good argumentation to compare the relative quality of argumentation by each team in order to determine a winner. This judge tries to avoid imposing a framework for judging the debate but recognizes that it is his or her role as an expert on argumentation to evaluate the relative quality of competing arguments. For example, the evaluator of argument would compare the competing claims of debaters based on such criteria as quality of sources, logical support for claims, sufficiency of data, and warrant in support of claims. If no judging philosophy emerges as clearly implicit in the debate, this judge may decide to select any one of the philosophies to use as the basis for decision. The evaluator of argument is most comfortable recognizing their superior knowledge of debate and of the topic, and feel obliged to consider the quality of in-round arguments based on both the arguments launched by the opponents in the debate and by their own evaluation of the quality of argumentation based on factors external to the debate.

G. Current Practice

As indicated earlier, the division of judges into paradigms is now archaic, as most judges have developed their own more individualized approaches combining some of the theoretical precedents. Although each debate judge has a unique approach, in general, they currently fall into one of two main camps.

The more traditional group of debate judges works to compare competing advocacy (whether policy or critical philosophical positions) based on the arguments, evidence, and clash as presented in the debate; works to remove itself from personal bias and involvement; and favors decisions based on the content of the argumentation over the delivery of the message. This group works to keep a complete and accurate flow sheet to record the debate and after the debate may examine evidence for precise wording. There is a preference among most of these judges for arguments about the concrete nature of the policies being debated, and an acceptance that the arguments are offered as hypothetical. They are comfortable with the notion of switch-sides debating, which debaters learn from the process of defending and opposing all sides of any issue. The judge is an observer of the educational game that is an academic debate, whose job is to promote the educational experience by fairly deciding the debate based on the content of argumentation.

A newer trend in debate judging could be characterized as more **activist** and interactive in nature. Judges in this approach see themselves as active participants in the debate process, and view the debate not as a game, but as an act. The performances of the debaters are extensions of themselves and their advocacy, which has importance in the lives of the participants in and out of the debate context. To some extent, this paradigm considers the unique skills expressed by the debaters, as well as their ability to engage their audience and exemplify ethical and right behavior. These judges are less likely to evaluate a text of the debate, but are more holistic in their evaluations. They are also more interested in form: The activist approach has incorporated music, rap, video, personal narrative, and dramatic performance. Activist judges are likely to consider themselves social critics, extending their critique of social structures and hierarchy to the activity of debate, which by its technical nature serves to exclude participation. A consistent measure for the activist approach to debate and debate judging is inclusion of repressed and underrepresented groups in the debate activity.

H. Significance to the Debater

We have considered six different historical judging philosophies and two general descriptions of contemporary judging practice, but these are hardly the limit. In fact, there may be as many ways to judge a debate as there are judges. Because the debaters usually will not know the philosophy of the judge, the question arises: How can debaters adapt to the situation? There are two considerations. First, the debater should know argumentation theory and be prepared to argue that the judge should serve, for example, as an issues judge for "this" debate if the debater intends to argue the case on issues. Second, although judges have their preferences for specific judging philosophies, most judges are willing to consider arguments about judging philosophies from the debaters and apply the model most appropriate to a specific debate. John Cross and Ronald Matlon have found that "the majority of judges in the academic debate community view debates with extraordinary consensus regardless of their stated judging philosophies."[4] Although this observation was made some time ago, it is still a fairly accurate statement.

It is the judges' responsibility to communicate their predispositions, preferences, and paradigms to debaters before the debate. Many tournaments, including the CEDA National Tournament and the NDT, require that each judge's philosophy statement be available. Most intercollegiate debate judges post their philosophies publicly at Debate Results (http://commweb.fullerton.edu/jbruschke/web/Index.aspx) or Planet Debate (http://www.planetdebate.com/philosophies). One judge at the 1999 CEDA National Tournament wrote his philosophy as a rap (a portion is presented here):

> I decided to rhyme this/so check this verse/It's as accurate/as one page can get/If I'm judging you/this is what I'll do/ ... and if you don't like/ consider me a strike....
>
> In the round/I get down/and I flow every card/I listen hard/to your tags/extensions and cross-apps/If you'd like to win/then you better begin/with good analysis/and then evidence.
>
> Qualified warrants/for the claims you make/is where/most debaters make/the fatal mistake/Don't mistake my understanding/ of the issues you bring/you better hustle/in rebuttals/so your arguments/mean something/I mean/tell me about the way it comes together/or your speaker points/will look like/Rochester weather.[5]

Another, more traditional example of a judging philosophy statement is provided in the inset on pages 327–328.

In addition, judges may voluntarily offer the debaters guidance by telling them their philosophy prior to the debate. Debaters are always free to ask judges to discuss their preferences. Debaters may also find it helpful to talk to people who know the judges about their judging habits.

We have considered the major decision-making paradigms used in academic debate. You should be aware that in other forums the decision renderers often will have formulated decision-making paradigms they deem appropriate to the subject or occasion. Although these paradigms may not be as clearly stated or as precisely articulated as the paradigms for academic debate, they are important and advocates must discover them. When necessary, the advocate should be prepared to debate about the paradigm for decision making, as well as the issues and evidence relating to the resolution.

---

4. Cross and Matlon, "An Analysis of Judging Philosophies," p. 123.
5. Myron King, "Judging Philosophy Rap Sheet," in CEDA National Judging Philosophy Booklet, Southern Illinois University, 1999. Reprinted with permission.

Judging Philosophy

Kris Willis
Director of Debate
The University of Florida
Years coaching: 10 (19 total years in the activity)

Debate is a game. It should be fun and educational.
Please be nice to each other.

I will judge the debate you want to have to the best of my abilities. I would say you are better to debate what you are good at debating, than change for me in the back of the room. I do, however, have some predispositions and beliefs regarding debate that you should know. Absent a framework set-up during the debate, I will default policymaker. I prefer to watch debates with good evidence and oriented around a policy action.

Theory Debates: I do not like to watch theory debates because they are generally blippy taglines and impossible to flow. Having said that, I understand the importance and strategy of engaging in a theory debate. I recognize that sometimes it is what you got. If you go for theory in the debate, go deep and slow to analyze the debate. Continuing to read front-lines with no depth of explanation will be bad for you. Try to make the debate about in-round implications and not centered around potential abuse or "how" debate should be in the future. In general, if you haven't caught on by the descriptions, I tend to find education arguments more persuasive than fairness arguments. But fairness is important.

Framework/Performance (or the like) debates: If the debate is a debate about framework or how I should evaluate the debate, please don't forget to talk about the other arguments in the debate. In other words, there should be something "productive" that comes with the way you want me to vote. Debates about how we should debate are interesting, but make sure you engage in some sort of debate as well. Reading scripted/blocked out front-lines is very unimpressive to me. Make it about the debate at hand.

Topicality: I do not vote for T very often but I do think it is a voting issue. If you read a T argument make sure to talk about "in-round" implications and not just potential abuse arguments. With the case list, disclosure, and MPJ, I do not find potential abuse arguments very compelling. Linking the T to other arguments in the debate and showing the affirmative is being abusive by avoiding core negative ground in the debate is what works best. Discussions about predictable literature outside of the in-round implications do not carry much weight because in most instances the negative knew about the case and research a good strategy. The exception is when an affirmative breaks a new 1AC, then the negative should be allowed to make potential abuse arguments—they didn't get disclosure and the case list to prepare. I generally prefer depth-over-breath education claims.

Disadvantages: I like them. The more specific the better. The link is very important. Please make evidence comparisons during the debate. I dislike having to call for 20+ cards to access uniqueness on a Politics DA (etc.) when they are highlighted down to one or two lines. Read the longer, more contextual cards than the fast irrelevant ones. I tend to not give a risk to the DA. You need to win the components to the DA to have me weigh it against the affirmative.

Counterplans: I do not like Consult CPs, please choose another type of CP. PIC and Agent CPs are OK, but are better when you have contextual literature that justifies the CP. Advantage CPs are cool. Affirmatives should not be able to advocate the permutation; however, theory abuse arguments can be used to justify this action. Condo is OK, but you shouldn't go for contradictory arguments in rebuttals.

Judging Philosophy (Continued)

Case Debates: I like case debates; however, these debates tend to turn into "blippy extensions" and force me to read cards to understand the arguments and/ or nuances of the case debate. Debaters should make these explanations during the debate and not rely on me to read the cards and make it for you. I tend to try and let the debater arguments carry weight for the evidence. Saying extend Smith it answers this argument is not a compelling extension. Warrants are a necessity in all arguments.

Critiques: I generally consider these arguments to be linear DAs, with a plan meet need (PMN) and sometimes a CP (often abusive) attached at the end. Yes, I will vote for a K. When I was in Graduate School I read a lot of this literature and so I liked these debates. Now that I am 10+ years removed from Grad school, I tend to see bad debates that grotesquely mutate the author's intent. This is also true for framework debates. Your K should have as specific literature as possible. Generic K's are the worst, as are bad generic affirmative answers. While I think condo is OK, I find Performative Contradiction arguments sometimes persuasive (especially if discourse is the K link)—so try not to engage in this negative (or affirmative).

General things you should know:

1. I like switch-side debating. While you are free to argue this is bad, it is a strong disposition I have to the game. **Read-Affirmatives should have a plan of action and defend it. However, because of this I usually give more "latitude" to affirmatives on permutations for critical arguments when they can prove the core action of the affirmative is a good idea.

2. Potential abuse is not very persuasive. Instead, connect the abuse to in-round implications.

3. Engage in good impact analysis. The worst debates to judge are ones where I weigh the impacts without the debaters doing the work in the speeches.

4. Research: I am a big believer that what separates "policy debate" pedagogically from other forms of debate and makes it a better form to engage in is the research and argument construction that flows from it. Hence, I like good arguments that are well researched.

5. Don't steal prep-time! If you are paperless, prep stops when you hand the jump-drive to your opponents, not when you say I am ready.

V. FUNCTIONS OF THE JUDGE'S DECISION

A. Reporting the Decision

Traditionally, the written ballot provided the primary means of communicating the judge's decision to the tab room, and in some settings still serves that function. In other tournament environments, ballot information is reported electronically. Either way, the ballot provides the results of the debate to those administering the competition and to the debaters. Results include the decision (which side won), speaker points (each debater is usually rated on a numerical scale for their performance), rank (in many tournaments involving team debate, debaters are ranked as to which was the best, second best, and so on in the debate). Speaker points typically (although not universally) are awarded on a scale of 0–30 points, where 30 is the best possible score, and points may be given in tenths (so, 27.5 or 28.2 are possible scores). Speaker point ties are usually discouraged or prohibited. Ranks, which reflect 1 for the best, 2 for the second best, and so on), should be consistent with the points (so the debater receiving 28.2 speaker points would receive a higher rank (that is, a lower number) than the debater receiving 27.5 points). In some cases, teams may tie on total points awarded, and although it is unusual, the team receiving lower points may win the judge's decision. There is usually a requirement that this "low point win" is indicated as such upon the ballot.

B. Explaining and Justifying the Decision

In the oral comments and, when available, the written comments, it is important for the judge to explain as clearly as possible their reason for decision. This process improves the quality of decisions. As judges know they will be called upon to explain their decision; they may work harder not only to make reasoned, careful, thoroughly considered and rational decisions, but also prepare their statements explaining the decision carefully and clearly. They may work harder to make a good decision when they know they will be called upon to defend it. The integrity of the competitive process and the quality of the educational experience are facilitated by clearly offered, well-supported explanations and discussions. Experienced judges take pride in their ability to communicate clearly their reasons for decision.

C. Serving as an Educational Tool

Judges' comments offer the opportunity for proactive experiential learning. Question and answer often becomes discussion, and student debaters engage with educator judges in mutually beneficial ways. Few other educational contexts offer the complete and open review of ideas, performance, and skill development leading to personal growth and change. The comments of the judge enable lessons to be learned and integrated into practice. They reinforce good argument practice and correct poor practice. Written records are helpful for later discussion and review by debaters with their own coaches and teachers.

Although forensic directors ordinarily do not judge intercollegiate debates involving teams from their own schools, they will judge many debates between their own students as they prepare for intercollegiate debates. The evaluations given at this time are often the most valuable part of the students' education. Usually time is available for a much more detailed critique than is possible in other circumstances. Because the directors have seen the student's debate many times, often over a period of several years, they have considerable knowledge about their students' abilities and limitations and more insight into each student's problems than does a judge who sees the student only once.

EXERCISES

1. Write your philosophy of judging.
2. View a debate (in class, online, at a tournament), and write a ballot for the debate.
3. Assign class members different philosophies of judging (skills, issues, policy, tabula rasa, hypothesis testing, activist). View a debate together, and staying true to your assigned philosophy, write a ballot explaining your decision, role-playing the approach.
4. Read judging philosophies at Planet Debate or Debate Results.

16

....

Debate as Public Speaking

D ebate is a form of communication. This may seem obvious, but is too often forgotten by its practitioners. Of course, to suggest that debate is communication begs the question, "what is communication?" A simplistic conception of communication might offer an interpretation such as "the transfer of information from one person to another." In fact, life would likely be less complicated if we could transfer information directly from one to another. If, for example, when we have thoughts, feelings, and ideas we wish to transfer to another person, we could simply plug a USB cable into each other's heads and "sync" the information, we would encounter far less misunderstanding and be much more efficient in avoiding and resolving conflicts. A more useful definition of communication is *the interactive and subjective process through which meaning is constructed and shared understanding is sought.*

Our understandings are shaped by the unique personal processes which formed and embedded our thoughts, feelings, and ideas. We interpret the representations of others' understandings through the perceptual screens built by our own life histories, cultures, knowledge, and prior understandings. Communication is a sloppy process! It begins when someone engages in an active process to become aware of some set of thoughts, feelings, and ideas and chooses to express them, for some reason, to another. To do so, they select a set of symbols (in debate, these are mostly words) to represent their thoughts, feelings, and ideas (arguments?). It must be recalled that these symbols are arbitrary, abstract, and ambiguous. They are not the things they represent and, at best, they offer a range of meaning rather than a singular, shared precise meaning. Once the symbols are selected, the originator of the communication (the source) also selects the channel they will use to present their message to others. In debate, that channel is usually the spoken word, or *public speaking*. The person or persons for whom the message is intended pay attention to the message (not a given!) and interpret it in their own way, affected by selective exposure, perception, and

---

Miniglossary

Antithesis   The juxtaposition of contrasting ideas using parallel structure.

Communication   The interactive and subjective process through which meaning is constructed and shared understanding is sought.

Confirmation   The pattern of communication by which we recognize the existence, importance, and value of the other person.

Connotative meaning   The personal, often emotional, interpretation of language.

Denotative meaning   The literal, relatively objective meaning of language as shared within a language community.

Disconfirmation   The pattern of communication in which we ignore or dismiss the other, emphasizing difference and explicitly or implicitly (often without recognition) expressing power over the other (person).

Extemporaneous speaking A style of speaking using limited preparation in which the speaker carefully words and plans some portion of the speech and speaks from an outline or notes, but makes spontaneous remarks and speaks with a conversational, informal tone.

Impromptu speaking   A style of speaking reflecting no preparation wherein the speaker is spontaneous, informal, and conversational in tone.

Metaphor   A figure of speech making implicit comparisons of unlike things.

Nonverbal communication   Characteristics of physical and vocal delivery that convey meaning to another person.

Public speaking   The oral expression of a message from one person to one or more persons where one is primarily the speaker and the other(s) represent an audience and the speaker offers a continuous and largely uninterrupted oral message.

Verbal communication   The use of language to influence, inform, teach, and inspire.

---

retention. This is to say that people attend to things in which they have an interest, perceive them according to their own screens, biases, and predispositions, and recall that which seems most relevant or consistent with their prior understandings. Debate strives to minimize the range of meaning inherent within the communication process and to maximize shared understanding; however, it is inevitable that participants in any communication process will personalize their understanding of the symbols, arguments, and reasoning expressed. Debate also provides tools to minimize the distortive influences of selectivity and bias. However, it must be remembered that debate, in all its forms, by definition, is a form of communication.

While debate does occur in informal settings including interpersonal communication, as well as in mass media and mediated communication, the focus of most of this text is debate in the channel of oral, spoken communication, that is, public speaking. Public speaking is *the oral expression of a message from one person to one or more persons where one is primarily the speaker, and the other(s) represent an audience and the speaker offers a continuous and largely uninterrupted oral message.*

It is pertinent to recognize that while technological changes are offering new opportunities, most academic debate, as all public speaking, is synchronous. It occurs in real time within a shared space. E-mail, for example, is asynchronous, meaning that the sender and receiver (debater and judge) need not respond to one another immediately or be in the same place.

You may recall Aristotle's definition of rhetoric, "the faculty for observing, for any given case, the available means of persuasion." Aristotle's challenge to the speakers to select their arguments and to construct their message specific to "the given case" points to his focus on audience adaptation. This also recognizes the reality of communication as a cooperative enterprise between speaker and audience, wherein messages must be constructed with the process in mind. The effective speaker understands and relates to their audience, crafting their message to what they know and can anticipate about the audience prior to presentation, developing a relationship with them upon presentation, and adapting the message to feedback received as the presentation progresses. To be an effective debater *demands* that one be an effective public speaker. This chapter explores effective public speaking.

I. PUBLIC SPEAKING ANXIETY

The first barrier faced by most beginning speakers is their fear or nervousness about speaking publically. Most people experience a normal and natural nervousness when confronted with the need to speak publically, and fear of public speaking is consistently found to rank among the most common fears. According to public speaking expert Stephen Lucas,

> Some of the greatest public speakers in history have suffered from stage fright, including Abraham Lincoln, Margaret Sanger, and Winston Churchill. The famous Roman orator Cicero said: "I turn pale at the outset of a speech and quake in every limb and in my soul." Oprah Winfrey, Conan O'Brien, and Jay Leno all report being anxious about speaking in public. Early in his career, Leonardo DiCaprio was so nervous about giving an acceptance speech that he hoped he would not win the Academy Award for which he had been nominated. Eighty-one percent of business executives say public speaking is the most nerve-wracking experience they face. What comedian Jerry Seinfeld said in jest sometimes seems literally true: "Given a choice, at a funeral most of us would rather be the one in the coffin than the one giving the eulogy."[1]

In fact, even though she is one of the most successful recording artists of recent years, Adele says that she experiences terrible stage fright. "I'm scared of

---

1. Lucas, S. L., *The Art of Public Speaking*, 10th ed. (New York: McGraw-Hill, 2009), pp. 9–10.

audiences," she says. "One show in Amsterdam I was so nervous I escaped out the fire exit. I've thrown up a couple of times. Once in Brussels I projectile vomited on someone. I just gotta bear it."[2]

Experiencing a stage fright for most people need not preclude their successful performance. Certainly, such an anxiety should not make you feel abnormal or weird! The goal of the nervous speaker, however, should *not* be to overcome their nervousness. In fact, it is sometimes observed that a healthy anxiety will boost performance, both in preparation and in presentation. And at worst, it is helpful to recall that most nervousness is invisible to the audience. The goal of the nervous speaker should be to learn to cope with their anxiety such that it does not interfere with their ability to achieve their speaking objectives (winning debates!). Effective speakers will remember the adage "what does not kill you makes you stronger!" They will discover that with experience, they will learn which coping skills work best for them, and so, seek out frequent opportunities to speak in front of audiences and judges. Some additional strategies include:

- Be prepared! Thorough preparation will help to produce confidence. This includes careful preparation of notes, briefs, manuscripts, and other materials with the speaking context in mind.

- Focus on meaning! Of course, style and delivery will impact reception of the content; however, your goal is to have your judge or audience favorably evaluate your arguments and ideas, *not* you! So maintain a focus on the substance of the debate or speech and the desired objectives.

- Achieve physical relaxation! Physiological and psychological well-being are intrinsically intertwined; you will feel more calm if you can achieve physical relaxation. Deep breathing relaxation exercises, being well rested, avoiding hard-to-digest foods or carbonated drinks, and working out prior to speaking can all help the speaker cope with the situational anxiety of speaking.

- Plan a great opening! If you get your audience on your side from the beginning of a speech, the rest of the speech will feel more positive.

- Treat it as a conversation! Whenever possible, make eye contact with audience members one at a time, focusing on their positive reactions and engagement between you and the individual audience member rather than on the totality of your performance to what can seem like a multi-headed monster.

- Breathe! Long, slow deep breaths can benefit your speaking in many ways, one of which is to force an effective pause and reduce the anxiety producing urgency of the moment. Also, you need oxygen, and deep breaths will help you feel better.

- Smile! And work smiles into your material. A more comfortable mood, helped by a more friendly atmosphere will contribute to anxiety reduction.

---

2. "Adele Opens Up About her Inspirations, Looks and Stage Fright in New Rolling Stone Cover Story," *RS* All Access, 2011. Retrieved from http://www.rollingstone.com/music/news/adele-opens-up-about-her-inspirations-looks-and-stage-fright-in-new-rolling-stone-cover-story-20110413.

Elements of Effective Speaking

- Delivery
- Support
- Organization
- Involvement
- Language
- Sensory aids

II. THE ELEMENTS OF EFFECTIVE PUBLIC SPEAKING

Martin Luther King, Jr., John F. Kennedy, Ronald Reagan, Barack Obama, Steve Jobs, Pat Riley, Anthony Robbins, Hillary Clinton, and Sarah Palin are all known for their public speaking skills, however, each is completely unique. Imagine the powerful emotions and metaphor of Dr. King delivered by the homespun and personable President Reagan; the affect would certainly be different, and each of their strengths diminished. Effective public speaking is, in part, a consequence of finding individual strengths and skills unique to the speaker and shaping them to the needs presented by the situation. What works for one individual or context will not fit another speaker or set of circumstances. So applying one set of criteria to all speakers is inappropriate. You must find your own voice and method. Nonetheless, there are some general categories of speaking skills which will help guide the speaker. Each impacts the other in a synergistic manner, like different ingredients to a stew. The elements of effective public speaking are delivery, support, organization, involvement, language, and sensory aids.

A. Delivery

The importance of delivery in oral communication has been stressed ever since Aristotle pointed out, "Success in delivery is of the utmost importance to the effect of the speech."[3] Modern students of communication theory confirm this classical dictum. For example, James McCroskey examined a number of experimental studies and concluded, "Good delivery allows the rhetorically strong message to have its normal effect. Poor delivery tends to inhibit the effect of a verbal message."[4] Once we have composed a rhetorically strong message, we have to deliver that message in a way that will obtain the desired decision from our audience. Of course, a strong delivery is necessary, but not sufficient to debate or speech success. Delivery is the means to the ultimate end of having

---

3. Aristotle, *Rhetoric*, III, p. 1.
4. James C. McCroskey, *An Introduction to Rhetorical Communication* (Englewood Cliffs, N.J.: Prentice Hall, 1968), p. 208.

an audience listen to and act upon your case. It ensures that the message is received, but does not impact the quality of the message itself. When one orders a pizza for delivery, if the pizza arrives hot and fresh to your door, it tastes no better if it is delivered in a beautiful and new sports car, or a beat-up, rusty pick-up truck. As long as the vehicle does not break down, you are simply happy to have your meal. In a like manner, as long as the speaker's delivery is able to help the audience follow and understand the content of the message, it has done its part. However, effective delivery does enable the speaker to convey meaning, especially emotional content, not achievable through words alone.

1. Methods of Delivery. The four methods of delivery available to the speaker are impromptu, extemporaneous, manuscript, and memorization. To some extent, the speaker's approach to delivery is dictated by the unique demands of the speaking occasion and its context. Each of the methods reflects both a type of speech or occasion and a style of content and tone.

a. Impromptu Speaking. When, as happens often in any debate, a speaker is called upon to speak off-the-cuff, offering spontaneous, unscripted remarks in response to a question or argument offered by another, they are engaged in impromptu speaking. In impromptu speaking contests, participants are given a topic and expected to make a speech about that topic almost immediately. When a student is called on to speak in class, or a member of the PTA, a fraternity, or the student government speaks up in a meeting, their speaking is impromptu. Such speaking tends to be unstructured and unpolished, but genuine and natural. There is, however, a difference between the circumstance of impromptu speaking and an impromptu style. An impromptu style conveys spontaneity. When speakers are very familiar with their material and accustomed to speaking about it, even when their remarks are offered without formal preparation, they may seem to be somewhat scripted. While this is *not* detrimental, it does mark a distinction in tone and style between an impromptu and an extemporaneous approach. Impromptu style is the most interactive and personal approach to speech presentation. As it is the least pre-scripted, it offers a genuine believability, and offers the greatest opportunity to adapt a message to immediate audience reactions. Of course, it may also be somewhat difficult to understand or follow, as impromptu speakers are likely to have limited organization and more influencies or verbal clutter ("uhs" and "uhms," "likes" and "ya' knows"...) than more prepared approaches.

b. Extemporaneous Delivery. An extemporaneous speech is given from an outline or fairly substantial speaker's notes. It is more prepared than an impromptu speech, but not completely prepared. In extemporaneous speaking contests, speakers are given a topic and allowed up to 30 minutes to prepare their presentation. Thus, the extemporaneous speech is a type of prepared speech. In delivering the extemporaneous speech, the speaker neither reads from a manuscript nor memorizes their entire speech; however, neither are they completely spontaneous. They will use notes and read short quotations or other bits of prepared verbatim material. They may even memorize a few short speech passages. The extemporaneous tone is prepared and organized, but offers opportunity for spontaneity. The speaker uses a "read/don't read" approach, reading some bits of quoted or carefully written material and referencing their outline, then breaking away for portions of impromptu style.

The extemporaneous method provides almost all the advantages found in other methods of delivery and few disadvantages. Its greatest advantage lies in the fact that it is both prepared and flexible, allowing the speaker to plan exactly what she wants to say and how she wants to say it. Thus all the advantages of case building and speech composition can be brought to bear in the extemporaneous speech. In addition, because the speech is planned but not "carved in stone," it can be modified to adapt to the situation and to the statements of previous speakers. Because the speaker can watch the audience closely during the speech, she can gauge the listeners' reaction and adapt the speech to their response.

The extemporaneous method has few disadvantages. It does have a greater possibility of error than do manuscript or memorized speeches, but careful preparation can minimize this risk. When the time element is critical, as in a radio or television speech, the extemporaneous method may pose some problems for the beginning speaker. It is more difficult to control the time with this method than with the manuscript or memorized speech. Experienced speakers, however, develop an excellent sense of time, and academic debaters know their time limits and can track their time with the use of timers. The repeat guests on TV talk shows are those who, among other things, have learned to adapt to the strict time requirements while retaining the spontaneity of the extemporaneous method. Political candidates, who have to make numerous speeches every day at the height of a campaign, usually develop "The Speech"—a block of material in which they can present their views extemporaneously in as little as 5 minutes or extend them to as much as 20 minutes, as the occasion requires. After the first affirmative speech, almost all debaters, be they students or senators, use the extemporaneous method of delivery. Only extemporaneous delivery provides for the carefully prepared on-the-spot adaptation and refutation so essential to effective debate while maintaining organization and adherence to the flow sheet.

The extemporaneous method most frequently makes use of notes, where the speaker writes keywords and phrases, making maximum use of abbreviations. Ronald Reagan used index cards in the mid-1950s when he was touring the country as a spokesman for General Electric. He continued to use the same method during his presidency.[5] A similar method is used for television shows, although the cards are much larger and usually are placed off camera.

c. Manuscript Delivery.   In using the manuscript method, the speaker prepares his speech carefully, writing it out in full, and reading it to the audience. The advantage of the manuscript is that it provides the opportunity, even under pressure of the debate or speaking occasion, for the speaker to say exactly what he wants to say in exactly the way he wants to say it. When minimizing the possibility of error

---

5. Ronald Reagan, *An American Life* (New York: Simon & Schuster, 1990), p. 130.

is the prime consideration, the manuscript speech is generally used. In delivering a State of the Union message or other major state addresses, all U.S. presidents, even those who are brilliant extemporaneous speakers, use the manuscript method. A slip of the tongue in such a situation would be too dangerous; it might lead to a domestic or international crisis. The first affirmative constructive is often a manuscript speech. A manuscript style of delivery reflects a higher level of formality and precision of speech than either impromptu or extemporaneous styles. It does offer a greater opportunity to employ eloquent writing styles and figures of speech as evidenced by the speeches of John Kennedy and Martin Luther King, Jr. Such careful scripting is difficult to command spontaneously or with limited preparation. With practice, a speaker can master reading from a script or teleprompter in a relatively seamless manner, employing nonverbal emphasis, eye contact, dramatic effect, and even a natural conversational tone when appropriate.

The disadvantages of the manuscript method include the lack of flexibility and the difficulty of reading the manuscript effectively. Because the manuscript is prepared in advance, it does not provide for adjustments to the situation, to previous speeches, or to audience reaction. Furthermore, the manuscript often becomes a barrier between the speaker and the audience when the speaker's objective is to establish rapport with the audience. Audiences would rather have the speaker talk *with* them than read *at* them. Ronald Reagan, the "Great Communicator," made the same point when he wrote, "I've always believed that you can't hold an audience by reading a speech."[6] It is a temptation when writing a speech, to write for a visual reading by an audience, rather than to maintain a quality of orality in language style. Skilled speakers, when they find it necessary to use a manuscript, often plan their delivery in such a way as to create the impression that they are frequently departing from the manuscript.

Portions of the speech under the advocate's complete control—that is, when there is little or no need or opportunity for adaptation—should reflect the maximum skill in speech composition. The first affirmative speech in team topic policy debate, for example, provides the greatest opportunity for advocates to say precisely what they want to say in precisely the way they want to say it and to deliver their carefully chosen words with maximum effectiveness. The well-planned first affirmative speech should be a masterpiece of composition and delivery. The issues, the contentions, the transitions, the analysis, the evidence,[7] and the summaries—all should be polished to perfection so that they will be recorded on the judge's flow sheet and lodged in the minds of the audience precisely as the speaker wants them to be. The well-written and well-delivered first affirmative speech is a graceful, forceful, highly literate, lucid, cogent statement that should be a powerful factor in advancing the affirmative's case. Portions of subsequent speeches, including argument and position briefs, and even overviews and underviews (introductions and conclusions) may also be written out by well-prepared debaters, but it must be remembered that debate demands clash, and

---

6. Reagan, *An American Life*, p. 130.
7. Again the admonition: Evidence may be edited to eliminate extraneous material, but the advocate must scrupulously preserve the author's intent.

that it is more than reading prepared scripts. After the first speech, effective debaters must adapt their prepared materials with spontaneous applications and explanations specific to the discussion as it is occurring in the unique context of the specific debate.

When preparing the physical manuscript, the speaker should consider ease of use during the speech presentation. The reading copy of the manuscript should be a carefully prepared document of professional quality. The rough draft will be covered with corrections, and reading from a manuscript in that condition is too difficult. (Of course, if you prepare your manuscript on a computer, the task becomes much simpler.) A professional quality manuscript is easier to read, and its appearance adds to the speaker's credibility. It can help the speaker achieve more effective delivery and increase the impact on the arguments. The manuscript should be typed on 8½ × 11-inch paper with 1½ inch margins on both sides. Double spacing makes it easier to read and allows space for last-minute changes. Underlining, capitalization, highlighting, phonetic spelling of difficult words, and dashes or slash marks to indicate pauses make it easier to deliver the speech effectively. The speaker should leave extra space at the bottom of a page rather than break a key sentence between two pages. It is best to begin a new argument or thought at the top of a new page rather than near the bottom of a page, as page flipping provides a natural pause and should coincide with intended pauses in delivery.

d. Memorized Delivery.   Speakers rarely memorize entire speeches, except as naturally occurs from repetition of presenting manuscript or extemporaneous speeches or speech segments. However, this method is still expected in many speaking contests. Outside the contest situation, however, most advocates do not feel they have time to memorize a speech—except, of course, when "The Speech" is used as in political campaigns. The memorized speech is, in fact, a manuscript that has been committed to memory. It provides all the advantages of the manuscript method, as well as the additional advantage that the manuscript is not present. Memorization also provides the maximum opportunity for polished presentation. With this advantage, however, comes a potential disadvantage.

Inexperienced speakers who memorize their speeches often appear stilted, artificial, and lacking in spontaneity. The speech may tend to seem robotic, and does not engage interaction with and reaction to the audience. Further disadvantages of the memorized speech include the time necessary for memorization, the lack of flexibility, and the possibility that the speaker may forget a portion of his or her speech. Many speakers, however, do find it beneficial to memorize speech segments.

Methods of Delivery

- Impromptu
- Extemporaneous
- Manuscript
- Memorized

2. Qualities of Effective Delivery.   Remember that speech delivery is necessary but not sufficient to effective speaking. Delivery serves the purpose of focusing and guiding audience understanding and attention to the content of the arguments, evidence, issues, and positions presented by the speaker. While in some ways, as in conveying personal emotions, nonverbal expression may *be* the message, the focus of a debate is almost entirely the content of cases and clash; therefore, effective delivery exists to complement, frame, and emphasize the material presented.

The importance of nonverbal communication is stressed by modern students of communication theory. Kenneth Hance and his colleagues maintain that "the ideas and feelings that we want to express to our audience are determined as much by nonverbal behavior and vocal signals as they are by the words we use."[8] And Randall Harrison has estimated that "in face-to-face communication no more than 35 percent of the social meaning is carried in the verbal messages."[9] Much of the remaining 65 percent of social meaning comes from the delivery of nonverbal messages.

It is important in delivering a speech to recall that written and spoken communication have different characteristics. When reading from the page, an audience can reread, underline, highlight, make margin notes, and reread again! They are on their own time, guided by punctuation, center and side headings, numbers, font manipulation (bold, italics, underline, size changes), paragraph indentation, and so on. When hearing a speech, it occurs in the speaker's time and needs to make sense, and be recordable as presented. The speaker provides punctuation, separation of ideas, and emphasis almost entirely through changes in their voice and expression. Effective delivery, therefore, is essential in enabling the listener to follow and understand the material of the speech, preventing the presentation from being received as nothing more than a barrage of words and noise. Delivery allows the listener to understand the organization and ideas presented. In addition, effective delivery builds credibility for the speaker and their arguments through dynamic and sincere presentation and can help to engage the audience in the material and develop a positive relationship between speaker and audience. Finally, effective delivery makes the speech more interesting, keeping the listener awake and attentive. It is also important to recognize that delivery is personal, no two people will have the same presentation, and that effective delivery is culturally specific. The advice offered in this text is based on standards for effective delivery in the dominant culture within North America. However, the wise speaker should learn the specific idiosyncrasies of their audience and the meaning they attach to delivery characteristics.

---

8. Kenneth G. Hance, David C. Ralph, and Milton J. Wiksell, *Principles of Speaking*, 3rd ed. (Belmont, Calif.: Wadsworth, 1975), p. 250.
9. Randall Harrison, "Nonverbal Communication: Explorations into Time, Space, Action and Object," in *Dimensions in Communication*, 2nd ed., eds. James H. Campbell and Hal W. Hepler (Belmont, Calif.: Wadsworth, 1970), p. 285.

a. Physical Attributes of Speech Delivery.   The speaker's body provides part of the vehicle by which they deliver their message. Physical characteristics of delivery include eye contact, physical movement, gestures, and facial expressions. Some may reference such nonverbal communication as "body language." While we are familiar with this colloquial term, and certainly recognize its importance, physical attributes are *not* language. Language consists of shared symbols (like words) which have a fairly precise shared and understood meaning among a group of users. Nonverbal communication is *more* important than verbal in most contexts; however, it rarely has a defined, agreed upon, and explicit meaning among a language community. Therefore, it is not language.

Debaters relying on prepared manuscripts, briefs, and other materials, and speaking to judges who are often writing or typing to maintain their flow sheet too often forget to make eye contact with their audience. This is a mistake. We communicate a tremendous amount through our eyes and through facial expressions from the area surrounding our eyes. Eye contact conveys emphasis, emotion, sincerity, and confidence and builds a relationship between speaker and receiver. It allows the speaker to gauge the reactions of the audience, and adapt the message accordingly. Effective eye contact is extended gaze, maintained long enough for both parties to be aware of it, but not so long as to leave out other audience members or make the primary parties to the eye contact uncomfortable. Effective eye contact is *not* scanning the audience, looking at a spot on the back wall, the ceiling, or the floor. Of all the characteristics of delivery, eye contact is the most culturally specific. Many cultures have rules limiting eye contact or assigning different meaning to it; however, within the dominant North American cultures, direct eye contact is considered a positive characteristic of effective public speaking.

Debaters and most public speakers should limit their physical movement so as to allow the audience to maintain focus on their face and eyes. Effective speakers maintain a stance with feet comfortably apart allowing their weight to be evenly balanced on both feet, and a comfortable upright posture maximizing height. This, along with keeping the shoulders square to the audience, keeps the speaker's head relatively still (not bobbing, looking down, or swaying side to side), allowing audience focus on the speaker's eyes and the area immediately around their eyes. This also maintains a command of attention and authority over the audience and allows the speaker's voice to project and resonate. Remember that the speaker's mouth is like a stereo speaker and should point toward listeners without obstruction. Good posture enables the speaker to breath from their diaphragm (belly breathing), enabling powerful and resonate voice projection. Deep breathing also helps reduce the physiological consequences of nervousness. This is not to say that the speaker should stay still as a statue; however, movement should be purposeful—it should aid in communicating with the audience. The way the speaker approaches the lectern, for example, is important. If he approaches the lectern with a confident step and takes possession of the rostrum with quiet authority, ethos is enhanced. Movements should be easy, economical, and purposeful, yet apparently spontaneous. The speaker should not remain in a fixed position behind the lectern or rooted to one spot on the rostrum as if inanimate. He might move away from the lectern and closer to the audience to emphasize a major issue; he might move from one side of the rostrum to the other to make a transition from one issue to another. But movement should never compete with the case for the attention of the audience. A story, which just might be true, is told of a young prosecuting attorney who lost his first case in a burglary trial, although he had ample evidence that the accused was guilty. The novice lawyer was so nervous that, in presenting his evidence, he continually paced to and fro before the judge. This pacing so attracted the attention of the jury that they concentrated on estimating how many steps he took in each direction and how many miles he walked in the course of the trial, rather than following the case he was attempting to present.

Gestures, movements of the hands and arms, are most effective when complementing or framing statements. They should be natural and small, generally between the waist and shoulder. Avoid repetitive or awkward gestures. We communicate emotions most effectively through our facial expressions. Appropriate matching of the desired emotion with the speaker's expression can increase ethos and pathos for the speaker's message. Facial expressions should be consistent with the attitude being expressed. While smiles can help create a more engaged audience and help relax the speaker and all participants, when telling the narrative of the gruesome amputations of child soldiers, or rape and murder of refugee communities, a more appropriate serious and horrified expression would be better than a smile. Experienced communicators such as Brian Williams or Katie Couric can convey a world of meaning by a tilt of an eyebrow, a toss of the head, a curl of the lip, or a slight change of expression. And, of course, others are constantly trying to "read" our facial expressions. After a news conference, for example, reporters often tell us that the president or the secretary of state looked "pleased" or "tense," "confident" or "worried."

b. Vocal Attributes of Speaker's Delivery. The voice is a powerful instrument used as subtly and powerfully by the effective speaker as a musician uses her instrument. While it is possible to separate out a list of vocal characteristics including rate, pitch, volume, and tone, the key for the speaker is to offer variety. Listeners often complain of a speaker's "monotone"; however, they are not really referring only to tone, but to all the vocal qualities. Pitch is how high or low your voice sounds, as manipulated by frequency of vocal cord vibrations. Higher pitch generally connotes a greater degree of excitement and is associated with persuasiveness, but should be reserved for limited statements or portions of a speech. The high impact, high pitch portions of a speech lose their impact if the entire message is of high pitch. It is also hard to listen to. Inflection refers to the variation of pitch when speaking.

Rate includes not just the speed of speaking, but the use of pauses to generate emphasis and variation. Conversational speech averages between 120 and 150 words per minute. Many people slow down when they begin to speak for an audience. Famous speakers have ranged from 90 to 190 words per minute, publishers advise readers for audio books to read at approximately 180. We can comprehend as quickly as 500 words per minute, and experienced academic debaters debating for expert debate judges often work to speak as fast as they can. The gap between our ability to listen and the slower pace of most speakers can cause the attention of audience members to drift; however, consistently fast delivery requires more effort than many audiences may exert. For most audiences, it is not advisable to follow the lead of experienced tournament debaters, although faster speech (within the acceptable range of 150–200 wpm) tends to be perceived as more persuasive. It is always important, however, in any context, to insert pauses and to vary rate for interest and emphasis! Silent pauses allow audiences to absorb what they have just heard and to prepare for what is to come, as well as to create drama or comedic timing. Within the dominant North American culture, it is better to be too loud than not loud enough. The speaker is well advised to make sure that audience members in the back row can hear, and to watch nonverbal feedback to ensure appropriate volume levels. It is more persuasive to be louder, but as with all vocal qualities, it is important to vary the volume. "Punch" keywords, taglines, and impact statements by pausing before them and increasing volume while saying them. Tone is a term that combines vocal qualities to express a level of commitment or to generate a feeling about the material. Vocal variation to express anger, excitement, enthusiasm, sincerity, and other qualities are expressions of tone. When asked "how can I sound more sincere about my case?" one debater was told, "well, the best way to sound sincere is to be sincere, so find a case, or at least some support materials, you can believe in!" It is also important for the speaker to be understood. Correct pronunciation is the generation by the speaker of the generally accepted way a word or name is expected to sound.

Mispronunciation results in misunderstanding and reduced credibility of the speaker. Articulation is the ability or effort of the speaker in making each syllable and word audible and clear, enunciation is the clarity or distinctiveness of sequences of words and sentences. Effective speakers practice to over-exaggerate each sound, avoiding the common practices of running words together, dropping vowels or consonants, or mumbling.

3. Speaking in Academic Debate. The experienced intercollegiate debate judge is a specialized audience. Each individual has different biases, and it is worthwhile to consider the judge's philosophy statement and ask him or her about delivery preferences. But also remember as well that these judges are used to distinct styles of delivery. Intercollegiate tournament debate delivery requires some special considerations, especially the team-topic evidence-based debate style:

1. *Vary the rate.* When you are relying on reading prepared material, rewarded for having more material than your opponents, and timed, it is natural that you will begin to read and speak more quickly. Intercollegiate debaters may speak at a very rapid pace, in excess of 300 words per minute. Judges are accustomed to listening to and "flow sheeting" very fast delivery if it is clear. Developing the ability to speak, or read, at such a fast pace is not easy. It is critical to maintain clarity and to enunciate at any speed. It is also important to remember to pause, use effective emphasis, and vary nonverbal vocal qualities. Introductions, conclusions, and transitions offer good opportunities to slow the pace for effect. Even simple and brief pauses assist the listener.

2. *Make eye contact.* If the judge is keeping a flow sheet scrupulously, the debater may see little more than the top of his or her head. Although continuous eye contact is impossible for the debater reading briefs and referring to the flow sheet, it is important to make eye contact when possible. The best opportunities for this are in the opening and closing to a speech. Effective eye contact commands attention and demonstrates confidence. In addition, it is important for the debater speaking (and the debater sitting at a desk) to watch the judge closely for any reaction to arguments made.

3. *Show energy, sincerity, and enthusiasm.* Debaters are salespersons selling their advocacy. Effective debaters display passion for their advocacy and present themselves with confidence and competence. One of the most exciting aspects of debate is its high energy level. It is better to be a little too loud than too quiet, and nonverbal behaviors demonstrating sincerity and commitment to the advocate's positions will enhance the presentation. Many debaters make the mistake of sitting to speak, bending over their notes, or hiding behind mountains of boxes. Tournament debaters should use proper posture to influence the judge's perception of their confidence and authority. Straight posture also facilitates deeper breathing, allowing debaters to enhance the projection and resonance of their voice and even their rate.

4. *Behave with courtesy and professionalism.* Perceptions begin to form before the debate begins, when the judge first sees the debaters. Their behavior during their opponents' speeches, their partners' speeches, and the cross-examination, as well as after the debate, can have powerful subliminal effects on the judge's evaluation.

5. *Avoid distracting mannerisms.* Repetitive gestures, tapping of feet or pens, gasping for breath—all diminish the potential impact of the debater's presentation. Speech delivery and composition involve many considerations. As in many other contexts, the great art is to conceal the art. As advocates our purpose is to win a decision. We use the arts of speech communication to help attain this objective. Avoid verbal clutter. The word "like" may be the greatest enemy to the credibility of today's college student. Influences are expected, but work to reduce "uhms" and "uhs."

6. *Be confident and controlled during cross-examination periods.* Do not busy yourself with preparation for the next speech or arrangement of materials at your

---

Speaking in Academic Debate

- Vary the rate
- Make eye contact
- Show energy, sincerity, and enthusiasm
- Behave with courtesy and professionalism
- Avoid distracting mannerisms
- Be confident and controlled during cross-examination periods

desk. Look the judge in the eye as much as possible and demonstrate confidence and mastery of the situation and the material. Shake hands at the end of the debate.

B. Support

Speeches are built on the quality of their support material. Support comes in a number of forms including narratives, various types of quotations, analogies and metaphor, statistics, factual observations, definitions, explanations, descriptions, even alternative forms like visual communication and music. But why do we need support? What functions does it serve to the advocate? Anyone focused on debate as a form of speech knows that support serves to make one's claims believable. This credibility or proof function is the first reason to present support. In addition, the wise speaker remembers that proof has no meaning if the listener does not understand the situation or the claim. So a second reason to use support is to make one's ideas clear. Finally, and most often forgotten, support can make the speech more interesting, engaging, entertaining, or meaningful. Some forms of support are better at achieving one of these functions than others, some are better at achieving other functions and it is rare that any item of support will accomplish all three. For example, the dramatic narrative of the death of Trayvon Martin may well involve the audience in a speech advocating the reform of "stand-your-ground-laws," but the unique and uncertain circumstances of the Martin case put into question the validity of the example as *proof*, and the confusing nature of the facts in the case limit its value in making the case regarding stand-your-ground laws any more *clear*. So the narrative should be used to accomplish the interest function of support, but the speaker may wish to supplement it with expert testimony from legal sources clearly explaining the implications of the law, and statistics about the hundreds of prior cases involving SYG in order to evidence the generalizability of certain criteria of the case. So the rules for providing support are to provide a variety of types of support, and to layer the support so as to achieve all three necessary functions of support. Layering implies that for a single claim, the advocate provide multiple forms of proof. In an academic debate, most of the proof comes in quoted format, but within the quotes are a variety of types of support. It is up to the speaker to ensure that all three functions of support are accomplished. In speaking, depth often means variety of support for a few points, rather than quantity of points.

Grounds, in Toulmin's basic model of argument, are what you have to go on, or the starting point of argumentation. Of course, grounds represent support. We have also said that evidence is the raw material of debate.

C. Organization

The type and context of the speech will determine the nature of organization required, but it is always valuable to ensure that speech organization is logical and clear. The test of logic means that the progression of arguments makes sense to the listener and is chosen for a reason. *Logical* organization follows an established pattern appropriate to the nature of material, audience, and objectives. Some examples of patterns are cause to effect, problem to solution, most important to least important, and least important to most important. For debaters constructing speeches on a policy topic, the problem to solution format generally makes sense and can be made more specific using the stock issues of inherency, harm, solution, respectively. Inherency to harm is a sort of cause to effect pattern. The stock issues of definition to designation provide a reasonable pattern for fact and value cases.

Speech organization should also be *clear*. This means that the speech employs an outline that is shared with the audience. Recalling that spoken communication does not offer the audience the same tools as written communication, such as lists, numbers, and punctuation, effective speakers use previews, signposts, and reviews to aid the audience in following, recording, and remembering their organization. Tell them where you are going, tell them where you are, and tell them where you have been. Previews are statements telling the audience what is to come, such as "In my speech, I will tell you about the causes of the immigration crisis, I will identify some of its impacts on our society, and I will offer a possible solution for your consideration." The signpost is a statement which tells the audience, for example, "First, let's consider the failure of U.S. Immigration policy to create a system where visas are considered in a timely and fair manner." The review should not retell the speech, but simply and succinctly restate the ideas addressed, "In this presentation, I have told you about some of the factors contributing to an immigration crisis, I have discussed the harmful consequences of this failure, and I have offered a partial solution to the problem." Internal summary reviews and effective segue transition statements can also help make statements clear. In debate, speakers must prioritize word economy, and knowing that judges will be carefully recording the debate on their flow sheets, they may reduce some of the repetition required when taking the three-step approach to clear organization. However, they should not forget the "roadmap" which is, in fact, a preview of the speech to come offered before the beginning of each speech. Speakers should also be careful to clearly signpost and reference their arguments and place them within the organizational structure of the debate.

D. Involvement

Effective communication is the achievement of shared understanding, accomplished through the building of identification between speaker and listener. The communication process is interactive and cooperative, demanding the positive participation of the listener. The degree to which the speaker can engage the listener, relating the importance of values and concepts to their personal experience and person, largely determines the effectiveness of the message. The speaker can build involvement and thus increase the listener's investment in the subject through a number of means. First, the speaker will need to rely on audience knowledge and adaptation to relate to the self system and feedback of the listener. Based on what the speaker knows and can surmise about the listener, they can offer relevant stories and comparisons, select appropriate and fitting language, select arguments, policies, and positions which relate to the biases, preferences, or experiences of the listener. For example, if the audience is made up of football fans, the speaker may wish to compare passing their proposal to winning the Super Bowl. Second, the speaker should use dynamic and energetic delivery and work to establish nonverbal immediacy through eye contact, facial expression, inviting tone, and reducing the distance between himself and the listener. Third, the speaker should use appropriate vocabulary for their audience. Jargon may be appropriate, and even increase credibility of the user, but often may need to be defined and exemplified. Fourth, the speaker should find ways to engage participation of the listener. This may occur through rhetorical questions or personal references and applications to the listener. When allowed by the context, gimmicks and games can offer real opportunities for real participation.

E. Language

Words have power! The Delivery section of this chapter discussed nonverbal communication, and the importance of the vehicle (body and voice) which delivers the message. But the message itself is your use of *verbal* communication, the use of language to influence, inform, teach, and inspire. Words can generate enthusiasm or apathy, inclusion or hatred, understanding and, unfortunately, misunderstanding. Effective language choice defines the memorable and impactful speaker. Recall that words are symbols, representations constructed to convey the thoughts, feelings, and ideas of the initiator of communication. As such, they are *arbitrary* sets of sounds devised to stand for something from which they are quite separate. Onomatopoeia, wherein words sound like the thing they are meant to represent, may offer something of an exception. However, even hearing words like "splash," "bang," or "pop" offers an experience separate and different from the real experience of hearing the bursting of a balloon or a rock tossed into a pond. Words are *abstract*, removed from the thing they are meant to represent. The concreteness or specificity of language can reduce or enlarge the level of abstraction; for example, saying that Sean is a person is more abstract than saying that Sean is a female, a girl, a 6-year-old girl, a happy 6-year-old girl who loves soccer, a goalie, and so forth. Finally, words are *ambiguous*, offering a range of meaning. What time is 6:00? Is 5:59:31 considered 6:00? What about 6:00:59? This may depend on whether you rely on the digital clock on your cell phone, or on the hands of your analog wrist watch. Words have meanings that are both denotative and connotative. Denotative meanings are the best understood within a language community. They are literal, relatively objective, limited by personal perception, and shared by the people who use them. The definition found in a dictionary is the denotative definition. A denotative definition for the word "dog" is offered by *Merriam-Webster Dictionary Online*[10] as "a highly variable domestic mammal (*Canis familiaris*) closely related to the gray wolf."

---

10. Merriam-Webster, *Merriam-Webster Dictionary* (January 1, 2012). Retrieved from http://www.merriam-webster.com/.

Public Speaking Guidelines for Effective Use of Language

- Oral language style
- Simple and clear
- Appropriate for audience
- Eliminate clutter
- Memorable and meaningful
- Inclusive

The personal meaning invoked in an individual user of the word, however, may be quite different. For some, "dog" represents a warm and fuzzy thought of their loyal companion; for others, the same word evokes a reaction of fear and a memory of a vicious animal attack. The personal, often emotional, interpretation of language is its *connotative* meaning. Effective speakers are well aware of the dynamic and deep power of language to convey precise meanings as well as personal reactions. To do so, we advise the effective speaker to follow some simple, sometimes contradictory, and often difficult guidelines.

1. Use Oral Language Style. The difference between written and oral language style may be as stark as the difference between English and Spanish. Effective spoken word is crisp and dynamic, simple yet vibrant, understandable and memorable in real time. Speech writing is an especially challenging process. Our default when writing is often to be too intricate and complex, often passive and subtle, and too wordy for oral presentation (probably for written communication as well). These tendencies to overwrite are magnified by writing with a computer. Work to "speak the speech" *not* "write the speech"! Stunk and White in *The Elements of Style* advise the writer not to overwrite. They warn, "Rich, ornate prose is hard to digest, generally unwholesome, and sometimes nauseating. If the sickly sweet word, the overblown phrase are your natural form of expression, as is sometimes the case, you will have to compensate for it by a show of vigor, and by writing something as meritorious as the Song of Sons, which is Solomon's."[11] Oral language style uses informal, animated language, simple sentence structure, personally tailored messages using active voice and first person, and repetition. This is not to say that the speaker should revert to slang or colloquial language use. The public speaking context should be natural and offer a tone of conversation and personal interaction, but be more formal and professional than actual conversation.

2. Be Simple and Clear. Work for vivid descriptions and clear and easily understood explanations, keeping in mind that "less is more." Too many adjectives or

---

11. Strunk, W., and White, E., *The Elements of Style*, 4th ed. (New York: Longman, 2000), p. 72.

excessive redundancy can obscure the intended meanings and increase the challenge of listening. However, when it is important for the listener to have a precise understanding, the speaker should provide enough description to create that understanding. For example, to suggest that the South Florida day was "hot" may not achieve the desired understanding; there are many types of "hot" in Miami. A hot January day may be 78 degrees, sunny, dry, and breezy, whereas a hot August day might be 90 degrees, humid, still, and oppressive with afternoon thunderstorms looming. Reducing the level of abstraction helps to make meanings more clear. Creating word pictures enabling the listener to experience the objects, people, places, or events described can be achieved if language is sufficiently concrete and vivid. Effective descriptions and explanations begin with careful observation. If the speaker does not perceive the richness and detail of a thing, they cannot convey it to others. The speaker must observe and share appropriate detail, but not unnecessary detail.

3. Use Appropriate Language.   The speaker must first know their audience and the language capabilities and familiarities of the audience. Don't take for granted that the audience is familiar with technical language and jargon. Jargon is the special language that develops within a professional, occupational, vocational, cultural, or other in-group that is understood within the group but not familiar to those outside the group. Within a group, jargon becomes efficient and effective shorthand, as much of the vocabulary offered in this textbook. For those unfamiliar with the jargon, it is a barrier to understanding. Speakers may enhance their own credibility by using limited jargon; if each time a potentially unfamiliar concept or term is offered, they define and exemplify the term. Familiar and personable language, which is direct and informal, helps to build audience identification and involvement, benefiting the speaker. Plain talk is preferable to a lay audience.

4. Eliminate Clutter.   Stephen Lucas has called cluttered speech "a national epidemic."[12] Strunk and White wisely advise the writer to omit needless words, "Vigorous writing is concise. A sentence should contain no unnecessary words, a paragraph, no unnecessary sentences, for the same reason that a drawing should have no unnecessary lines and a machine no unnecessary parts. This requires not that the writer make all sentences short of avoid all detail and treat subjects only in outline, but that every word tell" (p. 23). The speaker should carefully edit and review so as to avoid redundant explanations and adjectives, and strike phrases, which do not add meaning. Most importantly, avoid filler words, ("like," "really," "very," "ya' know," "knowhatI'm sayin," "knowhatI-mean," "whatever..."). These meaningless utterances will diminish the speaker's credibility and increase the difficulty of understanding the message.

5. Use Memorable and Meaningful Language.   You probably recognize these words:

"Four score and seven years ago ..."

---

12. Lucas, *The Art of Public Speaking*, p. 229.

"Ask not what your country can do for you, ask what you can do for your
country ..."

"I have a dream ..."

These famous words spoken by some of our great leaders are part of our lexicon.
They were powerful and memorable. They were crafted with style such that
they made an important point to the immediate listeners of the respective
speeches, but they also lasted with importance in our collective memory. Peggy
Noonan, speechwriter for President Reagan, observed that "style enhances substance; it gives substance voice, it makes a message memorable, it makes policy
clear and understandable."[13] Style may be accomplished in part through the use
of speech devices.

a. Metaphor.   When Winston Churchill compared the reach of the Soviet Union
to an "iron curtain" over Eastern Europe, Martin Luther King Jr. compared our
founding documents (the Declaration of Independence and the Constitution) to
a bad check marked insufficient funds, and cold war politicians referred to the
"cancer of communism," they were each employing the powerful use of metaphor. These implicit comparisons of unlike things sometimes reach archetypal
and subliminal influence (the "shining city on a hill," "the dark abyss of ignorance," "unending tides of the oceans") based on their comparison to shared
human experience; other times they are more specific, as was Dr. King's comparison of the promise of rights to a bounced check. In each case, they help the listener understand a new concept through their complete and innate understanding
of an old one. Use of metaphor is psychologically powerful and often memorable.

b. Parallelism.   Repetition or similar structure of one or more sentences can be an
effective way to help an audience attend to and recall a theme or common root
idea to a series of implications. In her speech to the 2008 Democratic National
Convention, Senator Hillary Clinton repeated the phrase "I will always ...":

> I will always remember the single mom who had adopted two kids with
> autism. She didn't have any health insurance; and she discovered that
> she had cancer. But she greeted me with her bald head, painted with my
> name on it, and asked me to fight for health care for her and her
> children.

> I will always remember the young man in a Marine Corps t-shirt who
> waited months for medical care, and he said to me, "Take care of my
> buddies. A lot of them are still over there." And then, "Will you please
> take care of me."

> And I will always remember the young boy who told me his mom worked
> for the minimum wage, that her employer had cut her hours. He said
> he just didn't know what his family was going to do.

---

13. Noonan, P., *On Speaking Well* (New York: Collins, 1991), p. 78.

I will always be grateful for everyone from all 50 states, Puerto Rico and the Territories, who joined our campaign on behalf of all those people left out and left behind by the Bush Administration. [14]

c. Antithesis. When astronaut Neil Armstrong stepped on the moon in 1969, he uttered the now famous words, "One small step for (a) man, one giant leap for mankind." This represents antithesis, the juxtaposition of contrasting ideas using parallel structure. Such language choice can offer meaningful and memorable rhetoric. Of course, President Kennedy's famous use of antithesis in his inaugural speech ("ask not what your country can do for you...") is an example of antithesis, as is Kennedy's quote, "Let us never negotiate out of fear, but let us never fear to negotiate." While such figures of speech are not easy to construct, they are beneficial to the speaker.

d. Additional Figures of Speech. These may include alliteration (the repetition of initial consonant sounds, such as "the deed was downright dastardly!"), rhyme, rhythm, and omission. How can a speaker or speech writer enhance their use of literary device to create more effective speeches? One should read great literature and listen to (read) great speeches, with attention focused on what made them memorable and meaningful. Poetry may be quoted or approximated by the effective speaker, with an aim of generating more pleasing language use.

6. Be Inclusive. The old adage, "sticks and stones can break my bones, but words will never hurt me," may be reassuring to a child defending himself after being called hurtful names. However, it simply is not true. Words not only have the power to convey meaning, to lift spirits, to empower and to inspire, they also have the power to hurt and to dismiss people as unimportant or worse. When we acknowledge a person as valuable and worthy of our attention, we are participating in communication of *Confirmation.* When we say hello, compliment a person, use their name or title, and go to the trouble to consider the cultural implications of our statements to them we have confirmed their existence and importance. *Disconfirmation* is the pattern of communication in which we ignore or dismiss the other, emphasizing difference and explicitly or implicitly (often without recognition) expressing power over the other (person). Confirmation is not only an ethically preferable practice, it also contributes to a greater level of success in speaking, debating, and interacting. To be a willing listener, open to others as equals within a communication setting, is to empower their voice and bring them into the conversation. For advocates, speakers, debaters, and communicators seeing to generate shared understanding and to investigate and solve problems, it is beneficial to invite all voices. The power of words to repress is as compelling as the power of words to liberate. It is essential that speakers and debaters use—to the best of their ability—language that is inclusive,

---

14. Clinton, H., *Democratic National Convention Keynote Address*, delivered August 26, 2008, INVESCO field at Mile High stadium, Denver, Colorado. Retrieved from http://www.americanrhetoric.com/speeches/convention2008/hillaryclinton2008dnc.htm.

nonoffensive, and culturally appropriate. Insensitive reference to people based on their victimization, difference, or foreign cultural ethnicity or group identification may cause you to think of them as "others" and therefore less important or less understandable than you or groups you belong to.

Language and labels which serve to identify negative characteristics of stereotypes, and which intentionally or inadvertently demean or diminish people based on culture or characteristic, placing them in hierarchically inferior positions, are disconfirming, therefore ethically wrong and pragmatically poor communication. A prevalent example is use of gendered language, as in the generic "he" or "mankind," referring to all people, but explicitly only recognizing males. Such generic reference relying on male referents should be avoided. Cultural or other group references meant to identify and highlight biases against groups should be avoided. Referring to someone as "gay" or "retarded" may be perceived and received so as to repress and demean people who self-identify as GLBTQ (gay, lesbian, bisexual, transgender, questioning/queer) or disabled, especially if these labels are used to negatively describe behaviors of people who are not gay or disabled, but whose behavior is being negatively judged. The challenge for the speaker is to recognize what may be received as unwelcome labels or descriptors and avoid unwanted, disrespectful, or damaging use, choosing communication behaviors which are confirming rather than disconfirming.

F. Sensory Aids

The appropriateness of sensory aids, most commonly computer-produced visual aids, depends on the context for speaking. In most educational and business environments, however, use of computer-generated visual aids has become the norm in contemporary practice. When used effectively, sensory aids help make a presentation more interesting and entertaining, help the audience understand, follow, and remember it, and make it easier for the speaker to present their ideas. When used ineffectively, sensory aids can become a distraction to the presentation, a barrier to effective engagement, and a logistical problem for the speaker. The sense of taste may be employed by a speech on cooking by a famous chef, and auditory aids (audio recordings, use of music and musical instruments) and even tactile or olfactory aids are occasionally utilized by innovative speakers. However, the focus of this section will be on the most common form of sensory aids, which are visual aids.

Visual aids may be objects, models, posters, flip charts, chalk boards, or marker boards, but the most common type of visual aids are computer projected, using PowerPoint, Prezi, or other presentation software. Visual aids primarily serve other functions of speechmaking already discussed. Text-based aids may serve as signposts, or organizational aids, helping an audience follow the outline structure or a list of concepts or terms to be discussed by the speaker. Other uses of text aids are to provide brief definitions or explanations and to display quotes. Graphic aids may include the visual representation of statistics (in charts, graphs, or tables), maps, diagrams, flow charts, organizational charts, or photographs.

Some visual aids embed brief video segments. The key to effective presentation of visual aids is to allow them to assist the listener in following, understanding, and enjoying the speech, but keep them from becoming the speech. Public speaking is a valuable method of addressing an audience because it generates a relationship between the speaker and the audience, and it is interactive. When the visual aid presentation becomes the speech, the speaker becomes unnecessary. Most speakers using PowerPoint or other presentation technology use too much visual aid and not enough speaking. These are some useful guidelines for use of visual aids:

1. *Limit the number of slides.* A good formula to determine the maximum number of slides to use is to determine the length of the speech in minutes, divide in half, and add one. So a 10-minute speech should have no more than six slides.

2. *Limit the amount of text on any single slide.* Use no more than six lines of text. Use keywords or phrases, not sentences, and limit any single line to no more than 40 characters. Use large font size (no smaller than 30 point fonts), use upper and lower case letters, and a simple font style.

3. *Not too busy.* One picture is better than four on a single slide; use simple charts and graphs, omitting data points and gridlines; use simple maps that outline an area but do not provide secondary roads and unneeded detail.

4. *Visible only when you are talking about it.* Organize the slide show such that slides, bullet points, list items, and so forth appear on mouse click at that point in your speech at which you want attention focused on the slide.

5. *Contrast and design.* The slide will look better on your monitor than projected on the screen. Text and background must have substantial contrast so that audience members can read the text. Include art on each slide, or design such that they are aesthetically pleasing and interesting.

6. *Don't face the screen! Keep your eyes on the audience.* If you do not have a monitor in front of you, this may mean you need to print the slides so you can hold them in front of you and read them while the audience views them on the screen.

7. *For a reason.* Include the slide only if it serves an important function in the presentation. If you don't need it, omit it.

8. *Don't stand in front of the projected image.*

An effective speech combines the elements of effective speaking (delivery, support, involvement, organization, language, and when relevant, sensory aids). Debaters, like all speakers, face a specialized environment where they must consider and analyze the unique demands of the speaking occasion and adapt appropriately; however, they should always recall that their challenge is to use verbal and nonverbal communication to persuade an audience, usually the debate judge, to their side, and that all the characteristics of effective speaking apply to the debater just as they do to the political candidate on the stump or the student government president at a convocation.

Guidelines for Visual Aids

- Limit the number of slides
- Limit the amount of text on any single slide
- Not too busy
- Visible only when you are talking about it
- Contrast and design
- Don't face the screen
- For a reason
- Don't stand in front of the projected image

EXERCISES

1. Breathing from the diaphragm. Good breathing for all public speaking requires the speaker to stand up straight and breathe from the diaphragm: belly breathing. When speakers are nervous or in a hurry, they usually take quick breaths off the top of their lungs. To work to fix this, hold a chair chest high in front of you, arms straight out (no resting the chair on anything, against one's chest, etc.). Put a brief on the seat of the chair and read it: Breathe from your diaphragm as you read out loud. Now put down the chair and reread the brief. Continue alternating until you start to notice the physical difference in your breathing process.

2. Hold a pen or pencil in your teeth and read a brief out loud.

3. Read a brief aloud, adding the "a" sound between each word.

4. Read a long section of quoted material aloud, backwards.

5. As fast as you can, but with emphasis, read any book by Dr. Seuss. Suggestions for this exercise are *Oh Say Can You Say, The Butter Battle Book, Oh The Thinks You Can Think, There's A Wocket in My Pocket*, and *Fox in Socks*, but any book by Dr. Seuss is excellent.

6. Read a debate brief, but with exaggerated emotion and feeling.

17

Formats in Academic Debate

The variety of styles and approaches to academic debate provide a wonderful range of diverse experience. New debate event structures emerge and old events change in their rules and expectations as creative students and educators find new ways to employ competitive debate practice. While retaining the essential values of debating from ancient times, today's debate constructs offer many examples of the rapid pace of adaptation to contemporary interests. This chapter reviews a number of popular formats for debate as practiced in intercollegiate competition. The format is the agreed-upon framework for the debate, identifying the order and length of speeches along with a limited number of procedural rules. Some debate tournaments, organizations, or sponsors offer content-based rules, but all establish formats for debate.

Competitive academic debate in tournament settings is practiced in a variety of formats, sponsored by numerous organizations, and enjoyed by many students representing diverse interests, organizations, and institutions. If you are reading this text as support for a course on debating, you may be participating in classroom debates that model one or more of these formats, or your experience may be quite different. While every format shares the application of argumentation to the comparison of competing claims and support, and most formats call for a decision to be made about a proposition, each offers its own special nuance and strategy, philosophical priority, and educational objective.

Formats substantially impact the nature of debate and the experience of participation. Working with a partner as a two-person debate team offers a substantially different experience than does one-on-one debate, or working with teams

---

Miniglossary

Format   The agreed-upon framework for the debate, identifying the order and length of speeches along with a limited number of procedural rules.

Point of order   In academic parliamentary debate, a debater asks the speaker (judge) to consider a violation of the rules of debating by their opponent.

Point of information   In academic parliamentary debate, a debater asks direct questions of their opponent, if recognized, during the opponent's speech.

Point of personal privilege   In academic parliamentary debate, a debater may ask the speaker (judge) to consider comments or behavior of their opponents as inappropriate, insulting, or otherwise offensive.

---

of five debaters. Cross-examination engages direct interaction and some formats offer participants the responsibility to "support" their opponent's arguments.

I. FORMATS OF DEBATE

The various formats of academic debate tend to have certain common elements: (a) Both sides must have an equal number of speakers; (b) both sides must have an equal or similar length of time to speak; and (c) the affirmative generally speaks first and last (although even these rules are not universal, as you shall see). The first National Developmental Conference on Forensics recommended that "more frequent use of alternative events and formats in forensics should be encouraged, and indeed, students now may choose from many approaches to debate." One thing that all formats have in common is a limit on time. Most debate formats prescribe a precise length for all speeches (for example, a 9-minute first affirmative constructive speech in CEDA/NDT debate).

A. Cross-Examination
Format (CEDA/NDT)

The most widely used format in intercollegiate evidence-based team topic policy debating is that practiced by the CEDA and the NDT. This policy debate format has evolved, with the addition of designated cross-examination periods and preparation time, and the reallocation of time so as to make the rebuttal speeches longer in relation to constructive speeches (current practice is to have 9-minute constructive speeches and 6-minute rebuttals, a change from the practice of 25 years ago when constructives were typically 10 minutes and rebuttals 5.) The most popular current organization of this format, as utilized in NDT/CEDA practice, is as follows:

Cross-Examination Debate Format	
First affirmative constructive	*9 minutes*
Cross-examination by second negative	*3 minutes*
First negative constructive	*9 minutes*
Cross-examination by first affirmative	*3 minutes*
Second affirmative constructive	*9 minutes*
Cross-examination by first negative	*3 minutes*
Second negative constructive	*9 minutes*
Cross-examination by second affirmative	*3 minutes*
First negative rebuttal	*6 minutes*
First affirmative rebuttal	*6 minutes*
Second negative rebuttal	*6 minutes*
Second affirmative rebuttal	*6 minutes*
Preparation time	*10 minutes per team per round*

You will notice that in this format, the first and last speeches belong to the affirmative, the side supporting the proposition. This offers the advantages of primacy and recency, and enables the affirmative a substantial advantage. Having the first speech allows the affirmative the opportunity to define the ground for the debate, and having the last rebuttal enables the affirmative to have the last word, capitalizing on any failures of their opponents to fall short of fulfilling the burden of refutation. Of course, having the final opportunity to leave a lasting impression and be last heard and last flowed is a strategic advantage. These affirmative advantages are offset by the negative's block. Sides alternate during the constructive speeches, then switch order, giving the negative two consecutive speeches in the middle of the debate, termed the negative block. This means 15 minutes of negative argumentation, interrupted only by the 3-minute cross-examination period, must be answered by the affirmative in the 6-minute first affirmative rebuttal. This makes it very difficult for the affirmative to meet their burden of refutation, and sets up what many consider the most difficult speech in the debate (the 1AR).

Another feature of this format is that it allows for an organized use of preparation time during the debate. Some formats discourage or disallow any preparation time. The use of preparation time during the course of the debate should, nonetheless, be carefully planned. Preparation time is finite, tracked throughout the debate. Each precious minute used is then gone, and will not be replaced. So debate teams should strategically manage their use of preparation time. Generally, no preparation time should be used before the cross-examination periods, and debaters not engaged in the cross-examination question and answer roles should use that time for their own preparation. The first negative speaker may wish to use a few minutes to help prepare their 1NC speech, especially to consult with their partner; however, as much of the argumentation presented by that speaker will be prepared in brief form prior to the debate, and because they can use the preceding cross-examination period to prepare, the 1NC should not require much time. Similarly, the 2AC should not require very much preparation time. The negative will need to coordinate their strategy prior to the negative block, and make sure that they carefully answer all 2AC arguments, so some time may be used prior to the 2NC. Limited or no preparation time should be needed before the 1NR. The first affirmative rebuttalist must be certain to answer all arguments advanced by the negative team in the negative block, so some time may be helpful. A team is in good shape if they have at least half of their preparation time available to prepare for their last rebuttal speech.

Finally, CEDA/NDT debate is conducted on a policy proposition announced to all participants long before the debate and even the debate tournament. Debaters conduct in-depth research and formulate evidenced cases, briefs, and files of prepared materials on the topic long before they arrive at the tournament or begin the debate. They read their material during the debate, and are expected to reference quoted material.

While CEDA/NDT does not establish content-based rules for debate practice, the same format and topic are debated by tournaments sanctioned by the ADA, which does offer more restrictive guidance governing the nature of debate practice within the 9-3-6 format.

B. Lincoln–Douglas Format

The Lincoln–Douglas format is a two-person debate, named in honor of Abraham Lincoln and Stephen Douglas for their seven famous campaign debates held during the 1858 Senate race in Illinois. Like CEDA/NDT debate described earlier, NFA style Lincoln–Douglas debate does focus on a policy proposition announced well in advance of the debate event, and debaters read prepared materials and quote evidence during the debate. They engage in cross-examination and are able to use some preparation time during the debate.

The organization of this format as practiced by the NFA is as follows:

Lincoln–Douglas Format	
Affirmative constructive	*6 minutes*
Cross-examination by negative	*3 minutes*
Negative constructive	*7 minutes*
Cross-examination by affirmative	*3 minutes*
Affirmative rebuttal	*6 minutes*
Negative rebuttal	*6 minutes*
Affirmative rebuttal	*3 minutes*
Preparation time	*4 minutes*

The NFA Rules for Lincoln–Douglas debate prescribe a judging paradigm based on evaluation of the traditional stock issues (harm, inherency, and solvency) and affirmative defense of a topical plan. Negative arguments may include a single competitive counterplan, disadvantages, topicality, and on-point arguments related to the stock issues. New arguments are disallowed during the rebuttal speeches, and evidence must be fully cited. Delivery is to be "pleasant, comprehensible, and persuasive in tone," and rules are such that excessively rapid delivery is discouraged.[1]

C. Mock Trial Format

The mock trial format emulates trial court debating. In mock trial debate the emphasis is on debate and argumentation skills and on cross-examination. This differs from moot court debate, widely used in law schools, which is concerned with the sometimes highly technical rules of procedure and which may emulate the appellate court rather than the trial court.

Instead of a proposition, the mock trial debaters are provided with the facts of a legal case. If the case is a criminal one, the affirmative becomes the prosecution and the negative becomes the defense; if the case is a civil suit, the affirmative is the plaintiff and the negative is the defendant. For example, the 2006–2007 national case debated by the American Mock Trial Association is as follows:

Case Summary

On January 2nd, 2005, off-duty police officer Jamie Conmey heard a radio transmission came over dispatch saying that two suspects had just robbed Joe's Corner Store. The description said that the perpetrators were wearing white T-shirts and blue jeans, appeared to be teenagers, and had taken the cash in a brown paper bag. Officer Conmey put on the siren and started searching the neighborhood surrounding the store. Officer Conmey saw a teenager dressed in a white shirt and jeans climbing a fence in an alleyway. Officer Conmey pulled over and told the teenager to come down. The teenager stopped climbing the fence but did not come down. Seconds later, Officer Conmey shot the teenager in the side. Officer Conmey claims to have seen a gun; however, no weapon was found at the scene. The teenager was rushed to the hospital as quickly as possible, where the teenager almost immediately fell into a coma—a state in which the teenager remains today.

The teenager was Max Jeffries. Max's parents, Sean and Leigh Jeffries, filed suit against the Polk County Police Department, alleging that the actions of Officer Conmey, who committed suicide shortly after the incident, and thus the Polk County Police Department, deprived Max Jeffries of Jeffries' constitutional rights to due process of law. In addition, the Jeffries allege that through its policy, custom, and practice, the Polk County Police Department deprived Max Jeffries of Jeffries' rights to due process of law. The Jeffries allege that as a result of the actions of Officer Conmey and the Polk County Police Department, their child experienced life-threatening

---

1. National Forensic Association, http://www.nationalforensics.org/lincoln-douglas-debate/ld-rules.

injuries, and as such they are entitled to damages. This case has been bifur-
cated and as such damages are not to be considered in this same proceeding.

Students follow a format modeling a real trial. Teams in the AMTA consist of six to
eight students. They are governed by a set of rules of procedure and rules of evidence
for the fictional jurisdiction of Midland. Time is limited to the following format:

Mock Trial Format	
Opening	5 minutes per side
Direct examinations of all three witnesses (combined)	25 minutes per side
Cross-examination of all three witnesses (combined)	25 minutes per side
Closing arguments	9 minutes total—max of 5 minutes may be reserved for Plaintiff's rebuttal

This format is a popular exercise in argumentation and debate classes. Members
of the class are assigned the various roles, including attorneys, defendants, judges,
juries, and witnesses. Both sides are limited to the information about the case provided by the instructor. No additional information may be introduced into the
mock trial. In the format shown below, suitable for classroom application, substitute plaintiff's attorney for prosecuting attorney, if the case is a civil one.

For more information about mock trial debate, visit the American Mock
Trial Association at http://www.collegemocktrial.org/welcome/welcome.php.

Classroom Mock Trial Format	
Judge gives background information and outlines the procedure.	3 minutes
Prosecuting attorney outlines the case.	3 minutes
Defense attorney outlines the defense.	3 minutes
Prosecuting attorney calls three witnesses and questions each one for four minutes.	12 minutes
Defense attorney may cross-examine witnesses, asking each a maximum of three questions.	6 minutes
Defense attorney calls three witnesses and questions each one for four minutes.	12 minutes
Prosecuting attorney may cross-examine witnesses, asking each a maximum of three questions.	6 minutes
Defense attorney sums up and makes final plea.	3 minutes
Prosecuting attorney sums up and makes final plea.	3 minutes
The judge instructs the jury.	
The jury votes.	

D. Academic Parliamentary Format

1. Academic Parliamentary Debate.   Intercollegiate tournament competition in parliamentary debate has grown exponentially in recent years. Parliamentary debate tournaments and activities are held under the auspices of the National Parliamentary Debate Association (NPDA) and the American Parliamentary Debate Association (APDA). National championships and even a world championship of parliamentary debate are held.

In the British (and World Debate) format, the debate consists of four teams of two speakers, called *factions*, with two factions on either side of the case. The format is as follows:

Worlds Debate Format

---

1. Prime Minister
2. Opposition Leader
3. Deputy Prime Minister
4. Deputy Opposition Leader
5. Member for the Government
6. Member for the Opposition
7. Government Whip
8. Opposition Whip

Each debater is allowed to speak for seven minutes, and the others may offer points of information during the speeches.

Academic parliamentary debate as practiced in the APDA and NPDA involves two 2-person teams. They receive their topics 15 minutes before the debate round is to begin. The emphasis is on logic, reasoning, general knowledge, and presentation skills rather than evidence use and debate technique. Use of preprinted materials and evidence is not allowed.

The topics for the 2010 NPDA National Championship tournament were as follows:

Round	Resolution
1	In the case of health care, an imperfect bill is better than no bill at all.
2	The British Houses of Parliament are preferable to the U.S. Houses of Congress.
3	Ground the drones.
4	TH should run the Race to the Top.
5	The Roman Catholic church should establish new standards for ordination into the priesthood.
6	The USFG should amend the internal revenue code to eliminate tax exemptions for religious institutions in the United States.
7	The EU should expel Greece from the Euro Zone.

8	The Arab league members should intervene to stabilize Yemen.
Quad Octas	The USFG should mandate daily recess for all primary school students.
Triple Octas	The USFG should replace the federal income tax with a federal value added tax.
Double Octas	The USFG should nationalize domestic Internet infrastructure.
Octas	Tim Geithner should go.
Quarters	The BRIC countries should adopt a common currency.
Semis	The U.S. Supreme Court should reverse its decision in Citizens United vs. the Federal Election Commission.
Finals	President Barack Obama is this generation's President Jimmy Carter.

While academic parliamentary debate does not include dedicated periods for cross-examination, participants may request points of information, points of order, and points of personal privilege. These are described in the 2012 NPDA National Championship Tournament Rules for Debating and Judging.[2]

a. Constructive and Rebuttal Speeches.   Introduction of new arguments is appropriate during all constructive speeches. However, debaters may not introduce new arguments in rebuttal speeches except that the proposition rebuttalist may introduce new arguments in his or her rebuttal to refute arguments that were first raised in the second opposition constructive. New examples, analysis, analogies, and so on that support previously introduced arguments are permitted in rebuttal speeches.

b. Points of Information.   A debater may request a point of information—either verbally or by rising—at any time after the first minute and before the last minute of any constructive speech. The debater holding the floor has the discretion to accept or refuse points of information. If accepted, the debater requesting the point of information has a maximum of 15 seconds to make a statement or ask a question. The speaking time of the debater with the floor continues during the point of information.

c. Points of Order.   Points of order can be raised for no reason other than those specified in these Rules of Debating and Judging. If at any time during the debate, a debater believes that his or her opponent has violated one of these Rules of Debating and Judging, he or she may address the Speaker of the House with a point of order. Once recognized by the Speaker of the House, the debater must state, but may not argue for, the point of order. At the discretion of the Speaker of the House, the accused may briefly respond to the point

———

2. http://www.forensicstournament.net/tournamentdocs/734-012NPDAInvite_Final.pdf.

of order. The Speaker of the House will then rule immediately on the point of order in one of three ways: (1) point well taken, (2) point not well taken, or (3) point taken under consideration. The time used to state and address a point of order will not be deducted from the speaking time of the debater with the floor. A point of order is a serious charge and should not be raised for minor violations.

d. Points of Personal Privilege.   At any time during the debate, a debater may rise to a point of personal privilege when he or she believes that an opponent has personally insulted one of the debaters, has made an offensive or tasteless comment, or has grievously misconstrued another's words or arguments. The Speaker will then rule on whether or not the comments were acceptable. The time used to state and address a point of personal privilege will not be deducted from the speaking time of the debater with the floor. Like a point of order, a point of personal privilege is a serious charge and should not be raised for minor transgressions. Debaters may be penalized for raising spurious points of personal privilege.

The format is as follows:

Parliamentary Tournament Format	
First proposition constructive	7 *minutes*
First opposition constructive	8 *minutes*
Second proposition constructive	8 *minutes*
Second opposition constructive	8 *minutes*
Opposition rebuttal by first speaker	4 *minutes*
Proposition rebuttal by first speaker	5 *minutes*

Debaters in NPDA parliamentary debate receive their proposition and are allowed 15 minutes to prepare before the debate begins, but no preparation time during the debate. The government presents a case. The debaters first define the terms of the proposition and set their framework for the debate. They may choose to offer a policy interpretation measured by cost-benefit analysis or a value interpretation measured by designated criteria. In outline form, the first proposition (the first speaker) offers the government case. The first opposition then offers refutation, which may include a challenge to the definitions and framework offered by the government. The debate continues much as a team topic policy debate, but without formal cross-examination periods.

While a debater is speaking (except during the first and last minute of their speech), an opponent may rise to a point of information, similar to a cross-examination question. The speaker may choose to recognize the questioner and answer the question or not.

For more information about parliamentary tournament debate, visit the National Parliamentary Debate Association website at http://www.parlidebate. org/. To learn about the British Parliamentary Debate Format and the World

University Debating Championships, visit http://parliamentarydebate.blogspot.
com/2007/08/british-parliamentary-debate.html and http://flynn.debating.net/
colmmain.htm.

2. Applied Parliamentary Debate.   Applied parliamentary debate is a specialized format involving the use of special procedures. This format is considered
separately in Chapter 19.

E. Ethics Bowl

Another format for competitive argumentation is the Intercollegiate Ethics Bowl,
sponsored by the Association for Practical and Professional Ethics. A national
championship tournament has been held since 1997. In advance of the competition, a number of cases or scenarios posing ethical dilemmas are announced. At
the competition, two competing teams of three to five members are presented
with one of the cases. A moderator frames a question about the case, and after a
2-minute period during which the team members may confer, the first team
offers a 10-minute response to the question. More than one member may participate in this speech, but only one may speak at a time. The other team then has
1 minute to confer, and then responds with a 5-minute speech. After a 1-minute
period for conference, the first team answers the response with a 5-minute
speech. Teams may elect to support or oppose the positions offered by their
opponents. The first team then answers up to 10 minutes of questions posed by
the round's judges. A second case is then offered, and the teams reverse sides and
repeat the same process. Judges score the teams and determine a winner based on
the following criteria:

- Clarity and intelligibility
- Avoidance of ethical irrelevance
- Identification and discussion of central ethical dimensions
- Deliberative thoughtfulness[3]

An example of an ethics bowl case from the 2012 tournament is offered as
follows:

> In 2009, the Family Smoking Prevention and Tobacco Control Act
> became law. It requires, among other things, that cigarette packages
> have more explicit and dramatic health warnings, and display emphatic
> health warning messages and graphic, color images meant to discourage
> smoking. The Food and Drug Administration (FDA) posted thirty-six
> images on the Internet from which the agency will select nine for use
> on cigarette packages. Among the messages is "Smoking can kill you,"
> and the images include a rotting lung, a diseased mouth, and a corpse.

---

3. Association for Practical and Professional Ethics, http://www.indiana.edu/~appe/2012-
Championship%20Rules.pdf.

Business Week (November 10, 2010), quoted FDA Commissioner Dr. Margaret A. Hamburg: "When the rule takes effect, the health consequences of smoking will be obvious every time someone picks up a pack of cigarettes."

Critics claim the packaging insults, embarrasses, and humiliates smokers and discriminates against them. They also claim that government should not impose its views about label content and that the legislation violates cigarette companies' rights to free speech.

Supporters of the governmental approach claim that the traditional warning labels on cigarette packages have been much too small to offset the emotional appeals and glamorization of smoking in advertising. They also point to studies documenting the effectiveness of more explicit warnings. On the basis of these findings, many other countries have mandated that more package surface area be devoted to health warnings.

Ethics Bowl competitions offer students the opportunity to apply ethical and philosophical criteria in an argumentative setting requiring effective presentation skills, critical thinking, knowledge and understanding of ethical and philosophical theory, quick thinking under pressure, and teamwork. For more information, rules, samples cases, and history of Ethics Bowl, visit http://www.indiana.edu/~appe/ethicsbowl.html.

EXERCISES

1. Organize a debate using each of the formats (Policy Debate, Lincoln–Douglas, NPDA Parliamentary, BP Parliamentary) identified, but on the same proposition. Compare the strengths and weaknesses of each. This is obviously a long-term project.

2. Visit the Ethics Bowl website http://www.indiana.edu/~appe/ethicsbowl. html, and choose a case for analysis. Apply ethical constructs discussed in Chapter 5 to the case. Conduct an ethic's bowl round.

18

....

Political Campaign Debates

Presidential debates are the paramount example of applied debate. Smith has described them as the "Rhetorical Superbowl."[1] They become the focal point of presidential campaigns and have sometimes been the decisive factor in determining the winner of the election. For days in advance of each presidential debate, the media feature the coming event. The debates usually are carried on all major networks in the United States and are widely broadcast around the world, and they are viewed by more people than any other campaign-related communication. For days after a debate the media continue to feature news about it, first trying to determine who "won" and then assessing the impact of the debate on the campaign. Following the model of presidential campaign debates, candidates for elected office at every level from mayor to U.S. Senate are now likely to participate in public campaign debates prior to Election Day. Of course, the bulk of commentary and academic research about campaign debates has focused on debates at the presidential level and, therefore, this chapter will also focus its discussion of political debates on the top level of campaign debates.

Presidential debates are a relatively new tradition in American history. In 1959, a group of speech professors led by Austin Freeley began[2] to organize the Committee on Presidential Campaign Debates to call on the candidates for the presidency to meet in debate in the tradition of Abraham Lincoln and Stephen Douglas. Initially the committee consisted of all the past presidents of the American Forensic Association. The movement quickly gained momentum and was endorsed by the AFA, Delta Sigma Rho–Tau Kappa Alpha, and the

---

1. Smith, C. A., *Presidential Campaign Communication: The Quest for the White House* (Cambridge, UK: Polity Press, 2010), p. 147.
2. Freeley, A., "The Presidential Debates and the Speech Profession," *Quarterly Journal of Speech* [serial online], February 1961; 47(1):60. Available from: Communication & Mass Media Complete, Ipswich, MA. Accessed June 17, 2012.

Ohio Association of College Teachers of Speech. These organizations named additional members to the committee. Senator John F. Kennedy promptly endorsed the proposal, as did all the potential candidates in 1960 except for Vice President Richard Nixon. The idea of presidential debates quickly captured the public's imagination. Soon editorials, columns, and articles appeared in support of the idea. Television networks indicated their willingness to cooperate.

September 26, 1960, brought the first presidential debate between Kennedy and Nixon. Four debates were held during the campaign; the first, which Kennedy "won," was judged to be the most important. The *New York Times* called the debates *the really decisive factor* in the election. Since 1960, presidential candidates have participated in 27 televised general election campaign debates, and there have been 8 debates involving the candidates for vice president. While aside from primary debates and surrogate debates, there were no presidential debates prior to 1960, and there were no presidential debates in 1964, 1968, or 1972, debates have been held during every election year since 1976 and are now a central feature of every presidential election campaign. While it is not required by law that debates occur, in the current environment it would take a very unusual set of circumstances to prevent debates from taking place.

The presidential debates have an interesting, tangled background of law and legal fiction. Under Federal Communication Commission rules, it was illegal for the networks to sponsor such debates. The "equal-time" rule required the networks to give equal time to all presidential candidates. In 1960, for example, 16 legally qualified candidates ran for the office of U.S. president (including one who campaigned in an Uncle Sam suit on the platform "Drop the Bomb"). Naturally the networks would not consider giving equal time to 16 candidates, nor would the major candidates consider sharing a platform with unknown candidates who had no chance of winning. The problem was solved when Congress passed legislation suspending the equal-time requirement for 60 days in 1960. The debates won widespread public approval, and the public demanded more presidential debates in 1964, 1968, and 1972. But the candidates in those years (including Nixon, who once remarked that he had flunked debating in the Electoral College) didn't want to debate, and their allies in Congress found a convenient way to avoid the pressures for debate. Both the House and the Senate passed bills suspending the equal-time law during the campaign, which allowed the senators and representatives to report to their constituents that they had voted in favor of presidential debates. However, because the House bill and the Senate bill differed in the number of days for which the law was suspended, the bills were referred to a Joint Conference Committee, where they quietly died.

In 1976 the League of Women Voters found a way to have presidential debates without the need to suspend the equal-time law. The league invited the major candidates to debate. The league was not subject to the equal-time law, and the networks maintained that the debates were a news event—not something sponsored by the networks—and thus not subject to the equal-time law. President Gerald Ford and Governor Jimmy Carter accepted the invitation to debate. Scholars generally described them as "eminently forgettable."

During the 1980 presidential campaign, President Carter declined to meet with Ronald Reagan and third-party candidate John Anderson in a three-way debate. Reagan agreed to debate Anderson and won points for being a "good sport"; Carter, conversely, lost points for being a "bad sport." Later in the campaign Carter, apparently reluctantly, agreed to meet Reagan in one debate.

After the election, supporters of both Reagan and Carter and many independent commentators cited the debate as the "turning point" in the election and a major factor in Reagan's landslide victory.

After the 1984 conventions, the League of Women Voters invited Reagan and Walter Mondale for a series of debates. Mondale, sorely needing the visibility the debates would give him, eagerly accepted. Reagan, enjoying a 20-point lead in the polls, was advised not to give Mondale the visibility and status the debates would bring. However, apparently remembering the "poor sport" charge that had hurt Carter in 1980, Reagan agreed to two presidential debates and one vice-presidential debate. (The first vice-presidential debate was between Senators Bob Dole and Walter Mondale in 1976.) Mondale was generally credited with winning the first debate, in which Reagan was perceived as being tired and unsure of himself. In the second debate, Mondale was credited with winning the issues, but Reagan, returning to his customary style that had won him the title of "the Great Communicator," clearly carried the burden of communication and won the decision of the voters.

Since 1988, presidential debates have been under the sponsorship of the Commission on Presidential Debates. (The commission, organized in 1987 by the Democratic and Republican National Committees, had taken over the sponsorship of the debates.) The format might be described as a highly specialized type of joint press conference. However, the presidential debates did have some important elements of real applied debates. Each candidate was allotted equal time, each had an opportunity for rebuttal, and each made a closing statement. Although the format fell short of a real debate, it did provide the American voters with their only opportunity to see and hear the candidates on the same platform at the same time as they responded to the journalists and to one another.

Presidential debates are now a firmly established part of the American political scene. In 1992 there were three presidential debates and one vice-presidential debate. That year marked the first three-way presidential campaign debates. Although Ross Perot was not expected to win the election, he commanded far larger public support than Anderson had in 1980, and both major-party candidates treated him as if he were an 800-pound bantam rooster, nodding at his arguments, smiling at his country homilies, and laughing at his jokes. Neither George Bush nor Bill Clinton came close to challenging him on a single point, obviously hoping that his supporters might switch to them on Election Day. This debate was noteworthy as well for its format. Clinton had, in the Democratic primary debates, been successful utilizing a "town hall format," in which audience members provided questions to be addressed by the debaters.

In 1996 two presidential debates and one vice-presidential debate were held. The second presidential debate in 1996 was held using the town hall format.

While respondents did not proclaim a clear winner, it was generally thought that Clinton won by not losing: Dole would have needed to score a knockout to catch up in the polls. He did not.

In 2000, George W. Bush was reluctant to agree to participate in the debates, then agreed to one debate, and finally to three (along with a vice-presidential debate). The debates were all too close to call, according to media and post-debate polls. Whether such a conclusion was reflective of the closeness of the campaign or the actual debates was unclear. In the first debate, October 3, 2000, at the University of Massachusetts, Amherst, Vice President Gore was criticized for being too aggressive, although generally perceived to be more knowledgeable and competent. In the second debate, October 11, at Wake Forest, Gore seemed strained to appear nicer, and the debate was close but cordial. In the third debate, October 17, at Washington University in St. Louis, the debaters seemed to agree more than disagree. All three debates were moderated by Jim Lehrer with the same format: single moderator; candidates questioned in turn with 2 minutes to answer; 60-second rebuttal; 2-minute closing statements. Approximately 46.6 million people watched the first debate, with about 37.5 million watching the second and third debates. As with the election itself, the debates were too close to call.

In 2004, President Bush and Senator John Kerry participated in three debates. The first was limited to questions of foreign policy, and was moderated by Jim Lehrer of PBS News. The candidates stood at podiums and answered the moderator's questions. The second debate involved domestic and foreign policy questions, and was moderated by Charlie Gibson of ABC News in a town hall format, engaging audience questions. The third and final debate, intended to focus on domestic policy, was moderated by Bob Schieffer of CBS News, and returned the candidates to podiums as in the first debate. Approximately 62.4 million viewers watched the first debate, 46.7 million the second, and 51.1 million watched the third debate. Vice-presidential candidates Dick Cheney and John Edwards also participated in a nationally televised debate, moderated by Gwen Ifill of PBS News, with both candidates seated at a table. Approximately 43.5 million viewed the vice-presidential debate. Most observers felt that Senator Kerry did the better job of debating during the first debate; the second debate was considered fairly even, and post-debate polls indicated a majority of viewers considered Kerry the winner of the third debate. The 2008 general election debates again featured three debates between the candidates, Senators Barack Obama and John McCain, and a vice presidential debate between Senator Joe Biden and Governor Sarah Palin. The most watched of the four debates was the vice presidential debate, with 69.9 million viewers tuning in.

Presidential debates have come to dominate the landscape of the Democratic and Republican Parties' primary campaigns. During the 2008 primaries, as many as 8 Democratic contenders for their party's nomination and 11 Republican candidates participated in 47 debates. Although many of the debates offered traditional opportunities for candidates to answer moderators' questions, new formats included the YouTube debates, engaging online contributors in a sort of cyber–town hall debate, and debates translated into Spanish language and moderated by Spanish-language news anchors. Sponsors of debates included Logo, a TV network targeted to lesbian, gay, bisexual, and transgender communities. The YouTube debates presented candidates with video questions contributed through the Internet service YouTube in a wide range of creative presentations, personalizing the questions in unique ways. During the 2012 primaries, as many as 9 GOP candidates participated in 27 debates (since President Obama ran as an unopposed incumbent, there were no Democratic Party debates).

The upcoming sections of this chapter will consider the formats for campaign debates, the functions served by and the strategies for debates within the campaigns, the effects and impacts of debates, a review of debate highlights since 1960, and a look at the future for campaign debates.

I. FORMAT

Perhaps the most notable political campaign debates in American history occurred during the Illinois Senate race of 1858, involving incumbent Senator Stephen Douglas and challenger Abraham Lincoln. While the series of seven debates did not address a formally framed proposition per se, the key issue of the day and of the campaign was the expansion of slavery into the new territories. Each debate consisted of three speeches: the first 60 minutes long, the response 90 minutes, and the closing rebuttal 30 minutes. There were no moderators, only Lincoln and Douglas. The clash was reportedly robust, and the depth of argumentation and support substantial. Although the debates were held in seven Illinois communities, newspaper reports and transcripts of the debates were widely disseminated, helping Lincoln's rise to national recognition. While Douglas held his senate seat, Lincoln was thrust into the national debate. The Lincoln–Douglas debates were substantial and represented excellence in debate practice. Nonetheless, many years passed before nationally important campaign debates reemerged, facilitated by the growth of electronic media, especially television.

In 1948, during the Republican primary in Oregon, candidates Thomas Dewey and Harold Stassen faced each other in a debate broadcast nationally by all three radio networks. An audience of between 40 and 80 million listeners heard Dewey and Stassen debate the question, "Should the Communist Party be outlawed?" This was one of the few issues upon which the candidates disagreed. Dewey opposed the proposition. The debate again reflected the value of focusing on a single issue and encouraging direct clash, although Dewey managed the context more successfully, winning the debate and ultimately, the nomination. As explained by Jamieson and Birdsell, "Because the debate was able to deal at length and in depth with a clearly defined issue of importance to the public, and because time was allotted for rebuttal, the format invited illumination of the issue and the candidates' stands on it. The candidates' differences on outlawing the Communist party were clarified and defended, their intellects publicly exercised in revealing ways. Dewey won on issue and image and with that the primary and his party's nomination."[3]

In 1956 Democratic primary candidates Adlai Stevenson and Estes Kefauver debated for a national television audience. The hour-long debate was broadcast by ABC television from WTVJ in Miami during the Florida primary. The format allowed 3-minute opening statements; questions and 5-minute closing statements with questioning by moderator Quincy Howe covering a range of domestic and foreign policy questions. The debate was not much of a debate, as there was little clash. The debaters agreed on most of the policy questions raised.

The pattern and general format for subsequent presidential debates was established by the 1960 Kennedy–Nixon debates, labeled (wishfully) by Robert Sarnoff of NBC as the "Great Debates." The campaigns negotiated extensively along with the television networks to establish guidelines governing format and broadcasting arrangements. All subsequent debates have engaged memoranda of understanding (MOU) between the candidates, detailing the nature of the debates, staging, and other concerns. Every conceivable detail, from camera angles to room temperature to whether the debaters may use notes or have water glasses is covered in these lengthy agreements. As observed by Minnow and Lemay, "Whatever one thinks of the candidates' memoranda of understanding, it is unrealistic to expect the campaigns not to negotiate. Even Lincoln and Douglas exchanged letters discussing the terms of their debate."[4] The number and length of debates, subjects to be addressed, whether there will be opening and/or closing statements, length of answers, follow-ups, responses, use of notes or written materials, moderator(s), panelists, staging (podiums, seated, stools, and so on), time and date of the debate, and other concerns are agreed upon and set out in the MOU. There has not been another topic debate since Dewey and Stassen in 1948. Kennedy and Nixon agreed upon four one-hour debates. The first addressed domestic issues, the fourth, foreign policy, with the middle two a mix of both. Debaters stood at podiums and, in the third debate, a split-screen telecast was used, with Nixon and the panelists in a Los Angeles studio and Kennedy in New York. Each debate featured a moderator and three or four panelists. The first and the last debates gave the candidates eight-minute opening statements and three-minute closing statements, with two-and-a-half minutes to answer each question and up to a minute-and-a-half for rebuttals. The middle two debates allowed no opening or closing statements. This basic format, characterized by limited answers to a series of questions asked by journalist moderators and/or panelists, has become the dominant model for political campaign debates. The most significant innovation to this basic framework occurred in the second presidential debate in 1992 when Republican incumbent George H. W. Bush, Democratic nominee Bill Clinton, and independent candidate Ross Perot participated in a moderated town hall format, wherein audience members

3. Jamieson, K. H., & Birdsell, D. S., *Presidential Debates: The Challenge of Creating an Informed Electorate* (Oxford: Oxford University Press, 1988).
4. Minow, N. N., & Lamay, C. L., *Inside the Presidential Debates: Their Improbable Past and Promising Future* (Chicago: University of Chicago Press, 2008).

asked questions of the candidates. (This debate was also notable for the inclusion of a third party participant: the only time this has occurred.) One of the three presidential debates in 1996, 2000, 2004, 2008, and 2012 has also selected a town hall format.

In Chapter 1, we defined debate as "the seeking of a reasoned judgment on a proposition." By this measure, presidential debates as they have been and are currently practiced, with the exception of the 1948 Oregon primary debate, are not debates at all as they do not address a single, clearly stated proposition nor do they call for a reasoned judgment beyond "vote for me!" J. Jeffery Auer described the 1960 debates between Richard Nixon and John F. Kennedy as "counterfeit debates" as they only met one of five criteria essential to a debate. First, he argued that a debate offers confrontation. In debate terms, the clash provided by fulfillment of the burden of refutation, or rejoinder, is missing. When there is any significant direct confrontation, it is provided by a moderator or panelist, not the opposing debater. Second, a debate offers advocates equal and adequate time to address each argument. The time limits on answers and severe limitations on time or ability to offer rebuttal and follow-up mean adequate time is not provided for any substantive development of argumentation. The third criteria, evenly matched debaters, was met; however, the fourth criteria, that the debate address a stated proposition, was obviously not met. Finally, debates call for a decision on the proposition or an audience vote. Presidential debates as exemplified by the 1960 debates did not call for such a decision. Bitzer and Reuter applied the same set of criteria to the 1976 debates between Carter and Ford with the same conclusion, "Auer's judgment of the Kennedy–Nixon debates could have been written with equal justice of the Ford–Carter debates. They fell far short of the conception of 'genuine' debate."[5]

In many ways, then, the great potential of presidential debates has been unrealized. Formats entertain a range of unrelated questions from journalists rather than focus on a clearly stated proposition; candidates do not confront each other, and rules for time and questioning enable debaters to provide brief responses without the need to defend them from extensive refutation or the opportunity to develop argumentation in significant depth. Debates become exercises in parallel oratory, where competitors share a stage but are allowed to escape meaningful comparison of ideas, policies, philosophies, and reasoning. This is not to suggest that presidential campaign debates are completely without merit, as will be discussed later. However, it is certain that they do not provide the potential benefit that would be possible to voters, democracy, and the political process if genuine debates were to take place.

II. FUNCTIONS AND STRATEGIES

Political campaign debates function as one part of the larger political campaign, thus all functions of the campaign are served by debates. These functions are

5. Bitzer, L., & Reuter, T., *Carter vs. Ford the Counterfeit Debates of 1976* (Madison: University of Wisconsin Press, 1980), p. 11.

wide and varied. Campaigns are important in facilitating the election of democratic leaders by creating an informed electorate, by mobilizing political participation, and by generating public discourse about the principles, values, and policies which contribute to civic organization and problem solving. Campaign communication facilitates direct involvement by citizens in the decision making which impacts governance and daily life. The openness of campaign communication engenders and enables a sense of legitimacy and faith in elections and government. Debate is particularly well suited to inform citizens and offer them depth of understanding about issues and candidates.

In 2008 and 2012, participation in primary debates has grown substantially, offering free exposure for numerous candidates, increasing the choices available to voters and offering opportunities for increased participation. The general election debates between each party's nominees are likely to be the most watched events of the never-ending campaign. Arguments, positions, themes, slogans, and personal styles which have been refined and tested through months, even years, of primary debates, stump speeches, town hall meetings, political advertising, convention speeches, interviews and appearances, social networking, blogging and microblogging, generation of print advertising and direct mail, and so much more are brought to their biggest stage in the presidential debates.

Trent, Friedenberg, and Denton identify three phases of political debate strategies: pre-debate, during the debate, and post-debate. Pre-debate strategies begin with lowering the expectations for one's performance and raising the expectations of the opponent. This prepares the campaign to claim success when their candidate's (low) expectations for debate performance are met or exceeded, and it allows campaigns to spin a good performance by the opponent as expected; therefore, not a new reason to support that candidate. In preparing for the debate, campaigns will seek to identify their target audience(s) and plan appeals and positions, even delivery styles and language, which might be more persuasive to that specific group. Surprisingly, these targets will include groups who do not represent the center or base of support for the candidate, as they may represent undecided or uninformed potential voters. The third step in pre-debate strategy is the same step classroom and tournament debaters conduct: Practice! Campaigns are likely to suspend other activities in preparation for upcoming debates to prepare answers to anticipated questions and, using surrogate stand-ins for the opponents and moderators or questioners, rehearse for the debates.

During-debate strategies begin with relating policy advocacy and issue development to an overall theme. The theme offers an identifiable and positive explanation, which reflects a coherent narrative for current circumstances, an underlying philosophy, and a vision for the future. The second strategy to be employed during the debate is developing an image, which involves three potential steps: (1) development of leadership style, (2) personification, and (3) identification. Leadership style is a function of image, and may be revealed through charisma, dynamism, and positive excitement or through a careful, serious, measured, and thoughtful tone. In addition, leadership style is revealed in advocacy of what policy initiates the candidate would prioritize and by what means he or she would seek to implement them. For example, an activist style is proactive, whereas a passive style may be more cautious. Personification refers to the personality revealed by the candidates as well as their personal qualifications and inclinations, especially in direct comparison or juxtaposition to their opponent. Identification is an essential function of communication. We support those whom we perceive to be like us, those who share our values, life experience, and perceptions. In building identification, the candidate appeals to commonality with his or her target audience and seeks to portray the opponent as "out of touch" or different from the citizen voter.[6]

Smith adds four additional strategies for the debaters to employ during the debate. First, he argues that it is strategically advantageous to "hold your opponent accountable for unpopular things." This may be accomplished by associating (for example) an incumbent opponent with circumstances of the status quo which are problematic, or charging an opponent who has a seemingly inconsistent record of public statements or votes with flip-flopping. Next, the debater is well advised to counter the worst personal charges of their opponent through language, argumentation, and demeanor. For example, if one's opponent has suggested that you are inexperienced and thus not knowledgeable enough to solve problems in a given area, an informed and detailed answer offered coolly and calmly with detail and insight will alleviate concerns. The next suggestion is the first inclination of the classroom or tournament debater: to counterpunch. This is to answer and extend arguments made and to capitalize on opponents' mistakes or failures to answer. The fourth new strategy offered by Smith is to "control the dramatistic appeal of the candidate's narrative." This step involves making effective choices about the narrative offered so as to employ language and focus appropriately to best satisfy the rhetorical needs of the situation. Finally, careful use of language through powerful and impactful words, phrases, and sentences helps the candidate control the sound bites that are repeated after the debate (even during the debate via microblogging tools like Twitter!).[7]

Post-debate success begins immediately with "spin," the positive interpretation of the candidate's performance in the debate. Of course, victory is measured against the previously lowered expectations, and proclaimed based on the positive responses of key surrogates and viewers as well as campaign insta-polls. Important moments from the debates will be recreated and clipped in speeches and especially in produced spot advertisements, and distributed by e-mail, Facebook, Tumblr, and numerous other outlets. As the impact of the debates will be magnified by opinion leaders and media, the campaigns will quickly reinforce their success with these important gatekeepers through post-debate appearances, e-mails, and other communications.

---

6. Trent, J. S., Friedenberg, R. V., & Denton, J., *Political Campaign Communication: Principles & Practices*, 7th ed. (Lanham, MD: Rowman & Littlefield, 2011).
7. Smith, C., *Presidential Campaign Communication: The Quest for the White House* (Malden, MA: Polity Press, 2010).

III. EFFECTS AND IMPACTS

As they are embedded within the mass of communication activities that make up a presidential campaign, it is difficult to isolate the impact of debates on voters and viewers. Of course, this difficulty has not prevented many from measuring and studying these effects. It is clear that presidential debates generate large audiences, with over 60 million viewers generally watching. More people are impacted indirectly by news and media coverage and interpersonal conveyance of opinion and information, and dissemination of debate information through political advertising. Entertainment media, including the parodies of *Saturday Night Live* and comedic coverage by the *Daily Show* and other late night talk programming generates an indirect, but substantial, impact of the debates.

It is likely that presidential debates reinforce the predispositions of most viewers, that they generate interest in the candidates and the campaigns, and that they may either shift some voters or win over undecided voters. Arguments and issue positions expressed by candidates in debates are discussed by journalists in their coverage and political commentary, and thus the debates serve to set the agenda for subsequent discourse. Debates serve to inform voters, and especially to help them associate issue positions with the candidates that hold them. They may also change viewers' images of candidates, especially when the candidates are not previously well known. For example, the 1960 debates have been credited with raising the public estimation of young Senator Kennedy such that he appeared, and was thought of, as "presidential" as a result of his participation in the debates. Senator Obama faced the same scrutiny in 2008.

Trent et al. argue that the debates "freeze the campaign." Since other functions of the campaigns may be put on hold during the period of the debates, the opinions, preferences, and predispositions of informed voters may be hardened in the absence of other campaign communication, at least during the period of the debates.[8] Trent also argues that the debates help to boost confidence in democracy, through the engagement of public discourse, a reduction in distrust and cynicism, and an inclusion of a national audience. Therefore, faith in the transparency and legitimacy of public decision making and confidence in democracy is enhanced. The debates may also serve as a test of the candidate in a high pressure environment and, due to the range of study and preparation required, may help prepare the candidate for the job they are seeking.

In 2008 and 2012, the number of primary debates grew exponentially. This phenomena created opportunities for experimentation with formats and changed the course of the campaigns in many ways. With as many as 10 candidates participating in a debate, each debater had to fight to secure and occupy time in the debate. The shortage of time and opportunity for rebuttal and follow-up was even more pronounced than in the general election debates, usually involving only two participants. With such limited time available, the power of the moderator was increased as she would select which candidates would receive a

---

8. Trent, J. S., Friedenberg, R. V., & Denton, J., *Political Campaign Communication: Principles and Practices*, 7th ed. (Lanham, MD: Rowman & Littlefield, 2011).

question. With so many debates to prepare for, candidates and their campaigns were overwhelmed by the debates. Of course, the debates offered free media exposure for otherwise marginal candidates, increasing participation and possibly, the duration of some candidacies. Perhaps most important was the opportunity for repetition. With so many debates to provide opportunities for practice and adjustment, the candidates who survived the primaries would be well prepared for the general election debates.

IV. A BRIEF HISTORY OF PRESIDENTIAL DEBATES

(Note: All material quoted directly from the debates came from unofficial transcripts posted by the Commission on Presidential Debates at http://www.debates.org/index.php?page=debate-transcripts.)

Vice President Richard M. Nixon versus Senator John F. Kennedy, 1960

Four debates were held, each lasted an hour. It is somewhat surprising that Nixon agreed to the debates, since as the standing vice president, he was viewed more experienced and qualified by most than the young and inexperienced junior senator from Massachusetts. However, polling indicated the race very close, and Nixon felt if he refused to participate, that refusal would cause voters to reject him. The first debate was the most noteworthy, and has been the most discussed. It is likely that it helped put Kennedy in the White House. Kennedy spent the two days prior to the debate reviewing materials prepared for him by his campaign aides, practicing for the debate and resting. Nixon reviewed materials but did not practice for the debate or work with his aides. Nixon had been ill, refused the typical makeup instead putting a product called "Lazy Shave" on his face, and looked haggard. Kennedy was young, rested, charismatic, handsome, and comfortable with the camera. Nixon sweated in front of the cameras, and his five o'clock shadow contributed to a less appealing look. Kennedy spoke directly through the camera to his audience while Nixon addressed Kennedy directly. This debate would allow 8-minute opening statements, and Kennedy went first. In his opening, he set the tone for the debate, going on the attack, but offering thematic oratory. Nixon's opening statement refuted Kennedy's point by point. While nothing in the content particularly stands out from the first Nixon–Kennedy debate, Kennedy clearly mastered the television medium and the debate format more effectively than did Nixon. Kennedy looked better and approached the content of the debate eloquently, but without relying on direct refutation. Nixon spent much more time attacking the arguments of Kennedy on-point. It seemed Nixon was more interested in "winning the debate" than in speaking to the American public about policy and issues. Kennedy clearly did a better job of navigating the television medium.

Most measures indicate that Kennedy benefitted more than Nixon from the first debate. It is mythological that those who saw the debate on television preferred Kennedy, while those who listened on radio preferred Nixon. This is not clear. While one study did indicate that those hearing the debate on radio found the debate a tie, and studies do indicate that those watching the debate on television thought Kennedy "won," the radio studies measured a smaller and different demographic: rural audiences (where access to television was less likely). Kennedy succeeded in the first debate by establishing himself as credible, competent, and "presidential."

While the remaining three debates had large audiences, they reflected less audience change than the first.

Governor Jimmy Carter versus President Gerald Ford, 1976

During the 1964, 1968, and 1972 elections, no presidential debates were held. Smith identifies seven criteria which are important in considering whether or not to debate. The first is the question, "Is there an incumbent president in the debate?" Incumbents enjoy the legitimacy of holding the office, and assuming they are ahead, stand to lose ground by sharing a stage with the challenger, thus granting the challenger legitimacy and exposure. In 1964 and 1972, incumbent presidents (Lyndon Johnson and Richard Nixon) stood for reelection and did not stand to gain by participating in debates. The second criteria is the question, "Is the election likely to be close?" The 1968 election saw Nixon ahead of his challengers. Third, "Is our candidate a good debater?" Fourth, "Are there only two candidates?" This was an issue in 1968, with the presence of Governor George Wallace of Alabama running on an Independent ticket. Fifth, "Will we be able to control the important variables?" and sixth, "Do we have clear strategic goals for the debate?"[9]

In July of 1976, incumbent president Gerald Ford trailed Governor Jimmy Carter of Georgia by more than 30 percentage points. Having some experience debating in his congressional campaign, and realizing the need to challenge Carter, Ford announced in his acceptance speech at the Republican National Convention that he was eager to debate Carter. Carter quickly took up the challenge and the debates were organized. There were three presidential debates and the first ever vice presidential debate (between Senator Walter Mondale and Senator Bob Dole). The formats allowed for follow-up questions by the moderators, and the venues were public auditoriums rather than TV studios. The most memorable thing about the first debate was the 27-minute delay in which the audio on stage went dead. The cameras, however, remained on, so the viewing public watched the two candidates stand awkwardly and silently at their respective podiums for nearly a half hour. The first debate addressed domestic policy and offered President Ford the opportunity to defend his pardoning of

9. Smith, C. *Presidential Campaign Communication: The Quest for the White House* (Malden, MA: Polity Press, 2010).

Richard Nixon in the wake of the Watergate scandal. The second debate was about foreign policy, and one of the more famous gaffes in presidential debate history was offered by Ford when he said, "There is no Soviet domination of Eastern Europe, and there never will be under a Ford administration." When the surprised questioner, Max Frankel, followed up with "I'm sorry … did I understand you to say, sir, that the Soviets are not using Eastern Europe as their own sphere of influence in occupying most of the countries there?" Ford responded with "I don't believe … that the Yugoslavians consider themselves dominated by the Soviet Union. I don't believe that the Romanians consider themselves dominated by the Soviet Union. I don't believe that the Poles consider themselves dominated by the Soviet Union. Each of these countries is independent, autonomous, it has its own territorial integrity, and the United States does not concede that those countries are under the domination of the Soviet Union." By any obvious measure, Ford's statements did not seem to be factually accurate, and news reports following the debate were primarily about them. Although the debates were described as boring, with Ford appearing dull and Carter awkward, polls reflected a boost for Carter after each of the debates. Carter said later that "if it hadn't been for the debates, I would have lost. They established me as competent on foreign and domestic affairs and gave the viewers reason to think that Jimmy Carter had something to offer."[10] Of course, the vice presidential debate performance of Ford's running mate, Senator Bob Dole, also helped Carter. Dole's stoic sense of humor and deadpan delivery of quips won him little support. His biggest gaffe was, in answer to a question about Watergate, "I figured out the other day: If you added up the killed and wounded in Democrat wars this century, it would be about 1.6 million Americans enough to fill the city of Detroit." Senator Mondale responded with "I think Senator Dole richly earned his reputation as a hatchet man."

Governor Ronald Reagan versus Congressman John Anderson; Governor Ronald Reagan versus President Jimmy Carter, 1980

Facing a failing economy, the Iranian hostage crisis, a primary challenge from Senator Edward Kennedy of Massachusetts, and the credible independent candidacy of Representative John Anderson, President Jimmy Carter entered his 1980 bid for reelection facing significant challenges. After a contentious series of republican primaries, the GOP nominated Governor Ronald Reagan. Republican Congressman John Anderson elected to run as an independent candidate. In September, the League of Women Voters extended invitations to Carter, Reagan, and Anderson to participate in a three-way debate. As the incumbent, Carter stood to lose from the three-way format, with both Anderson and Reagan focusing their attacks on the administration. Carter would agree to a three-way debate only after debating Reagan first. Seeing the advantage of

---

10. Witcover, J., *Marathon: The Pursuit of the Presidency, 1972–1976* (New York: New American Library), p. 576.

Anderson's participation, Reagan would not agree to the compromise, and so a debate was planned including Reagan, Anderson, and an empty chair. Ultimately, the empty chair was not included, and a debate involving Reagan and Anderson was held on September 21. While the candidates had originally agreed to allow limited candidate-to-candidate questioning, that format innovation was removed shortly before the debate. The debate offered Reagan the opportunity to reduce concern that he was too conservative and radical for the country, as he focused on an optimistic tone and positive campaign themes. His personality and humor positively impacted his image, and he concluded with "For 200 years, we've lived in the future, believing that tomorrow would be better than today, and today would be better than yesterday. I still believe that. I'm not running for the presidency because I believe that I can solve the problems we've discussed tonight. I believe the people of this country can, and together, we can begin the world over again. We can meet our destiny—and that destiny to build a land here that will be, for all mankind, *a shining city on a hill*. I think we ought to get at it." Anderson had been criticized for his condescending, professorial tone, which tended to be evident in the debate. While Anderson tended to be more specific in issue development, Reagan delineated his themes in an engaging and moderate tone. After the debate, Anderson's support diminished such that poll numbers did not warrant his invitation to the next debate.

With Anderson no longer included, and his support slipping, President Carter agreed to debate Reagan in a single debate one week before the election. Memorable moments in the debate were supplied by Reagan. Carter attempted to portray Reagan as dangerous in his policies on nuclear weapons, and too conservative and unresponsive to particular constituencies. Reagan's manner and wit served him well, and he delivered the best lines. When Carter accused Reagan of opposing Medicare, Reagan responded with "There you go again," suggesting that the charge was old and tired. In his closing remarks, Reagan asked, "Are you better off than you were four years ago?" Carter's gaff was to refer to a conversation he had with his daughter, Amy, "I had a discussion with my daughter, Amy, the other day, before I came here, and to ask her what the most important issue was. She said she thought nuclear weaponry, and the control of nuclear arms." This comment was not received positively and attracted post-debate criticism. In all, despite a competent job by President Carter, Reagan benefited more from the debate by offering a positive and optimistic vision, by presenting himself as tempered and reasonable, and by alienating some fear that he would be dangerous as a president.

President Ronald Reagan versus former Vice President Walter Mondale, 1984

Two presidential debates and one vice presidential debate were held in 1984. Entering the election of 1984, Reagan's approval ratings were quite high, and he had a large lead in the campaign. The debates offered Mondale an opportunity to make up ground, and while they provided some help, it was insufficient to challenge the popular president. The first debate addressed domestic policy. A primary focus was the growing budget deficit. Mondale employed Reagan's line from the 1980 debate against him: "Mr. President, you said, 'There you go again.' ... You remember the last time you said that? ... You said it when President Carter said you were going to cut Medicare, and you said, 'Oh, no, there you go again, Mr. President.' And what did you do right after the election? You went out and tried to cut $20 billion out of Medicare. And so when you say, 'There you go again,' people will remember this, you know ... And people will remember that you signed the biggest tax increase in the history of the United States ... You've got a $260 billion deficit. You can't wish it away."[11] Mondale was well reviewed for an effective rhetorical performance, and President Reagan was described by some viewers as appearing tired and occasionally confused. In the second debate, about foreign policy, Reagan's most likely vulnerability would be his age and vitality. While Mondale could not gracefully, and likely would not have addressed these concerns in the debate, one of the questioners, Henry Trewhitt of the Baltimore Sun, did, with this exchange:

MR. TREWHITT: Mr. President, I want to raise an issue that I think has been lurking out there for 2 or 3 weeks and cast it specifically in national security terms. You already are the oldest president in history. And some of your staff say you were tired after your most recent encounter with Mr. Mondale. I recall yet that President Kennedy had to go for days on end with very little sleep during the Cuban missile crisis. Is there any doubt in your mind that you would be able to function in such circumstances?

THE PRESIDENT: Not at all, Mr. Trewhitt, and I want you to know that also I will not make age an issue of this campaign. I am not going to exploit, for political purposes, my opponent's youth and inexperience. [Laughter and applause] If I still have time, I might add, Mr. Trewhitt, I might add that it was Seneca or it was Cicero, I don't know which, that said, "If it was not for the elders correcting the mistakes of the young, there would be no state."

MR. TREWHITT: Mr. President, I'd like to head for the fence and try to catch that one before it goes over, but I'll go on to another question.

While the debate provided substantive exchanges illustrating their competing approaches to military and foreign policy approaches, the "Youth and inexperience" line was the most memorable, and likely, the most impactful moment of the debate. The vice presidential debate between Vice President George H. W. Bush and Congresswoman Geraldine Ferraro was historic in that it involved

---

11. Debate Transcript October 7, 1984. The First Reagan–Mondale Presidential Debate. Commission on Presidential Debates. http://www.debates.org/index.php?page=october-7-1984-debate-transcript.

the first female candidate for that office the opportunity to take the stage. Congresswoman Ferraro contributed one of the more memorable moments of the debate with her response to Bush on covert activities, "Let me just say, first of all, that I almost resent, Vice President Bush, your patronizing attitude that you have to teach me about foreign policy. I've been a member of Congress for six years; I was there when the embassy was held hostage in Iran, and I have been there and I've seen what has happened in the past several months; seventeen months of your administration."[12]

Vice President George H. W. Bush versus Governor Michael Dukakis, 1988

Two presidential debates and one vice presidential debate were held in 1988. The first Bush–Dukakis debate was uneventful and received limited post-debate coverage. Bush accused Dukakis of being too liberal, and Dukakis criticized Bush for his choice of the inexperienced Senator Dan Quayle as his running mate. The debate addressed values, drugs, and health care among other issues. Perhaps the most important point established in the debate was not done so by either debater, but by Peter Jennings in asking the following question:

> JENNINGS: Good evening, Mr. Vice President, Governor. Governor, one theme that keeps coming up about the way you govern—you've both mentioned leadership tonight, so I'd like to stay with that for a second. The theme that keeps coming up about the way you govern is passionless, technocratic.
>
> DUKAKIS: Passionless?
>
> JENNINGS: Passionless, technocratic, the smartest clerk in the world. Your critics maintain that in the 1960s your public passion was not the war in Vietnam or civil rights, but no-fault auto insurance. And they say in the 1970s you played virtually no role in the painful busing crisis in Boston. Given the fact that a president must sometimes lead by sheer inspiration and passion, we need to know if this is a fair portrait of your governing or if it is a stereotype. And if it isn't fair, give us an example of where you have had that passion and leadership that sometimes a president needs?

In the debate, Dukakis answered the question effectively and Bush rejected the notion that Dukakis was without passion. However, the question of Dukakis's passion was raised in a more memorable fashion in the second debate, as initiated by CNN's Bernard Shaw in a famous exchange, "Governor, if Kitty Dukakis were raped and murdered, would you favor an irrevocable death penalty for the killer?" Dukakis replied, "No, I don't, Bernard. And I think you

---

12. Debate Transcript October 11, 1984. The Bush-Ferraro Vice-Presidential Debate. Commission on Presidential Debates. http://www.debates.org/index.php?page=october-11-1984-debate-transcript.

know that I've opposed the death penalty during all of my life. I don't see any evidence that it's a deterrent, and I think there are better and more effective ways to deal with violent crime." The question was meant to give Dukakis an opportunity to show his emotional side, but his answer seemed to reinforce the notion planted in the first debate, that he was without passion. In a parody of the debate on the comedy program, *Saturday Night Live*, Jon Lovitz played Dukakis, telling himself "I can't believe I'm losing to this guy!" referring to George H. W. Bush, who bumbled and stumbled through both the real debate and the skit.

In the vice presidential debate, veteran Senator Lloyd Bentsen faced first-term and inexperienced Senator Dan Quayle. A major part of the democratic strategy was to place the focus on Quayle's lack of qualifications. Bentsen said, "This debate tonight is not about the qualifications for the vice presidency. The debate is whether or not Dan Quayle and Lloyd Bentsen are qualified to be president of the United States." When asked what he would do if he became president, Quayle suggested that "I have as much experience in the Congress as Jack Kennedy did when he sought the presidency." Bentsen's response was sharp and evoked a loud response from the live audience, "Senator, I served with Jack Kennedy, I knew Jack Kennedy, Jack Kennedy was a friend of mine. Senator, you are no Jack Kennedy." Quayle responded, "That was really uncalled for, Senator," to which Bentsen continued, "You are the one that was making the comparison, Senator, and I'm one who knew him well. And frankly I think you are so far apart in the objectives you choose for your country that I did not think the comparison was well-taken."

President George H. W. Bush, Governor Bill Clinton, Businessman Ross Perot, 1992

Four debates were held in 1992, three presidential debates and a vice presidential debate. For the first time, three candidates lined up in each of the debates. Also for the first time, a town hall format, entertaining questions from audience members was employed (in the second presidential debate). The Bush campaign considered Clinton vulnerable on issues of character, and sought to attack on that basis in the debates. In the first debate, Clinton and Bush attacked each other, while Perot, in a plain-spoken style with humor and wit emphasized his themes: government gridlock, national debt, and the influence of lobbyists. A majority polled after the debate picked Perot as the winner. The second debate introduced the town hall debate, wherein the candidates stood or sat on stools or walked around a stage surrounded by audience members, and answered questions offered by the audience. A particularly meaningful question, asked by an audience member, had a profound impact on the debate. The questioner asked, "Can we focus on the issues and not the personalities and the mud? I think there's a need, if we could take a poll here with the folks from Gallup perhaps, I think there's a real need here to focus at this point on the needs." Clinton answered, "I agree with him." The questioner then followed up with "Could we cross our hearts? It sounds silly here but could we make a commitment? You know, we're not under oath at this point but could you make a commitment to the citizens of the US to meet our needs, and we have many, and not yours again? I repeat that. It's a real need, I think, that we all have." Bush's answer seemed to hedge. He said he agreed in principle, but his first response was "I think it depends how you define it." Perot was unequivocal, "just no hedges, no ifs, ands and buts. I'll take the pledge because I know the American people want to talk about issues and not tabloid journalism. So I'll take the pledge and will stay on the issues." When asked "How has the national debt personally affected each of your lives?" Bush's answers were, "I think the national debt affects everyone...." then, "I'm sure it has, I love my grandchildren.... I want to think that they're going to be able to afford an education...." and "I'm not sure I get—help me with the question and I'll try to answer it." Perhaps the most discussed moment of the debate was a result not of an argument or statement, but a simple gesture. During the debate, Bush was caught by the camera and observed by the viewing audience looking anxiously at his watch. He seemed uncomfortable, disengaged, and anxious for the debate to end. The third debate tended to return to the pattern of the first debate, with Clinton and Bush exchanging barbs and attacks while Perot rose above the fray. The vice presidential debate involved Senator Al Gore (D), Vice President Dan Quayle (R), and Admiral William Stockdale. While Gore and Quayle engaged each other in an intense brawl characterized by interruptions and verbal attacks, Admiral Stockdale seemed ill prepared and unbelieving. In his introduction, he said, "Who am I? Why am I here? I'm not a politician—everybody knows that. So don't expect me to use the language of the Washington insider.... Why am I here tonight? I am here because I have in my brain and in my heart what it takes to lead America through tough times." Of the vigorous exchanges between Quayle and Gore, Stockdale commented, "I feel like I'm an observer at a ping pong game, where they're talking about well, you know, they're expert professional politicians that massage these intricate plots and know every nuance to 'em."

Senator Robert Dole (R) versus President Bill Clinton (D), 1996

The two presidential debates and the vice presidential debates of 1996 may have been most notable for their lack of notoriety. By 1996 presidential debates had become routine. Clinton's reelection campaign was going smoothly, and he was well ahead going into the debates. While the 1988 and 1992 campaigns, and the debates, had been contentious, negative, and at times, personal, the debates of 1996 were decidedly polite and respectful. This was true despite the feeling by the Dole campaign that Clinton was potentially vulnerable to character questions. President Clinton began the first debate with a tribute to Dole and a promise, "I want to begin by saying again how much I respect Senator Dole and his record of public service and how hard I will try to make this campaign and this debate one of ideas, not insults." Dole agreed to focus on issues. When prompted by moderator Lim Lehrer with the question, "Senator Dole, we've talked mostly now about differences between the two of you that relate to policy issues and that sort of thing. Are there also significant differences in the more personal area that are relevant to this election?", Dole answered, "Well, my blood pressure is lower, my weight, my cholesterol, but I will not make health an issue in this campaign. So I think he's a bit taller than I am. But I think there are personal differences. I mean, I'm not I don't like to get into personal matters. As far as I'm concerned, this is a campaign about issues." Clinton successfully set the agenda for the debate with his allusion to Reagan's famous challenge of 1980. Clinton said, "We are better off than we were four years ago. Let's keep it going." While Dole challenged that premise, and much of the debate was about just that, polls indicated that voters tended to agree.

The second debate, on October 16, 1996, between Clinton and Dole received the lowest viewership for a presidential debate in history. Only 36.3 million people watched. The debate was broadcast opposite a major league baseball playoff game between the St. Louis Cardinals and the Atlanta Braves. Following the town hall format established in the second 1992 debate, but with only two participants, the tone of the debate was tempered by the audience and the context. One concern about Dole was his age (76), as expressed by an audience question from a college student, "...concerning you, Mr. Dole. All the controversy regarding your age. How do you feel you can respond to young voices of America today and tomorrow?" Before reviewing issues relevant to young voters, Dole answered, "Well, I think age is very—you know, wisdom comes from age, experience and intelligence. And if you have some of each— and I have some age, some experience and some intelligence—that adds up to wisdom. I think it also is a strength. It's an advantage." Famously, Clinton followed up with the statement which was the most often quoted debate line after the debates, "I can only tell you that I don't think Senator Dole is too old to be president. It's the age of his ideas that I question."

Many expected Vice President Al Gore and Senator Jack Kemp to serve as surrogate "attack dogs" in their debate. Of course, Gore had established an aggressive persona in his debate in 1992 with Dan Quayle. Kemp, a retired football quarterback for the Buffalo Bills, was known to be assertive as well. However, the tone and content of their debate was also respectful and focused primarily on policy issues. Gore opened with "I think we have an opportunity tonight to have a positive debate about this country's future. I'd like to start by offering you a deal, Jack. If you won't use any football stories, I won't tell any of my warm and humorous stories about chlorofluorocarbon abatement." Kemp responded, "It's a deal. I can't even pronounce it."

Vice President Al Gore versus Governor George W. Bush, 2000

The three debates between Vice President Al Gore and Governor George W. Bush in 2000 could be described in a word as *acrimonious*. Much of this tone of tension was due to the style and nonverbal communication of Gore. In the first debate, he was animated. During the debate, he was noticed sighing heavily and appearing exasperated while Governor Bush spoke. In the second debate, Gore was subdued; however, in the third debate, he was aggressive, even belligerent. It was during this third debate, a town hall debate, that while Bush was making a response, Gore walked over to him, approaching closely so as to invade the personal space of Bush and threaten what Bush described as a body or chest bump. In 2000, the country enjoyed the prospect of a substantial and long-term budget surplus. Much of the content of the debates centered around what to do with the surplus. In the first debate, Gore compared his plan with that of Bush, "Under Governor Bush's tax cut proposal, he would spend more money on tax cuts for the wealthiest 1% than all of the new spending that he proposes for education, health care, prescription drugs and national defense all combined. Now, I think those are the wrong priorities. Now, under my proposal, for every dollar that I propose in spending for things like education and health care, I will put another dollar into middle class tax cuts. And for every dollar that I spend in those two categories, I'll put $2 toward paying down the national debt.... And I also think it's very important to go to the next stage of welfare reform...." Gore emphasized the importance of protecting Medicare, "under my plan I will put Medicare in an iron clad lockbox and prevent the money from being used for anything other than Medicare." To this, Bush responded, "... look, this is a man who has great numbers. He talks about numbers. I'm beginning to think not only did he invent the Internet, but he invented the calculator. It's fuzzy math." The terms "lockbox" and "fuzzy math" became the most often-quoted language from the debates.

The debates also revealed a predisposition later realized under the Bush presidency. On foreign policy, in the second debate, Bush said, "The coalition against Saddam has fallen apart or it's unraveling, let's put it that way. The sanctions are being violated. We don't know whether he's developing weapons of mass destruction. He better not be or there's going to be a consequence should I be the president. But it's important to have credibility and credibility is formed by being strong with your friends and resolute in your determination." Jim Lehrer asked of Governor Bush, "Saddam Hussein, you mean, get him out of there?" and Bush responded, "I would like to, of course, and I presume this administration would as well. We don't know—there are no inspectors now in Iraq, the coalition that was in place isn't as strong as it used to be. He is a danger. We don't want him fishing in troubled waters in the Middle East. And it's going to be hard, it's going to be important to rebuild that coalition to keep the pressure on him." In the vice presidential debate, Cheney posited that "...it's unfortunate we find ourselves in a position where we don't know for sure what might be transpiring inside Iraq. I certainly hope he's not regenerating that kind of capability, but if he were, if in fact Saddam Hussein were taking steps to try to rebuild nuclear capability or weapons of mass destruction, you would have to give very serious consideration to military action to—to stop that activity. I don't think you can afford to have a man like Saddam Hussein with nuclear weapons in the Middle East."

While the presidential debates were acerbic at times, the vice presidential debate was surprisingly peaceful. After negative polling from the first debate, former defense secretary Dick Cheney and Senator Joe Lieberman had been warned against attacking or belligerent debate styles as producing unwanted audience effects. Although the most common single word evident in their answers was "disagree" in their debate, these disagreements were expressed in a consistently civil and respectful tone. The debaters were seated at a table for the debate, an arrangement Cheney credited for making the exchanges less contentious. In a memorable exchange, Cheney won the laugh lines while Lieberman again referenced Reagan's 1980 challenge of "are you better off...?"

> LIEBERMAN: Dick Cheney must be one of the few people who think nothing has been accomplished in the last eight years. Promises were made and promises were kept. Has Al Gore—did Al Gore make promises in 1992? Absolutely. Did he deliver? Big time. If I may put it that way. That's the record. Look at the 20—look at the 22 million new jobs. Look at the 4 million new businesses. Look at the lower interest rates, low rate of inflation, high rate of growth. I think if you asked most people in America today that famous question that Ronald Reagan asked, "Are you better off today than you were eight years ago?" Most people would say yes. I'm pleased to see, Dick, from the newspapers that you're better off than you were eight years ago, too.

> CHENEY: I can tell you, Joe, the government had absolutely nothing to do with it. (LAUGHTER) (APPLAUSE)

> MODERATOR: This question is to you.

> LIEBERMAN: I can see my wife and I think she's thinking, "I wish he would go out into the private sector."

> CHENEY: I'm going to try to help you do that, Joe.

Gallup analysis indicates that the 2000 debates did have an impact on voter's behaviors. According to Gallup,

> ...across the entire 2000 debate period, the race shifted from an 8-point lead for Gore to a 4-point lead for Bush. Other campaign factors may have come into play to cause this, but Gallup analysts at the time assigned at least some of the shift to the debates themselves. Gore had been consistently ahead in the race (among registered voters) for most of September and October prior to the first debate, whereas Bush generally remained in the lead in most Gallup polling after the third and final debate. (The race tightened up in the last few days before Election Day, with Gore moving into a 1- to 2-point lead among registered voters.) Gore won the popular vote, but he might also have won the Electoral College vote had his 8-point pre-debate-period lead not slipped away in the last few weeks of the campaign.[13]

13. Saad, L. (2008, September 25). Retrieved from http://www.gallup.com/poll/110674/ Presidential-Debates-Rarely-GameChangers.aspx?version=print.

President George W. Bush versus Senator John Kerry, 2004

The campaign debates of 2004 did not produce any particularly memorable zingers or gaffes but they did provide the opportunity to recognize substantial and substantive differences in the philosophies and positions of the President and Senator Kerry. They were the first debates held during wartime (wars were ongoing in Iraq and Afghanistan) and the competing narratives offered stark differences in their interpretations of the role of the United States in the world, the role of the president in a democratic government, and the difference between what it meant to be liberal or conservative.[14] Three presidential debates and one vice presidential debate were held. The first of the presidential debates was held at the University of Miami. Much of the debate centered on the decision to invade Iraq, the progress of the war effort, and what Bush portrayed as inconsistency by Kerry in his support for the war. These issues were layered and nuanced. Kerry argued that the initiation of the war on Iraq by the president was "a colossal error of judgment." His reasons included that the invasion was insufficiently supported by a coalition of allies, that "we had Saddam Hussein trapped" and that he (Hussein) was not linked to the attacks of 9/11. Kerry argued that "Saddam Hussein didn't attack us. Osama bin Laden attacked us. Al Qaeda attacked us," to which the President responded defensively, "... of course I know Osama bin Laden attacked us. I know that."

Kerry also argued that war had been initiated without an exit plan or plan to "win the peace," and that Iraq served as a diversion from the War on Terror, which was centered in Afghanistan with Osama bin Laden, and that the wars were being mismanaged by the administration. Kerry said, "... Iraq is not even the center of the focus of the war on terror. The center is Afghanistan, where, incidentally, there were more Americans killed last year than the year before...." Bush responded, "...of course, Iraq is a central part in the war on terror. That's why Zarqawi and his people are trying to fight us. Their hope is that we grow weary and we leave...." Kerry's response was, "The president just talked about Iraq as a center of the war on terror. Iraq was not even close to the center of the war on terror before the president invaded it." President Bush defended the war actions based on resolute and decisive actions. Eleven times he referred to the "hard work" necessary to defend the nation, "We've done a lot of hard work together over the last three and a half years. We've been challenged, and we've risen to those challenges. We've climbed the mighty mountain. I see the valley below, and it's a valley of peace. By being steadfast and resolute and strong, by keeping our word, by supporting our troops, we can achieve the peace we all want." This statement stood in juxtaposition to Kerry's statement, "I believe in being strong and resolute and determined. And I will hunt down and kill the terrorists, wherever they are. But we also have to be smart.... And smart means not diverting your attention from the real war on terror in Afghanistan."

---

14. Majdik, Z., Kephart III, J., & Goodnight, G., "The Presidential Debates of 2004: Contested Moments in the Democratic Experiment," *Controversia*, 2009; 6(1): 13–38.

As for Kerry's alleged inconsistency, Bush charged, "I think what is misleading is to say you can lead and succeed in Iraq if you keep changing your positions on this war. And he has. As the politics change, his positions change. And that's not how a commander in chief acts." Kerry replied, "I wasn't misleading when I said he was a threat. Nor was I misleading on the day that the president decided to go to war when I said that he had made a mistake in not building strong alliances and that I would have preferred that he did more diplomacy. I've had one position, one consistent position, that Saddam Hussein was a threat. There was a right way to disarm him and a wrong way. And the president chose the wrong way." Bush then followed with, "The only thing consistent about my opponent's position is that he's been inconsistent. He changes positions. And you cannot change positions in this war on terror if you expect to win."

If there was a gaffe in the first debate it was Kerry's statement that "no president, through all of American history, has ever ceded, and nor would I, the right to preempt in any way necessary to protect the United States of America. But if and when you do it, Jim, you have to do it in a way that passes the test, that passes the *global test* where your countrymen, your people understand fully why you're doing what you're doing and you can prove to the world that you did it for legitimate reasons." In the debate, Bush only responded that he did not know what the *global test* meant; however, after the debate, as pointed out by Majdik et al., "it was the global test that became the punch line, eliciting that the senator, underneath his glib debating style, had betrayed his multilateralism ... inclinations. The phrase appeared to be a godsend for the republicans. A **global test** was just the opposite of the strong-willed version of leadership championed by the Bush campaign."[15] Interestingly, Bush lost the nonverbal communication battle in debate 1 by adopting some of the behaviors while off camera which had hurt his opponent, Al Gore, in the 2000 debates. Bush tended to appear annoyed and dismissive of Senator Kerry. Bob Shrum quoted newspapers as describing the president as *agitated, unhappy, distracted, scowling*, and *grimacing*. He also leaned over the podium.

The vice presidential debate followed. The debate between Vice President Dick Cheney and Senator John Edwards was as tense and confrontational as the 2000 vice presidential debate had been relaxed and congenial. The two sparred contentiously on the Iraq war and other policy issues, while Edwards sought to defend Kerry and attack the president. The debate got personal when Cheney attacked Edwards's record in the senate, "And Senator, frankly, you have a record in the Senate that's not very distinguished. You've missed 33 out of 36 meetings in the Judiciary Committee, almost 70 percent of the meetings of the Intelligence Committee. You've missed a lot of key votes: on tax policy, on energy, on Medicare reform. Your hometown newspaper has taken to calling you 'Senator Gone.' You've got one of the worst attendance records in the United States Senate. Now, in my capacity as vice president, I am the president of

15. Majdik, Z., Kephart III, J., & Goodnight, G., "The Presidential Debates of 2004: Contested Moments in the Democratic Experiment," *Controversia*, 2009; 6(1): 13–38.

Senate, the presiding officer. I'm up in the Senate most Tuesdays when they're in session. The first time I ever met you was when you walked on the stage tonight." Edwards later claimed that this charge (that they had not met) was false. In the debate, he defended his record, "That was a complete distortion of my record. I know that won't come as a shock." In response to a question about same-sex unions, Edwards made reference to Cheney's daughter Mary, "... let me say first that I think the vice president and his wife love their daughter. I think they love her very much. And you can't have anything but respect for the fact that they're willing to talk about the fact that they have a gay daughter, the fact that they embrace her. It's a wonderful thing. And there are millions of parents like that who love their children, who want their children to be happy." Although seething, Cheney remained cool, and when given the opportunity by moderator Gwen Ifill to respond, he said, "Well, Gwen, let me simply thank the senator for the kind words he said about my family and our daughter. I appreciate that very much." Ifill replied, "That's it?" Cheney confirmed, "That's it." And Ifill continued, "OK, then we'll move on to the next question."

Going into the second debate, a town hall debate, Bob Shrum, Kerry campaign advisor, identified two priorities. First, Kerry must "retain the quality of strength and [be] presidential while connecting with the audience." The second priority identified by Shrum was to "raise the salience of domestic issues, the question of who will fight for the middle class."[16] Liz Cheney, daughter of Vice President Dick Cheney and advisor to the Bush–Cheney 2004 campaign, identified three objectives for Bush–Cheney (for all debates). First, they sought to "demonstrate ... a forward-leaning agenda"; second, to "demonstrate that [they] had a coherent strategy to win the global war on terror, and for [them], that included the war on Iraq." And their final goal was to "pass the living room test and to make clear to the people watching that they would feel comfortable having [them] in their living rooms for the next four years."[17] The second debate included 21 references to taxes, 24 references to health care, and substantial discussion of faith and cultural values issues. When asked about funding for abortions, Kerry positied, "... I cannot tell you how deeply I respect the belief about life and when it begins. I'm a Catholic, raised a Catholic. I was an altar boy. Religion has been a huge part of my life. It helped lead me through a war, leads me today.

But I can't take what is an article of faith for me and legislate it for someone who doesn't share that article of faith, whether they be agnostic, atheist, Jew, Protestant, whatever. I can't do that." The third debate covered a wide range of issues, but with a focus on domestic and values issues, from immigration, to abortion, social security, health care, taxes, jobs, education, trade, gun control, affirmative

16. Shrum, B., "Debate Strategy and Effects." In K. H. Jamieson (Ed.), *Electing the President 2004: The Insider's View* (Philadelphia: The University of Pennsylvania Press, 2006), pp. 114–123.

17. Cheney, L., "Debate Strategy and Effects." In K. H. Jamieson (Ed.), *Electing the President 2004: The Insider's View* (Philadelphia: University of Pennsylvania Press, 2006), pp. 123–130.

action, faith, and the Defense of Marriage Act. In reference to this last issue, Moderator Bob Schieffer asked each of the candidates, "Do you believe homosexuality is a choice?" Bush answered "You know, Bob, I don't know. I just don't know. I do know that we have a choice to make in America and that is to treat people with tolerance and respect and dignity. It's important that we do that." Kerry's answer was much discussed and may have cost him when he said, "We're all God's children, Bob. And I think if you were to talk to Dick Cheney's daughter, who is a lesbian, she would tell you that she's being who she was, she's being who she was born as. I think if you talk to anybody, it's not choice."

In each of the 2004 presidential debates, Kerry was declared the winner by insta-polls. However, the post-debate spin each time favored Bush. So without significant zingers, and with the only gaffes being Edwards's and Kerry's (poorly received) references of the vice president's daughter and her sexual orientation, Bush seemed to benefit more from the debates than did Kerry.

Senator John McCain v. Senator Barack Obama, 1984

The presidential and vice presidential debates of 2008 were historic for some of the same reasons the entire campaign and the election were historic. The Democratic candidate, Senator Barack Obama, was the first person of color nominated by a major party, and Governor Sarah Palin, the vice presidential nominee for the Republican Party, was only the second woman to be nominated by a major party as candidate for that position. In addition, during the primaries, candidates participated in 47 debates, providing a unique "practice season" for Obama, his running mate, Senator Joe Biden, and the republican nominee for president, Senator John McCain. Surprisingly, of the three presidential and one vice presidential debates, viewership was highest for the vice presidential debate, placing substantial focus on the least well known and least conventional of the candidates, Governor Palin. Interventions into Iraq and Afghanistan continued along with the War on Terror against Al Qaeda, and as the debates neared, a major financial crisis emerged. On the week of the first scheduled presidential debate, the senators rushed to Washington to respond to the financial crisis by crafting what would become the Emergency Economic Stabilization Act of 2008, the law which established TARP, the Troubled Asset Relief Program. This legislation originally authorized federal expenditures of $700 billion (later reduced) to purchase "toxic" assets and equities and to make funds available to major financial institutions so that credit would remain available and the economy could continue to operate. McCain announced that he had suspended his campaign and suggested that the first debate be delayed. Some tentative agreement was reached on Thursday, allowing Obama and McCain to travel to Mississippi for the Friday, September 26th debate.[18] The Bill was signed on October 3.

Obama held a lead in the polls going into the debates. However, as the relatively young and inexperienced senator, a part of his objective was to appear

---

18. "Bailout Collapse Endangers Presidential Debate," *Associated Press Worldstream* (September 26, 2008 Friday 6:32 AM GMT). Retrieved from www.lexisnexis.com/hottopics/lnacademic.

presidential and qualified in contrast to the veteran legislator, McCain. Obama had campaigned against the unpopular outgoing President George W. Bush and attempted to tie his opponent, as the Republican nominee and veteran senator, to the failed policies of the Bush administration. That strategy would continue into the debates. McCain walked a tightrope between the incumbent strategy of endorsing the Bush legacy to maintain support of the GOP base, and embracing a challenger strategy of differentiating himself from recent republican policy in favor of new directions. Indeed both Obama and McCain offered platforms of change.

The first debate, originally intended to address issues of foreign policy, began with a series of questions regarding the financial crisis and the bailout plan. The formats had been tweaked to encourage more direct interaction and development of arguments. As Jarman explained, "The Commission on Presidential Debates (2007) proposed a major innovation for the 2008 debates. Consistent with prior calls to improve the quality of the debates, the Commission proposed that each focus on a single area (foreign policy or domestic policy) and be divided into eight ten-minute segments." The moderator would then follow up with questions designed to create direct engagement of the candidates with each other on the segment topic, with the goal to increase the informative value of the debates.[19] The first question addressed the Economic Recovery Plan. Moderator Jim Lehrer asked, "Gentlemen, at this very moment tonight, where do you stand on the financial recovery plan?" Obama offered a four-prong test:

> Number one, we've got to make sure that we've got oversight over this whole process; $700 billion, potentially, is a lot of money. Number two, we've got to make sure that taxpayers, when they are putting their money at risk, have the possibility of getting that money back and gains, if the market—and when the market returns. Number three, we've got to make sure that none of that money is going to pad CEO bank accounts or to promote golden parachutes. And, number four, we've got to make sure that we're helping homeowners, because the root problem here has to do with the foreclosures that are taking place all across the country.

While the tests offered by Obama were not likely to be controversial, he was able to introduce himself as involved in the legislative process and qualified on the most threatening issue at hand. He also introduced an important theme of his campaign, Wall Street versus Main Street, and the connectedness of McCain and the Bush legacy. He argued, "... although we've heard a lot about Wall Street, those of you on Main Street I think have been struggling for a while, and you recognize that this could have an impact on all sectors of the economy. Now, we also have to recognize that this is a final verdict on eight years of failed economic policies promoted by George Bush, supported by Senator McCain." Obama was

---

19. Jarman, J. W., "The Effects of Format Changes on Viewers' Perceptions of Arguments Made by Obama and McCain in the 2008 Presidential Debates," *Conference Proceedings— National Communication Association/American Forensic Association* (Alta Conference on Argumentation), 2010, pp. 202–210.

also able to remind viewers of a recent gaffe by McCain in what set up a humorous exchange, while Lehrer attempted to encourage direct confrontation by the candidates:

OBAMA: …10 days ago, John said that the fundamentals of the economy are sound.

LEHRER: Say it directly to him.

OBAMA: I do not think that they are.

LEHRER: Say it directly to him.

OBAMA: Well, the—John, 10 days ago, you said that the fundamentals of the economy are sound. And….

MCCAIN: Are you afraid I couldn't hear him? (LAUGHTER)

LEHRER: I'm just determined to get you all to talk to each other. I'm going to try.

McCain answered in part by breaking from the recent policies of Bush and the Republican Party. He argued that "…we Republicans came to power to change government, and government changed us." He developed his consistent theme of controlling government spending, arguing that as "a fundamental difference between myself and Senator Obama. I want to cut spending. I want to keep taxes low. The worst thing we could do in this economic climate is to raise people's taxes." He charged that earmarks (individual spending projects passed by Congress) serve as "… a gateway to out-of-control spending and corruption" and proposed a "spending freeze on everything but defense, veteran affairs and entitlement programs." Obama responded that "The problem with a spending freeze is you're using a hatchet where you need a scalpel," and defended the importance of certain underfunded programs including education. Obama continued to link McCain and Bush, arguing to McCain, "John, it's been your president who you said you agreed with 90 percent of the time who presided over this increase in spending. This orgy of spending and enormous deficits you voted for almost all of his budgets." McCain's defense was to celebrate his persona as a "maverick" who did not fall in line with party policy. "It's well-known that I have not been elected Miss Congeniality in the United States Senate nor with the administration. I have opposed the president on spending, on climate change, on torture of prisoner, on—on Guantanamo Bay. On a—on the way that the Iraq War was conducted. I have a long record and the American people know me very well and that is independent and a maverick of the Senate and I'm happy to say that I've got a partner that's a good maverick along with me now." Issues discussed included Iraq, Afghanistan, the nature of engagement with world leaders, including rogue leaders, Russia, Energy and Homeland security. While both campaigns had worked to raise the expectations of their opponents, Obama seemed to meet or exceed expectations for his performance, establishing himself as credible and "presidential."

The vice presidential debate followed, on October 2, and drew the most attention of the four debates. This was due in part not only to scheduling, but also to the drama of the participation of Sarah Palin. The Alaska governor was a surprise selection by McCain as running mate. Relatively unknown on the national stage, Palin quickly garnered attention through nationally televised interviews with journalists Charles Gibson and Katie Couric. In both, she committed gaffes, which brought into question her preparedness and qualifications for national office. Also impacting negative attention toward Palin was an ongoing parody of her by *Saturday Night Live* comedian Tina Fey. Despite this negative attention, Palin was dynamic and personable, a fiery speaker in favor of conservative reform with the capacity to excite audiences with her folksy and direct manner. She offered an attractive and younger complement to the McCain ticket and generated genuine enthusiasm as well as criticism. Her opponent would be veteran Senator Joe Biden. While Palin's challenge in the debate was to establish herself as credible, Biden's goal was to attack the McCain candidacy as a continuation of failed Bush and Republican party policy, and to avoid making Palin a hero by patronizing her. He also had a history of misspeaking, so it was important for him to avoid gaffes. The debate offered the potential for high drama as well as comedy. Expectations for Palin could not have been much lower, while Biden's credibility as a debater was quite high prior to the debate.

What materialized was a success for both candidates. Biden was competent and persuasive in defending Obama and attacking McCain. He avoided gaffes and was careful not to speak down to Palin. Palin was homespun. She avoided gaffes by sticking to her themes and talking points; therefore, exceeding the (admittedly low) expectations for her performance.

Interestingly, the moderator for the debate was Gwen Ifill of PBS. It was released on the day prior to the debate that she had authored a book, *The Breakthrough: Politics and Race in the Age of Obama* to be released on inauguration day, January 20, thus causing a potential conflict of interest as her book sales might be enhanced if Obama succeeded and won the election. Post-debate review of Ifill was complimentary and evenhanded.

Keeping the tone folksy, Palin began the debate by addressing Biden, "Hey, can I call you Joe?" She worked to separate McCain and herself from linkage to Bush–Cheney with, "I've joined this team that is a team of mavericks with John McCain, also, with his track record of reform, where we're known for putting partisan politics aside to just get the job done…. We're tired of the old politics as usual. And that's why … we need to send the maverick from the Senate and put him in the White House, and I'm happy to join him there." To the charge that McCain's foreign policy would be a continuation of that of Bush, Palin continued, "Positive change is coming…. Reform of government is coming. We'll learn from the past mistakes in this administration and other administrations…. That's what John McCain has been known for in all these years. He has been the maverick. He has ruffled feathers." Biden replied, "Look, past is prologue, Gwen. The issue is, how different is John McCain's policy going to be than George Bush's? I haven't heard anything yet … let's talk about the maverick John McCain is. And, again, I love him. He's been a maverick on some issues, but he has been no maverick on the things that matter to people's lives."

Palin worked to reveal herself as an experienced reformer with connected-ness to common folk. She argued, "I think a good barometer here, as we try to figure out has this been a good time or a bad time in America's economy, is go to a kid's soccer game on Saturday, and turn to any parent there on the sideline and ask them, "How are you feeling about the economy?" She continued her folksy identification with "... let's commit ourselves just every day American people, Joe Six Pack, hockey moms across the nation, I think we need to band together and say never again. Never will we be exploited and taken advantage of again by those who are managing our money and loaning us these dollars," and "I think we need a little bit of reality from Wasilla Main Street there, brought to Washington, DC.... Just every day, working-class Americans saying, you know, government, just get out of my way."

Biden responded in part by revealing his own working-class background, "... all you've got to do is go down Union Street with me in Wilmington or go to Katie's Restaurant or walk into Home Depot with me where I spend a lot of time and you ask anybody in there whether or not the economic and foreign policy of this administration has made them better off in the last eight years. And then ask them whether there's a single major initiative that John McCain differs with the president on ... walk with me in my neighborhood, go back to my old neighborhood in Claymont, an old steel town or go up to Scranton with me. These people know the middle class has gotten the short end. The wealthy have done very well. Corporate America has been rewarded. It's time we change it. Barack Obama will change it." Palin responded with one of her more oft-quoted lines, "Say it ain't so, Joe, there you go again pointing backwards again. You prefaced your whole comment with the Bush administration. Now doggone it, let's look ahead and tell Americans what we have to plan to do for them in the future ... our schools have got to be really ramped up in terms of the funding that they are deserving. Teachers needed to be paid more. I come from a house full of school teachers. ... and here's a shout-out to all those third graders at Gladys Wood Elementary School, you get extra credit for watching this debate." Ifill later said, "Everybody gets extra credit tonight."

On energy, Palin touted both her environmental protection and promotion of oil resources in Alaska, but most memorably said, "The chant is 'drill, baby, drill.' And that's what we hear all across this country in our rallies because people are so hungry for those domestic sources of energy to be tapped into." And on taxation, Palin argued "I do take issue with some of the principle there with that redistribution of wealth principle that seems to be espoused by you. Barack's plan to tax increase affecting only those making $250,000 a year or more, you're for-getting the millions of small businesses that are going to fit into that category." Biden contrasted the term "redistribution with 'fairness,' We don't call a redistri-bution in my neighborhood Scranton, Claymont, Wilmington, the places I grew up, to give the fair to say that not giving Exxon Mobil another $4 billion tax cut this year as John calls for and giving it to middle class people to be able to pay to get their kids to college, we don't call that redistribution. We call that fairness number one. Number two fact, 95 percent of the small businesses in America, their owners make less than $250,000 a year. They would not get one single solitary penny increase in taxes, those small businesses."

Post-debate polls confirmed that Biden was perceived to have done the best job of debating and seemed more qualified to serve as president, that both exceeded expectations, and that Palin was more likable.[20] Ninety-five percent of those polled said they believed Ifill to be fair.

The second presidential debate was a town hall debate, and was considerably more contentious in tone than the first debate. Obama continued to link McCain to the unpopular Bush administration, "I think everybody knows now we are in the worst financial crisis since the Great Depression…. And I believe this is a final verdict on the failed economic policies of the last eight years, strongly promoted by President Bush and supported by Senator McCain…." McCain suggested that Obama's tax proposals were unclear, arguing, "… nailing down Senator Obama's various tax proposals is like nailing Jell-O to the wall." In a reference to McCain's campaign bus, Obama responded "…we're not going to solve Social Security and Medicare unless we understand the rest of our tax policies. And you know, Senator McCain, I think the "Straight Talk Express" lost a wheel on that one." In an odd reference, McCain offered an unusual reference to Obama when he said, "… it was an energy bill on the floor of the Senate loaded down with goodies, billions for the oil companies, and it was sponsored by Bush and Cheney. You know who voted for it? You might never know. That one [referencing Obama]." An hour of the hour and a half debate focused on domestic policy and the economy.

On the day of the third debate, scheduled to cover domestic policy, the Dow Jones Industrial Average dropped 733 points, the second biggest one-day point loss ever. McCain was significantly behind in the polls, and needed an outstanding and novel performance in the debate to gain ground. While McCain started strong, by the end of the debate, perception was that Obama had survived the McCain attacks. The debaters clashed over issues of abortion rights, taxes, health care, and the economy and regulation. Obama continued to attempt to connect McCain to the unpopular administration of President Bush. In one of his most memorable lines, McCain responded "Senator Obama, I am not President Bush. If you wanted to run against President Bush, you should have run four years ago. I'm going to give a new direction to this economy in this country."

McCain attempted to attack the character of Obama by raising questions about his association with ACORN (Association of Community Organizations for Reform Now) and Bill Ayers associated with the radical group, the Weather Underground. McCain made the ACORN association. "We need to know the full extent of Senator Obama's relationship with ACORN, who is now on the verge of maybe perpetrating one of the greatest frauds

---

20. CNN, "Debate Poll Says Biden Won, Palin Beat Expectations," *CNN Politics.Com.* N.p., 2008, Web. 9, July 2012.

in voter history in this country, maybe destroying the fabric of democracy." Obama responded in part, "ACORN is a community organization. Apparently what they've done is they were paying people to go out and register folks, and apparently some of the people who were out there didn't really register people, they just filled out a bunch of names. It had nothing to do with us. We were not involved. The only involvement I've had with ACORN was I represented them alongside the U.S. Justice Department in making Illinois implement a motor voter law that helped people get registered at DMVs." Regarding the attempted association with Bill Ayers, Obama explained, "Mr. Ayers has become the centerpiece of Senator McCain's campaign over the last two or three weeks. This has been their primary focus. So let's get the record straight. Bill Ayers is a professor of education in Chicago. Forty years ago, when I was 8 years old, he engaged in despicable acts with a radical domestic group. I have roundly condemned those acts. Ten years ago he served and I served on a school reform board that was funded by one of Ronald Reagan's former ambassadors and close friends, Mr. Annenberg. Other members on that board were the presidents of the University of Illinois, the president of Northwestern University, who happens to be a Republican, the president of the *Chicago Tribune*, a Republican-leaning newspaper. Mr. Ayers is not involved in my campaign. He has never been involved in this campaign. And he will not advise me in the White House. So that's Mr. Ayers."

Significant in the third debate was McCain's reference to a plumber named Joe Wurzelbacher. He became the narrative in support of each side's tax proposals, often referred to as "Joe the Plumber." McCain introduced the situation, "Joe wants to buy the business that he has been in for all of these years, worked 10, 12 hours a day. And he wanted to buy the business but he looked at your tax plan and he saw that he was going to pay much higher taxes. You were going to put him in a higher tax bracket which was going to increase his taxes, which was going to cause him not to be able to employ people, which Joe was trying to realize the American dream ... when Senator Obama ended up his conversation with Joe the plumber—we need to spread the wealth around. In other words, we're going to take Joe's money, give it to Senator Obama, and let him spread the wealth around." Obama's explanation in reply was, "...the conversation I had with Joe the plumber, what I essentially said to him was, "Five years ago, when you were in a position to buy your business, you needed a tax cut then. And what I want to do is to make sure that the plumber, the nurse, the firefighter, the teacher, the young entrepreneur who doesn't yet have money, I want to give them a tax break now...Not only do 98 percent of small businesses make less than $250,000, but I also want to give them additional tax breaks, because they are the drivers of the economy. They produce the most jobs." Joe the Plumber became well known through the use of his case as an illustration of the impact of policy changes by Obama and McCain, but it seemed to fail McCain in the debate based on the reactions of viewers in post-debate polls and analysis.

V. THE FUTURE OF CAMPAIGN
DEBATES AS DEBATES

Presidential debates are now an essential component of campaign communication. While they do not follow formats focusing direct clash as in academic or parliamentary debate, they do offer unique opportunities to test the candidates and their ideas in a simultaneous public forum under the scrutiny of large and interested audiences. An example of the link between academic policy debate and political campaign debates may be seen in the successful work of Brett O'Donnell, former director of debate for Liberty University. O'Donnell built the Liberty University debate team into a national championship program in the ADA, CEDA, and the NDT. Since that, he has coached President George W. Bush in his debates against John Kerry in 2004, as well as Senator John McCain, Representative Michelle Bachmann, and Governor Mitt Romney. He has been credited with significant contributions to the rise of Representative Bachmann early in the GOP primary debates in 2011, and with assisting Romney in successful performances during the Florida GOP primary debates in 2012. He was called the "The Candidate Whisperer" by the *Washington Post*.[21] Mark McKinnon, advisor to Bush and McCain, observed in the same article that debates "are often the best and sometimes only shot to make a broad impression .... Michele Bachmann used her first debate to break out of the pack and win the Iowa straw poll. And during the last debate, she furiously attacked Rick Perry at every turn with great discipline and got herself back on the map. And I assume Brett gets a good degree of credit for both." Mark Wittington of Yahoo reported of O'Donnell's work with Romney in Florida, "Mitt Romney's two solid debate performances in Florida are credited with turning around his campaign, which in turn earned him a double-digit win in that state's primary. Brett O'Donnell is credited with helping Romney sharpen his debate skills."[22]

Campaign debates may help to inform the viewing public, prepare the candidates for office, and guide future debate and policy. It is likely that they are the most direct merger of academic and applied debate, and are certainly among the most meaningful, and, they are likely to continue to be a critical and routine feature of campaign communication. Presidential debates will be replicated at every level of campaign activity with similar results. Primary debates in 2012 were instrumental in winnowing the field of republican candidates and in sharpening the talking points and presentation skills of Governor Romney entering the general election campaign. While the debates indeed do offer a valuable exercise in participatory democracy, they should be appreciated for what they

21. Gardner, Amy, "The Candidate Whisperer: The Man Behind Michele Bachmann," the *Washington Post* [Sheffield, Iowa] 21 September 2011, n. pag. Print. http://www.washingtonpost.com/lifestyle/style/the-candidate-whisperer-the-man-behind-michele-bachmann/2011/09/21/gIQARXgEmK_story.html.
22. Wittington, Mark. "Romney Debate Coach Fired for Being Too Good at His Job." *Yahoo! News* (04 February 2012), n. pag. Print. http://news.yahoo.com/romney-debate-coach-fired-being-too-good-job-184700169.html.

are without criticism for what they are not. They are *not* games or contests, and are not focused on particular decision making about a proposition. By most measures, they are *not* debates. They offer too much opportunity for candidates to avoid in-depth discussion and direct clash. However, for viewers and pundits to ask "who won?" is to ask the wrong question. Rather, focus should be placed on "what did we learn?" And in each debate, opportunities to learn about the candidates, their philosophies, and their ideas emerge.

EXERCISES

1. Visit http://www.pbs.org/newshour/debatingourdestiny/teacher_guide. html, discuss "debate: helpful or useless?"

2. Visit http://www.pbs.org/newshour/debatingourdestiny/index.html, match the debate quotes.

3. Test your presidential debate knowledge at http://edition.cnn.com/2008/ POLITICS/09/24/debate.quiz/index.html.

4. Read a transcript of a debate and/or view the debate at http://www. debates.org/index.php?page=debate-history.

   a. Prepare a flow sheet of the debate. On what issues did the most substantive clash occur? What arguments were "dropped" by either debater?

   b. Identify the most important issues addressed by the candidates. Which candidate "won" the debates on each (be sure to justify your evaluations)?

   c. Which debater made the best opening statement? Which made the best closing statement? Justify your evaluation.

   d. Based on your analysis of the arguments as presented, which candidate "won" the whole debate? Why?

5. If available in your library, view the following videotape: *Debating Our Destiny: 40 Years of Presidential Debate*, MacNeil/Lehrer Productions in association with the Commission on Presidential Debates, WETA, and Thirteen/ WNET. Washington, D.C.: MacNeil/Lehrer Productions, Alexandria, VA: Distributed by PBS Video, © 2000. Or read the transcript of the program at http://www.pbs.org/newshour/debatingourdestiny/dod_full_transcript. html. Also, view Debating our Destiny II, available at http://www.pbs.org/ newshour/debatingourdestiny/index.html.

6. View or read any presidential or VP debate and write a ballot, answering the question "who did the better job of debating?" and defending your answer.

7. In what ways was the third 2008 presidential debate between Obama and McCain like an academic debate? In what ways was it different? Would a different format have created a better debate? In what ways? Why?

8. Visit the following websites:

    The History of Televised Presidential Debates at http://www.museum.tv/
    debateweb/html/index.htm
    Commission on Presidential Debates at http://www.debates.org/
    Create a timeline tracing the history of presidential campaign debates. Note
    significant occurrences on the timeline.

9. In 2000, Ralph Nader, the Green Party candidate for president, was not
    invited by the Commission on Presidential Debates to participate in the
    presidential debates. Should the standard for participation in presidential
    debates be reconsidered to include third-party candidates? Write an essay
    defending your answer. You may wish to visit: Open Debates at http://
    opendebates.org/.

10. If you had been able to coach any of the candidates for their presidential or
    vice-presidential debates, how would you have advised them to change their
    argumentation on any of the issues raised? Prepare a briefing book to guide
    the candidate debaters (for an example, visit http://www.heritage.org/
    research/features/issues/).

11. Create a debate at Generation Engage, www.generationengage.org.

12. Prepare a question for a YouTube debate.

19

Applied Parliamentary Debate

Applied parliamentary debate refers to the use of parliamentary procedure as a set of guiding principles and rules for debate within organized bodies for the purpose of decision making. This kind of debate occurs in governmental bodies, civic organizations, clubs, and professional and work groups. Whenever a group finds it necessary or desirable to hold a formal debate in which decisions are made, some rules for that debate may be provided to ensure order, efficiency, and impartiality. Rules for parliamentary debate are intrinsically democratic, focusing debate and decision making in a fair way such as to ensure that all voices are heard and that substantial minorities are not shut out of the discussion and decision process. The law courts have special rules for debates conducted in the courtroom; the governing body of each city, town, or village conducts its debates under a special set of rules, as do the state legislatures and Congress; civic, social, and business organizations have special sets of rules governing debate. Parliamentary debate permits a large number of persons to participate and provides a means for a large group to reach a decision.

Parliamentary debate derives its name from the parliaments of Britain, but the details of parliamentary debate, however, vary from one group to another. The rules of debate for the British Parliament are different in many ways from the rules of debate in the U.S. Congress. The rules of debate in the Senate, for example, are far too complicated and specialized for general use by other organizations. In fact, they are different in important respects from the rules of debate in the House of Representatives. The NPDA, APDA, and World's debating competitions offer special rules for academic parliamentary debating (see Chapter 17). The foundational model for Applied Parliamentary Procedure is the historical text *Robert's Rules of Order*, now in its 11th edition.[1] This is the source upon

---

1. Robert, H. M. I., Evans, W. J., Honemann, D. H., and Balch, T. J. *Robert's Rules of Order*, revised 11th edition (Philadelphia: Da Capo Press, 2011).

which the National Association of Parliamentarians bases its opinions and instruction.[2] According to the "Official Robert's Rules of Order Website,"

> [General] Henry Martyn Robert was an engineering officer in the regular Army. Without warning he was asked to preside over a public meeting being held in a church in his community and realized that he did not know how. He tried anyway and his embarrassment was supreme. This event, which may seem familiar to many readers, left him determined never to attend another meeting until he knew something of parliamentary law.
>
> Ultimately, he discovered and studied the few books then available on the subject. From time to time, due to his military duties, he was transferred to various parts of the United States, where he found virtual parliamentary anarchy, since each member from a different part of the country had differing ideas of correct procedure. To bring order out of chaos, he decided to write *Robert's Rules of Order....*

All well-conceived rules of parliamentary debate have a common nature and certain common purposes, including the following:

1. *Parliamentary debate provides for the orderly and efficient conduct of business.* It does so by considering one matter at a time and by disposing of each matter before going on to another.

2. *Parliamentary debate assures a decision.* It does so by requiring that every motion be acted on in some way. Once a motion has been introduced, it must be passed, defeated, or postponed. A postponement, of course, is a decision not to pass a motion at the present time.

3. *Parliamentary debate protects the rights of the majority.* It does so by providing that the decisions of a sufficient number of members must prevail.

4. *Parliamentary debate protects the rights of the minority.* It does so by giving the minority many important privileges. For example, any member, without the necessity of securing a second, has the right to be heard on many important matters; only two members are required to introduce any motion; and one-third of the members plus one can exercise important restraints.

5. *Parliamentary debate is impartial.* Because the rules of procedure apply equally to all members, each member has an equal right to be heard and has equal voting power.

6. *Parliamentary debate serves to focus discussion.* At any moment during a rule-based parliamentary debate, discussion is relevant and germane to the item under consideration, whether it be the substance of a motion or the procedure upon which the motion will be considered. This ensures efficient (if seemingly cumbersome), relevant, and organized debate about the key points to be decided.

---

2. http://parliamentarians.org/procedure.php?cid=107 (May 20, 2012). Retrieved from National Association of Parliamentarians.

I. SOURCES OF PARLIAMENTARY DEBATE RULES

Although often based on Robert's Rules of Order which is frequently referenced as a reference or source, most organizations design their own unique set of rules for discussion. Thus, parliamentary debate in general has no one set of universally applied rules, although a body of commonly accepted practices and some legal requirements tend to be recognized. As has been indicated, the two branches of Congress do not debate under the same rules. (Note the "filibuster rule" which allows Legislators in the US Senate to prevent consideration of pending legislation with the support of 40 of 100 votes, while the House of Representatives has eliminated such an option). The faculty and student governments of a university undoubtedly operate under different rules of parliamentary debate; and even two different clubs probably conduct their debates under somewhat different rules. Where, then, do the rules of parliamentary debate for each body come from? Members of each group must adopt or create their own rules. If the decisions made by the group are of particular importance—for example, the decisions of a legislative body or a corporation—prudence dictates that those conducting the meeting have on hand expert parliamentarians familiar with general usage and attorneys familiar with the special laws applicable to the particular organization. For example, state laws, which differ considerably from one state to another, often dictate the methods of voting that have to be used by corporations. For the average group, however, the problem is simpler. It is usually enough that its members follow one set of commonly accepted practices and make provision for their special needs. The rules of parliamentary debate for the average group come from five sources: (1) the constitution of the organization, (2) the bylaws of the organization, (3) the standing rules of the organization (which are recorded in the minutes of the organization), (4) the agenda of the meeting (although not necessary, an agenda is often convenient), or (5) another stipulated source.

With the exception of national and state legislative bodies, few organizations attempt to write their rules of parliamentary debate in full. Rather, most organizations provide a set of rules to take care of their most obvious needs and special requirements and then stipulate some source as the basis for rules not otherwise provided. Small groups, for instance, could stipulate the rules presented in the table on pages 406–407 as the source of their rules, or reference a source such as the National Association of Parliamentarians, or Parliamentary Procedure online. Larger[3] groups, or groups likely to be confronted with complicated problems, would select one of the various books devoted entirely to parliamentary procedure as the stipulated source of their rules.

Sometimes the special requirements of an organization make it desirable to set aside common usage in parliamentary practice. Groups that meet annually or infrequently might take from the motion to adjourn its customary privileged status and give it the lowest possible priority. This provision is usually unnecessary

---

3. *Parliamentary Procedure Online.* (n.d.). Retrieved from http://parlipro.org/.

for groups that meet weekly, but it is often advisable for groups that meet only at infrequent intervals or in situations in which a hastily passed motion to adjourn might seriously inconvenience the organization. Although deviations from common practice are sometimes desirable or necessary, they should be made rarely and only after careful consideration of all their implications.

II. THE ORDER OF BUSINESS

The usual order of business for an organization using parliamentary procedure follows a clear, logical pattern.

1. *Call to order.* The call to order is usually a simple announcement by the chair: "The meeting will be in order" or "The National Convention of the Democratic [or Republican] party is now in session."

2. *Roll call.* A roll call is taken only if one is required by the rules or customs of the organization. A roll call is a useful device in a larger organization; most smaller organizations find it unnecessary. The roll call may be helpful in identifying the percentage of eligible voting members present at the meeting to confirm the representatives' ability to do business on behalf of the organization or group (that is, a "quorum" may be necessary) and to clarify the number of votes required to establish a majority or super majority.

3. *Reading of the minutes of the previous meeting.* The minutes are usually read by the secretary in smaller organizations, although this reading may be omitted by unanimous consent. Larger organizations and many smaller organizations find it convenient to have the minutes printed or duplicated and distributed to the membership. Once the minutes have been presented, they may be corrected, amended, or accepted.

4. *Reports of standing committees.* Most organizations have various committees that are established by the constitution or whose duties continue for a long period of time, such as the executive committee or the finance committee. These committees report at this time.

5. *Reports of special committees.* Most organizations also have various committees that are appointed to serve for a shorter period of time or to deal with a specific issue, such as a special fund-raising committee or the committee to recommend a site for next year's convention. These committees report at this time.

6. *Unfinished business.* Unfinished business is that business not completed at the previous meeting. For example, if a motion was on the floor at the time the previous meeting adjourned, that motion now comes before the assembly as unfinished business. A motion that was postponed at a previous meeting, by a motion to postpone temporarily or "lay on the table," may be brought before the assembly at this time by a motion to resume consideration to "take from the table." The motion to postpone to a particular time often specifies that the motion shall come before the assembly as unfinished business at the next meeting.

7. *New business.* Once the unfinished business has been disposed of, the floor is open to new business.

8. *Miscellaneous.* The last matter of business includes announcements and other miscellaneous items that may come before the group, such as "The executive committee will meet at eight o'clock" or "Members wishing to obtain tickets for the annual outing should see Debbie Jones after this meeting."

9. *Adjournment.* Once the business of the meeting is completed, the chair may ask for a motion to adjourn. Such a motion may, however, be introduced earlier.

Larger organizations, or organizations that have many items of business to consider, find it convenient to prepare an agenda. An *agenda* is a special order of business, drawn up in advance of the meeting, that takes precedence over the usual order of business. The agenda may be changed by passage of a motion setting a special order of business. The agenda often includes a detailed statement of the order in which reports will be presented and motions considered. When an organization's meetings extend over more than one day, it is desirable to indicate ahead of time which matters will be considered on each day.

III. PRESENTATION OF MOTIONS

Motions are proposals for consideration of the group. When motions are in order, a member who wishes to make a motion must first obtain recognition from the chair. To gain recognition, the member rises and addresses the presiding officer: "Mr. Chairman" or "Madam Chairwoman." (If the constitution of the organization provides for a chairperson, the form of address is then "Mr. Chairperson" or "Ms. Chairperson.") The chair grants recognition by addressing the member; "Tina" would suffice in an informal group, and "Ms. Smith" or "The delegate from Massachusetts" in a more formal group. If the member's name is not known, the chair may ask, "Will the member state her name?" The member replies, "Tina Smith, delegate from Massachusetts." In granting recognition, the chair replies, "The chair recognizes Ms. Smith from Massachusetts" (the chair always speaks in the third person and never says, "I recognize....").

When several members seek recognition at the same time, the chair must decide which one to recognize. In granting recognition, the chair should consider the following factors:

1. Priority should be given first to the maker of the motion.

2. Priority should be given alternately to speakers favoring and opposing the motion if they are known to the chair. If the chair does not know which speakers favor or oppose the motion, he or she may state, "The chair will recognize a speaker favoring [or opposing] the motion."

3. Priority should be given to a member who has not spoken previously.

4. If none of the other considerations apply, the chair should, when possible, recognize the member who first sought recognition.

Once a member has gained recognition, he or she states the motion by saying, "I move that...." In many organizations a member is required to give the secretary a written copy of the motion at the time it is introduced. The secretary has the privilege, should it be necessary, of interrupting a member to request a restatement of the motion so that it may be entered into the minutes accurately.

Before a main motion may be debated, it must be seconded by another member. Any other member, without the necessity of being recognized, may state, "I second the motion." If the motion is not seconded immediately, the chair may ask, "Is there a second?" If there is no second, the chair announces, "The motion is lost for lack of a second." The motion is then no longer before the assembly, and a new motion is in order. If the motion is seconded, the chair announces, "It has been moved and seconded that...." and then recognizes the proposer of the motion to speak on that motion.

IV. PRECEDENCE OF MOTIONS

In the interests of order and efficiency, a definite order of precedence of motions is followed. As shown in the table on pages 406-407, the main motion has zero, or lowest, precedence, because it may be introduced only when no other business is before the house. Once a main motion is before the house, any of the other motions, when appropriate, may be applied to it. The highest precedence—1—is given to a motion to fix the time of the next meeting, and the other privileged motions follow this motion in precedence. The incidental motions rank after the privileged motions in precedence but have no precedence among themselves; they are considered in the order in which they arise. The subsidiary motions follow the incidental motions in precedence and have a definite order of precedence among themselves. The table of precedence lists the motions most often used in parliamentary debate and the preferred rules applying to these motions. Some of the rules may be modified by special circumstances.

V. PURPOSES OF MOTIONS

The four types of motions—main, subsidiary, incidental, and privileged—have different purposes, as outlined in detail here.

A. Main Motions

Main motions bring substantive proposals before the assembly for consideration and decision. Main motions are the core of the conduct of business; they are the most important and most frequently used motions. Main motions are the plan by which the maker of the motion seeks to attain an objective. This may be very simple, such as a motion directing the treasurer to pay a small sum to the Scholarship Fund, or very complex. If the motion is other than very simple, you will

Table of Precedence of Parliamentary Motions

Once a main motion is before the meeting, any of the following motions, when appropriate, may be made. In the following table the motions are arranged from the strongest—1—to the weakest—0. A stronger motion takes precedence over any weaker motion and becomes the business before the meeting.

Precedence Number	Interrupt Speaker?	Require a Second?	Debatable?	Vote Required?	Amendable?	Subject to Referral to Committee?	Subject to Postponement?	Subject to Reconsideration?
Privileged Motions								
1. Fix time of next meeting	No	Yes	No	Maj.	Yes[1]	No	No	No
2. Adjourn	No	Yes	No	Maj.	No	No	No	No
3. Recess	No	Yes	No	Maj.	Yes	No	No	No
4. Question of privilege	Yes	No	No	Chr.	No	No	No	No
Incidental Motions								
Incidental motions are of equal rank among themselves; they are considered in the order they are moved.								
5. Appeal decision of the chair	Yes	Yes	Yes	Maj.	No	No	Yes	Yes
5. Close nominations	No	Yes	No	2/3	Yes	No	No	No
5. Division of the house	Yes	No	No	None	No	No	No	No
5. Object to consideration	Yes	No	No	2/3	No	No	No	No
5. Parliamentary inquiry	Yes	No	No	None	No	No	No	No
5. Point of order	Yes	No	No	Chr.	No	No	No	No
5. Suspension of rules	No	Yes	No	2/3	No	No	No	No
5. Request for information (Will the speaker yield for a question?)	Yes	No	No	Chr. or speaker	No	No	No	No
5. Withdraw a motion	No	No	No	Maj.	No	No	No	No

Subsidiary Motions

6. Postpone temporarily (lay on the table)	No	Yes	No	Maj.	No	No	No	No
7. Vote immediately (previous question)	No	Yes	No	2/3	No	No	No	No
8. Limit or extend debate	No	Yes	No	2/3	Yes	No	No	No²
9. Postpone to a specified time	No	Yes	Yes	Maj.	Yes	No	No	No
10. Refer to the committee	No	Yes	Yes	Maj.	Yes	No	No	No
11. Refer to the committee of the whole	No	Yes	Yes	Maj.	Yes	No	No	No
12. Amend an amendment	No	Yes	Yes	Maj.	No	Yes	Yes	Yes
13. Amend	No	Yes	Yes	Maj.	Yes	Yes	Yes	Yes
14. Postpone indefinitely	No	Yes	Yes	Maj.	No	No	No	No

Main Motions

Main motions are of equal rank among themselves. They have zero precedence since they may not be considered when any other motion is before the house.

0. General main motion	No	Yes	Yes	Maj.	Yes	Yes	Yes	Yes
0. Reconsider	Yes	Yes	Yes	Maj.	No	No	Yes³	No
0. Rescind	No	Yes	Yes	2/3⁴	Yes	Yes	Yes	Yes
0. Resume consideration (take from table)	No	No	No	Maj.	No	No	No	No
0. Set special order of business	No	Yes	Yes	2/3	Yes	No	No	Yes

1. Although the motion is not debatable, the amendment may be debated.
2. Motion may be renewed after a change in the parliamentary situation.
3. May be postponed to a specified time only.
4. Only a majority is required if previous notice has been given.

find it helpful to review the "Basic Plan Format" in Chapter 11. Main motions include the following:

General main motion: To bring new business before the meeting.

Reconsider: To stop all action on a motion previously voted until the motion has been reconsidered. This motion may be made by any member (unless the rules of the organization specifically establish some limitation), but it may be made only on the same day as the original motion was passed or on the next business day of a convention—not at the next weekly or monthly meeting or at the next convention. A motion to reconsider cannot be applied to a matter that has left the assembly. For example, if a motion has been passed directing the treasurer to pay $50 to the Scholarship Fund and if the treasurer has already paid that money, the motion cannot be reconsidered. If carried, the motion to reconsider places the motion previously voted on in the exact status it had before it was voted on. If defeated, the motion to reconsider may not be renewed.

Rescind: To cancel an action taken at some previous meeting. This motion may be made at any time when other business is not before the meeting; it cannot be applied to a matter that has left the assembly.

Resume consideration (take from the table): To bring a temporarily postponed motion (a motion that had been laid on the table) before the meeting in the same state that the motion held before it was postponed temporarily.

Set special order of business: To set a date or time at which a certain matter will be considered.

B. Subsidiary Motions

Subsidiary motions are alternative aids for changing, considering, and disposing of the main motion. Consequently they are subsidiary to the main motion. Examples of subsidiary motions include the following:

Postpone temporarily (lay on the table): To postpone consideration of a matter. This device may be used to allow more urgent business to come before the assembly or to allow time for some members to gather additional information before voting. It is also a way of "sidetracking" a matter in the hope that it will not be taken up again.

Vote immediately (previous question): To close debate and bring the matter before the meeting to an immediate vote.

Limit or extend debate: To set or extend a limit on debate on a matter before the meeting.

Postpone to a specified time: To delay action on a matter before the meeting until a specified time.

Refer to committee: To refer a matter before the meeting to a committee. If applied to an amendment, this motion also takes the main motion with it. It may be used to secure the advantage of having the matter studied more carefully by a small group or to delay action on the matter.

Refer to the committee of the whole: To refer a matter to the committee of the whole, in order to debate the matter "off the record" and in the greater informality of the committee of the whole.

Amend an amendment: To amend an amendment to a motion before the meeting. Most organizations find it advisable to prohibit an amendment to an amendment.

Amend: To change a motion. A motion to amend may take any of four forms: (1) amend by striking out, (2) amend by substitution, (3) amend by addition, or (4) amend by dividing the motion into two or more parts.

Postpone indefinitely: To suppress the main motion to which it is applied without the risk of adopting the main motion. This device is sometimes used to identify, without the risk of adopting the motion, who favors and who opposes it.

C. Incidental Motions

Incidental motions arise only incidentally out of the business before the assembly. They do not relate directly to the main motion but usually relate to matters that are incidental to the conduct of the meeting. Types of incidental motions include the following:

Appeal decision of the chair: To secure a reversal of a ruling by the chair.

Close nominations: To prevent nomination of other candidates. Voting is not limited to those candidates who have been nominated.

Division of the house: To require a standing vote.

Object to consideration: To prevent consideration of a matter.

Parliamentary inquiry: To allow a member to ascertain the parliamentary status of a matter or to seek parliamentary information.

Point of order: To demand that the chair rule on an alleged error, mistake, or violation of parliamentary procedure.

Suspension of rules: To suspend rules to allow procedure contrary to certain rules of the organization.

Request for information: To allow a member to ask the chair—or, through the chair, the speaker who has the floor—for information on a matter before the meeting.

Withdraw a motion: To prevent action on a motion before the meeting.

D. Privileged Motions

Privileged motions have no direct connection with the main motion before the assembly. They relate to the members and to the organization rather than to substantive proposals. They deal with matters so urgent that they are entitled to immediate consideration. Privileged motions would be main motions except for their urgency. Because of their urgency, they are given the privilege of being considered ahead of other motions that are before the house. Privileged motions include motions to do the following:

Fix time of next meeting: To fix a time at which the group will meet next.

Adjourn: To close the meeting. This motion is also used to prevent further consideration of a matter before the meeting.

Recess: To suspend the meeting temporarily.

Question of privilege: To request the chair to rule on a matter relating to the privileges of the assembly or the privileges of an individual member.

VI. UNANIMOUS CONSENT

To expedite business on a routine or obviously desirable matter, any member may ask that approval for a certain course of action be given by unanimous consent. The chair will ask, "Is there any objection?" and then, if no objection is made, will announce, "Hearing none, it is so ordered." If any member objects, the required parliamentary procedure must be followed.

EXERCISES

1. List the organizations to which you belong that conduct their business through parliamentary debate. Evaluate the effectiveness of each group in parliamentary debate. Identify differences in rules and procedures for debate between or among these groups.

2. From your experiences in groups that conduct their business through parliamentary debate, can you recall an instance when the will of the majority was defeated by a minority better versed in parliamentary procedure? Prepare a brief report of this instance.

3. Select a motion for parliamentary debate, and hold a debate on this proposition in class.

4. Conduct a debate using the same arrangement suggested in Exercise 3. This time, by prearrangement with your instructor, select a small group of students who will seek to secure passage of the motion; select a second small group of students who will seek to defeat the motion. The majority

of the class will be uncommitted on the proposition at the start of the debate.

5. Conduct a debate using the same arrangement suggested in Exercise 4. This time, the supporters of the motion will be instructed to use every possible parliamentary motion in order to "railroad" the passage of the motion. The opponents of the motion will be instructed to use every possible parliamentary motion in order to obstruct or defeat passage of the motion. The class will probably encounter some difficult problems in this exercise. In working your way out of these problems—with some help from the instructor, who will serve as parliamentarian when needed—you will gain practical experience in parliamentary procedure.

6. Arrange to conduct a model congress in class. Elect a speaker and a clerk. Your instructor will serve as parliamentarian. Before the class meets, each student will prepare a bill on a subject that would be suitable for consideration by the Congress of the United States at the present time. Prepare enough copies of your bill for each member of the class and for your instructor. Distribute copies of your bill at the first meeting of the class as a model congress. Prepare bills in the following form:

   a. They must be printed, duplicated, and double-spaced on a single sheet of white, 8½ × 11-inch paper.
   b. The first line will consist of these words: "Congress Bill Number."
   c. The second line will consist of these words: "by [your name]."
   d. Commencing with the third line, the title of the bill must be stated, beginning with the words "AN ACT" and containing a statement of the purpose of the bill.
   e. The text of the bill proper must begin with the words "BE IT ENACTED BY THE MODEL CONGRESS." The material following must begin with the word "That." Each line of the material that follows must be numbered on the left margin of the page, beginning with "1."
   f. Every section will be numbered commencing at "1." No figures will be used in the bill except for the numbers of sections and lines. No abbreviations will be used.
   g. The following form is an illustration of the prescribed form for drafting bills.

Congress Bill Number_____
by Rick Rogers
AN ACT to make the United States energy independent by the year 2020.
BE IT ENACTED BY THE MODEL CONGRESS

1. Section 1. That the federal excise tax on gasoline be
2. increased by twenty-five cents a gallon effective thirty days
3. after this bill becomes law.
4. Section 2. That the federal excise tax on gasoline be
5. increased by an additional twenty-five cents a gallon
6. effective one year from the date this bill becomes law.
7. Section 3. That gasoline purchased for agricultural and
8. fishery purposes be exempt from this tax.
9. Section 4. That the ...

20

Public Debating

What defines a debate as "public" is primarily its audience. Most academic debates occur in small classrooms with few observers. They are typically heard by one or a panel of judges who are expert debate judges and strive to focus, in making their decisions, on the quality of evidence, argumentation, and clash presented, as tracked in a technical and systematic fashion on their flow sheets. Even in many applied debates—as courtroom judge trials, congressional, and applied parliamentary debates—the audiences are decision makers who are knowledgeable experts about the topics and the procedures. However, an extremely rewarding format for debates is the wide range of debate styles that occur for the benefit of a public audience. These audiences differ from those in expert or specific context debates because they tend to have more members who are less trained or experienced in evaluating debates. If decisions are to be made, they are less likely to be made on the basis of technical points of debating, but rather on general impressions and feelings about the propositions under discussion. The contract debates depicted in the movie *The Great Debaters* and *Presidential Campaign Debates* are examples. Public debates may occur in classrooms, in the blogosphere, in public auditoriums, or on television. They can be informational, entertaining, engaging, inspiring, dramatic, and spirited. This chapter offers several formats for public debates, and some tips for approaching them.

I. PUBLIC DEBATE FORMATS

When considering a public debate, planners generally are not limited by prescribed formats. Many events invent their own format, based on the nature of their needs and logistics. Just as with political campaign debates, participants must first agree on their format. Setting comes first, and will vary based on the

---

Miniglossary

Public debate   A type of academic or special debate in which the audience is made up of individuals who are not experts in debate.

Town Hall debate   A type of public debate in which a moderator or chair and two debate teams address two sides of a proposition and invite audience participation prior to determination of a winner.

Long Table debate   A type of public debate involving three two-person teams on each side of a question, alternating speeches by side such that each participant speaks once, and utilizing some rules of parliamentary debate, including points of information.

---

room or location used, the size of the audience, the number of debaters participating, and the desired outcomes of the debate. Should the speaker stand at a podium? This may be necessary if it is important that the speaker speak into a microphone or be in front of a fixed camera. Debaters may speak to their audience while seated or be able to move freely on a stage or floor. How many teams, how many debaters per team, order of speakers, length of speeches, nature of questioning periods, or rules for questions if allowed, whether to include audience questions, and many other factors must be decided. In addition, announcement of a proposition in advance of the event will generally help to attract an audience. Will the debate be moderated, and if there will be questions asked, as in political campaign debates, how will be questions be chosen and presented?

While policy debate, academic parliamentary debate, or Worlds debate formats may be adapted for public debates, the only limits on format tend to be the creativity of the planners. Some formats currently in use for reoccurring public debate events include the following.

A. Town Hall Format

The town hall format has been used at annual conventions of the National Communication Association, the Southern States Communication Association, and the Florida Communication Association, to name a few, to debate issues of professional interest. A variation has become commonplace in the presidential campaign debates (Chapter 18). This format may be used for any matter of interest to the participants and audience. A popular variation for campus debates provides for a student and a faculty member to serve as "kickoff" speakers for the motion and another student–faculty team to serve as "kickoff" speakers against the motion. (See the following format items 3–6.)

The town hall format may be organized as follows:

1. The chair opens the debate by announcing the motion before the house and reviewing the rules of procedure.
2. The chair introduces each of the four kickoff speakers in order.

3. The first advocate gives a 7-minute speech moving the adoption of the motion.

4. The second advocate gives a 7-minute speech opposing the motion.

5. The third advocate gives a 7-minute speech moving the adoption of the motion.

6. The fourth advocate gives a 7-minute speech opposing the motion.

7. The floor is then open to audience members, who may speak for no more than 3 minutes. The chair recognizes speakers alternately for and against the motion. Preference should be given to those who have not previously spoken.

8. The debate proceeds in this manner for usually not more than 60 minutes. The chair then permits each of the kickoff speakers to summarize the arguments, first against and then for the motion. The summary speeches last no more than 3 minutes each.

9. The chair calls for a division of the house (a vote) and announces the result.

The town hall format also has some special procedural guidelines:

1. All action on the floor is channeled through the chair. It is the prerogative of the chair to exercise his or her judgment in any action not explicitly covered in these regulations.

2. Any speaker except the maker of the motion may be interrupted at any time if a member wishes to call attention to a violation of the rules by "rising to a point of order" or wishes to question the speaker "on a point of information." The speaker may refuse to answer the question or even to give the member a chance to ask it. But he or she cannot refuse to yield for points of order. The time involved in stating the point of information is not charged against the speaker; the time consumed in giving the information is.

3. Only these points of order will be considered: Objections to the behavior of an audience member and objections that the speaker's remarks are irrelevant.

4. The timekeeper will give each speaker a 1-minute warning and a termination signal. Members must conclude their remarks on receiving the second signal.

5. Unused time may not be passed to a speaker on the same side.

6. The resolution before the house may not be amended.

The town hall format also has some special seating arrangements. Those favoring the motion at the beginning of the debate seat themselves to the chair's right; those opposed, to the chair's left. A section is provided for the undecided. If, as a result of the debating, at any time the sentiment of a member changes, the member then moves from undecided to decided or across the aisle and sits with the side he or she now favors.

B. Long Table Format

Since 2001, James Madison University in Harrisonburg, Virginia, has held a competitive public debate tournament in which audiences (not expert debate judges) help to determine event winners. Their format, referred to as the "long table format," is similar to the Worlds debating format. This is a portion of the event description from the 2012 Tournament.

Competition Format: The debate uses a "long table" format. This is a public debate. Last year there was an audience of around 500 people for the final round; preliminary rounds were smaller (audiences of 20–30 people). The "long table" format features three (two-person) teams on each side of the question. Speeches start with the affirmative and alternate between the affirmative and negative throughout the debate. Teams are randomly assigned to sides and speaker positions. In other words, if a team is selected to be the first affirmative, they will give the first two affirmative speeches in the debate. The first and last speeches on each side of the question are uninterruptible. Any member of the opposing team may interrupt the speeches in the middle of the debate in order to ask the speaker to yield to a question. Speakers are not required to answer these questions (although not answering questions may cause the audience to think that the speaker is "dodgy"). Please see the example format below for more information. You can view the 2010 final round at: http://www.jmu.edu/debate/madisoncup/2010. shtml.

Jury Adjudication Procedure: A three- to seven-member panel, or jury, will adjudicate the debate. Juries will be comprised of local residents, students, professors, distinguished JMU alumni, and special invited guests. At the completion of the debate, the panel will adjourn to discuss, deliberate, and decide upon the winners as a group. The jury votes for (two-person) teams, not sides of the question. In other words, first place could go to an affirmative team, while second place could be awarded to a negative team.

Example Debate Format: The 2004 final round proceeded as follows:

1st Affirmative Speech (Wake Forest #1): (4 minutes) uninterrupted

1st Negative Speech (George Mason #1): (4 minutes) uninterrupted

2nd Affirmative Speech (Wake Forest #2): (5 minutes) The first and last minute of the speech are uninterruptible. In the 2nd–4th minutes of the speech any opposition debater may ask the speaker to yield to a question. The speaker may accept or decline the question.

2nd Negative Speech (George Mason #2): (5 minutes) The first and last minute of the speech are uninterruptible. In the 2nd–4th minutes of the speech any opposition debater may ask the speaker to yield to a question. The speaker may accept or decline the question.

3rd Affirmative Speech (Georgetown # 1): (5 minutes) The first and last minute of the speech are uninterruptible. In the 2nd–4th minutes of the speech any opposition debater may ask the speaker to yield to a question. The speaker may accept or decline the question.

3rd Negative Speech (James Madison #1): (5 minutes) The first and last minute of the speech are uninterruptible. In the 2nd–4th minutes of the speech any opposition debater may ask the speaker to yield to a question. The speaker may accept or decline the question.

4th Affirmative Speech (Georgetown #2): (5 minutes) The first and last minute of the speech are uninterruptible. In the 2nd–4th minutes of the speech any opposition debater may ask the speaker to yield to a question. The speaker may accept or decline the question.

4th Negative Speech (James Madison #2): (5 minutes) The first and last minute of the speech are uninterruptible. In the 2nd–4th minutes of the speech any opposition debater may ask the speaker to yield to a question. The speaker may accept or decline the question.

5th Affirmative Speech (Mary Washington #1): (5 minutes) The first and last minute of the speech are uninterruptible. In the 2nd–4th minutes of the speech any opposition debater may ask the speaker to yield to a question. The speaker may accept or decline the question.

5th Negative Speech (Towson #1): The first and last minute of the speech are uninterruptible. In the 2nd–4th minutes of the speech any opposition debater may ask the speaker to yield to a question. The speaker may accept or decline the question.

6th Affirmative Speech (Mary Washington #2): (4 minutes) Uninterrupted

6th Negative Speech (Towson University #2): (4 minutes) Uninterrupted

The event website is available at http://www.jmu.edu/debate/madisoncup/.

C. Trojan Web Debates, University of Southern California

The University of Southern California Annenberg Digital Debate Initiative (ADDI), operated through the Trojan Debate Team, now sponsors an online debate tournament. The spring 2012 event is described below.

> The Trojan Web Debates will take place entirely online. Debaters will debate asynchronously in a one-on-one format by uploading a series of video speeches to YouTube, and then submitting the URL of their responses to the tournament director. The tournament director will compile the video submissions into a running video playlist for each debate—thus to follow the debate, competitors watch the playlist to which they are assigned. Every competitor will take part in two preliminary rounds of debate between April 2nd and April 6th. The top 25% of competitors (based on speaking points and win/loss records) after round two will qualify for an additional two rounds of competition between April 9th and April 13th. All debates will take place in English.
>
> At the start of the tournament each debater will be randomly assigned to two debates—one in which they will propose a political party that they believe presents the best options for the future, and one in which they will refute the political party suggested by their

opponent. Judging will take place at the conclusion of all speeches for week 1. Assignments will be delivered to competitors and judges via e-mail and posted via our Facebook page.

Students will be assigned to propose a political party in one debate (the role of proposition speaker) and oppose the party chosen by their opponent in another debate (the role of opposition speaker). When each schedule is released students will have their sides selected for them. Debaters will be expected to adhere to the following time constraints and format:

Proposition speaker's opening speech: 4 minutes

Opposition speaker's opening speech: 5 minutes

Proposition speaker's rebuttal: 3 minutes

Opposition speaker's rebuttal and closing remarks: 4 minutes

Proposition speaker's rebuttal and closing remarks: 2 minutes

Please note: Debaters whose videos are more than 30 seconds longer than the maximum length for any given speech will forfeit their debates.

The website for the Trojan Web Debates can be accessed at http://usctrojan debate.com/page/current-addi-events with a link to the USC Facebook page, offering updates on current status of events.

D. We the Students, University of Miami

Broadcasting students at the University of Miami in Coral Gables, Florida, produce an online interactive debate program involving student debaters on either side of an announced topic, addressing questions offered by the in-studio host as well as e-mailing or texting viewers. The program description:

We the Students is the nation's first interactive debate show. College debaters from top schools around the country participate in engaging interactive debates on today's most compelling issues. The show is streamed LIVE on the show's website, and incorporates live comments and questions from an online audience.

The website for the University of Miami, We the Students Program, is http://umtv.miami.edu/shows/we-the-students.

II. PUBLIC DEBATE TIPS

While any audience and context generates its own unique demands, and thus most rules for public debating must emerge organically from the event itself, some general guidelines are outlined below.

A. Know Your Audience

While by its nature, rhetorical argumentation demands that the speaker adapt his or her message to their audience, in debate before expert or experienced judges,

---

Tips for Public Debating

- Know your audience.
- Use effective public speaking.
- Tell stories.
- Find a theme and repeat it.
- Compare and contrast.
- Maintain a positive focus.
- Employ Commonplaces.
- Plan and prepare introductions and conclusions.
- Limit preparation time.
- The debate is always ON.
- Ask and Answer questions effectively.
- Don't tell the audience what to do; don't treat the flowsheet as a holy grail.
- Impact arguments in as personal a way as possible.
- Avoid debate jargon and reference to the game.

---

the judges will also work to adapt to the debaters. And, as discussed in Chapter 15, judges provide detailed descriptions of their judging philosophies to debaters prior to competition. The public audience has no such inclination. So based on prior research, demographic analysis, audience feedback, and educated guessing, the debaters are well advised to shape their performance and message to their audience. Debaters should consider the level of formality or potential for interaction with their audience, the likely values and attitudes of the audience, and audience interests and concerns. Debaters should provide necessary information to give context to their audience, but not spend time telling the audience what they already know. References and allusions must be relevant to and make sense to the audience based on knowledge and experience, and persuasive appeals should not stray far from belief and value systems.

B. Use Effective Public Speaking

While in most competitive academic debates, judge(s) will employ their knowledge and skill in debate and their knowledge about the topic to evaluate the debate while working to turn off their personal biases about the subject, no such practice will likely be employed by the lay audience. Expert judges are more likely to separation form from content, with a primary focus upon the quality of content guiding their decision rendering. Lay audiences will not easily make such a distinction, and thus their judgment will be based on an overall impression blending presentation and argumentation. All the characteristics of effective speaking (as reviewed in Chapter 16) are, thus, very important. While the most important characteristic is fit, delivery should be extemporaneous or impromptu, with very limited use of manuscript style. Reading, with the possible exception of brief quoted material, will drive a wedge between debater and audience. Debaters should find an appropriate tone for the context while building connectedness with audiences through sustained eye contact. They should express energy, sincerity, and conviction through vocal variation, movement, and facial expression. Confidence and familiarity with material will lead to ethos, helping to persuade the audience.

C. Tell Stories

The key here is more than just injecting some cute or meaningful anecdotes into a presentation. Effective proof achieves the purposes of making concepts clear to listeners and keeping them interested in addition to the obvious function of *proving* the point. Expert debate judges in evidence-based contexts are trained to focus on quoted evidence to establish logical support for debaters' arguments. This quoted evidence generally tends to be in the form of expert observation, conclusion, or explanation (quotes and testimony), statistics and results from empirical academic research, and factual description from journalistic or other reporters. It strives to maintain a rational objectivity and accomplish the proof function of support. Stories help to develop clarity and engagement. In her appropriately named book, *Whoever Tells the Best Story Wins*, Annette Simmons observes that "Storytelling transports people to different points of view so they can reinterpret or reframe what your facts mean to them."[1] Joanna Slan identified seven benefits to the speaker to using stories as support:

1. Stories get an audience listening.
2. Stories offer entertainment.
3. Stories provide a change of pace.
4. Stories teach but do not preach.
5. Stories bond the speaker and the audience.
6. Stories remind us of who we are.
7. Stories enhance memorability.[2]

D. Find a Theme and Repeat It

Audiences may be taking notes, but they are not likely to be flowing the debate in detail. They will track the debate and recall it holistically, one speech at a time. The debate proceeds for the lay audience in more of a vertical fashion than a horizontal one; in other words, each speech stands as an artifact of its own without detailed consideration of item by item, line by line clash.

---

1. Simmons, A., *Whoever Tells the Best Story Wins: How to Use Your Own Stories to Communicate with Power and Impact*, 1st ed. (New York: American Management Association, 2007), p. 14.
2. Slan, J., *Using Stories and Humor: Grab Your Audience* (Boston: Allyn and Bacon, 1998), pp. 19–25.

The audience will not award you an argument because your opponents "drop" it, or fail to respond. So the goal of an audience debater is less to win the game of debating and more to persuade an audience and leave them with a clear and positive memory of one or a few important themes or points. In the 2010 New York gubernatorial race, fringe candidate Jimmy McMillan made a name for himself by repeating at every opportunity the mantra of his party, "The rent is too damn high!" While he did not win, audiences remembered his point. An effective organizational approach in many public debates is to use organizational aids to *preview* a set of points to be made. "In this speech, I will tell you the three reasons why importation of foreign oil must stop immediately…," *signpost* the points as presented (My **FIRST** point is that reliance on relatively cheap foreign oil commits slows our transition to renewable energy…), and *review* the points in summary (So, the three reasons we must stop importation of foreign oil now are….).This provides clarity and repetition to the audience. If the ideas are constructed around a simple theme and worded in parallel structure, such an approach enhances audience memory through redundancy.

E. Compare and Contrast

The key for the debater is to present their arguments and positions in juxtaposition to their opponent's positions, offering reasons why theirs are better, but not relying on the audience to maintain a flowsheet. The effective advocate can increase the power of their own positions by diminishing the acceptability of their opponents' claims and improving their own.

F. Maintain a Positive Focus

Audiences appreciate comparisons, and will be entertained by hearty and spirited exchanges, but do not generally render decisions based on direct line-by-line clash as do expert judges. They like to make their own comparisons (and inevitably will do so), so the debater should spend more energy and time working to build up their own positions than tearing down their opponents'.

G. Employ Commonplaces

The sophists in ancient Greece used chunks of memorized materials, at the ready use of the speaker, to make points when appropriate. Familiarity with these portions of familiar materials helps the speaker appear competent and comfortable with their arguments. When political candidates give stump speeches, they rely on repeating portions of "the speech" while injecting new material and appropriate transitions and linking materials into the speech. These repeated bits of a speech, or planned and practiced portions of cases or arguments are commonplaces, and can be very useful to the public debater. Identify likely arguments you will need to or be able to make, prepare a number of minispeeches, practice and put them to memory for use in debates.

H. Plan and Prepare Introductions and Conclusions

The introduction should begin by gaining the positive attention of one's audience. The conclusion should reinforce the speaker's theme by providing psychological closure for the message. Introductions set the table for the speech, preparing the audience for engaged and supportive listening and establishing a positive relationship with them. Of course, it is the first impression generated, at least for that speech, and thus has importance of primacy. Effective attention getters include startling statistics, quotations or statements, and rhetorical questions. They should be brief, no more than 15 percent of speaking time. It is critical that the introduction be delivered well, so the speaker should set it to memory or deliver extemporaneously, maintaining 100 percent eye contact and emphatic and dynamic style. The conclusion may tie in to the attention getter, foreshadow what is to come as the debate proceeds, or offer a call to action. Like the introduction, the conclusion should be brief, no longer than 10 percent of speaking time, and should be planned and practiced.

I. Limit Preparation Time

Tournament debate offers scheduled preparation time, however, in audience debates, down time may diminish the credibility of the next speaker. Speakers should be ready to respond seemingly spontaneously, without any lengthy silent time while preparing.

J. The Debate is Always *ON*

Assume the audience is always watching, even when opponents or partners are speaking. So while sitting at the table of desk, listing to other speeches, and preparing for their own upcoming speeches, the debater should appear confident and determined, organized and calm. Reactions are noted, and may have important persuasive impact, so the slightly raised eyebrow or quizzical expression during an opponent's speech can provide just as much effective counterargumentation as direct response during a speech.

K. Ask and Answer Questions Effectively

Just as in participating in cross-examination (Chapter 13), asking and answering questions is an opportunity for the debate to make points. Do not grand stand, steal time, or make speeches, but do use the opportunity to provide strong support for your positions. Focus on asking questions you perceive the audience would like to ask themselves, and offer answers based not on strategy, but based on persuasive force over the audience.

L. Don't Tell the Audience What to Do; Don't Treat the Flowsheet as a Holy Grail

Tournament debate judges may be open to appeals by debaters to "vote for our side because our opponents dropped topicality." Such rules of the game will be far less compelling to the lay audience. Of course, one may argue that "since our opponents have not addressed the proposition, as our definitions of the term 'energy' have established, they have not proved that the proposition is true." Audiences will not award you an argument they do not find compelling, simply because your opponents failed to address it, nor will they forget an important argument made early in the debate even if it was not extended. Debaters should use notes or a flow to track the debate for their own purposes, but need not refer to it in a debate where the audience is not participating in flowing.

M. Impact Arguments in as Personal a Way as Possible

Impact in an audience debate is personal. Does the audience feel the pain of the dislocated refugees of war discussed in the affirmative's case? Do they recognize the implications of energy shortages for their own lives? It is the challenge of the debaters to persuade through the establishment of meaningful and important consequences or measures understood cognitively and emotionally by the audience.

N. Avoid Debate Jargon and Reference to the Game

Intuitively, the audience may be considering the components of a prima facie case, the competition of a counterplan, or the possible link turn to a disadvantage. But they don't know the words or theory behind such concepts. This becomes a problem for well-prepared debaters who are so familiar with debate conventions and language that they take it for granted. While debate rules and jargon provide shortcuts for debate practice, they only work if the participants are qualified and familiar with them. Audiences will not respond well to debate words and rules, but can be persuaded by the concepts if offered with explanations and accessible language.

EXERCISES

1. Have a debate on an announced proposition using a town hall format.
2. Have a debate on an announced proposition using a long table format.

APPENDIX **A**

Debate Quick Start

EVIDENCE-BASED TEAM TOPIC POLICY DEBATE

This set of steps assume that you will be debating in a standard Cross-Examination format (see Chapter 17) and that you will be assigned a proposition for debate.

1. With your partner, *analyze the proposition*. Who is the *agent* of action called for (U.S. federal government)? What is the prescribed *action*? Is there an *object* of the action identified? Are any qualifications limitations or directions placed upon the action?

2. *Review what you know about the topic* and *expand your knowledge* about the topic with general reading. Brainstorming, a Google search, and even Wikipedia may be helpful at this stage (for general information only). Some good starting places are CQ Researcher Plus Archive (especially the Pro/Con page), Opposing Viewpoints in Context, and ProCon (http://www.procon.org/).

3. *Prepare the first affirmative speech.* This means you will be advocating the action identified by the proposition and you will be the first to speak. You will need to prepare a complete first affirmative speech. Begin with a sentence outline, and then gather evidence (published quotes and statistics) to support your claims. To gather evidence, conduct database research, ideally through your college or university library. Collect and save quotes and quoted material as you would if you were writing a paper. The following five points make up a template to be filled in.

   a. Identify the *harm.* This is an imperfection marked by urgency, the harmful condition or "bad stuff," which will be addressed by the plan. For example, childhood obesity is threatening the lives and well-being of nearly 20 percent of American children.

b. Identify the *inherency*. This is reason the harm is likely to continue into the future. For example, public schools facing budget shortfalls have reduced physical activity by cutting physical education courses and serve high calorie, low quality food which is less expensive to the school.

c. Identify a *plan*. Be specific. This is your operational interpretation of propositional action, the action you will advocate. It is probably more specific than the action of the proposition, but must be a topical interpretation of that proposition. You should look for "solvency advocates," experts who advocate the affirmative program and provide evidence that it will work and have benefits. For example, the affirmative may advocate the programs of Michelle Obama that schools should engage increased mandatory physical activity by students, better healthy food options, and nutrition and health training.

d. Prove *solvency*. This is evidence to prove that implementation of the plan will achieve advantages and will reduce the harm identified earlier. For example, when a similar program was implemented in Everytown, USA, obesity was reduced to less than 5 percent, with associated reductions in diabetes, heart disease, cancer, and their related medical costs.

e. Prove *advantages*. List and prove the benefits of implementing your plan. For example, you may argue that reducing obesity results in higher test scores and academic achievement, ultimately increasing employment and contributions to society.

f. *Write it out.* Fill in the outline, supported with evidence, being careful to use signposts to make claims clear. Be efficient with words, utilizing enough explanation and transition to make your case easy to understand and record, but no more than necessary to do so. The most important part of the speech is the evidence.

4. *Prepare the affirmative defense.* Anticipate possible negative arguments to each of the points in your first affirmative speech. Brainstorm and record 3–5 answers to each possible argument and prepare response briefs, lists of evidenced arguments you can read in response to possible opposing arguments. Anticipate off-case arguments; disadvantage, topicality, counterplan, or critical arguments the negative may argue against your plan. Brainstorm and record 8–10 answers to each possible argument and prepare response briefs, lists of evidenced arguments you can read in response to possible opposing arguments.

5. *Prepare the negative strategy and materials.* Anticipate possible affirmative interpretations to the proposition, including as many plans as you can think of. For each, prepare a set of answers, and prepare a set of your own arguments.

a. *Mitigate or turn the harm.* Considering possible harms to be forwarded by the affirmative, create a set of evidenced answers to those harms which either deny the existence or the impact of the harm, reduce the existence or the impact of the harm, or argue that the harm is in fact not a bad thing, but a good thing, or that it leads to something good (case turn). For example, the statistics on childhood obesity are overblown and exaggerated, many obese children outgrow the condition, and the attention brought by discussion of childhood obesity has drawn attention to increased healthy food items at fast food restaurants and in schools, and more attention has been given to nutrition and activity, which are good things.

b. *Mitigate the inherency.* Be prepared to read prepared arguments that the inherency has been misdiagnosed or that the problem is not likely to continue at the same magnitude into the future and that a major policy is not necessary. For example, you may argue that the more important contributing causes to obesity are marketing and popularity of fast food and video games, but that recent attention to obesity has shifted behavior such that healthier lifestyle habits are being adopted.

c. *Challenge solvency.* Be prepared to read evidenced arguments that the specific affirmative proposal will not work, that it will not reduce the harm, or that it will be circumvented. For example, changing healthy eating and exercise habits at school do not succeed out of school.

6. Prepare negative *off-case positions.* These challenge the affirmative premises, but do not provide on-point argumentation to the affirmative case as presented. They constitute a sort of "negative case."

a. Argue *topicality.* Build arguments, based on your definitions and interpretation of the proposition, that the plan is not really a legitimate interpretation of the policy action called for in the proposition.

b. Make *disadvantage* arguments. These arguments point to the harmful side effects, or unintended and undesirable consequences of the plan. Every policy action has costs: disadvantages weigh those costs. For example, the 70-point White House plan to fight obesity costs money, and might divert attention from cognitive learning programs in school. And with increased physical activity will come increased sports injuries, including concussions.

c. Advocate a *counterplan.* A counterplan is a policy action, different from the status quo *and* different from the plan. It may be a superior way to solve the affirmative harms (or gain the affirmative advantages), implementation of which cannot logistically coincide with the affirmative plan (that is, mutually exclusive), or the counterplan uniquely avoids the disadvantages of the plan while attaining the advantages. For example, rather than implementing school programs and in order to achieve the advantage of reducing obesity without increasing cost, the government ought to censor fast food and junk food advertising.

7. Start the timers!

APPENDIX B

....

An Affirmative Case

"Resolved: The U.S. federal government should remove restrictions
on the possession and use of marijuana."

A year ago, in 2011, Chris Bartkowicz was sentenced to five years in prison, to be
followed by an additional 8 years of probation, and mandatory drug and mental
health programs. Why? For operating a licensed business as a caregiver in the state
of Colorado. What sort of care was he giving? He was growing marijuana for
medical use as allowed by state law in Colorado. According to Rob Reuteman
in a 2010 CNBC report, "The case against licensed marijuana grower Chris
Bartkowicz ... epitomizes the face-off between state and federal enforcement of
marijuana laws.... After all marijuana—while decriminalized in Colorado—is still
against United States law."[1]

Prohibition against marijuana use has failed. Seventeen states and the District
of Columbia have legalized the medical use of marijuana, 14 states have decriminalized possession of small amounts of marijuana, and more Americans support
legalization now than ever. As many as 8 states have legislation pending to legalize
and regulate the sale of marijuana. Gallup polls in 2011 found that "A record-high
50% of Americans now say the use of marijuana should be made legal." According
to the National Institute on Drug Abuse, "Marijuana is the most commonly
abused illicit drug in the United States." The National Survey on Drug Use and
Health in 2009 found that "16.7 million Americans aged 12 or older used marijuana at least once in the month prior to being surveyed, an increase over the rates

---

1. Reuteman, R., "The Confused State of Pot Law Enforcement, Marijuana and
Money," *A CNBC* Special Report, 20 April, 2012, http://www.cnbc.com/id/36179498.

reported in all years between 2002 and 2008." The advocacy group National Organization for the Reform of Marijuana Laws (NORML) claims that marijuana is the third most popular recreational drug in America, behind only alcohol and tobacco. Some states have decriminalized marijuana's use; some have made it legal for medicinal use; and some officials, including former U.S. Surgeon General Joycelyn Elders, have called for legalizing its use. A Gallup survey last year found that "70% favored making it legal for doctors to prescribe marijuana in order to reduce pain and suffering."[2]

Despite all this, enforcement remains robust and federal law continues to prohibit the growth and sale of any marijuana. According to NORML, "Our country's war on drugs places great emphasis on arresting people for smoking marijuana. In the last decade, 6.5 million Americans have been arrested on marijuana charges, a greater number than the entire populations of Alaska, Delaware, the District of Columbia, Montana, North Dakota, South Dakota, Vermont and Wyoming combined. In 2010, state and local law enforcement arrested **853,838** people for marijuana violations. Annual marijuana arrests have nearly tripled since the early 1990s, and are the highest number ever recorded by the FBI. As has been the case throughout the 1990s, the overwhelming majority of those charged with marijuana violations in 2010—**758,593** Americans (88%)—were for simple possession. The remaining **99,815** individuals were for "sale/manufacture," an FBI category which includes marijuana grown for personal use or purely medical purposes. These new FBI statistics indicate that *one marijuana smoker is arrested every 37 seconds in America.* Taken together, the total number of marijuana arrests for 2010 far exceeded the combined number of arrests for violent crimes, including murder, manslaughter, forcible rape, robbery and aggravated assault."[3]

It is for these reasons, that we, the affirmative, support the proposition that the U.S. federal government should remove restrictions on the possession and use of marijuana. We support implementation of H. R. 2306, the Ending Federal Marijuana Prohibition Act of 2011 as introduced on June 23, 2011, by Congressmen Frank, Paul, Conyers, Lee, Polis, and Cohen. This law would remove federal prohibition, but not restrict states prohibition on use, possession, or sale of marijuana, and would enable regulation of commerce in marijuana. It would remove marijuana as a drug identified by Schedule 1(c).

We begin our analysis with:

Contention 1. Inherency. The Federal Government Prohibits the Growth and Sale of Any Marijuana.

A document published by the Drug Enforcement Agency in 2011 indicated that "Marijuana is properly categorized under Schedule 1 of the Controlled Substances Act … the DEA targets criminals engaged in the cultivation and trafficking of

2. Newport, F., "Record-High 50% of Americans Favor Legalizing Marijuana Use," Gallup.com. Gallup, Inc., 2011. Web. 26 Jul 2012, http://www.gallup.com/poll/150149/Record-High-Americans-Favor-Legalizing-Marijuana.aspx.
3. NORML, "War Against Marijuana Consumers," 2012, http://norml.org/legal/item/war-against-marijuana-consumers?category_id=740.

marijuana.... On October 19, 2009 Attorney General Eric Holder announced formal guidelines for federal prosecutors in states that have enacted laws authorizing the use of marijuana for medical purposes. The guidelines, as set forth in a memorandum from Deputy Attorney General David W. Ogden, makes clear that the focus of federal resources should not be on individuals whose actions are in compliance with existing state laws, and underscores that the Department will continue to prosecute people whose claims of compliance with state and local law conceal operations inconsistent with the terms, conditions, or purposes of the law. He also reiterated that the Department of Justice is committed to the enforcement of the Controlled Substances Act in all states and that this guidance does not 'legalize' marijuana or provide for legal defense to a violation of federal law."[4] While some people have interpreted these guidelines to mean that the federal government has relaxed its policy on "medical" marijuana, this in fact is not the case. Investigations and prosecutions of violations of state and federal law will continue. These are the guidelines DEA has and will continue to follow.[5]

Thomas Moran observed the general law enforcement commitment to enforcing these ineffective statutes in the *Washington and Lee Journal of Civil Rights and Social Justice* in 2011, "... Governments commit billions of dollars each year to stymieing drug use and drug flow, and the amount increases every year. Further, in the last decade, the percentage of money allocated to law enforcement has grown yearly while the percentage of money allocated to drug abuse prevention and research has contracted. Of this money, funding toward marijuana prevention represents approximately twenty percent of the total funds. Adding even more weight to the criticisms against spending, law enforcement and interdiction against marijuana has proved largely inefficient. For instance, the Office of Management and Budget, in its most recent assessment, graded the Drug Enforcement Agency (DEA) a mediocre 'adequate.' While the DEA earned a one hundred percent score for its purpose, it only received twenty-six percent for its results. Yet, in the face of such exorbitant spending and less-than-stellar law enforcement efforts, marijuana use in this country seems to be more popular than ever, represented by the 25,085,000 individuals aged twelve and older who used marijuana in 2007."[6]

It seems entirely likely, therefore, that prohibition of marijuana by the U.S. federal government will continue into the future, that enforcement will continue, and that use will continue. Unfortunately, the negative consequences of enforcement are substantial, as we see in:

Contention 2. Harm. Federal Prohibition of Marijuana Is Detrimental.

4. Memorandum from Deputy Attorney General David W. Ogden to the United States Attorneys, "Investigations and Prosecutions in States Authorizing the Medical Use of Marijuana" and Department of Justice Press Release 09-1119, October 19, 2009.
5. Drug Enforcement Agency 2011—January 2011, "The DEA Position on Marijuana," http://www.justice.gov/dea/marijuana_position.pdf.
6. Thomas J. Moran, "Just a Little Bit of History Repeating: The California Model of Marijuana Legalization and How it Might Affect Racial and Ethnic Minorities," *Washington and Lee Journal of Civil Rights and Social Justice*, 557 (2011), http://scholarlycommons.law.wlu.edu/crsj/vol17/iss2/8.

Norm Stamper, former Seattle police chief, observed that "not only is cannabis the biggest cash crop in … 12 states, it's in the top three in 30 states, the top five in 39. In fact, marijuana is the greatest revenue producer of all agricultural products grown in the U.S. With production values of roughly $36 billion annually, the cultivation of marijuana is permanently entrenched within and integrally connected to the U.S. economy. And it's illegal. Which guarantees obscene, untaxed profits and full employment for demonstrably evil and greedy people; criminal records attached to the lives of tens of millions of Americans; fractured families; inflated risks for cops; widespread discrimination against young, poor, and black and brown people; exploitation and despoilment of thousands of acres of national park lands; open-air drug markets and deflated property values; public corruption; a brutal and bloody war raging in Mexico, now spilling over into the U.S.; abridgement of our civil liberties; and the squandering of tens of billions of taxpayer dollars."[7]

First, *marijuana enforcement increases crime by creating and fueling the black market.* Congressman Ron Paul, co-sponsor of the Ending Federal Marijuana Prohibition Act of 2011, has observed that, "The illegality of drugs is, in fact, the Number One factor that keeps profits up for dealers and cartels, and ensures that organized crime dominates the market…. This is nothing new or unique to drugs, but a predictable outcome of prohibition. During alcohol prohibition, Al Capone and others involved in organized crime made fortunes taking advantage of the dangerous and lucrative underground market the laws had created. Every time law enforcement makes another bust, profits rise for the remaining suppliers. These types of economic forces are insurmountable for law enforcement, but make for very good business for dealers and cartels. For the rest of us, however, it is a disaster. The war on drugs keeps our prisons full to bursting at great expense to taxpayers, but also at great danger to the public at large when the real criminals, the murderers, the rapists, the child molesters, are let out to make room for non-violent drug offenders. We imprison more of our population per capita than Russia or China ever have…. The War on Drugs skews the priorities of law enforcement to the detriment of the public."[8]

And the *crimes perpetuated by the criminalization of marijuana trade are worse,* including violence. According to the New Hampshire Civil Liberties Union, "Those who benefit the most from prohibition are organized crime barons, who derive income from the illegal drug trade. Indeed the criminal drug laws protect drug traffickers from taxation, regulation and quality control. Those laws also support artificially high prices and assure that commercial disputes among drug dealers and their customers will be settled not in courts of law, but with automatic weapons in the streets and neighborhoods across the nation.

---

7. Norm Stamper, "Former Seattle Police Chief, Legalization Will Reduce Crime, Free Up Police Resources, Marijuana and Money," *A CNBC* Special Report, 20 April, 2012, http://www.cnbc.com/id/36201668.
8. "End Insanity of The War on Drugs—Start With Decriminalizing Marijuana at the Federal Level, Marijuana and Money," *A CNBC* Special Report, 20 April, 2012, http://www.cnbc.com/id/36267220.

Today's drug prohibition has spawned a culture of drive-by shootings, kidnappings, murder and other gun-related crimes. Just as people who were drunk did not commit most of the 1920s violence, people who are high on drugs do not commit most of the drug-related violence today."[9]

Marijuana prohibition costs law enforcement resources. Research discussed by Allen St. Pierre, Executive Director NORML, in 2006 reveals that "Increased marijuana enforcement is associated with greater fiscal and social costs. State and local justice costs for marijuana arrests are now estimated to be $7.6 billion, approximately $10,400 per arrest. Of this total, annual police costs are $3.7 billion, judicial/legal costs are $853 million, and correctional costs are $3.1 billion. In both California and New York, state fiscal costs dedicated to criminal marijuana law enforcement annually total over $1 billion for each state."[10]

And while law enforcement officers are forced to spend substantial time and energy enforcing marijuana laws, the money and nature of the trade lead to too many *opportunities for corruption*. A paper by the Drug Policy Alliance revealed that "In recent years there have been a number of high-profile drug-related police scandals, from the 'Rampart' scandal in California to the Tulia disgrace in Texas. Unfortunately, for every police corruption case that makes national headlines, dozens go unreported. A 1998 report by the General Accounting Office concluded that 'recent newspaper accounts, commission reports, academic studies, and other literature we reviewed suggest that today there are more opportunities than in the past for drug-related police corruption.' The GAO reported that from 1993 to 1998 the FBI opened at least 400 state and local police corruption cases that were drug-related, leading to the conviction of over 300 officers. It's not hard to understand how the drug war breeds police corruption. The consensual nature of the drug trade makes it very hard to produce evidence against willing buyers and sellers. Fabricating evidence, lying on the stand, and conducting illegal searches have become routine police practices."[11]

In addition, *marijuana prohibition laws embody racism*. Martin Carcieri, Associate Professor of Political Science at San Francisco State University, wrote in 2011, "... the drug war's disparate impact on racial minorities in all phases of the criminal justice system is well documented ... marijuana prohibition has long been motivated largely by racism."[12] As Sloman adds, "the first users of marijuana—that is, the first people to smoke cannabis for mostly recreational purposes—were members of minority groups.... [S]tate after state enacted some form of prohibition against the non-medical abuse of the drug. California in

9. "Government Drug Prohibition," New Hampshire Civil Liberties Union, July 2012, http://www.nhclu.org/drug-prohibition.php.

10. Allen St. Pierre, Executive Director NORML, 2005, *Crimes of Indiscretion*, http://norml.org/library/item/executive-summary.

11. Drug Policy Alliance, *Police, Drugs, And Corruption: A Review of Recent Drug War-Related Scandals in Five States and Puerto Rico*, 2002, http://www.drugpolicy.org/docUploads/police_corruption_report.pdf.

12. Carcieri—Associate Professor of Political Science at San Francisco State University, 10 February 2011, "Obama, the Fourteenth Amendment, and the Drug War," *Akron Law Review*, http://www.uakron.edu/dotAsset/1820641.pdf.

1915, Texas in 1919, Louisiana in 1924, New York by 1927—one by one most states acted, usually when faced with significant numbers of Mexicans or Negroes using the drug." As Booth elaborates, "the press and 'concerned citizens' took up the call, driven not only by their zeal but also by their anti-Mexican attitudes, which were strengthened during the Depression when jobs were scarce and migrants seemed to be stealing work from the white work force. The Mexicans were accused, without any justification, of spreading marijuana across the nation. State marijuana laws were often used as an excuse to deport or imprison inno-cent Mexicans...." "Although they had been using marijuana for years, it was not until 1938 that [Federal Bureau of Narcotics Director Harry] Anslinger finally came to realize the link between jazz musicians and the drug.... Once the association dawned on him, he set about going after the entertainment industry in general and jazz musicians specifically. They fitted nicely into his rac-ist agenda: if they were not black, they were whites who had come under and been corrupted by black influence...." Concern was not only voiced about the fate of women in black hands: there was a worry that the young might also come under their spell, this given credence by the arrest, in August 1951, of the first white teenager found in possession of marijuana. Cannabis, the black man's nar-cotic, was widely regarded as more dangerous than heroin or cocaine, not because of its potential for addiction but for its facilitation of multi-racial sexual communication. "Beyond the drug war's racially disparate impact, then, there is evidence that racism has long been a dominant motive behind U.S. marijuana prohibition."

St. Pierre reported, "The social costs of criminal marijuana enforcement include demographic impacts and their effects on society. Marijuana possession and sales arrest disproportionately impact young males as well as black adults. These disproportionate impacts nurture alienation from the rule of law. Among the demographic groups most adversely impacted, males age 18 are 0.7% of the population and 3.1% of annual marijuana users, but comprise 8.1% of all mari-juana possession arrests. Males aged 24 to 29 are 4% of the population and 9.7% of annual marijuana users, but comprise 13.7% of all possession arrests. Black adults account for 8.8% of the population, 11.9% of annual marijuana users, and 23% of marijuana possession arrests. Overall, 25% of marijuana possession arrests are of people age 18 or younger, and 74% are for people under the age of 30. Marijuana users who are white, over 30 year old, and/or female are dis-proportionately unaffected by marijuana possession arrests. Maybe of greater note and indicative of an unintended consequence in the U.S. government's mari-juana policy-making: Over one million teenagers in the U.S. sell marijuana."[13]

In order to offer the states the opportunity to reduce these harms, we advo-cate passage of the Paul–Frank Bill H. R. 2306, the Ending Federal Marijuana Prohibition Act of 2011, and believe it will achieve the following solvency and subsequent advantages.

---

13. Allen St. Pierre, Executive Director NORML, 2005, *Crimes of Indiscretion*, http://norml.org/library/item/executive-summary.

Contention 3. Solvency. Removal of Federal Prohibition Offers States the Opportunity to Solve the Harms of Criminalization of Marijuana.

First, it is important to recognize that affirmative action is essential to achieving the benefits of prohibition removal. The California Medical Association observed this in 2011, "Because cannabis remains an illegal substance at the federal level, it is currently impossible to adequately evaluate or regulate the substance nationally. The charge of this technical advisory committee was to consider whether appropriate regulation or taxation is technically irrelevant absent the federal legalization of cannabis because, in order to consider supporting a taxation or regulatory scheme, cannabis must first be legalized. Merely decriminalizing cannabis on a state-by-state basis is not sufficient because illegal substances would not be regulated at the federal level, which is where most of the regulation of labeling, quality control, safety, etc. of, for example, alcohol and tobacco takes place."[14]

Of course, the Bill does not legalize marijuana, it only removes the federal prohibition on it. As when prohibition of alcohol was lifted, it would be up to the individual states to decide their position on marijuana and establish appropriate regulations. Ryan Tracy wrote in the *Wall Street Journal* that "[the] bill ... would end the federal prohibition on marijuana, leaving it up to each state to set marijuana policy. The bill, designed to limit the federal government's role in enforcing marijuana laws, would allow states to legalize, regulate, and tax the drug, ... Mr. Frank emphasized that it 'is not a legalization bill.' According to the release, 'The legislation would limit the federal government's role in marijuana enforcement to cross-border or inter-state smuggling, allowing people to legally grow, use or sell marijuana in states where it is legal.'"[15] Recall that a number of states have or are contemplating liberalizing their marijuana laws and that increasingly Americans support such action!

We believe that passage of the Ending Federal Marijuana Prohibition Act will achieve a number of significant advantages.

Advantage 1 is *economic*. Removing prohibition and the resulting increase in regulation and taxation provides a positive benefit in resources. Jeffrey A. Miron, Professor of Economics at Harvard University, conducted a study in 2005. He concluded that budgetary impacts would be beneficial to government budgets, "If marijuana were legal, enforcement costs would be negligible and governments could levy taxes on the production and sale of marijuana. Thus, government expenditure would decline and tax revenue would increase. This report estimates the savings in government expenditure and the gains in tax

---

14. California Medical Association, "Cannabis and the Regulatory Void, Background Paper and Recommendations," *California Medical Association State Report*, 2011, http://www.cmanet.org/files/pdf/news/cma-cannabis-tac-white-paper-101411.pdf.
15. Tracy, R. "Joint Effort? Barney Frank, Ronpaul Team up on Marijuana Bill" (2011, June 20). Retrieved from http://blogs.wsj.com/washwire/2011/06/22/joint-effort-barney-frank-ron-paul-team-up-on-marijuana-bill/.

revenue that would result from replacing marijuana prohibition with a regime in which marijuana is legal but taxed and regulated like other goods. The report is not an overall evaluation of marijuana prohibition; the magnitude of any budgetary impact does not by itself determine the wisdom of prohibition. But the costs required to enforce prohibition, and the transfers that occur because income in a prohibited sector is not taxed, are relevant to rational discussion of this policy.... The budgetary implications of legalization exceed those of decriminalization for three reasons. First, legalization eliminates arrests for trafficking in addition to eliminating arrests for possession. Second, legalization saves prosecutorial, judicial, and incarceration expenses; these savings are minimal in the case of decriminalization. Third, legalization allows taxation of marijuana production and sale. This report concludes that marijuana legalization would reduce government expenditure by $7.7 billion annually. Marijuana legalization would also generate tax revenue of $2.4 billion annually if marijuana were taxed like all other goods and $6.2 billion annually if marijuana were taxed at rates comparable to those on alcohol and tobacco."[16] Miron's report was endorsed by Milton Friedman and 500 economists, as reported in *Forbes* in 2005, "Milton Friedman leads a list of more than 500 economists from around the U.S. who today will publicly endorse a Harvard University economist's report on the costs of marijuana prohibition and the potential revenue gains from the U.S. government of legalizing it and taxing its sale. Ending prohibition enforcement would save $7.7 billion in combined state and federal spending, the report says, while taxation would yield up to $6.2 billion a year."[17]

The 2011 analysis by Keith Yost projects the potential savings at half a trillion dollars over 10 years, "*If* these assumptions are correct, and *the government ended prohibition* and then levied an excise tax on marijuana equal to 60 percent of the end retail value (an exclusive tax rate of 150 percent), then *consumption of marijuana would remain unchanged* relative to the status quo. Suppliers would sell the drug at half of the pre-legalization price and receive $20 billion, the government would apply taxes and collect $30 billion, and the end price to the consumer would rise, but any loss of demand would be offset by the demand increase from decriminalization. This is a high tax rate, but not so high as to invite a resumption of black market activity—in Europe, many countries tax cigarettes at an exclusive rate of 300 percent, and little black market activity exists. New revenues are not the only budgetary effect of ending prohibition. In addition, *legalization would end significant outlays on law enforcement and incarceration.* Jeffrey Miron PhD '84, an economist at Harvard, has studied the budgetary effects of marijuana prohibition and estimated the federal and state *savings from the legalization of marijuana to be $13.7 billion annually.* This is consistent with California's experience with decriminalization—a reform which has reduced its

---

16. Miron, J., Professor of Economics, Harvard University, June 2005, "The Budgetary Implications of Marijuana Prohibition in the United States," Marijuana Policy Project, http://www.prohibitioncosts.org/wp-content/uploads/2012/04/MironReport.pdf.
17. Quentin Hardy, "Milton Friedman: Legalize It!" *Forbes* (2005, February 6), http://www.forbes.com/2005/06/02/cz_qh_0602pot.html.

marijuana law enforcement costs by 75 percent. Assuming a further three percent annual growth rate in tax revenues and enforcement cost-avoidance, the *total savings over a 10-year window from legalizing marijuana come to an even $500 billion.*"[18]

Legalization could also generate badly needed jobs. Offering the example of California, Michael Vitiello, Professor at Pacific's McGeorge School of Law, wrote in 2009, "... marijuana is a significant part of California's economy; ... as (a supporter) stated, 'it's time to bring this major piece of our economy into the light of day...." Beyond these significant savings, proponents contend that legalizing marijuana would "declaw powerful and violent Mexican drug cartels." "... Some proponents analogize to the post-Prohibition era, when legalizing alcohol weakened the power of mobsters around the country... In addition to undercutting the drug cartels, legalizing marijuana may reduce corruption among law enforcement officials in the United States as well. Finally, the medical marijuana experiment seems to have worked. That is, many Americans and especially Californians have seen that marijuana can be made available, regulated and used responsibly ... the proponent literature includes an even rosier picture of the post-legalized world. For example, NORML, the best known and probably oldest organization advocating legalization, makes some sweeping claims about the benefits flowing from legalization.... California NORML ... argues that beyond retail sales of marijuana, the total economic impact should include 'spin-off industries such as coffeehouses, tourism, and industrial hemp.' ... Analogizing to the wine industry, that organization argues that legalized marijuana could generate three times as much economic activity as its retail sales. 'If the marijuana industry were just one-third the size of the wine industry, it would generate 50,000 jobs and $1.4 billion in wages, along with additional income and business tax revenues for the state.' ... It estimates that industrial hemp could become a business comparable to the $3.4 billion cotton industry in California.... Meanwhile, hemp is better for the environment than is cotton. Growers need fewer pesticides for hemp than for cotton and the fields are virtually weed free after harvest."[19]

Advantage 2 is *improved regulation and crime control*. According to Tiffany Walden in 2012, "open drug regulation has the potential to decrease organized crime activity as it did with alcohol in the 1920s?" 'In Monterrey and Mexico City, you have the high-end business community saying "this is crazy. We can't deal with these levels of violence anymore,"' said Ethan Nadelmann, executive director of the Drug Policy Alliance, an organization promoting alternatives to the current drug policy in America. 'Mexico is like Chicago during the days of prohibition and Al Capone times 50.' This January the Mexican government updated its drug-related violence numbers to 47,515 killings since late 2006,

18. Yost, K., Economist for the Boston Consulting Group, 14 October 2011, "Getting Out of the Red: Legalize It," MIT: The Tech, http://tech.mit.edu/V131/N44/yostgotr.html.
19. Vitiello, M., Professor at Pacific's McGeorge School of Law, September 2009, "Legalizing Marijuana: California's Pot of Gold?," Selected Works, http://works.bepress.com/cgi/viewcontent.cgi?article=1003&context=michael_vitiello.

the *New York Times* reported. Capone's alcohol wars resulted in more than 300 deaths throughout the late 1920s, according to reports at the time of his death. Nadelmann argued that President Richard Nixon's War on Drugs initiative is a failure, causing the increase in drug-related violence all over the world. He spoke at Roosevelt University's Illinois Consortium on Drug Policy and Students for Sensible Drug Policy program Tuesday. Nadelmann presented a 'right of access' legalization model to spur discussion. In a drug-ideal world, every person would have the legal right to use a small amount of drugs and obtain these drugs from a single authorized source. This legally regulated source would produce all the drugs and be held accountable for the quality of each drug. 'Organized crime would lose 90 to 95 percent of its profits because everybody would just prefer to go to this other source rather than the black market,' said Nadelmann, founder of the Drug Policy Alliance. 'People would know exactly what they would get.' Folks in favor of legalization agree that large drug cartels thrive financially because of prohibition and its creation of a high-demand underground product, leading to more competition between rival organizations. 'People who don't have access to a system to address their grievances with each other result to violence,' said Morgan Fox, communications manager at the Marijuana Policy Project, a group focused on the decriminalization of marijuana use.... Gierach, a current board member of Law Enforcement Against Prohibition, said that ending drug prohibition would eliminate the profit motive that is the main driver of the illegal drug industry's success. Even with the money gone, he said that drug cartels wouldn't completely go away. 'Eliminate the source of money that buys the guns,' he said."[20]

Professor Miron argues that marijuana legalization solves violence, corruption, stigma, racism, and economy. In a 2012 article, he wrote, "Legalization will move the marijuana industry above ground, just as the repeal of alcohol prohibition restored the legal alcohol industry. A small component of the marijuana market might remain illicit—moonshine marijuana rather than moonshine whiskey—but if regulation and taxation are moderate, most producers and consumers will choose the legal sector, as they did with alcohol. Legalization would therefore eliminate most of the violence and corruption that currently characterize marijuana markets. These occur because, in underground markets, participants cannot resolve disputes via non-violent mechanisms such as lawsuits, advertising, lobbying, or campaign contributions. Instead, producers and consumers in these markets use violence to resolve disputes with each other and bribery or violence to resolve disputes with law enforcement. These features of 'vice' markets disappear when vice is legal, as abundant experience with alcohol, prostitution, and gambling all demonstrate. Legalization would result in numerous other benefits. Medical marijuana patients would no longer suffer legal limbo or social stigma from using marijuana to treat nausea from chemotherapy,

---

20. Walden, T., Northwestern University—Medill School of Journalism, February 9, 2012, "Marijuana for Everyone: Those in Favor of Legalization Ponder Its Effect on Organized Crime," *Medill News*, http://news.medill.northwestern.edu/chicago/news.aspx? id=200073.

glaucoma, or other conditions. Infringements on civil liberties and racial profiling would decline, since victimless crimes are a key cause of such police behavior. Quality control would improve because sellers could advertise and establish reputations for a consistent product, allowing consumers to choose low or high-potency marijuana. Legalization would also generate budgetary savings for state and federal governments, both by eliminating expenditures on enforcement and by allowing taxation of legalized sales. I recently estimated that the net impact would be a deficit reduction of about $20 billion per year, summed over all levels of government."[21]

Advantage 3 is *preservation of freedom*. According to Michael Huemer, Professor of Epistemology, Ethics, and Metaethics at CU-Boulder in 2004, "Individuals have a right to use drugs. This right is neither absolute nor exceptionless; suppose, for example, that there existed a drug, which, once ingested, caused a significant proportion of users, without any further free choices on their part, to attack other people without provocation. I would think that stopping the use of this drug would be the business of the government.... Indeed, it seems that if there is anything one would have rights to, it would be one's own body. This explains why we think others may not physically attack you or kidnap you. It explains why we do not accept the use of unwilling human subjects for medical experiments, even if the experiments are beneficial to society—the rest of society may not decide to use your body for its own purposes without your permission. It explains why some believe that women have a right to an abortion—and why some others do not. The former believe that a woman has the right to do what she wants with her own body; the latter believe that the fetus is a distinct person, and a woman does not have the right to harm its body.... But drug use seems to be a paradigm case of a legitimate exercise of the right to control one's own body. Drug consumption takes place in and immediately around the user's own body; the salient effects occur inside the user's body. If we consider drug use merely as altering the user's own body and mind, it is hard to see how anyone who believes in rights at all could deny that it is protected by a right, for (a) it is hard to see how anyone who believes in rights could deny that individuals have rights over their own bodies and minds, and (b) it is hard to see how anyone who believes in such rights could deny that drug use, considered merely as altering the user's body and mind, is an example of the exercise of one's rights over one's own body and mind. Consider two ways a prohibitionist might object to this argument. First, a prohibitionist might argue that drug use does not merely alter the user's own body and mind, but also harms the user's family, friends, co-workers, and society ... no one should be permitted to drive or operate heavy machinery while under the influence of drugs that impair their ability to do those things; nor should pregnant mothers be permitted to ingest drugs, if it can be proven that those drugs cause substantial risks to their babies ... in the great majority of cases, drug use does not harm anyone in

21. Miron, J., Professor of Economics, Harvard University, May 27, 2010, "Marijuana Legalization in California," *The Harvard Crimson*, http://www.thecrimson.harvard.edu/article/2010/5/27/marijuana-legalization-use-alcohol/.

any relevant ways—that is, ways that we normally take to merit criminal penalties—and should not be outlawed. Second, a prohibitionist might argue that drug use fails to qualify as an exercise of the user's rights over his own body, because the individual is not truly acting freely in deciding to use drugs. Perhaps individuals only use drugs because they have fallen prey to some sort of psychological compulsion, because drugs exercise a siren-like allure that distorts users' perceptions, because users don't realize how bad drugs are, or something of that sort. The exact form of this objection doesn't matter; in any case, the prohibitionist faces a dilemma. If users do not freely choose to use drugs, then it is unjust to punish them for using drugs. For if users do not choose freely, then they are not morally responsible for their decision, and it is unjust to punish a person for something he is not responsible for. But if users do choose freely in deciding to use drugs, then this choice is an exercise of their rights over their own bodies."[22]

Advantage 4 is *medical use.* Research has proven marijuana to be a safe and effective medicine. Jon Gettman, Ph.D., former president and national director of the National Organization for the Reform of Marijuana Laws, in a 2002 document in DrugScience.Org, reported, "Studies have shown the long-term use of cannabis to be safe. In contrast to many other medicinal drugs, the long-term use of cannabis does not harm stomach, liver, kidneys and heart. The Missoula Chronic Clinical Cannabis Use Study examined the effects of long-term and legal medical marijuana use."[23] Russo et al. (2002) demonstrated that regular use of cannabis for more than 10 years does not cause major harm to patients: "The Missoula Chronic Clinical Cannabis Use Study was proposed to investigate the therapeutic benefits and adverse effects of prolonged use of 'medical marijuana' in a cohort of seriously ill patients. Use of cannabis was approved through the Compassionate Investigational New Drug Program (IND) of the Food and Drug Administration (FDA). Cannabis is obtained from the National Institute on Drug Abuse (NIDA), and is utilized under the supervision of a study physician. The aim of this study is to examine the overall health status of 4 of the 7 surviving patients in the program. This project provides the first opportunity to scrutinize the long-term effects of cannabis on patients who have used a known dosage of a standardized, heat-sterilized quality-controlled supply of low-grade marijuana for 11 to 27 years. [...]

Results demonstrate clinical effectiveness in these patients in treating glaucoma, chronic musculoskeletal pain, spasm and nausea, and spasticity of multiple sclerosis. All 4 patients are stable with respect to their chronic conditions, and are taking many fewer standard pharmaceuticals than previously. [...] Mild changes

---

22. Huemer, M., Professor of Epistemology, Ethics, and Metaethics at CU-Boulder, 2004, "America's Unjust Drug War," The New Prohibition, http://spot.colorado.edu/~huemer/drugs.htm.
23. Gettman, J., DrugScience.Org, "Safety for Use: Documented Safety of Long Term Cannabis Use," http://www.drugscience.org/sfu/sfu_longterm.html; Gettman cites Russo E., Mathre M. L., Byrne A, Velin R., Bach P. J., Sanchez-Ramos J., Kirlin K. A., "Chronic Cannabis Use in the Compassionate Investigational New Drug Program: An Examination of Benefits and Adverse Effects of Legal Clinical Cannabis." *J Cannabis Ther* 2002; 2(1): 3–58.

in pulmonary function were observed in 2 patients, while no functionally significant attributable sequelae were noted in any other physiological system examined in the study, which included: MRI scans of the brain, pulmonary function tests, chest X-ray, neuropsychological tests, hormone and immunological assays, electroencephalography, P300 testing, history, and neurological clinical examination. [...] These results would support the provision of clinical cannabis to a greater number of patients in need. We believe that cannabis can be a safe and effective medicine with various suggested improvements in the existing Compassionate IND program."[24]

The Missoula Chronic Clinical Cannabis Use Study resulted in several important conclusions and recommendations:

1. "Cannabis smoking, even of a crude, low-grade product, provides effective symptomatic relief of pain, muscle spasms, and intraocular pressure elevations in selected patients failing other modes of treatment."

2. "These clinical cannabis patients are able to reduce or eliminate other prescription medicines and their accompanying side effects." "Clinical cannabis provides an improved quality of life in these patients."

3. "The side effect profile of NIDA cannabis in chronic usage suggests some mild pulmonary risk."

4. "No malignant deterioration has been observed."

5. "No consistent or attributable neuropsychological or neurological deterioration has been observed."

6. "No endocrine, hematological or immunological sequelae have been observed."

7. "Improvements in a clinical cannabis program would include a ready and consistent supply of sterilized, potent, organically grown unfertilized female flowering top material, thoroughly cleaned of extraneous inert fibrous matter."

8. "It is the authors' opinion that the Compassionate IND should be reopened and extended to other patients in need of clinical cannabis."

9. "Failing that, local, state and federal laws might be amended to provide regulated and monitored clinical cannabis to suitable candidates."[25]

Lester Grinspoon, M.D., Emeritus Professor of Psychiatry at Harvard Medical School, wrote in an August 17, 2003, article published in the *Boston Globe*, "Doctors and nurses have seen that for many patients, cannabis is more useful,

24. Russo, E., Mathre, M. L., Byrne, A., Velin, R., Bach, P. J., Sanchez-Ramos, J., & Kirlin, K. A., "Chronic Cannabis Use in the Compassionate Investigational New Drug Program," *Journal of Cannabis Therapeutics*, 2(1), 2002. doi: 10.1300/J175v02n01_02.
25. Russo, E., Mathre, M. L., Byrne, A., Velin, R., Bach, P. J., Sanchez-Ramos, J., & Kirlin, K. A., "Chronic Cannabis Use in the Compassionate Investigational New Drug Program," *Journal of Cannabis Therapeutics*, 2(1), 2002. doi: 10.1300/J175v02n01_02.

less toxic, and less expensive than the conventional medicines prescribed for diverse syndromes and symptoms, including multiple sclerosis, Crohn's disease, migraine headaches, severe nausea and vomiting, convulsive disorders, the AIDS wasting syndrome, chronic pain, and many others."[26]

Finally, it should be noted that marijuana is safer than all alternatives, according to Stephen Sidney, M.D., Associate Director for Clinical Research at Kaiser Permanente. He wrote in a September 20, 2003, editorial published in the *British Medical Journal*:

> No acute lethal overdoses of cannabis are known, in contrast to several of its illegal (for example, cocaine) and legal (for example, alcohol, aspirin, acetaminophen) counterparts.[27]

And, finally, legalization is not likely to significantly increase use, as explained by Dr. Myron in 2012, "The one impact of legalization that might be undesirable is an increase in marijuana use, but the magnitude of this increase is likely to be modest. The repeal of alcohol prohibition in the U.S. produced about a 20 percent increase in use, while Portugal's 2001 de facto legalization of marijuana did not cause any measurable increase; indeed, use was lower afterward. Across countries, use rates for marijuana show little connection to the strictness of the prohibition regime. The Netherlands has virtual legalization, for example, yet use rates do not greatly differ from those in the United States. An increase in marijuana use, moreover, is not necessarily bad. If the ballot initiative passes, people who would like to use marijuana but abstain due to prohibition would be able to consume responsibly; legalization would allow them to enjoy marijuana without fear of arrest or incarceration and without concern over quality. Some new users might generate adverse consequences for themselves or others, such as driving under the influence, but most irresponsible users are disregarding the law and consuming already. Legalization will not, of course, eliminate all negatives of marijuana use. But just as the harms of alcohol prohibition were worse than the harms of alcohol itself, the adverse effects of marijuana prohibition are worse than the unwanted consequences of marijuana use. Legalization is therefore the better policy."[28]

So for all these reasons, we advocate the proposition and hope you will support the affirmative in this debate!

(Thank you to Gerald Cowen for his assistance.)

---

26. ProCon.org., "What are Physicians' Views on Medical Marijuana?"
MedicalMarijuana.ProCon.org. (2008, June 17). Retrieved from http://medicalmarijuana. procon.org/view.answers.php?questionID=000086.
27. ProCon.org., "Can Marijuana Use Cause Death?" MedicalMarijuana.ProCon.org. (2008, May 30). Retrieved from http://medicalmarijuana.procon.org/view.answers.php? questionID=000231.
28. Myron, Professor of Economics, Harvard University, 27 May 2010, "Marijuana Legalization in California," *The Harvard Crimson*, http://www.thecrimson.harvard.edu/ article/2010/5/27/marijuana-legalization-use-alcohol/.

EXERCISES

1. This is a long case. Review the case and "highlight down" (edit) the text such that it is an appropriate length to be presented in 9 minutes. You will need to shorten some cards by highlighting keywords and/or phrases, and select some materials (evidence and/or arguments) to be omitted during the first speech. You may also wish to add material including your own explanations and rhetoric. Once prepared, practice reading the case with enthusiasm and emphasis.

2. Prepare a preflow of the case.

3. With a partner, read the case and alternate asking and answering cross-examination questions.

4. Research and prepare a negative strategy and give a 1NC in response to the case.

5. With classmates, research and prepare affirmative and negative briefs, positions, and support materials and conduct an entire debate beginning with the 1AC.

APPENDIX C

....

Debate and Technology

Academic debaters, as all students, rely on use of computers and digital technology to practice their art. They use computers to conduct research, organize and file information, flow, communicate with other debaters, tabulate debate tournaments, record their debates, and even time their speeches. While years ago, debaters recorded their evidence on index cards to be filed in recipe boxes, and flowed on art pads with multicolored pens, today's academic debate exercise is conducted with complex data access programs and multiple computers. The quantity of data and challenge of recording and accessing information in the computer era create exciting possibilities and new challenges. In fact, debates take place online. Much of the rationale for traveling across the country to compete in intercollegiate debate tournaments is based more on the enjoyment of learning gained through travel and the pleasure of meeting new people in new places than it is based on necessity. Of course, even with face to face, real time, real place debating, much reliance on computer-assisted debating is evident. Some resources are identified below to assist the debate in organizing the digital debate.

Debate Synergy
http://georgetowndebateseminar.wikispaces.com/Hoya+Template.

DigiDebate™ 1.0
http://www.digidebate.com/.

Verbatim Paperless Debate
http://paperlessdebate.com/.
http://paperlessdebate.wikispaces.com/.

Open Caselist
http://68.233.253.124/xwiki/wiki/opencaselist/view/Main/WebHome.

Debate Results Tabroom Management
http://commweb.fullerton.edu/jbruschke/Web/CATDownloads.aspx.

Tabroom.Com
https://www.tabroom.com/index/index.mhtml.

APPENDIX **D**

Debate Propositions

NATIONAL INTERCOLLEGIATE DEBATE
PROPOSITIONS (NDT)

Following is a list of the national intercollegiate debate propositions from the academic year 1920–1921 to 1995–1996.[1]

1920–1921

(Men) Resolved: That a progressive tax on land should be adopted in the United States. (Men) Resolved: That the League of Nations should be adopted. (Women) Resolved: That intercollegiate athletics should be abolished.

1921–1922

Resolved: That the principle of the "closed shop" is unjustifiable.

1922–1923

Resolved: That the United States should adopt the cabinet-parliamentary form of government.

1923–1924

Resolved: That the United States should enter the World Court of the League of Nations as proposed by President Harding.

1924–1925

Resolved: That Congress should be empowered to override, by a two-thirds vote, decisions of the Supreme Court which declare acts of Congress unconstitutional.

1925–1926

(Men) Resolved: That the Constitution of the United States should be amended to give Congress power to regulate child labor. (Women) Resolved: That the United States should adopt a uniform marriage and divorce law.

1926–1927

(Men) Resolved: That the essential features of the McNary–Haugen bill be enacted into law.[2] (Women) Resolved: That trial by jury should be abolished.[3] Resolved: That the Volstead Act should be modified to permit the manufacture and sale of light wines and beer.[4]

1927–1928

Resolved: That the United States should cease to protect, by force of arms, capital invested in foreign lands, except after formal declaration of war.

1928–1929

Resolved: That a substitute for trial by jury should be adopted.

1929–1930

Resolved: That the nations should adopt a plan of complete disarmament, excepting such forces as are needed for police purposes.

1930–1931

Resolved: That the nations should adopt a policy of free trade.

1931–1932

Resolved: That the Congress should enact legislation providing for the centralized control of industry.

1932–1933

Resolved: That the United States should agree to the cancellation of the interallied debts.

1933–1934

Resolved: That the powers of the president of the United States should be substantially increased as a settled policy.

1934–1935

Resolved: That the nations should agree to prevent the international shipment of arms and munitions.

1935–1936

Resolved: That the Congress should have the power to override, by a two-thirds majority vote, decisions of the Supreme Court declaring laws passed by Congress unconstitutional.

1936–1937

Resolved: That Congress should be empowered to fix minimum wages and maximum hours for industry.

1937–1938

Resolved: That the National Labor Relations Board should be empowered to enforce arbitration of all industrial disputes.

1938–1939

Resolved: That the United States should cease the use of public funds (including credits) for the purpose of stimulating business.

1939–1940

Resolved: That the United States should follow a policy of strict economic and military isolation toward all nations outside the Western Hemisphere engaged in armed international or civil conflict.

1940–1941

Resolved: That the nations of the Western Hemisphere should form a permanent union.

1941–1942

Resolved: That the federal government should regulate by law all labor unions in the United States.

1942–1943

Resolved: That the United States should take the initiative in establishing a permanent federal union with power to tax and regulate commerce, to settle international disputes and to enforce such settlements, to maintain a police force, and to provide for the admission of other nations which accept the principles of the union.

1943–1944

Resolved: That the United States should cooperate in establishing and maintaining an international police force upon the defeat of the Axis.

1944–1945

Resolved: That the federal government should enact legislation requiring the settlement of all labor disputes by compulsory arbitration when voluntary means of settlement have failed.

1945–1946

Resolved: That the policy of the United States should be directed toward the establishment of free trade among the nations of the world.

1946–1947

Resolved: That labor should be given a direct share in the management of industry.

1947–1948

Resolved: That a federal world government should be established.

1948–1949

Resolved: That the federal government should adopt a policy of equalizing educational opportunity in tax-supported schools by means of annual grants.

1949–1950

Resolved: That the United States should nationalize the basic nonagricultural industries.

1950–1951

Resolved: That the noncommunist nations should form a new international organization.

1951–1952

Resolved: That the federal government should adopt a permanent program of wage and price controls.

1952–1953

Resolved: That the Congress of the United States should enact a compulsory fair employment practices law.

1953–1954

Resolved: That the United States should adopt a policy of free trade.

1954–1955

Resolved: That the United States should extend diplomatic recognition to the communist government of China.

1955–1956

Resolved: That the nonagricultural industries should guarantee their employees an annual wage.

1956–1957

Resolved: That the United States should discontinue direct economic aid to foreign countries.

1957–1958

Resolved: That the requirement of membership in a labor organization as a condition of employment should be illegal.

1958–1959

Resolved: That the further development of nuclear weapons should be prohibited by international agreement.

1959–1960

Resolved: That Congress should be given the power to reverse decisions of the Supreme Court.

1960–1961

Resolved: That the United States should adopt a program of compulsory health insurance for all citizens.

1961–1962

Resolved: That labor organizations should be under the jurisdiction of antitrust legislation.

1962–1963

Resolved: That the noncommunist nations of the world should establish an economic community.

1963–1964

Resolved: That the federal government should guarantee an opportunity for higher education to all qualified high school graduates.

1964–1965

Resolved: That the federal government should establish a national program of public work for the unemployed.

1965–1966

Resolved: That law enforcement agencies in the United States should be given greater freedom in the investigation and prosecution of crime.

1966–1967

Resolved: That the United States should substantially reduce its foreign policy commitments.

1967–1968

Resolved: That the federal government should guarantee a minimum annual cash income to all citizens.

1968–1969

Resolved: That executive control of U.S. foreign policy should be significantly curtailed.

1969–1970

Resolved: That the federal government should grant annually a specific percentage of its income tax revenue to the state governments.

1970–1971

Resolved: That the federal government should adopt a program of compulsory wage and price controls.

1971–1972

Resolved: That greater controls should be imposed on the gathering and utilization of information about U.S. citizens by government agencies.

1972–1973

Resolved: That the federal government should provide a program of comprehensive medical care for all citizens.

1973–1974

Resolved: That the federal government should control the supply and utilization of energy in the United States.

1974–1975

Resolved: That the power of the presidency should be significantly curtailed.

1975–1976

Resolved: That the federal government should adopt a comprehensive program to control land use in the United States.

1976–1977

Resolved: That the federal government should significantly strengthen the guarantee of consumer product safety required of manufacturers.

1977–1978

Resolved: That United States' law enforcement agencies should be given significantly greater freedom in the investigation and/or prosecution of felony crime.

1978–1979

Resolved: That the federal government should implement a program which guarantees employment opportunities for all U.S. citizens in the labor force.

1979–1980

Resolved: That the federal government should significantly strengthen the regulation of mass media communication in the United States.

1980–1981

Resolved: That the United States should significantly increase its foreign military commitments.

1981–1982

Resolved: That the federal government should significantly curtail the powers of labor unions in the United States.

1982–1983

Resolved: That all U.S. military intervention into the internal affairs of any foreign nation or nations in the Western Hemisphere should be prohibited.

1983–1984

Resolved: That any and all injury resulting from the disposal of hazardous waste in the United States should be the legal responsibility of the producer of that waste.

1984–1985

Resolved: That the U.S. federal government should significantly increase exploration and/or development of space beyond the earth's mesosphere.

1985–1986

Resolved: That more rigorous academic standards should be established for all public elementary and/or secondary schools in the United States in one or more of the following areas: language arts, mathematics, natural sciences. (Narrow) Resolved: That more rigorous academic standards should be established for all public elementary and/or secondary schools in the United States in the subject of mathematics.

1986–1987

Resolved: That one or more presently existing restrictions on First Amendment freedoms of press and/or speech established in one or more federal court decisions should be curtailed or prohibited. (Narrow) Resolved: That one or more presently existing national security restrictions on First Amendment freedoms of press and/or speech established in one or more federal court decisions should be curtailed or prohibited.

1987–1988

Resolved: That the United States should reduce substantially its military commitments to NATO member states. (Narrow) Resolved: That the United States should reduce substantially its nuclear military commitments to NATO member states.

1988–1989

Resolved: That U.S. foreign policy toward one or more African nations should be substantially changed. (Narrow) Resolved: That U.S. foreign policy toward South Africa should be substantially changed.

1989–1990

Resolved: That the federal government should adopt an energy policy that substantially reduces nonmilitary consumption of fossil fuels in the United States. (Narrow)
Resolved: That the federal government should reduce nonmilitary consumption of fossil fuels in the United States by expanding the use of nuclear power.

1990–1991

Resolved: That the United States should substantially change its trade policy toward one or more of the following: China, Hong Kong, Japan, South Korea, Taiwan.

1991–1992

Resolved: That one or more U.S. Supreme Court decisions recognizing a federal Constitutional right to privacy should be overruled.

1992–1993

Resolved: That the United States should substantially change its development assistance policies toward one or more of the following nations: Afghanistan, Bangladesh, Burma, Bhutan, India, Nepal, Pakistan, Sri Lanka.

1993–1994

Resolved: That the commander-in-chief power of the U.S. president should be substantially curtailed.

1994–1995

Resolved: That the federal government should substantially change rules and/or statutes governing criminal procedure in federal courts in one or more of the following areas: pretrial detention, sentencing.

1995–1996

Resolved: That the U.S. government should substantially increase its security assistance to one or more of the following: Egypt, Israel, Jordan, Palestinian National Authority, Syria.

NATIONAL INTERCOLLEGIATE DEBATE
PROPOSITIONS (CEDA)

Following is a list of the national intercollegiate debate propositions (CEDA) for the academic years 1971–1972 to 1995–1996.[5]

1971–1972

Resolved: That the United States should withdraw all its ground combat forces from bases located outside the Western Hemisphere.

1972–1973

(1st Semester) Resolved: That the penal system in the United States should be significantly improved. (2nd Semester) Resolved: That the United States should seek to restore normal diplomatic and economic relations with the present government of Cuba.

1973–1974

(1st Semester) Resolved: That "victimless crimes" should be legalized. (2nd Semester) Resolved: That the United States should reduce its commitment to Israel.

1974–1975

(1st Semester) Resolved: That the federal government should grant amnesty to all those who evaded the draft during the Vietnam War. (2nd Semester) Resolved: That American television has sacrificed quality for entertainment.

1975–1976

Resolved: That education has failed its mission in the United States.

1976–1977

Resolved: That legal protection of accused persons in the United States unnecessarily hinders law enforcement agencies.

1977–1978

Resolved: That affirmative action promotes deleterious hiring practices.

1978–1979

Resolved: That a U.S. foreign policy significantly directed toward the furtherance of human rights is desirable.

1979–1980

Resolved: That compulsory national service for all qualified U.S. citizens is desirable.

1980–1981

(1st Topic) Resolved: That protection of the national environment is a more important goal than the satisfaction of American energy demands. (2nd Topic) Resolved: That activism in politics by religious groups harms the American political process.

1981–1982

(1st Topic) Resolved: That unauthorized immigration into the United States is seriously detrimental to the United States. (2nd Topic) Resolved: That the American judicial system has overemphasized the rights of the accused.

1982–1983

(1st Topic) Resolved: That a unilateral freeze by the United States on the production and development of nuclear weapons would be desirable. (2nd Topic) Resolved: That individual rights of privacy are more important than any other constitutional right.

1983–1984

(1st Topic) Resolved: That U.S. higher education has sacrificed quality for institutional survival. (2nd Topic) Resolved: That federal government censorship is justified to defend the national security of the United States.

1984–1985

(1st Topic) Resolved: That the method of conducting presidential elections in the United States is detrimental to democracy. (2nd Topic) Resolved: That the United States is justified in providing military support to nondemocratic governments.

1985–1986

(1st Topic) Resolved: That significant government restrictions on coverage by U.S. media of terrorist activity are justified. (2nd Topic) Resolved: That membership in the United Nations is no longer beneficial to the United States.

1986–1987

(1st Topic) Resolved: That improved relations with the Soviet Union are a more important objective for the United States than increased military preparedness. (2nd Topic) Resolved: That regulations in the United States requiring employees to be tested for controlled substances are an unwarranted invasion of privacy.

1987–1988

(1st Topic) Resolved: That continued United States covert involvement in Central America would be undesirable. (2nd Topic) Resolved: That the American judicial system has overemphasized freedom of the press.

1988–1989

(1st Topic) Resolved: That significantly stronger third-party participation in the U.S. presidential elections would benefit the political process. (2nd Topic) Resolved: That increased restrictions on the civilian possession of handguns in the United States would be justified.

1989–1990

(1st Topic) Resolved: That violence is a justified response to political oppression. (2nd Topic) Resolved: That the trend toward increasing foreign investment in the United States is detrimental to this nation.

1990–1991

(1st Topic) Resolved: That government censorship of public artistic expression in the United States is an undesirable infringement of individual rights. (2nd Topic) Resolved: That the U.S. Supreme Court, on balance, has granted excessive power to law enforcement agencies.

1991–1992

(1st Topic) Resolved: That U.S. colleges and universities have inappropriately altered educational practices to address issues of race or gender. (2nd Topic) Resolved: That advertising degrades the quality of life in the United States.

1992–1993

(1st Topic) Resolved: That the welfare system exacerbates the problems of the urban poor in the United States. (2nd Topic) Resolved: That United Nations implementation of its Universal Declaration of Human Rights is more important than preserving state sovereignty.

1993–1994

(1st Topic) Resolved: That U.S. military intervention to support democratic governments is appropriate in a post–cold war world. (2nd Topic) Resolved: That the national news media in the United States impair public understanding of political issues.

1994–1995

(1st Topic) Resolved: That throughout the United States, more severe punishment for individuals convicted of violent crime would be desirable. (2nd Topic) Resolved: That the United States should significantly increase the development of the earth's ocean resources.

1995–1996

(1st Topic) Resolved: That the United States should substantially change its foreign policy toward Mexico. (2nd Topic) Resolved: That the United States should substantially change its foreign policy toward Mexico.[6]

NATIONAL INTERCOLLEGIATE DEBATE PROPOSITIONS (NDT AND CEDA)

Following is a list of the national intercollegiate debate propositions (NDT and CEDA) for the academic years 1996–1997 to 2007–2008.

1996–1997

Resolved: That the U.S. federal government should increase regulations requiring industries to decrease substantially the domestic production and/or emission of environmental pollutants.

1997–1998

Resolved: That the U.S. federal government should substantially increase its security assistance to one or more of the following Southeast Asian nations: Brunei Darussalam, Myanmar (Burma), Cambodia, Indonesia, Laos, Malaysia, Philippines, Singapore, Thailand, Vietnam.

1998–1999

Resolved: That the U.S. federal government should amend Title VII of the Civil Rights Act of 1964, through legislation, to create additional protections against racial and/or gender discrimination.

1999–2000

Resolved: That the U.S. federal government should adopt a policy of constructive engagement, including the removal of all or nearly all economic sanctions, with the government(s) of one or more of the following nation-states:

Cuba, Iran, Iraq, Syria, North Korea.

2000–2001

Resolved: That the U.S. federal government should substantially increase its development assistance, including increasing government-to-government assistance, within the Greater Horn of Africa.

2001–2002

Resolved: That the U.S. federal government should substantially increase federal control throughout Indian Country in one or more of the following areas: child welfare, criminal justice, employment, environmental protection, gaming, resource management, taxation.

2002–2003

Resolved: That the U.S. federal government should ratify or accede to, and implement, one or more of the following: The Comprehensive Nuclear Test Ban Treaty; The Kyoto Protocol; The Rome Statute of the International Criminal Court; The Second Optional Protocol to the International Covenant on Civil and Political Rights aiming at the Abolition of the Death Penalty; The Treaty between the United States of America and the Russian Federation on Strategic Offensive Reductions, if not ratified by the United States.

2003–2004

Resolved: That the U.S. federal government should enact one or more of the following: Withdrawal of its World Trade Organization complaint against the European Union's restrictions on genetically modified foods; A substantial increase in its government-to-government economic and/or conflict prevention assistance to Turkey and/or Greece; Full withdrawal from the North Atlantic Treaty Organization; Removal of its barriers to and encouragement of substantial European Union and/or North Atlantic Treaty Organization participation in peacekeeping in Iraq and reconstruction in Iraq; Removal of its tactical nuclear weapons from Europe; Harmonization of its intellectual property law with the European Union in the area of human DNA sequences; Rescission of all or nearly all agriculture subsidy increases in the 2002 Farm Bill.

2004–2005

Resolved: The U.S. federal government should establish an energy policy requiring a substantial reduction in the total nongovernmental consumption of fossil fuels in the United States.

2005–2006

Resolved: The U.S. federal government should substantially increase diplomatic and economic pressure on the People's Republic of China in one or more of the following areas: trade, human rights, weapons nonproliferation, Taiwan.

2006–2007

Resolved: The U.S. Supreme Court should overrule one or more of the following decisions:

- *Planned Parenthood v. Casey*, 505 U.S. 833 (1992);
- Ex parte Quirin, 317 U.S. 1 (1942);
- *U.S. v. Morrison*, 529 U.S. 598 (2000);
- *Milliken v. Bradley*, 418 U.S. 717 (1974).

2007–2008

Resolved: That the U.S. federal government should increase its constructive engagement with the government of one or more of: Afghanistan, Iran, Lebanon, the Palestinian Authority, and Syria, and it should include offering them a security guarantee(s) and/or a substantial increase in foreign assistance.

2008–2009

Resolved: that the United States Federal Government should substantially reduce its agricultural support, at least eliminating nearly all of the domestic subsidies, for biofuels, Concentrated Animal Feeding Operations, corn, cotton, dairy, fisheries, rice, soybeans, sugar and/or wheat.

2009–2010

Resolved: The United States Federal Government should substantially reduce the size of its nuclear weapons arsenal, and/or substantially reduce and restrict the role and/or missions of its nuclear weapons arsenal.

2010–2011

Resolved: The United States Federal Government should substantially increase the number of and/or substantially expand beneficiary eligibility for its visas for one or more of the following: employment-based immigrant visas, nonimmigrant temporary worker visas, family-based visas, human trafficking-based visas.

2011–2012

Resolved: The United States Federal Government should substantially increase its democracy assistance for one or more of the following: Bahrain, Egypt, Libya, Syria, Tunisia, Yemen.

2012–2013

Resolved: The United States Federal Government should substantially reduce restrictions on and/or substantially increase financial incentives for energy production in the United States of one or more of the following: coal, crude oil, natural gas, nuclear power, solar power, wind power.

NATIONAL INTERCOLLEGIATE DEBATE
PROPOSITIONS (NEDA)[7]

Following is a list of the national intercollegiate debate propositions (NEDA) from spring 1997 to spring 2012.

Spring 1997

Resolved: The Central Intelligence Agency should be eliminated.

Spring 1998

Resolved: The United States should abolish the use of peer jurors.

Fall 1998

Resolved: Corporate emphasis on profit is excessive.

Spring 2000

Resolved: The federal government should significantly increase the use of privately operated prisons.

Spring 2001

Resolved: The United States should significantly decrease its dependence on foreign oil.

Fall 2001

Resolved: A national missile defense system would be beneficial to the security of this nation.

Spring 2002

Resolved: The United States should substantially expand its efforts to prevent terrorism.

Fall 2002

Resolved: Civil liberties are being inappropriately eroded.

Spring 2003

Resolved: The U.S. federal government should significantly increase its citizens' access to affordable health care.

Fall 2003

Resolved: U.S. corporations are insufficiently loyal to American workers.

Spring 2004

Resolved: The United States should significantly reduce its foreign military commitments.

Fall 2004

Resolved: Separation of church and state is being inappropriately eroded.

Spring 2005

Resolved: The United States should substantially reform public secondary school education.

Fall 2005

Resolved: Wal-Mart's business practices are detrimental to the United States.

Spring 2006

Resolved: Nonviolent crimes should not carry prison sentences.

Fall 2006

Resolved: U.S. foreign policy inappropriately emphasizes military action over diplomacy.

Spring 2007

Resolved: The U.S. Government should significantly increase the acceptance of immigrants.

Fall 2007

Resolved: Corporations exert undue influence over public policy.

Spring 2008

Resolved: The U.S. federal government should make adequate and affordable medical care available to all U.S. citizens.

Fall 2008

Resolved: Americans overvalue athletic competition.

Spring 2009

Resolved: The U.S. federal government should significantly limit the authority of the Department of Homeland Security.

Fall 2009

Resolved: The United States is overreliant on China.

Spring 2010

Resolved: The United States should significantly reform the welfare system.

Fall 2011

Resolved: Political parties are bad for effective government in the United States.

Spring 2012

The U.S. prison system should significantly increase programs to rehabilitate inmates.

NATIONAL INTERCOLLEGIATE LINCOLN–DOUGLAS DEBATE PROPOSITIONS (NFA)[8]

1992–1993

Resolved: That the terms of federal legislators should be limited to a specific duration.

1993–1994

Resolved: That the U.S. federal government should significantly alter laws for immigration into the United States.

1994–1995

Resolved: That the federal government should significantly reform the U.S. public welfare system.

1995–1996

Resolved: That participation in one or more of the six principal bodies of the United Nations should be significantly restricted by altering the U.N. charter and/or rules of procedure.

1996–1997

Resolved: That the U.S. Department of Education should require the implementation of more rigorous methods of teacher and/or student performance evaluation in secondary school systems.

1997–1998

Resolved: That the U.S. federal government should significantly change its foreign policy toward Taiwan.

1998–1999

Resolved: That the U.S. federal government should significantly increase its regulation of electronically mediated communication.

1999–2000

Resolved: That the U.S. federal government should increase restrictions on the development, use, and/or sale of genetically modified organisms.

2000–2001

Resolved: That the U.S. federal government should significantly increase restrictions on civil lawsuits.

2001–2002

Resolved: That the U.S. federal government should significantly alter its policy for combating international terrorism.

2002–2003

Resolved: That the U.S. federal government should significantly increase assistance to U.S. residents living below the poverty line.

2003–2004

Resolved: That the U.S. federal government should substantially increase environmental regulations on industrial pollution.

2004–2005

Resolved: That the U.S. federal government should significantly reform the criminal justice system.

2005–2006

Resolved: That the U.S. federal government should adopt a policy to increase the protection of human rights in one or more of the following nations: Tibet, Bhutan, Afghanistan, Nepal, Myanmar, Thailand, East Timor, Indonesia, Philippines, and/or Pakistan.

2006–2007

Resolved: That the U.S. federal government should adopt a policy to significantly increase the production of energy from renewable sources.

2007–2008

Resolved: That the U.S. federal government should substantially increase assistance to the Greater Horn of Africa in one of the following areas: economic development, human rights protection, or public health.

2008–2009

Resolved: The U.S. federal government should substantially increase its constructive engagement with Cuba.

2009–2010

Resolved: That the U.S. federal government should substantially reform domestic transportation infrastructure.

2010–2011

Resolved: The U.S. federal government should substantially reform the provision of mental health services to the chronically mentally ill.

2011–2012

Resolved: The U.S. federal government should substantially change its trade policy and/or practices with the People's Republic of China.

2012–2013

Resolved: The U.S. federal government should substantially increase assistance for organic and/or sustainable agriculture in the United States.

NOTES

1. See George McCoy Musgrave, *Competitive Debate: Rules and Techniques*, 3rd ed. (New York: Wilson, 1957), pp. 143–145, for a list of intercollegiate debate propositions from 1920–1921 through 1956–1957; and E. R. Nichols, "The Annual College Question," *Debater's Magazine* (December 1947), pp. 206–207, for a list of intercollegiate debate propositions from 1922–1923 through 1947–1948. Announcements issued by the Committee on Intercollegiate Debate and Discussion give the current NDT debate proposition.
2. Listed in Musgrave, *Competitive Debate*, pp. 143–145.

3. Musgrave, *Competitive Debate*, pp. 143–145.
4. Listed in Nichols, "The Annual College Question," pp. 206–207.
5. The list of CEDA propositions from 1971 through 1985 was furnished by Jack H. Howe, executive secretary of CEDA. Announcements by CEDA give the current CEDA propositions.
6. In December 1995 the CEDA topic ballot included a number of new topics and the fall topic. The membership elected to repeat the fall topic.
7. Posted by the NEDA at http://www.neda.us/.
8. Posted by the NFA at http://www.nationalforensics.org/lincoln-douglas-debate.

APPENDIX **E**

Debate Bibliography

The following bibliography for the debate student and the debate educator was originally adapted from the excellent bibliography prepared by Steven Hunt. In addition, you may wish to visit the following websites:

American Forensics Association (AFA)
  http://www.americanforensics.org/

American Parliamentary Debate Association (APDA)
  http://www.apdaweb.org/

Canadian University Society for Intercollegiate Debate
  http://www.cusid.ca/

Commission on Presidential Debates
  http://www.debates.org/

Critical Animal Blog
  http://www.criticalanimal.blogspot.com/

Cross Examination Debate Association (CEDA)
  http://www.cedadebate.org/

Debate Central
  http://www.debate.uvm.edu/

Debate Results
  http://www.commweb.fullerton.edu/jbruschke/web/index.aspx

DebateVision
  http://www.debatevision.com/

Forensic Friend (from Whitman College)
  http://www.wcdebate.com/forensicfriend.htm

Global Debate: News about Debating on Planet Earth
  http://globaldebateblog.blogspot.com/

International Debate Education Association (IDEA)
  http://www.idebate.org/

International Public Debate Association (IPDA)
  http://www.ipdadebate.info/constitution–bylaws.html

National Association of Urban Debate Leagues
http://www.urbandebate.org/index.shtml

National Debate Tournament (NDT) home page
http://www.wfu.edu/NDT/

National Educational Debate Association (NEDA)
http://www.neda.us/

National Forensic Association Lincoln–Douglas home page
http://www.nationalforensics.org/lincoln-douglas-debate

National Parliamentary Debate Association (NPDA)
http://www.parlidebate.org/

Open Debates
http://www.opendebates.org/theissue/

Planet Debate
http://www.planetdebate.com/

Rebecca Moore Howard Bibliography on Argumentation
http://www.rebeccamoorehoward.com/bibliographies/argument-and-argumentation

Tab Room on the PC
https://bearspace.baylor.edu/Richard_Edwards/www/TRPC_Software.html

The English-Speaking Union
http://www.esu.org/

The National Debate Project
http://www.nationaldebateproject.org/

Wake Forest University Guide to Debate Pedagogy (Links)
http://groups.wfu.edu/debate/MiscSites/PedegogyArticles.htm

Wake Forest University Guide to Debate Theory (Links)
http://groups.wfu.edu/debate/MiscSites/DRGArticles/DRGArtiarticles Index.htm

A SELECT BIBLIOGRAPHY ON DEBATE THEORY

I. Overview of Key Debate Theory Resources

Top Eight Sources for Debate Theory

It is very difficult to get a comprehensive vision of debate theory because the sources are difficult to find. There are a wide variety of forensics organizations separately publishing debate materials. Most debate materials are not well indexed or indexed at all.

1. *Argumentation and Advocacy*, formerly *Journal of the American Forensic Association* (referred to as *JAFA*), http://www.americanforensics.org/publications-and-research/argumentation-/argumentation-and-advocacy.
2. Textbooks on argumentation and debate
   Corbett, Edward P. J., and Rosa A. Eberly. *The Elements of Reasoning*, 2nd ed. Boston, MA: Allyn and Bacon, 2000.
   Govier, Trudy. *A Practical Study of Argument*, 6th ed. Belmont, CA: Wadsworth, 2005.
   Herrick, James A. *Argumentation: Understanding and Shaping Arguments*, 3rd ed. State College, PA: Strata, 2007.

Inch, Edward S., and Barbara Warnick. *Critical Thinking and Communication: The Use of Reason in Argument*, 6th ed. Boston, MA: Allyn and Bacon, 2010.

Johnson, R., and A. Blair. *Logical Self-Defense*. New York: International Debate Education Association, 2006.

Johnson, S. L. *Winning Debates: A Guide to Debating in the Style of the World University Debating Championships*. New York: International Debate Education Association, 2009.

Massey, J. *Critical Debaters Handbook*, 2011. DOI: Soonerdebate.com.

Meany, J., and K. Shuster. *Art, Argument, and Advocacy, Mastering Parliamentary Debate*. New York: International Debate Education Association, 2002.

Meany, J., and K. Shuster. *On That Point: An Introduction to Parliamentary Debate*. New York: International Debate Education Association, 2002.

Rieke, R., M. Sillars, and T. Peterson. *Argumentation and Critical Decision Making*, 8th ed. Boston, MA: Pearson Education, Inc., 2013.

Rybacki, K. C., and D. J. Rybacki. *Advocacy and Opposition: An Introduction to Argumentation*, 7th ed. Boston, MA: Allyn and Bacon, 2012.

Snider, A. *Code of the Debater*. New York: International Debate Education Association, 2008.

Trapp, R. *The Debatabase Book*, 4th ed. New York: International Debate Education Association, 2009.

Weston, Anthony. *A Rulebook of Arguments*, 3rd ed. Indianapolis, IN: Hackett, 2000.

3. *Contemporary Argumentation & Debate: The Journal of the Cross Examination Debate Association*, formerly *CEDA Yearbook*, http://cedadebate.org/CAD/index.php/CAD/index.

4. Thomas, David A., and Jack Hart, eds. *Advanced Debate: Readings in Theory, Practice, and Teaching*, 4th ed. Lincolnwood, IL: National Textbook, 1992.

5. *The Forensic* of PKD, http://www.pikappadelta.com/theforensic.html.

6. *Speaker and Gavel* of DSR-TKA, http://www.mnsu.edu/cmst/dsr-tka/speakerandgavel.htm.

7. SCA/AFA Conferences on Argumentation, http://altaconference.org/proceedings.html (There have been 16 biannual conferences since 1979.)

8. *National Forensic Journal* of NFA, http://www.nationalforensics.org/national-forensic-journal.

Other Important Sources

Griffin Research, Berkeley, CA. Used to publish debate theory booklets.

Championship Debates and Speeches, annual national final transcripts of final rounds of NDT, CEDA, and so on.

Philosophy and Rhetoric, http://www.psupress.org/Journals/jnls_pr.html.

II. Bibliographies

Bartanen, Michael. "Works Cited." In *Teaching and Directing Forensics*. Scottsdale, AZ: Gorsuch Scarisbrick, 1994. Pp. 179–184.

———, and David Frank. "Select Bibliography: Scholarly Materials on Value Theory and Value Argument." In *Nonpolicy Debate*, 2nd ed. Scottsdale, AZ: Gorsuch Scarisbrick, 1994. Pp. 51–53.

Berube, David. *Non-Policy Debating*. Lanham, MD: University Press of America, 1994. Pp. 351–370.

Brownlee, Don. *Coaching Debate and Forensics (Annotated Bibliography)*. Annandale, VA: SCA, 1988.

————, Julia Johnson, and Mike Buckley. "A Bibliometric Analysis of the CEDA Yearbook." *CEDA Yearbook* 12 (1991): 108–120.

Church, Russell T. "A Bibliography for Argumentation and Debate for 1975–76, 1977–78, and 1979." In various editions of *JAFA*.

————, and David C. Buckley. "Argumentation and Debating Propositions of Value: A Bibliography." *JAFA* 19 (Spring 1983): 239–250.

Conklin, Forrest. "A Bibliography for Argumentation and Debate." Published annually in *JAFA*, 1968–1973.

Cureton, Robert D. "A Bibliography for Argumentation and Debate." Published annually in *JAFA*, 1972–1974.

Hansen, Hans V. "An Informal Logic Bibliography." *Informal Logic* 12(3) (Fall 1990): 155–183.

Houtlosser, P. P. "Bibliography Argumentation Studies 2002." *Argumentation* 18(4) (2004): 501–518.

Hunt, Steven B. "A Select Partially Annotated Bibliography for Directing Forensics: Teaching, Coaching, and Judging Debate and Individual Events." *The Forensic* 81(2) (Winter 1996): 1–40.

Jensen, J. Vernon. "Bibliography on Argumentation." *Rhetoric Society Quarterly* 19 (1989): 71–81.

Johnson, Ralph H., and J. Anthony Blair. "A Bibliography of Recent Work in Informal Logic." In *Informal Logic: The First International Symposium*, ed. J. Anthony Blair and Ralph H. Johnson. Inverness, CA: Edgepress, 1980. Pp. 163–172.

Louden, Allan, "Non-Presidential Political Debates, Selected Bibliography," http://www.wfu.edu/~louden/Political%20Communication/Bibs/NonPresDebates.htm.

Louden, Allan, "Presidential Political Debates, Selected Bibliography," http://www.wfu.edu/~louden/Political%20Communication/Bibs/DEBATES.html.

Pfau, Michael, David Thomas, and Walter Ulrich. *Debate and Argument: A Systems Approach to Advocacy*. Glenview, IL: Scott, Foresman, 1987. Pp. 313–323.

Sproule, J. Michael. "The Roots of American Argumentation Theory: A Review of Landmark Works, 1878–1932." *JAFA* 23 (Fall 1986): 110–115.

Steadman, Clarence. "An Index to *The Forensic* 1915–1990." *The Forensic* 75(4) (Summer 1990): 1–30.

Tindell, J. H. "Argumentation and Debate Textbooks: An Overview of Content and Focus." *Argumentation & Advocacy* 35(4) (1999): 185.

Towne, Ralph, Robert M. Smith, and Thomas Harris. "Recommended Debate Texts and Handbooks: A Survey." *Speaker and Gavel* 11(3) (Jan. 1974): 52–54.

Trapp, Robert, and Janice Schuetz, eds. "Bibliography." In *Perspectives on Argumentation: Essays in Honor of Wayne Brockriede*. Prospect Heights, IL: Waveland Press, 1990. Pp. 315–338.

III. Values of Debate

Aden, Roger. "Reconsidering the Laboratory Metaphor: Forensics as a Liberal Art." *National Forensic Journal* 9 (Fall 1991): 97–108.

Bartanen, Michael. "The Educational Benefits of Forensics." In *Teaching and Directing Forensics*. Scottsdale, AZ: Gorsuch Scarisbrick, 1994. Pp. 3–5.

Bennett, William H. "The Role of Debate in Speech Communication." *The Speech Teacher* 21 (Nov. 1972): 281–288.

Bradley, Bert E., Jr. "Debate: A Practical Training for Gifted Students." *The Speech Teacher* 7 (Mar. 1959): 134–138.

Brockriede, Wayne. "College Debate and the Reality Gap." *Speaker and Gavel* 7(3) (Mar. 1970): 71–76.

———. "The Contemporary Renaissance in the Study of Argument." In *Argument in Transition: Proceedings of the Third Summer Conference on Argumentation*, ed. David Zarefsky, Malcolm O. Sillars, and Jack Rhodes. Annandale, VA: SCA, 1983. Pp. 17–26.

Chandler, Robert C., and Jeffrey Hobbs. "The Benefits of Intercollegiate Policy Debate Training to Various Professions." In *Argument in Controversy: Proceedings of the Seventh SCA/AFA Conference on Argumentation*, ed. Donn Parson. Annandale, VA: SCA, 1991. Pp. 388–390.

Clark, Ruth Anne, and Jesse G. Delia. "'Topoi'and Rhetorical Competence." *Quarterly Journal of Speech* 65(2) (Apr. 1979): 187–206.

Clevenger, Theodore. "Toward a Point of View for Contest Debate." *Central States Speech Journal* 12 (Autumn 1960): 21–26.

Colbert, Kent. "The Effects of Debate Participation on Argumentativeness and Verbal Aggression." *Communication Education* 42(3) (July 1993): 206–214.

———. "Replicating the Effects of Debate Participation on Argumentativeness and Verbal Aggression." *The Forensic* 79(3) (Spring 1994): 1–13.

———, and Thompson Biggers. "Why Should We Support Debate?" *JAFA* 21(3) (Spring 1985): 237–240.

DeLancey, Charles A. "The Values of Forensics Activities to Speech Communication Programs in Liberal Arts Colleges." *Association for Communication Administration Bulletin* (47) (Jan. 1984): 56–57.

Douglas, Donald. "Toward a Philosophy of Forensic Education." *JAFA* 8 (Summer 1971): 36–41.

Dowling, Ralph. "Arguers as Lovers: Implications for Forensics." *Communication Education* 32 (Apr. 1983): 237–241.

Farrell, Thomas B. "The Tradition of Rhetoric and the Philosophy of Communication." *Communication* 7(2) (1983): 151–180.

Freeley, Austin J. "An Anthology of Commentary on Debate." *The Speech Teacher* 10 (Jan. 1961): 44–47.

Goodnight, G. Thomas. "The Re-Union of Argumentation and Debate Theory." In *Dimensions of Argument: Proceedings of the Second Summer Conference on Argumentation*, ed. George Ziegelmueller and Jack Rhodes. Annandale, VA: SCA, 1981. Pp. 415–432.

Heymann, Philip, and Jody Heymann. "The Fate of Public Debate in the U.S." *Harvard Journal of Legislation* 33 (Summer 1996): 511–526.

Hill, Bill. "Intercollegiate Debate: Why Do Students Bother?" *Southern Speech Communication Journal* 48 (Fall 1982): 77–88.

Hobbs, Jeffrey Dale, and Robert C. Chandler. "The Perceived Benefits of Policy Debate Training in Various Professions." *Speaker and Gavel* 28 (1991): 4–6.

Hollihan, Thomas, and Patricia Riley. "Academic Debate and Democracy: A Clash of Ideologies." In *Argument and Critical Practices: Proceedings of the Fifth SCA/AFA Conference on Argumentation*, ed. J. W. Wenzel. Annandale, VA: SCA, 1987. Pp. 399–404.

Hunt, Steven B. "The Values of Forensics Participation." In *Intercollegiate Forensics*, ed. T. C. Winebrenner. Dubuque, IA: Kendall Hunt, 1994. Pp. 1–19.

Jones, Kevin T. "Cerebral Gymnastics 101: Why Do Debaters Debate?" *CEDA Yearbook* 15 (1994): 65–75.

Kay, Jack. "Rapprochement of World 1 and World 2: Discovering the Ties Between Practical Discourse and Forensics." In *Argument in Transition: Proceedings of the Third Summer Conference on Argumentation*, ed. David Zarefsky, Malcolm O. Sillars, and Jack Rhodes. Annandale, VA: SCA, 1983. Pp. 927–937.

Kruger, Arthur. "Debate and Speech Communication." *Southern Communication Journal* 39 (Spring 1974): 233–240.

Kully, Robert D. "Forensics and the Speech Communication Discipline: Analysis of an Estrangement." *JAFA* 8 (Spring 1972): 192–199.

Leeper, Karla, and Dale Herbeck. "Policy Debate as a Laboratory for Teaching Argument Skills." *Forensic Educator* 6 (1991–92): 23–28.

Littlefield, Robert S. "An Assessment of University Administrators: Do They Value Competitive Debate and I. E. Programs." *National Forensic Journal* 9(2) (Fall 1991): 87–96.

Matlon, Ron, and Lucy M. Keele. "A Survey of Participants in the National Debate Tournament, 1947–1980." *JAFA* 20 (Spring 1984): 194–205.

McBath, James. "Rationale for Forensics." In *American Forensics in Perspective: Papers from the Second National Conference on Forensics*, ed. Donn Parson. Annandale, VA: SCA, 1984. Pp. 5–11.

McGlone, Edward L. "The Behavioral Effects of Forensics Participation." *JAFA* 10 (Winter 1974): 140–146.

McGough, M. "Pull It Across Your Flow." *The New Republic* (Oct. 10, 1988): 17–19.

McGuckin, Henry E., Jr. "Forensics in the Liberal Education." *Western Journal of Speech Communication* 34 (Spring 1970): 133–138.

Morello, John T. "Intercollegiate Debate: Proposals for a Struggling Activity." *Speaker and Gavel* 17(2) (Winter 1980): 103–107.

Nobles, W. Scott. "Tournament Debating and Rhetoric." *Western Journal of Speech Communication* 22 (Fall 1958): 206–210.

Norton, Larry. "Nature and Benefits of Academic Debate." In *Introduction to Debate*, ed. Carolyn Keefe, Thomas B. Harte, and Larry E. Norton. New York: Macmillan, 1982. Pp. 24–40.

Pearce, W. Barnett. "Forensics and Speech Communication." *Association for Communication Administration Bulletin* (7) (Apr. 1974): 26–32.

Ritter, Kurt. "Debate and a Liberal Arts Education: The Forensics Program at the U. of Illinois." *Speaker and Gavel* 14(4) (Summer 1977): 72–84.

———. "Debate as an Instrument for Democracy." *Speaker and Gavel* 8(3) (Spring 1976): 41–43.

Rohrer, Dan M. "Debate as a Liberal Art." In *Advanced Debate: Readings in Theory, Practice, and Teaching*, 3rd ed., ed. David A. Thomas and Jack Hart. Lincolnwood, IL: National Textbook, 1987. Pp. 7–14.

Rowland, Robert, and Scott Deatherage. "The Crisis in Policy Debate." *JAFA* 24 (Spring 1988): 246–250.

———. "A Defense of Rational Argument." *Philosophy and Rhetoric* 28(4) (1995): 350–364.

———. "The Practical Pedagogical Function of Academic Debate." *Contemporary Argumentation and Debate* 16 (1995): 98–108.

———, and John E. Fritch. "The Relationship Between Debate and Argumentation Theory." In *Spheres of Argument: Proceedings of the Sixth SCA/AFA Conference on Argumentation*, ed. Bruce E. Gronbeck. Annandale, VA: SCA, 1989. Pp. 457–463.

Sellnow, Deanna. "Justifying Forensics Programs to Administrators." *National Forensic Journal* 11 (Winter 1994): 1–14.

Thomas, David A. "Forensics Shock: Making Forensics Relevant to Tomorrow's Higher Education." *Speech Teacher* 13 (Sept. 1974): 235–241.

Trapp, Robert. "The Need for an Argumentative Perspective in Academic Debate." *CEDA Yearbook* 14 (1993): 23–33.

Treadaway, Glenda. "A Pedagogical Rationale for Re-Establishing Complementary Debate and Individual Events Programs." In *Proceedings from the Pi Kappa Delta Development Conference: Re-Formulating Forensics for the New Century*, ed. Scott Jensen. Lake Charles, LA: McNeese State University, 1995. Pp. 17–24.

Windes, R. R., Jr. "Competitive Debating, the Speech Program, the Individual, and Society." *Speech Teacher* 9 (Mar. 1960): 99–108.

Winebrenner, T. C. "Reaffirming the Role of Argumentation Theory in Academic Debate." *The Forensic* 79(2) (Winter 1994): 1–9.

Zarefsky, David. "Keynote Address." In *Dialogue in the Forensic Community: Proceedings of the Conference on Forensic Education*, ed. Jack Kay and Julie Lee. Kansas City, MO: National Federation of State High School Associations, 1990.

IV. Debate and Critical Thinking

Beckman, V. "An Investigation of Their Contributions to Critical Thinking Made by Courses in Argumentation and Discussion in Selected Colleges." Unpublished Ph.D. dissertation, University of Minnesota, 1955.

Blair, J. Anthony. "Teaching Argument in Critical Thinking." *The Community College Humanities Review* 5 (1984): 19–30.

Brembeck, W. "The Effects of a Course in Argumentation on Critical Thinking." *Speech Monographs* 16 (1949): 172–189.

Colbert, Kent. "The Effects of CEDA and NDT Debate Training on Critical Thinking Ability." *JAFA* 23(4) (Spring 1987): 194–201.

———. "Enhancing Critical Thinking Ability Through Academic Debate." *Contemporary Argumentation and Debate* 16 (1995): 52–72.

———. "The Debate–Critical Thinking Relationship: Isolating the Effects of Self-Selection." Paper presented at the SCA Convention, San Antonio, TX, 1995.

Cross, G. "The Effects of Belief Systems and the Amount of Debate Experience on the Acquisition of Critical Thinking." Unpublished Ph.D. dissertation, University of Utah, 1971.

Follert, V., and Kent Colbert. "An Analysis of the Research Concerning Debate Training and Critical Thinking Improvements." ERIC Document Reproduction Service #ED 238 058, 1983.

Frank, D. "Teaching High School Speech to Improve Critical Thinking." *The Speech Teacher* 18 (1969): 296–302.

Greenstreet, Robert. "Academic Debating and Critical Thinking: A Look at the Evidence." *National Forensic Journal* 11 (1993): 13–28.

Gruner, Charles, Richard Huseman, and James Luck. "Debating Ability, Critical Thinking Ability, and Authoritarianism." *Speaker and Gavel* 8(3) (Mar. 1971): 63–65.

Hill, Bill. "The Value of Competitive Debate as a Vehicle for Promoting Development of Critical Thinking Ability." *CEDA Yearbook* 14 (1993): 1–22.

Huseman, Richard, Glenn Ware, and Charles Gruner. "Critical Thinking, Reflective Thinking, and the Ability to Organize Ideas: A Multi-Variate Approach." *JAFA* 9 (Summer 1972): 261–265.

Jackson, T., ed. "The Effects of Intercollegiate Debating on Critical Thinking." Unpublished Ph.D. dissertation, University of Wisconsin, 1961.

Katula, R., and C. Martin. "Teaching Critical Thinking in the Speech Communication Classroom." *Communication Education* 33 (1984): 160–167.

Perella, Jack. *The Debate Method of Critical Thinking*. Dubuque, IA: Kendall Hunt, 1983.

Powell, Robert G. "Critical Thinking and Speech Communication: Our Critical Strategies Are Warranted NOT!" *Journal of Applied Communication Research* 20(3) (Aug. 1992): 342–347.

Sanders, Judith, Richard Wiseman, and Robert Gass. "Does Teaching Argumentation Facilitate Students' Critical Thinking?" *Communication Reports* 7(1) (Winter 1994): 27–35.

Whalen, Shawn. "Intercollegiate Debate as a Co-Curricular Activity: Effects on Critical Thinking Skills." In *Arguments in Controversy: Proceedings of the Seventh SCA/AFA Conference on Argumentation*, ed. Donn Parson. Annandale, VA: SCA, 1991. Pp. 391–397.

V. Books on Argumentation and Debate

Adler, Mortimer. *Dialectic*. New York: Harcourt, Brace, 1929.

Anderson, Jerry M., and Paul J. Dovre, eds. *Readings in Argumentation*. Boston, MA: Allyn and Bacon, 1968.

Bartanen, Michael, and David Frank. *Non-Policy Debate*, 2nd ed. Scottsdale, AZ: Gorsuch Scarisbrick, 1994.

———. *Teaching and Directing Forensics*. Scottsdale, AZ: Gorsuch Scarisbrick, 1994.

Benoit, William, Dale Hample, and Pam Benoit, eds. *Readings in Argumentation*. New York: Foris, 1992.

Berube, David. *Nonpolicy Debating*. New York: University Press of America, 1993.

Branham, Robert James. *Debate and Critical Analysis: The Harmony of Conflict*. Hillsdale, NJ: Lawrence Erlbaum, 1991.

Campbell, Cole. *Competitive Debate*. Chapel Hill, NC: Information Research Associates, 1974.

Capp, Glenn R., and Thelma Capp. *Principles of Argumentation and Debate*. Englewood Cliffs, NJ: Prentice Hall, 1965.

Corcoran, Joseph. *An Introduction to Non-Policy Debating*. Dubuque, IA: Kendall Hunt, 1988.

Cox, J. Robert, Malcolm O. Sillars, and Gregg B. Walkers, eds. *Argument and Social Practice: Proceedings of the Fourth SCA/AFA Conference on Argumentation*. Annandale, VA: SCA, 1985.

Ehninger, Douglas, and Wayne Brockriede. *Decision by Debate*, 2nd ed. New York: Harper & Row, 1978.

Ericson, J. M., and J. J. Murphy, with Bud Zeuschner. *The Debater's Guide*, revised ed. Carbondale, IL: Southern Illinois University Press, 1987.

Fadely, Dean. *Advocacy: The Essentials of Argumentation and Debate*. Dubuque, IA: Kendall Hunt, 1994.

Foster, William T. *Argumentation and Debating*. Boston, MA: Houghton Mifflin, 1932 [1908]. A classic.

Freeley, Austin J. *Argumentation and Debate: Critical Thinking for Reasoned Decision Making*, 9th ed. Belmont, CA: Wadsworth, 1996. Probably used in more college debate classes than any other text from the 1960s to today.

Gronbeck, Bruce E., ed. *Spheres of Argument: Proceedings of the Sixth SCA/AFA Conference on Argumentation*. Annandale, VA: SCA, 1989.

Hollihan, Thomas A., and Kevin Baaske. *Arguments and Arguing: The Products and Process of Human Decision Making*. New York: St. Martin's Press, 1994.

Jackson, Sally, ed. *Argumentation and Values: Proceedings of the Ninth SCA/AFA Conference on Argumentation.* Annandale, VA: SCA, 1995.

Kahane, Howard. *Logic and Contemporary Rhetoric,* 5th ed. Belmont, CA: Wadsworth, 1988.

MacRae, Duncan. *Policy Indicators: Links Between Social Science and Public Debate.* Winston-Salem: University of North Carolina Press, 1985.

Makau, Josina M. *Reasoning and Communication: Thinking Critically About Arguments.* Belmont, CA: Wadsworth, 1990.

McBath, James., ed. *Forensics as Communication: The Argumentative Perspective.* Skokie, IL: National Textbook, 1975. Critical to developing a sound debate coaching philosophy.

McKerrow, Ramie, ed. *Argument and the Postmodern Challenge: Proceedings of the Eighth SCA/AFA Conference on Argumentation.* Annandale, VA: SCA, 1993.

McPeak, J. *Teaching Critical Thinking: Dialogue and Dialectic.* New York: Routledge, 1990.

Parella, Jack. *The Debate Method of Critical Thinking.* Dubuque, IA: Kendall Hunt, 1986.

Parson, Donn, ed. *American Forensics in Perspective: Papers from the Second National Conference on Forensics.* Annandale, VA: SCA, 1984.

———, ed. *Argument in Controversy: Proceedings of the Seventh SCA/AFA Conference on Argumentation.* Annandale, VA: SCA, 1991.

Patterson, J. W., and David Zarefsky. *Contemporary Debate.* Boston, MA: Houghton Mifflin, 1981.

Perelman, Chaim, and Lucie Olbrechts-Tyteca. *The New Rhetoric: A Treatise on Argumentation.* Trans. John Wilkinson and Purcell Weaver. Notre Dame, IN: University of Notre Dame Press, 1969. Along with Toulmin's *Uses of Argument,* should be familiar to all serious students of argumentation and debate.

Pfau, Michael, David A. Thomas, and Walter Ulrich. *Debate and Argument: A Systems Approach to Advocacy.* Glenview, IL: Scott, Foresman, 1987.

Reinard, John. *Foundations of Argument: Effective Communication for Critical Thinking.* Dubuque, IA: Brown & Benchmark, 1991.

Rhodes, Jack, and Sara Newell, eds. *Proceedings of the Summer Conference on Argumentation.* Annandale, VA: SCA, 1980.

Rieke, Richard D., and Malcolm O. Sillars. *Argumentation and the Decision Making Process,* 4th ed. Reading, MA: Addison-Wesley, 1996.

Roden, Sally, ed. *Commitment to Forensic Education: The Challenge to the Twenty-First Century: Proceedings of the 1991 PKD Professional Development Conference.* Conway: University of Central Arkansas, 1991.

Thomas, David, and John Hart. *Advanced Debate: Readings in Theory, Practice, and Teaching,* 4th ed. Lincolnwood, IL: National Textbook, 1992.

———, and Stephen Wood, eds. *CEDA Twentieth Anniversary Assessment Conference Proceedings.* Dubuque, IA: Kendall Hunt, 1993.

Thompson, Wayne. *Modern Argumentation and Debate: Principles and Practices.* New York: Harper & Row, 1971.

Toulmin, Stephen. *The Uses of Argument.* Cambridge: Cambridge University Press, 1958.

Ulrich, Walter. *Judging Academic Debate.* Lincolnwood, IL: National Textbook, 1986.

Warnick, Barbara, and Edward S. Inch. *Critical Thinking and Communication: The Use of Reason in Argument,* 2nd ed. New York: Macmillan, 1994.

Weiss, Robert O. *Public Argument.* New York: University Press of America, 1994.

Wenzel, Joseph, ed. *Argument and Critical Practices: Proceedings of the Fifth SCA/AFA Conference on Argumentation.* Annandale, VA: SCA, 1987.

Williams, David, and Michael Hazen, eds. *Argumentation Theory and the Rhetoric of Assent.* Tuscaloosa: University of Alabama Press, 1990.

Winebrenner, T. C., ed. *Intercollegiate Forensics*. Dubuque, IA: Kendall Hunt, 1994.

Winkler, Carol, William Newman, and David Birdsell. *Lines of Argument: Core Volume, Lines of Argument: Policy Argument, and Lines of Argument: Values Argument*. Dubuque, IA: Brown & Benchmark, 1993.

Zarefsky, David, Malcolm O. Sillars, and Jack Rhodes, eds. *Argument in Transition: Proceedings of the Third Summer Conference on Argumentation*. Annandale, VA: SCA, 1983.

Ziegelmueller, George, and Jack Rhodes, eds. *Dimensions of Argument: Proceedings of the Second Summer Conference on Argumentation*. Annandale, VA: SCA, 1981.

———, and Jack Kay. *Argumentation: Inquiry and Advocacy*, 3rd ed. Boston, MA: Allyn and Bacon, 1997.

VI. Prima Facie Cases and Stock Issues

Giffin, Kim, and Kenneth Magill. "Stock Issues in Tournament Debates." *Central States Speech Journal* 12 (Autumn 1960): 27–32.

Herlitz, Georg Nils. "The Meaning of the Term 'Prima Facie'." *Louisiana Law Review* 55(2) (Nov. 1994): 391–408.

McCroskey, James, and Leon R. Camp. "A Study of Stock Issues Judging Criteria and Decisions in Debate." *Southern States Communication Journal* (Winter 1964): 158–168.

Scott, Robert. "On the Meaning of the Term 'Prima Facie' in Argumentation." *Central States Speech Journal* 12 (Autumn 1960): 33–37.

Tuman, Joseph S. "Getting to First Base: Prima Facie Arguments for Propositions of Value." *JAFA* 24(2) (Fall 1987): 84–94.

Young, Gregory, and Paul Gaske. "On Prima Facie Value Argumentation: The Policy Implications Affirmative." *CEDA Yearbook* 5 (1984): 24–30.

VII. Presumption and the Burden of Proof

Brydon, Steven R. "Presumption in Non-Policy Debate: In Search of a Paradigm." *JAFA* 23(2) (Summer 1986): 15–22.

Burnett, Nicholas. "Archbishop Whately and the Concept of Presumption: Lessons for Non-Policy Debate." *CEDA Yearbook* 12 (1992): 37–43.

Cronkhite, Gary. "The Locus of Presumption." *Central States Speech Journal* 17 (Nov. 1966): 270–276.

Hill, Bill. "Toward a Holistic Model of Presumption in Non-Policy Debate." *CEDA Yearbook* 10 (1990): 22–32.

———. "An Evolving Model of Presumption for Non-Policy Debate." *CEDA Yearbook* 15 (1994): 43–64.

Lichtman, Allan, and Daniel Rohrer. "Critique of Zarefsky on Presumption." In *Proceedings of the National Conference on Argumentation*, ed. James Luck. Fort Worth, TX: Texas Christian University, 1973. Pp. 38–45.

Podgurski, Dwight. "Presumption in the Value Proposition Realm." *CEDA Yearbook* 4 (1983): 34–39.

Rowland, Robert C. "The Function of Presumption in Academic Debate." *CEDA Yearbook* 13 (1992): 20–24.

Sproule, J. Michael. "The Psychological Burden of Proof: On the Evolutionary Development of Richard Whately's Theory of Presumption." *Speech Monographs* 43(2) (June 1976): 115–129.

Thomas, David. "Presumption in Nonpolicy Debate: A Case for Natural Presumption Based on Current Nonpolicy Paradigms." In *Advanced Debate: Readings in Theory, Practice, and Teaching*, 4th ed., ed. David Thomas and John Hart. Lincolnwood, IL: National Textbook, 1992. Pp. 220–242.

Vasilius, Jan. "Presumption, Presumption, Wherefore Art Thou Presumption." *CEDA Yearbook* 1 (1980): 33–42.

VIII. Research

Adams, Tyrone, and Andrew Wood. "The Emerging Role of the World Wide Web in Forensics: On Computer-Mediated Research and Community Development." *The Forensic* 81(4) (Summer 1996): 21–35.

Bart, John. "Is There an Exit from the Information Superhighway? The Dangers of Electronic Research." *Forensic Educator* 9(1) (1994–95): 28–31.

Harris, Scott. "Databases in the Marketplace of Academic Debate: A Response to Tucker." *Argument and Advocacy* 32(1) (Summer 1995): 41–45.

Herbeck, Dale, ed. "Computer Mediated Research." *Forensic Educator* 9(1) (1994–95).

Pitt, Carl Allen. "Upgrading the Debater's Research Methods." *Speaker and Gavel* 7(2) (Jan. 1970): 44–46.

Rhodes, Jack, and Glenda Rhodes. "Guidelines for Library Services to College and High School Debaters." *Reference Quarterly* (Fall 1987): 87–94.

Scheckles, T. F. "Applications of Computer Technology in Intercollegiate Debate." *Speaker and Gavel* 23 (1986): 52–61.

Stafford, Shane, and Brian Lain. "Hitchhiking on the Information Superhighway: Research on the Net." In *Debaters' Research Guide*, ed. Wake Forest University Debate. Winston-Salem, NC: Wake Forest University, 1994. Pp. A10–A15, http://groups.wfu.edu/debate/MiscSites/DRGArticles/Stafford&Lain1994Immigration.htm

Tucker, Robert. "Argument, Ideology, and Databases: On the Corporatization of Academic Debate." *Argumentation and Advocacy* 32(1) (Summer 1995): 30–40.

Wood, Stephen C. "Threads: An Introduction to Forensic E-Mail." *The Forensic* 80(2) (Winter 1995): 18–29.

IX. Argumentation Theory, Dialectics, Logic and Reasoning, and Proof Standards as Applied to Debate

Aden, Roger. "The Enthymeme as Postmodern Argument Form: Condensed, Mediated Argument Then and Now." *Argument and Advocacy* 31(2) (Fall 1994): 54–63.

Adler, Mortimer. *Dialectic*. New York: Harcourt, Brace, 1929.

Anderson, Ray Lynn, and C. David Mortenson. "Logic and Marketplace Argumentation." *Quarterly Journal of Speech* 53 (Apr. 1967): 143–151.

———. "The Limits of Logic." *JAFA* 7 (Spring 1970): 71–78.

Aristotle. *The Rhetoric of Aristotle*. Trans. Lane Cooper. New York: Appleton-Century-Crofts, 1932.

Bator, Paul G. "The Good Reasons Movement: A Confounding of Dialectic and Rhetoric." *Philosophy and Rhetoric* 21(1) (1988): 38–47.

Benoit, William. "Aristotle's Example: The Rhetorical Induction." *Quarterly Journal of Speech* 66 (Apr. 1980): 182–192.

———. "On Aristotle's Example." *Philosophy and Rhetoric* 20(4) (1987): 261–267.

Billig, Michael. *Arguing and Thinking: A Rhetorical Approach to Social Psychology.* Cambridge: Cambridge University Press, 1987.

Blair, J. Anthony, and Ralph H. Johnson. "Argument as Dialectical." *Argumentation* 1 (1987): 41–56.

Brockriede, Wayne. "A Standard for Judging Applied Logic in Debate." *The AFA Register* (Spring 1962): 10–14.

———. "Arguers as Lovers." *Philosophy and Rhetoric* 5 (Winter 1972): 1–11.

———. "The Contemporary Renaissance in the Study of Argument." In *Argument in Transition: Proceedings of the Third Summer Conference on Argumentation,* ed. David Zarefsky, Malcolm O. Sillars, and Jack Rhodes. Annandale, VA: SCA, 1983. Pp. 17–26.

———, and Douglas Ehninger. "Toulmin on Argument: An Examination and Application." *Quarterly Journal of Speech* 46 (Feb. 1960): 44–53.

Brooks, Richard O. "Legal Studies and Liberal Arts: Outline of Curriculum Based upon the Practical Syllogism." *The Legal Studies Forum* 10(1) (Winter 1986): 97–120.

Clarke, Ruth Anne, and Jesse G. Delia. "'Topoi' and Rhetorical Competence." *Quarterly Journal of Speech* 65(2) (Apr. 1979): 187–206.

Conley, Thomas M. "The Enthymeme in Perspective." *Quarterly Journal of Speech* 70 (May 1984): 168–187.

Consigny, Scott. "Dialectical, Rhetorical, and Aristotelian Rhetoric." *Philosophy and Rhetoric* 22(4) (1989): 281–287.

Copi, Irving. *Informal Logic.* New York: Macmillan, 1986.

Delia, Jesse G. "The Logic Fallacy, Cognitive Theory, and the Enthymeme: A Search for the Foundations of Reasoned Discourse." *Quarterly Journal of Speech* 56 (Apr. 1970): 140–148.

Douglas, Rodney B., and Carroll Arnold. "On Analysis of Logos: A Methodological Inquiry." *Quarterly Journal of Speech* 55 (Feb. 1970): 22–32.

Ehninger, Douglas. "Argument as Method: Its Nature, Its Limitations, and Its Uses." *Communication Studies* 37 (1970): 101–110.

Epstein, William. "The Classical Tradition of Dialectics and American Legal Education." *Journal of Legal Education* 31(3–5) (Summer/Fall 1982): 399–423.

Fisher, Walter R. "Rationality and the Logic of Good Reasons." *Philosophy and Rhetoric* 13(2) (Spring 1980): 121–130.

Golden, J. L., and J. J. Pillotta, eds. *Practical Reasoning in Human Affairs.* Dordrecht, Holland: D. Reidel, 1986.

Goodnight, G. Thomas. "The Re-Union of Argumentation and Debate Theory." In *Dimensions of Argument: Proceedings of the Second Summer Conference on Argumentation,* ed. George Ziegelmueller and Jack Rhodes. Annandale, VA: SCA, 1981. Pp. 415–432.

Gottlieb, Gordon. *The Logic of Choice.* New York: Macmillan, 1968.

Hamer, David. "The Civil Standard of Proof Uncertainty: Probability, Belief, and Justice." *Sydney Law Review* 16(4) (Dec. 1994): 506–536.

Hample, Dale. "Teaching the Cognitive Context of Argument." *Communication Education* 34 (July 1985): 196–204.

———. "Argument: Public, Private, Social and Cognitive." *JAFA* 25 (Summer 1988): 13–19.

Hollihan, Thomas A., and Pat Riley. "Academic Debate and Democracy: A Clash of Ideologies." In *Argument and Critical Practices: Proceedings of the Fifth SCA/AFA Conference on Argumentation,* ed. J. W. Wenzel. Annandale, VA: SCA, 1987. Pp. 399–404.

Hunt, Everett. "Dialectics: A Neglected Method of Argument." *Quarterly Journal of Speech* 7 (June 1921): 221–232.

Iseminger, Gary. "Successful Argument and Rational Belief." *Philosophy and Rhetoric* 7 (1974): 47–57.

Jamieson, Kathleen Hall. *Eloquence in an Electronic Age.* New York: Oxford University Press, 1988.

Kennedy, George, ed. and trans. *Aristotle on Rhetoric: A Theory of Civic Discourse.* New York: Oxford University Press, 1991.

Klumpp, James. "Keeping Our Traditions Straight: Working with the Intellectual Modes of Argumentative Studies." In *Argument in Controversy: Proceedings of the Seventh SCA/AFA Conference on Argumentation,* ed. Donn Parson. Annandale, VA: SCA, 1991. Pp. 33–38.

Lakoff, George, and Mark Johnson. *Metaphors We Live By.* Chicago: University of Chicago Press, 1980.

Lichtman, Allan J., and Daniel M. Rohrer. "The Logic of Policy Dispute." *JAFA* 16 (Spring 1980): 236–247.

Miller, Gerald R. "Some Factors Influencing Judgments of the Logical Validity of Arguments: A Research Review." *Quarterly Journal of Speech* 55 (Oct. 1969): 276–286.

Mills, Glen E., and Hugh Petrie. "The Role of Logic in Rhetoric." *Quarterly Journal of Speech* 54 (Oct. 1968): 260–267.

Mortenson, C. David, and Ray L. Anderson. "The Limits of Logic." *JAFA* 7 (Spring 1970): 71–78.

Nelson, William F. "Topoi: Evidence of Human Conceptual Behavior." *Philosophy and Rhetoric* 2 (Winter 1969): 1–11.

Newman, Robert P. "Analysis and Issues—A Study of Doctrine." In *Readings in Argumentation,* ed. Jerry M. Anderson and Paul J. Dovre. Boston, MA: Allyn and Bacon, 1968. Pp. 166–180.

Nothstine, William L. "Topics as Ontological Metaphor in Contemporary Rhetorical Theory and Criticism." *Quarterly Journal of Speech* 74 (May 1988): 151–163.

Perelman, Chaim, and Lucie Olbrechts-Tyteca. *The New Rhetoric: A Treatise on Argumentation.* Trans. John Wilkinson and Purcell Weaver. Notre Dame, IN: University of Notre Dame Press, 1969.

Petrie, Hugh. "Does Logic Have Any Relevance to Argumentation?" *JAFA* 6 (Spring 1969): 55–60.

Pierce, Donald C. "The History of the Concept of Stasis." *The Forensic* 72 (1987): 75–81.

Pinto, Robert C., and John Anthony Blair. *Reasoning: A Practical Guide.* Englewood Cliffs, NJ: Prentice Hall, 1993.

Powers, John M. "On the Intellectual Structure of the Human Communication Discipline." *Communication Education* 44(3) (July 1995): 191–222.

Pruett, Robert. "Dialectic: A Starting Point for Argument." *Ohio Speech Journal* (1970): 42–47.

Rescher, Nicholas. *Dialectics: A Controversy Oriented Approach to the Theory of Knowledge.* Albany: State University of New York Press, 1977.

———. *Rationality: A Philosophical Inquiry into the Nature and the Rationale of Reason.* New York: Oxford University Press, 1988.

Rowland, Robert C. "Argument Fields." In *Dimensions of Argument: Proceedings of the Second Summer Conference on Argumentation,* ed. George Ziegelmueller and Jack Rhodes. Annandale, VA: SCA, 1981. Pp. 56–79.

———. "On Defining Argument." *Philosophy and Rhetoric* 20 (1987): 140–159.

———, and John E. Fritch. "The Relationship Between Debate and Argumentation Theory." In *Spheres of Argument: Proceedings of the Sixth SCA/AFA Conference on Argumentation,* ed. Bruce E. Gronbeck. Annandale, VA: SCA, 1989. Pp. 457–463.

Self, Lois. "Rhetoric and Phronesis: The Aristotelian Ideal." *Philosophy and Rhetoric* 12 (Spring 1979): 130–145.

Sunstein, Cass. "On Analogical Reasoning." *Harvard Law Review* 106(3) (Jan. 1993): 741–793.

Shiffrin, Steven. "Forensics, Dialectic, and Speech Communication." *JAFA* 8 (Spring 1972): 189–191.

Toulmin, Stephen. *The Uses of Argument.* Cambridge: Cambridge University Press, 1958.

———, Richard Rieke, and Allan Janik. *An Introduction to Reasoning.* New York: Macmillan, 1979.

Trapp, Robert. "The Need for an Argumentative Perspective for Academic Debate." *CEDA Yearbook* 14 (1993): 23–33.

Warnick, Barbara. "Judgment, Probability and Aristotle's Rhetoric." *Quarterly Journal of Speech* 85 (Aug. 1989): 299–311.

Zarefsky, David. "The Role of Causal Argument in Policy Controversies." *JAFA* 8 (Spring 1977): 179–191.

X. Evidence

Benson, James A. "The Use of Evidence in Intercollegiate Debate." *JAFA* 7 (Spring 1971): 260–270.

Dresser, William R. "Studies of the Effects of Evidence: Implications for Forensics." *The AFA Register* (Fall 1962): 14–19.

———. "The Impact of Evidence on Decision Making." *JAFA* 3(2) (May 1966): 43–47.

Gregg, R. B. "The Rhetoric of Evidence." *Western Speech* 31 (Summer 1967): 180–189.

Hobbs, Jeffrey. "Surrendering Decision Authority from the Public to the Technical Sphere of Argument: The Use of Evidence in Contemporary Intercollegiate Debate." *The Forensic* 80(1) (Fall 1994): 1–6.

Huff, Darrell. "How to Lie with Statistics." *Harper's Magazine* (Aug. 1950): 97–101.

Insalata, S. John. "The Persuasive Use of Evidence in Formal Argument." *The Forensic* (Mar. 1960): 9–11.

Kazoleas, Dean C. "A Comparison of the Persuasive Effectiveness of Qualitative Versus Quantitative Evidence." *Communication Quarterly* 41(1) (Winter 1993): 40–51.

Kellermann, Kathy, and Allan Louden. "Coping with Statistics in Debate." In *Debaters' Research Guide*, ed. Wake Forest University Debate. Winston-Salem, NC: Wake Forest University, 1979. Pp. 12–21, http://groups.wfu.edu/debate/MiscSites/DRGArticles/KellermannLouden1979ForPol.htm.

———. "The Concept of Evidence: A Critical Review." *JAFA* 16 (Winter 1980): 159–172.

Luchok, Joseph, and James C. McCroskey. "The Effect of Quality of Evidence on Attitude Change and Source Credibility." *Southern Speech Communication Journal* 43(4) (Summer 1978): 371–383.

McCroskey, James. "A Summary of Experimental Research on the Effects of Evidence on Persuasive Communication." *Quarterly Journal of Speech* 55 (Apr. 1969): 169–176.

Newman, Robert P., and Dale R. Newman. *Evidence.* New York: Houghton Mifflin, 1969.

———, and Keith R. Sanders. "A Study in the Integrity of Evidence." *JAFA* 2(1) (Jan. 1965): 7–13.

Reinard, John C. "The Empirical Study of the Persuasive Effects of Evidence: The Status After Fifty Years of Research." *Human Communication Research* 15(1) (Fall 1988): 3–59.

Sanders, Gerald H. "Misuse of Evidence in Academic Debate." In *Advanced Debate*, ed. David A. Thomas. Skokie, IL: National Textbook, 1975. Pp. 220–227.

Sanders, Keith. "Toward a Solution to the Misuse of Evidence." *JAFA* 3(1) (Jan. 1966): 6–10.

Scott, Robert L. "Evidence in Communication: We are Such Stuff." *Western Journal of Speech Communication* 42(1) (Winter 1978): 29–36.

Spiker, Barry K., Tom Daniels, and Lawrence Bernabo. "The Quantitative Quandry in Forensics: The Use and Misuse of Statistical Evidence." *JAFA* 19 (Fall 1982): 87–96.

Winebrenner, T. C. "Authority as Argument in Academic Debate." *Contemporary Argumentation and Debate* 16 (1995): 14–29.

XI. The Affirmative, Comparative Advantage, and Criteria Cases

Brock, Bernard. "The Comparative Advantages Case." *Speech Teacher* 16 (Mar. 1967): 118–123.

Chesebro, James W. "The Comparative Advantage Case." *JAFA* 5(2) (Spring 1968): 57–63.

———. "Beyond the Orthodox: The Criteria Case." *JAFA* 7 (Winter 1971): 208–215.

Fadely, L. Dean. "The Validity of the Comparative Advantage Case." *JAFA* 4(1) (Winter 1967): 28–35.

Flaningam, Carl D. "Concomitant vs. Comparative Advantages: Sufficient vs. Necessary Conditions." *JAFA* 18(1) (Summer 1981): 1–8.

Lewinski, John, Bruce Metzler, and Peter L. Settle. "The Goal Case Affirmative: An Alternative Approach to Academic Debate." *JAFA* 9 (Spring 1973): 458–463.

Lichtman, Alan, Charles Garvin, and Jerry Corsi. "The Alternative Justification Affirmative: A New Case Form." *JAFA* 10 (Fall 1973): 59–69.

Ware, B. L., Jr., and William B. English. "A Comparison of the Need Plan and the Comparative Advantage Approach: There Is a Difference." *Kansas Speech Journal* (Spring 1973): 4–11.

Zarefsky, David. "The Traditional Case Comparative Advantage Case Dichotomy: Another Look." *JAFA* 6(1) (Winter 1969): 12–20.

XII. Negative Approaches to Debate

Brewster, B. "Analysis of Disadvantages: Scenarios and Intrinsicness." In *Debaters' Research Guide*, ed. Wake Forest University Debate. Winston-Salem, NC: Wake Forest University, 1984. Pp. 14–16, http://groups.wfu.edu/debate/MiscSites/DRGArticles/Brewster1984Poverty.htm.

Cragan, John, and Donald Shields. "The Comparative Advantage Negative." *JAFA* 7(2) (Spring 1970): 85–91.

Hemmer, Joseph J., Jr. "The Comparative Advantage Negative: An Integrated Approach." *Speaker and Gavel* 13 (Winter 1976): 27–30.

Hemphill, Dwaine R. "First Negative Strategies: A Reevaluation of Negative Division of Duties." In *Argument in Transition: Proceedings of the Third Summer Conference on Argumentation*, ed. David Zarefsky, Malcolm O. Sillars, and Jack Rhodes. Annandale, VA: SCA, 1983. Pp. 883–892.

Patterson, J. W. "The Obligations of the Negative in a Policy Debate." *The Speech Teacher* 11 (Sept. 1962): 208–213.

Solt, Roger. "Negative Fiat: Resolving the Ambiguities of Should." *Argumentation and Advocacy* 25 (Winter 1989): 121–139.

Thomas, David, and Jerry M. Anderson. "Negative Approaches to the Comparative Advantages Case." *Speaker and Gavel* (May 1968): 148–157.

———. "Response to Cragan and Shields: Alternative Formats for Negative Approaches to Comparative Advantage Cases." *JAFA* 8 (Spring 1972): 200–206.

XIII. Criteria

Berube, David. "Parameters for Criteria Debating." *CEDA Yearbook* 11 (1990): 9–25.

Broda-Bahm, Ken. "Community Concepts of Argumentative Legitimacy: Challenging Norms in National-Circuit CEDA Debate." *The Forensic* 79(3) (Spring 1994): 26–35.

Brownlee, Don. "Approaches to Support and Refutation of Criteria." *CEDA Yearbook* 8 (1987): 59–63.

Cole, Mark, Ronald Boggs, and Kevin Twohy. "The Functions of Criteria in Nonpolicy Argumentation: Burdens and Approaches." *CEDA Yearbook* 7 (1986): 36–42.

XIV. Kritiks/Critiques

Broda-Bahm, Ken. "Meaning as Language Use: The Case of the Language-Linked Value Objection." *CEDA Yearbook* 12 (1991): 67–78.

———, and Thomas L. Murphy. "A Defense of Critique Arguments: Beyond the Resolutional Question." *CEDA Yearbook* 15 (1994): 20–32.

Moris, Eric, and John Katsulas. "Pro and Con: The Relevance Irrelevance of the Critique to Policy Debate." *Forensic Educator* II(1) (1996–97).

Roskoski, Matt, and Joe Peabody. "A Linguistic and Philosophic Critique of Language Arguments." Paper presented at the SCA Convention, Chicago, Nov. 1, 1992.

Shanahan, William. "Kritik of Thinking." In *Debaters' Research Guide*, ed. Wake Forest University Debate. Winston-Salem, NC: Wake Forest University, 1993. Pp. A3–A8, http://groups.wfu.edu/debate/MiscSites/DRGArticles/Shanahan1993HealthCare.htm.

Shors, Matthew, and Steve Mancuso. "The Critique: Skreaming Without Raising Its Voice." In *Debaters' Research Guide*, ed. Wake Forest University Debate. Winston-Salem, NC: Wake Forest University, 1993. Pp. A14–A18, http://groups.wfu.edu/debate/MiscSites/DRGArticles/ShorsMancuso1993.htm.

Solt, Roger. "Demystifying the Critique." In *Debaters' Research Guide*, ed. Wake Forest University Debate. Winston-Salem, NC: Wake Forest University, 1993. Pp. A8–A12, http://groups.wfu.edu/debate/MiscSites/DRGArticles/Solt1993Health.htm.

———. *The Anti-Kritik Handbook*. Denton, TX: Paradigm Research, 1995.

XV. Topicality

Adams, N., and T. Wilkins. "The Role of Justification in Topic Analysis." *CEDA Yearbook* 8 (1987): 21–26.

Allen, Mike, and Nancy Burrell. "A Pragmatic Theory of Topicality." In *Argument and Social Practice: Proceedings of the Fourth Conference on Argumentation*, ed. Robert J. Cox, Malcolm O. Sillars, and Gregg Walker. Annandale, VA: SCA, 1985. Pp. 854–861.

Berube, David. "Debating Hasty Generalization." In *Advanced Debate: Readings in Theory, Practice and Teaching*, 3rd ed., ed. David Thomas and Jack Hart. Lincolnwood, IL: National Textbook, 1987. Pp. 483–489.

———. "Parametric Topicality: An Analysis and a Rebuttal." *CEDA Yearbook* 12 (1991): 12–26.

———. "What Killed Schrodinger's Cat?: Parametric Topicality, That's What." *CEDA Yearbook* 12 (1991): 12–26.

———. "Parametrical Interpretation: Issues and Answers." *Contemporary Argumentation and Debate* 16 (1995): 30–51.

Bile, Jeffrey. "When the Whole Is Greater Than the Sum of the Parts: The Implications of Holistic Resolutional Focus." *CEDA Yearbook* 8 (1987): 8–15.

———. "Propositional Justification: Another View." *CEDA Yearbook* 9 (1988): 54–62.

Cross, Frank. *Debating Topicality*. San Francisco, CA: Griffin Research, 1987.

Dudczak, Craig. "Topicality: An Equal Ground Standard." *CEDA Yearbook* 10 (1989): 12–21.

Hastings, Arthur. "On the Meaning of Should." *Speaker and Gavel* 4(1) (Nov. 1966): 8–10.

Herbeck, Dale A., and John P. Katsulas. "The Affirmative Topicality Burden: Any Reasonable Example of the Resolution." *JAFA* 21 (Winter 1985): 133–145.

———. "The Case Against the Problem Area: A Response to Ulrich." *Forensic Educator* 4 (1989–90): 8–11.

Hingstman, David. "Topicality and Division of Ground." In *Framing Policy Dialectic in Argument and Social Practice: Proceedings of the Fourth SCA/AFA Conference on Argumentation*, ed. J. Robert Cox, Malcolm O. Sillars, and Gregg Walker. Annandale, VA: SCA, 1985. Pp. 841–853.

Hynes, Thomas J., and Walter Ulrich. "The Role of Propositions in Forensic Argument." In *Argument and Social Practice: Proceedings of the Fourth SCA/AFA Conference on Argumentation*, ed. J. Robert Cox, Malcolm O. Sillars, and Gregg Walker. Annandale, VA: SCA, 1985. Pp. 827–840.

Madsen, Arnie, and Al Louden. "Jurisdiction and the Evaluation of Topicality." *JAFA* 24(2) (Fall 1987): 73–83.

———. "The Jurisdiction/Topicality Analogy." *Argumentation and Advocacy* 26(4) (Spring 1990): 141–154.

———, and Robert C. Chandler. "When the Whole Becomes a Black Hole: Implications of the Holistic Perspective." *CEDA Yearbook* 9 (1988): 30–37.

———. "Further Examination of Resolutional Focus." In *Spheres of Argument: Proceedings of the Sixth SCA/AFA Conference on Argumentation*, ed. Bruce Gronbeck. Annandale, VA: SCA, 1989. Pp. 411–416.

McBath, James, and Joseph Aurbach. "Origins of the National Debate Resolution." *JAFA* 4(3) (Fall 1967): 96–103.

Murphy, Thomas L. "Assessing the Jurisdictional Model of Topicality." *Argumentation and Advocacy* 26 (Spring 1990): 145–150.

Parson, Donn W. "On Being Reasonable: The Last Refuge of Scoundrels." In *Dimensions of Argument: Proceedings of the Second Summer Conference on Argumentation*, ed. George Ziegelmueller and Jack Rhodes. Annandale, VA: SCA, 1981. Pp. 532–543.

———, and John Bart. "On Being Reasonable: The Last Refuge of Scoundrels Part II: The Scoundrels Strike Back." In *Advanced Debate: Readings in Theory, Practice, and Teaching*, ed. David Thomas and Jack Hart. Lincolnwood, IL: National Textbook, 1989. Pp. 130–138.

Rhodes, Jack, and Michael Pfau. "Resolution of Example: A Reply to Herbeck and Katsulas." *JAFA* 21 (Winter 1985): 146–149.

Sherwood, Ken. "Claim Without Warrant: The Lack of Logical Support for Parametric Topicality." *CEDA Yearbook* 15 (1994): 10–19.

Ulrich, Walter. "The Nature of the Topic in Value Debate." *CEDA Yearbook* 5 (1984): 1–6.

———. "The Nature of the Problem Area." *Forensic Educator* 4 (1989–90): 5–7.

XVI. Counterplans

Branham, Robert J. "Roads Not Taken: Counterplans and Opportunity Costs." *Argumentation and Advocacy* 25 (Spring 1989): 246–255.

———, ed. "The State of the Counterplan." *JAFA* 25 (special issue) (Winter 1989): 117–191. A key to modern counterplan theory.

Dempsey, Richard H., and David N. Hartmann. "Mirror State Counterplans: Illegitimate, Topical, or Magical?" *JAFA* 22 (Winter 1985): 161–166.

Fadley, Dean. "Fiat Power and the Mirror State Counterplan." *Speaker and Gavel* 24 (Winter 1987): 69–76.

Gossett, John. "Counterplan Competitiveness in the Stock Issues Paradigm." In *Dimensions of Argument: Proceedings of the Second Summer Conference on Argumentation*, ed. George Ziegelmueller and Jack Rhodes. Annandale, VA: SCA, 1981. Pp. 568–578.

Herbeck, Dale, John Katsulas, and Karla Leeper. "A Permutation Standard of Competitiveness." *JAFA* 22 (Summer 1985): 12–19.

———. "The Locus of Debate Controversy Re-Examined: Implications for Counterplan Theory." *Argumentation and Advocacy* 25 (Winter 1989): 150–164.

———, and John Katsulas. "Point of Theory: Counterplan Competitiveness." *The Forensic Quarterly* (Fall 1985): 46–48.

Hill, Bill. "Counterplans: Requirements, Presumption and Study." In *Debaters' Research Guide*, ed. Wake Forest University Debate. Winston-Salem, NC: Wake Forest University, 1980. Pp. 2–7, http://groups.wfu.edu/debate/MiscSites/DRGArticles/Hill1980ConsumerSafety.htm.

Hynes, Thomas J., Jr. "The Counterplan: An Historical and Descriptive Study." Unpublished M.A. thesis, University of North Carolina at Chapel Hill, 1972.

———. "The Studies Counterplan: Still Hoping—A Reply to Shelton." *JAFA* 21 (Winter 1985): 156–160.

———. *Debating Counterplans*. San Francisco, CA: Griffin Research, 1987.

Kaplow, Louis. "Rethinking Counterplans: A Reconciliation with Debate Theory." *JAFA* 17(4) (Spring 1981): 215–226.

Katsulas, John, Dale Herbeck, and Edward M. Panetta. "Fiating Utopia: A Negative View of the Emergence of World Order Counterplans and Futures Gaming in Policy Debate." *Argumentation and Advocacy* 24 (Fall 1987): 95–111.

———. "Fiating Utopia, Part Two: A Rejoinder to Edwards and Snider." *Argumentation and Advocacy* 24 (Fall 1987): 130–136.

Lane, Gina. "The Justification of Counterplans in Nonpolicy Debate: A Skeptical View." *CEDA Yearbook* 15 (1994): 33–42.

Lichtman, Allan, and Daniel M. Rohrer. "A General Theory of the Counterplan." *JAFA* 12 (Fall 1975): 70–79. A classic early article on counterplan theory.

Madsen, Arnie. "General Systems Theory and Counterplan Competition." *Argumentation and Advocacy* 26 (Fall 1989): 71–82.

Mayer, Michael. "Epistemological Considerations of the Studies Counterplan." *JAFA* 19 (Spring 1983): 261–266.

———, and J. Hale. "Evaluating the Studies Counterplan: Topicality and Competitiveness." *Speaker and Gavel* 16 (Summer 1979): 67–72.

Nebergall, Roger E. "The Negative Counterplan." *Speech Teacher* 6 (Sept. 1957): 217–220.

Panetta, Edward M., and Steven Dolley. "The Topical Counterplan: A Competitive Policy Option." *Argumentation and Advocacy* 25 (Winter 1989): 165–177.

Perkins, Dallas. "Counterplans and Paradigms." *Argumentation and Advocacy* 25(3) (Winter 1989): 140–149.

Shelton, Michael W. "In Defense of the Study Counterplan." *JAFA* 21 (Winter 1985): 150–155.

Solt, Roger. "Counterplan Competition: Permutations and Beyond." In *Debaters' Research Guide*, ed. Wake Forest University Debate. Winston-Salem, NC: Wake Forest University, 1985. Pp. 18–23, http://groups.wfu.edu/debate/MiscSites/DRGArticles/Solt1985Water.htm.

Thompson, Wayne N. "The Effect of the Counterplan upon the Burden of Proof." *Central States Speech Journal* 13 (Autumn 1962): 247–252.

Ulrich, Walter. "The Legitimacy of the Counter Procedure Counterplan." *JAFA* 23 (Winter 1987): 166–169.

Unger, James. "Investigating the Investigators: A Study of the Study Counterplan." *Debate Issues* 12 (Feb. 1979): 1–8.

Walker, Gregg B. "The Counterplan as Argument in Non-Policy Debate." *Argumentation and Advocacy* 25 (Winter 1989): 178–191.

XVII. Counterwarrants

Ganer, Patricia. "Counterwarrants: An Idea Whose Time Has Not Come." In *Dimensions of Argument: Proceedings of the Second Summer Conference on Argumentation*, ed. George Ziegelmueller and Jack Rhodes. Annandale, VA: SCA, 1981. Pp. 478–484.

Hunt, Steven B., and Greg Tolbert. "Counter-Warrants: A Method for Testing Topical Justification in CEDA Debate." *CEDA Yearbook* 6 (1985): 21–28.

Keeshan, Marjorie, and Walter Ulrich. "Critique of the Counter-Warrant as a Negative Strategy." *JAFA* 16(3) (Winter 1980): 199–203.

Mayer, Michael. "Extending Counter-Warrants: The Counter Resolutional Counterplan." *JAFA* 19 (Fall 1982): 122–127.

Paulsen, James W., and Jack Rhodes. "The Counter-Warrant as a Negative Strategy: A Modest Proposal." *JAFA* 15 (Spring 1979): 205–210. The article that started counter-warrant theory.

Rhodes, Jack. "A Defense of the Counter-Warrant as Negative Argument." In *Dimensions of Argument: Proceedings of the Second Summer Conference on Argumentation*, ed. George Ziegelmueller and Jack Rhodes. Annandale, VA: SCA, 1981. Pp. 485–493.

———. "Counter-Warrants After Ten Years." In *Spheres of Argument: Proceedings of the Sixth SCA/AFA Conference on Argumentation*, ed. Bruce Gronbeck. Annandale, VA: SCA, 1989. Pp. 406–410.

XVIII. Inherency

Benoit, William L. "The Nature and Function of Inherency in Policy Argumentation." *Speaker and Gavel* 19 (Spring 1982): 55–63.

Cherwitz, Richard A., and James W. Hikins. "Inherency as a Multidimensional Construct: A Rhetorical Approach to the Proof of Causation." *JAFA* 14(2) (Fall 1977): 82–90.

Cox, J. Robert. "Attitudinal Inherency: Implications for Policy Debate." *Southern Speech Communication Journal* 40 (Winter 1975): 158–168.

Dudczak, Craig. "Inherency in Non-Policy Propositions: Rediscovering the Lost Issue." In *Argument and Critical Practices: Proceedings of the Fifth SCA/AFA Conference on Argumentation*, ed. Joseph Wenzel. Annandale, VA: SCA, 1987. Pp. 371–378.

———. "Inherency as a Stock Issue in Non-Policy Propositions." *CEDA Yearbook* 9 (1988): 15–22.

Flaningam, Carl D. "Inherency and Incremental Change: A Response to Morello." *JAFA* 20 (Spring 1984): 231–236.

Goodnight, Tom, Bill Balthrop, and Donn W. Parson. "The Problem of Inherency: Strategy and Substance." *JAFA* 10 (Spring 1974): 229–240.

Ling, David, and Robert V. Seltzer. "The Role of Attitudinal Inherency in Contemporary Debate." *JAFA* 7 (Spring 1971): 278–283.

Morello, John T. "Defending the Present System's Capacity for Incremental Changes." *JAFA* 19 (Fall 1982): 115–121.

Parson, Donn W. "Response to a Critique of the Problem of Inherency." *JAFA* 12(1) (Summer 1975): 46–58.

Pfau, Michael. "The Present System Revisited. Part One: Incremental Change." *JAFA* 17 (Fall 1980): 80–84.

———. "The Present System Revisited. Part Two: Policy Interrelationships." *JAFA* 17 (Winter 1981): 146–154.

Schunk, John. "Farewell to Structural Change: The Cure for Pseudo-Inherency." *JAFA* 14(3) (Winter 1978): 144–149.

———. "Affirmative Fiat, Plan Circumvention, and the Process Disadvantage: The Further Ramifications of Pseudo-Inherency." *Speaker and Gavel* 18(3) (Spring 1981): 83–87.

XIX. Cross-Examination

Beard, Raymond S. "Legal Cross-Examination and Academic Debate." *JAFA* 6 (Spring 1969): 61–66.

Cirlin, Alan. "Evaluating Cross Examination in CEDA Debate: On Getting Our Act Together." *CEDA Yearbook* 7 (1986): 43–50.

Clevenger, Kenneth. "Cross-Examination for Trial Defense Counsel." *Army Lawyer* (Jan. 1992): 9–10.

Coverstone, Alan. "Rediscovering the Lost Art of Cross-Examination." *Debaters' Research Guide*. Winston-Salem, NC: Wake Forest University, 1992. Pp. A3–A6.

Durst, John E., Jr. "Cross-Examination." *Trial Lawyers Quarterly* 19(3) (Fall 1988): 29–42.

Fuge, Lloyd, and Robert P. Newman. "Cross Examination in Academic Debating." *The Speech Teacher* 5 (Jan. 1956): 66–70.

Hartje, Jeffrey H. "Cross-Examination: A Primer for Trial Advocates." *American Journal of Trial Advocacy Annual* 10 (1987): 135–179.

Henderson, Bill. "A System of Teaching Cross-Examination Techniques." *Communication Education* 27 (Mar. 1978): 112–118.

Larson, Suzanne. "Cross-Examination in CEDA Debate: A Survey of Coaches." *CEDA Yearbook* 8 (1987): 33–41.

Lewis, David L. "Cross-Examination." *Mercer Law Review* 42(2) (Winter 1991): 627–642.

Lisnek, Paul. "Direct and Cross-Examination: The Keys to Success." *Trial Diplomacy Journal* 18(5) (Sept.–Oct. 1995): 263–269.

Miller, Thomas, and E. Caminker. "The Art of Cross-Examination." *CEDA Yearbook* 3 (1982): 4–15.

Ulrich, Walter. "Vitalizing Cross-Examination Debate: A Proposal." *JAFA* 18 (Spring 1982): 265–266.

Younger, Irving. "A Letter in Which Cicero Lays Down the Ten Commandments of Cross-Examination." *Law Institute Journal* 61(8) (Aug. 1987): 804–806. See also Younger's excellent videotape on the ten commandments of cross-examination.

Ziegelmueller, George. "Cross Examination Reexamined." In *Advanced Debate: Readings in Theory, Practice and Teaching*, ed. David Thomas and Jack Hart. Lincolnwood, IL: National Textbook, 1987. Pp. 66–74. Also in *Argument in Transition: Proceedings of the Third Summer Conference on Argument*, ed. David Zarefsky, Malcolm O. Sillars, and Jack Rhodes. Annandale, VA: SCA, 1983. Pp. 904–917.

XX. Rhetoric and Persuasion in Debate: Public Debates, Style, and Speaking Rates

Bartanen, Kristine, and Jim Hanson. "Advocating Humane Discourse." *The Forensic* 80(1) (Fall 1994): 16–21.

Carpenter, Ronald H. "Style and Emphasis in Debate." *JAFA* 6(1) (Winter 1969): 27–31.

Cathcart, Robert. "Adopting Debate to an Audience." *Speech Teacher* 5 (Mar. 1956): 113–116.

Christopherson, Merrill G. "The Necessity for Style in Argument." *Speech Teacher* 9 (Mar. 1960): 116–120.

Colbert, Kent. "Speaking Rates of NDT Finalists from 1968–1980." *JAFA* 18 (Summer 1981): 73–76.

———. "A Quantitative Analysis of CEDA Speaking Rates." *National Forensic Journal* 6 (Fall 1988): 113–120.

———. "A Study of CEDA and NDT Finalists' Speaking Rates." *CEDA Yearbook* 12 (1991): 88–94.

Cox, E. Sam, and W. Clifton Adams. "Valuing of Tournament Debate: Factors from Practitioners and Administrators." *The Forensic* 80(4) (Summer 1995): 7–12.

Friedman, Robert P. "Why Not Debate Persuasively?" *Today's Speech* 5 (1957): 32–34.

Giffin, Kim, and D. A. Warner. "A Study of the Influence of an Audience on the Rate of Speech in Tournament Debates." *The Speaker* (1962).

Hill, Bill. "Improving the Quality of CEDA Debate." *National Forensic Journal* 4 (Fall 1986): 105–121.

McBath, James H., and Nicholas M. Cripe. "Delivery: Rhetoric's Rusty Canon." *JAFA* 2(1) (Jan. 1965): 1–6.

McGough, M. "Pull It Across Your Flow." *The New Republic* (Oct. 10, 1988): 17–19.

Murrish, Walter. "Training the Debate in Persuasion." *JAFA* 1(1) (Jan. 1964): 7–12.

Olson, Donald O. "A Survey of Attitudes on the Spread." *Speaker and Gavel* 8(3) (Mar. 1971): 66–69.

Peterson, Owen. "Forum Debating: 150 Debates Later." *Southern Speech Communication Journal* 47(4) (Summer 1982): 435–443.

Stelzner, Hermann G. "Tournament Debate: Emasculated Rhetoric." *Southern Speech Communication Journal* 27 (Fall 1961): 34–42.

Swinney, James P. "The Relative Comprehension of Contemporary Tournament Debate Speeches." *JAFA* 5(1) (Winter 1968): 16–20.

Vasilius, Janet M., and Dan DeStephen. "An Investigation of the Relationship Between Debate Tournament Success and Rate, Evidence, and Jargon." *JAFA* 15 (Spring 1979): 197–204.

Voor, John B., and Joseph M. Miller. "The Effect of Practice upon the Comprehension of Time-Compressed Speech." *Speech Monographs* 32 (1965): 452–454.

Weiss, Robert O. "The Public Presence of Forensics." *Speaker and Gavel* 23(1) (Fall 1985): 23–28.

XXI. Debating Judging and Debate Paradigms

Allen, Mike, and Kathy Kellermann. "Using the Subjective Probability Model to Evaluate Academic Debate Arguments." *Argumentation and Advocacy* 25 (Fall 1988): 93–107.

Balthrop, William V. "Citizen, Legislator, and Bureaucrat as Evaluators of Competing Policy Systems." In *Advanced Debate: Readings in Theory, Practice, and Teaching*, 2nd ed., ed. David Thomas. Skokie, IL: National Textbook, 1979. Pp. 402–418.

———. "Argumentation and the Critical Stance: A Methodological Approach." In *Advances in Argumentation Research*, ed. J. Robert Cox and Charles Willard. Carbondale, IL: Southern Illinois University Press, 1982. Pp. 238–258.

———. "The Debate Judge as Critic of Argument." *JAFA* 20 (Summer 1983): 1–15.

Bartanen, Michael. "The Case for Using Nontraditional Judges in Forensics Contests." *Argumentation and Advocacy* 30(4) (Spring 1994): 248–254.

Benoit, William, S. R. Wilson, and V. F. Follert. "Decision Rules for the Policy Metaphor." *JAFA* 22 (Winter 1986): 135–146.

Boileau, Don M., Jon Fitzgerald, David Ling, and Dan P. Millar. "A Debate Judge Certification Test: Development and Operation on a State-Wide Scale." *Communication Education* 30(4) (Oct. 1981): 414–420.

Branham, Robert J., and Thomas Isaacson. "The Ascent of Policy Making: Academic Debate from 1970 to 1980." *Speaker and Gavel* 17 (Fall 1979): 5–10.

Brey, James. "A Descriptive Analysis of CEDA Judging Philosophies, Part I: Definitive Acceptance or Rejection of Certain Tactics and Arguments." *CEDA Yearbook* 10 (1989): 67–77.

———. "An Analysis of CEDA Judging Philosophies, Part II: Accepting Certain Tactics and Arguments with Reservations." *CEDA Yearbook* 11 (1990): 72–79.

Brydon, Steven. "Judging CEDA Debate: A Systems Perspective." *CEDA Yearbook* 5 (1984): 85–88.

Buckley, David C. "A Comparison of Judging Paradigms." In *Argument in Transition: Proceedings of the Third Summer Conference on Argumentation*, ed. David Zarefsky, Malcolm O. Sillars, and Jack Rhodes. Annandale, VA: SCA, 1983. Pp. 858–870.

Cirlin, Alan. "Judging, Evaluation, and the Quality of CEDA Debate." *National Forensic Journal* (Fall 1986): 81–90.

Clevenger, Theodore, Jr. "Toward a Point of View for Contest Debate." *Central States Speech Journal* 12 (Fall 1960): 21–26.

Corsi, Jerome R. "Zarefsky's Theory of Debate as Hypothesis Testing: A Critical Re-Examination." *JAFA* 19 (Winter 1983): 158–170.

Cox, J. Robert. "A Study of Judging Philosophies of the Participants of the National Debate Tournament." *JAFA* 11 (Fall 1974): 61–71.

———, and Julia T. Wood. "The Effects of Consultation on Judges/Decisions." *The Speech Teacher* 24 (Mar. 1975): 118–126.

Crawford, C. B., and Willis M. Watt. "Argument Supporting the Requirement for Debate Judging Philosophy Statements at the PKD National Tournament." *The Forensic* 80(2) (Winter 1995): 1–10.

Cross, John D., and Ronald J. Matlon. "An Analysis of Judging Philosophies in Academic Debate." *JAFA* 15 (Fall 1978): 110–123.

"Debate Paradigms." *JAFA* 18 (special forum) (Winter 1982): Pp. 133–160.

Dempsey, Richard H., and David J. Hartmann. "Emergent Voting Criteria and the Judicial Impotence of Critics." *Argumentation and Advocacy* 22(3) (Winter 1986): 167–175.

Fisher, Walter R. "The Narrative Paradigm: In the Beginning." *Journal of Communication* 35(4) (Fall 1985): 74–89.

Freeley, Austin J. "Judging Paradigms: The Impact of the Critic on Argument." In *Dimensions of Argument: Proceedings of the Second Summer Conference on Argumentation*, ed. George Ziegelmueller and Jack Rhodes. Annandale, VA: SCA, 1981. Pp. 433–447.

Gass, Robert H., Jr. "The Narrative Perspective in Academic Debate: A Critique." *Argumentation and Advocacy* 25 (Fall 1988): 78–92.

Giffin, Kim. "A Study of the Criteria Employed by Tournament Debate Judges." *Speech Monographs* 26 (Mar. 1959): 69–71.

Gill, Mary. "Knowing the Judge: The Key to Successful Debate." *CEDA Yearbook* 9 (1988): 96–101.

Hanson, C. T. "What Are the Options? The Philosophy of Using Ballots." *The Forensic* 73(3) (May 1988): 1–5.

Henderson, Bill, and David L. Boman. "A Study to Determine If Debate Judges' Judging Philosophy Statements Are Consistent with Their Later Related Ballot Statements." *JAFA* 19 (Winter 1983): 191–198.

Hollihan, Thomas A. "Conditional Arguments and the Hypothesis Testing Paradigm: A Negative View." *JAFA* 19 (Winter 1983): 171–178.

———, Kevin T. Baaske, and Patricia Riley. "Debaters as Storytellers: The Narrative Perspective in Academic Debate." *JAFA* 23 (Spring 1987): 184–193.

Hufford, Roger. "Toward Improved Tournament Judging." *JAFA* 2(3) (Sept. 1965): 120–125.

Corsi, J. R. "Special Forum: The Hypothesis Testing Paradigm I. Zarefsky's Theory of Debate as Hypothesis Testing: A Critical Re-Examination". *JAFA* 19 (Winter 1983): 158–170.

Klump, James F., Bernard L. Brock, James W. Chesebro, and John F. Cragan. "Implications of a Systems Model of Analysis on Argumentation Theory." *JAFA* 11 (Summer 1974): 1–7.

Lichtman, Alan, Daniel M. Rohrer, and Jack Hart. "Policy Systems Revisited." In *Advanced Debate: Readings in Practice and Teaching*, ed. Thomas, David A. Lincolnwood, IL: National Textbook, 1987. Pp. 231–240.

McAdoo, Joe, ed. *Judging Debates*. Springfield, MO: Mid-America Research, 1975.

Miller, Gregory R. "The Forensics Critic as an Ideologue Critic: An Argument for Ideology as a New Paradigm for Academic Debate." *CEDA Yearbook* 10 (1989): 71–80.

———, John Gates, and Paul Gaske. "Resolving Paradigmatic Disputes as a Pre-Debate Issue: A Modest Proposal." *Speaker and Gavel* 26 (1988): 37–43.

Parson, Donn W. "Root Metaphors and Terministic Screens: Another Look at Paradigms." In *Argument in Transition: Proceedings of the Third Summer Conference on Argumentation*, ed. David Zarefsky, Malcolm O. Sillars, and Jack Rhodes. Annandale, VA: SCA, 1983. Pp. 792–799.

Rowland, Robert C. "Debate Paradigms: A Critical Examination." In *Dimensions of Argument: Proceedings of the Second Annual Conference on Argumentation*, ed. George Ziegelmueller and Jack Rhodes. Annandale, VA: SCA, 1981. Pp. 448–475.

———. "Standards for Paradigm Evaluation." *JAFA* 18 (Winter 1982): 133–140.

———. "Tabula Rasa: The Relevance of Debate to Argumentation Theory." *JAFA* 21 (Fall 1984): 76–88.

———. "The Debate Judge as Debate Judge: A Functional Paradigm for Evaluating Debates." *JAFA* 20 (Spring 1984): 183–193.

———. "On Argument Evaluation." *JAFA* 21 (Winter 1985): 123–132.

———. "A Defense of Rational Argument." *Philosophy and Rhetoric* 28(4) (1995): 350–364.

Smith, Mark. "To Disclose or Not to Disclose." *CEDA Yearbook* 11 (1990): 88–94.

Snider, Alfred C. "Games Without Frontiers: A Design for Communication Scholars and Forensics Educators." *JAFA* 20 (Winter 1984): 162–170.

Thomas, David A., ed. "Forum on Policy Systems Analysis." *JAFA* 22 (Winter 1986): 123–175.

Ulrich, Walter. "An Ad Hominem Examination of Hypothesis Testing as a Paradigm for Evaluation of Argument." *JAFA* 21 (Summer 1984): 1–8.

———. "Debate as Dialectic: A Defense of the Tabula Rasa Approach to Judging." *JAFA* 21(2) (Fall 1984): 89–93.

Wright, Tim, et al. "What Are the Characteristics of the Ideal Debate Judge?" *Speaker and Gavel* 7(4) (May 1970): 143–145.

Zarefsky, David, and Bill Henderson. "Hypothesis Testing in Theory and Practice." *JAFA* 19 (Winter 1983): 179–185.

———. "Reflections on Hypothesis Testing: A Response to Ulrich." *JAFA* 21 (Summer 1984): 9–13.

XXII. Ethics

Note: See AFA and CEDA ethics codes.

Church, Russell. "The AFA Code: Work Left Undone." *JAFA* 9 (Winter 1973): 378–379.

Day, Dennis. "The Ethics of Democratic Debate." *Central States Speech Journal* 17 (Feb. 1966): 5–14.

Duffy, Bernard. "The Ethics of Argumentation in Intercollegiate Debate: A Conservative Appraisal." *National Forensic Journal* I (Spring 1983): 65–71.

Fisher, Daryl. "Should a Coach Research and Develop Arguments for Debaters?" *Forensic Educator* 1 (1987): 15–16.

Inch, Edward S. "Forensics, Ethics, and the Need for Vision." In *PKD Proceedings of the 1991 Professional Development Conference: Commitment to Forensic Education: The Challenge to the Twenty-First Century*, ed. Sally Roden. Conway: University of Central Arkansas, 1991. Pp. 47–57.

Klopf, Donald, and James McCroskey. "Ethical Practices in Debate." *JAFA* 1 (Jan. 1964): 13–16.

Muir, Star. "A Defense of the Ethics of Contemporary Debate." *Philosophy and Rhetoric* 26(4) (1993): 277–295.

Murphy, Richard. "The Ethics of Debating Both Sides." *Speech Teacher* 6 (Jan. 1957): 1–9.

Newman, Robert P., and Keith R. Sanders. "A Study in the Integrity of Evidence." *JAFA* 2 (Jan. 1965): 7–13.

Rieke, Richard D., and David H. Smith. "The Dilemma of Ethics and Advocacy in the Use of Evidence." *Western Journal of Speech Communication* 32 (Fall 1968): 223–233.

Sanders, Keith R. "Toward a Solution to the Misuse of Evidence." *JAFA* 3 (Jan. 1966): 6–10.

Snider, Alfred C. "Ethics in Academic Debate: A Gaming Perspective." *National Forensic Journal* 2 (Fall 1984): 119–134.

Thomas, David A. "The Ethics of Proof in Speech Events: A Survey of Standards Used by Contestants and Judges." *National Forensic Journal* 1 (Spring 1983): 1–17.

Ulrich, Walter. "The Ethics of Forensics: An Overview." In *American Forensics in Perspective*, ed. Donn Parson. Annandale, VA: SCA, 1984. Pp. 13–22.

Watkins, Lloyd, ed. "Ethical Problems in Debating: A Symposium." *Speech Teacher* 8 (Mar. 1959): 150–156.

XXIII. Value Debate

See materials on value debating and CEDA. See especially CEDA yearbooks 1980 to present. See also materials on nonpolicy debate and L–D value debate, as well as Aristotle's enthymeme, Toulmin, Perelman, and informal logic.

Allen, Mike, and Lisa Dowdy. "An Analysis of CEDA and NDT Judging Philosophies." *CEDA Yearbook* 5 (1984): 74–79.

Bartanen, Michael. "The Role of Values in Policy Controversies." *CEDA Yearbook* 3 (1982): 19–24.

———, and David Frank. "Creating Procedural Distinctions Between Values and Policy Debate: The Issues Agenda Model." *The Forensic* (1983): 1–9.

———. "Application of the Issues Agenda Paradigm to Speaker Duties in Value Debates." *CEDA Yearbook* 8 (1987): 42–51.

———. *Debating Values*. Scottsdale, AZ: Gorsuch Scarisbrick, 1991.

Boggs, Ronald. "Comparing Values: A Review of Analytical Value Hierarchies." *CEDA Yearbook* 8 (1987): 27–32.

Church, Russell, and David Buckley. "Argumentation and Debating Propositions of Value: A Bibliography." *JAFA* 19 (Spring 1983): 239–250. An excellent values debate bibliography.

———, and Charles Wilbanks. *Values and Policies in Controversy: An Introduction to Argumentation and Debate*. Scottsdale, AZ: Gorsuch Scarisbrick, 1986.

Cirlin, Alan. "On Negative Strategy in Value Debate." *CEDA Yearbook* 5 (1984): 31–39.

Cole, Mark, Ronald Boggs, and Kevin Twohy. "The Function of Criteria in Non-Policy Argumentation: Burdens and Approaches." *CEDA Yearbook* 7 (1986): 36–42.

Corcoran, Joseph. *An Introduction to Non-Policy Debating*. Dubuque, IA: Kendall Hunt, 1988.

Dobkin, Milton. "Social Values and Public Address: Some Implications for Pedagogy." *Western Speech Communication Journal* 26 (Summer 1962): 140–145.

Fisher, Walter. "Toward a Logic of Good Reasons." *Quarterly Journal of Speech* 64 (Dec. 1978): 376–384.

———. "Rationality and the Logic of Good Reasons." *Philosophy and Rhetoric* 13 (Spring 1980): 121–130.

———. "Debating Value Propositions: A Game for Dialecticians." In *Dimensions of Argument: Proceedings of the Second Summer Conference on Argumentation*, ed. George Ziegelmueller and Jack Rhodes. Annandale, VA: SCA, 1981. Pp. 1014–1030.

Flaningam, Carl. "Value-Centered Argument and the Development of Decision Rules." *JAFA* 19 (Fall 1982): 107–115.

Gaske, Paul, Drew Kugler, and John Theobold. "Judging Attitudes and Paradigmatic Preferences in CEDA Debate: A Cumulative and Construct Validity Investigation." *CEDA Yearbook* 6 (1985): 57–66.

Gronbeck, Bruce. "From Is to Ought: Alternative Strategies." *Central States Speech Journal* 19 (Spring 1968): 31–39.

Hample, Dale. "Testing a Model of Value Argument and Evidence." *Communication Monographs* 44(2) (June 1977): 106–120.

Henderson, Bill. "Theoretical Implications of Debating Non-Policy Propositions." *CEDA Yearbook* 1 (1980): 1–8.

Hill, Bill, and Richard W. Leeman. "Developing Fields Dependent Criteria in Non-Policy Debate." *The Forensic* 79(3) (Spring 1994): 14–25.

Hollihan, Thomas. "An Analysis of Value Argumentation in Contemporary Debate." *Debate Issues* 14 (Nov. 1980): 7–10.

———, Patricia Riley, and Curtis C. Austin. "A Content Analysis of Selected CEDA and NDT Judges' Ballots." In *Argument in Transition: Proceedings of the Third Summer Conference on Argumentation*, ed. David Zarefsky, Malcolm O. Sillars, and Jack Rhodes. Annandale, VA: SCA, 1983. Pp. 871–882.

Howe, Jack. "CEDA's Objectives: Lest We Forget." *CEDA Yearbook* 2 (1981): 1–3.

———, and Don Brownlee. "The Founding Principles of CEDA." In *Twentieth Anniversary Assessment Conference Proceedings*, 1993, ed. David Thomas and Stephen Wood. Dubuque, IA: Kendall Hunt, 1993. Pp. 249–262.

Kennedy, George. *Aristotle on Rhetoric: A Theory of Civic Discourse*. New York and Oxford: Oxford University Press, 1991.

Kluckhorn, Clyde. "The Evolution of Contemporary American Values." *Daedalus* (Spring 1958): 78–109.

Louden, Allan, and Curtis Austin. "CEDA vs. NDT: A Dysfunctional Myth." *CEDA Yearbook* 4 (1983): 6–12.

Matlon, Ronald J. "Analyzing and Debating Propositions of Value in Academic Forensics." *Journal of Communication Association of the Pacific* 6 (July 1977): 52–67.

———. "Debating Propositions of Value." *JAFA* 14 (Spring 1978): 194–204.

———. "Propositions of Value: An Inquiry into Issue Analysis and Locus of Presumption." In *Dimensions of Argument: Proceedings of the Second Summer Conference on Argumentation*, ed. George Ziegelmueller and Jack Rhodes. Annandale, VA: SCA, 1981. Pp. 494–512.

———. "Debating Propositions of Value: An Idea Revisited." *CEDA Yearbook* 9 (1988): 1–14.

Micken, Kathleen, and Patrick Micken. "Debating Values: An Idea Revitalized." *CEDA Yearbook* 14 (1993): 54–71.

Miller, Gerald. "Questions of Fact and Value: Another Look." *Southern States Speech Journal* 28 (Winter 1962): 116–122.

Perelman, Chaim. "How Do We Apply Reason to Values?" *Journal of Philosophy* LII (Dec. 22, 1955): 797–802.

———. *The Idea of Justice and the Problem of Argument*. New York: Humanities Press, 1963.

———, and Lucie Olbrechts-Tyteca. "Value Judgments, Justifications, and Argumentation." *Philosophy Today* 6 (Spring 1962): 45–50.

———. *The New Rhetoric: A Treatise on Argumentation*. Notre Dame, IN: University of Notre Dame Press, 1969.

Rescher, Nicholas. *Introduction to Value Inquiry*. Englewood Cliffs, NJ: Prentice Hall, 1969.

Rokeach, Milton. *Beliefs, Attitudes, and Values*. San Francisco, CA: Jossey-Bass, 1976.

———. *Understanding Human Values*. London: Free Press, 1979.

Rowland, Robert C. "The Philosophical Presuppositions of Value Debate." In *Argument in Transition: Proceedings of the Third Summer Conference on Argumentation*, ed. David Zarefsky, Malcolm O. Sillars, and Jack Rhodes. Annandale, VA: SCA, 1983. Pp. 822–836.

Self, Lois. "Rhetoric and Phronesis: The Aristotelian Ideal." *Philosophy and Rhetoric* 12 (1979): 130–136.

Sillars, Malcolm O. "Audiences, Social Values, and the Analysis of Argument." *Communication Education* 22 (Nov. 1973): 291–303.

———, and Patricia Ganer. "Values and Beliefs: A Systematic Basis for Argumentation." In *Advances in Argumentation Theory and Research*, ed. J. Robert Cox and Charles A. Willard. Carbondale, IL: Southern Illinois University Press, 1982.

Steele, Edward, and Charles Redding. "The American Values System: Premises for Persuasion." *Western Speech Communications Journal* 26 (Spring 1962): 83–91.

Stevenson, Charles L. *Facts and Values*. New Haven, CT: Yale University Press, 1963.

Sumner, L. W. "Value Judgments and Action." *Mind* 77 (July 1968): 383–399.

Toulmin, Stephen. *An Examination of the Place of Reason in Ethics*. Cambridge: Cambridge University Press, 1950.

Tuman, Joseph. "Getting to First Base: Prima Facie Arguments for Propositions of Value." *JAFA* 24(2) (Fall 1987): 84–94.

Ulrich, Walter. *Debating Value Resolutions*. Berkeley, CA: Griffin Research, 1988.

Wallace, Karl. "Substance of Rhetoric: Good Reasons." *Quarterly Journal of Speech* 49 (Oct. 1963): 239–249.

Warnick, Barbara. "Arguing Value Propositions." *JAFA* 18(2) (Fall 1981): 109–119.

Wentzel, Joseph. "Toward a Rationale for Value Centered Argument." *JAFA* 13 (Winter 1977): 150–158.

Werkmeister, W. H. *Man and His Values*. Lincoln, NE: University of Nebraska Press, 1967.

———. *Historical Spectrum of Value Theories*. Lincoln, NE: Johnsen, 1973.

Williams, Robin M. *American Society: A Sociological Interpretation*, 3rd ed. New York: Knopf, 1970.

Wood, Stephen, and John Midgley. *Prima Facie: A Guide to Value Debate*. Dubuque, IA: Kendall Hunt, 1989.

Zarefsky, David. "Criteria for Evaluating Non-Policy Argument." *CEDA Yearbook* 1 (1980): 9–16.

XXIV. Lincoln–Douglas Debate

Grice, George L., and Edwin W. Knaak. *Lincoln–Douglas for Novices*. San Antonio, TX: Texas Group, 1985.

Howard, Derek V., Cheri Brussee, Halford Ryan, and Michael W. Shelton. "Lincoln–Douglas Debate." *National Forensic Journal* 14(2) (special issue) (Fall 1996): 1–68. Concerns L–D at NFA tourneys.

Kemp, Robert. *Lincoln–Douglas Debating*. Clayton, MO: Alan, 1984.

Luong, Minh. "Defining the Role of Presumption in Lincoln–Douglas Debate." *NFL Journal* 2 (1992): 1–16.

Minch, Kevin, and Timothy Borchers. "A Philosophy for Judging NFA Lincoln–Douglas Debate." *National Forensic Journal* 14(2) (Fall 1996): 19–36.

Morris, Charles E., III, and Dale Herbeck. "Lincoln–Douglas: An Educational Exercise." *National Forensic Journal* 14(2) (Fall 1996): 1–17.

Pollard, Tom, and Diana Prentice, eds. *Lincoln–Douglas Debate: Theory and Practice*. Lawrence: University of Kansas Press, 1981.

Williams, David E. "Educational Criteria in Forensics: An Argument for Lincoln–Douglas Debate." *National Forensic Journal* 14(1) (Spring 1996): 60–70.

XXV. Parliamentary Debate

See the new annual *Parliamentary Debate* and articles on parliamentary debate by Robert Trapp and Steve Johnson.

Bailey, R. J. "Adding Communication to Debate: A Look at Parliamentary Debate as a Complement to Cross-Examination Debate in Intercollegiate Debate." *Parliamentary Debate* 1 (1992): 25–37.

Bingle, Donald. "Parliamentary Debate Is More Serious Than You Think: Forensics at the University of Chicago." *Speaker and Gavel* 15(2) (Winter 1978): 36–42.

———. "What About Research?: How to Be Well Read." *Parliamentary Debate* 4 (1996): 3–13.

Johnson, Tom. "Full of Sound and Fury? The Role of Speech in Parliamentary Debate." *Speaker and Gavel* 1(3) (Mar. 1964): 88–92.

O'Neill, Daniel. "Recollections of University Parliamentary Debater: Irish Style." *The Forensic* 71(3) (Spring 1986): 66–69.

Sheckels, Theodore, Jr., and Annette Warfield. "Parliamentary Debate: A Description and a Justification." *Argumentation and Advocacy* 27 (Fall 1990): 86–96.

Trapp, Robert. "Parliamentary Debate as Public Debate." *Argumentation and Advocacy* 32(2) (Fall 1996): 85.

Williams, David E., J. Brent Hagy, and Ali McLane-Hagy. "Introducing Parliamentary Debate in the Argumentation and Debate Course." *The Forensic* 82(1) (Fall 1996): 16–21.

XXVI. Research in Forensics

The following studies represent only a small sample of research in forensics. For more information, see M.A. theses and Ph.D. dissertations, ERIC, papers from NCA and regional speech communication conventions, and so on. Names in forensics associated with quantitative research are fairly few in number but would include Mike Allen, Kenneth Andersen, Kent Colbert, Paul Dovre, Don Faules, Kim Giffin, C. T. Hanson, Bill Hill, Ed Hinck, Brenda Logue, Mike Mayer, John Reinard, and Wayne Thompson.

Anderson, Kenneth. "A Critical Review of the Behavioral Research in Argumentation and Forensics." *JAFA* 10 (Winter 1974): 147–155.

Bennett, William B. *The How To's of Library Research.* Taos, NM: Championship Debate Enterprises.

Colbert, Kent. "Speaking Rates of N.D.T. Finalists from 1968–1980." *JAFA* 18 (Summer 1981): 73–76.

———. "The Effects of CEDA and NTA Debate Training on Critical Thinking Ability." *JAFA* 12 (Spring 1987): 194–201.

———. "A Quantitative Analysis of CEDA Speaking Rates." *National Forensic Journal* 6 (Fall 1988): 113–120.

———. "The Effects of Debate Participation on Argumentativeness and Verbal Aggression." *Communication Education* 42(3) (July 1993): 206–214.

———. "Replicating the Effects of Debate Participation on Argumentativeness and Verbal Aggression." *The Forensic* 79(3) (Spring 1994): 1–13.

———. "Enhancing Critical Thinking Ability through Academic Debate." *Contemporary Argumentation and Debate: The Journal of the Cross Examination Debate Association* 16 (1995): 52–72.

Douglas, Donald G. "A Need for Review: Forensic Studies in Contemporary Speech Education." *JAFA* 8 (Spring 1972): 178–181.

————. "The Status of Historical Research in Argumentation." *JAFA* 10 (Winter 1974): 156–174.

Dovre, Paul, and John Wenburg. "Historical-Critical Research in Debate." *JAFA* 2 (May 1965): 72–79.

————. "Measuring Refutation Skills: An Exploratory Study." *JAFA* 4 (Spring 1967): 47–52.

————. "Experimental Research in Forensics: New Resources." *JAFA* 8 (Summer 1971): 47–51.

Giffin, Kim, and D. A. Warner. "A Study of the Influence of an Audience on the Rate of Speech in Tournament Debates." *The Speaker* (1962).

Gruner, Charles, Richard Huseman, and James L. Luck. "Debating Ability, Critical Thinking Ability, and Authoritarianism." *Speaker and Gavel* 8(3) (Mar. 1971): 63–65.

Harris, Edward, Richard Kropp, and Robert Rosenthal. "The Tournament as Laboratory: Implications for Forensic Research." *National Forensic Journal* 4 (Spring 1986): 13–22.

Herbeck, Dale, Brenda J. Logue, B. Christine Shea, Kevin W. Dean, Joseph M. Callow, Arnie Madsen, David Bickford, Roger C. Aden, Jack Kay, Donn W. Parson, Raymie E. McKerrow, James F. Klumpp, Don M. Boileau, Sharon Porter, Phillip Voight, Susan Stanfield, Kathleen M. German, Mary Umberger, David P. Brandon, Linda Carter-Ferrier, Judith M. Forsythe, Mary M. Gill, and Daniel Mills. "Forensics Research." *National Forensic Journal* 8 (Spring 1990): 1–103. Probably the best recent whole journal dedicated to forensic research.

Hunt, Steven B., and Edward S. Inch. "The Top Fifty Forensics Programs in the U.S.: A Twenty Year Retrospective." Paper presented at the Annual Meeting of the Western States Communication Association, Albuquerque, NM, Feb. 12–16, 1993. This study also listed on and available from ERIC.

Huseman, Richard, Glenn Ware, and Charles Gruner. "Critical Thinking, Reflective Thinking, and the Ability to Organize Ideas: A Multivariate Approach." *JAFA* 9 (Summer 1972): 261–265.

Jensen, Scott. "A Survey Analysis of Regional and National Programs and Competitive Trends in Collegiate Forensics." *The Forensic* 78(4) (Summer 1993): 1–10.

Klumpp, James F. "Wading into the Stream of Forensics Research: The View from the Editorial Office." *National Forensic Journal* 8 (Spring 1990): 77–86.

Littlefield, Robert S., Timothy L. Sellnow, Ann Burnett Pettus, Mary Ann Danielson, C. Thomas Preston, Jr., Edward A. Hinck, Robert C. Chandler, Don R. Swanson, Sheryl A. Friedley, Raymond Bud Zeuschner, Don R. Swanson, Gary C. Dreibelbis, Paul Gullifor, and Bruce B. Manchester. "Forensics as a Laboratory in Communication Studies." *National Forensic Journal* 10 (special issue) (Spring 1992): 49–82.

Logue, Brenda, and B. Christine Shea. "An Examination and Criticism of Forensic Research: The Last Five Years, 1984–1988." In *Spheres of Argument: Proceedings of the 6th SCA/AFA Conference on Argumentation*, ed. Bruce Gronbeck. Annandale, VA: SCA, 1989. Pp. 449–456.

Mayer, Mike, and Vince Meldrum. "The Effects of Various Time Limits on the Quality of Rebuttals." *JAFA* 23 (Winter 1987): 158–165.

McBath, James, Michael Bartanen, and John Gossett. "Research in Forensics." *ACA Bulletin* (Apr. 1979): 5–9.

McGlone, Edward L. "The Behavioral Effects of Forensics Participation." *JAFA* 10 (Winter 1974): 140–146.

McKerrow, Raymie E. "Evaluating Research in Forensics: Considerations of the Tenure and Promotion Process." *National Forensic Journal* 8 (Spring 1990): 73–76.

Pitt, Carl Allen. "Upgrading the Debater's Research Methods." *Speaker and Gavel* 7(2) (Jan. 1970): 44–46.

Porter, Sharon. "Forensics Research: A Call for Action." *National Forensic Journal* 8 (Spring 1990): 95–103.

Semlack, William D., and Donald C. Shields. "The Effect of Debate Training on Students Participating in the Bicentennial Youth Debates." *JAFA* 13 (Spring 1977): 192–196.

Stepp, Pamela, and Ralph B. Thompson. "A Survey of Forensics Activity at Selected Colleges and Universities in the United States, 1987." *National Forensic Journal* 6 (Fall 1988): 121–136.

Walwik, Theodore J. "Research in Forensics: An Overview." *JAFA* 6 (Spring 1969): 43–48.

XXVII. Women and Minorities in Forensics

Bartanen, Kristine. "Developing Student Voices in Academic Debate Through a Feminist Perspective of Learning, Knowing, and Arguing." *Contemporary Argumentation and Debate* 16 (1995): 1–13.

Bruschke, Jon, and Ann Johnson. "An Analysis of Differences in Success Rates of Male and Female Debaters." *Argumentation and Advocacy* 30(3) (Winter 1994): 162–173.

Crenshaw, Carrie. "Dominant Form and Marginalized Voices: Argumentation about Feminism(s)." *CEDA Yearbook* 14 (1993): 72–79.

Friedley, Sheryl, and Bruce Manchester. "An Analysis of Male/Female Participation at Select National Championships." *National Forensic Journal* 3 (1985): 3–12.

———. "An Examination of Male/Female Judging Decision in Individual Events." *National Forensic Journal* 5 (Spring 1987): 11–20.

Hayes, Michael T., and Joe McAdoo. "Debate Performance: Differences Between Male and Female Rankings." *JAFA* 8 (Winter 1972): 127–131.

Johnson, Ann, and Jon Bruschke. "A Research Agenda for the Study of Women in Debate: A Framework and Preliminary Analysis." In *Argument and the Postmodern Challenge: Proceedings of the 8th SCA/AFA Conference on Argumentation*, ed. RaymieMcKerrow. Annandale, VA: SCA, 1993. Pp. 55–60.

Loge, Peter. "Black Participation in CEDA Debate: A Quantification and Analysis." *CEDA Yearbook* 12 (1991): 79–87.

Logue, Brenda. "CEDA Male/Female Participation Levels: A Research Report." *CEDA Yearbook* 7 (1986): 64–75.

Murphy, John M. "Separate and Unequal: Women in the Public Address Events." *National Forensic Journal* 7 (Fall 1989): 115–125.

Nadler, Marjorie Keeshan. "The Gender Factor in Selecting Extra-Curricular Activities." *National Forensic Journal* 3 (Spring 1985): 29–36.

Pettus, Ann Burnett, and Mary Ann Daniels. "Coaching Intercollegiate Debate and Raising a Family: An Analysis of Perspective from Women in the Trenches." *National Forensic Journal* 11 (Winter 1994): 47–53.

Rogers, Jack. "Interrogating the Myth of Multiculturalism: Toward Significant Membership and Participation of African Americans in Forensics." *The Forensic* 80(4) (Summer 1995): 21–30.

Simerly, Greg, Ro Bites, and L. Scott. "Strategies to Achieve Cultural Diversity in Intercollegiate Debate." *Speech and Theatre Association of Missouri Journal* 22 (1992): 28–34.

Stepp, Pam, Greg Simerly, and Brenda Logue. "Sexual Harassment in CEDA Debate." *Argumentation and Advocacy* 31 (1994): 36–40.

Szwapa, C. "Sexual Harassment and Gender Discrimination in NDT Debate." *Argumentation and Advocacy* 31 (1994): 41–44.

XXVIII. Evidence and Ethics in Forensics

Bart, John. "Is There an Exit from the Information Superhighway?: The Dangers of Electronic Research." *Forensic Educator* 9(1) (1994–95): 28–31.

Benson, James A. "The Use of Evidence in Intercollegiate Debate." *JAFA* 7 (Spring 1971): 260–270.

Church, Russell. "The AFA Code: Work Left Undone." *JAFA* 9 (Winter 1973): 378–379.

Duffy, Bernard K. "The Ethics of Argumentation in Intercollegiate Debate: A Conservative Appraisal." *National Forensic Journal* 1 (Spring 1983): 65–71.

Kellerman, Kathy. "The Concept of Evidence: A Critical Review." *JAFA* 16 (Winter 1980): 159–172.

Klopf, Donald, and James McCroskey. "Ethical Practices in Debate." *JAFA* 1 (Jan. 1964): 13–16.

Newman, Robert P., and Keith R. Sanders. "A Study in the Integrity of Evidence." *JAFA* 2 (Jan. 1965): 7–13.

———, and Dale R. Newman. *Evidence.* New York: Houghton Mifflin, 1969.

Reinard, John C. "The Empirical Study of the Persuasive Effects of Evidence: The Status After Fifty Years of Research." *Human Communication Research* 15(1) (Fall 1988): 3–59.

Rieke, Richard, and David H. Smith. "The Dilemma of Ethics and Advocacy in the Use of Evidence." *Western Journal of Speech Communication* 32 (Fall 1968): 223–233.

Sanders, Keith R. "Toward a Solution to the Misuse of Evidence." *JAFA* 3 (Jan. 1966): 6–10.

Snyder, Alfred C. "Ethics in Academic Debate: A Gaming Perspective." In *Advanced Debate: Readings in Theory, Practice, and Teachings,* ed. David A. Thomas and Jack P. Hart. Skokie, IL: National Textbook, 1992. Pp. 15–29.

Spiker, Barry K., Tom D. Daniels, and Lawrence M. Bernabo. "The Quantitive Quandry in Forensics: The Use and Abuse of Statistical Evidence." *JAFA* 19 (Fall 1982): 87–96.

XXIX. Some Contemporary Debate Issues

Bruschke, Jon. "Debate Factions and Affirmative Actions." *Contemporary Argumentation & Debate* 25 (2004): 78–88.

English, Eric, Stephen Llano, Gordon R. Mitchell, Catherine E. Morrison, John Rief, and Carly Woods. "Debate as a Weapon of Mass Destruction." *Communication & Critical/Cultural Studies* 4(2) (2007): 221–225.

Godden, David M., and Douglas Walton. "A Theory of Presumption for Everyday Argumentation." *Pragmatics & Cognition* 15(2) (2007): 313–346.

Louden, Allan. "Debating Dogma and Division." *Contemporary Argumentation & Debate* 25 (2004): 40–42.

McGee, Brian R., Michael Bartanen, David M. Berube, Dale A. Herbeck, John P. Katsulas, and Linda M. Collier. "Whatever Happened to 'Value Debate'?: Reflections on Non-Policy Debating in CEDA." *Contemporary Argumentation & Debate* 23 (2002): 72.

Parcher, Jeff. "Factions in Policy Debate: Some Observations." *Contemporary Argumentation & Debate* 25 (2004): 89–94.

Rogers, Jack E. "Longitudinal Outcome Assessment for Forensics: Does Participation in Intercollegiate, Competitive Forensics Contribute to Measurable Differences in Positive Student Outcomes?" *Contemporary Argumentation & Debate* 23 (2002): 1.

———. "Graduate School, Professional, and Life Choices: An Outcome Assessment Confirmation Study Measuring Positive Student Outcomes Beyond Student Experiences for Participants in Competitive Intercollegiate Forensics." *Contemporary Argumentation & Debate* 26 (2005): 13–40.

Shuster, Kate. "Games, Which From a Long Ways Off Looks Like Flies." *Contemporary Argumentation & Debate* 25 (2004): 95–100.

Solt, Roger E. "Debate's Culture of Narcissism." *Contemporary Argumentation & Debate* 25 (2004): 43–65.

Warner, Ede, and Jon Bruschke. "'Gone on Debating:' Competitive Academic Debate as a Tool of Empowerment." *Contemporary Argumentation & Debate* 22 (2001): 1.

Zompetti, Joseph P. "Personalizing Debating: Diversity and Tolerance in the Debate Community." *Contemporary Argumentation & Debate* 25 (2004): 26–39.

APPENDIX **F**

Glossary of Terms in

Argumentation and Debate

Academic debate: Debate conducted under the direction of an educational institution for the purpose of providing educational opportunities for its students. The same as *educational debate.*

Academic parliamentary debate: A form of competitive academic debate practiced under the auspices of organizations including the National Parliamentary Debate Association and the American Parliamentary Debate Association.

Activist judge: Judges in this approach see themselves as active participants in the debate process, and view the debate not as a game, but as an act.

ADA: American Debate Association.

Add-on: When an affirmative speaker presents additional advantages after the initial presentation of a case.

Advantages: The benefits or gains that the affirmative claims will result from adopting its plan, which must be shown to outweigh the disadvantages.

Advocate: One who supports a position; to support a position.

AFA: American Forensic Association.

Affirmative: The side in a debate that argues in favor of the proposition.

Agency: The ability and opportunity for marginalized groups and individuals to resist domination.

Ambiguity: A fallacy, arises when the meaning of the word, phrase, or passage may reasonably be interpreted in two or more ways.

Analogy, figurative: A process of reasoning in which cases in different classifications are compared and inferred to be alike, for example, "used car dealers are like sharks."

Analogy, literal: A process of reasoning in which cases in the same classification are compared and inferred to be alike, for example, "New York is like Chicago."

Analogy, reasoning by: The process of making a comparison between two cases based on some identified similarity, and inferring that what is true in one case is true in the other.

Antithesis: The juxtaposition of contrasting ideas using parallel structure.

Anthropocentrism: A human-based ethic, considering the natural environment important as an instrument for the happiness and survival of humans.

APDA: American Parliamentary Debate Association.

Appeal to ignorance: A fallacy, wherein advocates maintain that something cannot be so because they, or the audience, have never heard of it.

Appeal to tradition: A fallacy, wherein support for an argument is based on customary and historical support for the argument.

Application: In debating a proposition of value case; the measure of effect in accepting the value, or concrete implication of the value.

Applied debate: Debate presented before a judge or audience with the power to render a binding decision on the proposition or to respond to the question or topic in a real way. (Compare with *academic debate*.)

Applied parliamentary debate: Debate conducted under the rules of parliamentary procedure (see Chapter 19).

Arguing in a circle: A fallacy, occurs when one assumes as a premise for the argument the very conclusion one intends to prove.

Argument, an: A potentially controversial statement, offering good reasons to believe it. Consists of a claim, supported by data and warrant.

Argumentation: Reason giving in communicative situations by people whose purpose is the justification of acts, beliefs, attitudes, and values.

Assertion: A claim offered without supporting evidence or reasoning.

Attitudinal inherency: A widely held belief, bias, or attitude that prevents the problem identified by the affirmative from being solved within the status quo.

Audience debate: A debate presented before and adapted to a lay audience. Usually the audience is not empowered to render a binding decision on the resolution.

Backing: (in Toulmin's model of argument) Additional evidence and reasoning advanced to support a warrant.

Bandwagon: A fallacy, wherein support for an argument is based on its popular support by a large number of people.

Benefits: See *Advantages*.

Block: A prepared group of arguments designed to support or refute a single point. May also refer to the negative block: the second negative constructive speech and the first negative rebuttal speech.

Blog: Literally a "Web Log," blogs began as a sort of online diary. They are websites or pages containing regular postings by authors and may include invited comments or articles by readers and guests.

Blurb: A one- or two-word argument, generally incoherent or incomplete, that lacks supporting evidence or analysis.

Boolean search operators: The words *and, or, not,* and *near* when used to define the relationships between keywords in a web search using a search engine.

Brainstorming: A method of shared problem solving in which all members of a group spontaneously contribute ideas. Individuals may use brainstorming by rapidly generating a variety of possible solutions.

Brief: An organized set of prepared arguments with supporting evidence; a prepared argumentative position or set of answers to an anticipated argument. Used interchangeably with *block*.

Burden of proof, a: The obligation to prove what one asserts. Applies to both the affirmative and the negative, as any advocate forwarding a claim must provide support sufficient to overcome the natural presumption against that claim.

Burden of proof, the: The risk of the proposition; the obligation of the affirmative, in order to overcome presumption, to give good and sufficient reasons for affirming a resolution.

Burden of refutation: In stock issues debate, the obligation of the negative to refute at least one of the issues of the affirmative. Otherwise the affirmative will prevail; the obligation of all debaters to refute arguments forwarded by their opponents, or the argument will be considered cogent for the weight of that argument. Failure to fulfill the burden of refutation results in the acceptance of the unrefuted argument. May also be called the *burden of rejoinder, burden of rebuttal,* or *burden of clash.*

Burden of rejoinder: See *Burden of refutation.*

Card: Debate jargon for a single item of quoted material used in support of an argumentative claim. A piece of evidence or evidence card. From the historical practice of debaters recording evidence on index cards.

Case turn: Offensive negative strategy designed to demonstrate that the needs identified by the affirmative are not needs but, in fact, benefits to the status quo; a negative turn-around argument, directed at the affirmative case claims.

Case: The operational strategy drafted by the advocates on one side of a proposition for the purpose of coordinating their reasoning and evidence and presenting their position with maximum effectiveness.

Casual evidence: Extrinsic proof or data, which is created without an effort being made to create it and is not designed for possible future reference.

Categorical imperative: According to the moral philosophy of Immanuel Kant, an unconditional moral law applying to all rational beings and independent of all personal desires and motives; representative of deontology or duty-based ethics.

Categorical syllogism: A syllogism in which the major premise is an unqualified proposition. Such propositions are characterized by words like *all, every, each,* and *any,* either directly expressed or clearly implied.

Causal reasoning: The process whereby one infers that a certain factor (a cause) is a force that produces something else (an effect).

CEDA: Cross Examination Debate Association.

Circumvention argument: The negative argument that the affirmative's plan won't work because many have the incentive and ability to check, evade, or otherwise defeat that plan—for example, gas rationing won't work because a widespread black market will develop.

Claim: (in Toulmin's model of argument) The conclusion we seek to establish by our arguments; the concise statement of the point we are making.

Clash: The obligation to respond to arguments that might harm one's position. (See *Burden of refutation.*)

Clear evidence: Proof that supports exactly what it is intended to support with precision and definitional clarity.

Coercion: The threat or use of force intended to limit the viable choices of action available to the person threatened.

Communication: The interactive and subjective process of symbol use through which meaning is constructed and shared understanding is sought.

Comparative advantage case: The affirmative argues that its plan will produce greater advantages than the status quo.

Competitive: Usually refers to the negative counterplan and requires that accepting the counterplan be a reason to reject the affirmative plan, either because it is mutually exclusive or because there is a net benefit to the counterplan over the plan. May also refer to any argumentative position, including the kritic (critique).

Conclusive proof: Evidence that is incontrovertible, either because the law will not permit it to be contradicted or because it is strong and convincing enough to override all evidence to the contrary and to establish the proposition beyond reasonable doubt.

Conditional argument: An argument that its arguers offer not as advocacy but as a tentative test or response which they may elect to abandon.

Conditional counterplan: Argument by the negative that it may abandon advocacy of the counterplan if certain conditions prevail.

Conditional syllogism: A syllogism in which the major premise deals with uncertain or hypothetical events. Usually identified by *if, assuming, supposing,* or similar terms, either expressly stated or clearly implied. Also known as the *hypothetical syllogism.*

Confirmation: The pattern of communication by which we recognize the existence, importance, and value of the other person.

Connotative meaning: The personal, often emotional, interpretation of language.

Constructive speech: The first and longer of the two speeches presented by a debater in an academic debate format, in which new evidence and new arguments for or against the proposition are presented. (See *Rebuttal speech.*)

Contention: Statement offered in support of an issue.

Corroborative proof: Strengthening or confirming evidence of a different character in support of the same fact or proposition.

Cost-benefit analysis: Comparing the advantages and disadvantages of a proposal and drawing a conclusion in favor of a position.

Counter value: A value claimed by the negative to be of greater importance than the principal value claimed by the affirmative.

Counterintuitive argumentation: Presentation of arguments that run counter to common thinking; the audience rejects in the first instance because they "know" it is wrong—for example, that employment causes harms.

Counterplan: A plan presented by the negative that is competitive with the affirmative's plan and is a superior policy alternative.

Criteria: The standard or the basis upon which a decision is to be made; a measure by which an impact is evaluated. A major issue in value debate; sometimes used in policy debate.

Critical theory: A theory of how cultural entities execute dominance and suppression of other cultural groups through their actions including communication.

Critical thinking: The ability to analyze, criticize, evaluate, and advocate ideas; to reason effectively; and to reach informed and careful conclusions based on sound inferences drawn from unambiguous statements of knowledge or belief.

Critique (kritic): A type of argument, usually initiated by the negative, which brings into question the language or behavior used in a debate or challenges the fundamental principles or premises upon which the affirmative case or proposition is built. Similar to a disadvantage argument.

Cross-apply: A request by the debater to the judge to apply previously stated evidence or argument to another point.

Cross-examination: The interactive process in debate, usually dedicated to designated and timed speech periods, wherein participants engage in the asking of questions and providing of answers pertinent to the arguments, cases, evidence, and other matters relevant to the debate. The 3-minute period, in a debate using the standard cross-examination format, following each constructive speech, during which opponents may question the constructive speaker.

Culture: The collective programming of the mind which distinguishes the members of one group or category of people from another; a set of norms and values shared by a group and handed down from generation to generation.

Data: (in Toulmin's model of argument) The grounds for an argument; evidence or what you've got to go on. In academic debate, usually in the form of evidence.

Debate: The process of inquiry and advocacy; the seeking of a reasoned judgment on a proposition.

Decision rule: A criteria or measure to aid in impact comparisons and upon which a judge may rely to select the winner of a debate.

Deduction: Argumentation that begins with a broad generalization and moves to a more specific application or conclusion.

Deep ecology: An ethical philosophy which measures the value of the natural environment as its own value, not as an instrument for the happiness or survival of humans.

Definition of terms: The advocate's supported interpretation of the meaning of the words in the proposition.

Definition, satisfactory: One that meets the minimal expectations of those who render the decision.

Degree of cogency: The extent to which an argument is both sound and intellectually compelling because it is well founded in fact, logic, or rationality.

Denotative meaning: The literal, relatively objective, meaning of language as shared within a language community.

Denying a valid conclusion: Advocate admits or cannot refute the premises of an opponent, yet denies the conclusion that logically follows from these premises.

Deontological ethics: An ethical approach that is process- or act-oriented, and is based on the notion that *actions* have moral value independent of their consequences, as contrasted with teleological ethics, which measure ethical actions based on their consequences.

Dialectic: A method of argumentation and reasoning in which interlocutors engage in a question and answer format in order to arrive at truth.

Direct evidence: That which tends to show the existence of a fact in question without the intervention of the proof of any other fact.

Direct questions: Call for a brief and concrete answer and are generally questions to which the questioner already knows the answer.

Disadvantages: The undesirable consequences that the negative claims will flow from the affirmative's plan. These must be shown to outweigh the advantages.

Disconfirmation: The pattern of communication in which we ignore or dismiss the other, emphasizing difference and explicitly or implicitly (often without recognition) expressing power over the other (person).

Disjunctive syllogism: A syllogism in which the major premise contains mutually exclusive alternatives. Usually indicated by such words as *either, or, neither, nor, but,* and *although,* either expressly stated or clearly implied.

Educational debate: Used interchangeably with *academic debate.*

Emotion: An internal state or condition attended to by pain or pleasure.

Enthymeme: (1) A truncated syllogism, in which one of the premises or the conclusion is not stated. (2) A syllogism based on probability, signs, and examples, whose function is rhetorical persuasion. Its successful construction is accomplished through the joint efforts of speaker and audience.

Ethical: Being in accordance with the accepted principles of right and wrong that govern the conduct of a profession or community.

Ethics: A set of constructs that guide our decision making by providing standards of behavior telling us how we ought to act.

Ethos: A mode of persuasion, the judgment the audience makes of the speaker based on character, sagacity, and goodwill.

Evaluator of argument: This judge recognizes the inevitability of intervention, but strives to determine the quality of logic, clash, and evidence presented by debaters in order to choose the superior case or argumentative advocacy.

Evidence aliunde: Evidence that explains or clarifies other evidence.

Evidence brief: A prepared argument, or set of arguments, complete with evidence.

Evidence: Consists of facts, opinions, and objects used to generate proof.

Example, reasoning by: The process of inferring conclusions from specific cases—an inductive approach to reasoning.

Existential inherency: The argument that because a problem exists it must be inherent in the status quo.

Extemporaneous speaking: A style of speaking using limited preparation in which the speaker carefully words and plans some portion of the speech and speaks from an outline or notes, but makes spontaneous remarks and speaks with a conversational, informal tone.

Extension: The continued discussion and development of an argument presented in an earlier speech as it progresses through the later speeches in a debate.

Extrajudicial evidence: Evidence that is not admissible in court; such evidence may be used outside the court.

Extratopicality: An advantage that is the result of a nontopical portion of the affirmative plan.

Fallacy: Any unsound mode of arguing, which appears to demand our conviction, and to be decisive of the question at hand, when in fairness it is not.

Fiat: The convention in academic policy debate that, for the sake of argument, participants may assume implementation of a reasonable policy. This allows debaters to focus on the question of whether a policy *should* be adopted and to avoid as irrelevant arguments about whether the policy *would* be adopted.

Flow sheet: A systematic set of notes recording the outline of a debate, with the arguments presented in each speech recorded in vertical columns and arranged so that a person can follow horizontally the flow of each argument as it evolves progressively through all the speeches in a debate.

Forensics: An educational activity primarily concerned with using an argumentative perspective in examining problems and communicating with people: rhetorical scholarship that takes various forms, including debate, public address, and the interpretation of literature. Usually organized as a competitive student activity.

Format: The agreed-upon framework for the debate, identifying the order and length of speeches along with a limited number of procedural rules.

Generic disadvantages: Disadvantages that may be applied to a number of possible affirmative plans.

Goals: In a value debate, the values expressed in the resolution or argued by the debaters.

Good reasons: Reasons that are psychologically compelling for a given audience, that make further inquiry both unnecessary and redundant—hence justifying a decision to affirm or reject a proposition.

Grammatical structure: Reasoning based on meaning distorted by incorrect or imprecise grammar.

Grounds: (in Toulmin's model of argument) Evidence and reasoning advanced to establish the foundation of a claim. Also called *data*.

Harm: The stock issue that identifies an imperfection within the status quo, marked by urgency and characterized by important deleterious consequences of inaction. The important problem that the affirmative claims exists in the status quo and requires remedy.

Hasty generalization: Argument from example in which the inference, or movement from specific example to generalization, is made on the basis of insufficient evidence, either nonrepresentative example(s) or an insufficient number of examples.

Headlining: The use of concise, precisely chosen words or short sentences to identify key points in the debater's speech. In academic debate the speakers often use numbers and letters to make their organization clear. Also called *taglining*.

Hegemony: The existence of dominance of one social group over another.

Hypothesis testing: A paradigm for academic debate in which the proposition is considered somewhat equivalent to a researcher's hypothesis in scientific method, such that the central focus of the debate is the proposition, to be measured against all possible alternative explanations, with negative arguments considered conditional by their nature but pertinent only to the extent that they are intrinsic to the affirmative's case.

Hypothetical syllogism: See *Conditional syllogism*.

Impact: A substantial measure of importance—the importance or relevance of an argument in a debate. (See also *Significance*.)

Impromptu speaking: A style of speaking reflecting no preparation, wherein the speaker is spontaneous, informal, and conversational in tone.

Incomplete comparison: A type of grammatical fallacy in which the point of comparison is missing or not clearly identified.

Indispensable proof: Evidence without which a particular issue cannot be proved.

Induction: Argument that begins with a specific case and moves to a broader generalization.

Inherency: The stock issue that identifies a probability for future harm, based in the embedded nature of the harm within the status quo and predicting that absent affirmative policy action, the harm will continue. The affirmative must prove that the significant harm it identifies is built into the essential nature of the status quo through legal structures and/or societal attitudes.

Intrinsic: A factor is intrinsic if it is embedded within the essential nature of a thing or is an inherent characteristic or consequence of the thing.

Intuitive acceptance of evidence: Evidence the audience accepts in the first instance because they "know" it is right—for example, that unemployment causes harms.

Irrelevancy: An argument in which proof is carried beyond its reasonable limits, and therefore does not pertain to the claim.

Issues: Critical claims inherent in the proposition. Questions identifying points of controversy.

Issues judge: A judge who focuses on the stock issues and requires the affirmative to win all the stock issues to win the decision.

Judicial debate: Debate conducted in the courts or before quasi-judicial bodies.

Judicial evidence: Evidence that is admissible in court.

Judicial notice: Evidence introduced into an argument without the necessity of substantiation; it is assumed to be so well known that it does not require substantiation.

Justification: Arguments to establish the reason for changing the status quo; the expectation that the affirmative address the unique importance and rationale for the proposition as worded.

Kritic: An argument that challenges the philosophical foundations, or applies ethical constructs to the opponent's advocacy and its implications. See *Critique*.

Leading questions: Questions that imply or contain their own answer and encourage that answer.

Link: The causal connection between the plan of action and the undesirable impact claimed. An essential component of a disadvantage argument.

Loaded language: Use of emotionally charged words in an effort to establish a conclusion without proof.

Loaded questions: Questions are based on prior assumptions, and are worded such that when the respondent answers the question directly, they are confirming the assumption.

Logos: A mode of proof based on the judgment the audience makes of the message itself, based in practical reasoning or logic.

Long table debate: A type of public debate involving three two-person teams on each side of a question, alternating speeches by side such that each participant speaks once, and utilizing some rules of parliamentary debate, including points of information.

Metaethics: The study of the inherent nature of ethical properties, including the basic foundations and assumptions upon which ethical premises are based.

Metaethics: The attempt to understand the metaphysical, epistemological, semantic, and psychological, presuppositions and commitments of moral thought, talk, and practice.

Metaphor: Comparison of unlike things, wherein a communicator seeks to establish common understanding about a new thing through its comparison to a known thing.

Mock trial debate: A form of academic debate that emulates trial court debating.

Modal qualification: The degree of cogency we attach to our claim.

Moot court debate: An academic form of judicial debate used by law schools to prepare students for courtroom debate.

Mutually exclusive: Means the negative's counterplan and the affirmative's plan cannot be adopted simultaneously. One measure of competitiveness.

NDT: National Debate Tournament.

NEDA: National Educational Debate Association.

Negative evidence: The absence of evidence that might reasonably be expected to be found were the issue in question true.

Negative: The side in a debate that argues against the resolution.

Net benefit: The negative claim that, when the advantages and disadvantages of the plan and counterplan are weighed, there is a net benefit in favor of its counterplan. The formula is CP > CP + P (adoption of the counterplan alone is superior to adoption of the counterplan plus the plan).

Non sequitur: A conclusion that does not follow from the premises or evidence on which it is based.

Nonformal debate: Debate that occurs in various contexts without formal or prearranged procedural rules.

Nonverbal communication: Characteristics of physical and vocal delivery that convey meaning to another person.

Normative ethics: The study of ethical action.

NPDA: National Parliamentary Debate Association.

Off-case: Negative arguments that, while not directly responding to the affirmative's case point by point, are offered as significant reasons for rejecting the case or plan—for example, countervalues, kritics, value objections, disadvantages, topicality arguments, and counterplans. They are organized and first presented by the negative.

On-case: Arguments that directly respond to the affirmative's case, on point, using the affirmative's organization.

Operational definition: A critical word or phrase (usually from the proposition) that is defined by its usage in the debate. In policy debate the affirmative's plan may be its definition of critical terms in the proposition.

Overview: A general argument offered at the beginning of a speech.

Parliamentary debate, academic: A form of competitive impromptu, off-topic tournament debate focusing on logic, reasoning, and presentation rather than evidence and technical debate strategy or jargon.

Parliamentary debate, applied: Debate conducted under the rules of parliamentary procedure.

Partial proof: Used to establish a detached fact in a series of facts tending to support the issue in dispute.

Pathos: A mode of proof based on emotional responses engendered within the listener.

Permutation: A test of competition of a counterplan offered by the affirmative. The hypothetical illustration of simultaneous adoption of plan and counterplan, or of simultaneous acceptance of plan and kritic.

Persuasion: Communication intended to influence the acts, beliefs, attitudes, and values of others.

Plan: The affirmative's proposed method of solving the problems claimed in the justification as needs or harms; their interpretation of the policy action called for by the proposition. It must produce the advantages claimed by the affirmative.

Planks: The major parts of a plan: agency, mandates, enforcement, funding and staffing, addendum.

Point of information: In academic parliamentary debate, a debater asks direct questions of their opponent, if recognized, during the opponent's speech.

Point of order: In academic parliamentary debate, a debater asks the speaker (judge) to consider a violation of the rules of debating by their opponent.

Point of personal privilege: In academic parliamentary debate, a debater may ask the speaker (judge) to consider comments or behavior of their opponents as inappropriate, insulting, or otherwise offensive.

Policy implications: In value debate the negative argument that deleterious policies will result if the affirmative's value is accepted.

Policymaker judge: A judge who contrasts the affirmative's and negative's policy systems and requires that the affirmative's policy system be viable and better than the negative's policy system in order to win the decision. This judge tends to evaluate competing policies on a basis of cost versus benefit.

Popular appeal: An advocate tries to win support for a position by maintaining that he or she is merely an "ordinary person" like everyone else.

Post hoc: Assuming a causal relationship where none has been proved because a condition exists after observation of another, supposed causal, condition.

Prearranged evidence: That which is created for the specific purpose of recording certain information for possible future reference.

Presumption: A predisposition favoring a given side in a dispute. Describes a psychological state in which listeners and decision makers are predisposed to favor or oppose one side of a debate or an argumentative position.

Presumptive evidence: Evidence that tends to show the existence of a fact by proving other, related facts.

Prima facie case: A case that in and of itself provides good and sufficient reason for adopting the proposition. It must provide effective issue statements to answer each of the stock issue questions.

Primary evidence: The best evidence that the circumstances admit; original or first-hand evidence that affords the greatest certainty of the matter in question.

Propaganda: The use of persuasion by a group (often a closely knit organization) in a sustained, organized campaign using multiple media for the purpose of influencing a mass audience.

Proposition: A statement of judgment that identifies the central issue in a controversy. May be a proposition of fact, value, nonpolicy, or policy.

Proposition of Fact: Descriptive claims addressing qualities of condition or causation.

Proposition of Policy: Advocative claims calling for action and including identification of an actor and the prescribed act.

Proposition of Value: Evaluative claims, identify qualities of relative goodness or badness of a thing or condition.

Pseudoargument: Fallacy created (by accident or design) by distortion, confusion, manipulation, or avoidance of the matters at issue or by substitution of matters not germane to the issue.

Pseudoquestion: An advocate asks an unanswerable, "loaded," or ambiguous question or series of questions, or asks a question based on a false assumption.

Psycho-facts: Beliefs that, though not supported by hard evidence, are taken as real because their constant repetition changes the way we experience life.

Public debate: A type of academic or special debate in which the audience is made up of individuals who are not experts in debate.

Public records: All documents compiled or issued by or with the approval of any governmental agency.

Public speaking: The oral expression of a message from one person to one or more persons where one is primarily the speaker, and the other(s) represent an audience, and the speaker offers a continuous and largely uninterrupted oral message.

Public writing: A frequently used source of evidence that includes all written material, other than public records, made available to the general public.

Qualitative significance: The compelling nature of a harm as diminished quality of life or denial of some important value.

Quantitative significance: Numerical, observable, and concrete measure of the harm.

Quasi-policy proposition: A proposition that expresses a value judgment about a policy.

Rebuttal: Argumentation meant to overcome opposing evidence and reasoning by introducing other evidence and reasoning that will destroy its effect. Also, the second speech by each advocate in an academic debate; evidence and reasoning introduced to weaken or destroy another's claim.

Rebuttal speech: The second and shorter of two speeches presented by a debater. New evidence and new argument may not be presented in such a speech. (See *Constructive speech.*)

Refutation: Argumentation meant to answer and overcome opposing evidence and reasoning by proving that it is false or erroneous.

Reliable evidence: Evidence from a trustworthy source, with a reputation for honesty and accuracy in similar matters and consistency in commenting on the matter.

Repeated assertion: An argument is presented as proof for itself.

Resolution: See *Proposition*.

Road map: Introductory remarks in which the debater states the order in which arguments will be presented.

RSS (Really Simple Syndication): A format for delivering regularly changing web content.

Search engine: A computer program that works to retrieve and prioritize information within a computer system.

Secondary evidence: Evidence that by its nature suggests the availability of better evidence in the matter in question.

Shallow ecology: An ethical philosophy that fights against pollution and resource depletion to maintain resources and standards of living for human quality of life.

Shells: Brief versions of arguments, usually presented by the negative side, to be expanded upon later in the debate.

Should: As used in policy debate, means that intelligent self-interest, social welfare, or the national interest prompts an action that is both desirable and workable. (See also *Fiat, Would*.)

Sign, reasoning by: The process of inferring relationships or correlations between two variables.

Significance: The degree of importance or impact attached to an issue. The advocate must prove that the essential elements of the case are quantitatively and/or qualitatively important. Also applies to the relative importance of an argument.

Signposting: See *Headlining*.

Skills judge: A judge who focuses on a set of debate skills—for example, analysis, reasoning, evidence, organization, refutation, and delivery—and awards the decision to the team that has done the best debating with regard to these skills.

Slippery slope argument: The argument that a seemingly harmless proposal in the affirmative's plan would be an irreversible first step leading inevitably to the most deleterious disadvantages.

Solvency: The ability of a plan to work and to reduce the harm identified by the affirmative.

Sophists: Teachers of rhetoric and other skills needed to participate in the civic life of ancient Greece.

Special debate: Debate conducted under special rules drafted for a specific occasion— for example, presidential campaign debates.

Special pleading: Urging that an exception be made to an accepted line of reasoning.

Spread: A large number of arguments, presented independently with minimal supporting evidence or analysis. The debater using a spread hopes to overwhelm the opponent's ability to respond to each.

Status quo: The existing state of things; the present system.

Stock issues: Those issues common to most debates on given types of propositions. In value debate, they are definitive and designative; in policy debate they include harm, inherency, and solvency.

Straw argument: Setting up an issue merely so it can be knocked down.

Structural inherency: Demonstrates that the harm is permanently built into the status quo; consists of law, court decisions that have the force of law, and societal structures.

Structured response: A pattern is established leading to an improper or unsupported conclusion.

Sufficient evidence: A fair preponderance of evidence.

Syllogism: A systematic arrangement of arguments consisting of a major premise, a minor premise, and a conclusion; dialectic structure for a deductive proof.

Tabula rasa judge: Literally, a blank slate, a judge who takes no position regarding expectations for the debate, and allows and expects the debaters to decide the theoretical framework for the decision. If no judging philosophy emerges in the debate, the judge may choose whatever judging philosophy seems most appropriate as a basis for the decision.

Teleological ethics: An ethical approach that is results oriented, and would focus on the good or bad consequences of an action or a decision.

Think tanks: Groups of experts who conduct research and prepare reports in support of their inquiry and advocacy concerning issues of various concerns including public and governmental policy, business, science, and education.

Time suck: An argument presented in anticipation that it will take longer for the opposing team to respond than for the presenting team to initially offer the argument. Such arguments are often dropped later in the debate, suggesting that the initiating team never seriously intended to develop them.

Topicality attack: An issue advanced by the negative that argues that the affirmative's plan is not an implementation of the policy action called for by the proposition, or that the affirmative interpretation of the resolution is incorrect.

Topicality: The state of conformity to the intent of the debate resolution. A plan is topical if it justifies the full intent of the resolution, the needs are solved, or the comparative advantages are gained as a direct result of the planks in the plan that implement the resolution.

Town hall debate: A type of public debate in which a moderator or chair and two debate teams address two sides of a proposition and invite audience participation prior to determination of a winner.

Turnaround argument: Converting a negative's disadvantage into an affirmative advantage. In common usage any statement that one turns against the originator.

Underview: An argument presented at the end of the speech or at the conclusion of argument on a specific issue.

Uniqueness: A necessary component of a disadvantage argument; the argument that absent the affirmative plan, the disadvantage will not occur.

Value applications: In value debate the negative argument that the values or quasi-policies advocated by the affirmative will not be applied to the problem.

Value objections: In value debate, the negative argument that undesirable consequences will flow from adoption of the affirmative's case. Similar to a disadvantage in policy debate.

Verbal communication: The use of language to influence, inform, teach, and inspire.

Verbalism: The abundant use of words without conveying much meaning.

Verifiable evidence: Evidence which may be authenticated, confirmed, and/or substantiated.

Virtues: Morally and ethically right habits of thought and behavior.

Voting issue: An issue claimed to be so important that by itself it justifies the judge's vote.

Warrant: (in Toulmin's model of argument) Evidence and reasoning advanced to justify the move from grounds to claim.

Wikis: The term "wiki" is Hawaiian for *quick*. Wikipedia is the most famous. Groups of readers contribute to the development of materials, including contribution of content as well as editing.

Workability: The issue, in policy debate, in which the negative argues that the affirmative plan is not feasible or practical, that it will not work. The affirmative argues the opposite.

Worlds debating: A format of debating involving four teams of two persons (known as "members"), a chairperson (known as the "Speaker of the House" or "Mister/Madame Speaker" and an adjudicator or panel of adjudicators in which debaters, without evidence or prepared materials, discuss a "motion" announced 15 minutes prior to the debate.

Would: In policy debate the argument that a certain policy would not be adopted; made irrelevant by fiat.

Index